Postwar Japan
1945 to the Present

Pantheon's Asia Library
New Approaches to the
New Asia

No part of the world has changed so much in recent years as Asia, or awakened such intense American interest. But much of our scholarship, like much of our public understanding, is based on a previous era. The Asia Library has been launched to provide the needed information on the new Asia, and in so doing to develop both the new methods and the new sympathies needed to understand it. Our purpose is not only to publish new work but to experiment with a wide variety of approaches which will reflect these new realities and their perception by those in Asia and the West.

Our books aim at different levels and audiences, from the popular to the more scholarly, from high schools to the universities, from pictorial to documentary presentations. All books will be available in paperback.

Suggestions for additions to the Asia Library are welcome.

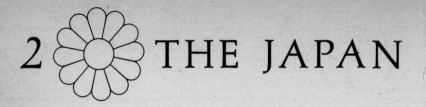

2 THE JAPAN

PANTHEON BOOKS *A Division of Random House*

READER

POSTWAR JAPAN

1945 to the Present

Edited, annotated, and with introductions by

JON LIVINGSTON, JOE MOORE, and FELICIA OLDFATHER

NEW YORK

Library of Congress Cataloging in Publication Data

Livingston, Jon, 1944–   comp.
Postwar Japan, 1945 to the present.

(Their The Japan Reader, 2)   (Pantheon's Asia Library)
Bibliography: pp. 581–82
    1. Japan—History—1945–   Sources.
I. Moore, Joe, 1939–   joint comp.   II. Oldfather,
Felicia, 1943–   joint comp.   III. Title.   IV. Series.
DS803.L57 vol. 2 [DS889]   952.04   73–12691
ISBN 0–394–48903–9
ISBN 0–394–70669–2 (pbk.)

Manufactured in the United States of America

9 8 7 6 5 4 3 2

Acknowledgments

Grateful acknowledgment is made to the following for permission to reprint previously published material:

British Journal of Industrial Relations: For "The Impact of Technological Change On Industrial Relations In Japan" by Sumiya Mikio, BJIR III:2 (July 1965); for "Japanese Wage Structure and Its Significance for International Comparison" by Masumi Tsuda, BJIR III:2 (July 1965).

Bulletin of Concerned Asian Scholars: For "American Labor and Japanese Unionists" by Herbert P. Bix, excerpted from "The Treaty System and the Japanese Military–Industrial Complex" by Herbert P. Bix, *Bulletin of Concerned Asian Scholars* II:2 (January 1970); for "The Eye of the Beholder" by John Dower, *Bulletin of Concerned Asian Scholars* II:1 (October 1969); for "The Historical Significance of the Japanese Textbook Lawsuit" by Ienaga Saburo, *Bulletin of Concerned Asian Scholars* II:4 (Fall 1970).

The Christian Science Monitor: For "Succession: A Japanese Game of Intricate Political Subtleties" by Elizabeth Pond, *Christian Science Monitor,* December 2, 1971. Copyright © 1971 The Christian Science Publishing Society. All rights reserved.

Columbia University Press: For excerpts from pages 180–87 of *Economic Development and the Labor Market in Japan* by Koji Taira, Columbia University Press, 1970.

Cornell University Press: For "Industrial Unionism" and "Japanese Trade Unionism" by Alice H. Cook, excerpted from *Japanese Trade Unionism* by Alice H. Cook (Ithaca, New York: New York State School of Industrial and Labor Relations, Cornell University, 1968).

Cornell University Press and Oxford University Press: For "Land Reform Laws" and "Japanese Rural Society" by Fukutake Tadashi, excerpted from *Japanese Rural Society* by Fukutake Tadashi.

The Current Digest of the Soviet Press: For "The U.S.S.R. and Japan: Possibilities in Cooperation" by V. Spandaryan, October 20, 1970, *The Current Digest of the Soviet Press* XXIII:42, pp. 41–2. Translation copyright © 1971 by The Current Digest of the Soviet Press, published weekly at The Ohio State University by The American Association for the Advancement of Slavic Studies.

The John Day Company, Inc., an Intext Publisher: For "Japan—Enemy or Ally?" by W. MacMahon Ball, excerpted from *Japan—Enemy or Ally?* by W. MacMahon Ball. Copyright © 1949 by the International Secretariat, Institute of Pacific Relations; for "Union Techniques," "SCAP and Government Employees, 1948," "General Strike Movement," "SCAP Policy Toward Labor Unions," and "Japanese

Labor, 1949–1950" by Miriam Farley, excerpted from *Aspects of Japan's Labor Problems* by Miriam S. Farley. Copyright © 1950 International Secretariat, Institute of Pacific Relations.

Editions Calmann-Lévy: For "Principal Characteristics of Small Firms," "Japanese Frugality," "The Great Trade Union Confederations: Sohyo and Domei," and "The Japanese Firm" by Hubert Brochier, excerpted from *Le Miricle Economique Japonais 1950–1970* by Hubert Brochier. Editions Calmann-Lévy, Paris, 1970.

Far Eastern Economic Review Ltd.: For "Old Pillars Fallen" by Nakamura Koji, *Far Eastern Economic Review* (August 7, 1971), pp. 49–50; for "Straddling the San Clemente Fault" by Nakamura Koji, *Far Eastern Economic Review* (March 4, 1972), pp. 27–8; for "Tanaka on Top" by Nakamura Koji, *Far Eastern Economic Review* (July 8, 1972), pp. 14–15.

Foreign Affairs: For "Education, Values, and Politics in Japan" by Marius B. Jansen, excerpted from *Foreign Affairs* XXXV:4 (July 1957). Copyright © 1957 by Council on Foreign Relations, Inc.

Fortune Magazine, Time, Inc.: For "How the Japanese Mount That Export Blitz" and "Japan Sets Out to Remodel Itself" by Louis Kraar, *Fortune* (March 1973). Copyright © 1973 by Time, Inc.

W. H. Freeman and Company: For "The Economic Growth of Japan" by James Abegglen, *Scientific American* (March 1970). Copyright © 1970 by Scientific American, Inc. All rights reserved.

Harper & Row Publishers, Inc., and Gabriel and Joyce Kolko: For "The Dodge Plan" by Joyce and Gabriel Kolko, excerpted from *The Limits of Power* by Joyce and Gabriel Kolko. Copyright © 1972 by Joyce and Gabriel Kolko.

Hill & Wang, a Division of Farrar, Straus & Giroux, Inc., George Allen & Unwin Ltd., and Albert Axelbank: For excerpts from pages 4–7, 16, 17, 55 from *Black Flag Over Japan* by Albert Axelbank. Copyright © 1972 by Albert Axelbank.

International Institute For Strategic Studies: For "Japan Trading and Investment Patterns" *Strategic Survey*, 1971, pp. 58–62. Copyright © 1972 The Internationl Institute For Strategic Studies, London.

Alfred A. Knopf, Inc.: For "A Regulated Press" by Richard Halloran, excerpted from *Japan: Images and Realities* by Richard Halloran. Copyright © 1969 by Richard Halloran.

Yasuhiro Kobayashi: For "Judging Tanaka's 'Remodeling Japan' Theory" by Yasuhiro Kobayashi, translated by Tomoko Moore, *Asahi Janaru* XIV:41 (October 10, 1972). Copyright © 1973 by Yasuhiro Kobayashi.

William Morrow & Company, Inc.: For excerpts from *Japan Diary* by Mark Gayn, pp. 87–90, 125–31, 226–32, 263–5, 328–34, 457–9. Copyright © 1948 by Mark Gayn.

New Left Review: For "The Student Left in Japan" by Gavan McCormack, *New Left Review* 65 (January–February 1971).

Newsweek: For "A Lawyer's Report on Japan Attacks Plan to Run Occupation," *Newsweek*, December 1, 1947. Copyright Newsweek, Inc., 1947; for "Needed: An Asian Policy" by George W. Ball, *Newsweek*, August 16, 1971. Copyright Newsweek, Inc., 1971.

Oxford University Press: For "Execution of Land Reform," "Rural Conservatism," "The Hamlet: Status, Dependence and Class," and "The Japanese Land Reform in Retrospect" by R. P. Dore, excerpted from *Land Reform in Japan* by R. P. Dore, published by Oxford University Press under the auspices of the Royal Institute of International Affairs.

Pacific Affairs, The University of British Columbia: For excerpts from pages 135–41 of *Land and Peasant in Japan* by Andrew J. Grad. Published by the International Secretariat, Institute of Pacific Relations, 1952; for "The Dispute Over

Japan's Police" by D. C. S. Sissons, *Pacific Affairs* XXXII:I (March 1959); for "Textbook Censorship in Japan: The Ienaga Case" by R. P. Dore, *Pacific Affairs* XLIII:4 (Winter 1970–1971); for "Beyond the Land Reform: Japan's Agricultural Prospect" by R. P. Dore, *Pacific Affairs* XXXVI:3 (Fall, 1963); for "The Role of the Bureaucracy in Japan" by John M. Maki, excerpted from *Pacific Affairs* XX:4 (December 1947).

Pacific Affairs and T. A. Bisson: For "The Constitution and the Retention of the Emperor," "April 1946 Elections," "April 1947 Elections," and "The Struggle on the Economic Front" by T. A. Bisson, excerpted from *Prospects For Democracy* in Japan by T. A. Bisson. Published by Macmillan Company, Inc. (1949) under the auspices of the Institute of Pacific Relations.

Pacific Affairs, The University of British Columbia, and R. P. Dore: For "The Japanese Land Reform in Retrospect" by R. P. Dore, *Far Eastern Survey* XXVII: 12 (December, 1958).

Pacific Affairs, University of British Columbia, and Miriam Farley: For "Labor Policy in Occupied Japan" by Miriam Farley, *Pacific Affairs* XX:2 (June 1947).

Pacific Affairs, The University of British Columbia, and Benjamin Martin: For "Japanese Mining Labor: The Miike Strike" by Benjamin Martin, *Far Eastern Survey* XXX:2 (February, 1961).

Pacific Community, the Jiji Press, Tokyo: For "Is Japan Changing Its Defense Policy?" by Martin Weinstein, *Pacific Community* 4:2, pp. 191–3.

Penguin Books Ltd., For "Growth of Japanese Armed Forces" by Jon Halliday and Gavin McCormack, excerpted from pages 79 and 86 of *Japanese Imperialism Today* by Jon Halliday and Gavin McCormack. Copyright © 1973 by Jon Halliday and Gavin McCormack.

Princeton University Press: For "Education: Japan" by R. P. Dore, excerpted from *Political Modernization in Japan and Turkey,* edited by Robert E. Ward and Dankwart A. Rustow, Princeton University Press, 1968; for "Combine Dissolution: Severing Personal Ties," "Pentagon and Shift in Occupation," "Antitrust in Japan," and "The U.S. Reorients Its Economic Policy in Japan" by Eleanor Hadley, excerpted from *Antitrust in Japan* by Eleanor M. Hadley. Copyright © 1970 by Princeton University Press; for "The Rise of Kishi," "Protest in Tokyo: The Security Treaty Crisis of 1960," and "The Great Debate" by George R. Packard III, excerpted from *Protest in Tokyo: The Security Treaty Crisis of 1960* by George R. Packard III. Copyright © 1966 by Princeton University Press.

The Progressive Magazine: For "Leftward Turn in Japan" by Albert Axelbank, *The Progressive* (Madison, Wisconsin), February, 1973.

The Royal Institute of International Affairs: For "Japanese Politics and the Approach of Prosperity" by Ronald Dore. Originally appeared in *The World Today,* July, 1961.

The Science Council of Japan and Solomon B. Levine: For "Japan's Labor Problems and Labor Movement 1950–1955" by Solomon Levine, reprinted from supplement to *Labor in Modern Japan* by Okochi Kazuo, Economic Series #18, March 1958.

Stanford University Press: For "Occupational Reforms in Local Government" by Kurt Steiner, excerpted from Ch. 4, 5, and 6 of *Local Government in Japan* by Kurt Steiner. Copyright © 1965 by the Board of Trustees of the Leland Stanford Junior University.

The University of California Press and The Regents of the University of California: For excerpts from *The Purge of Japanese Leaders Under the Occupation* by Hans H. Baerwald, pp. 78–80, 82–90. Published in University of California Press Publications in Political Science 8 (1959); for "American Business and the Zaibatsu" by T. A. Bisson, excerpted from *Zaibatsu Dissolution in Japan* by T. A. Bisson. University of California Press, 1954; for "Japanese Blue Collar," "Unity and Clevage Among Workers," and "The Worker and the Union" by Robert E. Cole, excerpted from *Japanese Blue Collar: The Changing Tradition* by Robert E. Cole, University of California Press, 1971.

University of California Press, The Regents of the University of California, and R. P. Dore: For "The Japanese Socialist Party and 'Structural Reform' " by R. P. Dore, *Asian Survey*, I:8 (October 1961). Copyright © 1961 by The Regents of the University of California.

The University of Chicago Press: For "Elections" by Richard K. Beardsley, John W. Hall, and Robert E. Ward, excerpted from *Village Japan* by Richard K. Beardsley, John W. Hall, and Robert E. Ward (University of Chicago Press, 1959).

The University of Illinois Press and Solomon B. Levine: For "Enterprise Union-ism" by Solomon B. Levine, excerpted from "Unionization of White-Collar Em-ployees in Japan" by Solomon Levine, from *White-Collar Trade Unions,* edited by Adolf Sturmthal (University of Illinois Press, 1967).

University of Michigan Press, Paul S. Dull, and Shuichi Sugai: For "Maeda Shoichi: A Case Study of a Japanese Political Boss" by Paul S. Dull and "The Japanese Police System" by Shuichi Sugai, both excerpted from *Five Studies in Japanese Politics,* edited by Robert E. Ward (University of Michigan Press, 1957).

Yale University Press: For "Socialist Taste of Power and Decline," "Labor and the 'Red Purge,' " "Socialist Parties and the Peace Treaty," "Socialist Schism." "Frustrations of the Opposition," "Labor and Electoral Support," and "Socialist Support From Middle and Other Strata" by Allan B. Cole. George O. Totten, and Cecil Uyehara, excerpted from *Socialist Parties in Postwar Japan* by Allan B. Cole, George O. Totten, and Cecil Uyehara. Copyright © 1966 by Yale University; for "Big Business in Japanese Politics," "Ikeda's Rise to Power," "Japanese Business Federations," "What is Zaikai?" and "Role of the Bureaucracy" by Yanaga Chitoshi, excerpted from *Big Business in Japanese Politics* by Yanaga Chitoshi. Copyright © 1968 by Yale University.

To my parents

J.L.

To my parents and my wife, Tomoko

J.M.

To my parents

F.O.

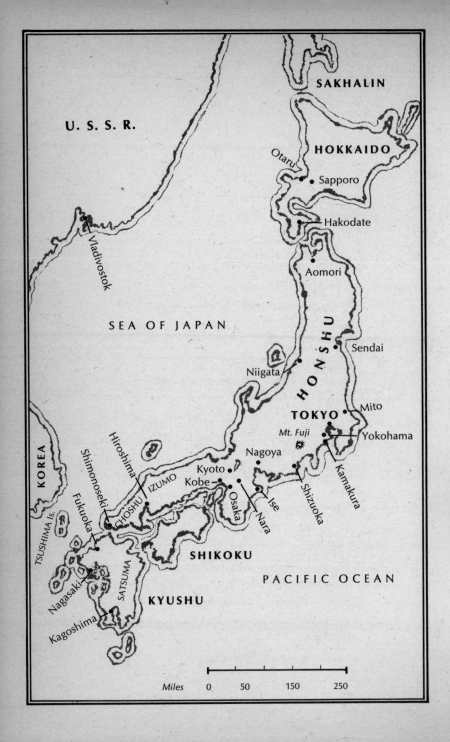

SAKHALIN

U. S. S. R.

HOKKAIDO

Otaru

Sapporo

Hakodate

Vladivostok

Aomori

SEA OF JAPAN

HONSHU

Sendai

Niigata

TOKYO

Mito

Mt. Fuji

Yokohama

Nagoya

Kamakura

KOREA

Hiroshima

Kyoto

Shimonoseki

IZUMO

Kobe

Shizuoka

Fukuoka

CHOSHU

Osaka

Ise

TSUSHIMA Is.

Nara

SHIKOKU

PACIFIC OCEAN

Nagasaki

SATSUMA

KYUSHU

Kagoshima

Miles   0   50   150   250

Contents

Preface

THERE ARE numerous translations of modern Japanese fiction and beautiful books about Japanese art and architecture. In recent years, there has also been a growing number of books on modern Japanese history. Yet ironically this sheer quantity is becoming an obstacle to understanding, making it hard to know even where to begin. To most Americans Japan remains unknown or paradoxical —the United States' westernized partner in Asia, a startlingly beautiful country with highly developed aesthetic tastes, and a new "yellow peril," flooding markets with "made in Japan" trademarks and threatening American jobs. *The Japan Reader* is designed to bring together in an introductory and readable form information essential to understanding Japan now scattered among a myriad of books and publications. Particular emphasis is placed on Japanese social and economic questions, two of the most important, if little understood, aspects of modern Japan.

Japan emerged from centuries of isolation, rapidly industrialized, fought and lost a world war, and then recovered to take a position as a world power—all in a brief hundred years. Yet after this enormously varied period of historical upheaval and change, Japan is often viewed simply as the "success story of Asia"—the only nonwhite nation to become a powerful, industrialized, modern state. Numerous writers, determined to discover how Japan broke from the supposed Third World norm, compare it with China, Latin America, India, and even Israel. Others view Japan as a successful "imitator" and duplicator of Western methods, an Oriental stepchild of the Western world.

In these volumes we seek not only to understand "how," but to raise the issue of "success" itself. Because the Japanese achievement has been an ambiguous one, we have sought to clarify the costs as well as the gains.

The problem is partly one of vantage point. Having sought and won parity with the Western imperial powers at the close of the nineteenth century, Japan itself became imperialist. It succeeded in industrialization, partially at least, at the expense of its weaker Asian neighbors, and its perceptions of strategic and economic needs ultimately led it into World War II. Can the Japan of late August 1945, the conclusion of Volume I, be called a modern-day success story?

Viewing Japan as a successful modernizer, moreover, raises at least as many problems as it clarifies. If the establishment of a dynamic industrial state and strong army constitutes modernization, then Japan was as modern as most of the Western nations in this century. Yet often when Westerners apply this perspective to Japan, they envision a state with social, intellectual, and institutional structures comparable to those of an advanced Western capitalist nation. Whatever falls outside this idealized model is viewed as quaint or exotic, or dismissed as anachronistic or "dysfunctional." Thus much of the richness and significance of Japan's road to economic development is lost, the roots of its social conflicts distorted, and its culture crudely simplified.

Postwar Japan has been touted as the only successful implantation of Western-style democracy in Asia. Such claims are usually made largely on the strength of Japan's parliamentary and political party system without questioning how such institutions really function in Japanese society, or considering where and how economic and political decisions are made. Knowledge of the historical origins of the present system is crucial, for power today is still largely restricted to the descendents of prewar parties with their strong ties to the bureaucratic and business elites.

About Japan's postwar "economic miracle" there are few apparent doubts: Japan has managed to sustain a growth rate of around ten percent in its Gross National Product for more than twenty years. Yet this economic expansion also has unattractive features: pollution of staggering proportions, glaring economic inequalities, poor working conditions. Control over the Japanese economy by the zaibatsu conglomerates remains powerful, and Japan's industry, finance, and trade are today as much as ever the preserve of a tightly knit oligopoly. In this reader we pose questions about the cost to Japan of this economic surge and explore new political challenges to the status quo emerging in popular movements around issues of ecology, education, and militarism.

The Japan Reader is arranged chronologically in six major sections, four in Volume I and two in Volume II. There are topical divisions within each section so that, for example, one can turn to a section on the Japanese labor movement during the American occupation period. The first volume ends with 1945: Japan met the West, achieved her goal of *fukoku kyōhei*—"rich country, strong army"— and finally lost a war when she tried to include China in her empire and challenged America's Pacific power. The second volume begins with the American occupation after World War II, and moves through the economic resurgence of the past two decades up to the present.

In assembling selections for the book, we sought materials that illustrated the central issues of modern Japanese history. We have used contemporary accounts, fiction, and documents, as well as more academic writing, including the work of such men as E. H. Norman and T. A. Bisson, whose lives and reputations were damaged by McCarthyism. The book is composed mainly of writings by Westerners and the best Japanese works available in English. Although, for reasons of time and resources, we decided against an anthology entirely of new translations from Japanese, we have included newly translated materials when nothing suitable could be found in English.

American readers should be reminded that in Japanese names the surname is followed by the given name. In the introductions to our selections we have used the Japanese order, but unfortunately there was no way to standardize names used in the selections themselves. In each volume, we have included a chronology, a brief bibliographical guide to further reading, and notes about the authors of our selections. Most selections have been abridged and footnotes have been removed. We thank all those who have given permission to use their writings.

Finally, we wish to acknowledge that the origins of this book lie in the Committee of Concerned Asia Scholars, to which the three of us belong. This is our first full-length effort dealing with Japan, but it is obviously only a beginning in our effort to understand Japan, whose future is crucial for Southeast Asia and China as well as for the United States.

I.

The American Occupation
1945–1952

✿ JAPAN EMERGED from World War II defeated militarily, severely damaged by bombing, and occupied by a foreign invader for the first time in history. Even before Japan surrendered unconditionally to the Allies in August 1945, the United States had decided that the occupation would be under American control. General Douglas MacArthur, head of the occupation administration in Tokyo (SCAP), largely ignored the eleven-nation Far Eastern Commission. The Soviet Union, Britain, and Australia, among others, protested in vain. From the beginning the occupation bore a thoroughly American stamp.

General MacArthur, in his highly individualistic style, set out to make the authoritarian society into a democratic one. Like many other Americans, he genuinely believed that if Japanese society had been organized along Western democratic lines, Japan would not have embarked on the road to militarism in the 1930s. Though the accuracy of this perception can be challenged, it nonetheless set the stage for a series of sweeping reforms in the first years of the American occupation. Demilitarization was begun by purging important military leaders and by dismantling much of Japan's war industry, army, and navy. Lesser purges, aimed at business leaders who had cooperated in Japan's overseas expansion, eventually reached 200,000 people. The emperor, however, was not deposed, despite strong pressures for his removal and bitter disputes over the consequences of his retention.

In the first two years after the war a surge of democratic

activities, strikes, and new ideas swept Japan. The land reform, plans for zaibatsu dissolution, reparation proposals, educational reform, the promulgation of a new constitution, all illustrate a wide-ranging attempt to transform the country. Communists and other political opponents of the prewar government were released from jail, and political life blossomed as civil liberties and labor organizations and political freedom were strongly supported by influential occupation authorities.

The pace and depth of reform differed in various areas and were conditioned by numerous forces—the economic crisis which followed wartime destruction, recurrent debates over the financial costs of the occupation to the Americans, struggles among competing Japanese groups. Within SCAP itself, there had long been individuals opposed to radical restructuring and splits over policy were evident throughout this period.

Two aspects of occupation policy, however, deserve particular emphasis for they ultimately set important limits on the nature and scope of the occupation reforms. First, unlike the occupation of Germany where each Allied power established a military government to administer its zone, in Japan the existing civil government was used to carry out occupation policy. This created an internal contradiction throughout the course of the occupation: a major component of the Japanese elite was expected to democratize and purge both the country and itself. Secondly, American foreign policy considerations led not only to initial American control, but to major external restraints on the scope of reforms. As American-Russian relations deteriorated and the power of the Chinese communists grew, the need for a dependable Pacific ally took increasing precedence over the commitment to democratize Japan.

General MacArthur's decision to ban the general strike planned by labor unions for February 1, 1947, marked a major shift in occupation policy. This "reverse course" eventually included backsliding in political reforms, the effective reconstruction of many prewar industrial and financial combines, and attacks on the left wing of the Japanese labor movement. Although other important reforms were not dismantled, forces opposed to the sweeping nature of the early occupation period now became dominant.

Within Japan, conservative groups supported these new policies for their own reasons. For many prewar industrialists and politicians, this was a chance to regain their former influence and wealth, and the conservative elite that dominated the Japanese government throughout the occupation happily joined in suppressing the new democratic forces in labor groups and in the left-wing political parties. Economic retrenchment in 1949 and 1950 undoubtedly reinforced the conservatives' position, while the purge machinery was used to weaken the communist movement. By the time full sovereignty was restored to Japan in 1952, the conservatives had recovered much of their prewar influence in government and business.

1. *Administration of the Occupation*

✿ AFTER THE SURRENDER of Japan in August 1945, General Douglas MacArthur was designated the Supreme Commander for the Allied Powers for the Occupation and Control of Japan (SCAP). SCAP also refers to the occupation bureaucracy as a whole. The SCAP mandate, seen below in sections of the United States Initial Post-Surrender Policy for Japan, was a broad one.

The initial American attitude was punitive in intent: Japan was to be deprived of her ability to make war. This meant the dismantling of war industries, the purging of officials thought to be responsible for Japanese militarism, and the democratization of Japanese society. The authority of SCAP was limited by the decision to use the existing Japanese government to administer the country, but MacArthur could force the Japanese legislature to make his plans law. Moreover, the language of the directive implied that the Japanese might even use force to overthrow their government without being stopped by Mac-Arthur.

*Basic Initial Post-Surrender Directive**

PART I—ULTIMATE OBJECTIVES

August 29, 1945

The ultimate objectives of the United States in regard to Japan, to which policies in the initial period must conform, are:

(*a*) To insure that Japan will not again become a menace to the United States or to the peace and security of the world.

(*b*) To bring about the eventual establishment of a peaceful and responsible government which will respect the rights of other states and will support the objectives of the United States as reflected in the ideals and principles of the Charter of the United Nations. The United States desires that this government should conform as closely as may be to principles of democratic self-government but it is not the responsibility of the Allied Powers to impose upon Japan any form of government not supported by the freely expressed will of the people.

These objectives will be achieved by the following principal means:

(*a*) Japan's sovereignty will be limited to the islands of Honshu, Hokkaido, Kyushu, Shikoku, and such minor outlying islands as may be determined, in accordance with the Cairo Declaration and other agreements to which the United States is or may be a party.

(*b*) Japan will be completely disarmed and demilitarized. The authority of the militarists and the influence of militarism will be totally eliminated from her political, economic, and social life. Institutions expressive of the spirit of militarism and aggression will be vigorously suppressed.

* "Basic Initial Post-Surrender Directive," *Political Reorientation of Japan, Report of the Government Section, Supreme Commander for the Allied Powers* (Washington, D.C.: U.S. Government Printing Office, 1949), vol. 2, Appendix A:11, pp. 423–426.

(*c*) The Japanese people shall be encouraged to develop a desire for individual liberties and respect for fundamental human rights, particularly the freedoms of religion, assembly, speech, and the press. They shall also be encouraged to form democratic and representative organizations.

(*d*) The Japanese people shall be afforded opportunity to develop for themselves an economy which will permit the peacetime requirements of the population to be met.

PART II—ALLIED AUTHORITY

1. MILITARY OCCUPATION

There will be a military occupation of the Japanese home islands to carry into effect the surrender terms and further the achievement of the ultimate objectives stated above. The occupation shall have the character of an operation in behalf of the principal Allied powers acting in the interests of the United Nations at war with Japan. For that reason, participation of the forces of other nations that have taken a leading part in the war against Japan will be welcomed and expected. The occupation forces will be under the command of a Supreme Commander designated by the United States.

Although every effort will be made, by consultation and by constitution of appropriate advisory bodies, to establish policies for the conduct of the occupation and the control of Japan which will satisfy the principal Allied powers, in the event of any differences of opinion among them, the policies of the United States will govern.

2. RELATIONSHIP TO JAPANESE GOVERNMENT

The authority of the emperor and the Japanese government will be subject to the Supreme Commander, who will possess all powers necessary to effectuate the surrender terms and to carry out the policies established for the conduct of the occupation and the control of Japan.

In view of the present character of Japanese society and the desire of the United States to attain its objectives with a minimum commitment of its forces and resources, the Supreme Commander will exercise his authority through Japanese governmental machinery and agencies, including the emperor, to the extent that this satisfactorily furthers United States objectives. The Japanese government will be permitted, under his instructions, to exercise the normal powers of government in matters of domestic administration. This policy, however, will be subject to the right and duty of the Supreme Commander to require changes in governmental machinery or personnel or to act directly if the emperor or other Japanese authority does not satisfactorily meet the requirements of the Supreme Commander in effectuating the surrender terms. This policy, moreover, does not commit the Supreme Commander to support the emperor or any other Japanese governmental authority in opposition to evolutionary changes looking toward the attainment of United States objectives. The policy is to use the existing form of government in Japan, not to support it. Changes in the form of government initiated by the Japanese people or government in the direction of modifying its feudal and authoritarian tendencies are to be permitted and favored. In the event that the effectuation of such changes involves the use of force by the Japanese people or government against persons opposed thereto, the Supreme Commander should intervene only where necessary to ensure the security of his forces and the attainment of all other objectives of the occupation.

3. Publicity as to Policies

The Japanese people, and the world at large, shall be kept fully informed of the objectives and policies of the occupation, and of progress made in their fulfilment.

Part III—Political
1. Disarmament and Demilitarization

Disarmament and demilitarization are the primary tasks of the military occupation and shall be carried out promptly and with determination. Every effort shall be made to bring home to the Japanese people the part played by the military and naval leaders, and those who collaborated with them, in bringing about the existing and future distress of the people.

Japan is not to have an army, navy, air force, secret police organization, or any civil aviation. Japan's ground, air, and naval forces shall be disarmed and disbanded and the Japanese Imperial General Headquarters, the General Staff, and all secret police organizations shall be dissolved. Military and naval matériel, military and naval vessels and military and naval installations, and military, naval, and civilian aircraft shall be surrendered and shall be disposed of as required by the Supreme Commander.

High officials of the Japanese Imperial General Headquarters, and General Staff, other high military and naval officials of the Japanese government, leaders of ultranationalist and militarist organizations, and other important exponents of militarism and aggression will be taken into custody and held for future disposition. Persons who have been active exponents of militarism and militant nationalism will be removed and excluded from public office and from any other position of public or substantial private responsibility. Ultranationalistic or militaristic social, political, professional, and commercial societies and institutions will be dissolved and prohibited.

Militarism and ultranationalism, in doctrine and practice, including paramilitary training, shall be eliminated from the educational system. Former career military and naval officers, both commissioned and noncommissioned, and all other exponents of militarism and ultranationalism shall be excluded from supervisory and teaching positions.

2. WAR CRIMINALS

Persons charged by the Supreme Commander or appropriate United Nations agencies with being war criminals, including those charged with having visited cruelties upon United Nations prisoners or other nationals, shall be arrested, tried, and, if convicted, punished. Those wanted by another of the United Nations for offenses against its nationals, shall, if not wanted for trial or as witnesses or otherwise by the Supreme Commander, be turned over to the custody of such other nation.

3. ENCOURAGEMENT OF DESIRE FOR INDIVIDUAL LIBERTIES AND DEMOCRATIC PROCESSES

Freedom of religious worship shall be proclaimed promptly on occupation. At the same time it should be made plain to the

Japanese that ultranationalistic and militaristic organizations and movements will not be permitted to hide behind the cloak of religion.

The Japanese people shall be afforded opportunity and encouraged to become familiar with the history, institutions, culture, and the accomplishments of the United States and the other democracies. Association of personnel of the occupation forces with the Japanese population should be controlled only to the extent necessary to further the policies and objectives of the occupation.

Democratic political parties, with rights of assembly and public discussion, shall be encouraged, subject to the necessity for maintaining the security of the occupying forces.

Laws, decrees, and regulations which establish discriminations on ground of race, nationality, creed, or political opinion shall be abrogated; those which conflict with the objectives and policies outlined in this document shall be repealed, suspended, or amended as required; and agencies charged specifically with their enforcement shall be abolished or appropriately modified. Persons unjustly confined by Japanese authority on political grounds shall be released. The judicial, legal, and police systems shall be reformed as soon as practicable to conform to the policies set forth in Articles 1 and 3 of this Part III and thereafter shall be progressively influenced, to protect individual liberties and civil rights.

◈ THE FATE of the Japanese emperor, Hirohito, was an open question until the new Japanese constitution was promulgated in March 1946. He was considered by many Americans, and by Washington's World War II allies, as a war criminal. At the same time, he had cooperated with SCAP and was still held in an exalted position by most Japanese.

George Atcheson was political advisor for the State Department in Tokyo and often wrote direct reports to President Truman. In addition to the emperor issue, the excerpts here provide a description of the response of the Japanese elite to the occupation, alternatives for U.S. occupation policy, and an analysis of the political situation at the beginning of 1946. They also reflect the broad range of SCAP activities during the occupation's first year.

The Acting Political Adviser in Japan (*Atcheson*) to President Truman*

TOKYO, November 5, 1945

. . . While many Japanese are still bewildered and apathetic, what resentment they feel is rather toward their own poor government and inept officials rather than toward us. Most of the so-called common people have had little background for political thinking; they are nevertheless generally in a mood for reform and change, and this is apparent from the ready manner in which they have absorbed the shocks of the various political directives. Contrary to most predictions, they were not horrified to learn that they may now discuss the emperor. They were startled when the emperor called on General MacArthur; but the humiliation over that was felt chiefly by the officials. It is not going too far to say that at least the urban people are even beginning to feel some hope that they will eventually have a better life—if their rather desperate economic problems can be solved.

There is naturally divergence between the attitudes toward American occupation and aims exhibited by the higher Japanese officials and the career bureaucracy, the intelligentsia, the men of big business, and "the common people." Practically all categories of Japanese show or pretend a desire to cooperate with our military, but the civil officials and bureaucracy are the least sincere and effective. There is an appalling lack of leadership, partially because the military backbone and driving force of the government is gone. And in any serious effort toward reform, cabinet ministers who may overcome their near incapacity to adapt themselves to the progress of events are confronted, often to the point of helplessness, by the obstructionism of the unregenerate and deeply

* U.S., Department of State, *Foreign Relations of the United States, 1945: The Far East* (Washington, D.C.: Government Printing Office), pp. 825–827.

entrenched bureaucrats. They carry out directives but seem incapable of solving many of the administrative and most of the serious economic problems with which the government is faced. We can probably expect a series of ineffective, short-term cabinets. . . .

There is, of course, more real liberalism among the intelligentsia than among other classes, but those deserving the name of liberal are almost all timid men timidly feeling their way, their spirits still chained by past repression, still haunted by undefined fears, still unable to realize that they are at last really free to speak and act. And among them, as among other classes, there are men who have merely (as the Japanese put it) repainted their signs. . . .

The big business people are among the most obvious sign-repainters. They are fundamentally conservative and reactionary; since the days of the Meiji restoration they and the military have been mutually dependent; but as their chief interest is the making of money they are inclined toward such reforms as will tend to stabilize the situation and get things back to some kind of business "normalcy." . . .

As for the emperor, there would certainly be advantages in having him continue in office until the constitution is revised and launched in order that revision may be expedited through his influence and given sanction under the existing legal framework. His abdication, if it occurs, will increase political instability in the government, and it may take a long time before an appropriately revised governmental structure takes solid root. But as between a long period of political confusion and the Imperial institution, the latter is undoubtedly the greater evil, and there seems little question that the Japanese people will never learn and follow the fundamental ways of democracy so long as the Imperial institution exists.

Japanese Democratic Political Situation (*Atcheson*)*

TOKYO, January 4, 1946

With the issuance today of a directive for the "denazification" of the bureaucracy, the basic preparatory actions for the democratization of Japan will have been taken. The arrest of major war criminals has been practically completed. The mandates for freedom of speech, press, and assembly, abolition of thought control, universal suffrage, dissolution of the zaibatsu, agrarian reform, collective bargaining by labor, disestablishment of Shinto, demilitarization of education—all are now on the record. These actions are not in themselves complete: the changes sought are too great to be accomplished by fiat. Among the most important of all, the constitution and its core—the emperor institution—have not yet been touched. But the scaffolding has been prepared; it remains to be seen what kind of structure is to be erected on it through revision of the constitution and the efforts of the Japanese themselves.

Those efforts will require our steady support and encouragement for a considerable time to come. Japan today, as is natural with its totalitarian background and after its recent demoralizing shock of defeat, is faced with a bankruptcy of capable, experienced, modern, and progressive political leadership.

The recently concluded Diet session proved the inability of most of the old political leaders to rise above their compromising (if not more tainted) pasts. . . .

The speed and completeness with which our final objectives can be realized will depend on the healthy development by the Japanese people of a democratic political consciousness. Japan's first postwar political party was inaugurated only two months ago. Since then four principal groups—Progressives, Liberals, Social Democrats, and Communists—have organized themselves and attained national importance. The "Progressives" are representatives

* U.S., Department of State, *Foreign Relations of the United States, 1946: The Far East*, vol. IX (Washington, D.C.: Government Printing Office), pp. 87–90.

of the past and wish no more change than necessary. The "Liberals" are by our standards conservative: their chief claim to liberalism is in impractical advocacy of a laissez-faire economy. The Social Democrats may be compared to the British Labor party. They have the backing of many intellectuals, are winning support among the middle class and organized labor, and appear at present to be the most promising group. The Communists are for complete abolition of the emperor institution, creation of a "republic," nationalization of land, and other traditional communist objectives—except that they espouse "democracy," private property, avoidance of class struggle.

Other minor political groups have not yet shown importance. A large number of small right-wing groups may become important if our control is greatly weakened or we lose our present goodwill and prestige, if the already severe economic hardship becomes desperation, or if communist expansion breeds violent political strife.

In this situation, there is obviously considerable encouragement for the Communists. Japan is groping for a new ideology to replace the shattered one which was so carefully and deliberately constructed during the years of military-feudal control. The old has been discredited and the new is attractive. Liberalism is vague and difficult to define. Communism is positive and concrete. It will be favored by the present serious economic insecurity. It will take at least moral encouragement from Soviet participation in control of Japan. But the popular hatred and fear of Russia and of communism will also be checks. The Communists as yet are too theoretical and too drastic for the political level of the people—particularly in their stand on the emperor. The great majority of the Japanese with whom I have talked do not expect them to become a dominant group in Japan. But they will grow stronger.

We must expect for some time, I believe, a situation in Japan which may be compared to that in postwar Italy. It is only natural that in the confusion, chaos, and demoralization, each group will try to salvage its own particular interests. However, the activities of the major parties are conducted against a background of at least four influential and favorable circumstances: (1) acceptance of the Potsdam Declaration—by the emperor—has committed the nation to some kind of democracy; (2) the old leaders who took the country into a war which ruined it are thoroughly discredited and hated; (3) even the conservatives desire, as a whole, to make a good showing toward fulfilling the terms they have accepted, if only so that they may the sooner be able to rejoin the family of "respectable" nations; and (4) there has been encouraging liberalization of the great and influential Japanese newspapers so that they have become sympathetic to, if not outright spokesmen for, groups such as the Social Democrats who sincerely wish to go further than merely "satisfying" occupational demands. . . .

One fundamental factor that we must not lose sight of in dealing with Japan is the inescapable relationship of politics and economics. In the dire straits of the Japanese people today, political development depends upon solution of the problems of food, shelter, and clothing. Today political education and experience in the practice of democracy are impeded by the preoccupation of the people with their economic distress. Left unsolved, these problems may encourage extremism of types we do not desire.

The courses for the future which are open to the United States (discounting drastic modification or restraint of our policy by the British, Soviet, and Chinese) depend to a large extent upon how much further effort we are prepared to put forth. If we are prepared to maintain for a period of years a large occupational force, if we are prepared to undertake that the Japanese shall have sufficient food, clothing, and shelter and be enabled to put their economy on its feet, if we are prepared—should that be necessary—to keep effective forces in Japan to take care of any contingency that might arise, then we can adopt a strongly aggressive political policy, try the emperor as a war criminal, and encourage the complete abolition of the emperor system. If we are not so prepared, we may do what we can and continue to proceed cautiously to give the Japanese the framework within which they may work out their own destiny—and then withdraw in due course and let them try it alone, whatever the result may be.

Decision hinges on the choice between these two admittedly oversimplified alternatives. The first is to my mind the ideal. I believe (and some of our allies may insist) that the emperor is a war criminal: even some Japanese argue that, if he had sufficient power to stop the war, he had the authority to prevent it. And I have not altered my opinion that the emperor system must disappear if Japan is ever to be really democratic.

But a number of circumstances seem to make the second, more

cautious policy the best for us to follow at this time. The speedy demobilization of our military forces is already creating handicaps. In this situation, in which we must continue to utilize the Japanese government for the administration of the country and the carrying out of reforms, there is no question that the emperor is most useful. He is obeyed by officials and the people at large. He manifests sincerity in wishing to aid in the accomplishment of our general objectives and is seemingly more anxious to be democratic than some of the people around him.

❃ ON MARCH 6, 1946, General MacArthur announced that the emperor and the government of Japan were presenting a constitution to the Japanese people. Coming a month before the April elections, this decided one issue: the emperor would remain. In one way, MacArthur's speech was misleading, since it implied some involvement of Japanese leaders in writing the new constitution. In fact, it is now generally regarded as having been forced on the government and translated into Japanese from the draft prepared by SCAP officials. A paradox of the constitution lies in the way it was passed down to the people from above. In this respect the event paralleled the promulgation of the Meiji constitution in 1889. Then, as in 1946, the constitution was presented as an act of good will on the part of the emperor.

*DOUGLAS MACARTHUR**
Statement on the Japanese Draft Constitution

March 6, 1946

It is with a sense of deep satisfaction that I am able today to announce a decision of the emperor and government of Japan to

* U.S., Department of State, *Foreign Relations of the United States, 1946: The Far East* (Washington, D.C.: Government Printing Office), pp. 132–133.

submit to the Japanese people a new and enlightened constitution which has my full approval. This instrument has been drafted after painstaking investigation and frequent conference between members of the Japanese government and this headquarters following my initial direction to the cabinet five months ago.

Declared by its terms to be the supreme law for Japan, it places sovereignty squarely in the hands of the people. It establishes governmental authority with the predominant power vested in an elected legislature, as representative of the people, but with adequate check upon that power, as well as upon the power of the executive and judiciary, to insure that no branch of government may become autocratic or arbitrary in the administration of affairs of state.

It leaves the throne without governmental authority or state property, subject to the people's will, a symbol of the people's unity. It provides for and guarantees to the people fundamental human liberties which satisfy the most exacting standards of enlightened thought.

It severs for all time the shackles of feudalism and in its place raises the dignity of man under protection of the people's sovereignty. It is throughout responsive to the most advanced concept of human relations—is an eclectic instrument, realistically blending the several divergent political philosophies which intellectually honest men advocate.

Foremost of its provisions is that which, abolishing war as a sovereign right of the nation, forever renounces the threat or use of force as a means of settling disputes with any other nation and forbids in future the authorization of any army, navy, air force, or other war potential or assumption of rights of belligerency by the state. By this undertaking and commitment Japan surrenders rights inherent in her own sovereignty and renders her future security and very survival subject to the good faith and justice of the peace-loving peoples of the world. By it does a nation, recognizing the futility of war as an arbiter of international issues, chart a new course oriented to faith in the justice, tolerance, and understanding of mankind.

The Japanese people thus turn their backs firmly upon the mysticism and unreality of the past and face instead a future of realism with a new faith and a new hope.

MARK GAYN*
Drafting the Japanese Constitution

TOKYO, March 6, 1946

All of us trekked to the premier's residence today, to the office of Wataru Narahashi, secretary of the cabinet, to hear the announcement of a new constitution. Narahashi is a stocky, bushy-haired, self-confident man in striped pants, black coat, and a stiff wing collar.

"The new constitution," he said, "is an epoch-making document. . . . In it, the emperor himself proclaims the people sovereign, as provided in the Potsdam Declaration. In it, we declare militarism is dead. . . . Through the adoption of this constitution, the emperor will become a symbol above the people, and people will also realize this is their government. . . ."

He answered some of our questions in fluent French. "We're in a very dangerous situation," he said, "and in order to avoid a bloody revolution, we must take revolutionary steps, such as this constitution. Some people say this is a government of peers. But I myself am a coal miner, and I began to work at the age of fourteen. I think I know what the people want."

. . . This is the story that went to the four corners of the earth— as yet another proof of Japan's cooperation and rapid advance toward democracy.

But there is a story behind the story, which Bob Cochrane, of the *Baltimore Sun,* and I are now piecing together. Like the new constitution itself, it belongs to the history of the occupation.

One night a month ago, key officers in General MacArthur's Government Section were told in extreme confidence that they would have to draft a new constitution for Japan. In an informal session at the Dai-Ichi Hotel, the broad outline of the document was sketched out. The next morning, General Whitney called his entire staff into the conference room.

"Ladies and gentlemen," he said solemnly, "this is an historic occasion. I now proclaim you a constitutional assembly."

* Mark Gayn, *Japan Diary* (New York: William Sloan Associates, 1948), pp. 125–131.

A former Manila lawyer, Whitney also is somewhat of an actor. In the speech he made, he alternated between solemnity, pathos, and political harangue. The most pressing issue of the hour in Japan, he said, is a new constitution. All the drafts prepared by the Japanese have been completely unsatisfactory, and the Supreme Commander—he pronounced it "Commahnder"—felt it was necessary for him to intervene. The Government Section was being given the assignment of drafting a new constitution. Extreme haste and secrecy would be necessary, so as to take the Japanese by complete surprise, and prevent them from organizing an effective opposition.

"I'm greatly flattered," Whitney said, "that the Supreme Commander considered the Government Section capable of drafting the constitution, and in such a short time. I asked the Supreme Commander if he wished to indicate the lines to be followed in drafting the new constitution, and the general replied he would leave the entire job to the expert judgment of this section—but with these three exceptions. . . ."

Whitney recited the three points which General MacArthur wanted to see in the new Japanese constitution:

(1) Japan was to renounce war forever, abolish her armed forces, and pledge never to revive them;

(2) While sovereignty was to be vested in the people, the emperor was to be described as a symbol of the state;

(3) The peerage was to be abolished, and the property of the Imperial household was to revert to the state.

The men who had taken part in the informal session the previous night were totally unprepared for the first point. All three points, however, provoked numerous questions.

"I assume from Point Two," said one questioner, "that the emperor would not be tried as a war criminal."

Colonel C. L. Kades, deputy chief of the section and a former Treasury Counsel, replied that he agreed with the assumption. General MacArthur, in his opinion, felt that the emperor had atoned for any past errors by his wholehearted support of the occupation.

"I would consider it a gross breach of faith," Whitney said, "if the emperor were to be tried as a war criminal after all the services he had rendered to the Allies."

Originally, it was intended to draft the new constitution in ten days. General Whitney had expressed his hope that it could be announced by the Japanese on February 22—George Washington's birthday.

At General Whitney's opening "constitutional assembly," teams were set up, each with the job of writing one or more chapters of the constitution. The team captains together formed a steering committee, which was to coordinate the work. There was a feverish study of American and European constitutions, but on the whole the new constitution followed the pattern of the old Meiji constitution which is to be discarded. Kades and Commander Alfred R. Hussey Jr., U.S.N., took on the job of drafting the preamble. There is good reason to believe that the provision renouncing war and armed forces was originally drafted by General MacArthur himself.

The entire job was finished in two weeks. On February 19, General Whitney sprang the constitution on the Japanese.

Cochrane and I have been unable to find out whether the meeting took place in the residence of Premier Shidehara or Dr. Jōji Matsumoto, the ultraconservative lawyer who was "revising" the old constitution. General Whitney took Colonel Kades and Commander Hussey along. When the three Americans entered the room, they were met by Matsumoto, Foreign Minister Shigeru Yoshida, and a slippery character named Shirasu, who was now vice-chief of the Central Liaison Office. We believed that Premier Shidehara and his cabinet secretary, Narahashi, were also present.

The Japanese apparently had been studying the Matsumoto draft before the Americans came in. Anyway, it was spread on a desk. The Americans later said the atmosphere was one of an anticipated horse trade. General Whitney strode to the table, looked at the papers on it, and said:

"Gentlemen, the Supreme Commander has studied the draft prepared by you. He finds it totally unacceptable. I've brought with me a document which has the approval of the Supreme Commander. I'll leave it with you for fifteen minutes, so that you can read it before we discuss it."

The three Americans then withdrew to the adjoining porch. Through the windows they could see the Japanese huddled over the document. Just about then, a U.S. bomber buzzed the house. It was a well-timed incident, even if General Whitney insisted that it had been unscheduled.

At the end of fifteen minutes, Shirasu came in to summon the Americans. As General Whitney reentered the room, he said dramatically:

"We've just been basking in the warmth of the atomic sunshine."

The Americans noticed that the Matsumoto draft had been removed from the desk, which now held only General Whitney's draft. The Japanese looked thunderstruck. Shirasu, who acted as interpreter, actually opened his mouth several times, but no sound came out.

The Japanese devoted the next few minutes to fishing for information in an effort to discover room for compromise. They argued that the American draft had gone far beyond anything that they had ever considered, and that it was totally un-Japanese in its tradition. Whitney replied firmly that General MacArthur would not consider any document which did not go as far, although he would be willing to consider minor modifications which did not violate the spirit of the American draft.

"If you are not prepared to sponsor a document of this type," he said, "General MacArthur will go over your heads to the Japanese people. But if you will support a constitution of this kind, General MacArthur will support you."

The Americans left after a few polite remarks. Hussey later wrote a detailed account of the interview for the record, and it was read to the staff at a general meeting. The memorandum emphasized that the Japanese had been taken by surprise, and the Americans therefore enjoyed a marked advantage.

The Japanese are excellent politicians, and the surprise did not last. As soon as they recovered from the shock they began to play for time. Their first move was a plea that, since they had seen the new constitution only in English, they could not properly evaluate it. Therefore, they insisted that the new Japanese constitution be translated into Japanese. A staff of Government Section interpreters worked all day Sunday, but when the translation was done the Japanese claimed that it was "simply not Japanese" in word or spirit. There was some more haggling over the wording.

· Time wasted away, and General Whitney finally informed the Japanese that Headquarters would announce the draft on its own, thus denying the government an opportunity to identify itself with the new constitution. The Japanese then capitulated. Today's announcement was the result.

The American constitution for Japan is not a bad constitution. Despite the doubletalk of the Japanese officials, it vests sovereign power in the people; it guarantees civil liberties; it provides for checks and balances on the government's actions.

What is wrong—disastrously wrong—is that this constitution does not come from the Japanese grass roots. It is an alien constitution foisted on the Japanese government, and then represented as a native product, when any Japanese high-school student simply by reading it can perceive its foreign origin.

The Far Eastern Commission has been aware of the dangers of an imposed constitution. During its recent visit here, it insisted on letting the Japanese themselves formulate their basic law and exacted an assurance from Headquarters that that would be done. Only a few weeks later, this promise was broken. The lame explanation by one of Whitney's aides was that the original undertaking was based on the assumption that the constitution was a long-range problem, "while the events have proved it a matter of immediate business."

And nothing in the constitution is more wrong than General MacArthur's own provision for the renunciation of armed forces. For no one who has read the morning papers or studied Japanese history can doubt that as soon as the occupation ends the Japanese under one pretext or another will re-create their army. That is as inevitable in Japan as earthquakes. By its very nature, the new constitution thus invites circumvention. No constitution in which fraud is inherent can survive.

What is more, the new constitution is being passed on to the Japanese through unclean hands.

What better illustration of this is needed than the fact that Japan's spokesman for a new democratic constitution today was a man who, by his own admission, was an agent of the Japanese Army in China? Wataru Narahashi, who may yet be the premier of Japan, reminded the voters in the "Tōjō elections" of 1942 that eighteen months before the attack on Pearl Harbor he "took part in the reconstruction of East Asia, and cooperated with the Japanese Army in North China." Today, by one of those incredible Japanese paradoxes, he decides who among the candidates running in next month's elections is a war criminal.

No one can fathom the motives of the Americans who have tailored the new constitution for Japan. One motive could be General MacArthur's desire to go down in history as the maker of Japan's basic law. Another could be the military man's belief that anything could be done through a military order—even a democratic constitution. And no one apparently has thought of the contradiction inherent in the idea that any constitution forced down a nation's throat could be democratic.

⚜ ANOTHER WRITER on the occupation, T. A. Bisson, felt that keeping the emperor even in a titular position could provide the cornerstone for the revival of a nationalist and militaristic Japan. Yet there were important steps made toward representative government in the new constitution. In the Diet, the elected Lower House in the parliament gained real power. The cabinet, formerly autonomous, was now directly responsible to the Diet. A vote of "no confidence," as in the British system, could force a new election. Seats in the Upper House were no longer held for life, and in many cases it lost its veto power over Lower House decisions.

T. A. BISSON*
The Constitution and the Retention of the Emperor

. . . Revisions of the constitution and its associated laws made the Diet, and more particularly the House of Representatives, the

* T. A. Bisson, *Prospects for Democracy in Japan* (New York: Macmillan, 1949), pp. 20–25.

"highest organ of state power." Long regular Diet sessions thus became necessary. The cabinet could summon extraordinary sessions on its own initiative, but was obliged to call such sessions on a vote of at least one-fourth of the total membership of either house. Legislation passed by the House of Representatives was no longer subject to the veto of the Upper House. On money bills and treaties, the Lower House could override an Upper House veto by a simple majority vote; on other matters, a two-thirds' majority was required. Revision of the Election Law enfranchised women and lowered the voting age from twenty-five to twenty. Amendments to the Diet Law brought the pay of Diet members up to that of top-ranking bureaucrats, enlarged the rights of private members and of minority groups, and empowered both houses of the Diet to hold open hearings on legislative measures, to subpoena witnesses, and to conduct investigations.

Under the revised constitution, furthermore, the cabinet was made collectively responsible to the Diet. The prime minister was to be appointed by the two houses and, in case of disagreement, the decision of the Lower House was to prevail. All cabinet ministers, including the prime minister, had to be civilians and a majority had to be members of the Diet. A no confidence vote in the Diet obliged the cabinet either to resign or to dissolve the House of Representatives within ten days and undergo the test of a new election. Either house could conduct investigations of the government, demand the presence and testimony of witnesses and access to official records, and require the presence of ministers to give answers or explanations. Cabinet orders—replacing Imperial ordinances—were permitted when necessary to execute provisions of the constitution or Diet enactments. Such orders, however, could not include penal sanctions unless specifically authorized to do so by the acts that they were designed to implement.

The foregoing brief summary is sufficient to indicate that far-reaching changes were made in the governmental structure of Japan to bring it in line with democratic principles and practices. In these matters the occupation was nevertheless dealing only with the institutional framework of Japanese political life. Beyond this lay the more fundamental and far more difficult problem presented by the strongly entrenched group interests that had controlled the old regime and were fighting vigorously to establish a similar control over the new.

THE EMPEROR'S ROLE

If one were asked to choose typical examples of the political problems confronting the occupation, the role of the emperor might well head the list. Under the old regime, the emperor was the keystone in a carefully constructed system of authoritarian government designed to meet the needs of the ruling oligarchy. Belief in the emperor's divinity was inculcated in the people of Japan by every means known to modern propaganda. Actions taken in his name had an authority far exceeding that of purely mundane governmental edicts. A repressive regime at home and an aggressive foreign policy were sold to the Japanese people as essential aspects of their "divine mission" to bring the world under the beneficent rule of the Son of Heaven. . . .

Under the aegis of the occupation, the emperor has conducted himself so circumspectly and shrewdly that his position now appears secure. During the early months of the occupation, he effectively assisted the occupation authorities in the task of demobilizing the Japanese armed forces. His public pronouncements and other actions contributed a great deal to the peaceful reception that greeted the occupation forces in Japan. On January 1, 1946, undoubtedly in response to a "suggestion" from Supreme Headquarters, the emperor also issued a statement to the Japanese people disavowing his divinity. On the whole, during this early period, he gave valuable support to the occupation authorities, although there were still grounds for questioning whether this support represented adequate compensation for the past, or complete assurance for the future.

Evidence presented at the war crimes trials in Tokyo during 1946–1947 proved conclusively that Emperor Hirohito had been an intimate participant in all the major decisions that led to the attack on Pearl Harbor. But this sort of evidence came out bit by bit, at a time when American public interest had shifted to Europe, and, while somewhat embarrassing to the occupation authorities, it received little publicity and had no noticeable effect on policy. By then the American authorities in Tokyo had decided that the emperor's services to the occupation were too useful to permit action to be taken against him, and they were under no pressure from American public opinion to reverse this decision.

The amended constitution sanctioned retention of the emperor as "the symbol of the state and of the unity of the people." But it vested sovereignty in the people and sought to limit the emperor's authority to the strictly ceremonial functions of a constitutional monarch. The list of state acts allotted to the emperor are to be performed "on behalf of the people" and "with the advice and approval of the cabinet." His wealth and estates have been largely transferred to the national treasury, leaving him dependent on appropriations voted annually by the Diet. The formerly independent and powerful Imperial Household Ministry has been reduced to the status of an Imperial House Office under the jurisdiction of the prime minister. On the Imperial House Council of ten members sit the heads of both houses of the Diet, the prime minister, and the chief justice of the Supreme Court.

With changes of this scope and character, it would seem that every precaution had been taken to ensure the establishment of a limited constitutional monarchy in Japan. It would nevertheless be premature to assume that the best possible course has been followed in dealing with the emperor system.

Retention of the emperor, even with the drastic modifications effected in his formal constitutional powers, has left the cornerstone of the old structure untouched, and facilitated the oligarchy's efforts to preserve its control. In Japan the tradition of "divine right" is still powerful, and there is no background of a popular struggle to limit monarchical power, such as we find in the West. The very fact that the occupation authorities have worked through the emperor is sufficient to encourage the Japanese people to continue their former dependence on the emperor, instead of striking out on a new and independent path. On November 3, 1946, when the new constitution was promulgated, the cheers of the crowds assembled in the Imperial plaza were raised to the emperor rather than to the constitution—an omen of the future if reactionary forces should succeed in establishing control over the new regime.

Since the surrender, the emperor has visited all thirty-two prefectures on the main island of Honshu, and received ovations from millions of Japanese who never saw him before. His tours about the country during 1947 alone cost about 300 million yen—forty times the sum appropriated by the Diet to cover his personal establishment. Prefectural, city, and local governments, as well as private organizations of many types, raised the funds to pay for his receptions, and helped to turn out the crowds that greeted him.

The sentiments of veneration expressed in these gatherings went far beyond those normally existing between a democratic-minded people and a constitutional monarch. In a Tokyo dispatch (December 17, 1947) the *New York Herald Tribune* correspondent, Allen Raymond, noted: "Japanese emperor-worship is like a stout tree that bends before a Western breeze but does not break. The carefully planned 'democratization' of the emperor bids fair to make him an even greater symbol of Japanese nationalism than ever before."

☯ ALTHOUGH A MEMBER of the ruling wartime triumvirate, with the military and the business elite, the Japanese government bureaucracy was spared the extensive occupation purging that hit the economic and military elites. John Maki, writing in late 1947, saw the carefully trained and chosen bureaucratic elite as a possible obstacle to democratizing Japan. Their power rested on the American decision to use existing governmental machinery during the occupation. This gave them numerous opportunities to manipulate policy differences within SCAP, as well as to obstruct occupation reforms.

JOHN M. MAKI*
The Role of the Bureaucracy in Japan

If any single organized group in Japan today possesses the power to prevent the creation of a peaceful, responsible form of government in that country, it is the bureaucracy. Neither the elimination and barring of influential bureaucrats from public office nor sweeping changes in the structure of Japanese government have yet been sufficient in themselves to alter the basic character of the bureauc-

* John M. Maki, "The Role of the Bureaucracy in Japan," *Pacific Affairs* XX:4 (December 1947), pp. 391, 392–393, 395–400.

racy. More than any other organized group in contemporary Japan it is rooted in Japan's presurrender past. . . .

It is a striking fact that nowhere in either American or Allied basic policy for Japan is the bureaucracy as a class mentioned as a target for the reforms necessary to achieve the establishment of a "peaceful and responsible government" in Japan. A relative unawareness of the significant political role of the bureaucrats, and the decision to continue the Japanese government as the machinery through which the occupation would operate, undoubtedly account for the absence of a definitely formulated antibureaucracy policy. But if occupation policy has been comparatively uninterested in the role of the bureaucracy, the bureaucrats have been subjected to moves intended to circumscribe their authority or to recast their role as a class so that they will relinquish their previous position in Japanese government. These moves, however, fall far short of the antimilitarist, antizaibatsu programs and cannot be expected to have even the possibly limited effectiveness of the latter. . . .

The strength of the bureaucracy in the past and its threat to the creation of a peaceful and responsible government in the Japan of tomorrow lie in two complementary sources: first, the bureaucracy has grown directly out of the Japanese theory of irresponsible government, and, second, it has enjoyed an existence as a governing class. The former constitutes the theoretical basis of its strength, and the latter the practical basis of its power.

One searches Japanese history in vain for either substantial or significant instances of the operation of responsible government within the accepted meaning of that term. Instances can be found of what might be termed "benevolent" government, that is, rule under which the general welfare of the ruled was considered, but these were local and the result of individual caprice. In every period of Japanese history, government was based on the principle of government of, by, and for the governing groups whether court nobility, feudal lords, or the modern militarist-zaibatsu-bureaucrat oligarchy. . . .

While the external factors of political tradition, the specific political situation, and the old constitution gave the bureaucracy great strength, its internal cohesion as a class, as an administrative elite, afforded it additional power. . . .

The bureaucrats (in other words, those who occupy positions of administrative or executive authority) constitute a relatively small group. It is estimated that there were about 4000 in 1945. Yet each member of this group shared a common training, a common tradition, a common ideology, and a common desire to monopolize what the group regarded as the skills of government. . . .

The decision taken by the United States (and concurred in by the Allies) to retain a Japanese government in power after the surrender, although it was to be completely under the control of the Supreme Commander for the Allied Powers, meant, in effect, that the bureaucracy would escape the fate to be dealt out to the militarists and the zaibatsu. This was no mere oversight nor a desire to appease certain potentially dangerous elements in Japan. . . .

The decision to retain a Japanese government in power solved the immediate and major problem of ensuring an effective administrative system under the occupation. At the same time, however, it created a long-term problem—a possibly retarding effect on the achievement of the basic objectives of the occupation through the unavoidable use of a bureaucracy which could neither understand nor bring itself effectively to cooperate in the development of a "peaceful and responsible government." There is no question but that the retention of the bureaucracy has added immeasurably to the success of the occupation. On the other hand, its retention has given Japan certain crucial advantages over the occupation that are often overlooked. The most concrete example is the Central Liaison Office, a brilliant administrative and political device that has undoubtedly been of major service to the Japanese government.

As far as is known, the Central Liaison Office is a purely Japanese creation, set up on the Japanese government's own initiative without prompting from the occupation. It was established on August 26, 1945, a week before the surrender instrument was signed, to handle relations between the Japanese government and the occupation authorities. It is under the jurisdiction of the Foreign Ministry, although it is not organically incorporated into the regular structure of the ministry, undoubtedly because it fulfills what is essentially a temporary function in Japan's foreign relations. The CLO was and is, however, an administrative necessity. Briefly described, it is the channel through which business between the occupation and the Japanese government is conducted. For example, directives from GHQ, SCAP (General Headquarters, Supreme Commander for the Allied Powers—that part of General MacArthur's headquarters in charge of occupation affairs), are transmitted to the Japanese government through the CLO; documents, information, and reports from the Japanese government to GHQ, SCAP, are transmitted through the CLO; all official appointments between occupation and Japanese officials are arranged by the CLO; and all translations of important documents are made or supervised by the CLO. Certain types of business are, of course, transacted informally without recourse in the CLO, but the initial contacts are invariably established by it. In addition, the CLO has jurisdiction over a nationwide network of Local Liaison Offices, which were established to perform liaison work between local military government teams and the Japanese local authorities.

The foregoing sketch indicates the great value of the CLO as an intelligence agency for the Japanese government. Not only is it privy to all matters currently of interest to GHQ, SCAP; it is also in a position to maintain at least informal dossiers on each and every official with whom it deals—and even a knowledge of the pro- or anti-Japanese attitudes of certain officials can be of great use to the Japanese government. Naturally, it is also in a key position to observe the individual and administrative rivalries and conflicts in GHQ, SCAP. Such specific information, in addition to an intimate knowledge of the general atmosphere prevailing at occupation headquarters, undoubtedly gives the Japanese government an accurate picture of the current aims, attitudes, and interests, as distinct from the long-range policy, of the occupation. . . .

The CLO is perhaps one of the most striking examples of the ingenuity, administrative awareness, and political shrewdness of the bureaucracy in its relations with the occupation. But the bureaucracy has other advantages of both immediate and long-range significance.

In spite of the operation of the purge and the routine shifts of personnel from one position to another, the bureaucracy has enjoyed the great advantage of a stable personnel as compared with that of the occupation forces. Demobilization, now an old and almost forgotten story, robbed the occupation of some of its most effective men within six months after its inception. In addition, American unwillingness to spend money on the administration of foreign areas, as well as the reluctance or inability of individual Americans to serve with the occupation at the cost of personal sacrifice, have undoubtedly prevented the assembling of a staff, military and civilian, as expert as a successful occupation would require. The stability of its own personnel has therefore given the Japanese government a great advantage, for it favors the achievement not only of relatively short-term objectives but of long-range aims as well.

Although several hundred bureaucrats (complete up-to-date figures are not available) were removed from public office and barred from government service, the bureaucrats were not made specific targets of the purge as were, for example, army officers and members of secret intelligence and police organizations connected with the services. Those bureaucrats who were purged were removed because of militaristic, ultranationalistic, or otherwise aggressive activities carried on outside of or in addition to their regular duties. Consequently, few bureaucrats have been purged simply because of their activities as bureaucrats.

In addition to that represented by continuity of personnel, the bureaucracy has another great advantage over the occupation: namely, a desire to preserve and to protect most of what it believes to be the essentials of the Japanese way of life and system of government, at the expense of a minimum of friction with the occupation and under as brief an occupation as possible. In other words, the Japanese bureaucrats as individual Japanese have a much greater conscious stake in the ultimate results of the occupation than do any members of the occupation forces.

Perhaps the greatest single advantage that the bureaucrats enjoy over the occupation is time. The occupation, the Japanese know, is bound to end eventually. To the bureaucrats the end of the occupation will signify freedom to operate as they wish, without the restraints and constraints that have been placed on them by the occupation. They may not act as they did in presurrender days, but they know that they will once more be in a position to govern Japan as they think it should be governed. Conversely, there are few good officials in the occupation who can rid themselves of the feeling that much of what they now hope will be permanent in the reform of Japan may vanish as soon as the occupation ends.

❀ THE HOME MINISTRY, although finally abolished in 1947, continued for the first two years of the occupation with some of its former functions, particularly leftist-watching. The Home Ministry had controlled the nationally centralized police, and it also held extensive powers over local governmental officers. It was thus a crucial organ of state power. In the following passage Mark Gayn speaks with a former Thought Control Police (*Tokkō*) official who has found a niche in the new regime. The man's position reflects the slowness of reform, the staying power of the bureaucracy, and the early SCAP support of anticommunist activities.

MARK GAYN*
Interview with Tokkō *Official*

TOKYO, November 27, 1946

A few days ago, I asked my friend, Chikosaburō Hayami, the cabinet adviser, what had happened to the men who once held high posts in *Tokkō,* or Thought Control Police. He smiled his usual vague smile and said he would find out. This morning he called up to ask if he could come to lunch "with a friend who knows a great deal about *Tokkō.*"

He came in with a small, trim man of about fifty, whom he introduced as "Shigenori Hata, chief of the Fourth Section of the Investigation Bureau in the Home Ministry."

He paused for effect. "Mr. Hata is a former *Tokkō* official."

At first Mr. Hata was cautious. He drank pineapple juice instead of whiskey, and he answered in monosyllables. But Hayami has a way of getting his friends to talk to me. By the time we sat at the table for lunch, Hata had begun to talk.

During the war—between 1941 and 1944—Hata served as

* Mark Gayn, *Japan Diary* (New York: William Sloan Associates, 1948), pp. 457–459.

chief of the Thought Control Division in the Tokyo Metropolitan
Police Board. He had about sixty men directly under him, and his
main job was hunting for Communists. When the Tōjō cabinet fell,
Hata was promoted to prefectural police chief, first in Kagawa and
then in Shiga.

I asked him the question that was on many minds during the
war: Had there been an antimilitarist underground in Japan after
Pearl Harbor?

Hata said that only the Communists had been active. While he
was in Tokyo, he said, he arrested between two hundred and three
hundred of them a year. By the time he left for Kagawa, the
number of Communists still at large had dwindled down to
"twenty or thirty, with about a thousand sympathizers." These
men were organized in tiny "cells" of four or five men each, and
since agitation for higher pay was forbidden the Communists
engaged either in agitation for "better working conditions" or in
petty sabotage.

"There were small fires," he said, "or something went wrong
with the machinery, or ammunition was found to be defective. But
all this was on a small scale, and it was difficult to find the cul-
prits."

Over coffee, Hata told us the story of *Tokkō* and its successful
efforts to retain power after Japan's surrender.

"Before the war," he said, *"Tokkō* was a hand-picked force. To
recruit it, the Home Ministry combed the field for bright men. They
were farmed out to other government departments. Membership in
Tokkō won for us special honors and privileges. A governor, for
instance, could dismiss his section chiefs at will. But he could do
nothing to a *Tokkō* man serving under him, for *Tokkō* people were
appointed from Tokyo.

"Take the year I went into *Tokkō,* for instance. There were fifty-
eight of us that year, all lawyers. We all came into the Home
Ministry at one time and were given special training. Then the
ministry scattered us. We served through the years of the China
Incident, the Great Far Eastern War, and the early days of the
occupation. We knew the purge directive was coming out in
October 1945, and we resigned beforehand.

"Today most of us are back in important posts. Some are in the
Ministry of Education. Others are in the Ministry of Welfare. These
include the chief of the Labor Division. Still others are in the

Ministry of Commerce. Several, including the chief of the Wood and Charcoal Section, are in the Ministry of Forestry and Agriculture."

The list grew. It was not amusing that the man in charge of charcoal rationing was a *Tokkō* man: charcoal is a Japanese housewife's only fuel for warmth or cooking, and it is a potent instrument of political pressure. It was even less funny that the man who watches over the growth of democratic labor unions is a man who once helped to destroy them.

"Two prefectural governors," said Hata, "are *Tokkō* alumni. Two or three *Tokkō* men who served in Korea through the war have now come back to key positions in the Home Ministry. Minor *Tokkō* officials, who had served in the provinces, have now been pulled back to Tokyo, to fill subordinate government jobs."

"Early this year," Hata said, "while he was still head of the Liberal party, Mr. Hatoyama started organizing an Anti-Communist League. It was doing nicely when Mr. Hatoyama was purged as a war criminal. For a while there was a hiatus. But now the Japanese Federation of Labor is making ready to launch a major anticommunist campaign. The federation is run by right-wing Social Democrats. They hope the campaign will help them to get rid of communist competition.

"In general, the anticommunist campaigns are significant. If a powerful ultranationalist movement reappears in this country it will begin as an anticommunist crusade. That's inevitable. But right now there's no integrated ultranationalist movement yet. Just numerous small groups of ex-servicemen and former nationalists who gather secretly in private homes and discuss the next step. They are in difficulty. In the past, the nationalists got their money from the army and from blackmail of big business. All this has now stopped. What's worse, there is a philosophical vacuum. Most of the men who once shaped nationalist thought are dead. Thus, the nationalist movement is still in ferment. It has a will; it has little money and no philosophy."

I asked Hata which government organs now kept an eye on the leftists—the communists, the labor movement, the farm unions.

"The job is divided," he said. "The Welfare Ministry, the Home Ministry, the Metropolitan Police Board." He thought a moment. "It was much better before," he said wistfully. "Then, everything was in our hands."

A little sharply, I said: "There are reports of a new purge. Aren't you afraid you might be purged too?"

"I don't think so," said Hata. "After all, my section has been set up at the request of your army."

⌬ THE PURGE of "undesirable personnel" from public life was aimed at preventing remilitarization and at encouraging the democratization of Japan. Stymied by Japanese leaders and the bureaucracy, its effectiveness was mixed. Only a few bureaucrats, but many high-level politicians, economic leaders, and military officials, were purged. Moreover, the delay in purging local government officials, lower-ranking business officials, and leaders in the information media helped consolidate the rule of the conservative Liberal and Progressive parties. The impact of the political purge fell mainly on the top leadership.

When the occupation became overtly more conservative— interested in economic recovery, not democratization—the purge originally aimed at the right wing was turned on the communists and other radicals. Meanwhile, many early purgees were being rehabilitated. The effect was to help reestablish the old elites with much of their former power.

HANS H. BAERWALD*
The Purge of Japanese Leaders Under the Occupation

TIMING OF PHASES

The timing of the various phases of the purge made its impact uneven during the years when it was operative. Its implementing phase reached the high-water mark in 1948. By May of that year

* Hans H. Baerwald, The Purge of Japanese Leaders Under the Occupation (Berkeley and Los Angeles: University of California Press, 1959), pp. 78–80, 82–90.

the Japanese government had designated some 200,000 purgees. Concurrently, their surveillance was in the hands of a fairly effective investigating agency. Before 1948, the impact that the purge might have had was limited by the fact that the designation process had not yet been completed. As a result, potential purgees still held positions of trust in public life. Furthermore, control over the activities of those designated had been practically nonexistent. During 1946, when the purge might have had its greatest influence on every important category of Japanese leadership, only personnel in the national government were affected by it. Subsequent to the summer of 1948, the purge became a holding operation.

The "reverse course" which dominated the formulation of policy during the occupation's later years (1948–1952) also influenced the implementation of the purge. Successive waves of appeals and rescinding of entire purge categories brought an ever-increasing group of purgees back into public life. . . . As a result of these reinstatements only 8710 persons were still purgees by the effective date of the peace treaty.

By contrast, in 1950 SCAP utilized the purge to remove from influence the leadership of the Japan Communist party. (In addition, some 20,997 Communists and fellow travelers lost their jobs in government, information media, and private industry in the period 1949–1951.) The occupation objective that Japan emerge from the period of tutelage with a leadership of moderates was compromised by the timing of the so-called "Red purge," for the latter coincided with the release from designation of the political extreme right.

Finally, the relatively short duration of time during which the purge was operative must be taken into consideration. General Whitney had stated in June 1948, "Final action taken under the purge program is regarded to be of a permanent nature for which the Allied powers will unquestionably hold future Japanese governments fully responsible." This statement was in consonance with the clause of the Potsdam Declaration upon which rested the whole superstructure of the purge program. A clause to this effect should have been included in the peace treaty in order to have made effective the permanency of the purge. This, however, was not done. As a result the Japanese government issued ordinances revoking the purge in its entirety, and these came into force the day after the peace treaty became official. . . .

BUREAUCRATS

The purge removed a relatively small group from the ranks of the bureaucracy; nearly 100 military or ex-military personnel were designated for every bureaucrat purged. Few of the purge criteria were specifically aimed at eliminating members of the civil service. Criteria purging cabinet ministers and high public officials affected 145 members of the senior civil service; criteria concerning political police and "thought" procurators affected 356 individuals; and those criteria concerning governors of occupied territories purged eighty-nine. The vast majority (1219) of bureaucrats fell under the so-called *Butokukai* (Military Virtue Society) criteria. Considerable controversy surrounded the inclusion of the *Butokukai* in the purge criteria. The organization's officers were for the most part police officials in the home ministry. Criteria purging its officials were among the very few designed to remove lower-echelon civil bureaucrats, in particular police personnel. Out of the total of 1809 bureaucrats purged, the *Butokukai* criteria accounted for sixty-seven percent. . . .

POLITICIANS

The impact of the purge on the political elite can best be seen by analyzing its effect on political party leadership. One category of purge criteria, that concerning the Imperial Rule societies, was the handle by which undesirable elements in the political elite were purged. Out of a total of 34,892 designated as purgees in this group, 34,396 had been national or prefectural officials of the Imperial Rule Assistance Association (*Taisei Yokusan Kai*) and its affiliates; 434 had been Diet members "recommended" to the voters by the Imperial Rule Assistance Political Society (*Taisei Yokusan Seiji Kai*) in the 1942 wartime election. The remainder (sixty-two) were leaders of the Communist party designated in 1950.

Leadership of the Progressive party was the most seriously affected by the purge in its initial stage. This party had held a majority of the seats (274 out of 466) in the pre-1946 election Diet. Only twenty-seven wartime Diet members who had joined the Progressive party upon the dissolution of the Imperial Rule Assistance Political Society (*Taisei Yokusan Seiji Kai*) remained un-affected by the initial purge order. . . .

The Progressive party initially attempted to reconstitute itself on the basis of its local organizational structure, which remained intact until the extension of the purge to local government officers in 1947. With the extension of the purge, some of the party leaders recognized that the party would have to reorganize itself and redefine its policy orientation if it were to survive as a force in Japanese politics. Consequently, one faction made a valiant attempt to revitalize the party by adopting a less reactionary platform. It was partly successful in ousting the entrenched leadership of Shidehara Kijūrō, and renamed the organization the Democratic party. It had to overcome the purge of four important reorganizers—Inukai Ken, Narahashi Wataru, Ishiguro Takeshige, and Chizaki Usaburō. The Central Screening Committee under the chairmanship of Matsushima had designated them within the three weeks just before the 1947 election. The widely held contention that these removals were motivated by political considerations was supported by two principal lines of argument. First, Shidehara resented the revolt within the Progressive party against his leadership, which had been headed by Ashida Hitoshi and the four individuals named above. Also, Yoshida was anxious to see a union between the two conservative parties (Liberal and Democratic); he believed that it could more readily take place if Shidehara's leadership remained unchallenged. In 1948, Shidehara and his faction did join a partial amalgamation of conservative forces entitled the Democratic-Liberal party.

The Liberal party, conservative party colleague of the Progressive party, initially sustained less formidable blows. Of its fifty members in the lame-duck session held over from the wartime Diet, only ten were purged. The party lost 198 individuals destined for high office in the years 1946–1948.

Hatoyama's designation as a purgee on the very day that a letter to SCAP from Premier Shidehara recommended him as the next prime minister was the most substantial loss suffered by the Liberal party. This instance of the purge of one man serves as an excellent example of the fact that the impact of the purge cannot be measured merely in numbers of individuals purged. The purge of a potential prime minister had far greater repercussions on politics than could the designation of thousands of Imperial Rule Society branch chiefs or the like. Yoshida Shigeru, upon whom Hatoyama conferred his mantle of leadership, regrouped Liberal party forces. He relied on a few old party bosses such as Ōno Bamboku but depended most heavily on ex-bureaucrats to fill party ranks. This was an astute move in terms of the purge, for the removal program did not cut too deeply into the ranks of Japan's professional officialdom.

What had been the career of Yoshida Shigeru, who replaced Hatoyama Ichirō? Yoshida, whose tenure as prime minister extended from April 1946 through April 1947 and from October 1948 to April 1952 (a total of fifty-five out of the occupation's eighty months), had had a long and varied career. He had been consul general in Mukden at the time of Marshal Chang Tso-lin's assassination. (No evidence has ever come to light indicating that he played a part in the marshal's demise.) Yoshida had also been vice-minister of foreign affairs in the Tanaka Giichi cabinet which had followed a "strong" (euphemism for expansionist) policy vis-à-vis China. Hatoyama had served as chief cabinet secretary in this cabinet, and this service was among the reasons given for his purge. Whether Yoshida should be included among those who had "played an active and predominant governmental part in the Japanese program of aggression" was the subject of considerable controversy. Yoshida was saved from the purge by the fact of his participation in the 1945 spring "peace plot" for which pains he was temporarily incarcerated by the gendarmerie (*kempeitai*). This is the only major difference between the careers of Yoshida and Hatoyama, with the exception that the former was a career bureaucrat and the latter a parliamentarian.

Of the major political parties, the Social Democratic party was least affected by the purge. To be sure, it sustained a heavy loss in experienced leadership percentage-wise, for ten of its seventeen representatives in the wartime Diet were disqualified from public office. In comparison to the conservative parties, which lost 206 and 198 major leaders respectively in the 1946–1949 period, the Socialists were decreased by only thirty-four individuals.... The more limited impact of the purge on the Social Democratic party is readily understandable in view of the emphases of the purge criteria. The majority of the Social Democrats had either been in prison or been *persona non grata* during the militarist era. Hence, few had held positions or participated in activities which would make them subject to the purge criteria. In fact, if any one political group gained by the purge, it was the Social Democratic party. From a wartime representation of seventeen in the House of Representatives (and a prewar high of thirty-six), the party won ninety-six seats in the 1946 election and 144 seats in 1947.

Until the summer of 1950, the Communist party leadership did not suffer any losses under the purge. Removals up to that time were militarists and ultranationalists, and during the wartime period Japanese Communists had been in prison or in exile. In June 1950, however, the Communist party leadership felt the full weight of the purge. As a result of these removals, in addition to other complex factors, the party lost all of its central committee and fifteen out of its total Diet membership of thirty-seven. . . .

Impact of the purge on the political elite, as represented by candidates for the national Diet, was substantial. In the 1947 election, however, two factors militated against the purge's encouraging the rise of a new leadership. First, the purge had not as yet touched the source of conservative party funds, namely, big business interests. Also, the conservative parties had on their side tradition and a vast network of local organizations manned by individuals similar in outlook to those purged. More than removing some members of the prewar and wartime political elite was necessary to equalize the contest between the established parties and those which became influential only during the postwar period.

However, within the conservative parties, certain changes in leadership did take place. How much of this change is directly attributable to the purge is open to question. The fact remains that it was because of Hatoyama's purge that Yoshida became prime minister. Neither differed on fundamentals to be sure; Hatoyama would have sought another replacement if they had. Nonetheless, whereas Hatoyama had been a parliamentarian, Yoshida had been a bureaucrat in the prewar era. Furthermore, Yoshida relied heavily on the ranks of professional officialdom to furnish Liberal party candidates, thereby channeling the search for new leadership into a source which was different from the parliamentarians who had supported Hatoyama. The latter's absence from the overt political scene for nearly six years and his acquisition of the premiership some eight years and a half after being initially considered for it, thus came at a crucial time. Not he, but Yoshida set the dominant tone of conservative party policies. This substitution, a direct result of the purge, made more difficult the continuation of a direct line between prewar and postwar leadership among the conservatives. Hence, though the purge did not play as significant a role as it might have in changing the personnel and outlook of the political elite of Japan as a whole, it did contribute to the rise of a different leadership in the conservative parties.

❀ GOVERNMENT FUNCTIONS in Japan at all levels were highly centralized under the prewar system. During the occupation SCAP sought to decentralize local government. Part of this job was negative—eliminating central organs of control, reducing the role of neighborhood groups. The rest of the task involved setting up decentralized organs, such as police stations and elected school boards, and trying to establish a financial base to support these institutions. Kurt Steiner discusses the efforts to change local government, police administration, education, and local finances. The changes were painfully slow, and the extent to which they significantly altered old patterns is still debated.

KURT STEINER*
Occupation Reforms in Local Government

Neither the Potsdam Declaration of July 26, 1945, nor the Presidential Policy Statement on Japan of September 6, 1945, required expressly that the democratization of Japan include the establishment of local autonomy. But when the Government Section of SCAP was established, on October 2, 1945, one of its functions was to make recommendations for the decentralization of the Japanese

* Kurt Steiner, *Local Government in Japan* (Stanford, Calif.: Stanford University Press, 1965), pp. 69–77, 90–96, 103–104, 108–113.

government and the encouragement of local responsibility. A policy of changing national–local relations in Japan had thus been decided upon in Tokyo before the occupation was one month old. A month later, on November 3, 1945, it was apparently sanctioned in Washington. The Joint Chiefs of Staff's Basic Initial Post-Surrender Directive for the Occupation and Control of Japan, forwarded to SCAP on November 8, 1945, stated: "Local responsibility for the local enforcement of national policy will be encouraged."

This was a somewhat cryptic sentence. It considered local entities only in their relation to the execution of national policy—a viewpoint that had been the bane of local self-government ever since the Meiji restoration. . . .

The enthusiasm for decentralization and local self-government was not shared throughout SCAP, however. The exigencies of war and its aftermath create a particularly unhealthy climate for the dispersion of governmental power. In the early years of the occupation the economic situation of Japan was critical and economic controls were essential, and it is not surprising that the SCAP sections in charge of this field of governmental activity were opposed to a weakening of these controls by limitations on the powers of the central government. But even later, when the economic crisis had passed, staff sections engaged in certain practical and ostensibly nonpolitical programs—public health, public safety, social security, development of natural resources, and so on—were often in favor of centralized controls for their particular projects.

Nevertheless, the occupation was publicly committed to the establishment of local autonomy, and we may now review the steps it took, or failed to take, in that direction.

As a new local government structure was erected, some parts of the old order were destroyed. The abolition of the regional superintendencies-general and the system of neighborhood associations did away with innovations of the immediate prewar and wartime periods. But the abolition of the Home Ministry struck at an institution with a history of seventy-five years, an institution which had occupied a position of great importance, second perhaps only to that of the army and navy, ever since Japan's emergence as a modern state.

In all three cases, the abolition was not ordered immediately but was the result of a series of developments. In regard to regional administration, the Japanese government requested on September 28, 1945, SCAP's permission to replace the superintendencies-general, created in anticipation of an invasion emergency, with regional administrative affairs bureaus. There was some feeling in SCAP in favor of immediate dissolution rather than replacement, but the opinion that the bureaus might prove useful in the application of necessary controls prevailed, and the permission was given. . . .

The abolition of the neighborhood associations raised a more delicate problem. When the war ended, the activities of these associations, including those of rationing and thought control, were at their height. Some of these activities ceased with the end of the war, but the continuation of controls on production and consumption held the system together. The Home Ministry, furthermore, considered the neighborhood associations an essential part of local government.

The first steps regarding these groups did not involve any change in their position. Not even the amendment of the basic local government laws in September 1946 affected their legal status. As before, the local executive could delegate administrative business to them. At the time, the Japanese government replied to a question in the Diet by stressing that neighborhood associations would remain the lowest branch of local administration and would play an important role in the execution of assigned national functions. Control by the local executive was retained and public subsidization continued.

But, in keeping with the demands of the hour, the government thought it necessary to create the appearance of a "democratization" of the neighborhood association system. The vice-home minister therefore instructed prefectural governors to encourage election or other methods of selection of officers of neighborhood associations that would reflect the will of the constituency. This step, which did not bring about a significant change in local leadership, failed to satisfy SCAP. The Japanese government was faced with the alternatives of either abolishing the neighborhood associations or else providing by law for the public election of their chiefs. At the time an extension of the original purge directive to local levels was under consideration. If the purge was to be extended to the level of the neighborhood association chiefs, their public election would have required the examination of the eligibility of some 220,000 persons. The Japanese government had various misgivings about the extension of the purge to the local level in general, but it particularly wanted to exclude the neighborhood association chiefs from it. It finally submitted a plan for the extension on October 21, 1946. The memorandum from the chief of Government Section, General Whitney, to the Japanese government, reviewing the government's plan, insisted on the free election of heads of block associations, but demanded screening only for "all holders of important executive policy-making positions in the local government, including chiefs of departments, bureaus, and sections in municipal and town governments." The demand for election was based of course on the governmental character of the neighborhood associations. In an effort to deny this basis, Prime Minister Yoshida described the neighborhood associations in his letter to General MacArthur of October 31, 1946 (which dealt with the extension of the purge) as "entirely voluntary associations." But this picture was hardly in accord with reality; membership remained compulsory as long as a person's residence had to be certified by neighborhood associations for rationing purposes, and as long as the actual distribution of rations was carried out by them. Yoshida's plea against the requirement of election of neighborhood association chiefs failed. The purge was extended to the local level by a series of Imperial ordinances of January 4, 1947. In regard to block associations, Imperial Ordinance No. 4 provided for the election of heads by universal adult suffrage. Reluctantly, the government thus reached its decision to divest the neighborhood associations of their public character in order to obviate the necessity for the election of their chiefs, which would otherwise have been part of the local elections scheduled for April 1947. . . . But while ostensibly stripping the neighborhood associations of their governmental functions, the government made it clear that it favored the continuation of the associations on a voluntary basis. The chief of the General Affairs Section of the Home Ministry's Local Affairs Bureau stated that only the character of the neighborhood associations as terminal administrative agencies had been abolished, and that this did not imply that the organizations had been a bad thing. He stressed that there existed no obstacle to their continuation as voluntary associations. A few days later Home Minister Ōmura released a statement in which he explained the abolition of the wartime system. He referred to the original evolution of the neighborhood associations through a natural and voluntary process. Then he mentioned that because of their ties with the Imperial Rule Assistance Association during the war they "were considered as a perpetuation of a system born of war whose aspects recall wartime regimentation and chauvinism." The alteration of the structure had been administratively unwise up to now in view of the exigencies of rationing, but now the "continuation of the present structure is considered not only contrary to the principle of local autonomy but may also permit unscrupulous individuals to exercise improper influence over the forthcoming elections." . . .

It is thus not surprising that the changes effected by the Home Ministry instructions did not go very deep. Repeated violations were reported in the press. A great many neighborhood associations thought it desirable to change their names—for instance, to "cooperative living guilds" (*seikatsu kyōdō kumiai*)—but otherwise they carried on as usual under the same leadership.

As the failure of the attempt to change the neighborhood associations into voluntary, democratic, and independent organizations became apparent, SCAP's attitude stiffened and its policy shifted toward compulsory abolition. A cabinet order "with teeth" was promulgated on May 3, 1947. All heads or assistant heads of *buraku* [village] associations who had held office continuously from September 1, 1945, until September 1, 1946, were barred for four years from any municipal office that had similar functions. Officials were forbidden to issue orders to the chiefs of either the original association or its successor and these chiefs were forbidden to issue orders to the membership. The prohibited acts and the refusal to issue rations to a consumer who was not a member of such an association were made punishable. All block associations, similar groups, and "liaison offices" formed after January 22, 1947, to take up the slack created by Home Ministry Instruction No. 4 were to be disbanded by May 31, 1947. The governors were given the task of liquidating those that did not disband voluntarily by the prescribed date. Thus the neighborhood associations were not simply to be deprived of their public character, but actually abolished. The wisdom of this step has been questioned on various grounds. To some, it seemed that if the associations had been stripped of their objectionable wartime features and placed under new leadership, they could have become a nucleus for real local self-government. Others were convinced that the "democratization" of the system was a hopeless task.

At any rate . . . the step was not successful. In rural areas, where the *buraku* was more firmly entrenched in the needs and customs of the community, it retained not only its social but also its political significance and, to some extent, its connection with the village office. In the cities, the abolition of the *tonarigumi* [neighborhood associations] and *chōnaikai* [block associations] was welcomed by many, especially among the intelligentsia. But here and there various organizations, voluntary only insofar as government regulation was replaced by social pressure or pressure by "bosses," took over some of their tasks, often with the aid of municipal subsidies of doubtful legality. . . .

The abolition of the Home Ministry was also the result of a lengthy development. To the decentralization-minded officials of SCAP's Government Section, the Japanese government existing at the time of the surrender was a monster that reached with thousands of tentacles into the home and private life of every individual Japanese. If the abolition of the neighborhood associations aimed at shortening the tentacles, the abolition of the Home Ministry was meant to strike at the very heart. It was more than a measure of administrative reorganization; its significance was primarily political. . . .

The Home Ministry officials had long been regarded—not only by foreign observers—as the very incarnation of Japanese bureaucracy, possessed of their own importance as pillars of the emperor's rule, disdainful of the masses of subjects who had to be governed, well aware of their strategic political position, tightly knit as a result of professional inbreeding and strict discipline, and generally opposed to changes in the existing social and political order. . . .

The Law Concerning the Abolition of the Ministry of Home Affairs and of the Imperial Ordinance Governing Its Organization and Other Ordinances and a second law providing for adjustment in other laws—such as a transfer of functions from the defunct home ministry to the various other "competent ministers"—were finally passed on November 28, 1947, by the House of Representatives and on December 8, 1947, by the House of Councilors. . . .

In the decentralization of police and education, the primary consideration was not that these are, by their nature, local functions. The centralized education system had been used for indoctrination in a narrow nationalism and the centralized police system had been used for the control of "dangerous thoughts." The decentralization of police and education was thus thought of primarily as a step in eliminating specific evils of the past and in preventing their recurrence, and only incidentally as a step in a general program of reallocating functions.

Certain police functions and organs were abolished at the very outset of the occupation. As was frequently the case, the Japanese government then sought to forestall more drastic action by SCAP by taking some action of its own. In early 1946 plans for improvement of the quality of the police and for its "democratization" by a system of civilian advisers were discussed. The new slogan for the police was "Respect human rights, keep alert, always be kind and popular." . . .

The Japanese cabinet submitted a draft plan . . . to SCAP on February 28, 1947. While loudly condemning the obviously dying past by the use of such phrases as "improper functions" and "excessive centralization," the plan was essentially a plea against "hasty reorganization of the fundamental system." It would have left control of the police force unchanged until "local government officials have demonstrated efficiency in self-government," at which time the police forces were to be reorganized "in cities with populations capable of supporting them" and controlled and operated by these local self-governing bodies. The government's preoccupation with "stabilizing the condition of the nation" and with the use of the police force as "the only stabilizing influence available to the Japanese government" is apparent throughout the plan, which also envisioned an increase in overall police strength from about 94,000 to 125,000.

The plan did not find favor with Government Section. In a lengthy memorandum for the record, dated July 17, 1947, Government Section set forth its objections and called for "decentralization of the police force without delay and not at the expiration of any period of probation."

The early part of 1947 was a period of momentous developments. After a general strike had been averted at the last minute by SCAP intervention, elections were called for and they brought the downfall of the Yoshida cabinet and the formation of a coalition cabinet under a social democratic prime minister, Katayama Tetsu.

As soon as the Katayama government was formed, the discussions on police reorganization were resumed. . . .

Government Section and G-2 cooperated closely in the drafting of the law, which was promptly passed on December 17, 1947.

The salient features of the Police Law were: (1) the division of police functions between the National Rural Police and the police of the autonomous entities; (2) the division of controls into operational and administrative controls in the case of the national police; and (3) the institution of Public Safety Commissions on all levels.

The national police was to be in charge of the police communications system, of criminal identification, and of police training. Otherwise its operations were limited to rural areas and to towns and villages with less than 5000 inhabitants. The autonomous police was to operate in cities, towns, and villages with more than 5000 inhabitants.

The control of matters relating to organization, budget, and personnel management of the police (administrative control) and control over the activities relating to maintenance of public order, prevention and suppression of crime, and traffic and judicial police affairs (operational control) were separated in the case of the National Rural Police. Administrative control was to be exercised at the national and regional level—the country being divided into six police regions—by the National Public Safety Commission and the directors of the police regions; operational control was to be exercised at the prefectural level by the prefectural public safety commissions. In the case of the autonomous police, both controls were lodged in the local entities, more specifically in the local public safety commissions.

The establishment of public safety commissions was intended to limit the control of the executive over the police, which had been so strong in the past. For this reason, the commissions were assured a certain independence of status. When the prime minister wanted to appoint a member of the national Public Safety Commission, he needed the consent of both houses of the Diet. The same was true for dismissals, which had to be for cause. Not more than two of the five members of the commission could belong to the same political party. The chairman of the commission was to be co-opted by its members. Similar provisions were made for the public safety commissions of prefectures, cities, towns, and villages, all of which consisted of three members.

As indicated earlier, there was a basic difference between the prefectural commissions and those of cities, towns, and villages: the former were within the framework of the national police, the latter outside it. For the autonomous police the chain of command ended, generally speaking, within the boundaries of the respective localities. Within those areas, local control was complete. Article 154 of the law stated explicitly: "There shall be neither administrative nor operational control by the National Rural Police over the police of cities, towns, and villages." Since a simple lack of authorization frequently failed to prevent national officials from interfering in local affairs, a provision of this type, making such interference clearly illegal, was perhaps not a superfluous precaution.

The decentralization of police raised great problems in dealing with large-scale internal unrest. Japan had been stripped of its army and had renounced the right to maintain land, sea, and air forces or other war potential. In cases of widespread internal unrest amounting to a state of emergency, the national government had no way to "call out the militia" for its suppression. Until the creation of the National Police Reserve Corps in 1950 it had to rely on the regular police. For this reason, the National Public Safety Commission was authorized to prepare and execute plans for integrating the police to cope with a state of national emergency, which was to be proclaimed, on the commission's recommendation, by the prime minister. The proclamation had to be ratified by the Diet within twenty days to remain valid. In such an emergency, the prime minister would assume control over the entire police system down to the autonomous police of towns and villages.

With some changes—including one in 1951 that led to the virtual abolition of the autonomous police on the town and village level—this police system of 1947 remained in force for seven years. . . .

In the field of educational reform, as in the field of police reform, some preliminary steps were taken shortly after the beginning of the occupation. These involved a ban on the spreading of militaristic and ultranationalistic thought, a purge of educators, a revision of texts, and the suspension of the teaching of certain courses, especially the course in morals (*shūshin*). The decentralization of the Japanese school system was recommended by the United States Education Mission, which stayed in Japan during March 1946. The mission suggested that prefectural and local administrative agencies, to be elected by popular vote, should be put in charge of educational functions, while the Ministry of Education, which had been in principal control of local schools, should in the future provide them only with professional and technical counsel. A Japanese Educational Reform Council, created in August 1946, approved these recommendations in general. The recommendations went far beyond the vague and timid steps, such as the establishment of local advisory councils, that had been under consideration by the ministry of education since the end of the war. . . .

The climax in the process of decentralizing education came with passage of the Board of Education Law, adopted on July 15, 1948. Its purpose was to free education from direct control by the Ministry of Education, to place responsibility for education on the local citizenry, and to make educational administration within the locality independent of the general local administration. For this purpose, boards of education were put in charge of all schools except private schools and higher educational institutions. Their control was to include, among other things, the curriculum, the selection of textbooks, and the hiring and firing of personnel. The members of the boards of education—seven in the case of prefectural boards, five in the case of municipal boards—were to be elected locally for terms of four years. The election was to be direct, except that one member of each board was to be elected indirectly by the assembly of the prefecture or municipality. The board members were made subject to the recall provisions of the Local Autonomy Law. The boards were given the power, not attributed to other commissions created by the occupation (such as the public safety commissions), to participate in the compilation of the budget, a function otherwise reserved to the chief executive. The Ministry of Education was to cease its direct supervision of education and became an advisory body, giving technical guidance. . . .

The five great weaknesses in the field of local finance, as the

Shoup Mission saw them, were: (1) the lack of a clear separation of functions; (2) the lack of a clear tax structure and the excessive control of local tax sources by the central government; (3) the insufficiency of financial resources of local bodies; (4) the arbitrariness and unpredictability of national subsidies and grants, the lack of equalization between richer and poorer areas, and the strain placed on local resources by the requirement that national payments be matched locally; and (5) the excessively severe limitations on the borrowing power of local authorities. . . .

The primary laws, which were enacted as a result of the Shoup report, were the Local Tax Law, the Local Finance Equalization Grant Law, and the Local Finance Commission Establishment Law. The first of these, the Local Tax Law, was submitted to the Diet in December 1949 and created tremendous agitation. The public was in no mood to countenance anything resembling an increase in taxes in any field after the austerity measures associated with the Dodge program. The opposition was strong against the new "value-added" tax and the new municipal property tax, which subjected machinery, tools, etc., to taxation and thus affected business, large and small. The political parties were not prepared to resist these pressures, and it may well be that the government was not eager to push the bill too hard for the sake of a reform about which it was not enthusaiastic. An almost unprecedented situation arose: the regular budget was delayed. It passed the House of Representatives on March 11, but was held up in the House of Councilors until April 3, 1950, three days after the beginning of the new fiscal year. The Local Tax Bill was finally passed by the Lower House on April 20, but only after the opposition walked out. Even then the Upper House did not go along. The Japanese suggested the idea of breaking the deadlock with a "Potsdam Declaration Ordinance," probably hoping that this would direct the criticism toward the occupation.

Instead, SCAP issued a statement on May 3, 1950, that the Diet had acted within its prerogatives. It became necessary to call a special Diet session to cope with the problem. . . .

During this time, the Shoup Mission returned to make another survey of the situation. It made recommendations for some amendments of the new law. It also found its system already endangered by certain measures contemplated by the government, such as a return to the old system under which disaster rehabilitation was to be borne in part by the local entities. There was a note of gloom in the mission's prediction that 1951–1952 would be a critical year for local finance. It felt certain that inadequate finances could kill local autonomy, but it believed that there were still ways to solve the problem. . . .

The effort to reallocate functions in accordance with the Shoup recommendations came to a close before Japan regained independence, and we shall dwell on it here as a melancholy epilogue to the occupation's endeavors to establish local autonomy.

The Local Administration Investigation Committee, which was to perform the vital task, was established by law in December 1949. Its chairman was Dr. Kambe Masao, a former mayor of Kyoto and professor of Kyoto University. Under SCAP auspices, three of the five members of the committee undertook a journey to the United States to inspect local administration there. Then the group settled down to do a prodigious amount of careful and painstaking work.

It submitted its first and principal report to the cabinet and to both houses of the Diet in December 1950. This report was based on the three principles for the redistribution of administrative affairs, as set forth in the Shoup report, namely:

> 1. So far as possible or practicable, the functions of the three levels of government should be clearly demarcated, and each specific function should be assigned exclusively to one level of government. The level of government would be then fully responsible for performing the function and for financing it from general funds.
> 2. Each function would be allocated to that level of government which is equipped by virtue of its size, its power, and financial resources to perform it efficiently.
> 3. In the interests of local autonomy each function would be given to the lowest appropriate level of government. Municipalities would have first priority in the sense that no function would be given to the prefecture or national government which could be performed adequately by municipalities. The prefecture would be given second priority, and the national government would assume only those functions which cannot be administered effectively under local direction.

The committee put its finger on almost every problem that had thwarted the development of local autonomy, and its report can be read with profit for an understanding of both the former and the present systems. It envisioned a more cooperative and less hierarchical relationship between the state and the local entities. "The state," it said, "should give no guardianlike attention to or have no solicitude about the performance of such [local] affairs." In local matters that might also have nationwide bearing, the state should be responsible for information, assistance, the adjustment of inequalities, and the maintenance of minimum standards. None of these should involve "authoritarian supervision."

National affairs were defined in accordance with specified criteria. The commission recommended that their delegation should be kept to a minimum and that the state should bear full costs in such cases. There was nothing equivocal in the parts of the report dealing with the participation of the state in the affairs of local bodies. A few quotations show the spirit:

> In regard to those affairs which are related exclusively to a particular local public body or its people and which have little effect upon other local public bodies or the nation as a whole, the state should have no part. Provisions should be made to preclude even the nonauthoritarian participation of the state, to say nothing of the enactment of laws establishing standards or making the performance of certain affairs obligatory. . . .
>
> The ill effects that may arise when the local public bodies neglect the execution of affairs or when the manner of execution is not appropriate should be criticized or corrected by the people of the local public bodies concerned through election or the system of various direct demands, or by arousing public opinion. The maintenance of the integrity of law should be made secure finally through the judicial system, and the state should be patient enough to refrain from hasty intervention and wait for the occurrence of the voluntary criticism of the people. . . .
>
> The so-called authoritarian supervision by the state in the form of permission, approval, authorization, direction, cancelation, alteration, subrogation, etc., which are the manners of state participation with the local public bodies, should be abolished as a matter of principle.

The committee advocated that the delegation of national affairs to the executives of local entities, or "agency delegation," be avoided, and spelled out exceptions to this rule. The entrusting of national affairs to local entities as such, or "entity delegation," should not be compulsory but should be made on the basis of agreement. In principle, state responsibilities should be performed by agencies of the state.

Prefectures were not considered to have a higher status than cities, towns, and villages in the hierarchy of local government, but it was envisioned that they would provide liaison between the state and the municipalities and adjust extraordinary inequalities among the municipalities. The report also made recommendations for increasing the efficiency of local administration, for rationalizing the scale of local public bodies, and for promoting cooperative relations among them.

These general observations were followed by particular recommendations regarding the various functions. The principal laws concerned were specified and the lines along which they should be amended were laid down. This was, indeed, the sort of overall review of laws affecting local government that had been planned, but not carried out, in 1947. As the foregoing outline will have shown, the report constituted a clean break with the prevalent bureaucratic thinking about national–local relations. It was a constructive and careful blueprint for a system of genuine local self-government. The reaction of the various associations of local public bodies was uniformly in sympathy with the report. Nevertheless, two undercurrents were noticeable in the words of praise: one was the doubt whether the government would show the necessary "enthusiasm" in implementing the recommendations; the other was a certain apprehension about the yet unexperienced situation in which local units would find themselves when the mass of delegations—and with it the mass of subsidies, insufficient as they were—would dwindle. Everyone agreed that the existing situation put local government in a squeeze and that certain steps were necessary, but there was little spirit of optimistic experimentation among the local leaders themselves.

When Prime Minister Yoshida submitted his appointments for the Local Administration Investigation Committee to the Diet, as the law required, he stated that the government intended to fully respect and implement their recommendations. But in fact, the Kambe report was shelved in all but a few minor recommendations. Some SCAP sections were as unwilling to insist on implementation as were their Japanese counterparts. The real problem, however, was the general trend of the times. Decentralization, along with democratization, had lost its importance as an occupation aim. The work of the Kambe committee should have been carried out in 1947, when the Local Autonomy Law was drafted. By 1950 it was too late.

The Kambe report was the flowering of the last rose in the Indian summer of local autonomy reform, which had begun with the Shoup Mission. With the imminent conclusion of the peace treaty and the departure of the occupation forces, the climate was no longer propitious for new reforms. The Indian summer was over.

☸ THE FIRST POSTWAR ELECTIONS were scheduled for April 1946. Popular sentiments against the old establishment were expressing themselves now that wartime censorship was over and civil liberties had been granted by MacArthur. However, Bisson argues there had not been time for reforms which would have changed the political system and thus the influence of the prewar elite. Thus the Liberals and Progressives, the two major prewar parties renamed and reconstituted, still had a firm grip on local political machines which elected candidates. They also had the financial resources of the zaibatsu interests behind them. In addition, the opposition parties lacked the time to create strong political organizations, and they could never get money from the business interests they opposed. Given this situation, the victory of the old guard in the 1946 elections was virtually inevitable.

T. A. BISSON*
April 1946 Elections

The seven months that elapsed between the beginning of the occupation and the holding of this first election on April 10, 1946, were of decisive significance in molding the postwar development of Japan. . . .

* T. A. Bisson, *Prospects for Democracy in Japan* (New York: Macmillan, 1949), pp. 32–35, 42–45, 47–48.

By the middle of September 1945, demobilization of the Japanese home armies was proceeding smoothly, and the whole operation was completed on October 15. The old ruling forces in Japanese society, doubtful as to how far General MacArthur was prepared to go, were on the defensive. The occupation was free to act at a time when its power to act was most unlimited. Vigorous popular stirrings against the old regime, evident from the early months, strengthened the opportunity for drastic action in the political sphere.

The first moves were promising. Directives issued in September 1945 freed the press from authoritarian restrictions, while vesting censorship in SCAP hands. These orders, however, did not disturb old-line control of the newspapers themselves, but left the workers to seek this needed reform through bitter union struggles against the owners that lasted through the first year of the occupation. ˙

A broader and more significant move, lifting restrictions on political, civil, and religious liberties, was taken on October 4 with the issuance of the Civil Liberties Directive. This brought about the release of political prisoners, abolition of the police system's thought control agencies, and the repeal of laws restricting freedom of thought, religion, speech, and assembly. Its major weakness lay in the failure to bar former thought control officials from government agencies other than those of the Home Ministry.

These initial moves, combined with the positive support accorded trade union organization and activity during the early months, constituted a notable installment on a bill of rights for the Japanese people. They opened the path for successful completion of the struggle for a democratic Japan which the people gave every evidence of being willing and anxious to conduct.

During these early months the people responded eagerly to every forward step taken by General MacArthur. They took immediate advantage of the Civil Liberties Directive. Overnight the press and radio were filled with vigorous attacks on the old regime, the wartime leaders, and the Shidehara cabinet. Six months later these sharp attacks on government policy became embarrassing to the occupation authorities, and they were gradually curbed through stricter radio control and support to old-line editors and publishers. In the fall of 1945, however, the air of Tokyo was electric with the unleashing of long pent-up emotions and suppressed resentments. Before the people were forced by the inflation to devote every spare moment to the scramble for food, they gave active political expression to these feelings in many directions.

In leading newspaper offices, during October–November 1945 and later, the working staffs conducted a strong drive against old-line editorial policy, which was subtly opposing SCAP's measures. Newspaper offices were rapidly unionized. In the strike at the *Yomiuri* office, its owner-publisher—a war criminal in Sugamo prison—was publicly exposed and forced to resign his control. In this action the *Yomiuri* strikers anticipated SCAP's purge in the publicity field—enforced in the summer of 1947—by nearly two years.

At this period, too, the first difficult phases of union organization were eased by the eager response of the workers. The equally difficult task of organizing the new opposition parties was also made easier by widespread popular support, shown by the nearly ten million votes cast for the Social Democrats in April 1946. When Sanzō Nosaka, the Japanese Communist leader who had organized his compatriots in China to fight the Japanese armies, returned to Japan by permission of SCAP, he received an ovation from the Tokyo populace.

Popular feeling at this period was bitterly critical of the old leaders who had led Japan into the war. Freedom of speech and the press gave it every opportunity to be heard.

The establishment of civil liberties, on the other hand, did not mean that the field was clear for an *equal* struggle between the old and new forces. Fifty years of indoctrination under the old regime left effects on patterns of thought and action that could not be wiped out in a few months that preceded the first election. This heritage was a fortress of the old Japan which the occupation could not take by storm. It might have been undermined more rapidly by social revolutionary disturbances, but this was prevented both by the peaceful transition to occupation control effected by the Japanese leaders and by the very "orderliness" of occupation procedures.

This factor increased the responsibility laid upon the occupation authorities. They were quite free, and under obligation, to sweep away a large assortment of advantages held by the old guard in the political struggle leading up to the election. These advantages included at least three prominent features: control of the government, control of the economy, and control of four great agencies of mass influence represented by the neighborhood units, the Agricultural Association, the Fisheries Association, and the labor boss system. . . .

Adding up the results of this brief survey of preelection measures, the score is shown to be none too favorable.

On the credit side can be placed such factors as the establishment of civil rights (to the extent not violated by the neighborhood unit or labor boss systems), the purge of the Diet membership inherited from Tōjō, and the right accorded trade unions to organize. A revised election law had enfranchised women, lowered the voting age, and set up a system of large constituencies with a plural vote that constituted a step toward proportional representation.

On the negative side was the overall ineffectiveness of the purge, and its inadequacies both in scope and timing. There was also the failure to shake the grip of zaibatsu firms and personnel on the business life of the country, which went on as before throughout this period. Even more noteworthy was the failure to destroy the strongholds of authoritarian influence represented by such agencies as the neighborhood units, the labor bosses, and the Agricultural Association.

During these preelection months the democratic opposition was vigorously attempting to build up sufficient organized strength to wage a successful campaign against the old-line parties. By the spring of 1946, trade union membership was growing rapidly, but at the end of March organized workers still numbered only about two million. The labor bosses probably controlled more workers than the trade unions at the time of the first election.

A comparable situation existed in the rural areas. The beginnings of an independent peasant union movement had appeared, but the number of farmers actually enrolled in the new unions by April 1946 totaled only a few thousand. These small farmers' unions faced a hopeless struggle against the powerful influence wielded throughout the countryside by hundreds of Agricultural Association branches.

The Shidehara cabinet and the old-line Diet members had watered down the first land reform bill until SCAP had to reject it and were continuing to stall for time on this vitally needed measure. Tenant–landlord relations thus continued as usual in the farm areas, except that the landlords were evicting tenants in anticipation of the eventual application of the land reform program.

The odds were no less unequal in the sphere of party organization. Throughout the war, even under Tōjō, the Minseitō and Seiyūkai leaders and party organizations had continued to exert influence in the Diet. After the surrender, . . . the same old-line party leaders organized two "new" parties named, in deference to the occupation's democratic objectives, the Progressive and Liberal parties. These "new" parties were firmly based on the old Minseitō and Seiyūkai party machines, respectively, which emerged virtually intact. The Diet purge dealt them one serious blow, but though damaging it was by no means fatal. It was countered by the usual method of substituting new faces for the old, including, in many cases, the nomination of candidates who were close relatives or associates of those who were purged—a loophole in the first purge directive that was never satisfactorily plugged.

Much more difficult organizational problems confronted the opposition. A number of the Social Democratic leaders had given full support to the militarist program in China and Greater East Asia. Their party machine, however, had largely disintegrated during the war, in contrast to the Minseitō and Seiyūkai organizations. The Communists were the one group that could point to a consistent record of opposition to Japanese militarism and the war. This factor helped them to muster popular support as soon as their leaders were released from prison. On the other hand, the Communist party organization had been almost completely shattered, even to its underground activities, by two decades of drastic police repression. Both parties, unlike the Liberals and Progressives, thus had to start virtually from scratch in rebuilding their organizations, and without the funds available to their opponents.

An even greater handicap was the split in the opposition ranks. The cleavage between the Social Democrats and the Communists confused their following and dispersed the concentrated strength needed to win against the overwhelming advantages enjoyed by their opponents. The cleavage was sharpened by the Communists' demand for abolition of the emperor system. This demand played into the hands of the right-wing Social Democratic leaders, who were the chief stumbling block in the way of joint action. In the end, these right-wing leaders swung the Social Democratic party to a program of support for the emperor system. Their policy on this question was completely vindicated, tactically if not in principle, when the SCAP-inspired constitution, entrenching the emperor in Japan's postwar political structure, was made public on March 6, 1946, at a crucial point in the election campaign.

The knowledge that General MacArthur favored retention of the emperor decided the question for the Japanese people. Even SCAP's prestige might not have been able to wean the Japanese people away from their dependence on the emperor, but time enough might have been given for at least some attempt at reeducation. The old guard was prepared to settle for Hirohito's abdication and his replacement by Crown Prince Akihito. Not even this was done. Publication of the draft constitution, together with a glowing public endorsement by SCAP, prejudged the issue and settled it out of court. Any claim that the April 1946 election gave the Japanese people a free chance to express their views concerning the new constitution and the retention of the emperor system was transparent pretense.

Partly as a result of developments on this question, the main forces of the people's opposition were mustered behind the Social Democratic party. This party, however, was itself badly split into right-wing and left-wing factions, with a wavering group in the middle. The right-wing Social Democratic leaders, only a few of whom were purged as ultranationalists at this period, were largely indistinguishable from the old-line Progressive or Liberal party politicians. The fact that these men controlled the party machinery led many Japanese liberals to question the Social Democrats' ability to head a genuinely democratic movement. The so-called "left-wing" faction, except for one or two individuals, was a moderate socialist group akin to the British Labor party, but its voice in party councils was small. . . .

Out of 466 seats in the House of Representatives, the old guard won approximately 325, counting in the allies of the Liberals and Progressives among the minor parties and independents. The Social Democrats won ninety-two seats, and the Communists five.

Considering the obstacles with which they had been confronted, the showing made by the parties opposing the old regime was a remarkable testimony not only to the people's demand for political change, but also to the extent of the opportunity missed by SCAP. For with all its shortcomings, the Social Democratic party came nearest to meeting the aspirations of Japanese liberal sentiment at that period, and, of all the political groupings in Japan, it was best fitted to extend active cooperation to SCAP in carrying through democratic reforms in the Japanese political and economic system.

As it was, the results of the 1946 election compelled SCAP, during the ensuing year, to rely for the fulfillment of its basic reform directives upon a cabinet headed by Shigeru Yoshida, whose close identification with the old ruling oligarchy has been noted, and upon a Diet in which the old-guard forces enjoyed an overwhelming majority. These reforms included such all-important measures as the revision of the constitution, the land reform program, laws affecting the Imperial House, local government reform, the House of Councilors' election law, tax reform, an antitrust act, and laws relating to wartime contract indemnities—all of which were dealt with by the three Diet sessions held during the Yoshida cabinet's term of office. Furthermore, the old guard's victory in this first election seriously handicapped SCAP's efforts to cope with the increasingly acute economic crisis. For in attempting to encourage the revival of industrial production and control inflation, SCAP had to work with and through the political representatives of the very forces that were passively resisting or actively sabotaging all measures of economic recovery.

Those who had warned that an early election would not produce a new leadership in Japan thus found their fears fully confirmed.

THE APRIL 1947 ELECTIONS resulted in a plurality victory for the Japan Socialist party (called in the following sections the Social Democratic party or SDP). This victory was a tribute to the opposition forces and to the economic chaos of the period. During the first few years of the occupation the Progressives and Liberals, the old prewar parties renamed, continued to have important advantages over the left-wing forces. The SCAP purge of local officials and the abolition of neighborhood groups were, for the most part, not in effect, leaving these and other conservative power bases intact. Furthermore, election procedures had been changed by the Diet to favor the conservatives. The authority of the conservatives was also increased by the implicit support of the Americans and by MacArthur's suppression of a general strike in February 1947. In the end, a plurality victory was not enough to change the status quo, and it was clear that conservative forces had not lost their prewar strength.

T. A. BISSON*
April 1947 Elections

Developments during the preceding year strengthened the opportunity afforded by these 1947 elections to place control of Japan's reformed governmental structure in new hands. The Yoshida cabinet not only refused to take measures to check the inflationary spiral but adopted policies that served to increase inflation. As a result, the living standards of the Japanese people were steadily undermined. Popular resentment against the conduct of government by the Liberal–Progressive coalition mounted to such heights that in March 1947, just before the elections, the Progressive party reorganized itself under the new name of the Democratic party in the hope of avoiding the expression of this disapproval at the polls. By April 1947, moreover, trade union membership exceeded five million, newly formed peasant unions embraced more than one million farmers, and the opposition parties had strengthened their organizations and extended the ties with their following. These were all great advantages, sufficient, it might have seemed, to assure a sweeping democratic victory at the polls. . . .

For the second election, the occupation authorities had in the making two notable moves: abolition of the neighborhood unit system, and extension of the purge into economic, publicity, and local government spheres. Delays in promulgating and enforcing the measures, occasioned by conflicts of opinion within GHQ,

* T. A. Bisson, *Prospects for Democracy in Japan* (New York: Macmillan, 1949), pp. 50–51, 53–57, 72–74.

largely neutralized their potentially favorable effects on the elections.

These moves had been given the fullest and most protracted consideration. They were intended to apply to the April 1947 elections. The effective date of abolition of the neighborhood unit system, however, was finally set as of April 1, or five days before the first election. Action thus came too late to prevent use of the system by the old-guard Liberal and Democratic (Progressive) parties during the campaign.

The economic purge, which has been attacked savagely in some quarters for its alleged severity, had actually affected only some 200 top officials in zaibatsu firms when the elections were held. By the end of July the number affected had risen to 296. Its effects on zaibatsu firms were no more severe than the earlier government purge, which covered only those officials above the rank of bureau chiefs. In most cases, the second-level zaibatsu executives had smoothly taken over from the removed corporation presidents and directors. The purge of newspapers, magazines, and the radio was not fully applied until the summer of 1947, when influential wartime publicists were removed from positions they had continued to hold during nearly two years of the occupation.

Once again the delayed application of the purge, which could have been a single concerted operation during the early period of the occupation, had ironical results. Four members of the Yoshida cabinet were eventually removed by the purge. But three of these ministers served throughout the Yoshida cabinet's thirteen months in office. One of them, Kawaii, had blocked the formation of a Labor Ministry and kept a tight rein on labor, while another, Ishibashi, had carried through the inflationary budget program. . . .

Abolition of the neighborhood unit system and extension of the purge had some effect, even though the moves came too late to be applied fully before the elections. Other needed steps were not taken at all. The Agricultural Association and the labor boss system were left untouched. An extended purge of the central bureaucracy's upper ranks was not made despite its obvious necessity. After the election this problem was tackled by the more drastic method of a complete dissolution of the Home and Justice Ministries, but such a method could not be applied so easily to the economic ministries, notably Commerce and Industry, where a house cleaning was equally needed.

Safeguards against the political influence of old and new business interests, many of whom were engaged in black-market operations where profits depended on continuance of the inflationary spiral, were weakest of all. The Yoshida cabinet was not interested in taking measures against the rapid concentration of wealth in the hands of these speculators. Zaibatsu dissolution was far from complete. The zaibatsu firms to which the economic purge had been applied were still running the business life of the country with virtually no change in policy, after providing replacements for their purged officers. . . .

In March and April, moreover, SCAP intervened directly on behalf of the old parties through press conferences and by granting Yoshida permission to revise the election law under which the previous general election had been conducted.

The press conferences, held several times a week during the March–April election campaign, were attended by thirty or more of the leading Japanese newsmen in Tokyo and thus received nationwide coverage. Most of the carefully prepared statements made by SCAP spokesmen to these conferences were exhortatory or dealt with election procedures. These were politically innocuous. On the other hand, statements such as that which challenged the electorate to choose between "two ways of life" were charged with political content, leaving no doubt in the minds of the Japanese people as to where SCAP stood. These politically motivated statements by SCAP were directed primarily at the Communists, but they also reacted against the Social Democrats, who were the sole opposition party with a popular following large enough to challenge the old guard successfully at the polls.

Even more decisive were the effects of the revised House of Representatives' Election Law, jammed through the Diet at the last moment over desperate resistance by the Social Democratic, National Cooperative, Communist, and minor party representatives in the lower house. SCAP might have refused permission for the introduction of this bill on the ground that it favored the Liberal and Democratic parties, but the authorization was granted.

Introduced on March 23, the bill was forced through the Lower House amid tumultuous scenes. The opposition mustered about two-fifths of the House of Representatives, far more than a minority to be recklessly overridden on a fundamental issue of this character, but it stood no chance against the Liberal–Democratic steamroller. Only SCAP could have protected the rights of the solid opposition minority that went down to defeat in this struggle. The bill was approved on March 31, after a four-day extension of the Diet session which brought adjournment to the eve of the elections.

The election law discarded the large-constituency, plural-ballot system that had governed the election of April 10, 1946. Fifteen months earlier, liberal Japanese sentiment had cordially welcomed SCAP's initiative on behalf of this system, which was regarded as a preliminary step toward full proportional representation. Now the Liberal–Democratic majority in the Diet reversed the process by returning to the small-constituency, single-ballot system of the old regime. The limits of the redefined constituencies were those within which the Minseitō and Seiyūkai organizations had functioned so successfully in the prewar and wartime periods. Combined with a return to the single ballot, the smaller constituencies severely handicapped the opposition parties which found their support chiefly in urban areas and among the trade unions. As the Liberal party politicians freely admitted in private, the smaller constituencies could be delivered more easily by the machine bosses at election time, and would thus reduce the margin held by the opposition in the cities. By the same token they increased the effectiveness, and so encouraged the use, of bribery and other illegal methods of influencing the voters. Once again, moreover, a move aimed ostensibly against the Communists had its most serious effect on the Social Democrats. . . .

The outcome of these elections, ostensibly designed to place democratic adherents in charge of Japan's reformed government structure, left a most disturbing impression.

In the national Diet, the old forces retained control of two-thirds of the Representatives and three-fourths of the Councilors. The pluralities of the Social Democrats in both Houses represented the biggest gain scored by the opposition in the elections, but the substantial old-guard majority barred constructive progressive action on vitally urgent matters even in the central government.

Out of forty-six prefectural governors the old guard controlled forty-two, of which twenty-seven were ex-governors appointed by the Home Ministry and five more were former Home Ministry bureaucrats. In their prefectural assemblies these governors controlled virtually every seat, since the Social Democratic assemblymen—only seventeen percent of the total—were concentrated in but four prefectures.

In the cities, well above eighty percent of the mayors were old-line choices. Even in the five big cities the old guard captured three mayors, to which the governor (instead of a mayor) of Tokyo Metropolis should be added. In towns and villages, its control of the local executives and assemblymen exceeded ninety-seven percent.

While there are bound to be honest differences of interpretation among students of Japanese affairs, the author maintains that the record of political developments in Japan during the first twenty months of the occupation warrants the following conclusions:

(1) The ease and speed with which the military surrender was accomplished led SCAP to underestimate the determination and skill with which the Japanese ruling oligarchy intended to fight for the preservation of its basic powers. As a result, the occupation authorities failed to recognize that the old guard's control over the political and economic life of the country could be broken only by swift and drastic action, extending far beyond the purge of a relatively small group of politicians, bureaucrats, and business leaders and the granting of civil liberties to the Japanese people. The initial directives were unquestionably admirable in purpose and scope, but the decision to continue to work through the existing governmental structure meant that the execution of these directives was entrusted to staunch supporters of the old regime, who were inherently opposed to democratic reforms. This decision not only gave the old guard ample opportunity to delay and weaken the proposed reforms but enabled them to pose before the Japanese people as the chosen representatives of the Allied powers. Given this dual advantage, it was not surprising that they succeeded in maintaining their customary dominance over the political and economic structure.

(2) The second conclusion concerns SCAP's attitude toward the all-important question of developing a new political leadership for Japan. All available evidence indicates that the occupation authorities came prepared to play the role of firm but benevolent guardians of a docile and oppressed people that had no conception of the meaning, much less the practice, of democratic rights and responsibilities. The general consensus of opinion was that the

majority of Japanese would be meek and apologetic and would willingly accept the tutelage of their liberators. As it turned out, however, the release of political prisoners from jail, the granting of free speech, freedom of the press, freedom of organization, and other rights produced a popular movement that startled the occupation by its vigor and independence, and by the far-reaching character of its demands for political and economic reform.

During the first few months of the occupation, SCAP directives did much to encourage the growth of this popular movement, which constituted the only organized opposition to the rule of the old regime. At the same time, however, the occupation authorities became increasingly disturbed by the "left-wing" character of the programs sponsored by the new political parties. And after the first election in April 1946, the emphasis of occupation policy was placed on controlling rather than encouraging the growth of the popular movement. Since the control mechanisms were all in the hands of the old guard, this shift in emphasis naturally facilitated their campaign to preserve their power. The result, as we have seen, was that the old guard's control over the new governmental structure remained virtually as complete as it had been under the old regime.

◦ THE ILL-FATED Socialist participation in the Katayama government after the 1947 elections was short lived. In February 1948, under pressure of economic difficulties, Ashida Hitoshi formed a new cabinet. The Socialists continued to participate in this cabinet, as controversy within their party on that and other issues raged. From 1949 on, weakened electorally and out of the cabinet, the Socialists moved toward criticism of the occupation. This was in response to the economic austerity of the Dodge Plan and the atmosphere of the Red purge. Socialists were uneasy about the purge, but disliked the influence of the Japanese Communist party (JCP) too much to protest it. Only after the occupation were the Socialists able to recover some of their electoral support.

COLE, TOTTEN, AND UYEHARA*
The Socialists' Brief Taste of Power

Disillusionment with bureaucratic ineptitude, popular identification of the conservatives with the discredited wartime regime, the attraction of a new force, and a feeling of desperation on the part of the people—all heaped unreasonable and naïve expectations on the SDP. As a symbol of the new era, and the only party that might be trusted to guide Japan toward democratic aims, the SDP had become the chief beneficiary of the prevailing mood. The ruling conservatives had been slow in enforcing the purge—even overlooking certain cabinet ministers—had maintained a more than friendly relationship with the chief director of the purge, and had crippled the Economic Stabilization Board. The confident SDP rejected a bid from the JCP for electoral cooperation. During the campaign, Socialists emphasized the deficiencies of the retiring Yoshida administration and advocated governmental control of coal mines and the fertilizer industry, taxation of wartime black-market profiteers, and suspension of interest payments on wartime government bonds.

To their own surprise the Socialists obtained a plurality with 143 members in the House of Representatives. The two conservative parties, Liberals and Democrats (with factional rearrangements, the Progressive party having changed its name), obtained 132 and 126, respectively. The People's Cooperative party had thirty-one members elected, while the JCP secured only four seats. The extent of discontent was thus indicated. But the tenacity, skill, and determination of conservative politicians was equally apparent.

SHARING POWER: THE KATAYAMA CABINET

"We shall struggle against the conservative reactionary camp and carry out a revolution through the Diet"—so spoke Tetsu Kata-

* Allan B. Cole, George O. Totten, and Cecil H. Uyehara, *Socialist Parties in Postwar Japan* (New Haven, Conn.: Yale University Press, 1966), pp. 15–17, 19–22, 25, 30–32.

yama, Chairman of the SDP, immediately after the elections from the balcony of the *Asahi* newspaper building to crowds assembled below. It proved to be no more than a bold gesture.

Should the SDP, with only a plurality in the Lower House, try to form a cabinet? Tension persisted between its left and right wings on this score. The left opposed participating in the government because of the difficult economic situation, the lack of an absolute majority, and slim hopes for a future Socialist government if it failed the first time. The right wing, on the other hand, felt that the SDP should participate in the government since the people had given the largest support to the Socialists; because the party must not seem to lack in political courage; because it should abide by parliamentary practices as the plurality party; and it was, they argued, the only party that could "save the masses" from postwar economic chaos. The Socialist predicament was accentuated by the overwhelming conservative majority, though split as it was into competing parties and jealous factions.

For a month the four main parties (the SDP, the Democrats, the Liberals, and the People's Cooperative party) worked toward a national unity government and a four-party policy agreement. The JCP was pointedly omitted. The left-wing Socialist leaders, Mosaburō Suzuki and Kanjū Katō—in order to placate the suspicions of the conservatives on account of their active role in the aforementioned labor offensives, and in a bid for possible participation in the government—made a dramatic anti-Communist declaration. Instead of accepting these gestures, however, the Liberals demanded that the SDP be purged of its left wing. This the Socialists refused to do, but they agreed to exclude them from cabinet posts, to reject the extreme left and right, to prevent leakage of state secrets, and to refrain from any action conducive to social unrest. With more concessions from the SDP than from the conservatives, a four-party policy agreement was concluded. The Socialists pledged not to demand a freeze of the "new yen" or suspension of interest payments on war bonds and acceded to a diluted version of their coal nationalization policy. Socialist policies for overcoming chronic inflation were also sacrificed. At the last minute, the Liberal party declared it would not participate in the government anyway. The Socialists, Democrats, and People's Cooperative party eventually formed an administration. While they were officially bound by the four-party agreement, the Liberal party as "friendly" opposition could not be counted on for much cooperation. The ratio of cabinet seats was seven each for the SDP and the Democrats and two for the People's Cooperatives. The Socialists held the portfolios of education, agriculture and forestry, justice, commerce, and industry, and in addition the directorship of the Economic Stabilization Board. Thus, for the first time in modern Japanese history, a Socialist (and incidentally a Christian), Tetsu Katayama, headed the government. He was also the first premier under the new constitution.

The Katayama cabinet inherited an intolerable crisis from its predecessor: the vicious wage–price spiral, the militant demands of labor, and the food problem. In retrospect, Katayama claims that there was only four days' supply of rice in government warehouses when he took office. The paramount mission of this cabinet was, therefore, the formulation and execution of effective economic policies. The premier made desperate appeals to the people to bear up under the crisis and to cooperate with the government. The economic measures adopted by the Socialist-led government were in line with the general requirements enumerated in a letter from General MacArthur to the previous prime minister, calling for strong economic controls. . . .

At the time the Katayama cabinet had been formed, the labor movement had supported the Socialist party. The conservative Federation of Labor (Sōdōmei) had promised the coalition government its unqualified support, while the Sambetsu (the CIU [Congress of Industrial Unions, the Communist-oriented labor federation]) had given approval upon condition that Socialist policies should continue to be effected. Labor disputes and strikes had temporarily decreased. The Sōdōmei had proposed a rally to "support the Katayama cabinet" but, at the insistence of the Sambetsu, this was changed to "encourage the SDP." The difference in the attitudes of these two major labor federations was significant. When the government announced its wage–price stabilization program, the Sōdōmei reluctantly gave its support to the government, but Sambetsu demanded the fulfillment of SDP promises and the abandonment of the four-party policy agreement. Although the government had initiated many institutional reforms in favor of labor, it was unable to curb the deteriorating economic situation. Labor became restive; disputes and strikes began to increase again. Because private employers were able to circumvent the government's wage–price stabilization program with impunity, the real wages of government workers began to lag. Negotiations became protracted and bitter. The Central Labor Relations Board urged the adoption of a compromise: the payment of 2.8 months of a government worker's salary to overcome the inflationary deficit. The government paid two months extra wages; only the 0.8 month's pay remained, but this was too great a problem for the SDP and the coalition government. . . .

Very few Socialists had had any experience as administrators when their party first participated in this coalition. Their leaders had lacked adequate opportunities to draft national administrative plans and policies. They had made few preparations; they had neither resources nor personnel to create long-range plans which would spark the imagination, enthusiasm, and initiative of a people suffering from manifold disaster. They had no strong, nationwide grass-roots organization to sustain them and no adequate grip on local government which was essentially conservative. Had the SDP not led the government at that time, however, democratization would not have progressed as far as it did. The immediate results were catastrophic for the party, but it can be argued that long-range benefits accrued to Japan by the participation of the SDP in the government at that time.

Unfortunately, the Katayama cabinet presided over the highest inflation rate yet. It faced an almost unmanageable situation. To raise production and hold down inflation simultaneously seemed impossible. In emphasizing the revival of basic industries, it gave industrial management and capital a breathing spell, and also restrained the demands and pressures of trade unions. It incurred the antipathy of farmers when it ordered compulsory collection of rice quotas to ease the food situation. When prices were controlled, black markets prospered. Taxes rose, unemployment spread, and scarcity prevailed. Efforts of the Socialists had the ironical effect of strengthening the entrenched bureaucracy because of necessary dependence on it for the formulation and enforcement of policies, in spite of their hopes for "socialistic planning and control."

Intertwined with these problems was the harassing experience of a coalition government with two divergent ideologies, capitalism and socialism, bound together by a vague policy statement. Socialist willingness to compromise was based on the illusion that eventually, through a cumulative process, their socialist objectives would be attained—an illusion that was completely shattered. This and the ensuing experience impressed upon the SDP the undesirability of a tenuous coalition with parties bent upon conserving capitalist interests. Furthermore, the SDP should not have expected to initiate a wholly socialistic program under a basically conservative, even though benevolently reformist, occupying power. There is no doubt that factional strife within the party and its coalition partners had its toll on the efficiency of governmental leadership; but, after all the criticism has been heaped on the Katayama government and the SDP, it is more than rhetorical to ask whether this tragicomedy was not virtually inevitable in the circumstances, the more so once the party decided to join the coalition. Socialists have since realized that there would be less excuse in the future if history in this regard should ever be repeated.

COALITION RENEWED: THE ASHIDA CABINET

The Liberal party, as the opposition, insisted that formation of a new cabinet should be its responsibility. Its leaders continued their refusal to participate in negotiations toward a new coalition. The Democrats, weakened by defections to this conservative rival, desired a four-party coalition. Officially, the SDP did not demand the premiership and declared it would support the Democrats if a policy agreement could be reached; but left-wing Socialists stubbornly demanded the redesignation of Katayama as premier. They feared the Liberals would revert to reactionary policies and call for an election which would result in Socialist defeat. Only after Katayama refused to accept their nomination did they concede and vote for Hitoshi Ashida, president of the Democratic party, as new premier. . . .

The Ashida cabinet lasted eight months. It had been unable to curb inflation or to achieve any great measure of economic recovery and had been saved from the onslaught of determined labor offensives only by the Supreme Commander's intervention. It had been rent by policy dissensions resulting in expulsions on the left, defections on the right. The gravitation of dissident Democratic splinters toward the newly formed Democratic–Liberal party had been disruptive. . . .

Shigeru Yoshida formed what was meant to be a caretaker government. Fearing losses, the SDP tried to postpone the elections. The party had grown more factionally fragmented; its organization was shattered. . . . The elections, held on January 24, 1949, resulted in the most severe electoral setback suffered by the SDP during the entire postwar period. From a plurality of 143 seats in the Lower House, it fell to forty-eight. Many Socialist cabinet ministers, including Katayama, Katō, and Nomizo, were defeated. The SDP polled only 4.1 million votes or thirteen percent of the total cast. On the other hand, the JCP elected thirty-five Representatives, attaining the peak of its postwar popularity. . . .

Between 1949 and 1951, Japanese Socialist attitudes toward the Allied (chiefly American) occupation's policy changed from oblique criticism to direct attack. Japan could not escape the repercussions of the Cold War. Occupation policy no longer emphasized reform but rather recovery and security. The land reform program had been virtually completed, but industrial and financial deconcentration, which had also been regarded as essential to democratization of Japanese economic and political institutions, was brought to a halt; gradual, later marked, reconcentration and revision of antitrust legislation became a contrary trend. SDP disillusionment with the United States was further deepened by the strict enforcement of the so-called "Dodge line," which called for a balanced budget, severe curtailment of credit from governmental banks, a single exchange rate, and retrenchment of personnel in governmental and private industries. The Socialist party, together with the principal labor unions and federations, grudgingly accepted these measures in principle but lamented what they called the "one-sided" sacrifices being forced on the mass of workers and small entrepreneurs. Recognizing that they had little power to prevent enforcement of this program, the SDP and allied unions did their best to mitigate resultant sacrifices. The right- and left-wing factions supported the unions to varying degrees in their successive offensives. While the left wing generally encouraged more militant tactics pointing toward a general strike, the right rejected any attempt to use this weapon.

When the Communists scored their spectacular electoral gains in 1949, they controlled a large segment of the labor movement, but since the abortive strike intended for February 1, 1947, the challenge to their influence had been gathering momentum. This was centered in the so-called democratization leagues, which were being established in various national unions, and the trend was accelerated by the violent resistance of Communist-dominated unions against the personnel retrenchment prescribed by the "Dodge line." When the JCP was criticized early in January 1950 by the Cominform for its somewhat conciliatory attitude toward the Japanese government and the American occupation, it shifted to a more "positive" policy of sabotage, violence, and militant strikes. This aroused criticism of Communist leadership in the labor unions and assisted the activities of the democratization leagues.

The American occupation authorities also took a strong stand against Communist elements in the unions and actively supported their purge. A series of directives in May and June 1950 culminated in drastic reduction of JCP influence in both the Diet and in the labor movement amid charges of grave disregard of civil liberties. On May 3, 1950, the third anniversary of the new Japanese constitution, General MacArthur suggested outlawing the JCP, but, for various reasons, even conservative leaders in the main preferred not to do so. On June 3 and 7, 1950, the Japanese government at the behest of SCAP purged twenty-four members of the JCP Central Committee from public office and seventeen editors from the party's organ, *Akahata* (*Red Flag*). On June 27, two days after the Korean War started, this newspaper was suspended. The nearby conflict seemed further to justify a thorough purge of Communist elements from the ranks of organized labor. From 1949 to the end of November 1950, this expulsion— the "Red purge"—eliminated 11,000 workers in private industry and 1200 in governmental service.

... [O]n June 4, 1950, the SDP had faced its first major national election since 1949. As previously intimated, all indications showed Socialist popularity to be on the rise again after the serious lapse. Party morale was given a boost when a Socialist won the governorship of Kyoto in April. Though barely recovered from its incipient rift earlier that year, the SDP campaigned for a comprehensive peace treaty and against the disinflationary financial policies of the Yoshida government. Virtual elimination of Communist opportunities caused the labor unions to concentrate support behind the SDP. It became the second largest party in the House of Councilors with sixty-one out of 250 seats. On the

prefectural level, Socialist candidates polled more votes than in
1947. . . . Only seventeen months following their disastrous defeat,
the Socialists regained a posture of some strength. They steadily
increased their Diet membership until a plateau was reached in
1958–1960.

2. Trust-Busting the Japanese Zaibatsu

INITIAL MOVES TO DISSOLVE THE ZAIBATSU: 1945–1947

❀ As THE END of the war approached, the business leaders of Japan—the key figures in the huge zaibatsu—began preparations for recovery after defeat. The war itself had not seriously limited the power of the zaibatsu as a central institution of militarism. Rather, as the Japanese military was smashed by the overwhelming power of the Allied forces, it declined in influence in Japan and left the zaibatsu and the bureaucracy in control. Business took steps to ensure its continuity as the principal elite in Japan. Records were destroyed, personnel were shifted to protect those involved in the war and to help transfer exclusive blame to the military. Economically, at the cost of inflation to the rest of the country, the zaibatsu were paid indemnities to cover their wartime losses. Further, they acquired large stocks of equipment for later disposal.

On September 6, 1945, President Truman approved a document on "Initial Post-Surrender Policy for Japan." In the section pertaining to economics, part of which is given below, the zaibatsu saw that their fears and defensive preparations were not in vain. This statement, suggesting a harsh economic policy, reflected the initial U.S. attitudes after the war and is typical of many that saw the zaibatsu as the source of Japanese militarism and their destruction as the occupation's top priority.

Basic Initial Post-Surrender Directive*

PART IV—ECONOMIC

1. ECONOMIC DEMILITARIZATION

The existing economic basis of Japanese military strength must be destroyed and not be permitted to revive.

Therefore, a program will be enforced containing the following elements, among others: the immediate cessation and future prohibition of production of all goods designed for the equipment, maintenance, or use of any military force or establishment; the imposition of a ban upon any specialized facilities for the production or repair of implements of war, including naval vessels and all forms of aircraft; the institution of a system of inspection and control over selected elements in Japanese economic activity to prevent concealed or disguised military preparation; the elimination in Japan of those selected industries or branches of production whose chief value to Japan is in preparing for war; the prohibition of specialized research and instruction directed to the development of war-making power; and the limitation of the size and character of Japan's heavy industries to its future peaceful requirements, and restriction of Japanese merchant shipping to the extent required to accomplish the objectives of demilitarization.

The eventual disposition of those existing production facilities within Japan which are to be eliminated in accord with this program, as between conversion to other uses, transfer abroad, and scrapping will be determined after inventory. Pending decision, facilities readily convertible for civilian production should not be destroyed, except in emergency situations.

2. PROMOTION OF DEMOCRATIC FORCES

Encouragement shall be given and favor shown to the development of organizations in labor, industry, and agriculture, orga-

* "Basic Initial Post-Surrender Directive to Supreme Commander for the Allied Powers for the Occupation and Control of Japan," *Political Reorientation of Japan, September 1945 to September 1948* (Washington, D.C.: U.S. Government Printing Office, 1949), pp. 78–79.

nized on a democratic basis. Policies shall be favored which permit a wide distribution of income and of the ownership of the means of production and trade.

Those forms of economic activity, organization, and leadership shall be favored that are deemed likely to strengthen the peaceful disposition of the Japanese people, and to make it difficult to command or direct economic activity in support of military ends.

To this end it shall be the policy of the Supreme Commander:

(a) To prohibit the retention in or selection for places of importance in the economic field of individuals who do not direct future Japanese economic effort solely towards peaceful ends; and

(b) To favor a program for the dissolution of the large industrial and banking combinations which have exercised control of a great part of Japan's trade and industry.

❀ THE ZAIBATSU LEADERS, realizing that the occupation was resolved to end their monopoly of Japanese economic life, decided to take the initiative in devising the plans for their own "dismemberment." Not surprisingly, the Yasuda Plan (submitted by the Yasuda zaibatsu) was hardly a complete dismemberment. Even so, the zaibatsu and the Japanese government were not hasty about implementing even limited reforms, and only the great power of MacArthur's position forced them through.

Despite much foot-dragging, the Yasuda Plan was put into effect in 1946, and the purge of business personnel which began then reinforced it. The significance of the Yasuda Plan is that although put forward as a zaibatsu proposal, it resulted in the formal dissolution of the largest zaibatsu. Further legislation, formulated in 1947, was necessary to prevent the zaibatsu from re-forming.

*The Yasuda Plan**

OFFICIAL JAPANESE PROPOSAL FOR HOLDING COMPANY
DISSOLUTION INCORPORATING THE YASUDA PLAN,
NOVEMBER 4, 1945

The firms of Mitsui Honsha, Yasuda Hozensha, Sumitomo
Honsha, and Kabushiki Kaisha Mitsubishi Honsha, hereinafter
referred to as the "holding companies," have been holding conversations with the minister of finance with a view to voluntary
dissolution in accordance with the desires of the Supreme Commander for the Allied Powers.

The following plan is proposed for your approval to govern the
dissolution of these firms and such other firms of similar character
as may volunteer for dissolution:

1. a. The holding companies will transfer to a Holding Company Liquidation Commission all securities owned by them and all
other evidences of ownership or control of any interest in any firm,
corporation, or other enterprise.

b. The holding companies will cease to exercise direction or
control, either directly or indirectly, of all financial, industrial,
commercial, or noncommercial enterprises whose securities they
own or of which they hold any other evidences of ownership or
control.

c. The directors and auditors of the holding companies will
resign all offices held by them in such holding companies immediately after the transfer of the securities and other evidences of
ownership . . . and cease forthwith to exercise any influence, either
directly or indirectly, in the management or policies of the holding
companies affected by this dissolution.

d. All members of the Mitsui, Yasuda, Sumitomo, and Iwasaki families will immediately resign all offices held by them in
any financial, commercial, noncommercial, or industrial enterprises and cease forthwith to exercise any influence, either directly

* T. A. Bisson, *Zaibatsu Dissolution in Japan* (Berkeley and Los Angeles:
University of California Press, 1954), pp. 241–244.

or indirectly, in the management or policies of the enterprises affected by this dissolution.

2. The Imperial Japanese government will establish a Holding Company Liquidation Commission whose functions, among others, shall be:

    a. To proceed with the liquidation of all property transferred to it by the holding companies as rapidly as feasible.

    b. To issue receipts to the holding companies in exchange for such transferred property. Such receipts will be nonnegotiable, nontransferable, and ineligible for use as collateral.

    c. Pending the final disposition of the transferred property, to exercise the voting rights incident thereto, but only to the extent necessary to insure proper methods of accounting and reporting and to accomplish changes in management, corporate practices, and such other changes as are specifically desired by the Supreme Commander for the Allied powers.

    d. To redeem such receipts, upon the final liquidation of the transferred property, by delivery to the holders thereof, bonds of the Imperial Japanese government. . . .

3. When the securities, or other property transferred to the Holding Company Liquidation Commission, are offered for sale, preference to purchase will be given to employees of the companies involved, and in case of corporate shares the number of such shares that may be purchased by any single purchaser will be limited in order to insure maximum democratization of ownership.

4. Neither the holding companies nor any member of the Mitsui, Yasuda, Sumitomo, or Iwasaki families will purchase or otherwise acquire title or ownership of, or any interest in, any of the transferred property when it is offered for sale by the Holding Company Liquidation Commission. . . .

DIRECTIVE ACCEPTING JAPANESE PROPOSAL UNDER TITLE
OF "DISSOLUTION OF HOLDING COMPANIES,"
SCAPIN 244, NOVEMBER 6, 1945

. . . 2. The plan proposed therein is approved in general and the Imperial Japanese government will immediately proceed to effectuate it. No disposition of any property transferred to the Holding Company Liquidation Commission will be made without the prior approval of the Supreme Commander. You will submit the legislation through which the Holding Company Liquidation Commission will be created to the Supreme Commander for approval. It should be clearly understood that full freedom of action is retained by the Supreme Commander for the Allied Powers to elaborate or modify the proposed plan at any time and to supervise and review its execution. . . .

5. It is the intention of the Supreme Commander to dissolve the private industrial, commercial, financial, and agricultural combines in Japan, and to eliminate undesirable interlocking directorates and undesirable intercorporate security ownership so as to:

a. Permit a wider distribution of income and of ownership of the means of production and trade.

b. Encourage the development within Japan of economic ways and institutions of a type that will contribute to the growth of peaceful and democratic forces. . . .

❀ ALTHOUGH THE Yasuda Plan to dissolve the four largest zaibatsu was accepted by MacArthur, the Japanese government continued quietly to obstruct and oppose the occupation authorities in economic policies. It was recognized that the Yasuda Plan was acceptable to the large zaibatsu because it offered the possibility that a thorough dissolution of combines would not reach below the very top levels of corporate ownership and would thus be relatively ineffective. Far more sweeping plans were then formulated by SCAP for massive removals of Japanese industrial plants. This approach is exemplified by the stiff measures proposed by American oil magnate Edwin Pauley, whose letter excerpted below is a brief summary of extensive plans for reparations known as the Pauley report. The full report is sweeping in its scope, listing specific pieces of Japan's industry to be given to countries in the Far East that Japan had ravaged during the Second World War.

EDWIN PAULEY*
Letter to General Douglas MacArthur and President Truman

TOKYO, JAPAN, December 6, 1945.

General of the Army Douglas MacArthur
    Supreme Commander for the Allied Powers

Dear General: 1. On the basis of all the material available, including the Japanese figures assembled for me by the Economic and Scientific Section of your headquarters, I have now been able to come to some decisions on interim reparations policy and interim removals from Japan on reparations account.

2. My decisions fall within the following very simple framework:

(1) In preparation for war, in aggression in China, and in war against the United Nations, Japan built up the most diversified and overexpanded industrial economy in Asia.

(2) In spite of extensive destruction, especially in the closing phases of the war, Japan retains more industrial capacity than she needs or has ever used for her civilian economy.

(3) The removal of the surplus, especially to neighboring Asiatic countries, will help to raise their industrial standards and all living standards without depressing the standards of Japan, since only excess capacities are at the moment in question.

(4) Interim removals will, in most cases, be below the total quantities that may eventually be allocated to reparations.

(5) A program of interim removals should be announced to other claimant nations immediately, and the successive actions of seizure, inventory, packing, and shipment should follow in the shortest possible time, in order to make both the framework of policy and the course of action uncompromisingly clear.

---

* Edwin Pauley, Letter to General Douglas MacArthur and President Truman, *Foreign Relations of the United States, 1945: The Far East,* vol. VI, 1945 (Washington, D.C.: U.S. Government Printing Office).

3. Accordingly, I am recommending to our government that plants and equipment be made available as soon as possible under a program of interim deliveries as follows:

(1) Half of the capacity for the manufacture of machine tools. I believe that this could most conveniently be done by seizing the twenty-seven most important machine-tool manufacturing plants, which produce almost exactly half of Japan's total. The list of these plants, which you may wish to examine before making your own decision on plants to be seized, is attached to this letter on a separate sheet.

(2) All tools and equipment located as follows:

> *a.* In army and navy arsenals, except for equipment useful solely for making arms, ammunition, and implements of war, which will be destroyed. It is estimated that these seizures should bring in not less than 70,000 machine tools, as well as other kinds of equipment.
> *b.* In the entire aircraft industry of Japan. It is estimated that this should bring in 220,000 machine tools.
> *c.* In all plants manufacturing ball and roller bearings.
> *d.* In all plants manufacturing aircraft engines.

(3) All equipment and accessories in twenty shipyards, to the extent that it is not needed for the repair of shipping essential to the occupation. . . .

(4) All steel making capacity in excess of 2,500,000 tons per year. Japan's admitted present steel capacity is in excess of 11 million tons, as compared with 1930, when Japan produced 2,300,000 tons of ingot and consumed only 1,700,000 tons of finished steel.

(5) A recommendation on pig iron will be sent to you later.

(6) All facilities for the production of magnesium, for the preparation of alumina and reduction to aluminum, other than those required for processing scrap, and all machinery and equipment used exclusively for finishing magnesium and aluminum such as strip mills, rolling mills, and extrusion presses.

(7) Half of the thermal (coal) electric generating plants of Japan. In selecting the half of the plants of this character which are to be left, I suggest that the thermal electric generating plants left to Japan should be selected primarily for their value as standby plants to supplement hydroelectric energy in areas of high consumption.

(8) All contact process sulfuric acid plants, except those necessary to recover waste gases from zinc, lead, copper, and other heavy metal smelters.

(9) The most modern large Solvay process soda-ash plant in Japan. (According to Japanese information made available by the Economic and Scientific Section, there are four of these from which to choose.)

(10) Twenty of the most modern large plants for the production of caustic soda and chlorine, either in diaphragm or in mercury cells. (According to the Japanese information relayed to me by your Headquarters, there are forty-one plants under this classification.) . .

5. I am sure that you will agree with me that, in the interest of disarming and demilitarizing Japan, as well as in order to avoid unnecessarily dislocating the Japanese economy when later removals become necessary—a situation which could easily be exploited to make Japanese workers feel that we are destroying peaceful industry—the sooner the reconversion program is geared into what may reasonably be anticipated as definitive reparations policy, the better will be our chances of successfully attaining all our objectives.

6. Under the policy now being pursued by the Japanese, I am inclined to think that the giant corporations will take over the country in spite of our program of breaking up the zaibatsu, and that it will be next to impossible to pry loose those machine tools which should be removed as a disarmament measure. If this happens, a most important sector of the Japanese war potential will remain functioning, integrated, and in the hands of those who ran it during the war. . . .

❀ NOT UNTIL JANUARY 1947 was an economic purge promulgated eliminating certain individuals from their jobs and positions of influence. The integral role of personal ties in the zaibatsu complexes meant that economic dissolution was not enough; the personnel had to change as well. The delay in implementing the economic purge, however, as well as the small number of people actually purged, reduced its potential impact. Below Eleanor Hadley surveys the opening year of the purge.

ELEANOR M. HADLEY*
Combine Dissolution: Severing Personal Ties

A study of ownership holdings . . . indicates how inadequately ownership alone tells the story of Japanese combine structures. In some of the core subsidiaries the Mitsui, Mitsubishi, and Sumitomo top-holding companies held no more than seven, thirteen, and seventeen percent, and the combine itself held no more than seventeen, thirty-six, and twenty-two percent ownership, yet these were described as "almost perfectly" under top-holding company control. To have "perfect" or "almost perfect" control of subsidiaries with low ownership holdings indicates the presence of other controls with unmistakable clearness. Among the most important of these other means of control were the officers.

The controls exercised over the officers were both traditional and modern. The officers were expected to demonstrate a feudal-like loyalty to the controlling families. However, to ensure that such loyalty was always in force, the families through their top-holding companies: directly or indirectly appointed all officers of the core companies; bound such hand-picked officers through contractual agreements to take virtually no action on their own; and provided numerous interlocks between the top-holding company and the core subsidiaries, and among the core companies. The interlocks with the top-holding company served the dual function of simplifying liaison and providing on the scene watchfulness to ensure that no officer would lose sight of the fact that he was but a servant of the families. Inasmuch as the goal of combine dissolution was to make the member firms of the combine businesses in their own right, businesses that would decide on their own questions of output, product lines, prices, technology, and investment, the need to eliminate the integration by officers who had spent a

* Eleanor M. Hadley, *Antitrust in Japan* (Princeton, N.J.: Princeton University Press, 1970), pp. 77–80, 82, 85–88, 92–94, 100, 102.

lifetime in obeisance to the larger whole appeared vitally important. In the Basic Directive the JCS [Joint Chiefs of Staff] had ordered MacArthur to remove key business figures, because it believed them to be active exponents of "militant nationalism and aggression," which it was the objective of the occupation to eliminate, not because such persons were a vital part of the combine structures, likewise an objective of the occupation to eliminate. . . .

The zaibatsu organizations combined the modern holding company with feudal loyalty. The families at the top were the superiors to whom staff of the entire organization owed fealty. The spirit of subordination of staff to superiors, and ultimately to the families themselves, began on the day the individual joined the combine. The device of company "loyalty oaths" was used to heighten awareness of this quality. Earlier the writer observed,

> . . . each employee upon assignment to his subsidiary in the case of designated companies, or upon directly entering the company in the case of nondesignated subsidiaries, swore an oath of loyalty and secrecy to the company, much as in this country one swears an oath of loyalty to the Constitution of the United States on entering government service. The oaths to the business companies committed the employee to complete obedience to the instructions of all senior officials, devotion to the company, a policy of secrecy concerning business information "large or small, trivial or important," observance of all company rules, and the pledge never to act independently on his own judgment. The oaths were of a standard form. The text of the type of oath in common use prior to the Allied occupation is translated below; it is followed by a translation of the new "democratic" form. In English the two forms reveal less difference than they show in Japanese, because the older oaths were written in extremely formal, literary Japanese, whereas the new ones are written in a style nearer to the colloquial, though employing, of course, honorific and humble forms. Thus, for example, in the new form the word "company" is still prefixed with an honorific (the honorable company), the word "I" . . . [appears in its humble form]. The literary style of the older form made that form a more solemn pledge, but it is evident that this would only be a matter of degree. The text of the older type oath is the form used by a subsidiary of Mitsubishi Mining, Southern Sakhalin Colliery and Railroad Company; the new form, that of Mitsubishi Mining itself.

Oath of the Southern Sakhalin Colliery and Railroad Company:
1. I shall never violate the orders of the president or the instructions of my senior officers.

2. I shall sincerely and assiduously perform my duties, never bringing loss to the company.

3. I shall never divulge to a third party any of the affairs of the company large or small, trivial or important.

4. I shall keenly bear in mind never to violate any of the rules of the company.

5. With respect to any business I transact I shall always follow the instructions of my senior official, never undertaking any transactions on my own judgment.

> I accept the foregoing oath.
> Year _____ Month _____ Day _____
> Permanent Residence _____
> Family Relationship (*i.e.* relationship to head of the house)
> _____
>
> Name _____
> Date of birth _____
> Southern Sakhalin Colliery and Railroad Company.

Employee Oath of Mitsubishi Mining:
Having come into the employ of this company, I pledge this oath.

1. I shall follow the rules of the company and the instructions of the chief under whom I work.

2. I shall at all times strive toward an increase in the business of the company and shall diligently attend to my duties.

3. I shall never divulge secrets of which I am informed in connection with my duties.

Year _____ Month _____ Day _____

> [Space for signature and seal]
> Mitsubishi Mining Company.

The zaibatsu families conceived staff loyalty in personal terms. Loyalty was not to be to the staff person's conception of the business interests of the subsidiary in which he worked, but personally to the families themselves. Not only did such loyalty preclude an officer responding to a more attractive offer from the outside— once a Mitsui man always a Mitsui man—but it required demonstrated personal fealty to the families. It could be said of all the zaibatsu organizations that the ultimate test of advance up the ladder to the most coveted positions of all, the presidency of the core subsidiaries and membership on the board of the top-holding company, rested on business ability only where it was conjoined to unquestioning loyalty to the families at the top. . . .

INTERLOCKING OFFICERSHIPS

To ensure unity of action among this hand-picked officership group, all of the combines relied on interlocking directorships. . . .

. . . It is evident that if such integration was to be eliminated, several steps must be taken. There would have to be exclusion of those symbols of feudal-like loyalty, the zaibatsu family members. There would have to be removal of key officers of the major subsidiaries from positions within the combines, officers who had spent their entire professional experience being trained to operate as a combine team. There would need to be prohibition of officer-interlocks among such companies. Headquarters spent almost three years taking these steps, by which time the objectives of the occupation had changed.

In the Yasuda Plan, which was put forward in early November 1945, zaibatsu family members offered to resign all positions in business, but the ordinance that made this offer legally binding, Imperial Ordinance 233, took several months to achieve, and by April 1946 the Japanese government was no longer feeling so overwhelmed by the catastrophe of August 1945. The ordinance did not include the offer by the family members to "resign all offices." It simply stated that the HCLC [Holding Company Liquidation Commission] would direct the affairs of the holding companies designated for dissolution, thereby superseding the families. Nothing was said about restricting family participation in companies not among the designated holding companies.

To correct the deficiency of the HCLC Ordinance, SCAP in July 1946 instructed the Japanese government to eliminate the influence of zaibatsu family members and their appointees from positions of business responsibility and cease appointment of interlocking officers. Five months later, in December 1946, the Japanese government amended Imperial Ordinance 233 to provide for exclusion of zaibatsu family members from business positions. . . . Three more months were to pass before the "authorizing" authority of the December action was given meaning by naming fifty-six persons as coming within the meaning of the December amendment. . . . Provision for the elimination of appointees took considerably longer; it was not until January 1948 that specific provision was made for their elimination.

THE ECONOMIC PURGE

The JCS [Joint Chiefs of Staff] had instructed MacArthur:

> You shall prohibit the retention in or selection for positions of important responsibility or influence in industry, finance, commerce, or agriculture of all persons who have been active exponents of militant nationalism and aggression, of those who have actively participated in the organizations enumerated in paragraph 5(g) of this directive, and of any who do not direct future Japanese economic effort solely toward peaceful ends. (*In the absence of evidence, satisfactory to you, to the contrary, you will assume that any persons who have held key positions of high responsibility since 1937, in industry, finance, commerce, or agriculture have been active exponents of militant nationalism and aggression.*)

This formulation complicated rather than helped MacArthur's task. The weakness of the JCS approach, as T. A. Bisson aptly stated, was, "It was premised not on conditions of . . . [concentration] in Japan's business system but on the system's association with militarists and aggression." Clearly certain Japanese business leaders had worked openly and actively with the militarists in promoting Japan's "New Order in Greater East Asia"—Fujihara Ginjirō, president of the Ōji Paper complex, historically within the Mitsui combine, and Sasaki Shirō, . . . a director of the Mitsui Holding Company and head of its "research department," were among them. But they were, in their outspokenness, more the exception than the rule.

What was more at fault in the business world was the system. More important than the collaboration of various business leaders in the country's military adventures . . . was the system of enterprise itself, Japan's system of private collectivism. It was the zaibatsu which, with the other power blocs within the country, the military (*gumbatsu*), and the bureaucracy (*kambatsu*), supported oligarchy in government and actively opposed individualism and civil liberties. It was this system which resulted in favored treatment to a handful of businesses and a lack of concern toward others. And it was this system that produced a stunted domestic market with the resulting additional pressure for overseas markets. The JCS directive called for a change in Japan's system of private collectivism, but failed to tie the action on personnel changes in the business world to the way in which the system had been put together.

THE MECHANICS OF THE PURGE

The economic purge promulgated January 4, 1947, grew out of the political purge a year earlier. That is, public service was expanded to include top positions in major companies in the "private" sector of the economy, if one can call "private" those combines which accounted for up to one-tenth of the paid-up capital of the nation's corporate and partnership businesses. Technically the purge came as a result of the expansion of the final paragraph of the January 4, 1946, directive, calling for the removal of "militarists and ultra-nationalists." The major part of the economic purge related to persons holding key positions in 245 major companies—160 companies in Japan and eighty-five companies outside Japan—between the outbreak of the war in China and the end of World War II. The key officers in these 245 companies, which this time included, appropriately enough, financial institutions, were automatically required to give up their positions and were barred from all public service, which in the case of private business organizations was taken to mean *designated positions in designated companies.*

If a purged businessman wished to accept a lower nonspecified position in his same company, or to accept a top position in a company that was not listed, either a nonlisted subsidiary in his own combine or in a company outside, he was free to do so, as well, of course, as to join a new company. While the first circumstance was a possibility, there was little likelihood, with Japan's strong sense of hierarchy, of its being used. Superiors cannot serve under inferiors. In fact, one cannot serve under an equal, as is demonstrated by the custom of resigning in the civil service when one's classmate reaches the position of undersecretary. Therefore, the chief avenue for business "purgees" was either to retire or shift to one of the thousands of companies not among the 245 listed ones. . . .

In a number of circles in Japan and in the United States the economic purge occasioned sharp criticism of the occupation. It even created dissension within the Headquarters staff. Headquarters by the second year of the occupation was divided on the advisability of the economic purge. Had it occurred in January

1946, at the time of the political purge, criticism would probably have been minor, but it did not, largely because of Japanese government obstruction and procrastination. By the second year the Cold War was emerging, and there were those who in their new concern with the threat of communism believed it expedient to forget the reform aspects of the occupation, even though these were the *raison d'être* of the occupation and even though in the longer run they provided the best defense against communist inroads. Most unfortunately of all, there was an ugliness creeping into the differences of view, an ugliness which Senator Joseph McCarthy was later to make synonymous with his name. Critics of the economic purge tended to impugn the motives of those who emphasized the integrating of combine officers. Thus at times it could happen that staff carrying out the orders of the JCS could for this reason find themselves coming to be regarded in the eyes of their own government as doubtful security risks. . . .

There is no easy answer as to what the consequences of the purge and related measures were, for history cannot be rerun so that we can know "what would have been if. . . ." Given the GNP record of the economy, it is clear, however, that the economy of Japan was far from being seriously damaged. In fact, some observers of the postwar scene assert that an element in the truly phenomenal growth of the economy has been the new managerial blood which the purges and reorganizations (financial and structural) brought about in the new business environment in which corporate officers have been able to be officers in fact rather than in name only.

The legal prohibitions restricting zaibatsu family members from business positions and the removals brought about by the economic purge and the Zaibatsu Appointees Law were in effect somewhat less than four years. While some depurging occurred in 1950, the principal part took place in 1951. In a May 3, 1951, memorandum to the Japanese government on the fourth anniversary of the postwar constitution, General Ridgway authorized the Japanese government "to review existing ordinances issued in implementation of directives from this headquarters, for the purpose of evolving through established procedures such modifications as past experience and the present situation render necessary and desirable." The Japanese government acted with vigor under its new independence. Professor Bisson states that by the end of

October 1951, "only eighty ... economic purgees were still under designation." Yasuba Yasukichi's figures are slightly different; he reports that by May 1951 "all but convicted war criminals were released." Zaibatsu family members' designations were canceled July 11, 1951, the day the Holding Company Liquidation Commission was dissolved.

❖ BY 1947, occupation reforms had still failed to extensively democratize Japan's economy—in large part because of delays in executing the economic purge—and the task was increasingly complicated by other factors. The delays in attacking the concentrations of ownership meant that business leaders were able to consolidate their position. Moreover, dissolution orders had never been sufficiently extensive. The changes in American–Russian relations also had immediate effects in Japan, as did the highly negative reaction of visiting American businessmen to the proposals. Many viewed with alarm the American government's support for policies abroad that would harm their interests if ever attempted at home. Some stressed the economic cost to the United States of running the occupation. Growing antagonism toward occupation policies led to a reorientation of SCAP officials' outlook. Instead of diminishing the economic capacity of Japan, the goal was now to make Japan a partner, and the earlier draconian approach on reparations to Allied nations was challenged.

T. A. BISSON*
The Struggle on the Economic Front

... [T]he occupation authorities were well aware of the necessity for far-reaching changes in the Japanese economic structure. But while they were drafting long-range reform programs, they were

* T. A. Bisson, *Prospects for Democracy in Japan* (New York: Macmillan, 1949), pp. 95–99.

also confronted with a current economic crisis that became steadily more acute as time went on, and it soon became apparent that the old guard was waging its shrewdest battle against the occupation on the economic front.

By the time the Katayama cabinet took office on June 1, 1947, Japanese industrial production was lagging far behind capacity, budget deficits were increasing, and the volume of currency in circulation was following the dizzy upward path of an inflationary spiral that had already reached ominous proportions. Price increases had far outstripped the rise in wage levels, and, with the majority of the Japanese people already living at a bare subsistence level, this decline in real wages had given rise to a continuous succession of bitter labor disputes.

Some critics of the occupation contended that this crisis was primarily due to the unsettling effects of economic reforms and purges, the uncertainties attending reparations policy, the cumbersome restrictions imposed on Japanese foreign trade, and the large requisitions of Japanese materials by the occupation forces.

In making these charges, however, they neglected to mention several pertinent points. If the Japanese economy was to be left under the control of the old business leaders, and if Japanese economic recovery was to depend on their activity, then the reforms and purges were obviously a mistake. But the official policy of the U.S. government, supported by the Far Eastern Commission, was to destroy the monopolistic powers of the old business combines. As far as reparations were concerned, virtually no removals of Japanese industrial plants had actually occurred, and here again it was the old business groups that were most disturbed by the prospect of such removals. With respect to foreign trade, it was extremely doubtful whether Japan, by its own free efforts, could have imported foodstuffs and raw materials in the amounts that had been supplied by the occupation.

Of the four criticisms leveled at the occupation, the last had the most substance. The occupation had unquestionably made heavy drafts on Japanese materials and labor for construction projects, without enforcing adequate controls. Though expected to foot the bill, the Japanese government made little if any attempt to keep down prices of materials or labor costs, and both contractors and labor bosses reaped large profits. These construction projects thus served to intensify the inflation, whereas under better control they might have provided a stimulus to legitimate production that would have at least partly offset their inflationary effects.

In reality, however, the economic crisis in Japan reflected the operation of a more broadly determining factor than any of those noted above. Stated in its simplest terms, this was the failure of the occupation to achieve a sufficiently rapid and thorough destruction of zaibatsu power, with the result that the leaders of these great combines were left in a position where they could effectively sabotage efforts to expand production and curb inflation.

The occupation authorities had instituted measures that were potentially dangerous to the position of the old ruling oligarchy, but they had been slow in actually limiting its powers and destroying its influence. For the first twenty-one months of the occupation, no real shift in governmental authority was perceptible. The zaibatsu dominated the business life of the country, while the economic purge was delayed. Until the Katayama cabinet took office, Japan's old-line bureaucrats and industrialists virtually monopolized the operational control of both the government and the economy. And it was during this period that the economic crisis developed. In fact that crisis had its real beginnings in the last two weeks of August 1945, when nearly fourteen billion yen were suddenly pumped into circulation, and the army and navy ministries transferred large stocks of commodities to zaibatsu firms. . . .

A major obstacle to the development of a healthy economy in postwar Japan, more serious than the occupation authorities could have realized, had thus been created even before they entered the country. But on the other hand, the broad facts of Japan's economic situation and the general lines of the reform measures required were both clear. Japan's industrial plant had suffered heavy damage, and the entire economy was in short supply. To obtain production of essential basic materials and consumer goods, strict allocations of materials to essential industries were obviously necessary. Prudent fiscal policies were also needed to channel available funds into essential production, to limit government expenditures, and to keep the use of printing press money at a minimum. Rice and other food collections had to be strictly administered to provide rations for the urban population and to keep food imports as low as possible. By applying a program along these lines, the occupation authorities could stimulate Japanese economic recovery, limit the drain on American resources, and at the same time satisfy the legitimate needs of the Japanese people.

Such a program, however, did not suit the requirements of Japan's business leaders, and they had the power to prevent its application. As the occupation began, the zaibatsu concerns had control of Japan's industrial plant and the bulk of her commodity stocks. The value of their tangible assets would appreciate with the advance of inflation and thus cushion the shock of any demands that the occupation authorities might lay upon them. On all economic matters they controlled the application of government policy, no matter how that policy might be influenced by SCAP. Their power included not only operational control of fiscal measures, but also the ability to block any program looking toward the controlled allocation of materials. On this vital front they were doubly protected. Available goods were largely in their hands, while the Commerce and Industry Ministry and the semiofficial allocations agencies, such as the control associations and special distribution control companies, were headed by their representatives.

From these vantage points, they even fought to secure government indemnities for the losses suffered in destruction and damage to their munitions plants. Such indemnities, calculated on the basis of wartime Diet enactments, totaled upwards of eighty billion yen, and their payment would have bankrupted the treasury and accelerated the march of inflation. The zaibatsu firms had made vast profits during the war, and it was obvious that by seeking indemnities they also hoped to escape the burden of paying for a war that they had lost by shifting the burden to the shoulders of the Japanese people.

Zaibatsu spokesmen nevertheless boldly pressed the issue in statements directed not only to the occupation but also to the public. In mid-November 1945, for example, Kiyoshi Goko, chairman of the board of directors of Mitsubishi Heavy Industries, made the following declaration:

> The main reason for the slowness in reconversion of war plants to civilian production is that the industrialists are reluctant to resume operation unless they are sure of operating on a paying basis. There are also some industrialists who are withholding resumption of operations because they are uncertain as to how much they will get as indemnities for their war plants. Total

suspension of indemnities would bring about a general breakdown of industries with a resultant decline in production and rise in the prices of commodities.

Against such threats, Supreme Headquarters could make little effective response, despite the overriding authority that it possessed. The fact was that real control of the Japanese economy did not rest with the occupation authorities. It rested with the old Japanese business leaders, working through the government and its semiofficial "control" agencies and associations. These men favored a laissez-faire policy that permitted, or even encouraged, the development of inflation. They were prepared to hoard their materials, operate in the black market, let the economy stagnate, and wait for the end of the occupation. Unless the occupation authorities could place new men in control of government and industry, they faced a hopeless task in seeking to reverse this economic trend.

ELEANOR M. HADLEY*
The Pentagon and Shifts in Occupation Policies

Not only by late 1947 had the continuation of the wartime alliance with the Soviet Union gone sour, but events in China were raising questions as to the soundness of the U.S.'s postwar policy of basing its Far Eastern policy on a friendly China. The Communist takeover of China did not occur until 1949 (it is to be noted that unlike the situation in Eastern Europe Communist control in China was accomplished by indigenous forces, not with Soviet armies). However, the military performance of the Kuomintang in 1947 and 1948 did not breed a sense of confidence in its ability to overcome the Communist forces. In fact, Mao's success in 1949 betrayed in a sense the whole meaning of the Pacific War. . . .

The product of these developments was that the Pentagon began to think quite differently about Japan. In fact, by the end of the

* Eleanor M. Hadley, *Antitrust in Japan* (Princeton, N.J.: Princeton University Press, 1970), pp. 132-133.

second year of the occupation it began to propose that Japan be promoted from "ex-enemy" to partner. Ex-enemy and partner call for quite different policies. With a partner one is concerned only with its foreign policies. With Japan as an ex-enemy the United States and its allies were worried about the internal political forces that had produced the foreign expansion. And a number of America's allies were not nearly so ready to forget the Pacific War.

In addition to the Pentagon's desire to effect a fundamental change in the character of the occupation in Japan, certain conservative spokesmen were urging a reversal—for different reasons. Businessmen, first permitted to enter Japan in August 1947, were dismayed at what they found. Believing, as they did, in the sanctity of private property in all circumstances, they could not bear to see legal and procedural niceties set aside, even temporarily, for the purpose of creating a competitive, free-enterprise environment. To criticize with effectiveness one needs knowledge of what one is criticizing. It was not until businessmen saw the situation with their own eyes that they acquired the knowledge needed for effective criticism. American political mores require everyone to denounce monopoly and cartels, which all conservative critics were careful to observe, but when this had been dispensed with they indicated in unmistakable terms their distaste for both the attempt to break up the giant combines and the measures being used to accomplish the objective.

T. A. BISSON*
American Business and the Zaibatsu

Apart from conditions in Japan, the occupation program was subject to influences from abroad, of which those from the United States counted most. Immediately after V-J Day, the excitement of the American people over Japan was at high pitch, and remained so for some weeks or months. Public opinion favored strong measures by the occupation, including action against the zaibatsu,

* T. A. Bisson, *Zaibatsu Dissolution in Japan* (Berkeley and Los Angeles: University of California Press, 1954), pp. 41–43.

as editorials of the period clearly indicated. . . . Later, the attention of the American public shifted to European affairs, domestic issues, or events in China.

American business formed a normal pressure group in respect to the occupation. Its interest in occupied Japan took a different course from that of the public, tending to grow stronger and more active instead of weaker. This was particularly true of the dissolution program, where nearly two years passed before the full scope of occupation enforcement became evident.

The interest of the American business group in the zaibatsu, as might be expected, was quite unlike that felt, for example, in the matter of land reform. Americans, whether businessmen, officials, or the public generally, displayed no particular concern for the fate of the Japanese landlord. He was an anachronism, anyway, and found no defenders in the United States. But the program to dissolve the Japanese combines was of direct concern to the American businessman. A blueprint for deconcentration of the big combine subsidiaries affected certain Japanese corporations with which former ties had existed, and in any event was something to watch, since it could be reexported to the United States.

An ambivalent pattern, however, could be traced in the pressures exerted by American business on the dissolution program. Two well-defined groups existed, with contrasting interests. Some American traders and manufacturers, with vivid memories of prewar Japanese competition, were not averse to having the occupation cut the zaibatsu combines down to size. Exporters representing important domestic industries in the United States, such as cotton textile, rayon, and ceramics manufacturers, sought actively to prevent the restoration of Japan's industrial exports. To importers, also, the strong position still held by the great zaibatsu trading companies early in the occupation was a disturbing factor in their own business operations.

American firms with prewar investments in Japanese industry formed an interest group, running counter to the traders and allied manufacturers, that was much less favorably disposed to the dissolution program. At the end of 1941 American corporations accounted for three-fourths of the total foreign capital invested in Japanese industry, aggregating 110 million yen scattered among thirty-three Japanese concerns. The largest single investment, of forty-seven million yen, was by General Electric, which held six-

teen percent of the paid-up capital of Tokyo-Shibaura Electric, a
firm linked to the Mitsui combine, though not one of its direct
subsidiaries. In smaller amounts, Associated Oil had invested in
Mitsubishi Petroleum, Westinghouse in Mitsubishi Electric, Owens-
Libby in Japan Sheet Glass (Sumitomo), American Can in Oriental Can (Mitsui), and Goodrich in Yokohama Rubber (Furu-
kawa). Many of these connections were resumed, and new ones
were formed, in postwar Japan.

Both American pressure groups were active in occupied Japan,
with the traders, certain American banking firms, and petroleum
companies most prominent. . . . Pressures were at first confined
mainly to Tokyo but they soon extended to Washington, where the
significant reversals of policy were eventually obtained. In the
showdown of 1947–1948, General MacArthur was found
staunchly defending implementation of a program, fully approved
not long before, that had meanwhile lost favor at home.

§ THE LAST STAGE of antimonopoly activity was a proposal
placed before the Far Eastern Commission in 1947. The logic
of the program to create a competitive free enterprise economy was clear: first deconcentrate the zaibatsu, then have an
antimonopoly law to maintain the new system. The law designed to dissolve the zaibatsu permanently into small competing companies was proposed in the "FEC 230" directive
prepared by the State–War–Navy Coordinating Committee
("SWNCC") in early 1947 and sent to the Far Eastern Commission. Passed in December 1947 by the Japanese Diet under
American pressure, this policy directive came under heavy
fire in the United States and was almost immediately withdrawn. At the time of its framing, however, it was seen simply
as a logical step to guarantee that the zaibatsu did not re-form
after the occupation was over. Hadley describes the course of
the directive during 1947, and the State Department memorandum gives the rationale for continuing the dissolution
process to its conclusion.

ELEANOR M. HADLEY*
State–War Mission on Japanese Combines

The State–War Mission submitted a comprehensive set of proposals for eliminating Japan's historical pattern of industrial organization in the capital-intensive sector of the economy. It was thought that combine dissolution embraced not only holding company dissolution but prohibition of interlocking directorates, dissolution of contractual and service arrangements, procedures for opening up combine patents, and dissolution of oversized operating companies. Because of the existence of strong business loyalties, the mission recommended that zaibatsu members and those close to them be divested of all corporate securities and be removed from participation in business for a ten-year period. Such persons were to be compensated for their property, but the mission cautioned against giving them enough to buy back their former position. It recommended a rapid liquidation of zaibatsu properties, preferably over a two-year period, and cautioned that sales should be screened to prevent cloaks for zaibatsu interests or formation of new excessive concentrations of economic power. The mission proposals in finance were curiously weak; somehow it never came to grips with a key element of the issue, the integral union of commercial banking with industrial and commercial undertakings.

Under the U.S. Commercial Code, commercial banks are not permitted to own on their own account stock in nonbanking companies, though they are permitted, of course, to own debt instruments. While calling for a virtual prohibition of intercorporate stock ownership among nonfinancial companies, which is far more stringent than anything in the United States, the mission did not recommend that banks be prohibited from holding stock in commercial and industrial corporations. Furthermore, it did not call for a separation of investment banking from commercial banking. . . .

* Eleanor M. Hadley, *Antitrust in Japan* (Princeton, N.J.: Princeton University Press, 1970), pp. 127–129, 110–111, 114–115.

In addition, and more generally, the mission called for the termination of "control legislation," including within the term government monopolies, legislation requiring government approval for the formation of new businesses, and repeal of the laws and ordinances establishing "control associations"—the semiprivate, semigovernment bodies with which Japan had handled wartime allocations. The mission said: "New government monopolies should not be established during the transition period except with the explicit consent of SCAP. The petroleum and alcohol monopolies, which were instituted for war purposes, should be terminated."

The mission urged a systematic review of all forms of subsidy, legal monopoly, trade preference laws, and termination of such as do not have a demonstrable public purpose. It called for enactment of an antitrust law and revision of the patent law, and offered several suggestions for making control of corporations by insiders more difficult, among which was the establishment of independent auditors. . . .

To prevent the re-formation of combines, the mission called for permanent legislation prohibiting intercorporate stockholdings, "with exceptions for banks, insurance companies, investment trusts, and possibly other types of financial institutions," prohibiting interlocking directorates, prohibition of intercorporate shareholding. It recommended that basic changes be made in Japan's income and inheritance taxes, and concluded with several proposals for creating Japanese support for the program. . . .

It was this document which, with relatively minor word changes by SWNCC, became, with State's transmittal of it to the Far Eastern Commission, FEC 230. . . .

The Deconcentration Law of December 1947 was not the product of GHQ, SCAP thinking alone. In view of subsequent charges it is important to keep in mind that the language of the proposed measure had been cleared with Washington through the Department of the Army before a vote was taken in the Japanese Diet, and that, in fact, it paralleled comparable legislation in Germany enacted almost a year earlier. . . .

The Japanese "Law for the Elimination of Excessive Concentrations of Economic Power" was finally passed by the Diet December 8, 1947, and promulgated ten days later. A SCAP release published in the *Nippon Times* for December 18, 1947, stated of the law:

> Its broad intention is to establish a reasonable basis for competition and freedom of enterprise through the elimination of those concentrations of economic power which stifled efficiency as well as freedom. . . . *It is essential to recognize that this Deconcentration Law is not intended to hamper large-scale production or to prevent efficiently integrated enterprises.* . . . Likewise it should be clear that the Deconcentration Law does not establish any maximum or minimum size for business enterprises and it is to be administered by weighing carefully the actual facts characterizing each company affected by the Law. . . . It should be stressed that the deconcentration program, of which the Deconcentration Law is a major part, is a partner of other programs for the economic recovery of Japan. . . .

The key provisions of the law were the two articles, 3 and 6. Article 3 read, in part:

> . . . an excessive concentration of economic power shall be defined as any private enterprise conducted for profit, or combination of such enterprises, which by reason of its relative size in any line or the cumulative power of its position in many lines, restricts competition or impairs the opportunity for others to engage in business independently, in any important segment of business.

Article 6 specified the criteria to be taken into account by the HCLC in publishing more detailed standards about what constituted an "excessive concentration of economic power." The article included:

(1) market position including how gained (independent growth or by means of mergers).
(2) number of subsidiaries.
(3) whether parent-company plants stand on their own or are tied together through common raw material purchases, intermediate goods production, or joint selling of final goods.
(4) history of monopolistic practices of the company. . . .

There was alarm and resistance to the Deconcentration Law from conservative groups in the United States, which were upset that such a program had been attempted. The Department of the Army reversed its position. Although the army approved the text of the law before a vote was taken in the Japanese Diet, three months later key officials of the department were able, in effect, to have the law negated. Such an about-face left MacArthur in an embarrassing and awkward position. And timing on the reversal was such that no insurance or banking companies were designated, though the need for a more competitive banking structure was more urgent than change among most of the industrial and commercial companies.

MEMORANDUM PREPARED IN THE DEPARTMENT OF STATE*
Dissolution of Excessive Concentrations of Economic Power in Japan (*Zaibatsu Program*)

. . . Until recently there has been general agreement in the government on the zaibatsu program. Several weeks ago, however, the Department of the Army raised certain questions. . . .

The exchanges of views between the Army and State Departments and between Washington and Tokyo have not answered, to the satisfaction of the Army Department, a number of questions which have been raised by the program. These questions seem to arise from a number of general apprehensions. The first of these is, apparently, that the program is "un-American." The specific objection is thought to be the fact that the compensation to be paid to former zaibatsu owners for their divested property is inadequate. It is inadequate and inevitably must be, for if full compensation were paid the former owners would retain the financial power to resume their former positions of economic domination. Certainly the objective of the program—the breaking of the identity of interest between monopolistic business and the totalitarian state by encouraging a system of free enterprise—is soundly American. As General MacArthur has pointed out . . .

[T]his program, if successful in transforming a small number of monopolistic combines into numerous competing units and in

* Memorandum Prepared in the Department of State, "Dissolution of Excessive Concentrations of Economic Power in Japan (Zaibatsu Program)," *Foreign Relations of the United States, 1947: The Far East,* vol. VI (Washington, D.C.: Government Printing Office).

bringing about widespread ownership of the instruments of production and trade, will erect a solid bulwark against the spread of ideologies or systems destructive of both free enterprise and political freedom under democratic capitalism.

Another fear appears to be that the program has been or may be carried too far. The basic directives, however, contain no instructions to SCAP to take extreme action. Criticism of the ordinance is apparently based on the fear that it might, however, be administered in too drastic a manner. It seems doubtful that General MacArthur, who as theater commander is responsible for implementation, would permit this.

The third fear is that the program may interefere with economic recovery. It is SCAP's conclusion, with which the Department of State agrees, that Japanese recovery would on the contrary be seriously jeopardized by delay in carrying out the program. As long as the divested securities of former zaibatsu concerns remain in the hands of the Japanese government, where they now are, opportunity for free enterprise is restricted and recovery is consequently hampered. A further important consideration is that delay would create uncertainty among Japanese businessmen and others as to whether we really intend to free them from the domination of the zaibatsu, and whether they may now assume positions of responsibility in the Japanese economy without fear of reprisal at the hands of resurgent zaibatsu interests. Finally, delay would prevent the reorganization of many technologically incongruous combines which, under their existing sprawling organization, cannot obtain intelligent guidance from this top management.

. . . General MacArthur has pointed out . . . that "involved in the failure or success of the program is the choice between a system of free competitive enterprise which goes hand in hand with political freedom and a socialism of one kind or another under which political freedom is a myth," and that "reopening the policy for discussion at this time might well result in altering not only procedural or policy matters but in sacrificing the essential objective."

REVERSE COURSE: 1947–1952

❧ THE GENERAL POLICY of the occupation in reforming Japan came into sharp conflict in 1947 with the new emphasis on recovery of Japan's economy as the Cold War led to new perceptions of Russian power, the Chinese revolution, and insurgency movements in Asia. The two different approaches for dealing with Japan proved irreconcilable, and splits erupted within both SCAP and Washington. What has become known as the occupation's "reverse course" in economic and political policies was quite evident by late 1947, when the final deconcentration proposals were under consideration. The opposing arguments were first publicly posed in *Newsweek,* excerpted below, where the occupation reforms were harshly attacked, and by Senator Knowland, in December 1947. Another example indicating the shift in thinking by top American officials is Secretary of the Army Royall's speech in early 1948, in which reform is clearly viewed as secondary to a self-sufficient Japanese economy.

Significantly, these attacks were begun in the United States, not Japan, and reflected a long-standing dispute over the proper occupation policy. The shift in U.S. policy was made clear to SCAP headquarters in Tokyo by the Draper-Johnston Mission in February 1948, discussed here by Hadley. Led by Under-Secretary of the Army William Draper, the mission was advised by a business group headed by Percy H. Johnston.

NEWSWEEK*
A Lawyer's Report on Japan
Attacks Plan to Run Occupation

Heretofore the purpose of an occupation has been to demilitarize the occupied country, restore order, and protect and conserve property until a peace treaty could be concluded. Demilitarization was deemed to have been accomplished when the conquered nation was physically disarmed. In Japan, however, it was decided that demilitarization included the complete reformation of the nation's ideology. One of the means for bringing that about has been the imposition of an economic theory which has, I believe, no counterpart anywhere else in the world. It is not communistic but it is far to the left of anything tolerated in this country. . . .

The economic advisers to those in authority are for the most part either former instructors at universities who have also served some years in one of the many bureaus in Washington, or recent college graduates. Few of these men have had any practical experience. The few businessmen in SCAP with real experience are not on the policy-making level.

DEMOCRACY REDEFINED

SCAP proposes to create in Japan what it terms a "democratic Japanese economy" and "to this end, it is desirable that the Japanese economy be reorganized and concentrations of economic power be eliminated at the earliest possible date." There is no definition in writing, as far as I have been able to learn, of what is meant by a "democratic Japanese economy," but, whatever that term may mean, in this instance it is proposed to distribute the wealth of Japan to the workers, farmers, and small traders through the medium of taxes, sales of valuable properties at nominal values, financial assistance, regimentation, and regulation. . . .

* "A Lawyer's Report on Japan Attacks Plan to Run Occupation," *Newsweek*, December 1, 1947, pp. 36–38.

This policy (as outlined in FEC 230) has been implemented by SCAP-sponsored Japanese laws such as the Enterprise Reconstruction and Reorganization Law (October 18, 1946) and the Labor Standards Law (April 5, 1947). SCAP also intends to have the Japanese government enact several other laws, one of which is sweeping and general in its terms and provides for breaking up companies on the ground of "excessive concentration of economic power." The policy has been further implemented by instructions, directions, and explanations given by various members of SCAP.

UNDEMOCRATIC OVERTIME

For example, take the Labor Standards Law. This forces on an impoverished Japan the same high standards enjoyed by American labor. . . .

Many labor contracts go far beyond such agreements in this country. The agreement between the Japanese company in which a well-known American company had a controlling interest and the company union, in addition to the usual provisions for a closed shop, hours, rights of dismissal, cost of living, wages, etc., states that part of the profits (not stating what part) shall be paid to the union, and the election and removal of directors, inspectors, and advisers of the company may be accomplished only after consulting the union.

BROKEN ECONOMY

But it is largely through the medium of the Enterprise Reconstruction and Reorganization Law and the law dealing with concentrations of economic power that the existing economy is to be destroyed and one radically different from ours is to be substituted.

These new laws require that Japanese corporations be broken into many small units. At first the idea of dividing companies into many small units was confined to the zaibatsu (family) holding companies and those in which the zaibatsu had substantial interests. Now under the theory of an "excessive concentration of economic power" the Antitrust and Cartels Division of the Economic and Scientific Section of SCAP has the power to destroy any single Japanese company. This is true even though the zaibatsu has no connection with such corporation.

Of course, the family holding companies should have been dissolved and their hold on Japan's economic life broken. But the manner in which this is now being done makes one wonder whether for Japan and the world the remedy may not prove worse than the disease.

BROKEN MEN

This purge is being used by us as a lethal weapon in the socialization of Japan. It is estimated that upwards of 200,000 Japanese have already been purged and over another 100,000 will shortly be added. . . .

Because of this purge both the Japanese government and businesses have been stripped of older men of ability and experience. Japanese banks are being run by former cashiers and assistant vice-presidents while business concerns are being directed by former plant managers and clerks. Young men hold the key positions in government. They are hard working, sincere, and intelligent but lack the experience so desperately needed at this time. . . .

SECOND THOUGHTS

There is grave danger that the entire Japanese economy may collapse with a sacrifice of a substantial part, if not all, of the good which the occupation of Japan from a military point of view has accomplished. The Japanese had been told by their military leaders that American troops would loot, rape, and kill. When they arrived and this did not happen and instead they conducted themselves in a truly admirable manner and showed a disposition to help, there was a complete reversal of feeling on the part of the Japanese. This fear quickly changed to enthusiasm for the occupation. As they began to realize how much better off they were in our hands than they would have been in those of Russia, they showed a real desire to cooperate and to carry out what the occupational government directed.

The restoration of law and order and the demilitarization and repatriation of troops were all most ably carried out under the most skillful, intelligent, and sympathetic leadership of General MacArthur. But the military phase of the occupation was completed months ago and was succeeded by the necessity of restoring the Japanese economy. In this respect the occupation to date has not only been a failure but it has sought to impose on the Japanese an economic system which is distinctly un-American. . . .

ON THE CUFF

Japan is costing the American taxpayers millions of dollars a year. Theoretically Japan is paying the costs of occupation. A military operation, at least with us, is always expensive, and in this instance it is particularly so on the basis that Japan is paying for it. Houses with large staffs of servants are demanded for officers and their families at rentals far below their cost to the Japanese government. Clubhouses and servants are supplied without cost to the members on the supposition that it is all on the Japanese, so why worry? Innumerable other extravagances of a similar nature constantly occur. It is true that most of these are paid for directly in yen by the Japanese government, which is given a corresponding credit against future reparations payments. But, in fact, the American taxpayer is paying in the form of millions of dollars' worth of food and other necessities to Japan.

Were economic conditions otherwise, I am convinced Japan would be a most attractive prospect for American industry and a fertile field for American capital. Whether Japan can be made such a place depends in my opinion upon the willingness of our government to do two things: First, put an end to the economic experiment being conducted in Japan. Second, replace the theorists now there with men of ability and experience who can restore Japan's economy.

THE TROUBLESOME FEC 230

One of the basic objectives of the American occupation of Japan has been to break up the zaibatsu, the great family monopolies that controlled most of the country's economic life and were used to finance Japanese aggression. However, it has never been the purpose of the American government to weaken the Japanese economy to the point where the maintenance of Japan would become a continual charge on the American taxpayer.

Last spring—against this background—State Department economists drew up an amazingly detailed document known as FEC 230. It was submitted to the Far Eastern Commission on May 12 and communicated to General MacArthur's headquarters. It was classified as confidential and its contents thus kept from the American public.

In September the new Under-Secretary of the Army William H. Draper Jr. visited Japan. Draper, who gained an outstanding reputation as economic adviser to General Clay in Germany, became aware of FEC 230 during this visit. He and other officials found FEC 230 not only provided for the abolition of the zaibatsu but also for a virtual destruction of Japanese business and the sale of its assets at nominal prices to selected purchasers, including Japanese labor unions, of which about one-half are Communist-dominated. On his return to Washington Draper warned the State Department that the application of the directive would make Japan a permanent ward of the United States.

A heated discussion on the future of FEC 230 is now going on between the Army and State departments. For the time being the document has been withdrawn from the FEC "for redrafting." Its application in Japan has been ordered suspended.

Newsweek has obtained a copy of FEC 230. Although the legal language of the following excerpts makes heavy reading, they reveal, as no condensation can, why FEC 230 has now been shelved and why it was kept secret in the first place.

DISSOLUTION

FEC 230 was based on the thesis that "the dissolution of excessive private concentrations of economic power is essential to the democratization of Japanese economic and political life." Such excessive concentrations were then defined as:

> Any private enterprise or combination operated for profit is an excessive concentration of economic power if its asset value is very large; or if its working force . . . is very large; or if, though somewhat smaller in assets or working force, it is engaged in business in various unrelated fields, or if it controls substantial

financial institutions and/or substantial industrial or commercial ones; or if it controls a substantial number of other corporate enterprises; or if it produces, sells, or distributes a large proportion of the total supply of the products of a major industry. . . .

DIVESTMENT

FEC 230 continued: "Excessive concentrations of economic power should immediately be dissolved into as many nonrelated units as possible. . ." Creditors, stockholders, managers, or any other individuals who have "exercised controlling power" in any excessive concentrations will be:

a. Divested of all corporate security holdings, liquid assets, and business properties;

b. Ejected from all positions of business or governmental responsibility;

c. Forbidden from purchasing corporate security holdings or from acquiring positions of business or governmental responsibility at any time during the next ten years.

SALE

In order to liquidate excessive concentrations FEC 230 provided for "Holding Company Liquidation Commission, a wholly public agency of the Japanese government operating under close supervision of SCAP. Especial care should be taken not to allow representatives of large-scale business, large-scale trade, or large-scale finance . . . to have any place on this commission." The individuals whose holdings are liquidated "shall be indemnified." However, FEC 230 carefully stated that no effort would be made to obtain a fair price for their holdings: "The overriding objective should be to dispose of all the holdings in question as rapidly as possible to desirable purchasers; the objective should be achieved even if it requires that holdings be disposed of at a fraction of their real value."

Furthermore,

a decided purchase preference, and the technical and financial aid necessary to take advantage of that preference, should be furnished to such persons as small or medium entrepreneurs and investors, and to such groups as agricultural or consumer cooperatives and trade unions. . . . All possible technical and financial assistance should be furnished the trade unions concerned.

SENATOR WILLIAM F. KNOWLAND*
Speech, December 19, 1947

. . . Mr. President, the Congress and the country are entitled to know the basic American policy being carried out by this government abroad.

In time of war, there is recognition of a need for withholding information as a security measure. However, in peacetime, government departments have used the classification of material as a means of keeping facts from both the Congress and the people. . . .

There are very few members of the Senate or of the House of Representatives who have seen the document FEC 230. It was issued under a confidential classification on the 12th of May. This document when presented to the Far Eastern Commission was the official statement of policy of the American government which was recommended for adoption by the Commission with respect to certain economic policies to be followed in Japan. . . .

Although I am in complete accord with the policy of breaking up cartels and trusts in both Germany and Japan, I believe that FEC 230 and other policies being followed in Japan go far beyond this.

If some of the doctrine set forth in FEC 230 had been proposed by the government of the U.S.S.R. or even by the labor government of Great Britain, I could have understood it. . . .

On Monday of this week a copy of FEC 230 came into my possession. I was so shocked by what I read that at the next meeting of the Appropriations Committee I requested Mr. Walton Butterworth, of the State Department's Far Eastern Division, to officially supply a copy of this document to the Senate Committee on Appropriations.

On December 17, in response to my request that a copy of the document be made available to the Appropriations Committee, the Department of State replied by stating that it did not have the authority to declassify the document as I had requested. . . .

The fact of the matter is that the policies laid down in FEC 230

* U.S., Congress, Senate, *Congressional Record,* 80th Cong., 1st sess., 1947, pp. 11686–11687.

are the policies which the government of the United States itself is advocating before the Far Eastern Commission. If anything, the other members of the Commission are apt to strengthen rather than to weaken its provisions.

While the document itself may have been temporarily withdrawn due to a controversy on the subject going on now within the American government, the fact remains that the policies and philosophies enunciated under FEC 230 are still playing an important part in the economic and political life of Japan.

A short time ago American occupation officials gave their tacit approval, if not their active support, to the adoption in the Japanese Diet of four bills which set up the laws and machinery to put into effect the type of economy outlined in FEC 230. These bills are: The economic decentralization bill, the Holding Company Liquidation Act, the special law to liquidate zaibatsu companies, and the act to nationalize the distribution of foodstuffs, liquors, and oil. The correspondent of one of the large American newspapers called the last of these bills the most socialistic ever attempted outside of Russia. . . .

Without any provision for a prelude of accusation, trial, or conviction for war crimes or other offenses, the American policy under FEC 230 is that all individuals who have exercised a controlling voice in the large economic organization of Japan as managers, stockholders, or creditors, or in any other capacity, should be divested of all corporate liquid assets and business property; ejected from all positions of governmental responsibility, and forbidden from purchasing corporation security holdings, or from acquiring positions of governmental responsibility at any time during the next ten years.

This document, however, goes far beyond even this arbitrary purge, and sets forth in the name of the American people and the American government a sort of bill-of-attainder doctrine by proposing further that all persons likely to act on behalf of any of the individuals above enumerated should be subjected to substantially the same restrictions, though slightly modified, as those mentioned above. In determining who such persons may be, American policy under FEC 230 provides that ties by blood, marriage, adoption, or past personal relationship should be taken into account in expanding the purge.

With reference to compensation to the former legal owners of zaibatsu interests, this very unusual and distinctly un-Anglo-Saxon philosophy is enunciated. Policies which validate the conveyance of all property rights from the legal owners are not to be modified to obtain any specified degree of compensation for the former owners. The overriding objective set forth is to dispose of all the holdings as rapidly as possible to desirable purchasers, and this objective is to be achieved even if it requires that holdings be disposed of at a fraction of their real value. . . .

Mr. President, it was unbelievable to me that such a document could be put forward as representing the policy of the government of which I am a part.

The time has long since passed when members of Congress can complacently stand aside and remain silent while policies are being carried out in the name of the government of the United States which are contrary to American standards of decency and fair play and are not in conformity with our own political, moral, or economic standards.

Mr. President, the Congress and the country should be told who the originator of this proposal is. It should be fully informed as to his background and the positions of trust he has held in various agencies of the government of the United States. The country and the Congress should be informed as to whether General Douglas MacArthur was consulted in advance regarding these economic policies being followed in the name of the American government in Japan, or whether he has been given directives from Washington which he has no choice but to carry out.

Mr. President, I believe that this matter is of such importance to the Congress and the country that I hope a full-scale investigation of these and other policies being followed in our name may be promptly carried out. I do not care whether this full-scale investigation is conducted by the Appropriations Committee or by the Foreign Relations Committee, but I do urge that one or both of these committees act separately or jointly and proceed immediately to get the full facts.

If we delay, the Congress and the country will be confronted in this as we have been in other matters with a fait accompli, and with no choice but to rubber stamp a policy contrary to our way of life. It would also be a way of life that even a future democratic Japan may find it difficult to change. In the last few years, we have found too often that it is not possible to unscramble eggs.

KENNETH C. ROYALL*
Speech, January 6, 1948

SPEECH BY KENNETH C. ROYALL, SECRETARY OF THE U.S.
ARMY, TO THE COMMONWEALTH CLUB, SAN FRANCISCO,
ON AMERICAN POLICY TOWARD JAPAN

To many American citizens—including myself—the most surprising development—and one of the most disappointing aspects of our victory over Germany and Japan has been the responsibility and cost which have been placed upon us in the matter of occupation. There were few who originally recognized the extent of this burden. And today every citizen of our country is justified in asking the "what" and the "why" of our occupation policies.

On this occasion I will speak specifically of Japan. Immediately after the surrender, the objectives of our policy were stated to be, first, "to insure that Japan will not again become a menace to the peace and security of the world," and, second, "to bring about the earliest possible establishment of a democratic and peaceful government which will carry out its international responsibilities, respect the rights of other states, and support the objectives of the United Nations."

The underlying idea was the prevention of future Japanese aggression—direct prevention by disarmament, and indirect prevention by creating a type of government unlikely to develop again the spirit of aggressive war. The real well-being of Japan—or her strength as a nation—was decidedly a secondary consideration: secondary to protection of ourselves against Japan, and secondary to payment of reparations to the victorious Allies for the damages inflicted upon them.

This attitude is clearly shown by the emphasis in the original directive, which stated in part: "Japan shall be permitted" (not encouraged but permitted) "to maintain such industries as will

* *Documents Concerning the Allied Occupation and Control of Japan, Volume Two (Political, Military, and Cultural)* (Japan: Division of Special Records, Foreign Office, 1949), pp. 4–10.

sustain her economy and permit the exaction of reparations . . . but not . . . enable her to rearm. . . . Access to, as distinguished from control of, raw materials shall be permitted. Eventual Japanese participation in world trade . . . shall be permitted." . . .

Action against the zaibatsu has proceeded vigorously, and its control has now been virtually abolished. Sixty-seven holding companies with 4000 subsidiaries and affiliates, have been marked for liquidation. The two largest holding companies—Mitsubishi and Mitsui—have been closed. Others of the larger ones have been almost wholly liquidated.

The Japanese government has been directed to prepare legislation prohibiting international cartels. Stringent antitrust and deconcentration legislation has been prepared and passed in part. A Holding Company Liquidation Commission has been established and is functioning in the supervision of the entire program. . . .

But the Department of the Army and the Department of State—which shares the policy responsibility of occupation—both departments realize that, for political stability to continue and for free government to succeed in the future, there must be a sound and self-supporting economy, and General MacArthur in command of the occupation can be depended upon to implement these policies.

We also realize that the United States cannot forever continue to pour hundreds of millions of dollars annually into relief funds for occupied areas, and that such contributions can end without disaster only when the occupied countries can pay for their own necessities with their own production and exports.

These factors have resulted in efforts to improve in many fields the economic situation in Japan. And with this increasing economic approach there has arisen an inevitable area of conflict between the original concept of broad demilitarization and the new purpose of building a self-supporting nation.

In the case of agriculture the two purposes do happen to run practically parallel. The breaking down of feudal holdings has ended a war-making influence. At the same time the wider division of lands tends to produce incentive on the part of the larger number of landowners and thereby to increase overall production.

But it is a different situation with manufacturing. The destruction of synthetic rubber or shipbuilding or chemical or nonferrous metal plants will certainly destroy the war potential of Japan, but such destruction may also adversely affect the peace potential.

The dissolution of the zaibatsu may present in itself no serious economic problem, but at some stage extreme deconcentration of industry, while further impairing the ability to make war, may at the same time impair manufacturing efficiency of Japanese industry—may, therefore, postpone the day when Japan can become self-supporting.

Such is our dilemma. It is clear that Japan cannot support itself as a nation of shopkeepers and craftsmen and small artisans any more than it can exist as a purely agricultural nation. We can expect a continuing economic deficit in Japan, unless there is at least some degree of mass industrial production.

Another borderline situation between demilitarization and economic recovery is presented in the case of personnel. The men who were the most active in building up and running Japan's war machine—militarily and industrially—were often the ablest and most successful business leaders of that country, and their services would in many instances contribute to the economic recovery of Japan.

What should we do about them now? We cannot afford to leave the Japanese war system intact nor forget that there is danger in retaining in power leaders whose philosophy helped bring on World War II. On the other hand we cannot afford to sterilize the business ability of Japan. . . .

We realize that deconcentration must stop short of the point where it unduly interferes with the efficiency of Japanese industry. Earlier programs are being reexamined—as for example the details of the program stated in the paper submitted some months ago to the Far Eastern Commission, and recently given wide publicity as FEC 230. . . .

The lines to be drawn are, of course, not always easy to draw, and as in the case of all decisions of importance one cannot be too dogmatic. There can be—and are likely to be—differences of opinion among sincere and informed people. Nor do I have any illusion that everything we do will be perfect.

But I can assure you that our decisions will be made with realism and with a firm determination of doing all possible to prevent Japan from again waging unprovoked and aggressive and cruel war against any other nation. We hold to an equally definite purpose of building in Japan a self-sufficient democracy, strong

enough and stable enough to support itself and at the same time to
serve as a deterrent against any other totalitarian war threats
which might hereafter arise in the Far East.

ELEANOR M. HADLEY*
The Draper-Johnston Mission and the Reverse Course

The Draper-Johnston Mission, whose role it was to underscore the
changed U.S. policy, served the purpose not only of reorienting
Headquarters to the new United States policy, but also reorienting
public thinking. Inasmuch as the mission, with no background on
the Far East, drew up its recommendations, including a new set of
reparation proposals, on the basis of two weeks in Japan, it is clear
that it did not come in search of information but rather a rostrum
from which to enunciate the new policy.

Technically, the visit was one by the Under-Secretary of the
Department of the Army, Mr. Draper, who was advised by a group
of big business representatives known as the Johnston Committee.
The Johnston Committee consisted of Percy H. Johnston, chairman of the Chemical Bank and Trust Company, Paul G. Hoffman,
formerly president of Studebaker, who had just been named administrator of the European Recovery Program, Robert F. Loree,
chairman of the National Foreign Trade Council and formerly vice-
president of the Guaranty Trust Company, and Sidney H. Scheuer,
senior partner of Scheuer and Company. However, the committee's report was to the secretary and was officially published as the
Johnston Report. Mr. Draper, who in civilian life was an investment banker with Dillon Reed, had been an economic advisor in
the Germany occupation before becoming under-secretary in
1947. He was influential in effecting a reversal of United States
decartelization policy in Germany, and now turned his attention to
United States policy in Japan.

The Johnston Committee saw the "problem" of Japan in 1948
as one of economic recovery. The focus on recovery (including

* Eleanor M. Hadley, *Antitrust in Japan* (Princeton, N.J.: Princeton University Press, 1970), pp. 144–146.

Japan as a site for foreign investment) suggests that in the committee's judgment other problems had essentially been met. Its concern with this issue is shown in the following excerpts from its report.

> The first economic need of Japan is increased production. . . . The Committee, therefore, looked into the present obstacles. . . . The three main deficiencies in the physical means available to Japan are: (1) lack of essential raw materials, (2) the bad condition of many existing factories, (3) the poor state of transport. . . .
> Despite all physical limitations, production could even now be at a higher level, were it not for other deterrent influences affecting adversely the desire to produce, work, plan and invest. . . .
> The threat of removal for reparations hangs over much of Japan's industry, especially heavy industry. . . .
> Another element of uncertainty derives from the changes being effected in the control of Japanese industry. A very large part of Japanese industry before the war was dominated either by the government or by private monopolistic groups. . . . [A] small number of family groups, through holding companies and controlled banks, owned and directed a large part of all Japanese industry, shipping and finance. . . .
> The period of uncertainty caused by this economic reform should be made short and the area of uncertainty lessened as rapidly as possible. The possible disturbing effect should be allayed by care not to hurt production, and by limiting reorganization to the minimum necessary to insure reasonable competition.
> Various obstacles to foreign investment remain which must be removed before any substantial flow of such investment can be anticipated. . . . (1) Protection of foreign investments from confiscation and discriminatory taxation, (2) reasonable freedom of export of dividends and profits, (3) a tax structure which would permit earning and payment of reasonable profits, (4) permission to foreign nationals to control enterprises proportionately to their investments.

The shift in the climate of opinion with respect to Japan in the change from ex-enemy to partner is clearly seen in the matter of reparation removals, for reparation policy was of course also integrally involved in the softening attitude. During the ex-enemy period, proposals for reparation removal were high; now that partnership was being considered, proposals were strikingly reduced. Any number of reparation-removal studies were made. The recommendations of three are cited—that of the Pauley Mission in the fall of 1945; the proposals made by Overseas Consultants,

Inc., during a five-month study in the fall of 1947 and into 1948 (with which Mr. Kauffman was associated); and Draper-Johnston Mission recommendations, in March 1948.

❀ UNLIKE THE DEVELOPING American reaction to the zai-batsu program, other nations continued to approve of it. As the "reverse course" progressed, many in Australia and Asia became dismayed. Both Ball and Mei below, Australian and Chinese respectively, expressed the bitter disappointment of many that the dissolution program was not carried out. For those nations that had been occupied or immediately threatened by the Japanese in World War II, a guarantee that this would not happen again appeared more important than the shifting strategic considerations of Washington and the growing opposition of American conservatives to occupation reforms. Ultimately, all such protests were ignored by SCAP and the United States government.

MEI JU-AO*
The Future of Japan

I went to occupied Japan on March 20, 1946, and left the country on June 4, 1949. With the exception of a few home visits to Shanghai which lasted seldom more than two weeks, my stay in Tokyo had been continuous for more than three years, thus giving me an excellent opportunity in watching how Japan fared in defeat and in recovery, how the Allied occupation was carried out, and how the American policy toward Japan underwent various stages of transformation until it finally crystalized into its present form. As a judge sitting on the bench of the I.M.T.F.E. (International Military Tribunal for the Far East) for the trial of top-ranking

* Mei Ju-ao, "The Future of Japan," *China Digest* VI:2 (January 2, 1949).

Japanese war criminals, my mission was unique and my work was heavy. But, being a Chinese, I could under no circumstances confine my interest to things purely judicial. Besides hearing and studying the case before the tribunal, which amounted almost to a complete story of Japanese aggression during the last twenty years, I have utilized every opportunity to observe for myself what was going on, both on the stage and behind the screen, in that sub-jugated empire, which for nearly fifty years had been China's deadly enemy. . . .

Let us begin with the first year, *i.e.,* from the signing of the Instrument of Surrender at Tokyo Bay on September 2, 1945, to September 2, 1946. . . .

On the part of the occupation authorities, certain measures of demilitarization, deconcentration, and democratization were initiated and carried out, in pursuance to the Four-Power Pots-dam Declaration and the American Initial Post-Surrender Policy Directive. The Allied Council for Japan and the International Mili-tary Tribunal for the Far East were established and started to function. Major Japanese war criminals were sent to trial and a purge was going on to screen and eliminate undesirable persons from public life. A new constitution, known to be a product of American authorship, was promulgated, and Japan had for the first time in her history a representative government based on universal suffrage. Although the real power and actual rein of the Japanese government were still in the hands of the old guard or the reactionary element, it appeared, however, that developments in Japan were heading toward the right direction. This enabled MacArthur, or the SCAP, *i.e.*, the Supreme Commander for Allied Powers, as he is officially called, to say in his first Post-Surrender Anniversary message that "A spiritual revolution ensued almost overnight, tore asunder a theory and practice of life built upon 2000 years of history and tradition and legend. . . . This revolu-tion of the spirit among the Japanese people represents no thin veneer to serve the purpose of the present. It represents an un-paralleled convulsion in the social history of the world." These conclusions are of course naïve, if not purposely misleading. When asked to comment on this SCAP's statement, a Japanese told me sarcastically, "The SCAP must be either day-dreaming or talking with his tongue in his cheek."

The second year of occupation, ending in September 1947, was rather uneventful, as far as the occupation policies were concerned. The eleven-nation FEC (Far Eastern Commission) at Washington issued to the SCAP on June 26, 1947, a comprehensive directive, called the Basic Post-Surrender Policy for Japan, which was in substance no more than a confirmation of the American Presidential Initial Post-Surrender Policy Directive of November 8, 1945. Occupation orders and instructions were issued out as a matter of routine on the part of the Allied authorities, while the Japanese were cleverly manipulating, undermining, and sabotaging them from behind.

It would be unjust to charge that the occupation authorities did not make some genuine efforts to push reform measures at this time. Ostensibly, some progress was made along every line—the land reform, the purge, the dissolution of the zaibatsu, the war crimes trials, the restitution and reparation. But the progress was slow, and in many cases the achievement was negligible. The chief cause for failure was the fact that the SCAP, in carrying out all the reforms, had to use and rely on the instrumentality of the Japanese government, which was overwhelmingly dominated by conservatives and old guards of the prewar-days type. These people knew how to obstruct each reform measure at its every turn and how to nullify its practical effort under the pretense of making earnest efforts of carrying it out.

This was a great mistake! But it was an inevitable result of American monopoly of the Allied occupation of Japan! The American authorities were always honored, praised, and flattered, but they were everywhere cheated and double-crossed. It must be noted here that among the American personnel there were at first a small number of eager New Dealers, energetic and progressive-minded. In due course of time, these persons were either dismissed or forced to resign and go back to America. They were replaced by men, mostly military underlings and "yes-men" of the SCAP, who had neither the vision, nor the ability, nor the enthusiasm, to see the reforms carried through. . . .

The third year, ending on September 2, 1948, is the turning point in the history of Japanese occupation. It represents a transitional period in the American policy vis-à-vis Japan.

. . . In a large measure the change was inspired by, as well as coordinated to, the newly inaugurated Truman Doctrine, Marshall Plan, and the 80th Congress atmosphere. Yet the outward reasons assigned by Americans were the Russian threat to her security and the ever-growing emancipation movement in China. However, an impartial observer would fail to see how could the peaceful Soviet Union or a newly emancipated China constitute a threat either to Japan or to America. Clearly it was America herself, who, seeing that her imperialistic designs in Asia and her ambition of world domination might possibly be frustrated by the emergence of a new China friendly to the Soviet Union, was quick to realize what Japan could mean and do for her when Japan is made her exclusive tool. Hence came the policy to feed Japan and make her strong. Reform or democratization of Japan was no more of concern to the Americans now. America was determined to ignore the Potsdam Declaration and to disregard the interests and fears of other Allies.

Following the publication of the Strike and Johnston reports, a new set of reactionary measures and activities began to gain way and flourish in the Japanese politics and economy. The occupation authorities were now practically set to destroy what little they had accomplished during the past two years; and the Japanese government, ever dominated by old-time politicians, financiers, and bureaucrats, was only too jubilant to assist and serve their American masters in carrying out works of this kind. . . .

The struggle between the two opposing forces characterizes the occupation of the fourth year, ending today. The result of the January election this year demonstrated most clearly that, while conservative and old guards still dominated Japanese politics, the Communists' strength has also increased by leaps and bounds. Not only had their Diet seats increased many times, but most of the trade union workers, government employees, progressive intellectuals, and even small industrialists, have all come to rally under their banner and look to them for leadership and cooperation in their common fight against oppression. They constitute now a formidable rival to the reactionary party in power—the so-called Liberal–Democratic, which is a great misnomer.

Since the beginning of this year until the present day, the fight between these two forces, or rather two groups of forces, has been going on incessantly. . . . The so-called Economic Deconcentration Program has been given up altogether, and the zaibatsu people are gaining once more their prewar prestige and power. The purge program has not only degenerated, but actually been made use of by the old guards as a political weapon against their liberal and progressive opponents. . . .

But to abolish the existing reforms, or to nullify their effect, constitutes only one part, the negative part, of the reactionaries' work. They have yet a positive mission to fulfill, and that is the revival of the old, fascist Japan, in order to qualify Japan as a competent and trustworthy American "watch-dog" in the Far East. . . .

Suffice it to say that a visitor to Japan today will not fail to gain the impression that she is tending to drift back to a state of affairs similar to that of her prewar days. A return to fascism seems to be the logical outcome of this tendency.

W. MACMAHON BALL*
Japan—Enemy or Ally?

I believe that the two most significant features of the situation at the end of 1947 were, first, the steadily returning confidence of the wealthy and powerful Japanese, whose interests SCAP's economic reforms appeared to threaten, and, second, a marked drop in the reformist impetus of GHQ. . . .

The loss of drive in GHQ's reform program has not been clear-cut and consistent, but the trend from 1945 to 1948 is unmistakable. The program SCAP outlined in 1945 and early in 1946 would, if completed, produce fundamental changes in Japan's economic organization, and a great shift in the balance of economic powers. Indeed, if only the two measures discussed in this chapter—land reform and the dissolution of the zaibatsu—were to be carried out thoroughly, they would amount to a social-economic revolution. There were officials in GHQ who planned and worked for this sort of revolution, and these Americans had the sincere support of a small group of Japanese radicals. But the senior officers in SCAP did not always share the reformist enthusiasms of their subordinates. General MacArthur's purpose in directing reform measures seems

* W. Macmahon Ball, *Japan—Enemy or Ally?* (New York: John Day Co., 1949), pp. 130–132, 133, 164–166, 167, 182.

to spring mainly from the desire to eliminate those features of Japan's economy that are inconsistent with the philosophy of American individualism. He tends to equate what is un-American and what is undemocratic. Land reform was a blow at feudalism; the zaibatsu program a blow at monopoly: both un-American concepts. But further than that General MacArthur seems reluctant to go. It is true that he has from time to time directed the Japanese government to enforce certain economic controls, but he is usually careful to express the view that controls are in themselves evil, and only necessary as temporary and exceptional measures. . . .

I am not suggesting that controls are necessarily reforms, nor that "socialism" is intrinsically superior to "individualism." It remains true that in several Allied countries, including the United Kingdom, Australia, and New Zealand, there are freely elected governments which believe that a controlled economy is consistent with democracy, and may, in certain economic circumstances, be necessary for democracy to survive. It is, therefore, interesting that General MacArthur, in his capacity as Supreme Commander for the Allied Powers, should warn the people of Japan that a regime of "private capitalism, based upon free competitive enterprise," is indispensable to their well-being. . . .

If SCAP's forced reliance on the Japanese government has been the main practical difficulty, there were other difficulties rooted deeper in Japan's character and history. A purge assumes that it is possible to separate the sheep from the goats; the "moderates" and "liberals" from the "undesirables," the innocent followers from the wicked leaders. No such dichotomy is possible in Japan. The nation is exceptionally homogeneous. Indoctrination in the ways of nationalism and war has permeated every stratum of society. You cannot change the outlook of a group—of a party, or a school, or a business—by dismissing its leaders. The new leaders will carry on the old tradition, though with great circumspection under the exigencies of the occupation. I am aware that this generalization needs qualification. There were real liberals and revolutionaries in Japan, mostly in jail. But they were too few and inexperienced in executive responsibility to assume leadership. . . .

Perhaps the most important question today is not whether the purge has succeeded, but whether the United States now wishes it to succeed. The plain fact is that American aims in Japan today are different from what they were at the surrender. The ideas behind the purge, certainly those behind the "purge extension," are an overlap from 1945. This comes out most clearly in connection with the economic purge. Since the middle thirties the privately owned industries of Japan have all been organized for war. For various historical reasons, the control of these industries has been highly centralized. All senior executives were, in a sense, involved in "monopolistic" or "militarist" enterprises. If, in accordance with the purge extension, they are to be removed from all positions of influence, this will deprive Japan of the managerial skill that would seem indispensable if she is to become the "workshop of East Asia" and a safe field for American loans and credits. There are many signs that Americans realize this, and Japanese leaders have been quick to exploit this situation. In December 1947 the Japanese government was able to announce that the purge was "virtually complete." . . .

America now aims to help Japan regain her prewar position as the workshop of East Asia. She seeks to do this in four main ways. First, she wants to permit Japan to retain industrial plants which the Allies had previously intended to remove as reparations. Second, she wants to give Japan direct financial help to restore her secondary industries, to reequip her plants, to secure overseas raw materials and overseas markets. Third, America wants to restore to the large Japanese business groups many of the freedoms of which SCAP had earlier intended to deprive them. And, fourth, she wants to contract some of the new freedoms which SCAP had previously given to Japanese trade unions. . . .

. . . There is no secret about the reasons for America's changed outlook. There is the simple and understandable wish to make Japan self-supporting and not a permanent burden on the American taxpayer. But the root motive is political. It is fear of Russia and communism. America desires a strong and prosperous Japan as a backing against the extension of Russian influence in the Far East and the growth of Japanese communism.

American policy in Japan is a regional expansion of her world policy. This policy crystalized in the first half of 1947. It was authoritatively formulated in the Truman Doctrine on March 12 and the Marshall Plan on June 5.

▦ ONCE MACARTHUR understood that economic deconcentration was to be reversed, policies changed rapidly. The Deconcentration Review Board became the instrument for easing controls on industrial concentration. Not surprisingly, once the new policy was clear, the Japanese weakened the antimonopoly law they had been forced to pass.

ELEANOR M. HADLEY*
The U.S. Reorients Its Economic Policy in Japan

Following the withdrawal of U.S. support for FEC 230 on March 12, 1948, together with the Report of the Draper-Johnston Mission later that month, MacArthur realized that the 325 companies designated under the Deconcentration Law were excessive and set about to effect large-scale releases. He now believed that only those concerns which were "interfering seriously with economic recovery" should be reorganized under the Deconcentration Law. A rather balder statement of the change in policy is to be found in a Headquarters memorandum of mid-April 1948 in which the new policy was summarized:

> (1) no banks were to be considered as excessive concentrations or reorganized under the Deconcentration Law; (2) no more than twenty companies were to be subject to reorganization under the Law [the final number was nineteen] and these were to be chosen on the basis that they were interfering with Japanese economic recovery; (3) all the rest were to be removed from designation with no less than 100 companies taken off in the first such action and, where necessary, be remanded to the Fair Trade Commission for surveillance.

Action followed swiftly. An announcement was made by SCAP on May 1, 1948, stating that the HCLC was releasing 194 industrial

* Eleanor M. Hadley, *Antitrust in Japan* (Princeton, N.J.: Princeton University Press, 1970), pp. 166–168, 171–174, 180, 197–200.

and distributive companies from continued designation under Law
No. 207.

> ... Fifty would be released as not actually constituting ex-
> cessive concentrations [that is, outright] and 144 others were
> regarded as relatively minor concentrations whose operations
> would continue under surveillance or concurrently with the ac-
> complishment of organizational readjustments such as divestment
> of certain subsidiary relationships and other action to remove
> monopolistic characteristics. The announcement emphasized that
> this list of 194 companies was an initial list and other removals
> would follow subject to the completion of investigation by the
> Holding Company Liquidation Commission.

On July 1, 1948, an additional thirty-one firms were removed from
designation, making a total of 225 firms that were removed from
the original designation of 325. The army historical report stated:
"Further action, by the [Holding Company Liquidation] Commission in respect to the canceling of company designations, was
momentarily deferred, however, so as to give the opportunity for
the Deconcentration Review Board, which had arrived in Tokyo
in May, to make further recommendations concerning the deconcentration program." ...

The members of the review board arrived in Tokyo in May
1948 and spent most of the first month familiarizing themselves
with their duties. On June 4 the board sent to MacArthur a
document entitled "Deconcentration Review Board—Basic Interpretation of Authority," in which the purpose of their review
was stated:

> The Deconcentration Review Board is to make an indepen-
> dent review of the Reorganization Order issued by the HCLC for
> the purpose of appraising the impact and effect of the deconcen-
> tration action upon the operating efficiency of the industrial, dis-
> tributive, insurance, or banking enterprise concerned, and its
> consequent effect upon the general industrial, financial, or com-
> mercial economy of the country.

Under "Findings," the board repeated MacArthur's instructions
that its sole criterion would be the effect of the reorganization plan
on the efficiency of the company and acknowledged the limits on
its authority in this way:

> The Deconcentration Review Board is specifically limited in
> its deliberations to the terms of reference previously set up ex-

cept as specifically called upon by direction in writing from the Supreme Commander for the Allied Powers for such other appraisals as he requires.

Having explicitly reiterated MacArthur's instructions governing creation of the Deconcentration Review Board (DRB) as the board's understanding of its responsibilities and jurisdiction in its memorandum to MacArthur, it ignored its terms of reference; not one of its judgments was determined on the basis of the effect of the reorganization plan on efficiency. Instead, the DRB in reviewing its first case, that of Nippon Soda, the holding-operating company of one of the lesser zaibatsu, enunciated "four points" which were to "guide" the HCLC in determining which companies were and which were not excessive concentrations. Various comments come to mind. The DRB had not been invited to Japan by MacArthur to determine what companies were excessive concentrations; it had been invited to determine the effect of the proposed reorganization plan of companies, deemed excessive by the HCLC working with ESS [Economic and Scientific Section], on economic recovery. Accordingly, in departing to this field, the DRB was leaving its area of responsibility and moving out into an area in which it had no formal authority. Secondly, as shall become apparent, having enunciated its "four points," the DRB used them only for eliminating companies. In none of the eleven cases in which it recommended structural reorganization did the DRB itself refer to them. . . .

The four points were the DRB's public expression of their views. A franker statement of its thinking is to be found in a memorandum circulated among DRB members: "It is becoming quite clear that the implementation of these laws is being carried on on a 'police-state' basis, bordering on (if not actually) the methods used by so-called communist states today."

THE HCLC AND THE FOUR POINTS

In the new climate of Washington opinion, MacArthur bowed completely to the wishes of the Deconcentration Review Board, and instructed the chief of the Economic and Scientific Section to hold a meeting of all interested persons for the purpose of explaining the DRB's four points to the HCLC. On September 11, 1948, representatives from the Economic and Scientific Section, Legal Section, and the members of the DRB met with the seven members of the Holding Company Liquidation Commission for the purpose of informing them of the DRB findings in the Nippon Soda case and acquainting them with the DRB's concepts of the deconcentration program. . . .

The news of the meeting was released to the press, together with the four points. On September 12, 1948, the *Nippon Times* carried a straight news story on it. However, other portions of the press, less under the influence of SCAP, were not slow to realize the implications of the announcement. The *Asahi Shimbun* on September 14, announced the news under a story captioned "Deconcentration—To Be Liberalized on Great Scale. Re-Investigation for Those Already Decided." The Central News Agency of China transmitted the following dispatch from its Tokyo office on September 17:

> The economic deconcentration law aimed at breaking the "zaibatsu" monopolies in Japan is on its way to the scrap heap. A most reliable source today opined that instead of reaffirmation of the Far Eastern Commission policy the four basic principles recently laid down by the SCAP deconcentration review board actually takes another step toward the law's complete abolition. He quoted a top-ranking holding company liquidation commission official as saying that the "law will eventually be scrapped in Japan as in Germany due to the fundamental change of the U.S. policy in the Far East." . . .

The board ended its activities in August 1949. At a press conference held on August third, the chairman of the DRB stated that the board had recommended a reorganization of nineteen major companies, and that, in his opinion, excessive concentration of economic power in Japan was completely broken and a condition for free competition in all fields had been created. By contrast, E. C. Walsh, Chief, Antitrust and Cartels Division of Headquarters, observed in late 1948: ". . . what was initially considered . . . a major objective of the occupation [had] become . . . a major embarrassment to the occupation. Without formally questioning the desirability or broad purposes of the policy, it was decided to take measures which would minimize the actions prepared for carrying out the policy. Facts of the last war faded . . . and conjectures [on] the next war took their place."

The Pentagon and conservative opinion had been successful in reversing U.S. antitrust policy in Japan. . . .

REVISION OF THE ANTIMONOPOLY LAW

Given the views of the Japanese government toward the original version of the Antimonopoly Law, it was predictable that it quickly responded to the change in American policy signaled by enunciation of the Deconcentration Review Board's four points of September 11, 1948. While it had taken MacArthur a year to get the Japanese cabinet to submit an antitrust bill to the Diet and a year and a half to get the law on the statute books—not to mention the additional months required for issue of the implementing cabinet orders—it took less than three weeks from the September 1948 publication of the four points for the Japanese government to announce its proposals for revision. The chairman of the Fair Trade Commission informed the Deconcentration Review Board that the Japanese government intended to amend the provisions of the law governing "corporate securities holdings, international contracts, multiple directorates, individual stockholdings, mergers and transfers of business." He said:

> As it was pointed out in your press release of September 11, 1948, I believe the time is now appropriate that the Antimonopoly Law be restudied and reconsidered in light of the basic principles of antitrust legislation as they are internationally recognized. While it is felt that there is no need for the Japanese Antimonopoly Law to be a translation of the American or Canadian antitrust legislation and that all reasonable improvements proved in experience to be practical and effective from an antitrust viewpoint should be incorporated, it is going a little too far when all provisions of the law are written for the sole purpose of enabling the strictest possible enforcement of the law. In light of the foregoing thought, reconsideration and amendment of our present law should be made as suggested above.
> . . . [I]t is the intention of our government to introduce into the coming extraordinary session of the Diet a bill covering the amendments to the Antimonopoly Law. . . . While certain proposals have been submitted [to the Headquarters], our government as well as this commission are of the opinion that the whole question of amending the present Antimonopoly Law must again be reconsidered in light of the newly indicated four basic principles for carrying out the deconcentration program under the Deconcentration Law. This commission, in coordination with

other ministries of our government, has drawn up a preliminary draft of our proposed amendments along the lines indicated above, which are attached herewith for your study and reference.

This revision resulted in the 1949 amendments. . . .

Amendment was achieved through Law No. 259 of September 1, 1953. The provision proscribing disparities in bargaining power was deleted. Resale maintenance was limitedly authorized (copyrighted books, records, and commodities "which are in daily use by the general consumer and easily identifiable by trademarks and other labels, in free competition with other similar commodities"). The flat prohibition on cartels was removed; instead, with the approval of the FTC, two types of cartels were authorized, depression and rationalization. Restrictions on intercorporate stockholding and interlocking multiple directorates were further modified. The stipulation that these not be attained by unfair methods of business was deleted, and the only restriction remaining was that the result would not be a substantial restraint of competition in any particular field of trade. Reporting of intercorporate stock ownership and interlocking directorates was required for companies whose assets were valued at 100 million yen (about $278,000). The Trade Association Law was repealed and some of the prohibited acts were incorporated in a new Article 8 in the Antimonopoly Law.

⚛ AFTER DRAPER returned from Japan in the spring of 1948, he asked Joseph Dodge, a conservative Detroit banker, to take over the Japanese economy. Dodge arrived in Japan in February 1949 and began a harsh program of deflation and budget-cutting. His program, known as the Dodge Line or Dodge Plan, was based on the nine-point stabilization plan proposed by the Young Commission, a group of fiscal experts who visited Japan in May 1948. With the power of economic dictator, Dodge forced through a tough program of deflation deliberately leading to mass unemployment. It hit small business, too, as it was reported at the time that one-third of the four million small businessmen in Japan (those employing less than thirty persons) closed their doors or merged with larger firms during 1949. The Kolkos argue that the policy, theoretically designed to make Japan self-supporting by 1953, in fact had Japan rapidly sliding into a depression by fall 1949.

JOYCE AND GABRIEL KOLKO*
The Dodge Plan

During the six months after Draper had asked him to go to Japan, Dodge studied the conditions of the country and in October 1948 sent Draper a memorandum on a Japanese recovery program which reinforced the Johnston and Young committee's concerns. In December, Dodge felt free to accept the post as director of the Japanese economy.

Washington now viewed the direction of the Japanese economy as a matter of great urgency. Truman met with Dodge on December 11 before the banker left for Japan. The President pointed out that the developments in China had compounded Japan's importance, and that the National Security Council considered the Japanese economy as one of the most important international issues it had to face at the time. It had decided unanimously that Dodge should take charge of the matter.

It is significant that the leading men of power in Washington chose Dodge, "without qualification or dissent," to deal with the most urgent economic problems for which the United States had direct responsibility—Germany and Japan. Dodge turned down as many jobs as he accepted, for he was asked to direct the economies of Korea and the Philippines as well, and his views colored the policies of the European Recovery Program. There was no old school tie in his relationships to Washington. The son of a poster painter, Dodge was a car salesman in 1917, and in the 1920s he entered banking at a very modest level to rise to president of the Detroit Bank in the next decade. But the positions that he held

* Joyce and Gabriel Kolko, *The Limits of Power* (New York: Harper and Row, 1972), pp. 521–524, 528.

during and after World War II were so critical that it is worth examining his views in some detail, for they were shared by the most important men in Washington of both the Democratic and the Republican parties.

A conservative, orthodox banker—"antediluvian," as some have said—Dodge held policies that inevitably led not to reconstruction of a complex industrial economy, supposedly essential to America's political, economic, and strategic goals, but to a balanced budget accompanied by severe economic depression. His random jottings on controlling inflation capture the essence of his approach. Dodge noted that an

> ... increase in unemployment will in turn lead to increased efficiency of labor and a greater production. ... A disinflation policy intends to bring the aggregate demands ... to slightly below the aggregate of supply. ... There should be no fear of mass unemployment. ... What is the combined cost of health, welfare, and education? ... Get the country into hard condition for the struggle in the export market. ... Radicals ... can't make it in a free society. ... Remedial actions are always unpleasant. ...

Virtually simultaneous with his arrival in Tokyo, SCAP introduced Dodge's program for economic stabilization which embodied these views and came to be known as the Dodge Plan. But even the Liberal party of Premier Yoshida, whose corrupt and reactionary policies had created the economic morass, found the negative social implications of Dodge's program to be politically unpalatable. Yoshida, however, overestimated his power and misjudged once more Washington's intentions regarding Japan. Convinced that United States interests were primarily strategic, he assumed that he held a trump card in securing continued subsidies for his economic policies by offering the United States a conservative, anticommunist bastion in Asia. When Washington ordered SCAP to introduce the nine-point stabilization program he sought to ignore the features which were politically unattractive. It therefore became necessary for Secretary of the Army Kenneth Royall to go to Tokyo in February 1949 to further reinforce the position of Dodge and his virtually dictatorial power over the Japanese economy. Royall sought to remedy the fact that too many in SCAP and the Japanese government had overemphasized Japan's strategic importance to the United States and now had to confront the fact that the primary American policy was to establish a conservative,

capitalist, but self-supporting economy by 1953. Paramount in
these considerations was the need to make Japanese goods more
competitive in the world markets and to put greater emphasis on
the production of hard capital goods for export, primarily to
Southeast Asia. This policy continued until the Korean War, for as
Dodge pointed out to the top administrators of the ECA, ". . . if
Japan is stabilized financially, she is not likely to be outpriced.
. . ." Yet until December 1949, despite extreme diplomatic pressure, no nation other than the United States accepted Japanese
traders. In October 1949 SCAP removed the price floors on exports, allowing the Japanese to lower prices as far as they wished
—in other words, to resume the "dumping" practices of the
prewar period to meet competition. Coming as it did in the midst
of a severe world recession and following the British devaluation,
the measure heightened international tension and increased British
demands that the Japanese be given access to their natural market
in China.

The nine-point program, while establishing the direction of
policy, still left specifics open to interpretation. It was not until
several months later that Dodge released more precise directives
on the implementation of the program. They elicited an immediate
protest from the labor division of SCAP for having ". . . disregarded
dangerous social, political, and economic consequences inherent in
them." But it was the labor division that was completely out of
tune with the current American aims. The reduction of government
subsidies in certain high-cost industries, encumbered with scarce
raw materials, guaranteed immediate layoffs, and wage reductions,
and the restrictions of credit were expected to have the same effect.
The Dodge Program proposed an increase in the price of essential
services, such as commuter trains and staple foods, coupled with
tight wage controls and other policies increasing unemployment.
Anticipating trouble from the workers, it proposed a ban on strikes
for all workers in private as well as public industries. The labor
division predicted there would be 1 to 1.5 million unemployed
government workers as a result, and mass unemployment in
private industry as well. Dodge, in principle, disapproved of
unemployment compensation, for ". . . there would be no incentive
to the individual to answer his own problem by seeking other
employment," and public works were "inflationary." The burden

of the entire program was placed squarely on the back of the working class, as in Germany and the Marshall Plan in general.

When again a member of SCAP raised the matter of the political implications of forcefully lowering the already minimal standard of living of the Japanese worker, Dodge responded, ". . . the standard of living has probably been permitted to go too high—cannot increase further—we cannot give them everything they want." At the same time, SCAP estimated with equanimity that removal of subsidies would result in a thirteen percent increase in staple food prices. The program also met strong objections from the Japanese conservatives, although they were perhaps more vocal than sincere. Nevertheless, even in private meetings with Dodge they pleaded for the abolition of the sales tax, one of their party's important slogans in the last election, as well as for the continuation of public works and, in particular, the new nine-year compulsory education program. Dodge adamantly rejected all pleas. Rather than expansion, he noted, "A completely realistic approach would suggest that public works should be eliminated entirely. . . ." In every instance where there was a choice between concessions to business and to workers, Dodge insisted on the former, despite even the arguments of Japan's conservative politicians.

By June 1949 Dodge had succeeded in his aim of a balanced budget for 1949–1950 and a single exchange rate for imports and exports, resulting by September in one of the most drastic shifts in economic history. And the Japanese economy, along with the rest of the capitalist world, was sliding into a depression. . . .

Given Washington's complete confidence in Dodge and his dictatorial powers in Tokyo, it is possible to perceive most clearly the type of society it sought to create in Japan. Despite the plethora of political rhetoric on stopping the spread of communism by raising the standard of living in a reconstructed world economy, when forced to decide on tangible options the United States committed itself to socially retrograde policies that even sectors of Japan's paternal ruling class thought too conservative. In reality, then, the real contours of America's reorientation of Japan from the inception took on an unmistakably reactionary shape.

By June 1950 the full impact of the Dodge "recovery" was apparent to all. Production at barely one-third the 1931 level, investment at one-half the 1949 level, and a nearly exhausted capital market all revealed what was in fact a critical depression. It is academic to speculate on the outcome of a continuation of America's recovery program, for the outbreak of the Korean War, as in Europe and the United States, reversed the process of economic stagnation. Paralleling the German experience, that bloody conflict provided the essential economic stimulus and actuated the Japanese economic "miracle" that has endured, despite periodic lapses, until this day.

3. The Japanese Labor Movement and the Occupation

❀ THE EARLY MONTHS of the occupation produced a great outburst of union activity. Democratization provided the political freedoms labor needed for organizing, labor leaders imprisoned during the war were released, and legislation created a legal status for unions. Labor organizations mushroomed, and their tactics were varied and imaginative, ranging from sitdown strikes to "production control."

MIRIAM FARLEY*
Labor Policy in Occupied Japan

In the field of labor the American blueprint is now fairly clear, though it took shape slowly. The first basic directive issued to General MacArthur by the American government, and made public on September 22, 1945, contained a broad mandate to promote democratic reforms but little specific guidance on labor policies, beyond the injunction to encourage democratic organizations in labor, industry, and agriculture, and a wide distribution of income and ownership. Labor policy, like so many others, had at first to be improvised. . . .

Labor experts on General MacArthur's staff have evolved for themselves a working philosophy which assumes that the working classes constitute, potentially, the strongest if not the only reliable base for a democratic regime in Japan. The middle class is numeri-

* Miriam Farley, "Labor Policy in Occupied Japan," *Pacific Affairs* XX:2 (June 1947), pp. 131–134.

cally, economically, and spiritually weak. The farm population is traditionally conservative and politically lethargic. The wage workers, who with their families form approximately forty percent of the population, have historically displayed more political consciousness and receptivity to new ideas than has any other important group. In prewar Japan labor organizations and parties were among the most vigorous and effective opponents of war and militarism and advocates of democratic change. Consistently oppressed and exploited in the past, labor has little or no stake in the old order and can be counted on to support the new one *provided* that it is given a positive incentive to do so. Democracy must, therefore, offer to Japanese workers freedom of expression and action and tangible improvement in their material conditions of life. . . .

What does "democracy" mean as regards labor's role in society and government's role in relation to labor? Labor experts of the Supreme Commander for the Allied Powers (SCAP), well versed in the theory and practice of labor relations, labor legislation, and labor administration in the United States, define it in terms of their own experience. Few of them knew much about Japan when they came to the country, although they have learned a good deal since. They naturally conceive of desirable goals for Japan in American terms: free trade unions, operating chiefly in the economic field; peaceful adjustment of labor-management issues by collective bargaining, aided by public or private agencies of conciliation and mediation; legislation to assure to workers minimum standards of health, safety, income, and economic security.

The first step toward these long-range goals was, obviously, the destruction of those barriers to progress erected by the *ancien régime*. This was accomplished, thoroughly on paper and to a large degree in practice, during the early months of the occupation. The SCAP directive of October 5, 1945, on Removal of Restrictions on Political, Civil, and Religious Liberties resulted in the abrogation of laws and ordinances restricting, for labor and other groups, freedom of speech, of the press, and of organization. The notorious "thought police" . . . was disbanded, its members were declared ineligible for other public offices, and a purge of undesirable elements was instituted among the remaining police personnel. Police control of labor administration, one of the worst evils of the

old regime, was attacked by transferring all labor functions from
the Home Ministry to the Ministry of Welfare. Repeated instructions were issued to the police to refrain from interference in labor
affairs, except to deal with criminal acts. The release of political
prisoners on October 18, 1945, liberated a number of old-time
labor leaders. Finally, Japan's vicious labor-front organization, the
Patriotic Industrial Association (Sangyō Hōkokukai, better known
as Sampō), which was the former government's chief agency for
the physical and spiritual regimentation of labor, was dissolved on
September 30, 1945.

The next step was positive encouragement of labor organization.
On October 11, 1945, General MacArthur publicly informed
Premier Shidehara that he would expect the Japanese government
to undertake certain reforms, including "encouragement of the
unionization of labor." In December, prodded by SCAP, the government prepared and the Diet passed the Trade Union Law, often
referred to as the Magna Carta of Japanese labor. A more
appropriate sobriquet would be "Japanese Wagner Act," for as the
new Japanese constitution repeats the language of America's
Founding Fathers, so the Trade Union Law is modeled on the
United States National Labor Relations Act of 1935. There are
marked differences, however, which reflect a determined rear-
guard action by Japanese bureaucrats to water down proposed
reforms—another familiar pattern in Tokyo. Like its American
counterpart, Japan's Trade Union Law guarantees the right of
trade union organization (except for policemen, firemen, and
employees of penal institutions), and its stated purpose is the
encouragement of collective bargaining. It protects the worker
against discharge or discrimination because of union activity. It
outlaws company unions in a backhanded and somewhat ambiguous manner, but lacks detailed restrictions on interference by
employers with union organization. It provides no machinery for
adjusting the claims of rival unions. To apply and enforce the law,
Labor Relations Committees are set up in Tokyo and in the
prefectures, representing equally labor, management, and neutral
opinion; the enforcement procedure, however, is weak and clumsy.
The law also contains detailed provisions requiring unions to
register with the proper authorities, and empowers the Labor Relations Committees to dissolve or remodel unions which do not meet

certain standards. While these powers can be used for the legitimate purpose of disqualifying company unions, they could also be used to harass, coerce, or dissolve legitimate unions. The weaknesses of the law are recognized by SCAP, and revision is hoped for at a later date.

A companion piece of legislation, passed by the Diet in September 1946, is the Labor Relations Adjustment Law. This, though also based on American precedents, provides a much more logical and comprehensive system for adjusting labor disputes than anything so far produced in the United States. Machinery is provided for conciliation, mediation, or arbitration, as the parties may select, under the auspices of the tripartite Labor Relations Committees. There is no compulsory arbitration. In certain industries affecting the public welfare, strikes are prohibited for a prescribed period, pending mediation. Strikes are also prohibited for government employees, but this does not affect operating employees of government enterprises.

While the Trade Union Law was welcomed by Japanese labor, the Labor Relations Adjustment Law, mild as it is, was strongly opposed by most of the unions, which regarded it as a government offensive against labor. The prohibition of strikes by government employees was, in particular, bitterly attacked. Labor opposition to the law was undoubtedly due not so much to a considered appraisal of its content as to a strong distrust of the Yoshida cabinet and a not unfounded fear that the law would be used to weaken the unions and to block legitimate aspirations of labor. . . .

. . . Weak, divided, and repressed before the war, snuffed out altogether in 1940, the Japanese labor movement has come back with astounding energy. Its phenomenal growth is probably unprecedented in world history, save possibly for the Chinese labor movement in 1925–1927. At its prewar peak, union membership was less than half a million. By December 1946 there were 17,163 registered unions with a total membership of 4,415,482, or approximately half of all nonagricultural wage workers in the country. While some unions are controlled by employers, and many rank-and-file members are not quite sure what a union is, still this is a remarkable expression of popular vitality.

The rapid growth in union membership has not been due to any concerted organizing drive. Most of the unions sprang up spontaneously at the local level. Within a few months movements for consolidation appeared. The first step was the consolidation of local units into national industrial unions; the second, consolidation of industrial unions into national labor federations. There are now two major federations, the Japanese Federation of Labor and the Congress of Industrial Unions, both of which were formally inaugurated in August 1946. Agitation to unite them in a single national federation of labor has come to nothing, nor, owing mainly to political differences, is it likely to succeed in the near future. Thus an organizational structure exists which can be and is being put to effective use. The organization is loose; it is fluid; its staying power has not yet been tested. But it is strong enough to make labor's voice heard, if not always heeded, in the councils of the nation.

MIRIAM FARLEY*
Union Techniques: Production Control

The techniques used by Japanese unions to enforce their demands were many and varied, often ingenious and imaginative. Outstanding of course was the strike, the classic weapon of labor, and to Japanese workers a cherished symbol of their new freedom. In the early days many workers went on strike out of sheer exuberance; such strikes were of course short-lived. Sometimes they were not properly strikes at all. In the fall of 1945 the telephone operators in Sendai "struck"; they remained at their switchboards, but persons calling the exchange were greeted with : *"Moshi moshi!* [Hello!] We are on strike! Long live democracy! Number, please?" Demonstrations and parades were extremely popular, and many devices were adopted to dramatize the workers' demands, as when actors went through a play in pantomime without speaking the lines. In some plants the employees decided to work only that number of hours for which they felt they were being fairly paid. There were hunger strikes, sitdown strikes, and many slowdowns, commonly called "sabotage.". . .

* Miriam Farley, *Aspects of Japan's Labor Problems* (New York: John Day Co., 1950), pp. 88–89, 92–95.

PRODUCTION CONTROL

The most interesting technique developed by Japanese workers, apparently without exact parallel elsewhere, was "production control," which became a subject of nationwide discussion and at one time aroused considerable alarm. In production control the workers, instead of striking, take over the plant and run it until management meets their demands or a compromise is reached. Any surplus of operating receipts over disbursements is banked to the credit of the employer. This method had much to recommend it in postsurrender Japan, for it did not interrupt production. It might be expected that efficiency would suffer, and this sometimes occurred, but an abundance of reliable testimony confirms the fact that in many cases output was greatly expanded, not only because the employees worked harder under their own leaders—this nearly always happened—but because they introduced administrative improvements. . . .

Production control was violently denounced by government spokesmen and others as an unwarranted invasion of the rights of private property. Unions defended it as a legitimate method of dispute. Since no precedents existed, controversy raged over its legality. The unions contended that it was a form of strike and therefore legal. The cabinet debated the question, issued several strong statements against production control, and endorsed the labor–management committee as an alternative. In the face of vigorous labor protests, however, the government backtracked and modified its unequivocal opposition. All sections of organized labor defended production control. SCAP remained carefully neutral, maintaining that the question should be decided by Japanese courts, or by legislation. But in a statement in the Allied Council on July 10, 1946, criticizing Russian proposals on labor policy, Mr. George Atcheson strongly condemned production control as confiscation of property without compensation.

❧ THE GREAT SUCCESS of SCAP in creating the conditions for unionization was soon perceived as a problem by some occupation authorities. While they had wanted unions, their image was of American ones, and the rash of strikes and demonstrations in early 1946 was viewed with fear by some. Thus an early ambiguity in SCAP attitudes became evident, and any antiunion sentiments of occupation officials expectably were seized upon by conservative members of the Japanese elite. The impact, for example, of MacArthur's warning to demonstrators on May 20, 1946, cannot be underestimated. He had absolute power—both to free union activity and to restrict it.

MARK GAYN*
Food Demonstrations and MacArthur's Warning

TOKYO, May 19, 1946

The political pot is boiling madly. Yoshida is still struggling to form a new cabinet. As fast as he picks his ministers, it is discovered that they are war criminals subject to the purge. Meanwhile, the food rationing machinery has bogged down. In the far north the distribution of food is thirty days behind schedule; in Tokyo, twelve. There are street-corner rallies, parades, mass meetings of protest. On Tuesday, eight hundred people demonstrated before the palace, demanding to know what the emperor was eating. On Friday, there were eight "food demonstrations" in front of rationing stations. Yesterday, twenty. There is a steady stream of marching men past the Diet and the premier's residence.

The climax came today with a "Give Us Rice" mass meeting. By ten o'clock on this bright, warm morning, there were at least 60,000 people at the imperial plaza. They had put three trucks together, and mounted tables on them for the speakers' platform. The chairman was the head of the Transport Workers' Union. But the meeting was actually run by a hard-looking man in corduroy knickers and a sports jacket. This was Katsumi Kikunami, an editorial writer for the *Asahi,* head of the Newspaper Union, and founder of the huge Congress of Industrial Unions. Grimly, he

* Mark Gayn, *Japan Diary* (New York: William Sloan Associates, 1948), pp. 226–232.

introduced a succession of speakers—union leaders, political workers, and just plain people.

One of these was a housewife of thirty-five, slim and plain looking and obviously undernourished. She came from a ward in which there has been no rice distribution in two weeks. She had a child strapped to her back, and as she denounced the police and the rationing officials, the child's wailing came clear and loud over the loudspeaker.

But most of the speakers talked of politics. They demanded Yoshida's resignation, a Popular Front, a new cabinet including workers and farmers. "We must use the privileges we've gained since the war," cried Suzuki, editor of the *Yomiuri,* "One of them is the right to make revolutionary changes that will produce a democratic government. A one-day general strike will force Yoshida out!"

Tokuda was the last to speak. He wheeled around on the table top, pointed at the palace, and shouted: "We're starving. Is he?" He denounced Yoshida and the war criminals in the Diet, but he saved his sharpest barbs for the emperor. "Last week," he said, "we went to the palace and asked to see the emperor. We were chased away. Is it because the emperor can say nothing but 'Ah, so. Ah, so?' " He mimicked the emperor. The crowd cheered wildly. . . .

The moat at this point is probably thirty feet wide, and a bridge crosses it to the massive gate in the palace wall. The bridge was now a no-man's-land. The crowd stood or sat at one end, while a force of palace guards, armed with staves, stood in front of the gate. Earlier, the crowd had come up to the gate, and in the melee a policeman was tossed into the moat, and some demonstrants were beaten. A delegation of twelve men had gone in three hours earlier, and the growing crowd was waiting for their return. While waiting, the demonstrants sang, or listened to pep talks by men who spoke from atop a small police kiosk.

Around four one of the delegates came out, and climbed on the booth. Both the emperor and the minister of the imperial household, he said, had refused to see the delegation. It was finally permitted to talk to a secretary, who said he would report to the minister, who would report to the emperor.

"Geez," said the delegate, in effect. "This is the first time I've been in the palace, and it's wonderful. Why, the lavatory there is better than the house I live in."

Half an hour later the rest of the delegation came out. It was led by Kikunami, who looked even grimmer than he had earlier in the day. One after another, the delegates climbed atop the kiosk to report their failure, to say they would come back in forty-eight hours, and to detail their discoveries in the palace. It appeared that they had gone through the palace kitchen, and had had a look at the emperor's cooking pots, refrigerators, and menu for tonight.

"What will you have for dinner?" they shouted to the crowd. "How much is there in your larder? Now hear what the emperor and his family will eat tonight. . . ."

They listed the dishes, and the kinds of food which came to the palace from the Imperial preserves—fresh milk daily, chickens, pigs, eggs, butter.

"This is what the emperor and his officials eat. Do you think they understand the meaning of the word 'hunger'?"

But the big show of the day was going on elsewhere. After this morning's meeting, a delegation went to the premier's residence to demand that Yoshida give up his job, and that hoarded food be distributed to the people. Yoshida refused to see the group. In an argument with a secretary, someone (it sounded like Tokuda to me) said, "All right, if he won't see us, we'll just sit here until he resigns." The delegation then made itself comfortable for a long stay, while the photographers' bulbs flashed, and reporters scribbled furiously.

The unorthodox "sit-down strike" came close to being the last straw. By late afternoon it had been estimated that 250,000 people in all had demonstrated in Tokyo, and the nerves of the politicians had become frayed. Yoshida's advisers spent most of the day with Hatoyama in his house, discussing, among other things, the tactics for meeting the public pressure.

Around seven in the evening the secretary came out and said to the delegates, "You can go home now. Mr. Yoshida has decided to give up the job."

It is possible that at this moment Yoshida was ready to give up—partly because he was having trouble finding ministers, partly in fear of what was beginning to look like a full-scale, nonviolent revolution. But Tokuda, the skeptic, would take no promises secondhand.

"We'll sit here," he said, "until Yoshida himself tells us he is giving up."

TOKYO, May 20, 1946

This morning General MacArthur issued a warning to the Japanese people.

"I find it necessary," he said, "to caution the Japanese people that the growing tendency toward mass violence and physical processes of intimidation, under organized leadership, present a grave menace to the future development of Japan.

"While every possible rational freedom of democratic method has been permitted and will be permitted . . . the physical violence which undisciplined elements are now beginning to practice will not be permitted to continue. They constitute a menace not only to orderly government but to the basic purposes and security of the occupation itself.

"If minor elements of Japanese society are unable to exercise such restraint and self-respect as the situation and conditions require, I shall be forced to take the necessary steps to control and remedy such a deplorable situation. . . ."

The statement had a startling effect. I could actually recall no American move that matched this pronouncement in its repercussions. There was consternation in union headquarters and in the offices of the left-wing parties. In conservative quarters, there was undisguised jubilation.

As soon as word of the statement reached the premier's residence, the "sit-downers" quietly left the building. All demonstrations scheduled for today, and for the rest of the week, have been canceled. The Japanese press, which thus far has been explaining that the people had no other way to change the government but to go into the streets, hastily backtracked.

The right-wingers in the Social Democratic party, who were being pushed into the Popular Front by the sight of the marching multitudes, now happily announced they needed time to reconsider the issue, "in the light of the new circumstances." Two left-wing leaders admitted to me privately the fight was lost.

And Yoshida, who may have wavered last night, no longer wavered this noon. He announced that he would have a cabinet ready by tomorrow, and indicated that Twiddledum, or Shidehara, would be in it. As clearly as any of us, Yoshida saw the statement for what it was—a prop for Yoshida.

MIRIAM FARLEY*
SCAP Policy Toward Labor Unions

As the Japanese unions grew rapidly in strength and began to develop political interests and militant tendencies, some American officials became alarmed over the unexpected vigor of the genie which they had released. Others, including those closest to labor activities, were much encouraged by the vigor of the Japanese response but felt that the situation had entered a new phase in which labor no longer needed stimulation but required sympathetic guidance to restrain undesirable tendencies. Opinions within SCAP were divided and policy was not always consistent.

The first clear note of warning was sounded by General Mac-Arthur in his public statement of May 20, 1946, in which he cautioned against "the growing tendency toward mass violence and physical processes of intimidation" by "disorderly minorities." This was generally taken to refer to public demonstrations by labor (mass meetings, parades, etc.), which had become increasingly common, culminating in the great May Day demonstrations throughout the country, in which at least a million persons took part, and the so-called Food May Day in Tokyo on May 19. With minor exceptions these affairs had been peaceful and orderly. There had been a demonstration at the prime minister's residence on April 7 demanding Shidehara's resignation, during which a slight scuffle occurred, several policemen were injured, and MPs intervened. On or about May 14 residents of Setagaya ward,

* Miriam Farley, *Aspects of Japan's Labor Problems* (New York: John Day Co., 1950), pp. 44–50.

Tokyo, had tried to force an entrance to the Imperial Palace grounds to protest to the emperor over the delay in issuing rice rations, but were prevented by the guards. During the Food May Day demonstration on May 19 a similar incident occurred at the palace in which several policemen were bruised and someone fell or was pushed into the moat, but emerged unharmed. A delegation of thirty, headed by Kyūichi Tokuda, the Communist leader, spent that night and part of the next day camping in the corridors of the prime minister's residence in an attempt to see Yoshida, who was then forming his cabinet.

There had, in fact, been dramatic and unorthodox methods of protest and slight disorders, but to speak of a "grave menace" to "the occupation itself" from "mass violence" was a considerable exaggeration. Most demonstrations represented merely exercise of the right, guaranteed by the Constitution of the United States, to assemble peaceably and petition for the redress of grievances. Unfortunately, MacArthur's statement was interpreted as a warning against all such demonstrations. Labor was somewhat confused, and in some cases . . . police took advantage of the statement to interfere with legitimate union operations. The incident put a temporary damper on labor activity; demonstrations almost ceased for a month or so, after which they were resumed with unabated vigor. MacArthur's statement appears also to have had the effect of intensifying the split between Socialists and Communists.

It is probable that a mixture of motives lay behind the May 20 statement, including SCAP's intense fear of communism and its extreme sensitivity to criticism. Another repercussion from May Day was a "manifesto" prepared by the committee which organized the May 1 Tokyo demonstration, and circulated to the members of the Allied Council, charging the Japanese police with various infringements of citizens' legal rights, especially in connection with the recent election. These charges were brought up by General Kuzma Derevyanko, the Russian representative, in the Allied Council meeting of May 29. Mr. George Atcheson, the American member, denied the accusations and charged that the manifesto appeared to be a translation from a foreign language, meaning Russian. The United States, he added, does not favor communism in Japan or elsewhere. . . .

Labor Division, in dealing with Japanese labor, adopted a

more conciliatory attitude than did Mr. Atcheson in dealing with the Russians. In August 1946 Theodore Cohen, then chief of Labor Division, addressed the inaugural conventions of the Japanese Federation of Labor and the Congress of Industrial Unions, reaffirming SCAP's friendly attitude but adding some words of advice. To the JFL Mr. Cohen said: "This inauguration of the postwar Nippon Rōdō Kumiai Sōdōmei is indeed an historic occasion. Democracy in action is always inspiring . . . the response of the Japanese workers to the opportunities opened to them by SCAP . . . has exceeded my most optimistic expectations. . . . Japanese labor unionists can play a vital role in the creation of the new Japan." He went on to stress the importance of full democratic participation by all union members in the work of the unions, and in a gentle warning against extreme demands, pointed out that "the well-being of the workers . . . is closely tied in with the essential soundness of the national economy." His speech to the CIU was similar in tone, with perhaps a shade more emphasis on good advice. Praising the Japanese unions for showing a sense of responsibility, he warned against abuse or dissipation of labor's strength. "Excessive diversion of union strength to outside activities better fulfilled by other organizations," he said, "can only handicap the efforts to improve the economic status of the Japanese workingman." This guarded language was correctly understood as a warning against "excessive" political activity by labor unions.

A similar evolution took place in SCAP's policy toward labor disputes. The initial policy was one of nonintervention. It was considered to be the responsibility of the Japanese government, through appropriate organs, to take any action needed to settle disputes. The theory was that the Japanese must learn to solve such problems for themselves. SCAP, however, reserved the right to intervene if it considered such action necessary. Up to the summer of 1946, according to an official report in June of that year: "In no instance have occupation troops been ordered to intervene in a labor dispute or been used to influence the settlement of a dispute or strike. Military intervention to maintain essential industries or services has at no time been necessary."

As regards strikes, SCAP policy was stated in a command letter to the armies of occupation dated November 17, 1945: "Strikes, lockouts, or other work stoppages which are inimical to the objectives of military occupation are prohibited. . . . A labor dispute 'inimical to the objectives of military occupation' is one which jeopardizes the safety of Allied troops, interferes with troop supply, disrupts public services or production necessary to the maintenance of public order, public service, and public health, or adversely affects other purposes of the occupation." This was interpreted as follows: "In practice, transportation, communication, coal mining, public utilities, repatriation service, and occupation forces' projects have been considered essential. This limitation has been communicated orally by Economic and Scientific Section, GHQ, SCAP, to the Japanese government, employers and labor unions on numerous occasions and has prevented several serious stoppages in those categories." The decision to prohibit a strike as inimical to the occupation was not left to the discretion of local military units but was supposed to be referred to SCAP. Actually, local units sometimes used their own judgment.

This policy was clear enough up to a point, but the question remained whether or not any given strike would be considered inimical to the occupation. No precise rules could easily be formulated, had General MacArthur tried to avoid the necessity of making such decisions. Hence the Japanese could never be quite sure of SCAP's intentions. The autumn of 1946 saw a wave of labor militancy expressed in many disputes and actual or threatened strikes, some of national importance. On August 27 the Supreme Commander issued a public warning that "strikes, walkouts, or other work stoppages which are inimical to the objectives of the occupation are prohibited." Subsequently, rumors that SCAP was preparing to crack down on strikers gained wide circulation. For example, a member of the electrical workers' union informed the writer that leaders of his union had been told by a Japanese official that, if the union should strike, its leaders would be arrested by the occupation forces. The source of such rumors cannot easily be traced. It is probable that some American officials, not necessarily those authorized to expound labor policy, expressed themselves privately to certain Japanese in terms which may well have been exaggerated with frequent repetition.

❋ IN THE SUMMER of 1946 labor was still gaining strength, and individual unions were organizing into larger groups. In August inaugural conventions were held for both Sōdōmei (JFL—Japan Federation of Labor) and Sambetsu (NCIU—National Congress of Industrial Unions). Sōdōmei's political links were to the Japan Socialist party, and Sambetsu's were to the Japanese Communist party. The two federations were divided on policy and tactics, with Sambetsu taking more militant positions. A third federation, the All-Japan Council of Labor Unions, was smaller than Sōdōmei and Sambetsu, and it sometimes served as a bridge between them.

A series of labor actions occurred in the fall of 1946. Although there were some gains, there were also some ominous signs, as powerful SCAP officials exerted influence in various situations. The events of the *Yomiuri* newspaper strike described below are a good example of this. Major Daniel Imboden, the chief of the SCAP Press Division, and Brigadier General Frayne Baker, the public relations officer, both worked to defeat the strike, successfully in the end. This strike also shows the divisions within SCAP headquarters on labor questions.

MARK GAYN*
Yomiuri Strike

.

TOKYO, July 11, 1946

Once again the *Yomiuri*, Japan's largest daily, has become a testing ground of our labor policies. This noon, after weeks of jockeying, 750 of its employees went on strike.

* Mark Gayn, *Japan Diary* (New York: William Sloan Associates, 1948), pp. 263–265, 328–334.

Spread over the strike lies the shadow of Major Daniel Imboden, chief of the Press Division. A few days ago, representatives of Baba, publisher of *Yomiuri,* called on Imboden and discussed the impending strike with him. Whatever it was that Imboden said, Baba immediately summoned members of his staff, one by one, told them Imboden was behind him, and asked them to sign a statement supporting his stand against the union. The Japanese Labor Relations Committee, one of our better efforts in the field of labor, indicated that it did not like the smell of the procedure. Baba then informed it that, "in the opinion of American authorities," the Labor Code was superseded by the "press code," drafted by Imboden.

Anyway, Baba hired some *gorotsuki,* or professional toughs, and waited for trouble. Walker and I went into the *Yomiuri* building this afternoon, and here were the *gorotsuki* standing guard at the door, and the walls were covered with the posters of both sides. We tried to see Baba, but he was out. We then went to the fourth floor, where the strike committee sat in session in a tiny room. Just outside of the door lay a large straw bag with 120 pounds of rice—a gift to the strikers. Summer is here, and most of the committee members were stripped to the waist and damp with sweat. At the head of the table, with his usual scowl, sat Kikunami, the *Asahi* editorial writer who is now forming the Congress of Industrial Unions.

The atmosphere in the small room changed from minute to minute, as messengers came in to report the latest news. Now it was word from the printing plant, where seven more men decided to join the walkout. The faces smiled, and there were shouts of Good, Good, and the warm air was saturated with confidence. But there was a glum silence when a report was brought in that Baba had called in key *Yomiuri* officials to discuss the formation of a company union.

Major Imboden is having a busy time. The liberal daily, *Mimpo,* ran an editorial saying Baba sought to dominate the Newspaper Union. Imboden warned the paper that the comment was "one-sided." Long under pressure from Imboden, the daily is gradually modifying its progressive policy or using doubletalk allowing it to say what it feels needs to be said, and yet escape Imboden's wrath.

The *Jimmin Shimbun* is a Socialist paper, with a circulation of

250,000. One of its editors told me Imboden had warned the
paper that it was following a "pro-communist policy," and gave it
until July 13 to change its ways, on fear of suppression. There was
much brave talk of free speech and of defying the major. But
courage oozed out. Yesterday's edition carried mostly innocuous
"literary news." From now on the paper will pretend it is living in
a nonpolitical Wonderland.

The *Hokkaidō Shimbun,* in Japan's extreme north, has just gone
through one of Imboden's famous purges. In all, fifty-nine union
members have been fired for being "Communist racketeers." The
union, of course, is broken up. Imboden's dark view of the daily
does not jibe with the official opinion of Headquarters, which less
than a month ago said the daily was "comparatively conservative,"
and noted its strong editorial attacks on communism. My Japanese friends tell me the paper was one of Japan's most reputable
provincial dailies. They think Imboden is simply union busting.

TOKYO, July 17, 1946

The *Yomiuri* strike is over, with the union defeated.

There really never was a fight. While the *Yomiuri* was on strike,
other units of the Newspaper Union merely watched the show. So
did other unions. And on the *Yomiuri* itself more than half the
workers stayed out of the strike. What sympathy they might have
had for the strikers shrank with each reminder by Baba, the publisher, that Headquarters was behind him.

Baba has formed a company union, and yesterday ordered its
members to drive the strikers out. Spearheaded by professional
toughs, the small army forced its way into the composing room
and threw the strikers out. Another force went up to the strike
headquarters on the fourth floor, beat up the union people, and
drove them out too. Dozens of Japanese policemen on the scene
watched the fun, but did not intervene.

When I left the building, a few printers caught up with me. They
said they wanted to tell the American people that fear alone impelled them to join the company union, and that their hearts were
still with the strikers. An old printer added:

"General MacArthur doesn't know what Baba is doing. Please
tell him. Tell him everything."

TOKYO, October 4, 1946

The *Yomiuri* is back in the news.

After four months of desperate maneuvering, Kikunami's Newspaper and Radio Workers Union went on strike today. Ostensibly it is seeking to force Baba, the publisher, to comply with the order of the Labor Arbitration Board to rehire the thirty-one men he fired in July. But no simple explanations ever apply to the *Yomiuri*. The union wants more than justice for thirty-one men. It is fighting for its own life.

With the help of General Baker and Major Imboden, the Japanese publishers are gradually destroying the union. Baba has set up a company union on his paper. Imboden has helped to break up the union on a daily in Japan's north. Now he has been moving in on the two great newspaper chains, the *Asahi* and the *Mainichi*. The union knows that it will be crippled if Imboden succeeds.

But even that is too simple an explanation. Neither Baker nor Imboden is an important man. Both are merely instruments of a policy which must inevitably destroy the progressive press in Japan. There is no longer any question of communism. Baker and Imboden are now after the moderates who find fault with the "new democracy" and its Japanese sponsors.

This time the Newspaper Union is better prepared than it was in July. It is not fighting alone. The newspaper strike will be a part of what labor calls "The October Offensive." Instead of calling a general strike, which might be banned by Headquarters, the unions will walk out in succession, each with a demand for a living wage. The second in the strike line are the coal miners. The third are the electrical workers.

Special care is being taken to give Headquarters no cause to break the strike. The printers will continue to set the army newspaper. The striking radiomen will stay on the job in the army stations. The Japanese papers will cease publication, but will issue special editions carrying the texts of any new American directives and reports of the war crimes trial.

Correspondents were told of the strike at a press conference called by the union. Two of them, noted for their antilabor views, very deftly tried to catch the union spokesman in an anti-American statement. The bait they dangled before him was a visit paid by Major Imboden to the *Asahi* plant. It seems that the good major said nothing; he just looked stern. But as soon as he left, the management started a rumor that Headquarters was planning to take over the plant, if the union went on strike.

The spokesman chose his words with care. "I've heard that Major Imboden visited the *Asahi,* but I don't like to say anything about it. Whatever we do is done to protect the workers' rights. It's also done with full respect for the occupation policies. . . . A state of uncertainty has prevailed in the *Asahi* since the major's visit. What worries us is not the suffering, but the solidarity of labor. Ours is a young union, and there are great outside pressures at work."

Later, in the gutted power plant which serves as strike head-quarters, we found out what some of the outside pressures are. The plant is a two-storey blackened shell. The strikers have strung out a few dim lights in it, built a ramshackle stairway, and put in old tables and benches. Now a "financial committee" was at work in a corner. In another, a committee was considering the problem of getting rice for the pickets. Artists were drawing posters, a mimeographing machine was turning out leaflets, messengers were rushing in and out. In the center sat the "Strike Direction Committee."

Fromm, Costello, and I came in just as a message arrived from a daily in southern Japan. After the workers voted to strike, the message said, a U.S. army sergeant came to the plant and announced that no strike would be allowed.

We were still there when two agitated delegates arrived from an interview with an American officer in the Radio Division of Head-quarters. He had told them bluntly, they said, that if the radio workers struck, he would throw them in jail.

"These are Headquarters orders. If you disobey, you'll suffer the consequences."

Such decisions are not easy to make. There was a ring of men around us now, dark and silent. They waited for the committee's ruling. Work elsewhere ceased, and more people came up. The members put their heads together, and whispered. Finally the chairman spoke up:

"We shall not in any way interfere with U.S. army broadcasts. All we want is to exercise our legal right to strike, given to us by General MacArthur. The radio strike will begin as scheduled."

Imboden's tour of the *Asahi* was a shrewd move, for the only axiom of this strike is, "As the *Asahi* goes, so goes the press." All the tremendous power that is seeking to break the strike—Headquarters, the Yoshida cabinet, the publishers—has now been concentrated on the *Asahi,* on the large auditorium on the top floor, where the workers have been closeted for nearly twenty-four hours in an effort to make up their minds. They had once decided to join the strike, but the fearful among them asked for a new debate.

At midnight, word came that the *Asahi* might reverse itself, and pull out of the strike. Hugh Deane, of the Allied Labor News, and I went to the *Asahi* building. We came into the closely packed hall just as a delegation of *Yomiuri* strikers was pleading passionately for support. The sentiment in that room was a tangible element, and we could see it sway this way and that as one speaker followed another. The last speaker put in words what was hidden deep in their minds:

"General MacArthur is opposed to strikes. He would not hesitate to close up the *Asahi* if we strike. You saw Major Imboden. . . ."

When the decision not to strike was finally announced, there was a period of silence. And the only sounds that were audible in the room were the sobs of men—both the victors and the losers. For even the men who opposed the strike said fear was their only counsel.

TOKYO, October 5, 1946

This morning the five million radios of Japan went silent. Despite the *Asahi's* decision last night, the radio workers decided to strike. The official heat is now on the *Mainichi,* whose workers have voted to walk out. A Japanese editor told me the *Mainichi* management was in conference with General Baker—presumably to map out strategy.

I went to the Labor Division of Headquarters to find out its stand on the strike. I found only a group of disheartened, frustrated men. Our policy in Japan has been based on the premise that a strong labor movement is the best guardian of democracy. The Labor Division was given the job of nursing the unions to strength. But back last spring, the Labor Division discovered that

strong labor was anathema to many powerful men in Headquarters. While the Labor Division was talking in pious phrases to
Japanese union leaders, counterintelligence agents were breaking
up labor demonstrations, Imboden had begun his campaign of
union-busting, General Baker had entered the picture. Men big and
small, from sergeants in remote detachments to General Willoughby, have begun to remake the U.S. labor policy for Japan.
From time to time, the Labor Division tried to assert its interest in
the subject. It was quickly slapped on the wrist. Its chief, Cohen, a
young man with a pathological fear of being labelled Red (though
Lord knows he is not), was no match for his tough military
opponents. At this point, not even Japanese labor pays much
attention to the Labor Division. It has learned at a bitter cost
where the real power lies in Headquarters.

"We had orders to stay out of this mess," an officer said. "We
also had orders not to talk to correspondents. Go away."

Thus, while Japanese labor fights its greatest battle in history,
and Imboden and Baker are engaged in what is known as "house-
breaking the labor movement," the Labor Division is hiding in a
neutral corner.

At noon, for the fourth time, the *Asahi* workers decided to
reconsider their decision. They filed back into the auditorium, and
began the argument anew. At this point the strike score stood:
forty newspapers throughout Japan for the strike, three against,
thirteen sitting on the fence. But the *Asahi* remains the heart of the
movement. As long as it is working, there is no real strike. If the
heart stops, other newspapers will shut their plants. The radio
workers are thus fighting it out on their own. The government
today threatened to set up an emergency transmitter, but discovered it could get no one to operate it. Baba, the *Yomiuri* publisher, meanwhile announced that he would start a campaign for a
chain of company unions in the newspapers of Japan.

In the afternoon, the Japanese police threw cordons around
every newspaper plant in Tokyo. Employees were allowed to leave
the buildings, but not to reenter. This meant that the mass meetings in half a dozen newspapers were isolated from each other. The
central strike committee countered with loudspeakers mounted on
trucks. The loudspeakers cruised in front of the *Asahi,* and roared

pleas to the workers to join the strike. Shortly after noon, American military police broke up one rally of radio workers, while the Japanese police dispersed another.

Later, a procession of sympathetic unions marched by the *Yomiuri* building. It sang lustily, and waved posters denouncing Baba, the Yoshida cabinet, and the so-called "depression firings." The *Yomiuri* doors were locked. The plant guards stood in the upper-storey windows and yelled insults and challenges.

The whole crew of correspondents was covering the parade. To all of us, whether we sympathized with Baba or the strikers, this shabby building was the testing ground of our policy for Japan. Every one of us knew of the secret moves being made by American officers to break up the strike. But we all wondered if these moves could be translated into positive action.

We got our answer. Sally and I were sitting in our jeep catty-corner from the *Yomiuri* building. A military policeman came up and asked my business. I pointed at the "Chicago *Sun,*" painted in foot-high letters on the jeep. He took down my name and the jeep number. He said, "Move on." I told him I would stay put and cover the procession. That ended the conversation.

But, meanwhile, in front of the *Yomiuri,* a hundred Japanese policemen and a unit of American MPs had gone into action. The procession was orderly. Then suddenly armed men were upon it, pushing the demonstrants, seizing the posters, breaking up the parade. The marchers did not resist. But as fast as one group was broken up, another one reformed its ranks somewhere else. Their own marshals kept them in line. The men and women fell into new ranks, and sang, and waved flags.

In the middle of it, Captain William Riley, who led the force of MPs, ordered American correspondents off the sidewalk. When Costello, whose leg bothered him, lagged behind, Riley threatened him with arrest. Costello, who is an extremely calm and competent individual, told the captain to go ahead and arrest him. Margaret Parton then pitched in:

"Yes, go ahead! And me too!"

Riley thought better of it.

At eight at night, the *Asahi* workers, for the third time, re-affirmed their decision to stay out of the strike. But this time, bitterness had broken through the walls of self-restraint. Few men now hid their resentment against the American policy. One after another, they rose to cry out their support for the strike, and to protest against a policy that filled them with fear.

"If I were allowed to talk of the Allied policy toward labor and the press," said a young *Asahi* reporter, "I could speak for three hours. There's much talk of a 'free press.' But how about the censorship which forbids us to criticize our own government?

"Headquarters gives us freedom to print all we like, but expects us to print only propaganda. Now it's trying to break up the *Asahi* and the *Mainichi*. Three months ago, Headquarters warned the *Yomiuri* of its 'inaccuracy.' After that the *Yomiuri* was destroyed. Now the *Asahi* is warned, and Major Imboden attacks us for publishing a story that has already been passed by the American censors."

After the meeting, men filed out of the building weeping. There was no need to tell the crowd waiting outside what had happened. The sobs told the story. I went down to the strike headquarters in the power plant. There were a few score men and women there, but the militant spirit was gone. The strikers are learning some bitter lessons. One of their leaders was discovered to be a government *agent provocateur,* who has been in constant touch with one of Yoshida's secretaries. I talked to Kikunami in a corner. He was utterly worn out. "The printers were with us," he said, "but the white-collar people were frightened. They need more education before they learn to stand up for their rights."

I was with Kikunami when the word came that the *Mainichi,* in a double-reverse, had again decided to strike. But few in this dark, gloomy barn were cheered. The *Mainichi* unit will reverse itself again when it learns of the *Asahi* vote.

❧ IN SPITE OF THE DIFFICULTIES in the fall 1946 strikes, plans moved ahead for strike actions in early 1947. The union organizations were cooperating with each other, and a unified plan developed for a general strike on February 1, 1947. SCAP tried to prevent the strike, proposing wage increases and threatening labor leaders. Finally, faced with the unions' refusal to call off the strike without an official SCAP command, MacArthur forbade it.

Although the occupation authorities had exhibited displeasure with various labor activities during 1946, MacArthur's action came as a shock. The Japanese left, and labor in particular, was put on notice that their latitude in instituting democratization efforts was relatively narrow. Not only did the order abort one of the most important labor strike attempts in Japanese history, but it also hinted at the "reverse course" that was increasingly manifest by the end of 1947.

MIRIAM FARLEY*
General Strike Movement

GOVERNMENT EMPLOYEES PREPARE FOR STRIKE

On January 1 the government employees' Joint Struggle Committee met to work out its strike plans. The strike date was subsequently set for February 1. It was stated that services to the occupation forces would be maintained and that the legal prohibition of strikes by government office workers, under the Labor Relations Adjustment Law, would be complied with. That the unions were at first thinking in terms of limited or gradual action is indicated by various reports. The railway workers planned to begin with business control, followed by strike action; there was some division of opinion as to whether food shipments would be permitted. The teachers, also, planned to try production control before proceeding to a strike.

The strike objectives, as announced on January 18, were: (1) minimum basic monthly salary of 650 yen, effective from December, (2) immediate payment of the balance of the year-end allowance, (3) immediate conclusion of collective bargaining agreements, (4) no unreasonable discharges, (5) no discriminatory treatment, (6) cash payment of all salaries and allowances, (7)

* Miriam Farley, *Aspects of Japan's Labor Problems* (New York: John Day Co., 1950), pp. 144–150, 152–153.

grant of "cold zone" allowances, (8) abolition of Labor Relations Adjustment Law, (9) abolition of income tax on wages, (10) raising exemption point of consolidated income tax to 30,000 yen, (11) payment of salaries during strike, (12) guarantees against police oppression of labor, (13) apology for Prime Minister Yoshida's references to labor in his New Year's message.

ALL LABOR JOINS IN

During January the movement gained in volume and velocity until it became virtually a dispute between the government and all of organized labor. On January 15 the All-Japan Joint Struggle Committee of Labor Unions was formed to support the government employees. It included some thirty unions and all three major federations, and represented about 4 million workers. The committee planned a joint struggle for common objectives, including a minimum wage, income tax revision, payment of all wages in cash, collective agreements, opposition to discharges, and establishment of a democratic government.

The committee was united on its general objectives but not on the question of tactics. Communists and other militant left-wingers pushed for a broad program of concerted nationwide strikes. The CIU supported such a program but the JFL and JCLU were opposed and the JFL eventually withdrew from the committee. . . .

BASES OF STRIKE MOVEMENT

Economic conditions were the basic cause of the growing unrest among wage and salary workers. Inflation was unchecked, prices were still rising, black markets flourished, and the resources of many families were approaching exhaustion. Not only government employees but all urban workers suffered increasingly great hardships with little visible hope of improvement, as production was still in the doldrums and the government seemed either unable or unwilling to take effective remedial measures.

Political motives were also present; in fact, economic and political goals cannot be dissociated. The more intelligent labor leaders realized that there was little point in merely fighting for wage increases while the inflationary spiral continued. Relief for the workers' hardships could come only from a concerted all-out attack on the nation's economic problems. Neither the Shidehara nor the Yoshida cabinet seemed to be capable of constructive action. There were also numerous complaints of specific abuses such as favoritism and corruption in the distribution of rationed supplies.

Beyond all this lay the fact that the people of Japan had been promised a new deal—summed up in the magic word "democracy"—and many of them believed they were not getting it. The militarists had gone but in its domestic aspect the Japanese government did not seem to have changed greatly. Few of the long-range reforms introduced by SCAP had yet produced any tangible effect on the lives of the people. A vague discontent fused with economic privation to produce widespread unrest. Under such conditions it was easy for Communist and other radical labor leaders to arouse the smoldering discontent of the rank and file with the slogan, "Down with the Yoshida cabinet—establish a people's government!" Moderate leadership tended to be swept aside or to join the bandwagon.

The big disputes in the fall of 1946—of seamen, miners, railwaymen, electrical workers, etc.—had been mainly fought for straight economic objectives. While union leaders made no secret of their dislike of the Yoshida cabinet, they refrained for the most part from raising political slogans, knowing that political action by labor was frowned on by SCAP and often identified with communist influence. In the winter offensive, opposition to the government was voiced openly, and resignation of the cabinet was generally understood to be the major strike objective, although it was not formally stated as such. This was rationalized on the ground that the government had taken the offensive by instituting a campaign to crush labor organization and to protect the profits of capitalists at the expense of the people's livelihood.

The government, for its part, although under pressure it had often given in to labor demands, was suspicious and hostile in its attitude toward the labor movement, which it regarded as a threat to public order, if not as a revolutionary conspiracy. In October, when the coal miners', Radio Tokyo, and electrical workers' disputes were at their height, Prime Minister Yoshida called the strike wave "a challenge to democratic government" and "a movement by small minorities aiming at the establishment of dictatorial government." On October 30 Yoshida spoke in similar terms at a conference of prefectural governors, condemning the tactics of the coal miners and electrical workers as a threat to economic reconstruction and hence to the life of the nation. The fall offensive was punctuated by similar statements by other government spokesmen. In a joint statement on October 12 the Liberal and Progressive parties reaffirmed their support of the prime minister and warned against strikes instigated by a "faction" to disrupt the economic and political situation.

It was at about this time that Mr. George Atcheson made his famous statement in the Allied Council that "the time has come when Japanese aims have become virtually identical with Allied aims." Although this sweeping language surprised many people in SCAP whose experience in dealing with Japanese officials did not support Mr. Atcheson's conclusion, it was endorsed by the State Department in Washington. Obviously this statement was helpful to the hard-pressed Yoshida government in its struggle against the demands of labor. This was not the only occasion when statements in the Allied Council, intended primarily as a defense of SCAP's record against Russian criticism, had the effect of strengthening conservative against progressive elements in Japanese politics.

In his New Year's message Yoshida used particularly strong language in speaking of labor. The main cause of low production, inflation, and unrest lay, he charged, in labor disputes instigated by "rebellious elements" . . . who hampered reconstruction, disturbed national unity, and sought to exploit economic conditions in order to seize political power. This speech aroused strong resentment in labor circles, especially the word *"futei,"* which has about the same connotations as "disloyal" or "subversive" in the United States.

By this time activists in the labor unions were definitely aiming at a nationwide strike movement of sufficient proportions to force the resignation of the Yoshida cabinet. The movement was one of peaceful protest. Although some of the strike supporters were too handy with their fists, there was no evidence of any plan for concerted violence or insurrection. The strike leaders do not seem to have had any very clear idea of the next step, if the campaign succeeded. There were vague demands for a government "based on the Social Democratic party." If they had anything more definite in mind, it was probably a government composed of Social Democrats, Communists, and other "popular" elements. Such a government, of course, would have had the support of only a small minority in the existing Diet.

By the middle of January events seemed to be working toward a showdown between the unions and the government. As tension mounted, an ugly incident occurred when, on January 21, Katsumi Kikunami, CIU head and active pro-strike leader, was attacked with knives and seriously wounded by two men who later surrendered to the police and identified themselves as members of Shin'ei Kinrō Taishūtō, a reactionary organization which openly threatened more attacks on labor leaders unless the strike were called off. Threatening anonymous letters were received by other union leaders. Home Minister Ōmura, deploring the incident, promised that the government would suppress terrorism.

SCAP TRIES TO PREVENT STRIKE

In the meantime SCAP, which was reluctant to interfere openly, was working quietly behind the scenes in an effort to head off the strike. Pressure was brought to bear on the government to induce it to concede some part of the union demands, and strong pressure was applied informally to induce the unions to call off the strike. . . .

Knowledge that SCAP intended, if necessary, to ban the strike may well have stiffened the backs of both parties. The government need not make too many concessions if SCAP were going to prohibit the strike in the end. On the other hand the union leaders need not back down before their followers by giving in to the government; submitting to SCAP's paramount power would involve no such loss of prestige. It was for this reason that the union leaders insisted on a written order from SCAP.

SCAP BANS STRIKE

On the afternoon of January 30 General Marquat again called in the union leaders and ordered them to call off the strike. They were told to report by the following day what steps they had taken. They requested a written order but were told that this was unnecessary. At 2:30 P.M. on the next day, nine-and-a-half hours before the deadline, no word of compliance had been received. General MacArthur therefore issued a formal order forbidding the strike. This action, he said, was being taken with the greatest reluctance, and on the ground that the strike would paralyze Japanese industry and might necessitate further Allied assistance to Japan. He did not, he said, intend otherwise to restrict the freedom of labor in pursuit of legitimate objectives or to influence the basic social issues involved; but the general tenor of his statement was strongly critical of the unions.

The news of MacArthur's order was received with bitter disappointment at strike headquarters. A few hotheads counseled defiance, but after a short discussion the strike committee submitted unconditionally. To ensure compliance Yashiro Ii, the committee chairman, broadcast news of General MacArthur's order by radio that evening. In a voice charged with emotion he told the workers: "We must comply" with SCAP's order, but urged them to continue the struggle by other methods. The strike movement collapsed completely. Except for one or two brief local stoppages, no attempt was made to challenge the SCAP order. . . .

❦ IN JULY 1948 government employees were negotiating a wage increase when General MacArthur sent a letter to Prime Minister Ashida proposing changes in the National Public Service Law. The effect was to reduce to virtually nothing the bargaining rights of government employees. The events of spring 1948 made final the increasingly visible drift of occupation policy away from democratization toward an emphasis on Japan as an economically strong and politically stable Cold War partner of the United States. MacArthur's letter was an indication of what this shift would mean for labor. The Ashida cabinet showed great haste in implementing the "suggestions," and in some places the letter was used to go even farther than MacArthur suggested. Naturally, great pressure was put on the Socialists in the cabinet to pull out of the coalition, but they stayed in at considerable cost to their reputation.

MIRIAM FARLEY*
SCAP and Government Employees, 1948

The government employees were far from satisfied with the wage agreement of March 1948. In June the National Council of Government and Public Workers' Unions presented a demand for an average wage of 5200 yen. They were also opposed to grievance machinery, wage ceilings, price increases, and reduction of personnel. The government offered 3791 yen, and in June submitted legislation to this effect to the Diet. The bill was passed on July 5, with the new wage scale retroactive to June 1. That this scale was still below the wage level prevailing in private industry was generally admitted. On July 7, after a month of negotiations, the union council called for mediation of the dispute by the Central Labor Relations Committee, to which the government finally agreed.

Mediation was thus under way, with strike tactics for the moment in abeyance, when the Supreme Commander threw a bombshell in the form of an open letter to Prime Minister Ashida, on July 22. Though dealing specifically only with labor relations in government service, SCAP's action profoundly affected the labor movement as a whole. In fact, according to the SCAP *Summation* for July, it "became the center of public interest and caused replanning of all political strategy."

In his letter the Supreme Commander proposed a revision of the existing civil service act, a postwar measure. Government employees, he said, are responsible to the whole people. No government employee has the right to strike or use other delaying tactics; by such action he forfeits his rights as a civil servant. Collective bargaining, he continued, is not applicable in public service, although public servants have the right individually or collectively to present their views and grievances. He thought that public enterprises such as railways, and the salt, camphor, and tobacco monopolies might

* Miriam Farley, *Aspects of Japan's Labor Problems* (New York: John Day Co., 1950), pp. 189–190, 192–193, 195–196, 203, 205–206.

be excepted from this rule, but they should be reorganized as public corporations. Finally, General MacArthur recommended that the National Public Service Law be revised in accordance with these principles.

Government employees, other than operating employees of public enterprises, were already debarred from striking under the Labor Relations Adjustment Law, although this provision had not been strictly enforced. The SCAP letter went further and denied them the right of collective bargaining which they had previously enjoyed. Moreover, the letter could be interpreted as depriving operating employees of the right to strike, at least temporarily and perhaps permanently.

Exactly what prompted this demarche by SCAP has never been fully explained. It was no doubt intended as a reprisal against communist tactics, which had been very troublesome, especially among government employees. It was, moreover, in line with the increasing emphasis on economic recovery which characterized United States policy toward Japan in 1948. Numerous official statements made clear the belief that the occupation's original aim of democratic reform must, if necessary, give way before the urgent need to place Japan's economy on a self-supporting basis. . . .

The cabinet lost no time in acting on General MacArthur's suggestions. On July 31 it issued an ordinance declaring that government employees (national and local) were debarred from exercising the right of "collective bargaining as usually understood with its coercive character supported by the strike threat." They or their organizations might present claims or grievances and discuss them with the appropriate authority. Current mediation proceedings affecting government employees were suspended, and the handling of labor relations in the civil service was transferred to the National Personnel Authority. Strikes or delaying actions were prohibited on pain of loss of civil service rights, 5000-yen fine or one year's imprisonment. The ordinance would continue in effect until the National Public Service Law had been revised by the Diet. The government also announced that all existing contracts with public employee unions were void, although clauses not incompatible with the ordinance would be observed. The cabinet's action, although temporary, thus went much farther than General MacArthur's proposal, which had not denied collective bargaining rights to employees of public enterprises. As a gesture of appeasement, government spokesmen announced plans to improve the welfare of public employees through better housing, clinics, sanatoria, etc., and said that consideration would be given to a salary increase.

Rightly or wrongly, the SCAP statement was generally regarded in Japan as the most serious blow yet dealt to organized labor as a whole. As on other occasions, various Japanese agencies took advantage of the atmosphere which it created to impose restrictions on labor activity unrelated to the issues dealt with by SCAP. A number of municipalities, for example, issued regulations limiting the holding of public meetings and demonstrations. . . .

The effect of SCAP's letter followed by the cabinet ordinance was to throw the whole labor movement into turmoil. All sections of organized labor viewed the new developments with alarm, but opinions on what line the unions should take under the new conditions were sharply divided. As criticism of the occupation was forbidden, it was impossible publicly to take issue with General MacArthur; but it was possible to criticize the government's interpretation of his words, and great ingenuity was shown in this direction.

Labor leaders, confronted by SCAP's bombshell, divided roughly into two groups: those who bowed to the inevitable, and those who did not. The former accepted, however unwillingly, the principles of the SCAP letter and sought to work within this framework, by legal methods, for the best possible terms. The latter condemned the government's action and sought to reverse or modify it, some by agitation and peaceful protest, others—chiefly communists— by strike action in defiance of the cabinet ordinance.

NEW LEGISLATION FOR GOVERNMENT EMPLOYEES

As the cabinet order was a temporary measure, great interest attached to the terms of the revised National Public Service Law, which the Ashida cabinet now set about drafting; the work was completed by the Yoshida cabinet. The process was accompanied by intense debate both inside and outside the cabinet, and frequent consultation with Government Section, GHQ. . . .

The bill to revise the National Public Service Law was introduced in the Diet on November 10, passed on December 1, and immediately promulgated. It was hailed by General MacArthur as "a major victory for those who seek integrity of representative government over those who would leave the government prey to minority subjugation."

As revised, the law provided that government employees might "join or refrain from joining" associations. They might designate, through such associations, representatives of their own choice to negotiate with the proper authorities about working conditions and employee welfare, but might not conclude a collective agreement with the government. Wages were not specifically mentioned among the subjects for negotiation. Elsewhere the law provided that "personnel of the service may present application to the [National Personnel] Authority relative to salary, wages . . . or working conditions" and request administrative action; this would permit individual adjustments but would not affect basic pay schedules. Such schedules were fixed by the Diet, and the National Personnel Authority was required to make recommendations to the Diet on this subject annually. As a concession to labor, the law provided that in fixing wage schedules account should be taken of the cost of living and prevailing wages. Government employees were prohibited from striking or engaging in delaying action or other dispute tactics, subject to penalties ranging up to 100,000-yen fine or three years' imprisonment.

⚛ THE UPROAR caused by the revision of the National Public Service Law brought increased factionalism to labor. The leadership of Sōdōmei, for example, was challenged from within by left elements, and in the Sambetsu organizations, the Democratization Leagues (Mindō) were fighting the Communists for control. These strongly anti-Communist labor groups gained in importance in 1949–1950, when the Communists were purged from labor unions. Supported by SCAP, the Mindō represented the American desire to have unions, but not Communist-dominated ones.

HERBERT P. BIX*
American Labor and Japanese Unionists

Stimulating Japanese rearmament has not been the only goal of
U.S.–Japan policy during the past two decades. Another part of
that policy has been enlisting the support of American labor
leaders to strengthen the hand of conservative Japanese unionists,
with the aim of maintaining the internal status quo in Japan. . . .

The American labor movement had among its top generals
during the prewar period men like George Meany, David Dubinsky, and Matthew Woll. Conservative on domestic matters, such
labor representatives more often than not supported chauvinistic
policies abroad as well. In the 1930s, for instance, Woll, an AFL
vice president, "was prominent in pushing 'labor pan-American-
ism'—the cultivation of labor leaders throughout the hemisphere
who would applaud U.S. incursions, including the various dispatches of marines. . . ." "Dubinsky and Woll," according to
Michael Myerson's recent study of the International Ladies Gar-
ment Workers Union, "formed a core of anticommunist militancy
in the AFL (and later the AFL–CIO)." During World War II they,
together with the embittered ex-Communist, Jay Lovestone, had
founded the American Labor Conference on International Affairs
(ALCIA) as a vehicle for their own reactionary brand of
unionism. . . .

In the early Cold War years American labor leaders were busy
trying to destroy the newly unified (October 1945) international
labor movement represented by the World Federation of Trade
Unions (WFTU), and create in its place a new anticommunist
labor international; at the same time they were also carrying the
Cold War to Asia where occupied and isolated Japan was a key
battlefield.

In January 1947 General MacArthur took two actions designed

---

* Herbert P. Bix, "The Security Treaty System and the Japanese Military–
Industrial Complex," *Bulletin of Concerned Asian Scholars* II:2 (January
1970), pp. 42–44.

to weaken the Japanese labor movement. He issued for political and ideological reasons a ban against a proposed general strike of government employees set for February 1, 1947, and he wrote a letter to Matthew Woll to get his organization's help in countering the leftist trend in the Japanese labor movement. On Woll's recommendation, James Killen, "a top official of the International Brotherhood of Pulp, Sulphite, and Paper Mill Workers," was sent to Japan and appointed chief of SCAP's . . . labor division. Under Killen's direction "democratization leagues" were set up as anti-communist cells within Japanese unions and an intensive effort was made to split the newly formed "National Liaison Council of Labor Unions" (Zenrōren). On July 22, 1948, the Japanese government, in response to an open letter from General MacArthur to Prime Minister Ashida, issued an ordinance "denying government workers not only the right to strike but also the right of collective bargaining." This drastic and unexpected action led Killen and several of his associates to resign their posts.

AFL cooperation with the occupation then took a different form. AFL agents working through SCAP put all of their efforts into getting Japanese unions to affiliate with the AFL and CIA-inspired anticommunist international labor federation that was then taking shape in Western Europe. In late 1949 and early 1950, SCAP stepped up its anticommunist witch hunt, purging all communist leaders from the unions. An all-out effort was made with strong AFL backing to bring organized labor under the control of the right-wing "socialists" through a new national labor center called Sōhyō.

♲ THE NINE-POINT stabilization plan soon to be administered by Joseph M. Dodge was enunciated in December 1948. It was an austerity program aimed at rapidly creating a self-sufficient capitalist economy. Its methods were harsh; deflation and unemployment were the conscious costs. The firing of workers—176,000 discharged from the government alone—was also used as an excuse to fire Communists and other radicals. Of course, this had a disastrous effect on the labor movement in membership. Yet the blow was even harsher, for the purge of radicals weakened labor militancy. Resistance to it was never mobilized, for the remaining labor leaders felt their own power would increase. Sambetsu was drastically weakened, and MacArthur finally suggested the outlawing of the Japan Communist party on Constitution Day in 1950, leading to the complete political purge of the party. The strengthened Democratization Leagues, Sōdōmei, and other labor unions finally joined in creating the General Council of Japanese Trade Unions (Sōhyō) in 1950.

The effects of the Dodge Plan and the political purge were apparent in the Sōhyō-led labor offensive in early 1950. Union leaders negotiated, behaved moderately, and yet obtained few gains. As the Korean War approached, economic and political conditions for labor activity were poor, and benefits were obtained more by fiat from above than struggle from below.

COLE, TOTTEN, AND UYEHARA*
Labor and the "Red Purge"

Disinflation and the "Red purge" were the two trends during 1949–1950 that threw the labor movement into confusion and retreat, with repercussions also on the temporarily discredited Social Democratic party. At SCAP insistence, governmental credit to enable deficit financing of industries was to cease; the Japanese economy was to be prepared to stand independently and to enter the competitive international market. This entailed indirect wage stabilization and reductions of both governmental and private industrial personnel. Occupation authorities tried to insist on a distinction between this painful readjustment, which affected more than 400,000 workers, and the political as well as labor purge of Communists plus extremist sympathizers, which gained momen-

* Allan B. Cole, George O. Totten, and Cecil H. Uyehara, *Socialist Parties in Postwar Japan* (New Haven, Conn.: Yale University Press, 1966), pp. 330–332.

tum after General MacArthur's Constitution Day speech in May 1950. But when SCAP opened the door to conservative renovationists, there was no adequate screening process before dismissals. By the end of that year, at least 11,000 labor leftists had been fired from more than twenty industries; more than 1000 lost jobs in governmental services and enterprises which had experienced the most militant labor activities, while similarly inclined unions in key private industries were also weakened. The process undoubtedly involved widespread disregard of basic civil and human rights.

Not only Communists but also other activists on the "struggle committees" of unions were dismissed, and usually this involved loss of their union membership. After the outbreak of the Korean War in June, "security risks" were fired from companies with "special procurement" contracts. Conservative bureaucrats and such organizations as the Japanese Federation of Employer Associations (Nikkeiren) tried to convert these trends into a full union-busting movement, but SCAP's Labor Division applied brakes. During the year beginning in June 1949, Japanese unions declined in number by more than 5500 and in membership by 880,000. The retreat slowed by the first half of 1951, and in the following twelve months mild recovery began. In fact, Japanese capitalism was by 1950 able to launch its first postwar offensive; SCAP held and tipped the balance decisively. The occupation had directed the purge of rightist nationalists in 1947–1949, and now the pendulum swung against the other extreme. . . .

The Socialist party did not actively oppose the purge, for its leaders realized that, with outside assistance, the way was being cleared for their domination of a large sector of the labor movement. With the blessings and active encouragement of the occupation, the democratized labor unions began moving toward the establishment of a common organization near the end of 1949. The Democratization Leagues, formation of the International Confederation of Free Trade Unions, and the labor offensive in March 1950 led to the creation of the General Council of Japanese Trade Unions (Sōhyō) in July 1950. It brought together about 3 million organized Japanese workers, many of whom had ousted their Communist leaders. Sōhyō, born of anticommunism, did not directly oppose the purging of labor ranks; rather it regarded this measure as inevitable in the circumstances, and it joined in denouncing the destructive tactics of the JCP.

MIRIAM FARLEY*
Japanese Labor, 1949–1950

The early part of 1949 saw labor struggling under the impact of the Dodge Plan and the new legislative restrictions on government workers. Split internally over the issue of proper tactics to cope with these issues, unions were not very effective.

In October 1949 this writer commented:

> Thus unions find themselves facing a difficult situation in the fourth year of the occupation. Along with extensive layoffs, unions charge that both the government and management are firing the most active trade unionists. For example, by July 18, 1949, the government announced that of the total railway workers discharged, 1699 were discharged "dishonorably," for displaying an "uncooperative" attitude toward the reduction program. This included all of the Communist members and most of the Communist sympathizers of the union's central committee, giving the right wing (Mindō) undisputed control. Of the once-militant communications workers union the *New York Herald Tribune* on August 14, 1949, reported that the government had dismissed 11,000 workers, and "thereby got rid of most of the strike committee of the leftist . . . union." With stricter economy imposed on both industry and government, negotiation for wage increases is in many cases impossible. Emphasis on increased production has tended to play into the hands of recalcitrant employers, who feel that pressure from both the Japanese government and the occupation will be brought to bear on striking unions. Unemployment is increasing. Some of the most militant unions, which often established patterns for wages and other benefits through their vigorous negotiation tactics, are now considerably circumscribed in their permissible actions by recent legislation.

Private industry, as well as the government, utilized the retrenchment programs to fire left-wing and Communist unionists, and the Democratization Leagues gave both active and passive support to these measures. . . .

* Miriam Farley, *Aspects of Japan's Labor Problems* (New York: John Day Co., 1950), pp. 227–229, 233–235, 237–239.

But some of the moderate labor leaders began to fear that these tactics might be extended to themselves. Thus it was reported that the anticommunist leaders were worried for fear that the same measures that ousted Communists and "sympathizers" might be extended to them. The article noted that there had been almost a year free of strikes because of what amounted to an "occupation ban" and went on to add that many workers had been fired for actions which were forbidden by the new laws but which are ordinary practice elsewhere.

The Labor Division reported in October 1949:

> To date anticommunist leaders have not protested recent unilateral dismissals of union officers and members by government and private industry because Communists were thereby eliminated. However, conservative unions are now building defenses in fear that similar action may be taken against aggressive but noncommunist leadership. National union leaders feel compelled to take this position in order to hold their following and by refusal of qualified men to accept union offices for fear of being marked for discharge.

This observation was made a few weeks after General MacArthur's reference to the "machinations of irresponsible leadership." . . .

It was thus not surprising to see these "moderate" leaders, under pressure from their membership over wages and job security, and apprehensive over new manifestations of reaction and repression, adopt a more militant policy toward the end of 1949. By early 1950, a steady deterioration of labor relations led to a threatened series of nationwide strikes in major industries, only averted, once again, by SCAP action. . . .

Government recalcitrance on the wage issue, plus the stiffened attitude of private employers, both backed up by the SCAP economic program, were sufficient to drive the "moderate" labor leadership to consideration of immoderate action. In January, Sōdōmei, the conservative federation closely allied with the Social Democratic party, established a Joint Central "Diet Struggle Committee," backed by the Social Democrats and composed of representatives of thirty-five noncommunist unions and two million workers, to press for wage increases for government workers.

By February 6, unions of government and private industry workers had, through this Diet Joint Struggle Committee, posted notice of a general strike warning which could involve "possibly five million workers." The correspondent who reported this went on to state: "The situation is made more difficult by the fact that the demand is put forward by a section of labor which has purged itself of Communist influence, has followed a moderate legal course of action in the past, and represents the type of unionism which the occupation most desires to support. The wage . . . recommendations . . . have come from two official quarters . . . the issue is extremely serious because it means that arbitration channels urged by the occupation as the only means of achieving better working conditions have broken down."

The unions pressed ahead despite warnings by Chief Cabinet Secretary Masuda that a "new policy" would classify "all strikes in any major industry—even a walkout by a single union" as a "general strike" and a "violation of the MacArthur order" of 1947. On March 7, the National Federation of Metal Miners called 60,000 workers out on strike. By March 12, 269,000 coal miners had struck for seventy-two hours and planned further stoppages. Kyōdō News Agency reported that nineteen steel mills closed as a result of the metal miners strike. Electric power cutoffs of from fifteen minutes to two hours occurred throughout all Japan. Seamen were holding limited strikes and "protest meetings" aboard vessels in the major harbors. Teachers, rail workers, and other government workers were participating "legally" by refusing to work overtime, by taking accrued leave, by strict observance of all safety rules, and by maintaining the bare minimum of performance standards required by law.

Thus, in the spring of 1950, after unions had been purged and had purged themselves of "irresponsible leadership," a combination of economic conditions and SCAP and Japanese government policies had been factors in creating what Lindesay Parrott described as a "situation . . . probably the most critical since General MacArthur issued his directive against a general strike of 1947." There was irony in the fact that not only had this developed under "noncommunist leadership" but that it represented action by unions representing five million of the 6,500,000 organized workers and thus had, if anything, a broader base than the 1947 strike. As a matter of fact, the two situations suggest that fundamental economic and political factors inherent in the Japanese postwar scene are more significant than the oversimplified reasons of "communist inspiration" that SCAP and other commentators have been inclined to cite as chief causes of major labor unrest during these years. . . .

The events which occurred rapidly and decisively on the eve of this particular "general strike" of "labor's offensive" of 1950 show at least what SCAP and the Yoshida cabinet did, if not what the precise reasoning and motives were. The situation, described by the *New York Times* dispatch of March 7 as "most critical . . . since 1947," grew more serious. On March 12, 1950, this same paper reported (somewhat vaguely) that "unions with a total membership of two million are striking, threatening to strike, or engaging in slowdowns, refusal of overtime work and other semi-strike tactics." It also reported later that the head of SCAP's Labor Division, immediately following an announcement that the coal miners union had called out 290,000 miners for a one week strike, had called a conference with the union leader, Takeo Mutō; the Labor Minister, Suzuki; and the CLRC chairman, Itsutarō Suehiro. Mr. Mutō told the press that the head of the Labor Division "had informed him that Allied Headquarters would not permit coal strikes . . . to last for more than the scheduled week since the 'national economy cannot stand continuation beyond that limit.' The announcement indicated that prolongation beyond this week would be met by other measures."

This same account reported that, following this meeting,

> the Japanese government with approval of Allied Headquarters today placed a curb on labor's "March offensive" for a new round of wage increases by ordering compulsory arbitration of a coal miners' strike which was held to be endangering the national economy. . . . The government action drove a wedge into the already weakening ranks of the "labor offensive," which is being stage managed by a "struggle committee" of Diet representatives claiming to represent 2 million workers opposed to the conservative cabinet's disinflation policy. . . . With coal miners ordered to accept compulsory arbitration the sole important labor offensive area is in the power industry. . . .

On March 30, the *New York Times* reported that the " 'labor offensive' of Japanese trade unions . . . virtually collapsed today. The electrical [power] workers union and management agreed to accept the arbitration plan of the CLRC." It was on March 7 that Chief Cabinet Secretary Masuda had said that a power strike would be a violation of the 1947 SCAP ruling. The *Times* account went on to state: "Efforts to compel a change in the government labor and financial policies thus may be said to have broken down." . . .

Several things are noteworthy about these developments. The unions had shown considerable restraint before launching this unsuccessful "offensive." The case of the railroad workers perhaps best illustrates what Japanese labor was able to achieve through the use of arbitration boards, courts, and other "legal" machinery. Government workers' wages were pegged in July 1948. As prices continued to rise, the union finally requested the Public Corporation Arbitration Committee to consider its request for a wage increase. This was on September 14, 1949. By May 1950, eight months later, following additional committee and court affirmation, wages for government workers had still not been appreciably improved.

In short, unions had been ignored to a large extent in their attempts to utilize the legally constituted restrictions of arbitration, and had been forcibly restrained from exerting economic and political pressure by strikes and other dispute tactics. Such minor concessions as had been granted had largely occurred by fiat.

Just what attitude the rank and file have toward the "moderate" leadership at this stage of developments is difficult to say, but it would not be surprising if confidence has weakened. On March 7, 1950, the *New York Times* had said: "What both the government and the Allied sources fear is that, even should the strikes be forcibly prevented, the unions would revert to Communist leadership unless league members [meaning Democratization League leaders] are able to show they have been able to produce benefits for the rank and file." The strikes were forcibly prevented, and benefits thus far have been meager.

❖ A CAPSULE ACCOUNT by Solomon Levine of the labor movement from the late 1940s to the early 1950s is presented below. Some of Levine's interpretations are controversial, such as his characterization of the "democratic" movement (Mindō) as "spontaneous rank-and-file revolts." There is considerable evidence of an early and continuing SCAP involvement in Mindō. Levine underscores the extent to which factional strife, encouraged by SCAP and abetted by management, sapped much of the strength of the union movement. So long as labor could be prevented from overcoming the narrow confines of isolated and therefore weak industrial unions and from forming a united front against the relatively united business community, the Japanese employer held the upper hand. Indeed, enterprise unionism (discussed in Part II, section 6) and a divided and weak national labor movement are quite possibly an enduring legacy of the occupation period.

SOLOMON LEVINE*
Japan's Labor Problems and Labor Movement, 1950–1955

In the five years after 1950, the Japanese labor unions hardly recovered from the blows they received in the economic retrenchment and disinflation of the Dodge Plan, the extirpation of left-wing elements through the "Red purge," and the revision of the postwar labor laws. Between 1949 and 1950 union membership, which had mushroomed at a phenomenal rate in the four years following the surrender, suddenly dropped by nearly a million. After that time, the number of members virtually stood still, losing almost another 850,000 between 1950 and 1951, and recovering slowly with an annual increase of 100,000 or 150,000 in the three years 1952, 1953, and 1954. By July 1954 the claimed membership stood at slightly less than six million, still almost one million below the high point reached in the early months of 1949. Moreover ... the degree of unionization failed to keep pace with the expansion of the industrial work force, declining from over forty-five percent in 1949 to less than forty percent by 1954.

* Solomon Levine, "Japan's Labor Problems and Labor Movement, 1950–1955," in Ōkochi Kazuo, *Labor in Modern Japan* (Tokyo: Science Council of Japan, 1958), pp. 87–100.

The distribution of trade-union membership by industry also showed little change during these years. Public utility workers and miners, with more than three-quarters of their numbers in unions, remained the most highly organized. Heavy concentrations still were to be found in large-scale private and government enterprises engaged in manufacturing, but the several million small and medium sized firms which abound in the Japanese economy continued to be almost completely unpenetrated by union organization. The number of basic union bodies—the equivalents of the American local union—suffered a sharp drop between 1949 and 1952 of about twenty percent, from more than 34,500 to fewer than 28,000. In the next three years, partly as the result of reorganizations and splits, there was a gradual recovery in the number of these units, so that by 1954 there were almost 31,500, which was still ten percent fewer than at the high point of postwar Japan's trade unionism.

These are net figures, however, and they hide a rather high rate of turnover that has been a constant phenomenon. Even during the period of greatest union expansion, in the year 1948–1949 for example, over ten percent of these unions disappeared. Thousands of basic units have been dissolved each year for one reason or another, but chiefly because of business failures and of apathy among rank-and-file workers. Still other thousands have been created each year. With the downturn of union growth, in 1949–1950, about twenty-five percent went out of existence, while each year since that time the dissolutions have averaged one-tenth or more of the total. Most of the turnover, both the disappearance of existing units and the creation of new ones, has occurred among the smaller enterprises and in the industrial sectors which have been least amenable to organization.

These statistics reflect the fact that, although unionism seems to be tenaciously established in certain parts of the industrial economy, in particular among the large, ex-zaibatsu undertakings and government operations, at best the labor movement has been on an organizational treadmill in this recent period. The unorganized workers, who form a majority of the nonagricultural wage earners, are for the most part . . . migratory-type laborers—those not permanently attached to the modern industrial structure of Japan. To understand the persistence of unionism in certain sectors and its failure to take hold in others requires an analysis of the predominant type of Japanese labor organization, the "enterprise" union. Before turning to this question, however, we shall look into the developments since 1950 in Japan's national trade union centers.

The demise of Sambetsu was almost complete by the beginning of the period under review. The change of emphasis in occupation policy from reform to recovery (in order to bolster Japan as an ally in the Cold War struggle), the revolt of political right-wing and neutralist groups against Communist leadership within the unions, the direct assault of the SCAP-sponsored "Red purge" upon the leftist elements, the mass discharges that followed the implementation of the Dodge line, the reemergence of management's status, and so forth, led to defections, splits, and, in general, a turn away from Sambetsu as the leading national federation in the Japanese labor movement. . . . In mid-1949 Sambetsu still could claim a membership of more than one million; a year later it had less than 300,000. By 1954 the once dominant Sambetsu center had a mere 13,000 adherents, found in two small national industrial unions. Allied with the Soviet-dominated World Federation of Trade Unions, Sambetsu has been openly communistic, and its rapid disintegration from a position of political influence paralleled the decline of the Japan Communist party during the same years.

Probably the most significant labor development after 1950 was the establishment and growth of an entirely new trade union center, the General Council of Trade Unions (Nihon Rōdō Kumiai Sōhyō Gikai), or, as commonly abbreviated, Sōhyō. Within this organization the principal problems of the organized labor movement in Japan were thrashed out in the following years. The origins of Sōhyō are found in the factors that led to the demise of Sambetsu. Sōhyō represented another attempt to establish the unified labor center which Sambetsu and Sōdōmei had failed to achieve earlier. Since Sambetsu was considered by noncommunist elements in the labor movement as the main obstacle to the development of a unified center, it was necessary to eliminate Sambetsu's position of dominance and to erect an organization which could accommodate all but the Communist groups. The impetus for the new federation came from at least three quarters. First, SCAP itself, after the Cold War had become a reality, encouraged the formation of an anticommunist center. This objective was helped along by SCAP prohibition of various strike tactics employed by Sambetsu—in particular the use of the general strike and of simultaneous regional and localized walkouts among government employees; by the enactment of new labor legislation, supported by the occupation, which denied strike and bargaining rights to government workers and set new standards for determining the legitimacy of unions; and directly by the elimination of left-wingers from leadership positions through the "Red purge."

The second spur to the development of a new unified center came from within Sōdōmei, which from the beginning had attempted to accomplish this very objective, only to fail on the two or three occasions where the possibility appeared promising. Sōdōmei, which had resurrected the prewar right-wing federation of the same name, was outspokenly allied with the new Socialist party, in particular its conservative faction, and within a year after the surrender it was engaged in open competition with the Sambetsu Communists to command the allegiance of the mushrooming labor unions. On the other hand, at some points Sōdōmei leaders had been willing to cooperate with Sambetsu, probably in the hope that they could thereby secure control of the latter's affiliates. Thus they joined with Sambetsu in planning and conducting the wage campaigns in the fall of 1946, which culminated in the general strike threat of February 1, 1947. When it became clear that Sōdōmei had failed to dominate this drive, it quickly withdrew in face of SCAP condemnations. Again, Sōdōmei agreed to enter a body known as the Zenkoku Rōdō Kumiai Renraku Kyōgikai, or Zenrōren, in the spring of 1947, which was to coordinate the efforts of all unions—Sambetsu, Sōdōmei, or unaffiliated—in achieving wage improvements for the organized workers. Within a year or so, however, Zenrōren, too, was clearly under Communist control and Sōdōmei pulled out to resume its direct attacks upon Sambetsu.

The third major force behind the establishment of Sōhyō came from spontaneous rank-and-file revolts, especially among the Sambetsu unions, to end dictatorial controls at the top and permit greater membership participation in union affairs. These took the form of so-called "democratization," or "Mindō" (Minshuka Undō) movements, beginning in late 1947 within the National Railway Workers' Union, which, although unaffiliated with either Sambetsu or Sōdōmei, was the center of the contest between the two and appeared to be inclined toward the Communists. A successful Mindō movement here gave rise to a rash of similar attempts in most other major unions within Sambetsu. The democratization groups even spilled over to Sōdōmei itself as protests grew that the right-wing center, although free from Communist domination, practiced the same dictatorial methods that existed in Sambetsu. In general the Mindō movement was less an effort to bring the Sambetsu unions into the Sōdōmei camp than an attempt to break away from political leadership and to set up a labor movement free from the dominance of any politically inclined groups.

The convergence of these three influences came to a head in 1949. Politically and organizationally, the groups involved were not of one mind, except that all agreed that some coordination of union activities was now urgently needed in the face of the Dodge Plan retrenchment and the requirements of the new labor law revisions. No doubt other factors were also at work to bring them together. By 1949 it was becoming clear that Japan would soon gain its independence, which could well mean the creation of a political vacuum in Japan after the withdrawal of SCAP controls. The organized labor groups, though loosely bound together, saw this as an opportunity to escape from restrictions supported by the conservative parties, for the first time since the discouraging election defeats the Socialists had suffered after their dismal failure in leading the government a year or two earlier. Also, since a line was being drawn at that time between labor of the free world and the iron curtain nations, with the planned establishment of the new International Confederation of Free Trade Unions to counter the Soviet-controlled WFTU, a fresh impetus was lent to the quick establishment of a noncommunist unified labor center in Japan.

However, in spite of the fanfare given to the foundation of Sōhyō in mid-1950, it rested on a shaky base. Its components were diverse. The groups ranged from Sōdōmei on the right (which itself suffered from divisions over ideology, politics, and organizational strategy) to the former Sambetsu industrial unions on the left, barely converted in many cases from communism. A spearhead in the original move to form Sōhyō was the Shinsambetsu, or New Sambetsu, which, while ideologically among the left Socialists, espoused pure industrial unionism and the cutting of all political ties. This group found it difficult to agree to working with right-wing Sōdōmei elements. In addition, many other unions which were willing to join—notably those which had clearly broken away from Sambetsu or which had never joined any federation but sought protection against changing economic conditions—embraced neutrality in ideological and political conflicts.

Thus, even though the newly established Sōhyō resolved initially to concentrate on pure trade unionism, to ally with the new ICFTU, and to reject Communist infiltration, it is clear that no single philosophy really dominated the new labor center, which was to become a field of contest for numerous competing influences. That Sōhyō's basic theme was unclear and unconvincing was seen in the fact that a majority of the unions preferred to remain outside and watch its development before deciding to affiliate; as a result, even as late as 1954 Sōhyō could claim only about half the membership of the organized labor movement. Sōhyō, like both of its predecessors, Sambetsu and Sōdōmei, thus did not represent the ascendancy of any dominant theme such as those which have given unity to labor movements in other countries. As events proved, it was to become the scene for the recurring ideological conflicts which have characterized the Japanese labor movement since its inception in the 1890s.

Although Sōhyō remained the largest labor center after 1950, its internal conflicts were sharp and it suffered from important defections. The first of these, which occurred almost immediately after Sōhyō was formed, was the withdrawal of Sōdōmei's right wing, precipitated by the insistence of Sōdōmei's left wing that the federation dissolve and lose its identity within the new Sōhyō. Inasmuch as the conservative wing of Sōdōmei did not fully agree with the proposal to establish industrial unions with great haste, a step which would do away with the nonindustrial types of organization it controlled, the Sōdōmei right preferred to walk out rather than yield. The New Sōdōmei, as it was called, took with it about 300,000 members and openly allied with the non-Marxist Right Socialists, who at that moment were on the brink of formally breaking with the Marxist left wing of the party over the issue of the proposed peace treaty. On the other hand, the New Sambetsu group with some 50,000 members also pulled out by 1952 for the opposite reason, that is, because of Sōhyō's failure to follow the tenets of pure industrial unionism and complete political neutrality.

4. Land Reform and Agriculture, 1945—1952

❀ RURAL POVERTY was one of the outstanding domestic issues of prewar Japan. Critics of the establishment deplored the misery of the Japanese countryside, and right-wing ideologists and activists concentrated their attention on the oppressed Japanese peasant as an abuse of the Japanese essence. The roots of rural poverty lay in two factors: surplus population and inequalities of land distribution. One of the most successful of the occupation reforms, land reform struck at the landlords, redistributed landholdings in small parcels to farmers, and drastically reduced the economic and political domination of landlords in the village.

FUKUTAKE TADASHI*
Land Reform Laws

. . . As soon as the war was over the contradictions of the landlord system inevitably came once more to the surface. Apart from anything else, it was necessary, in order to reconstruct industry destroyed by the devastating bombing raids and reestablish the capitalist economy, to break through the inflationary spiral exacerbated by the shortage of food. This meant ensuring compulsory deliveries of rice at low prices, and this in turn made it necessary to reduce the burden of rents on the cultivating farmers.

* Fukutake Tadashi, *Japanese Rural Society* (Tokyo: Oxford University Press, 1967), pp. 17–18.

In this way the government recognized that a reform of the land system was absolutely essential and attempted to carry through such a reform on its own initiative. In December 1945, soon after the defeat, the government placed before the Diet a bill to amend the Agricultural Land Adjustment Law. This is generally known as the first land reform. The measure allowed landlords to keep up to five hectares of their property, and envisaged the freeing of some forty percent of the tenanted area in the course of five years.

However, the Headquarters of the occupation forces had already in a "Memorandum on Land Reform" instructed the Japanese government to "break the economic bondage which has enslaved Japanese farmers through centuries of feudal oppression" and soon after the passage of the law it halted the execution of this first land reform and required the government to prepare a more thoroughgoing measure. The result was the "second land reform" which began the following year, 1946. It was a drastic reform, the like of which could hardly have been contemplated in prewar Japan.

Under the reform laws, all the land of absentee landlords and all leased-out land of village landlords in excess of one hectare was purchased by the state and resold to tenants. The practice, until then general, of paying rents in kind was forbidden, and cash payment was required. Moreover, rents were controlled; landlords could no longer demand rents at a level which had justly been described as feudal. This reform was practically completed within the short space of a little over two years and as a result the area of tenanted land, which before the war had been approximately fifty-three percent for rice land and forty percent for dry land, fell to below ten percent.

. . . [W]hereas only about thirty percent of farmers were owner-cultivators before the war, the figure is now seventy-five percent, and the proportion of farmers who rent all their land has fallen from around thirty percent to a mere three percent. In this way the dominance of the landlords in village society lost its material economic basis. The land reform may be considered, on the whole, to have succeeded in liberating Japanese farmers from "feudal oppression."

⚙ THE EXECUTION of the land reform was marked by pre-dictable difficulties. In the postwar confusion, administrative niceties such as trained officials, supplies, and communications facilities were not easily available. There were controversies over classifying land. Landlords tried to evict tenants in order to get more land for themselves. The local decisions on imple-mentation of the reform rested with the elected Land Commit-tees, and whether they were landlord- or tenant-dominated had a great effect on the results.

R. P. DORE*
Execution of Land Reform

The land reform program was not an easy one to carry out. It involved changes in the property rights of some six million families of whom over two million had every motive for trying to obstruct its purposes. It required considerable executive ability and conscien-tious integrity from over 36,000 paid officials, 115,000 ill-remunerated committee members, and some quarter of a million voluntary hamlet auxiliaries. And it implied a subversion of tradi-tional patterns of social relations which had held sway for decades or even centuries.

The immediate postwar period, though in one sense the only time when people were sufficiently bewildered and ready for change to make such a drastic measure possible, was in another sense the worst possible moment for the execution of a project on the scale of the land reform. Communication services were not yet working normally, there was a shortage of paper, many of the officials engaged in the work were half-starved, their offices were unheated, and the inflation was constantly leaving their salaries

* R. P. Dore, *Land Reform in Japan* (London: Oxford University Press, 1950), pp. 149–153.

behind in the rising tide of the cost of living. The latter was a cause of friction which certainly impeded the efficiency of the work of the reform. And so, too, did the smallness of the remuneration provided for elected Land Committee members, which may have deterred poorer farmers from accepting office and made those who did more susceptible to bribery.

There were technical difficulties too. Not even the most detailed law could be expected to deal adequately with all the complexities of Japanese agriculture. New problems were constantly arising. Did vegetable gardens on the former site of bombed-out buildings constitute agricultural land? When the owner of an apple orchard allowed other farmers the right to plant rows of vegetables between the trees in return for a cash payment, was the land owner-cultivated or tenant-cultivated? What was to be taken as the basis for the establishment of ownership rights in land? How far, for the purpose of calculating maximum permitted holdings, was resurveying to be carried out in order to check discrepancies between actual and registered areas? Such were some of the many problems which required elucidation as the reform proceeded. Altogether, from the time of the second land reform up to the end of 1950, a total of ten laws and amending laws had to be passed, thirty-one ordinances, and fifty-one ministerial regulations and orders having legal force were issued, together with no less than 120 ministry circulars of an elucidatory or supplementary nature, some of which made substantial changes in the interpretation of the law. It is hardly surprising that members of Land Committees and even full-time secretaries were not always very clear how the law stood at any particular time.

But however complete the law, in the very nature of the case its evasion—either by ignoring it or by the falsification of documents—was by no means difficult. A great deal was left to the discretion of local Land Committees, and whether the law was applied with conscientious thoroughness or with a laxity which amounted to a complete perversion of its purposes depended chiefly on the composition of these Committees. It depended also on the power structure of the villages and the general consensus of opinion which provided a background to their work, and on the extent to which control and guidance was exercised by prefectural officials and was exercised in the direction of unyielding adherence to the spirit and the letter of the law.

THE PROBLEM OF LANDLORD REPOSSESSION

The chief source of evasion and the chief cause of disputes lay in landlords' attempts to take tenanted land back into their own cultivation. The temptation was obvious enough. A landlord who had, say, hitherto lived off the proceeds of twenty *chō* of land leased out to tenants, cultivating none himself, was faced with the prospect of losing nineteen *chō* outright. Moreover, the remaining *chō* which he would be allowed to keep (provided he was resident in the village) would, under the new and stringent tenancy regulations, bring him very little profit. And as long as the tenants wished to continue cultivating, provided they paid the nominal rent and did not do anything which could be construed as a "breach of faith," he would never be allowed to take it back into his own cultivation. He would be faced with a sudden almost total loss of income and be forced to find a new means of livelihood in a disrupted postwar economy rife with unemployment and semistarvation. If, on the other hand, he could persuade some of his tenants to give up tenancy of some of his land and establish himself as an owner-cultivator of 3 *chō,* these 3 *chō* the law would permit him to keep. As a farmer of a bigger-than-average holding his livelihood would then be amply assured even if his income and his property were substantially reduced.

Again, a landlord who had some other means of livelihood—say a village official with a small holding of leased-out land—might have relied hitherto on the produce rents from this land for his family food supply. Now, with the banning of produce rents, even if he kept his small leased holding, he was faced with the loss of that food supply at a time when rice was difficult to obtain—and salaries were appallingly low. The temptation to get back enough land to grow his own rice was very strong.

But could tenants be found who were willing to give up not simply cultivating rights but cultivating rights which the law soon promised to translate into ownership rights, on part of a holding which was rarely of generous proportions in the first place? Very often they could. Tenants conditioned to listen to their landlords' instructions with respectful bows could not easily make the psychological break with their past which an outright refusal to return the land would require. Moreover, self-preservation often dictated compliance. Many depended on the landlord's permission to cut firewood and green fertilizer from his forest land. Reliance on the landlord's benevolence in times of acute economic distress was the only form of social security many tenants knew. Such a source of actual and potential benefits could not easily be offended, particularly in the uncertainties of the early stages of the reform when peasants, congenitally skeptical of all the actions of authority, could never be sure that today's law which promised to turn them into owner-farmers might not be replaced by a new one tomorrow which threatened to make them tenants again.

Altogether, according to one estimate by the Ministry of Agriculture, based on the reports of local authorities, in the ten months between the end of the war and June 1946 there were 250,000 cases of landlords reclaiming land from tenants, of which only 23,000, or less than a tenth, were disputed.

The law did not, and could not in the nature of the case, entirely forbid the return of land to landlords. There were numerous cases where families whose sons had been called up to the army had temporarily leased land to neighbors on the promise that it would be returned as soon as the men were demobilized. It was impossible legally to discriminate between such instances and others. What the law did do was to require the approval of local (Village and Town) Land Committees for all such return of tenanted land. . . .

Land Committees had, therefore, the power to forbid landlords to take back land if they thought that undue pressure was being put on the tenants to give it up; that the tenant was acting against his best interests by giving his consent; or that the landlord would not be as efficient a cultivator as the tenant. Alternatively they could agree to all such applications from landlords, quash objections from the tenants, and, either by applying "persuasion" to the tenant or by deliberately falsifying documents, prevent such objections from reaching the prefectural office to which the applications had to be sent for final approval.

Control over eviction was the touchstone of a Land Committee's efficiency. Where it was loose other abuses generally followed. Landlords who could use the threat of eviction freely were able to exact high black-market payments from the tenants whom they "allowed" to enjoy the benefits of the law. Even if eviction was kept within limits, where landlord-dominated committees allowed landlords freely to choose *which* plots of land they would relinquish to tenants and which they would retain as their one-*chō* allotment, the same effect could be achieved. In tenant-dominated committees, on the other hand, landlords who attempted such blandishments were given short shrift.

Other forms of evasion practised where the climate of the Land Committees was favorable to the landlords included the nominal transfer of land to relatives—the transaction being backdated— and the designation of owners who were in fact not resident in the village in November 1945 as resident-owners permitted to retain a reserved portion of tenanted land.

❉ SINCE THE WORK of the Land Committees was crucial to the reform, the postwar tenant organizations exerted much influence on the committees, where possible, to fight the traditional power of landlords. These rural mass organizations declined in influence with the end of the land reform. A major cause of this was the divisive actions taken by political forces which disliked the politics of the early Japan Peasant Union (Nichinō). First, in July 1947 a group of Nichinō anticommunists, with the blessings of the Japan Socialist party, formed a new group, Zennō. In August of the same year, worried about losing the village as a conservative political stronghold, the Liberal party formed its own group, Zennichinō. These divisions, as well as the end of the land reform and the persistence of rural conservative forces, contributed to the decline in peasant organizations in the late 1940s.

*ANDREW J. GRAD**
The Peasant Unions

Various groups interested in the peasants and their problems became active immediately after the surrender. Temporary asso-

* Andrew J. Grad, *Land and Peasant in Japan* (New York: International Secretariat, Institute of Pacific Relations, 1952), pp. 135–141.

ciations like the "Union of Cultivators" and the "Peasants' League" sprang up rapidly. Certain right-wing leaders of the Social Democratic party such as Genjirō Sugiyama, Rikizō Hirano, and others, who enjoyed freedom at the time of surrender, sought to revive the peasant unions. Though their ranks had been decimated by twenty years of suppression, Communist leaders, freed from prison in October 1945, also began to organize the peasantry. While a few of the postwar leaders had taken part in the activities of earlier decades, most of them were new.

The old problem at once arose in the new organization, Japan Peasant Union, as to whether the peasant unions should directly affiliate with a political party or should permit their members to decide party allegiance for themselves. Hisao Kuroda, remembering the bitter experience of the twenties, called for unity of the peasants and succeeded in bringing together the many disparate elements in one association, which grew rapidly. By January 1946 it already contained more than 60,000 members, by April 282,000 and by February 1947 it reached 1,200,000 members. When Japan Peasant Union (Nippon Nōmin Kumiai or Nichinō) held its first Congress, in February 1946, many of the occupation reforms were still incomplete. The Diet consisted largely of the Tōjō-approved members elected in 1942, the old constitution was still in force, the purge directive had been published but not yet applied, and the First Land Reform Act, passed by the Diet in December 1945, had been disavowed by SCAP. The Congress advocated the following reforms: elimination of feudal landlord influence in the villages, establishment of the basis for a democratic system, and organization of the peasants for both political and economic action. In addition to supporting land-tenure reform, the Congress declared that the peasant unions should win the confidence of the peasants by a sincere and energetic struggle for peasant interests in which all democratic organizations should be mobilized. A strong membership drive aimed at all peasants was stressed as the primary method of achieving the union's aims. . . .

The organizational task required much time and effort. In many villages the peasants were able to organize their own union. More often an organizer had to go to the villages, explain the aims and advantages of the organization, and invite peasants to join. At first the response might be small—only a few of the more advanced peasants would express a readiness to join. As work began, however, and the peasants saw that the new organization really had their interests at heart, many others would join, and soon the village union might have a hundred or more members. After the members had mastered the details of the organization, had established connections with the prefectural and in some cases with the national headquarters of the Peasant Union, and showed a certain degree of unity, solidarity, and enthusiasm in their activities, the task of the organizer had been completed. He then moved on to a new village where no organization existed or where for some reason the local union was weak and needed help.

The union accepted a principle based on bitter prewar experience: it was not to be the instrument of any political party, though its members were free to join any political party. Thus, while the union stood to the left of the general political alignment in 1945–1946, it did not formulate its position in precise terms. The political parties were, nevertheless, interested in winning over members of the union, and even the union itself. In that respect the Socialists, and especially the right-wing Socialists, were at first most successful. They formed a majority on the organizational committee and later on the central committee of the union. Since they had preserved their connections with the villages during and immediately after the war, they did not have to create a new organization so much as to adjust their old ties to the new situation.

The Communists faced an entirely different problem. At the surrender, they were either still in prison or else living far from their former residences, frequently under assumed names. Their old connections had been broken, and everything had to be organized anew. During the first year the Socialists were much more successful in their organizational activities among the peasants. Yet two factors helped Communists. Many Socialists, especially in the right-wing group, had been associated with the war and had joined the patriotic societies or ultranationalist organs, and were now compromised. Also, many Socialists had worked in the agricultural associations, which had a bad name in the countryside.

Thus the majority of the peasant unions were mildly pro-Socialist, though almost all of them contained a sprinkling of Communists. A substantial number, mainly those organized by the peasants themselves, were politically neutral, while a growing minority had some communist leanings. The last group was as a rule better organized and better run. These locals were members of the Japan Peasant Union (Nichinō). There were other unions . . . but from 1946 to 1948 Nichinō remained the most important. . . .

Especially important was the work undertaken by the union in respect to land reform. No reform of such scope and touching on so many vital interests could succeed unless the people at large were informed about its objectives and methods. Official efforts in this direction were far from adequate. A government representative would appear in a village, deliver a lecture, distribute some pamphlets, and then return to his office. The newspapers were more helpful, but their space was limited. Even the radio did not reach every village or peasant. When the second Reform Act was passed by the Diet, in October 1946, the union put forth great efforts to make the peasants familiar with its provisions through meetings and discussions.

Next came the struggle for election of the members of the land commissions. Again, without the persistent work of the union, the membership of these commissions would have been much less favorably disposed toward the tenants. In many cases, the union was able to advance tenant and owner-cultivator candidates from its own membership. Even more important was the task of watching the activities of the members of the land commissions once they had been elected. It was easy to show energetic activity during the election period, but much more difficult and more important to watch the actions of commission members from day to day and to encourage and help them. Here the Peasant Union made use of the right to recall representatives who, in the opinion of the majority of their electorate, had failed to fulfill their duty to the peasants. There were hundreds of cases of such recalls, and they helped the representatives to remember that they were on the land commissions to defend the interests of the peasants. . . .

Its Second Congress opened in February [1947] with a clash between right-wing Socialists and Communists. The Communists accused Rikizō Hirano of intrigues with the Yoshida cabinet on behalf of a coalition cabinet, and also attacked his position on the question of the use of force against the peasants. After three days of bickering and uproar, Hirano and twenty of his followers issued a demand for the formation of an anticommunist Peasant Union, withdrew from the Congress, and set about organizing a League for Renovation of the Peasant Union.

A statement issued by the Hirano group made various charges against the communists—that they had violated the mission and character of the Peasant Union, had packed the Congress with delegates who were not genuine representatives of the peasants, that they had engaged in abstract discussion that had no direct relation to peasant problems, and that they had brought Youth Guards to the Congress hall. The Hirano group, so they said, had "piled patience upon patience," but could no longer stand the fascistic, undemocratic, and arbitrary Communist actions; they "could not but come to the decision, in collaboration with people of the same mind, to eliminate completely the factional activities of the communists, and to develop a really democratic Peasant Union. . . ."

The results of the Congress did not bear out Hirano's accusations. The central committee elected by this Congress included eleven members who were anticommunists and "neutrals"—of these one, Ōnishi, died, and another, Murataka, fell under the purge directive—seven partisans of unity, including chairman Kuroda, and two Communists. If the Communists had dominated the Congress, it is doubtful that they would have shown such self-abnegation. . . .

On July 25, 1947, a congress of dissenters from Nichinō opened in Tokyo with great ceremony under the chairmanship of Minister of Agriculture Rikizō Hirano. In attendance were 1000 guests and representatives from thirty-eight prefectures. The leaders of the new organization included such men as Toyohiko Kagawa, a founder of the prewar Peasant Union, and Genjirō Sugiyama, a former chairman of Nichinō. Also present were sixty Socialist Diet members. Among the advisers of the new organization were Tetsu Katayama, president of the Socialist party and prime minister; Komakichi Matsuoka, speaker of the House of Representatives; Minister of Education Tatsuo Morita; and other leading figures.

The speeches delivered at the Congress, and the program adopted, charged that Nichinō was based on class principles, and urged the formation of a new union free of Communists and of those who tolerated them. Three principles were advanced as basic to the new organization (Zennō): anticommunism, antifascism, and anticapitalism. . . .

Zennō's main organizer was Rikizō Hirano, a right-wing Socialist who had strong nationalist and fascist connections before and during the war. In the Katayama cabinet, formed on June 1, 1947, Rikizō Hirano became Minister of Agriculture; this position strengthened his prestige among the conservative peasantry and helped him to influence union membership. His appointment received SCAP approval at a time when he was engaged in a bitter political struggle with Nichinō. Whatever the motivations behind it, Hirano's appointment as minister helped the Zennō that he was then in the process of organizing, but failed to destroy Nichinō, which survived the split and emerged from the struggle much stronger than Zennō, though weakened by continued inner struggles.

On November 3, 1947, Premier Katayama, anticipating Hirano's impending purge, dismissed him from the cabinet. Hirano was later purged and imprisoned for having tried to conceal his former association with the ultranationalist magazine *Kōdō* ("The Imperial Way"). This was a blow to Zennō.

ZENNICHINŌ

The Liberals and Democrats, constituting the two main conservative political parties, did not at first form any union of their own in opposition to Nichinō. Later, the rapid growth of Nichinō began to worry the Liberals. The elections showed that, in many cases, the traditional conservative hold on the peasants had weakened, and the opinion was expressed that, if the Liberals did not form a union of their own, they might lose the villagers, hitherto their most loyal supporters. As a result, in August 1947, the Liberal party organized the All-Japan Peasant Union (Zen Nippon Nōmin Kumiai) or Zennichinō, which was to unite all groups interested in agriculture—landlords, owner-cultivators, and tenants.

Zennichinō issued a manifesto welcoming the great economic and cultural changes in the villages, but emphasizing that

> for the healthy reconstruction of the countryside and for the advancement of its welfare it is necessary that all sincere and unbiased people should unite their forces on an all-village basis. These aims cannot be achieved by a peasant movement guided by radicals, intent only on destructive struggle and aiming at bringing commotion to our peaceful land. In order to achieve

this result we must organize a new union, fusing all farmers into one body, and through its efforts bring the land reform to a peaceful completion, contribute to the rational improvement of agricultural management, and raise the village culture. . . . Not asking whether one is a landlord, an owner-cultivator, or a tenant, in a spirit of mutual help, we shall form a strong organization and will strive to carry out the land reform, improve the methods of cultivation, and renovate agricultural management. . . .

Most of its aims and resolutions are similar to those adopted by other peasant unions, but there are noteworthy differences which acquire special importance from the fact that the party that sponsored them won an absolute majority in the Diet elected in January 1949. . . . Their Peasant Union, despite its name, is not an all-Japan organization, but only a combination of a number of prefectural unions, especially in those prefectures where the old Liberal party connections and traditions are especially strong. But, with some administrative help and such other measures as are available to the government authorities, this union may acquire an importance out of proportion to its present membership.

Worthy of note is the emphasis on the unity of all groups—landlords, owner-cultivators, and tenants. With the end of the land reform, only resident landlords will remain in the villages, and even these may lease out not more than one *chō* of land. Under the existing law, if they leave the village, they will lose even this one *chō*. Their rents will be fixed and their rights limited. Under such conditions, it is difficult to understand the emphasis on landlords, or to see what concern they have with peasant unions. To the Liberals, however, it is quite natural, since they have always represented the landlords and never wished to deprive them of land and influence. When they speak of the necessity to accelerate the land reform, they may not be entirely sincere.

Second, the emphasis is on reconstruction, "healthy" democracy, "healthy" cooperation, "healthy" amusements. Who is to determine what is healthy and what is not? Presumably the Liberal party, whose leaders are steeped in Japanese tradition and administrative practices.

Third, the new union is to aim at the speedy establishment of freedom of trade. This measure is certainly overdue. But will this include also freedom to trade in land? And freedom to import and export agricultural products?—a question of grave importance to the peasants. These questions remain unanswered, but the future character of Japanese agriculture and the welfare of millions of peasants depend upon the answers.

Fourth, mention of a rescue of the "pure agricultural spirit" is of great interest. Can this be the famous *Yamato damashii* [spirit of Japan] observed in action from 1931 to 1945, or is it something else?

In other words, the aims that Zennichinō proclaimed in August 1947 do not tell the complete story; they are merely guarded expressions that the Liberals found possible to publish at that time. Takeshi Yamazaki was selected the president of the new union and Kotarō Mori its vice-president. Other persons selected were of the same type: able, respectable businessmen who had had nothing in common with the interests of small peasants.

❀ THE LAND REFORM sought to destroy the ties of dependence, both personal and economic, which linked tenants to landlords in Japanese villages. It was effective in eliminating much of this structure, but some ties of economic dependence remained. Those who were left with insufficient land to live on were dependent on finding work from other farmers. Thus, although economic differences were much reduced, there was still a stratum economically above the others.

Dore below also points to a paradoxical result of the effort to create economically independent farmers: the diminishing of class differences increased local solidarity, thereby increasing the pressure on the individual to conform to local norms. Simultaneously, however, the leveling of class distinctions may also have led to more egalitarian organizations and communal projects.

R. P. DORE*
The Hamlet: Status, Dependence, and Class

... One of the chief functions of the land reform has been to reduce the dependence of one man on another in Japanese villages. It remains to consider in detail what forms of economic dependence still survive.

First of all, some tenancy remains. Although the total area of tenanted land is still now only ten percent of the total area and only five percent of farm families rent more than ninety percent of their land ... the actual *number* of farm-tenancy relations still remaining is large, particularly in districts where there were a large number of small landlords, rather than a few big ones, all of whom have retained a reserve portion of leased-out land. ...

Tenancy relations today do not imply the same degree of economic power of the landlord over the tenant. Legally the latter is secure in his tenure and rents are controlled at a low figure. Nevertheless, there are hamlets where the tenant could not be sure that the consensus of hamlet opinion would be with him if he held out for his rights ... and there are tenants for whom their few extra plots of tenanted land are sufficiently vital for them to pay more than the controlled rent and in other ways do all they can to make themselves agreeable to their landlords, in order to make it "humanly impossible" for him to ask for the land back. There are not many tenants today who are "kept alive by the grace and favor of" a landlord, but there are a good many who find it politic and necessary to "observe carefully the color of their landlords' faces."

A second source of economic dependence lies in the distribution of ownership of forest and grazing land. About a half of the total area is owned by private individuals. (Of the rest about thirty percent is nationally and thirteen percent municipally owned, and the remainder is in the hands of temples, shrines, and private companies.) Ownership is, on the whole, distributed quite widely. Forest area statistics ... suggest that the majority of Japanese

* R. P. Dore, *Land Reform in Japan* (London: Oxford University Press, 1959), pp. 371–378, 385–387.

farm households own at least some forest land, though most of these have only a tiny amount. There are a good number of farm families without such land, or with insufficient to meet their needs. . . .

Some owners of woodland make a point of allowing their less fortunate neighbors to gather firewood and green fertilizer and fodder from their land, and the latter put themselves under an obligation to their benefactors in doing so. The importance of this as a source of economic power is often overrated however. There are few villages in which one or two large landowners have a monopoly of all the nearby woodland, and if one owner tries to put pressure on his beneficiaries they can often turn to another. Many farmers do not use green fertilizer at all, in any case, or grow a manure crop, and it is possible to buy fodder and firewood in a way that it is not possible for a tenant to find a substitute for rented land. . . .

A third source of dependence lies in the fact that many households with not enough land of their own rely for extra income on the opportunity to work for their richer neighbors. Casual day labor is far more common than regular employment, but we may consider the latter first.

Such regular employment has been fairly common in the large holdings of the north. The traditional pattern was for a young unmarried man or woman to live as family servant employees in the employer's house, being given their keep and wages paid twice a year in the form of rice. The relationship was a familistic, rather than an economic contractual, one; if he served the family long and loyally enough the laborer would be set up as a branch *family* of his employer and might even take his employer's name. . . .

Nevertheless, there have been changes. In Ibaragi prefecture it was said that this form of employment had practically disappeared; people were unwilling to accept family servant conditions of service. The same story was repeated in the Shimane village. "I only got mine—straight from school—because he was an orphan," said one employer. In the Yamagata village a certain amount of traditional living-in employment remained, but conditions appeared to have changed somewhat. Employees now ate the same food as the family rather than the leftovers. Strict order of precedence in the taking of baths—with the employee last—was no longer observed. One employee was said to have left because he did not get enough sake with . . . meals. Wages are regulated by the village and are paid in cash. . . .

Much more common than this form of employment is irregular day labor, particularly concentrated in the busy season of rice planting and rice harvesting. . . .

Where there is more surplus labor than jobs in the village—and this is generally the case—such employment relations can be a powerful source of dependency relations, the more so since the element of personal paternalism is still strong; the employer provides two or three meals, in addition to the wage, with, in the case of a man, probably some sake or potato wine too in the evening. The employer's little extra in the form of food and drink, or sometimes wages slightly above standard rates, puts the employed under something of an obligation. And he makes certain that he fulfills that obligation—by working loyally, or by voting for his employer or his employer's friend in elections—in order to make sure that he is asked again.

Those many farmers whom the land reform left with smaller owner-occupier holdings than are necessary to make ends meet are likely, then, in some form or other to be dependent on the good offices of one or more of their richer neighbors. And although these modern relations of dependence are rarely so complete as formerly and rarely require the old attitude of humble deference, they do imply some diffuse obligation of a generalized nature, and they do affect the freedom with which dependents can, say, oppose their particular benefactors at hamlet meetings. Just as important, perhaps, as these particular personal relations of dependence is the general dependence of all the poorer strata on all the richer strata. It is the latter who, in addition to controlling most of the available job opportunities, also dominate the councils and committees which set the rates for day labor, can influence grants of public assistance, and determine the amount of village funds to be devoted to unemployment relief work on road repairs or riparian works—another important source of additional income for the poor farmer. . . .

One effect of the land reform has been to reduce the proportion of villagers who have, or have cause for having, smoldering resentments on such grounds as these. It has destroyed many and weakened many more of the relations of economic dependence which formerly provided a prop for autocratic power. It has also

by its redistribution of wealth brought greater equality of opportunity to occupy positions of leadership, and broadened the strata
of those who have no difficulty in feeling themselves full members
in good standing of the hamlet community. It has, to that extent,
strengthened the solidarity of the hamlet.

Herein lies something of a paradox. The democratization of
Japanese villages, as it was understood by the authors and pro-
moters of the land reform, involved a greater emphasis on the
dignity and independence of the individual. Insofar as tenancy
relations involving personal dependence on, and personal submission to, a landlord have been largely destroyed, one important
detraction from individual independence has been removed. Insofar, however, as the land reform has also strengthened the solidarity of the hamlet, it has increased the constraint on individual
choice exercised by the hamlet community, increased the pressure
on the individual to conform, and increased the demands made on
the individual to sink a part of his individuality in the group.

It would be only fair to state that this is not the universal view.
Some authorities consider, on the contrary, that the net effect of
these changes has been to reduce the solidarity of the hamlet.
Examples are cited of hamlets where unity was formerly assured
by authoritarian, coercive leadership and where the disappearance
of that leadership has led to disintegration, sometimes into factional groups which compete for positions of power, sometimes
taking the form of a decentralization which makes the smaller
neighborhood groups within the hamlet the effective focus of
communal action and sentiment. Often, however, these are transitional phenomena. Most hamlets, even those formerly autocrati-
cally led, have underlying patterns of egalitarian communal organization for certain purposes, and it may take time for these to
establish themselves over the whole range of hamlet organization
and fill the vacuum left by the disappearance of the traditional
authority. Also, many of these disintegrating hamlets are so, not
because of the equalization of wealth brought by the land reform,
but owing to other extraneous factors—urban influence, competitive marketing following the introduction of new commercial
crops, the growth of commuting subsidiary wage employments,
and so on. Factors such as these last being equal, on balance it
would seem that the effect of the land reform has been rather to
strengthen the solidarity of the hamlet—by reducing the number of

second-class citizens and making the individual's identification with the hamlet more positive and his acceptance of hamlet constraint more spontaneous. It is difficult to forget the quiet pride with which a formerly very poor tenant in the Yamanashi village spoke of his election as hamlet chief designate for the following year. He had, he said, long been saving up to buy a power thresher. He would now have to postpone his plan because being hamlet chief is "bound to be a bit expensive." He "belonged" to the hamlet in a way that he had never done in the days when it would have been unthinkable that he could ever become hamlet chief.

There is another paradox. Land reform and its effects apart, the solidarity of the hamlet tends to vary roughly in proportion to the degree of its isolation. The more isolated, solidary hamlets are often spoken of as the most "backward"—the strength of community sentiment itself, as well as the small degree of urbanization and the prevalence of old customs, being considered criteria of backwardness. Yet it seems, paradoxically, that of recent years it is these very "backward" hamlets which often exhibit the greatest innovating zeal. It is in remote fishing and mountain villages that one often finds the most active and successful family-planning movements, the most earnest young farmers' clubs, the greatest diffusion of rationalized kitchens, the brides' societies which discuss how to get on with mothers-in-law, the agreements to cut down unnecessary prestige expenditure on *rites-de-passage*. The reason is not difficult to seek. In such hamlets, in the Japanese phrase, *matomari ga ii*—they hang together. The more solidary hamlet provides a greater social energy for reforming leadership to work with and can mobilize a greater willingness to cooperate. The slogan "let us make ours a bright [*akarui*] hamlet" has greater appeal, and where it is accepted that each man is his brother's keeper it is easier to suggest to one's brother's wife that she should not have so many children.

SINCE THE FIRST postwar elections, the conservative parties have had the electoral support of the Japanese countryside. Why is this so, and what impact did the land reform have on postwar rural politics? At the most obvious level, the money coming to the local village government is dependent on ties with the ruling party, which has been conservative almost without exception since the war. Initially the conservatives won with their old rural power structure not yet dismantled. With the land reform, new bases for power arose. The richer men, often ahead of their neighbors in the ability to get education and political skills, had a significant leadership role, often as head of local agricultural cooperatives. Thus the old-style bosses still reproduced themselves. The tendency for village government to be linked into that of nearby towns has changed the closeness of village politics, but the voting tendencies remain the same. In general, having initially maintained their prewar rural base, the conservative parties developed new organizational ways of maintaining village support—even when their power is not exercised primarily in the interest of the farmers.

FUKUTAKE TADASHI*
Postwar Politics in the Countryside

The land reform . . . created a new and broader top stratum which contained not only landlords brought down from their commanding heights by the ending of tenancy relations and the declining importance of all kinds of patron–client ties, but also of owner-farmers and ex-tenants with large holdings. The status hierarchy was weakened, not least by the formation at the time of the land reform of farmers' unions which stood in declared opposition to the landlords. In a good many hamlets, it is true, the traditional slogans of hamlet unity and hamlet harmony did succeed in muting the class-conscious activities of the farmers' unions. Movements which sought to create a sense of class solidarity stretching beyond the confines of the hamlet were denounced as destructive

* Fukutake Tadashi, *Japanese Rural Society* (Tokyo: Oxford University Press, 1967), pp. 148–150, 179–183, 185–188, 191–195.

of hamlet harmony—hence the failure of the farmers' union movement to acquire a real class character and hence also its loss of direction and rapid decline after the land reform was completed. However, the very existence of the movement is proof that there was some stirring of resistance against the traditional status order, and the movement itself can share—along with the actual destruction of the landlords' power by the land reform itself—the credit for delivering a powerful blow to the traditional status system.

As a result the hamlet community, once so effective in smothering the development of class divisions, could no longer be so easily mobilized under the leadership of its upper stratum. At hamlet general meetings the poorer villagers too began to make demands and proposals reflecting their own particular interests. The post of hamlet chief became something to be avoided, and there was an increasing tendency for the post of *kumi* chief to be filled on a turn-and-turn-about regular roster. Even in the least developed districts there was no longer a group of hereditary hamlet councilors. Since the traditional authority no longer attached to those who occupied hamlet offices, they no longer could command the implicit obedience of hamlet residents. Hence it was not unnatural that even those in the upper stratum often came to consider involvement in hamlet affairs primarily as a waste of valuable time.

Nevertheless, it inevitably happens that it is the stratum of richer farmers who have to take these offices; a group of men, all much of a muchness in terms of their wealth and standing, who take these posts in turn. The payment attaching to these posts— usually a small allowance paid partly from hamlet funds and partly from the village office—is usually slight. Even for a job as onerous as that of hamlet chief it is little more than enough to keep him in cigarettes. This is now, in fact, the basis of his authority; the very fact that he has to make considerable personal sacrifices for very small reward restrains the villagers' criticism. The other source of his authority is the fact that he acts as the liaison man with the village authorities and with other organizations which transcend the hamlet. Nowadays, the hamlet chief is less the chief of the hamlet as a community than of the hamlet as a sub-unit of the administrative system. His work in this respect has come to make even greater demands on his time since the amalgamations of local government units. Hence a farmer who is fairly well-to-do and has a good number of supporting workers in his family is preferred for the job. The kind of man who has real power and the ability to dominate the hamlet is much more likely to become the village or town councilor, or a director of the agricultural cooperative. At any rate, the position of hamlet chief has lost its prestige; in some cases it has become a messenger-boy job that everyone has to take his turn at, and in few hamlets does anyone occupy the post for many years running. It has now become a job suitable for an old man who has practically handed his farm on to his son, and needs something to keep him from being bored with his retirement.

By contrast, younger men, who are in full control of their holdings and keenly interested in farming them better, are the ones who take on the job of chief of the agricultural practice union. Other offices, too, reflecting the separation between the hamlet community and functional associations, and reflecting also a general trend to avoid letting any one man have too many jobs, are likely to be widely distributed. Power ceases to be concentrated; there is no center of authority formed around the office of hamlet chief from which the activities of a united hamlet can be directed. In hamlets now more differentiated into farmers and part-time farmers, the holders of official positions now exercise leadership only within their circumscribed sphere. They may still be drawn predominantly from the upper strata, but they do not exercise anything like the same authoritarian dominance of the prewar leaders. In this sense the hamlet has become less capable of unified action.

But the upper strata still manage to maintain control over the hamlet for in most hamlets there is still no complete separation between the hamlet community as such and the functional associations it contains. As long as the two remain undifferentiated, these associations will not become the unadulterated special-purpose bodies they are supposed to be. Nor will it be easy to develop democratic patterns of leadership through elections designed to fit the man to his function.

. . . Mayors who had played the key role in the grass-roots war effort, and occupied *ex officio* the positions of divisional directors of the Imperial Rule Assistance Association, were purged from public office. Under the new system mayors were to be directly elected—and at a time when the land reform was creating turmoil in the villages. By virtue of their direct election the mayors occupied a stronger position than before the war. No longer simply the chairmen of the village councils, chiefly concerned with securing compromise agreements among the members of the council, they were now able to pursue positive policies of their own.

The councils, too, as a result of the structural changes brought in the villages by the land reform, were no longer dominated by landlords. Councilors were drawn from a much wider stratum of villagers, and men who had been part-tenants or even wholly tenants could get elected, if they had the ability. The voting age was lowered and women were given the vote. As a result it was possible for relatively young men to secure election, and there were even women councilors, though they were few in number.

These changes did not, however, imply a definitive change in the mechanisms of village politics. . . . [A] high proportion of mayors and village councilors were still drawn from the landlord stratum. And as we have seen, elections for the village council were still generally on a hamlet basis, and those elected were still expected to act as representatives of the interests of their hamlets. It is unnecessary to add that even after the dissolution of the tenancy system the interests of the hamlet were largely interpreted in terms of the interests of its richer members.

But even if mayors and councilors were often former landlords, they no longer formed a ruling stratum by virtue of their authority as landlords. If ex-landlords were heavily overrepresented, this was because as a result of their wealth they had received higher education and could claim to be better fitted in knowledge and experience than former tenants or part-tenants. Ability was a much more important prerequisite for office after than before the war, and it was no longer possible to be elected simply on the grounds of one's family's traditional standing or wealth. Since it was generally speaking only members of the upper strata who were able to develop those abilities, they naturally predominated among the officeholders, and in a situation in which political interests were defined in local hamlet terms rather than in class terms, it was still possible for them to promote their own interests under the guise of pursuing their hamlet's interest.

However, this kind of sleight-of-hand was no longer so easy after the dissolution of the landlord system. The attitudes of the voters had changed too, and they were no longer willing to bow submissively to authority and accept the compromises reached by the "powerful men." In those villages where the class tension developed in the course of the land reform had led to the forma-

tion of farmers' unions there were "movements for the democratization of village politics" and strong criticism of the "rule by
powerful men" which had replaced rule by the landlords. Even in
other villages councilors were under much stronger pressure from
their constituents to promote their hamlet's interest and the process of reaching acceptable compromises became more difficult.
The change in attitudes can be seen in the fact that village
authorities found it increasingly difficult to operate the system of
compulsory food deliveries which was carried over from the war
period. Village politics were no longer something remote and the
business of members of a superior landlord class; it was something
with which the ordinary villager was concerned and in which he
was involved. Those who held office knew that they could only
continue to do so if they provided real benefits for their electors.

Nevertheless these burgeoning trends of change in village politics did not develop satisfactorily. With the postwar extension of
the compulsory education period, towns and villages had to devote
the major part of their slender financial resources to the building of
new middle schools. As we have already seen, the financial
strength of local governments was not such as to permit them to
formulate any positive policies. Again, with the completion of the
land reform, the farmers' unions lost their immediate campaign
objective and began to disintegrate; the awakening sense of class
interest was once again submerged in the sense of hamlet community. And we have also seen already how the financial limitations
of local governments forced greater reliance on the self-government activity of the hamlets which further prevented the development of a proper appreciation of the function of local government.

The Political Structure of the New Towns
and Villages

Until the recent amalgamations most rural areas were included in
town or village administrations. And for most towns and villages,
consequently, local politics meant the politics of agriculture. With
the amalgamations the situation has changed considerably, since
rural areas of considerable size now come within the boundaries of
cities. Whereas before the amalgamation sixty-three percent of the
total population of Japan lived in towns and villages, the present
proportion has fallen to forty-five percent. Consequently, it is no

longer possible to discuss the political structure of rural areas
solely in terms of the politics of towns and villages. City administrations must come into the picture too. Equally an understanding
of the politics of towns and villages requires full attention to the
commercial and manufacturing elements found in their central
settlements. The power structure of rural areas, in other words, has
become much more complicated. One effect has been to reduce the
total number of local government councilors. For example, a village with a population of some 3000 people might formerly have
had a council of sixteen members. Now amalgamated with three or
four other such villages into a town of, say, 12,000 to 15,000
inhabitants, the total number of council members would be twenty-
six representing a big proportionate reduction. Moreover, among
the reduced number of councilors the proportion representing rural
areas is likely to decrease. This tendency is particularly marked
. . . in cities with very large commercial or manufacturing centers.
In the towns and villages farmers still predominate among members of the council, but if one takes into account the fact that
members from the commercial center are generally more influential, even a small drop in the proportion of farmer representatives
may have a considerable effect on local politics. In the new cities
the very sharp decrease shows that in these new mixed areas it will
be hard for agricultural interests to get a fair hearing.

   The nonfarmer members of these councils are for the most part
shopkeepers and owners of small businesses, but among them the
operators of construction and timber concerns very frequently
have a source of strength in rural areas inasmuch as they offer part-
time employment for poorer farmers. Such men are frequently at
loggerheads with the agricultural cooperatives and, organized as a
chamber of commerce, they are likely to promote the mercantile
interests of the urban center and prevent too much spending in the
rural areas. When there is a factory of some size in the district it is
likely to feel that it has a right to get its money's worth out of its
property tax contribution to municipal finances, and to seek to get
representatives of the firm elected to the council. These are also
likely to try to cut down on spending in rural areas. It is true that
the largest proportion of funds spent under the heading industrial
and economic affairs is preempted as counterpart funds for subsidies given by the Ministry of Agriculture and consequently spent
on agriculture, but, generally speaking, in most of the local

administrations newly created by the amalgamations the tendency in agricultural policy has been toward retrenchment.

Similarly, an increasing proportion of mayors have been non-farmers. Even if village mayors have never commonly been actual cultivators, this is a big change from the days when, as landlords, they could at least officially declare their occupation to be farming. Certainly few city mayors are now farmers. This means that for most rural people the mayor has become a somewhat remote figure. Gone are the days when it was always possible for a group of farmers to go along with their hamlet's councilor and plead personally with the mayor to do something about their problems. The mayor, particularly if he is a city mayor or a town mayor, is now somebody only to be approached by formal petitions through the council.

. . . [T]here are some new features of politics in the post-amalgamation local governments which one would hardly have found anywhere in the old. The first results from the fact that the voting situation has become more fluid since hamlets are no longer able to exercise the same control over their votes. It has consequently become possible for new types of local councilors to appear, men whose support comes from, for instance, a youth organization whose members are scattered over a wide area. Such men can act in relative freedom from hamlet or other regional interests, and generally they are men of a rather different mentality and outlook from the typical conservative boss.

Secondly, in those of the new cities and towns which contain numbers of organized workers, there have appeared a few councilors belonging to left-wing parties. Again, the trade unions which hitherto paid little attention to local government have recently revised their opinion of its importance, and formed regional union committees specially concerned with local government matters. Another new phenomenon, in towns and villages which contain large numbers of people in regular wage or salary employment, is the occasional formation of "employees alliances." Their motive is protest against the fact that they seem to pay a disproportionately large part of the taxes for, and receive a disproportionately small part of the benefits of, local government activity. As such they represent an attack on the principle that global interests of local residential districts should be the prior consideration. It has happened in the new cities, too, with the expansion of the municipal office, that officials have formed their own union and affiliated to the federation of local government workers.

If these two trends were to coalesce, the way would be opened for a worker–peasant alliance within the framework of local government. However, the way ahead is by no means easy. As a formal slogan the worker–peasant alliance sounds easy enough, but hitherto there have been few instances of successful achievement. There may have been momentary cooperation prompted by some particular incident, but it is rare for such alliances to last long.

The reasons are, firstly, that it is hard for new leaders to emerge from the farmer's side, or if they do emerge they are always likely to be converted into old-style bosses. The young men of the caliber to make new-style leaders usually have their own farm. Many of them are preoccupied with trying out new ideas such as cooperative management of their farms, and so have little time left to get into local government politics. Moreover, as the income differential between agriculture and other industries increases, able young men are increasingly unwilling to stay on the farm, and consequently the hopes of finding new leaders grow more and more dim. In these circumstances if a young man does attempt to take part in local government politics, the chances are that, finding few kindred spirits, he will receive a tough initiation from the old-style bosses, and eventually succumb to harsh reality and himself move in a conservative direction. He may intellectually appreciate the importance of alliance with the workers, but the difference in occupation makes this intellectual appreciation take second place to the realities of his situation.

From the workers' side, secondly, an important reason is that the unions, although they have begun to show a little interest, are still not very positively concerned with local government. The fact is that full-time workers are not very concerned about the district they live in, while those who are part-time workers and still draw some income from agriculture are given a certain security by the land they own and tend to be lukewarm toward union activities. The most insecure, the casual daily laborers, are less likely to be organized by the unions than by the owners of local construction firms. Where there are large factories in the area and a good number of workers on the city council they tend, in terms of city politics, to think of their firm's interests first. They, who from the point of view of income levels represent a labor aristocracy, seem not to have much appreciation of the troubles of farmers in their own city let alone the inclination to help them.

Thus, at present, local government remains largely in the hands of local political bosses whether from the villages or from the town areas. It is because of this, and because it is possible for a small number of people to settle matters, that thirty percent of the mayors of towns and villages are elected unopposed. It is because of this too that in elections for town and village councils, although there are only thirty percent more candidates than seats, voting ratios reach more than ninety percent. This high level of voting is not a reflection of a deep concern with local government matters; it is better seen as an index of the strength of the local bosses and of their ability to mobilize the votes of their respective districts. It is the overwhelming strength of these conservative independents in local government which produces parliamentary majorities for the Liberal Democratic party, and which produces the Socialist party's "inverted pyramid"—the phenomenon of diminishing representation the lower one goes in the local government scale, from one-third of the seats in the national Diet to a much smaller level in prefectural assemblies and almost no representation at all in local municipalities. . . .

In the postwar regime, the people were now declared to be sovereign. The farmers too were counted in the ranks of the sovereign people, and they ceased to be mere voting machines manipulated by the landlords, for tenancy relationships no longer gave the landlords the influence wherewith to direct their tenants' votes. Their votes were not perhaps completely freed from the influences exerted by the social pressures of the hamlet and consequently by the richer "powerful men" and village politicians who dominated hamlet opinion, but these influences did allow, and work upon, realistic judgments of advantage—that a vote for such-and-such a candidate would be in the interests of the hamlet or of the village. At least they no longer voted for any man just because he was backed by their landlord; they needed to be persuaded that there were advantages to be gained for their locality.

However, these new voting patterns do, in their final effect, give support to the conservative parties. At present, when the left-wing parties, of negligible importance before the war, have succeeded in securing a third of the Diet seats, the vast majority of rural votes

go to form a powerful basis of support for the majority conservative party which holds the other two-thirds. If one divides the
prefectures of Japan into agricultural and industrial prefectures
according to the proportion of their working population employed
in agriculture, the agricultural prefectures returned an overwhelming proportion of conservative Diet members. One can interpret
this as peasant conservatism causing the farmers to distrust a left-
wing party, their instincts of petty proprietorship making them
shun what they see as parties of the propertyless workers. However, one should not overlook the mechanisms which lie behind
these voting patterns.

Local government, which is of the most intimate concern to
farmers, is supported by equalization tax rebates and subsidies
from prefectural and central governments. Similarly, local government loans cannot be floated at will; permission is necessary, and
for the most part these loans depend on central government funds.
A slight change in the assessment basis for the equalization tax
rebate can have a very large effect on local government funds. The
size of the grants or subsidies received determines the funds available for industrial and economic development. Without loan issues
it is difficult to go ahead with the building of schools and municipal offices. For these reasons mayors and influential members of
the council must maintain close connections with members of the
prefectural assembly and the latter's ultimate patrons, members of
the national Diet. And it goes without saying that these Diet members have to be members of the government party if they are to
have any influence.

It is by utilizing these connections that towns and villages get
their municipal offices and their schools built and keep their roads
and their bridges in good repair. These are looked on as benefits
received through the efforts of the locally elected Diet members.
And it is by pointing out that the Diet members who have worked
so hard for local interests can be relied on to continue to do their
best in future that the local politicians can mobilize support for
them in elections. At the same time it is through these connections
with Diet members and the benefits they bring that mayors and
influential councilors can demonstrate the strength of their own
influence, and so ensure their own reelection.

However, Diet members cannot be absolutely certain of enough
votes for election simply by acting as brokers in this kind of peti-

tion politics. In an electoral system where constituencies elect between three and six members and where there are only two major parties, candidates of the dominant party must face competition from other candidates of their own party. If their role as mediators in the petitioning process is not enough to secure the loyalty of town and village mayors and influential councilors they must play a full patron's role, finding some way of lending their support to their clients in their own elections and contributing in some degree to their election expenses. And if, further, the hold which these local politicians have over the farmers' vote is less complete than that formerly enjoyed by the landlords, and if the voters are much more sensitively aware than they used to be of where their own material interests might lie, they must seek to retain the loyalties of even lower levels of local politicians, making contributions to their campaigns in town and village council elections, and generally nursing their constituencies by all the means available to them.

Thus Diet members create their own support societies, organizing them around a nucleus of prominent local politicians and spreading the net to embrace men of lesser influence. When they return to their constituencies they hold meetings of their support society and give parties to feast their members. They make donations to local societies, subscribe to local festivals, send their secretaries to act as tourist guides when parties of farmers come up to the capital, send wreaths to the funerals of local politicians, and help their sons to get jobs—in these little everyday matters no effort must be spared. Needless to say, the expense of thus nursing a constituency is of no mean order.

In return for all these favors the Diet member's lesser followers in the villages reinforce the mayor and the influential local politicians in explaining to the farmers just how much their patron is devoted to local interests. Sometimes, perhaps, the propaganda work will be assisted by the occasional drinking party. And when it comes to elections this network of local bosses, large and small, will be mobilized into full activity. Election expenses, as a consequence, are likely far to exceed the legal allowance.

And whence, one might ask, come these funds for elections and for nursing constituencies between elections? The obvious and simple answer is that the Liberal Democratic party itself, and also individually the leaders of factions within the party, extract money from the big capitalist firms. This is the mechanism through which the conservative party is able to afford the expenses of retaining power. The process is perpetuated by its ability, through its individual Diet members, to keep the local interests of the farmers primed with the benefits of petition politics, while in the field of government activity proper, they require these financial contributions by promoting policies attuned to the interests of monopoly capital. As long as the farmers are kept happy with the lollipops of local benefits, they fail to perceive the richer fare which is served up to the capitalists. Nor do they become conscious of the fact that these benefits, provided under the neutral guise of services to the whole community, by no means in fact benefit every member of the community.

It should be added, of course, that farmers today are not satisfied simply with local benefits. In matters of national policy, too, they show a sharp hardheadedness where their own interests are directly involved. The determination of rice prices is an example in point. Under the present food control system this is a matter of very great concern to the agricultural cooperatives, the majority of which depend for a good deal of their income on handling charges for the rice they collect on behalf of the government. Through the system of National Cooperative Federations the farmers exercise a good deal of political influence. The cooperatives are the farmers' pressure group, and their affiliated association, the Farmers' Political Alliance (*Nōmin Seiji Remmei*) represents for Diet members a reservoir of votes which they cannot ignore.

In their pressure group activities, the agricultural cooperatives —partly because they are basically economic organizations—are generally on the defensive. In order to protect the farm economy and consequently to strengthen the foundations of the cooperatives themselves, they seek to raise the price of rice, but they do not attempt to go further and press for policies which will ensure the future development and stability of agriculture. At the village cooperative level, the officials themselves are generally elected on a hamlet-representation basis, and since the cooperative's director is generally a conservative village politician it is inevitable that the officers of the National Federations should also have conservative connections. Moreover, the kind of connections which they forge with members of the government party under the necessity of negotiating from a defensive position prevent them from developing more positive pressure group action. . . .

The only possible substitutes are farmers' unions as explicitly political organizations. But, as we have already seen, since the end of the land reform the farmers' unions in the villages have either dissolved or lapsed into dormancy. The left-wing parties still have as supporting organizations a national system of farmers' unions, but at the local level they remain inactive. One reason for this is the lack of organizational power in the left-wing parties, but another reason is the lack on the part of farmers, caught up as they are in the political system described above, of any consciousness of the need for creating such organizations.

Hence, national policies are not designed to promote the farmer's welfare. Since the farmers are an important source of electoral support the Liberal–Democratic party always seeks in its policies to present an appearance of giving agriculture every consideration. In particular, as househeads have lost their authority in the family and ceased to be able to control the votes of their children, with a consequent tendency for votes of the younger generation even in rural areas to go to the left-wing parties, the party has recently been at great pains to speak of the need for modernizing agriculture and to stress its determination not to sacrifice the farmers' interests. Nevertheless national policies are in essence always attuned to the interests of big business, and when they speak of consideration for agriculture and for farmers there is always the proviso: insofar as this does not clash with business interests or hinder their development.

⚙ LOOKING BACK on the land reform in 1958, R. P. Dore comments here on developments since the occupation ended. The ruling Liberal–Democratic party, not eager to disturb its reestablished rural base, did not hesitate to ignore the efforts of dispossessed landlords to recoup some of their losses—for small farmers and part-tenants are a far larger bloc of votes now. The rural conservatism of post-land reform Japan, however, resting largely on structural features of Japanese politics, actually says little about the potential for change and technical innovation among farmers. In fact, innovation in agricultural techniques continued throughout the 1950s, while Japan also faced the continuing problem that Dore saw in 1958—a shortage of tillable land.

R. P. DORE*
The Japanese Land Reform in Retrospect

Many Western observers during the occupation, suspicious of the apparent smoothness with which the reform was carried out, predicted that, as soon as the occupation troops were gone, "the landlords would soon be back." They have been proved wrong. The only postoccupation legislation bearing on the land system has been the Agricultural Land Law of 1952 (designed by bureaucrats, but carried through the Diet by members of the conservative Liberal party), which had the express purpose of freezing the Japanese system of land tenure in the state in which it emerged from the land reform. The original maxima which the land reform imposed on the size of total holdings and on the area to be leased to tenants are still maintained, and elected farmers' committees supervise all land sales and tenancy changes to see that they are not exceeded. Tenants are still guaranteed complete security of tenure, landlords may not sell leased-out land except to the tenant if the tenant expresses a wish to buy it. Moreover, rents are still controlled: even the most recent increase in controlled rents, in 1955, still gave landlords only a one percent return on capital if land were valued at current prices—and from that rent the landlord had to pay taxes.

The reasons for the landlords' failure to make a comeback are fairly obvious. Postwar governments depend for their existence on a parliamentary majority and parliamentary majorities depend on votes. Conservative parties, moreover, depend disproportionately

* R. P. Dore, "The Japanese Land Reform in Retrospect," *Far Eastern Survey* XXVII:12 (December 1958), pp. 85–86, 88.

on rural votes. There is no incentive for a conservative party to sponsor measures which would favor the two and a quarter million ex-landlords or the million or so remaining landlords (who are less likely to vote for their opponents in any case) at the expense of alienating the nearly five million farm families who benefited from the land reform or the more than two million who share the remaining ten percent of tenanted land. The landlords and ex-landlords have not been inactive in recent years; they have formed large and vocal organizations to plead their case, but so far with little success.

They have two grievances. The first, affecting only the remaining landlords, concerns the current tenancy regulations. Perhaps the most unfortunate provision of the land reform law was that which permitted landlords to retain up to two-and-a-half acres of leased-out land. (It might have been better to abolish tenancy altogether and instead, perhaps, have permitted landlords who wished to become full-time farmers to reclaim a modicum of their leased land from tenants, in other words to have legalized and controlled the process which in fact went on in defiance of the law.) In 1950, at the end of the reform, there were a million-and-a-half such residual small landlords. The fact that the present laws permit them only a minimal rent income from this land is a minor irritant to those among them who have found some other satisfactory means of livelihood. But the fact that the law's guarantee of security of tenure also forbids them to take this land back into their own cultivation is a major source of resentment and frustration to those others among them who tried at the time of the land reform to turn themselves into owner-farmers and succeeded in getting only a small holding. About half the remaining landlords in 1950 were farmers with less than two-and-a-half acres of land in their own cultivation. They would dearly like to get their hands on the additional land which is nominally theirs but which brings them no profit, and there is a widespread feeling in the villages (shared by most people except tenants whose livelihood depends on using land which their landlord covets) that, if "ownership" means anything at all, it should surely mean the right to use land oneself.

Slowly this, the greatest cause of friction in Japanese villages today, is being eliminated. Sometimes the landlord decides to cut his losses and sell the land to the cultivating tenant—usually at about half the price paid for ownership and cultivating rights.

Sometimes, taking advantage of the remnants of his traditional landlord prestige and of the general feeling that ownership should mean something, the landlord has persuaded a reluctant tenant to give up tenancy. In a few notorious cases landlord organizations have made concerted attempts to force tenants to relinquish tenancy by devious methods of bribery and threats, though often a counter-revival of tenants' organizations and the activity of left-wing Diet members have nipped such attempts in the bud.

The landlord organizations formed in the last few years have, however, given their demand for revision of the current tenancy regulations only secondary place. Partly to avoid arousing opposition from tenants, they have been ostensibly less concerned with the grievance of *present* rump landlords than with the grievance of all former landlords, namely that the compensation paid during the land reform was unrealistically small. The main battle cry of the National Federated Association for State Compensation for Liberated Land, formed in 1954, and of the breakaway Federation of Land Reform Victims, founded in 1957, has, as their names indicate, been a demand for a measure of additional compensation. Their case has been seriously prejudiced by the decision of the Supreme Court on the land reform law in 1953. By a majority of twelve to four the court rejected the claim of the appellants that the land reform offended against the constitutional provision that private property could only be taken by the state on the payment of "just compensation." It held that the method used to calculate the amount of compensation was consistent with the general trend of public policy with regard to the regulation of land prices since long before the war's end. It added that the land reform, unlike other reforms of the occupation period, was not something which "could not possibly have come about except at the orders of the Allied powers."

Undaunted, the landlord organizations were extremely active in 1955 and 1956 in demonstrating, petitioning, and lobbying Diet members. They received a fair measure of support from Liberal–Democrat members (on the compensation issue, since there was no threat to the present interests of tenants, they could win friends without making enemies), but the Ministry of Agriculture, strongly supported by the Ministry of Finance, successfully resisted such political pressures as came from the party and issued strong statements on its own authority opposing all concessions to the compensation demand. The declining landlords' campaign revived somewhat as the May 1958 Lower House elections approached, and as an election gesture the party established a committee to study the whole question. The minister of agriculture, appointed after the elections in June, insisted, however, that while he would cooperate with the party's study, no compensation would be paid. Little has been heard of the landlord organizations since. . . .

Rural conservatism is a standard cliché of political analysis. But the fact that Japanese rural districts at present vote predominantly for conservative candidates does not necessarily imply a pervasive resistance to change of any sort. The technical progress of recent years has already been referred to, and the continued processes of urbanization and education are bringing gradual social changes too. Indeed, the whole history of Japanese villages over the past century has been one of continuous change, of slow but effective technical and social reform sponsored by paternal authority. In the immediate postwar period the rate of change was vastly accelerated. Moreover, the defeat and the purges destroyed the prestige of traditional authority, while the land reform struck at the roots of the system of economic dependence on which the authority of the landlords in particular has rested. Leadership moved to new groups. It was now youth organizations, demobilized soldiers and farmers' unions which took the lead in denouncing feudalism in the family, in organizing agricultural improvement societies and economic study groups, in insisting on the right of the individual to choose his own mate, in demanding open elections for village office and public scrutiny of budget accounts, in proposing modernized kitchens to lighten the burden of farm women, and cooperative ownership of machines to make a communal attack on poverty.

The initial burst of enthusiasm did not, of course, maintain itself for very long. Some of the more energetic leaders soon left the village for the towns again. The young tenant who led the fight for the brave new world ten years ago is now often the established local politician, prosperous owner of a large holding, who dines with the local Diet member and in return for the prestige which this confers rallies the voters to his flag. More traditional patterns of leadership have reasserted themselves, and, though the land reform's redistribution of wealth has placed many ex-tenants among the leaders and many ex-landlords among the led, once

again it is wealth and connections and seniority rather than reforming zeal which are the important qualifications for village
office. . . .

It is not easy to disentangle the effects of the land reform on
Japanese villages from the effects of the other manifold changes
which have taken place in Japan in the last thirteen years. It is
evident, however, that it has done a great deal to improve economic conditions, and that it has, while certainly making Japanese
villages safe for conservatism, changed the nature of the mechanisms by which conservative parties get their rural support and
changed it, moreover, in such a way as to give no encouragement
to ultranationalists of the prewar variety who might propose once
again to promote rearmament at the expense of agricultural subsidies. It also contributed, as one of the most stunning of the postwar changes which shook Japanese rural society by the ears, to a
considerable liberalization of village social structure and the patterns of family life. But the mere redistribution of land to the
cultivators could not affect the fundamental fact that there is not
enough land to cultivate. This is a problem for the Japanese
economy as a whole, for only a rapid increase in industrial and
commercial employments can absorb the underemployed labor
reserve on the land, and so ensure the villages a prosperity which
does not depend, as does the relative prosperity of 1958, on the
uncertain continuance of costly government protection.

II.

Resurgent Japan:
The Politics of Prosperity
1952–1973

⚙ FOR THE LAST TWO DECADES, Japan has been a continuing source of astonishment to the rest of the world. Poorer in natural resources than any other major power, Japan is nonetheless the fastest growing industrial nation, and economically the third most powerful country in the world.

This rise to world prominence in trade and industrial might was accomplished within the parameters of American Cold War foreign policy. In exchange for the end of the American occupation, Japan accepted the bilateral United States–Japan Mutual Security Treaty, placed itself under the military protection of Washington, agreed to adhere to an extensive embargo on trade with the People's Republic of China, diplomatically recognized Chiang Kai-shek as the government of China, and limited its dealings with the Soviet Union.

American wars, in Korea in the 1950s and Indochina in the 1960s, illustrate another consequence of United States foreign policy for Japan. Both wars gave major boosts to the Japanese economy. Japan served as an industrial and military supplier for America, and also had a golden opportunity to expand its investment and exports with American support. These developments, not surprisingly, were linked with American encouragement for the remilitarization of Japan and the rebuilding of a Japanese military establishment. Before the Peace Treaty was signed, American forces were fighting in Korea. MacArthur had the Japanese establish their Self-Defense Force, the beginning of a Japanese military, which was widely argued to be in direct contradiction to the "no war" clause (Article IX) of the Constitution forbidding rearmament. Two decades later, Japan has become a military power, and possesses the industrial base for nuclear weapons and a rapid expansion of its already sophisticated military equipment.

Since World War II, Japan has been ruled by a triumvirate of big business, political parties, and government bureaucracy. Although, as Part I shows, the bureaucracy was not greatly changed by the occupation reforms, business was shaken up temporarily. The old family-owned holding companies that were the lynchpin of the vast zaibatsu combines were formally dissolved by American antitrust efforts. Today these combines have been reconstituted in a more modern corporate form, somewhat like an American conglomerate, with banks assuming a central role in coordinating their varied elements. The Japanese government bureaucracy continues to function chiefly to fulfill the needs of big business, and the Liberal Democratic party is essentially its elected spokesman. The three legs of the triumvirate are thus tightly integrated and can work together with great efficiency.

Party politics, moreover, even in its American-reformed version, retains some major prewar characteristics. Local political machines, *jiban,* institutionalized the power of the conservatives' parliamentary parties through a patronage and pork barrel system which ensured loyal and dependable constituencies. By the end of the occupation period the conservative parties from prewar Japan—now reconstituted as the Democrats and the Liberals—had regained control over these local machines, a control that remains well into the early 1970s.

One enduring legacy of the American occupation, however, has been a spirit of popular resistance to the political and cultural recentralization sought by the Japanese government. Protests have been strong and consistent against attempts by the conservative parties to centralize and strengthen the Japanese police and to return to patriotic indoctrination in education. Some of the best publicized and most vehement opposition to government policies has been directed at the Japanese-American security treaty system.

These struggles, led by the Japanese labor movement, students, and the Socialist and Communist parties, have expressed determinedly pacifist and democratic feelings during several political crises since independence. Yet these groups have been severely limited both by political constraints imposed by the government and by their own internal weakness. Labor, for example, is faced with a hostile environment for organizing. In Japan industry-wide national unions, discussed in Parts I and II, are practically unknown. The large labor federations are composed of "enterprise unions," limited to a single plant or company. This disadvantage is compounded by the competition of "second" (essentially company) unions and by factionalism on the national level between opposing labor federations.

The left-wing parties have been constricted by government repression, their own factionalism, and the success of the conservative parties in the rural areas. The Socialists, split into two parties, still have a relatively small membership and are almost completely dependent on the labor unions for funds. The Japanese Communist party, unlike the Socialists, was forced underground during the purge of the left at the end of the occupation, and patiently rebuilt its urban political base after its legal reestablishment in the mid-1950s. Like the Japan Socialist party, it has had a political role mainly in major urban centers. By 1973, Socialists and Communists had elected mayors of Tokyo, Osaka, Kyoto, Yokohama, and Nagoya.

The most widely discussed developments in Japan in the last two decades have occurred in the economic sphere. Today Japan competes successfully in global markets, selling a wide assortment of industrial goods, especially those requiring high technological skill. In the crucial American and Western European markets, Japan's aggressive export strategy has provoked increasing antagonism, creating the possibility of open economic warfare.

Along with economic growth and wealth has been the appearance of a sizable middle class, a relatively new development for Japan. By 1973, Japanese per capita income had passed $3000 and the Gross National Product was over $300 billion. As in Western countries, the service sector of the economy is growing faster than manufacturing. Yet prosperity has been a mixed blessing for Japan. A country of small physical area and high population density, it has some of the world's worst pollution and congestion problems.

1. Foreign Policy

✿ THE OCCUPATION of Japan ended in 1952 after the signing of the Peace Treaty of San Francisco and the ratification of the accompanying United States–Japan security treaty. The two treaties, ostensibly returning Japan's sovereignty and re-admitting her to full diplomatic status, in fact tied Japan to American foreign policy for the next two decades. The Soviet Union, China, India, and other Asian nations strongly con-demned the security treaty and refused to sign the peace treaty, protesting the dangers of Japanese remilitarization and its resurgent economic strength. John Dower explores the politics and policies of the American occupation that led to this post-1951 alliance with the United States. Washington's attitudes are further illustrated in a selection from a National Security Council memorandum of 1951, prepared shortly before the two treaties were formulated.

One of the chief architects of the peace treaty, John Foster Dulles, sets forth some of the assumptions underlying Ameri-can postoccupation planning for Japan in his Congressional testimony on the security pact in 1952. The Yoshida letter indicates another aspect of American policy. By pressuring the Japanese prime minister against his better judgment to recog-nize the Nationalist government on Taiwan or face the defeat of the peace treaty in the United States Senate, Dulles was able to further tie Tokyo's foreign policy to the American contain-ment of China and lessen any possibilities for the resumption of the prewar patterns of trade that had existed between China and Japan. Japanese opposition to the peace treaty is voiced by members of the "Peace Study Group," which included some of Japan's leading intellectuals (Abe Yoshishige, Sadasukke Amano, Yoshio Nakano, Maruyama Masao, Shintarō Ryū, Gōrō Hani).

JOHN DOWER*
The U.S.-Japan Military Relationship

At war's end the Allied powers were unanimous in their agreement that Japan, like Germany, had to be prevented from ever again becoming a great military threat. This was particularly clear in American policy—in the plans approved for postsurrender Japan by the State-War-Navy Coordinating Committee; the double-kill of the terror bombing; the early claim to the mandated islands, Ryukyus, and Bonins as insurance against any future Japanese aggression; the near total demobilization of the Japanese armed forces and destruction of remaining Japanese artillery, warships, and aircraft; and in the sweeping fundamental reforms of the early occupation period, especially the no-war clause of the American-drafted constitution. To a considerable degree, American war and peace policy toward Japan in the 1940s operated in a Manichean dimension: both the Pacific War and the opening stages of the occupation which followed it were devoted to the eradication of evil. When evil was assigned new incarnations within two years of the end of the war, the morality play remained but Japan's role within it changed drastically. This metamorphosis began in 1947 and was transparent by 1948, and both in form and timing Japan's new guise bore striking parallels to the posture being assigned to occupied West Germany. The shift in occupation policy toward Japan was undertaken virtually unilaterally by the United States; for various reasons, almost all of the other wartime Allies were more or less opposed to the decision to rebuild Japan.

The so-called "reverse course" toward Japan had two faces, military and economic. And the military face in turn had two

* John Dower, "The Eye of the Beholder," *Bulletin of Concerned Asian Scholars* II:1 (October 1969), pp. 16–25.

sides: American military presence in Japan and the specter of a
resurgent, rearmed Japan. It is misleading to think of the military
relationship between the two countries as having begun with the
signing of the security treaty in 1951, for the United States has
maintained a military presence in Japan ever since September of
1945. More significantly, the formal decision to maintain this
presence indefinitely in post-treaty Japan appears to have been
agreed upon by the State Department as early as the winter of
1949—over half a year before the outbreak of the Korean War
and almost two years before the security pact was signed. The
American decision to encourage expansion of the Japanese paramilitary capability was made secretly by the National Security
Council in November, 1948, and the first positive steps toward
recruitment and training of a new Japanese army were initiated in
July 1950. In September 1951, when the peace treaty was being
signed in San Francisco, Japan already had four rough infantry
divisions undergoing training by American officers. Where did it all
really begin?

The official record is not open, but the first positive gesture
toward preparing Japan for a possible future military role against
the Soviet Union was taken in 1945, almost immediately after the
occupation began, under Major General Charles Willoughby. One
of MacArthur's two most influential aides in Japan, Willoughby
was reputedly called "my loveable fascist" by the Supreme Commander, and actually was to serve as an advisor to Franco after his
retirement from the Army in the early fifties. As chief of the
occupation's G-2 (Intelligence) section, Willoughby from the beginning opposed a hard policy toward Japan and in particular
succeeded in freeing from the purge certain key officers of the
former Imperial army and navy. If Willoughby's plans had carried
through, these men—approximately fifteen in number—would
have become the nucleus of the general staff of Japan's future
military establishment. They formed several noteworthy groups.
Intelligence personnel headed by Lieutenant General Seizō Arisue,
former chief of Military Intelligence for the General Staff, were
incorporated into G-2's historical section; they were key sources of
intelligence concerning Russian military dispositions in the Soviet
Far East. A second group headed by Colonel Takushirō Hattori,
Tōjō's former secretary and chief of the First Section of the
General Staff's Operations Division, managed the demobilization

boards through which some four million Japanese servicemen were returned to civilian life. The potential influence of these demobilization board personnel was greater than their number suggests, for by virtue of their position they maintained up-to-date files on the whereabouts of some 70,000 former career officers: the clerical work for demobilization could obviously function equally well for remobilization. In addition to tasks relating to their anticipated role, the favored officers also reputedly served G-2 as spies, submitting influential reports on labor movements and activities on the political left. . . .

Almost from the very beginning of the occupation, dispatches from correspondents in Tokyo reported the belief among ranking American officers there that Japan was to become the "springboard for the next operation." In late December 1945, MacArthur made clear his extreme displeasure at the inclusion of the Soviet Union in the essentially powerless Allied Council for Japan agreed upon by the Big Four at Moscow, and, from the opening sessions of the council the following March, all statements by the Soviet delegate were met with open hostility by the American representative. On August 30, 1946, under a headline reading "U.S. Army Foreseen Staying on Indefinitely in Japan," the *Baltimore Sun* printed an article by Russell Brines of Associated Press which opened with this lead paragraph:

> Although the military phase of the occupation is nearly completed, American forces may remain indefinitely in Japan to hold what is regarded here as the eastern anchor of a worldwide American line against the Soviet Union and communism.

Three days later, in an address marking the first anniversary of the formal Japanese surrender, MacArthur created an international stir by stating that the Japanese islands might become "a powerful bulwark for peace or a dangerous springboard for war." The impact of the Supreme Commander's remark was regarded as particularly significant since it coincided closely with statements by Secretary of State Byrnes, culminating in the famous speech at Stuttgart on September 8, which similarly suggested a reappraisal of American policy toward Germany. With few exceptions, the American press regarded MacArthur's speech as signaling a substantial change in American policy toward Japan, and writers such as Mark Gayn of the *Chicago Sun* expressed the view that Mac-

Arthur's increasingly obvious support of the conservative wing in Japanese politics "was an integral part of the pattern of our foreign policy. Our support of conservatives here [in Japan] was no different from our support of the Kuomintang in China or of the Dutch in the East Indies, or of the British in Greece and Iran." . . .

The failure of the Marshall Mission to China in early 1947 and the increasing certainty thereafter of communist victory in the Chinese civil war gave Japan added significance in the eyes of American strategic planners, as China joined the Soviet Union as the projected enemy in Asia. In the summer of 1948, Lieutenant General Robert Eichelberger, who had just retired as commander of the Eighth Army in Japan, announced his "personal" support for the creation of a 150,000-man armed Japanese constabulary. That fall, the National Security Council secretly approved, to the exact figure, the organization of such a "national police force" in Japan. Acting to a large extent on the recommendations of George Kennan, who had visited Japan in February and March of 1948, the NSC at the same time voted to strengthen Japan economically while easing off the pressure for continued fundamental reforms. Although Secretary of State Acheson and others thereafter urged MacArthur to begin to build up the Japanese "police" within the prescribed limits, the Supreme Commander refused to accede to these pressures for Japanese rearmament until after the outbreak of the Korean War.

General MacArthur's personal views on the strategic role Japan was to play in the Pacific were complex and enigmatic. From 1947 on, he was the leading advocate of an early peace treaty, and while supporting a continued strong military posture in Okinawa, for a long time he appears to have remained convinced not only that Japanese rearmament was inadvisable, but also that a post-treaty American military presence would be neither necessary nor desirable in the four main islands. His celebrated description of Japan as the "Switzerland of the East," for example, was made in 1949. In this respect, the general held one of the least militaristic American positions current on Japan in the late 1940s; George Kennan held a similar view concerning post-treaty U.S. military presence in Japan, but he was an earlier and firmer advocate of strengthening Japan's military capability than was the general. At the same time, however, MacArthur had described Japan as "the westernmost outpost of our defenses" as early as 1946, and in March 1949 he offered a more vivid (and racial) description of the Pacific sphere claimed by the United States:

> Now the Pacific has become an Anglo-Saxon lake and our line of defense runs through the chain of islands fringing the coast of Asia. It starts from the Philippines and continues through the Ryukyu archipelago which includes its broad main bastion, Okinawa. Then it bends back through Japan and the Aleutian Island chain to Alaska.

This was the vision that mattered, the image that caught hold. It is academic but nonetheless interesting to speculate how the United States would have responded if a famous Russian general had described the Pacific as a Sino-Soviet Pond, or if a prominent Chinese communist had defined China as an American power since the same waves that washed America's shores washed his country's as well. . . .

International pressures forced the U.S. government to announce in September 1949 that it would soon begin negotiating a peace settlement with Japan, but—like previous statements made in 1947—this proved to be largely a diplomatic charade. The key international issue in considering a peace treaty at this time was whether or not U.S. troops would be withdrawn from the country following the restoration of sovereignty to Japan. If so, then it was conceivable that an "overall peace" could be negotiated—that is, a treaty such as had been anticipated at war's end, involving all of Japan's former wartime enemies including the Soviet Union and other communist countries. If on the other hand the United States decided to hinge the treaty on the indefinite maintenance of U.S. forces in Japan in the post-treaty period, it was understood that this would be absolutely unacceptable to the Soviet Union. The best that could be hoped for then would be a "separate peace" involving Japan on the one side and the United States and its Cold War supporters on the other. The decision lay in the hands of the United States, and the U.S. position had become increasingly clear during the course of 1949. By the end of the year it was apparent that the United States did not contemplate a military withdrawal from Japan. In Kennan's words, a general consensus had emerged, at least within the State Department, that:

> while the treaty would not itself provide for the retention of American bases in Japan, it would be accompanied by a separate

agreement with the Japanese government sanctioning such an agreement; and that if all this was not agreeable to the Russians, as it obviously would not be, we would not hesitate to conclude both treaty and agreement without them.

As soon became apparent, even this separate-peace-with-American-hardware plan envisioned by the State Department was deemed too soft by the Joint Chiefs of Staff, Secretary of Defense Louis Johnson, and others. They opposed any peace settlement whatsoever in the foreseeable future, being, in the words of one scholar, "most reluctant to give up the secure base in Japan assured by the American command position obtaining under the occupation for the uncertainties involved in dealing with a once more sovereign Japan, no matter how friendly to the West." The viewpoint held by these leading spokesmen of the military establishment was of critical importance, because from the end of 1949 this group held the upper hand in government councils and successfully prevented any further significant activity on the part of the American government relating to a peace settlement with Japan—even a settlement contingent upon a bilateral U.S.–Japan military pact such as was eventually signed.

Other "defense considerations" on the part of the U.S. government contributed further to the uncertainty and fear in Asia concerning the future of Japan. In October 1949, Congress responded to the establishment of the People's Republic of China by appropriating $58 million for military construction on Okinawa, clearly revealing the projected role of this island bastion—which initially had been placed under special control by the U.S. military on the grounds that such control was necessary to prevent any future Japanese aggression. On April 2, 1950, Assistant Secretary of the Army Tracy Voorhees confirmed what had long been apparent by announcing that the United States would occupy the Ryukyus indefinitely. . . . Japan's military role in the Chinese civil war was openly established on June 27, 1950, when President Truman responded to the outbreak of hostilities in Korea by assigning the Seventh Fleet to the Straits of Taiwan, effectively preventing a communist invasion of Taiwan, and having the fleet operate out of Sasebo—thus making Japan, in the words of one Japanese commentator, "a forward military base for intervention in the Chinese communist revolution." . . .

To both China and the Soviet Union, on the other hand, this

situation was a matter of immense concern, as any survey of the press of the two countries from late 1949 reveals. They charged that the United States planned both a prolonged occupation and the rearmament of Japan; in November 1950, Tass made this more specific by asserting that the United States planned to continue the occupation for another thirty years while tripling the size of the paramilitary Japanese constabulary. These allegations as usual were dismissed as blatant propaganda, but they were in essence correct. In this respect, the role of John Foster Dulles is illuminating.

Dulles was appointed advisor to the State Department in April 1950 by President Truman in an endeavor to establish bipartisanship in foreign policy formulation. On May 18, he was assigned to negotiate a settlement with Japan, and it was in part due to his energetic endeavors toward this goal that the opposition of the Department of Defense was eventually overcome. As noted above, however, by the beginning of 1950 the real issue within the U.S. government was not whether American troops would remain in Japan, but whether they would remain in a Japan that was sovereign or still occupied, depending on whether State or Defense had its way. What mattered to the Communists was the military dimension, and in this respect the Tass assertion of a thirty-year occupation will be two-thirds of the way to vindication in 1970. Dulles never considered a nonmilitary settlement.

In the week prior to the outbreak of the Korean War, Dulles, General Bradley, and Defense Secretary Johnson all arrived in Tokyo to study and discuss the issue of Japan's future. The latter two men argued heatedly against any alteration of America's preeminent position in Japan, and, in a normally routine briefing organized by occupation officials, Johnson took the floor to deliver a fifteen-minute harangue attacking "the State Department crowd." In particular he leveled his guns, in the best tradition of Defense Department marksmanship, at Dulles and his "pacifistic" approach to world problems. On his own part, Dulles was meeting for the first time with Prime Minister Yoshida and applying his approach by urging the rearmament of Japan and raising the question of future U.S. bases in that country. In a reportedly unpleasant exchange, Yoshida refused to consider rearmament and remained noncommittal on the issue of bases. The incidents are particularly interesting because they were prelude, not response, to the Korean War.

The Korean War altered the equation, although by no means to the extent that Dulles desired. The first American divisions sent to Korea were taken from the occupying forces in Japan, and it was soon clear that by early September no substantial military force at all would remain in Japan. To protect both the bases in Japan and approximately one-quarter-million American dependants, the decision was reached to expand the existing Japanese police force by creating a 75,000-man National Police Reserve (NPR). By a top secret Basic Plan dating probably from the first week of July, it was made clear that the NPR was to be the nucleus of the future Japanese army. This violated Article 9 of the Japanese constitution, written in 1947, which stated that "land, sea, and air forces, as well as other war potential, will never be maintained." As a result both American and Japanese authorities were forced to extreme contortions to disguise the real nature of the NPR. Within the occupation bureaucracy, responsibility for building the new army was unorthodoxly placed under a specially created Annex of the Civil Affairs Section (CASA), while Japanese government officials steadfastly refused to admit that any more was involved than an expansion of the police. Even recruits to the NPR (some 400,000 applied for the first 75,000 openings) were not informed of the real nature of their new employment, and problems arose in such normally routine areas as the preparation of training manuals for the undercover army. Tanks, for example, were unpoliceman-like and consequently could not be mentioned by name; they rolled camouflaged through the manuals as "special vehicles." Despite these obstacles, CASA succeeded in training its NPR recruits in an arsenal of increasingly diverse and large-caliber weapons. In a recent account, Frank Kowalski, who was the American officer directly responsible for the creation of the new Japanese army between 1950 and 1952, describes the status of the NPR at the time of the San Francisco peace conference as follows:

> Although the force by this time had undergone nothing more advanced than battalion field exercises, the officers and troops had been given extensive individual and small unit training. Practically everyone in the battalions had actually fired carbines, M-1 rifles, machine guns, bazookas, and mortars. As individual

soldiers and members of small units the NPR men could have given a very creditable account of themselves. As battalions or infantry the NPR could, in the closing months of 1951, have put on a whale of a fight. Beyond that the capacity of the force for war was very limited, although in the opinion of many, the organization possessed a great potential for future development.

The NPR at this time was stationed in some thirty-seven camps throughout Japan. At approximately the same time, that is, between August and October 1951, previous barriers against the recruitment of former officers of the Imperial armed services were dropped. In Kowalski's words:

> Eventually 243 graduates of the Imperial army and navy academies, the younger men initially considered, were enrolled in the first Officer Training Course for de-purgees in the latter part of August 1951. In October 812 former Imperial captains, majors and Lt. colonels were brought into the NPR and ordered to attend a two month reorientation course. The door was now open for the former military to resume their interrupted careers.

The new Japanese military still fell far short of what Dulles envisaged, however, and repeatedly from the time of his second visit to Japan in January 1951 he continued to urge the Japanese to create a force of 300,000 to 350,000 men. At the San Francisco conference itself, according to Kowalski, Dulles allegedly offered U.S. financial support specifically directed to this end. Yoshida continued to resist these pressures, arguing that such rapid military expansion was both financially and socially impossible in Japan at that time. In addition, Yoshida's aides subsequently revealed that the old prime minister feared that if Japan did create a force meeting Dulles's specifications, the Japanese government would immediately be subjected to a new pressure to deploy part of that force in Korea—and this was unthinkable. In this regard, historians probably will have to temper the popular image of Yoshida as the arch-conservative on the Japanese political scene. Insofar as negotiation of the peace and security treaties is concerned, his stature may well increase as that of Dulles declines. . . .

The peace treaty signed by forty-nine nations in San Francisco in 1951 has been widely acclaimed for its brevity, clarity, and nonpunitive nature. In this it represented a strong contrast both to earlier treaty drafts prepared by the U.S. government and to various provisions for post-treaty control or restriction over Japan

proposed by other countries. For this reason it has been hailed as a
model of its kind and as clear evidence of American magnanimity.

The bilateral security pact signed only hours after the peace
treaty by the United States and Japan has been regarded by most
Americans as a similarly generous arrangement, for it has obvi-
ously enabled Japan to grow sleek under the protection of the
American nuclear umbrella. L. Mendel Rivers, chairman of the
House Armed Services Committee, recently expressed this bluntly:

> I will tell you one thing, just get it in your head right now: if
> there is any country getting by without paying their share, it is
> Japan.

The magnanimity concept, however, obscures both the strong
American self-interest which underlies support of the alliance, as
well as the many negative features of the relationship which have
given rise to legitimate resentment and fear among many Japanese.
It is obvious from his own statements that Dulles urged a generous
peace treaty because he was convinced that it was eminently
pragmatic to do so. Throughout the period when he was responsible for arranging the treaty, he constantly referred to the lesson
of Versailles: punitive peace settlements do not work. To this
extent, the Dulles accomplishment appears wise and statesmanlike.
At the same time, the end result of Dulles's accomplishment in
1951 was essentially a peace for Asia without Asians. The three
major countries of continental Asia—China, Russia, and India—
did not sign the treaty at San Francisco, nor did Burma or North
Korea. Australia, New Zealand, and the Philippines signed only
with misgivings. And if the peace treaty by itself was admirably
brief and nonpunitive, it nevertheless had no separate existence of
its own, but rather was contingent upon Japan's agreeing to a
military alliance with America: magnanimity under lock and key.
Moreover, the agreement to give American forces virtually free
rein in post-treaty Japan was not the only price the Japanese paid
for their sovereignty. As mentioned above, they were also expected
to rearm and constantly pressured to do so at a rapid rate.
Furthermore, they were forced to abandon hopes to restore natural
economic ties with Asia; most strikingly, Japan was not permitted
to normalize relations with the People's Republic of China.

Few persons now deny that the original United States–Japan
security pact was an unequal treaty in the fullest sense of that old

Western legal tradition for dealing with Asian countries. It was of course negotiated with Japan when that country was still under occupation and without sovereign rights. It violated the no-war provision (Article 9) of the Japanese constitution by stating in its preamble that Japan was expected to "increasingly assume responsibility for its own defense against direct and indirect aggression." More than this, however, the treaty forced Japan to agree to conditions of inferiority unmatched in any of the other forty-plus security treaties negotiated between the United States and other nations in the 1950s. In the 1960 Congressional hearings on the revised treaty, Secretary of State Christian Herter acknowledged that:

> ... there were a number of provisions in the 1951–1952 security treaty that were pretty extreme from the point of view of an agreement between two sovereign nations.

Exactly what these provisions were was subsequently outlined by J. Graham Parsons, Assistant Secretary of State for Far Eastern Affairs:

> The United States is permitted to use bases without consulting the Japanese government for actions in other parts of the Far East that might involve Japan in a war irrespective of Japan's interests.
> Second, the United States could bring into Japan whatever weapons she chose regardless of the wishes of the Japanese with regard to their own territory.
> Third, it provided for the intervention of U.S. forces in large-scale internal disturbances in Japan incompatible with the sovereign status of Japan.
> Fourth, there was no specific commitment by the United States to defend Japan in case of attack; the treaty provided she may defend Japan if she chooses.
> Fifth, it provided for a United States veto over any arrangements for the entry of the forces of a third power into Japan.
> Finally, there were no provisions for a termination of the treaty except by mutual consent.
> I might add that we have often seen the view expressed by the Japanese that this first treaty of 1951 was not one which was entered into by Japan voluntarily.

In addition to the above sources of tension, it should be noted that the really operative part of the pact, the so-called administrative agreement, was not negotiated until February 1952 and was never

subject to Diet or Senate approval. Moreover, the final decision of
the number and location of facilities to be used by the U.S. military in Japan was not settled until June 1952. Thus even in September 1951, neither the Japanese people nor the Japanese government itself were entirely clear as to exactly what they were
getting into—being ignorant of details such as the fact that sovereign Japan was to play host to 100,000 American troops, and that
within a few years America would attempt to introduce nuclear-
capable Honest John missiles to the main islands (a move
thwarted only by a strong outcry from the Japanese populace in
1955). On the American side, major responsibility for negotiating
the administrative agreement fell to special ambassador Dean
Rusk. Thus the two foremost architects of the American hard line
in Asia—Dulles and Rusk—were both intimately involved in the
initial formulation of America's Asian containment policy before
assuming the responsibilities of Secretary of State.

Some of the more blatant inequities of the 1951 agreement were
amended in 1960, but very fundamental differences of outlook
have remained. One of these concerns China. The statements of
key Japanese officials such as Yoshida reveal that up to the time of
the San Francisco conference, and for a short while thereafter, the
Japanese intended to normalize relations with the People's Republic of China once they were in a position to do so—that is, when
the occupation was formally ended through ratification of the San
Francisco treaty by, most importantly, the U.S. Senate. Yoshida
abandoned these plans only after it was made clear to him that
Congress, at the peak of its indignation over the "loss of China,"
would refuse to ratify the peace treaty unless Yoshida gave prior
guarantee that Japan would recognize only the Kuomintang
regime. Dulles visited Tokyo in December 1951 with Senators
John Sparkman and Alex Smith, Democrat and Republican representatives respectively of the Senate Foreign Relations Committee,
primarily to impress this fact upon Yoshida. The success of their
mission was revealed the following month with the publication of
the "Yoshida letter," in which the Japanese prime minister signed
his name to the American line on China. That so virulent an anticommunist as Yoshida had to be pressured into taking this position indicates how widely divergent the two countries were, and
still are, in their evaluation of the situation in Asia. With regard

to China, American "magnanimity" has forced Japan into a posture which many Japanese believe to be inimical to their real self-interest.

National Security Council Memorandum, May 17, 1951

With respect to Japan the United States should: . . .

. . . *d*. Pending the conclusion of a peace settlement continue to:

(1) Take such steps as will facilitate transition from occupation status to restoration of sovereignty.

(2) Assist Japan in organizing, training, and equipping the National Police Reserve and the Maritime Safety Patrol in order to facilitate the formation of an effective military establishment.

e. Following the conclusion of a peace settlement:

(1) Assist Japan in the development of appropriate military forces.

(2) Assist Japan in the production of low-cost military matériel in volume for use in Japan and in other noncommunist countries of Asia.

(3) Take all practicable steps to achieve Japanese membership in the United Nations and participation in a regional security arrangement.

(4) Establish appropriate psychological programs designed to further orient the Japanese toward the free world and away from communism.

* Department of Defense, *United States–Vietnam Relations, 1945–1967* [Pentagon Papers] (Washington, D.C.: U.S. Government Printing Office, 1971), V.B. 2 (*Justification of the War—Internal Commitments*), *The Truman Administration, 1945–1952*, Book 2 (1950 to 1952), pp. 434–435.

JOHN FOSTER DULLES*
Congressional Testimony on Japanese Peace Treaty

STATEMENT OF AMBASSADOR JOHN FOSTER DULLES,
PERSONAL REPRESENTATIVE OF THE PRESIDENT
ON THE JAPANESE PEACE TREATY

1. COMMUNITY OF FREE NATIONS NEEDS JAPAN

The first proposition I have to submit is this: The community of free nations needs Japan. Japan is not just a spot on the map that we see. Japan is a living community which can contribute largely to the happiness and well-being of others. . . .

Japan is the only important industrial nation of Asia. Its existing plants, at full capacity, can produce 10 million tons of crude steel each year and they can launch at full capacity 800,000 tons of ships each year. Japan, through its skills, industry, and its trade, cannot only achieve for itself a good measure of well-being, but can do so in ways which are going to help the other underdeveloped countries, particularly in Asia, themselves to develop better their resources and achieve for themselves a better well-being and a greater industrial capacity for themselves.

That is one side of the picture. When we look at the other side, we can see that if perchance Japan, instead of being one of the free nations, should become a captive Soviet country, that would involve a major shift in the present power position in the world today. Japan's capabilities could be exploited to give long-range overseas striking power to the vast human and natural resources which the Soviet Communists already control in Asia. Stalin, whose views on these matters certainly are not negligible, has said that with Japan, the Soviet Union would be invincible. . . .

The community of free nations needs to deny to the Soviet Union the chance to use Japan for evil and it needs for itself Japan's great capability for good.

* U.S., Congress, Senate, Committee on Foreign Relations, *Japanese Peace Treaty and Other Treaties Relating to Security in the Pacific,* 82d Cong., 2d. sess., January 21, 22, 23, and 25, 1952, pp. 5–8, 10–11, 28–29.

2. JAPAN NEEDS COMMUNITY OF FREE NATIONS

Now my second proposition is this: If the community of free nations needs Japan, so equally Japan needs the free world community.

Czarist Russia has been the historic enemy of Japan, and the Soviet Communists have enthusiastically taken over that role.

They have closed in on Japan, seizing its northern islands and their effort to conquer Korea has obviously been for the purpose of completing the encirclement of Japan. They have refused to repatriate the Japanese prisoners that they took. At the San Francisco conference, which several of you attended, we saw the Soviet Union give a preview of its real intentions as regards Japan, when it demanded that the peace treaty should give the Soviet Union in perpetuity the exclusive right to patrol the straits which surround Japan and even the home waters which divide the home islands of Japan.

The Japanese, now wholly disarmed, need collective security as is envisaged by the United Nations Charter. Without that, Japanese sovereignty would vanish in a matter of hours, and the new hopes and worthy ambitions which now inspire the Japanese people would be ruthlessly extinguished.

3. PEACE AND FREEDOM ESSENTIAL TO JAPAN

My third proposition is this: The mutual goals of Japan and the free community can be obtained only if Japan gets peace and freedom.

The Japanese are a proud and sensitive people. They have demonstrated the capacity to be a great people, although at times they have misunderstood the nature of true greatness.

They accepted, in defeat, the Potsdam surrender terms which were severe and they have scrupulously and honorably carried them out, and have lived up to every particle of those surrender terms. They expect, and rightfully expect, that their victors will be equally honorable and equally scrupulous. . . .

4. JAPAN A RELIABLE MEMBER OF COMMUNITY OF FREE NATIONS

My fourth proposition is this: Japan can be relied upon to be a dependable member of the community of free nations.

The Japanese are an intensely patriotic people who love their country and their distinctive culture and their civilization. They respect and revere their emperor and the stability and unity of the nation which he symbolizes.

The Japanese people, with their new privileges and dignities, and the industrial workers with their new bargaining powers, and the farmers who have now largely become owners instead of tenants, cherish the new rights and new opportunities which have come to them under the wise policies of the occupation and which are reflected in the new Japanese constitution and postsurrender legislation. All the Japanese people long fervently for lasting peace which will erase the awful horror of the last war. . . .

Now I do not deny, or try in any way to evade the fact, that the communist mainland has raw materials and markets which the Japanese could use to advantage. The communists can offer what looks like attractive economic bait to the Japanese people. But I feel completely confident that the Japanese people, before they bite on that bait, will be wary, knowing that this bait may be on a hook and that the hook may be on a line and that the line may run to Moscow. . . .

Concededly Japan's economic future involves uncertainties as indeed does the economic future of almost any country. But unless the free nations become irresponsible in their attitudes Japan will not be forced by economic conditions to aline itself with the communist mainland area or be forced to strengthen the communist military potential by its exports. . . .

I am able to see the possibility of a healthy Japanese economy without any large dependence upon the Asian mainland if Japan has continuing access to the markets primarily of Southeast Asia where there are large populations, and no problem about either the size of the market or the need of the market for such things as Japan can produce.

Also, in Southeast Asia there are sources of supply for most of the raw materials which Japan requires. . . .

Therefore, I do not think that we need to speculate about whether ten, fifteen, twenty, thirty, or fifty years from now Japan can be getting along without access to these markets because I think there will be conditions at that time which will enable Japan to have access to these markets. The problem that Japan faces and we face at the present time is a transitory problem and not a permanent problem.

As a transitory problem it surely can be dealt with and just as Japan's economy has enormously improved over the past six years without dependence on these markets, so I believe it can continue to improve for a period of years without dependence on these markets.

Surely the healthy and normal thing is that there should be contact between Japan and those markets, and I believe that our overall Far Eastern policies should have that as their objective and I believe it is an objective which can be achieved.

PRIME MINISTER YOSHIDA SHIGERU*
Letter, December 24, 1951

His Excellency JOHN FOSTER DULLES,
   The Department of State, Washington, D.C.
DEAR AMBASSADOR DULLES: While the Japanese Peace Treaty and the United States–Japan security treaty were being debated in the House of Representatives and the House of Councilors of the Diet, a number of questions were put and statements made relative to Japan's future policy toward China. Some of the statements, separated from their context and background, gave rise to misapprehensions which I should like to clear up.

The Japanese government desires ultimately to have a full measure of political peace and commercial intercourse with China which is Japan's close neighbor.

At the present time it is, we hope, possible to develop that kind

* U.S., Congress, Senate, Committee on Foreign Relations, *Japanese Peace Treaty and Other Treaties Relating to Security in the Pacific,* 82d Cong., 2d sess., January 21, 22, 23, and 25, 1952, pp. 9–10.

of relationship with the National Government of the Republic of China, which has the seat, voice, and vote of China in the United Nations, which exercises actual governmental authority over certain territory, and which maintains diplomatic relations with most of the members of the United Nations. To that end my government on November 17, 1951, established a Japanese Government Overseas Agency in Formosa, with the consent of the national government of China. This is the highest form of relationship with other countries which is now permitted to Japan, pending the coming into force of the multilateral treaty of peace. The Japanese Government Overseas Agency in Formosa is important in its personnel, reflecting the importance which my government attaches to relations with the national government of the Republic of China. My government is prepared as soon as legally possible to conclude with the national government of China, if that government so desires, a treaty which will reestablish normal relations between the two governments in conformity with the principles set out in the multilateral treaty of peace. The terms of such bilateral treaty shall, in respect of the Republic of China, be applicable to all territories which are now, or which may hereafter be, under the control of the national government of the Republic of China. We will promptly explore this subject with the national government of China.

As regards the Chinese Communist regime, that regime stands actually condemned by the United Nations of being an aggressor and in consequence, the United Nations has recommended certain measures against that regime, in which Japan is now concurring and expects to continue to concur when the multilateral treaty of peace comes into force pursuant to the provisions of article 5 (a) (iii), whereby Japan has undertaken "to give the United Nations every assistance in any action it takes in accordance with the charter and to refrain from giving assistance to any state against which the United Nations may take preventive or enforcement action." Furthermore, the Sino-Soviet Treaty of Friendship, Alliance and Mutual Assistance concluded in Moscow in 1950 is virtually a military alliance aimed against Japan. In fact there are many reasons to believe that the Communist regime in China is backing the Japan Communist party in its program of seeking violently to overthrow the constitutional system and the present

government of Japan. In view of these considerations, I can assure
you that the Japanese government has no intention to conclude a
bilateral treaty with the Communist regime of China.

Yours sincerely,
SHIGERU YOSHIDA

Statement by the Peace Study Group on Peace Settlement for Japan*

About a year ago we issued a statement in which we expressed our
common views on the problems of the cause of war and of the
basis for peace. Now we issue a statement again, this time on the
question of the peace settlement for Japan and the problem of
Japan's security after such settlement. For us, the gravity of these
problems is indeed paramount; and the manner in which they will
be settled is likely to determine the fate of our country for a long
time to come. With full awareness of shame for having been
unable to play a part for peace in deciding our own fate at the time
of the outbreak of the war, we have come to feel strongly that, this
time, it is up to us to do our best in shaping our own future. Thus
it is that we, the undersigned, led by the will to peace and the love
for our country, have decided to study these problems carefully
and, transcending the divergence of political beliefs, have finally
reached the common views on them.

Few will deny that the Allied occupation of Japan has given an
impetus to, and formed the basis for, the democratization of
Japan. Neither can it be denied, however, that the further progress
in the democratization of Japan will be possible only under the
responsibility and the initiative of the Japanese themselves. Furthermore, such progress requires as its necessary condition the
establishment of the free communication and sincere cooperation
with all the countries in the world, which Japan can hope to attain
through the final peace settlement. Thus, it is now the urgent

* "A Statement by the Peace Study Group on the Problem of the Peace
Settlement for Japan," in *Three Statements for World Peace* (pamphlet),
comp. Editorial Staff of *Sekai* (Tokyo, 1950), pp. 18-22.

necessity and desire of all the Japanese people that the final peace settlement be attained and the occupation be ended.

However, for the peace settlement to have real significance, it shall be complete both with respect to its form and content. Otherwise, even if the settlement is "peace" by name, its real content may only contribute toward aggravating the danger of a new war. Therefore, the peace settlement has to be necessarily complete and with all the countries concerned. It is patent enough that there exist in the world today such conflicts as make such an overall settlement difficult. But it is also true that we cannot but feel encouragement in the fact that there still lies underneath these conflicts the strong sense of international justice and morality, such as were exemplified in the International Military Tribunal. Furthermore, if we reflect upon the fact that we surrendered to all the Allied countries after accepting the Potsdam Declaration, it appears to us fully justified that we express our wish for the restoration of peaceful relations with all the Allied countries.

The above is the general conclusion we have come to. Before summarizing below the further points of agreement which we arrived at after thoroughgoing discussion in connection with the above, we feel called upon to point out two propositions which formed the premise for our discussion. They are: Firstly, that we are duty-bound to contribute to world peace in the spirit of the determination for peace as embodied in our Constitution. And secondly, that we earnestly desire that Japan attain her economic self-support at the earliest possible moment, thus becoming freed from the dependence on foreign countries.

1. Japan's economic self-support requires as its most important condition that Japan shall have broad, close, and free trading relations with Asiatic countries, in particular with China; and this condition, needless to say, can be met only through the establishment of the complete peace settlement. A partial or separate peace, as is being discussed today, would result in severing the natural relations which Japan sustains with China and other countries, and is most likely to lead to the situation of Japan's economic dependence or subjugation to a specific country. The loss of economic self-support will prepare the ground for the loss of political independence; and under such circumstances it cannot be expected that the living conditions of people will improve or that Japan can avoid becoming, against her will, a potential threat to

the peace of the world. We value Japan's economic and political independence more highly than the would-be advantages which a separate peace might appear to promise.

2. It is obvious enough that various discussions on the problem of the peace settlement arise out of the fact of the existence of "the two worlds." However, the fact that there are signs of tireless efforts being continued for the general adjustment betweeen "the two worlds" and specifically for the overall peace with Japan supports strongly our faith in the possibility of peaceful coexistence of "the two worlds" and also our hope for the overall peace settlement. If we are to be faithful to the spirit of peace in our Constitution, we are required to take a positive attitude in helping achieve the harmony of "the two worlds," instead of resigning ourselves to adjusting our thinking on the peace problem passively to the vicissitudes of international politics. We believe that our responsibility in contributing toward world peace is so much higher if we are to atone for our guilt in the last war. The so-called separate peace is likely not only to throw us onto one side of the two opposing camps, strengthening our tie with that side while leaving us still in the technical state of war with the other, but it may go further to the point of stimulating hostile relations with the other side, thus helping to deepen the chasm which unfortunately separates "the two worlds" today. This certainly is the last thing we wish to happen.

3. As for the question of Japan's security after the peace settlement, we favor the status of "inviolable neutrality" and at the same time we hope that Japan be admitted to the United Nations. The United Nations, as is clear from the express statement in its Charter, is the present-day crystalization of all the efforts toward peace for which humanity has striven since long past; and along with all the people in the world who pray for peace, we too wish to place great reliance and expectation upon this international body. The "Universal Declaration of Human Rights" adopted by the Third Session of the General Assembly of the United Nations calls for the guarantee, both internal and international, of various rights, especially of social and economic rights. This fact gives us the cause for great encouragement. It is obvious that both the status of inviolable neutrality and the admission to the United Nations presuppose the complete and overall peace. Such things as the mili-

tary agreement with a specific country or the leasing of bases for military purposes to a specific country—the possibilities which may accompany a separate peace or the de facto condition of separate peace—are, regardless under what pretext it may be, against the Preamble and the Article IX of our Constitution, and are likely to contribute towards the ruination of both Japan and the world. We are definitely opposed to such actions. The future of Japan, we believe, lies in practicing the spirit of peace to the utmost and in marching unflinchingly down the path of economic and political independence.

SUMMARY CONCLUSIONS

1. If we Japanese are to express any wish at all on the question of the peace settlement for Japan, there could be no other alternative but "the complete and overall peace."

2. The condition of economic self-support for Japan cannot be attained through a separate peace.

3. As for Japan's security after the peace settlement, we favor the status of inviolable neutrality and also would like to be admitted to the United Nations.

4. We stand opposed to giving military bases to any country under any pretext.

15 January 1950

☃ A POTENTIALLY serious opponent to the ratification of the peace treaty and the security pact was the Japan Socialist party. However, their strength was weakened by splits between left and right wings. Initially they disagreed about whether Japan should rearm, and then over whether a separate peace should be made with the United States and other nonsocialist countries. The final decision of the right Socialists to support the peace treaty but not the security pact showed their confusion. The treaty and the pact were indivisible, especially in U.S. eyes, for Japan got its "independence" in the peace treaty only on condition that she rearm and join the U.S. military system. In effect, Japan was told that independence would be withheld unless she became a military ally of the United States.

COLE, TOTTEN, AND UYEHARA*
Socialist Parties and the Peace Treaty

Official termination of the state of war and of the occupation had been delayed mainly by Soviet–American differences. American policy toward Japan had become less restrictive, and Chinese communist victories had forced reconsideration of the whole problem of noncommunist security in Asia. Negotiations, when renewed, bogged down between the Departments of Defense and State on touchy problems of national security and foreign relations. On April 6, 1950, John Foster Dulles was appointed consultant to Dean Acheson, who was then Secretary of State, to make a determined effort to negotiate a peace treaty between Japan and its recent enemies.

The Socialists reacted to each change in Allied policy. The Katayama government, for instance, had made a weak bid to represent the Japanese people at a peace conference; but food, inflation, and other economic matters were then far more pressing both on the cabinet and on the people. While the United States government was endeavoring to unify its own policies, the SDP began formulating its views regarding a settlement. It had early decided that Japan should (1) conclude one peace treaty with all its former enemies, (2) maintain neutrality, and (3) neither conclude military pacts with any one country, nor give military bases in Japan to any foreign country. It asked that special consideration be given to Japan because of its constitutional prohibition preventing participation in any sanctions against an aggressor. It is significant that these policies, generally referred to as the "three

---

* Allan B. Cole, George O. Totten, and Cecil H. Uyehara, *Socialist Parties in Postwar Japan* (New Haven, Conn.: Yale University Press, 1966), pp. 33–36.

principles of peace," were initially accepted by both wings of the party.

However, as the provisions of the expected treaty gradually became sharper issues both in Japanese national politics and in the SDP itself, the attitude the party should adopt became intimately linked to the question of party control. The seventh convention in 1951 not only reaffirmed the previously formulated three principles of peace but, at the insistence of the left wing, added a fourth opposing the rearmament of Japan. This faction believed that the United States was considering the peace treaty as only a preliminary step to a security treaty which would require Japan to rearm. They were emotionally, theoretically, and strategically opposed to any rearmament proposals. The right wing, however, forced the left into a lengthy debate on the merits of a separate peace and self-defense treaty. The former's position was, no doubt, strengthened in 1951 by General MacArthur's New Year statement to the Japanese people in which he referred to the inherent right of self-defense. A proposition to endorse that right suffered an overwhelming defeat, however, and was followed by the election of Suzuki as party chairman, although right-wingers were elected secretary-general and treasurer. The CEC was divided into fifteen members for the left wing, ten for the right, and five for the center.

The left-wing position was massively reinforced by its labor union supporters. Sōhyō, the Teacher's Union, the National Railway Workers Union, and others in convention all supported leftist policies. Religious leaders of several faiths, together with Sōhyō and other major national labor unions, formed a National Conference for Furthering the Peace. Initially, it excluded Communists but later was extensively infiltrated by them. The labor union front was by no means unanimous, since the Sōdōmei and moderate factions in certain other unions rather ineffectually opposed the movement's left wing. The Sōdōmei regarded a separate or partial peace treaty as inevitable but was relatively inactive in pressing its case.

In tenaciously sustaining its four principles of peace, the left SDP was conscious of compromises in the name of expediency at the time of the Manchurian Incident twenty years previously. Its leaders felt conscience-bound not to surrender to "reaction," this time in the form of the Western "imperialist" camp. They believed, furthermore, that peaceful coexistence was possible between the opposing communist and free world blocs and that only through general peace could they achieve their program of socialism in Japan. Outright alignment with the West would only jeopardize their position of neutrality. A rearmed nation, they reasoned, would not only offer a pretext for aggression against Japan but could easily involve Japan in highly undesirable foreign wars. Such an armed force would not be a national army but merely a mercenary one which might be used in the suppression of the Japanese working class—a fear not wholly without grounds in the light of historical experience. Left-wing Socialists aimed at achieving "positive" rather than "passive" neutrality, at creating a "third force" in world affairs. They further based their stand on postwar pacifist tendencies among the Japanese people, their revulsion against ultranationalism, and their fear of war in the nuclear age.

The right wing, on the other hand, viewed such policies as idealistic and claimed that, realistically—in the world of power politics—a separate peace was inevitable. So long as Japan sided with the West, strict neutrality was impossible. Communist aggression, direct or indirect, must be countered by some sort of self-defense. . . .

Unable to agree among themselves, they repeatedly procrastinated. In a speech on March 31, 1951, John Foster Dulles revealed the general contents of the proposed peace treaty. On August 15, the final draft was announced. On September 4, the treaty was signed in San Francisco. It had been negotiated, hotly debated in and outside Japan, and then signed, but the Socialists still could not agree on their attitude. From spring into the fall of 1951, when the treaty was ratified by the Diet, they inched painfully toward a decision. . . .

The right wing feared a convention; the left realized it would be defeated in the two highest party committees—the CEC and the Central Committee—where these decisions were being made. The apparently unavoidable eighth special convention was convened on October 23, 1951. The special session of the Diet called to approve the treaties was already in session. After seventeen hours of confusion, the Socialist convention split in two. The main factions continued their separate conventions in Buddhist temples, each claiming to be the "real" party, so they both used exactly the same name. In the Diet, left-wing Socialists voted against the treaties;

the right Socialists voted for the peace treaty and against the security treaty.

❀ THE REARMAMENT of Japan was accentuated by Mac-Arthur at the beginning of the Korean War—ostensibly for defense against potential threats of invasion from the Soviet Union and China. The most important result of the war spending, however, was the boost that was given to the Japanese economy during the war by U.S. procurement purchases. The largest part of this money was spent on arms, and in this way the Korean War gave birth to a new Japanese military-industrial complex. The end of the Korean War and the loss of the special procurement spending forced Japan to decide whether to continue rearming as the Americans wished. The conservative leadership agreed to do this, but not as rapidly as Washington desired.

One result was that while Japan profited from the Korean War and later procurement money spent inside the country, the Japanese government was reluctant to significantly expand the Self-Defense Forces. Tokyo was generally content to accept American protection under the treaty and its continued arms spending for Korea. Yet voices were heard in the 1950s in the United States arguing for Japan's speedy and complete rearming. The speeches excerpted below by Vice President Richard M. Nixon and Assistant Secretary of State Robertson represented a powerful element of official American opinion that favored a policy of remilitarization and argued against the early occupation policy of demilitarizing Japan.

HERBERT P. BIX*
The Security Treaty System and the Japanese Military–Industrial Complex

JAPAN'S PRESENT MILITARY POSTURE

Japan has rearmed and already possesses formidable military strength. A bare listing of facts about her Self-Defense Forces indicates why Japan is now rated sixth or seventh in the world in terms of actual military power.

The Ground Self-Defense Force (GSDF) is expected to have 180,000 men by 1971 with a volunteer reserve of over 30,000. While small, this army has a high proportion of officers and non-coms and could easily be expanded to millions if the constitution were revised and a conscription law enacted. Under the present Third Five Year Plan the GSDF has been equipped with Japanese-made small arms, antitank rockets, and heavy tanks. For anti-aircraft defenses it has automatic, radar-guided, 35 mm. Swiss-designed guns and several battalions of HAWK missiles. Its air support component is also being augmented with sixty Hughes reconnaissance and command helicopters and 106 Japanese-manufactured Bell-Iroquois troop-carrying helicopters.

Japan's Maritime Self-Defense Force (MSDF) is the third most powerful navy in the Pacific after those of the United States and the Soviet Union. According to the latest *Jane's* figures, it has nine diesel-powered submarines, twenty-six destroyers including one guided missile type, sixteen frigates, twenty fast patrol vessels, and 155 assorted support ships, motor torpedo boats, landing ships, and service craft. It also has an air component of 190 fighter aircraft and fifty helicopters. This naval arsenal will soon be beefed up and a naval reserve force started. MSDF contingency planning for the 1970s is said to call for the deployment of ships and aircraft to Singapore "to protect Japanese shipping in the

* Herbert P. Bix, "The Security Treaty System and the Japanese Military–Industrial Complex," *Bulletin of Concerned Asian Scholars* II:2 (January 1970), pp. 30–31, 33–37.

event of serious trouble in Hong Kong." The cruise of a Japanese flotilla squadron through the strategic Malacca Straits, between Malaysia and Sumatra, and its participation in naval maneuvers with Australian and Malaysian warships during the summer of 1969, was probably correctly judged as the "prelude to a future . . . Japanese naval presence in Southeast Asia."

The Air Self-Defense Force (ASDF), with 1530 aircraft, was recently rated by *Air Force* magazine as the most powerful in Asia after the United States and Russia. It has 200 F104Js, 300 F86D and F86F fighters, Nike-Ajax (surface-to-air) missiles, 400 jet trainers, and thirty large Sikorsky helicopters. The Nike-Hercules missiles which she is now manufacturing provide Japan with an option for a missile-type nuclear delivery system. "This, however, will not be the first or only nuclear delivery system that Japan possesses. The Japanese-manufactured EIKO (F104J), presently in service, can carry a nuclear bomb anywhere within a 700-mile radius. . . ." In the 1970s Japan will acquire a third nuclear delivery option as the F4E Phantom, a long-range fighter-bomber capable of carrying nuclear weapons, becomes the mainstay of the ASDF. It is interesting to note that the Japanese government in 1960

> . . . held that the ASDF could not be equipped with any kind of bomber aircraft; later it said that Japan could not possess fighter bombers with long flying range but could have such an aircraft whose cruising range was short; now the ASDF is in the process of acquiring a fighter bomber with a radius of 3700 kilometers. . . .

On the assumption that "offense is the best defense," her officers speak of building a 5000 plane air force, such as Japan had during World War II.

Needless to say, this military capability does not even begin to suggest Japan's economic potential for waging conventional war. That is to be seen in the fact that Japan has the third largest GNP in the world: 145 billion in 1968 and expected to reach from 500 to 800 billion by the end of the seventies. Moreover, it is the second largest steel producer in the world. Economically and militarily Japan is a giant among nations. Compared with two of her hypothetical adversaries—North Korea and China—she is not only a giant but an increasingly ominous threat in her own right. In the late forties and fifties China and North Korea viewed the

American domination of Japan as a serious threat to their own security; today they have good reason to place increasing stress on Japan itself and not just the United States presence there. . . .

THE JAPANESE MILITARY–INDUSTRIAL COMPLEX

Japan's modern defense industry was revived on a small scale as a repair industry for the occupation forces within a few years after the end of World War II. But for practical purposes the origins of the Japanese military–industrial complex can be dated from the start of the Korean War, when General MacArthur reluctantly ordered the illegal rearmament of Japan in the guise of an expansion of the National Police Reserve. At the same time, the American government initiated a "special procurements" program to meet the needs of its Japan-based Eighth Army and Fifth Air Force. Within one year, special procurements income from the construction of bases and the purchase of war materials had started Japan on the road to economic recovery and a more favorable balance of payments.

Two facts about the special procurements program need to be emphasized. One is that it did not end with the Korean War. Between 1951 and 1960, special procurements amounted to over $6 billion, an average of $600 million annually. Even as late as 1958–1959 they were "sufficient to pay for about fourteen percent of [Japanese] imports," an important boon for a country with a chronic balance of payments problem. . . .

The second fact to note about special procurements is that they started Japanese industry toward a military-industrial complex. SCAP had stopped Japanese industrial reparations removals when only 30 percent of designated confiscations had been carried out. Of the untouched plant, as much as 72 percent was directly related to the manufacture of weapons. By January 1951, eight months prior to the end of the occupation and the signing of the first Security Treaty, 80 to 90 percent of Japan's intact, war-related productive capacity was directly engaged in the manufacture of munitions and weapons.

As Japan's involvement in defense production deepened during 1952, conservative forces began to differ over how to meet the economic crisis that was anticipated with the ending of the Korean War. Representatives of the shipbuilding, fishing, and textile industries wanted to reestablish economic and political relations with the Soviet Union and the People's Republic of China. The more influential segments of the ruling class, however, regarded the defense sector even at this early date as crucial to Japan's continued economic growth. They argued that Japan could best weather the decline in Korean War spending by strengthening economic ties with the United States and developing defense production after regaining independence. In response to pressure of this sort, the Japanese government adopted its first postwar rearmament policy on November 10, 1952. Two days later, "as the first formal step toward underwriting Japanese rearmament," the U.S. signed a lend-lease agreement with Japan.

The key agreement of the period of the first American military alliance with Japan was the U.S.–Japan Mutual Defense Assistance Agreement (MDA), signed by the Yoshida government on March 8, 1954, after a year of lengthy negotiating. Yoshida himself, it should be noted, had desired the rearmament of Japan to follow rather than accompany the completion of economic reconstruction, and therefore disagreed with Dulles over the speed at which rearmament should proceed.

On the basis of the MDA, Japan's modern armed forces were organized: laws were enacted setting up the Japan Defense Agency (JDA), equivalent to a ministry of war in all but name, and the Self-Defense Forces; the police system was recentralized to bolster internal security; a Defense Secrets Protection Law was enacted; and other laws were passed to consolidate the defense industry.

. . . [T]he tempo of Japanese rearmament has never proceeded as fast as American policy-makers anticipated or desired. One reason for this has been the effectiveness of the left-led opposition, based on commitment to the principles of the constitution and reflecting the genuine sentiments of a large minority of the Japanese people. Perhaps an even more important reason has been the split within conservative ruling circles over the speed with which rearmament should proceed. The exit of the cantankerous Yoshida at the end of 1954, the bribery scandal involving the Liberal party's secretary-general, Satō Eisaku, and the growing strength of the Socialist opposition, all testified to the conservatives' difficulty with the rearmament question (as well as the problem of creating a stable political climate for business expansion).

Neither Yoshida nor his successor, Hatoyama Ichirō, responded satisfactorily to American pressure for rapid rearmament or were wholeheartedly devoted to American anticommunist planning for Asia. While Hatoyama sought to revise the constitution to expedite a "well-balanced" rearmament program, he also pushed ahead with plans to improve relations with the Soviet Union and the People's Republic of China. On the rearmament question, moreover, "the Hatoyama government insisted that it had to hold its defense budget for fiscal 1956 to $388 million, or only $20 million more than in fiscal 1955." According to Scalapino, the United States "considered this far too low and sought to use various forms of persuasion to get it raised...." When Hatoyama refused to budge, the American government increased its contribution of weapons and materials to the JDA to $150 million for 1957, or "thirteen times the previous amount ... in an effort to spur on Japan."

Hatoyama's diplomacy, consequently, was no more acceptable to the men behind rearmament and "defense production" pressure—which first emerged during the Korean War—than his overall policies were to American policy planners. The former saw the solution to their difficulties in a merger of the two conservative parties. By the end of 1955 the leaders of Japan's monopoly corporations, working through powerful business organizations such as the Federation of Economic Organizations (Keidanren), had succeeded in creating the Liberal Democratic party (LDP). This event marked the clear ascendancy of organized monopoly capitalism over Japanese political life, as well as a trend toward ever closer American–Japanese military and economic cooperation.

Not until the advent of Kishi Nobusuke, "former economic czar of Manchukuo, architect of prewar Japan's New Economic Order, Minister of Trade and Industry and Vice Munitions Minister in the Tōjō Cabinet," did the United States at last find its man in Tokyo. Kishi, an uncompromising anticommunist, was Japan's prime minister from 1957 until after the second military alliance was concluded with the United States in September, 1960. During his tenure, foundations were laid for the growth of a military–industrial complex tightly bound to American defense industry, closer ties with Taiwan, and the Japanese economic advance into Southeast Asia. . . .

RICHARD M. NIXON*
To the Japanese People

And so now the question arises: How does Japan fit into these general principles that I have mentioned? It is a key bastion in the defense of freedom in Asia. If Japan falls under communist domination, all of Asia falls. There is no question about it and from Japan's standpoint, if the rest of Asia falls under communist domination, Japan also will fall under communist domination; and therefore if Japan desires to be free, desires to be independent, it is essential that they work with the free nations in maintaining adequate defenses and adequate strength—strength which will insure that the communist aggression goes no further than it has already gone in this section of the world.

And that, of course, brings me to a second point. I had the opportunity to inspect some of the National Safety Forces here in Japan. They are in every respect excellent forces, well led, well trained, good men from top to bottom. Yet the leaders of those forces would be the first to admit that at the present time they are not adequate to defend Japan against aggression from abroad.

It must be admitted that the primary responsibility for Japan's defense must rest upon Japan and the Japanese people. It is true that there are grave problems. The nation's economic capabilities have been sapped by the war through which it has gone, but it is essential, if Japan is to survive as a free and independent nation, that we recognize frankly that its defense forces must be increased eventually to an adequate level; and I am confident that the people of Japan and the government of Japan are working toward that end, and they can count on the assistance which the United States is able to render in helping Japan to work toward that objective.

There are those who say the United States is taking a very inconsistent position about the rearmament of Japan. They might say: In 1946 who was it that insisted that Japan disarm? It wasn't

* Richard M. Nixon, "To the Japanese People," *Contemporary Japan* XXII:7–9 (1953), pp. 369–371.

the Japanese, although they were willing to embark on that program, but it was at the insistence of the United States that Japan disarmed.

Now if disarmament was right in 1946, why is it wrong in 1953? And if it was right in 1946 and wrong in 1953, why doesn't the United States admit for once that it made a mistake? And I'm going to do something that I think perhaps ought to be done more by people in public life. I'm going to admit right here that the United States did make a mistake in 1946.

We made a mistake because we misjudged the intentions of the Soviet leaders. It was an honest mistake. We believe now as we believed then in the principle of disarmament. We believe in peace; we believe that the nations should be able to live without huge armies and navies and air forces and stock piles and atomic bombs. But on the other hand, we recognize that disarmament under present world conditions by the free nations would inevitably lead to war and, therefore, it is because we want peace and we believe in peace that we ourselves have rearmed since 1946, and that we believe that Japan and other free nations must assume their share of the responsibility of rearming since 1946.

In other words, in 1946, both in the United States, in Japan and in most of the free world, we looked ahead to the future hoping against hope that it would be possible at long last to reduce the armaments of nations to a minimum level. But since that time, the communist threat has gained in power, wars have been begun—witness the one in Korea—and the threat has become so great that as we analyze it today we must change our opinion.

WALTER S. ROBERTSON*
The Need for a Strong Japan

We gave strong encouragement during the occupation to Japan's recovery from the war, advancing about $2 billion to that end. We moved to break up those overconcentrations, or monopolies, of

* U.S., Department of State, *American Foreign Policy 1950–55, Basic Documents* II (Washington, D.C.: Government Printing Office, 1957), pp. 2430–2435.

power—economic, political, and military—that had deprived the Japanese people of their rights and opportunities in the years before the war and had led Japan to disaster. . . .

If I may further condense the statement of our objective in the occupation, I should say that it was to promote the creation of a strong Japan, in the true and best sense of the word. Unfortunately, a cardinal element of strength was left out of our concept. We and our allies, including those who had been occupied by the Japanese army, did that which had come to be normal after total war: We totally disarmed the enemy. In addition, Japan with our encouragement renounced military forces in its constitution. It was not that we wished to leave Japan helpless in the face of deadly danger. On the contrary. We failed to recognize that there was such a danger or to realize what kind of world we were living in and were to live in. We put our faith in the partnership of the United Nations, which had been forged in a war against aggression. We did not discriminate against Japanese safety; we impartially rushed to disarm ourselves as well.

The Japanese are now entirely in command of their country. Our relations with them are those of collaboration between friends and equals. The American troops in Japan are there for the same reason and on the same basis as those in Western Europe—in recognition that the problem of defense against aggression today transcends nationality and does not permit any of us the luxury of living unto himself. As far as we are concerned, nothing in our relations with Japan today reflects the relationship of winner or loser, occupier or occupied. I trust that the great majority of Japanese feel this statement is true. . . .

Some Japanese, as well as some others in the Far East, are opposed to Japanese rearmament because they fear it would mean a recrudescence of the military caste in Japan. I believe they are too much influenced by the past. Just as we were thinking too much in terms of 1941 when we disarmed Japan, so those fearful of Japanese militarism today are, I believe, thinking in terms of May 1932 and February 1936, when vicious attacks were launched on the Japanese civil government by groups of army officers. It seems to us that the conditions of 1954 are distinctly different. The Japanese people are now possessed of the means required to prevent the accumulation of power in the hands of a military caste. They have free elections; they have a representative Diet; they have a free press; they have a constitution in which human rights are firmly embedded; and above all, they have the experience of the past ever before them.

To assume that, because Japan embarked on imperialist adventures in the past, she is likely to do so again is to take a hopeless view of human affairs. However much we may lament it, the fact is that many of the most respected members of the family of nations have yielded to imperialist urges in the past. Militarism, expansionism, aggressiveness are—we must conclude—not endemic with certain nationalities but epidemic under certain economic, social, and political conditions. We should be watchful not of particular races but of particular circumstances that cause nations to act in certain ways.

Japan has, of course, made a beginning in the development of the means to protect herself. In the future increase in the size of the Japanese defense forces, which the Japanese government has recognized is necessary, we have agreed to help by providing major items of land, sea, and air equipment. We may hope the time is not too remote when Japan—in the words of the security treaty of 1951—will be ready "to assume responsibility for its own defense" and we can bring our troops home. . . .

It is, of course, not in food alone that Japan is unable to supply her own needs. Japan is lacking in most of the natural resources required by an industrial nation, particularly coal and iron. These must be also bought from abroad. Japan must sell abroad in increasing amounts, but Japan's exports have been shrinking. Last year Japan's exports and its earnings from its shipping amounted to about $1⅓ billion while its imports stood at over $2⅓ billion. Almost nine-tenths of the difference was made up by U.S. expenditures in Japan incident to the Korean War and the stationing of American troops in Japan. Such expenditures by the United States will not go on indefinitely, however. The plain fact is that Japan is living beyond her earnings from normal sources by about a billion dollars a year. Japan must sell much more abroad. If she is unable to do so we shall be back in 1930—with differences that are apparent to us all.

Trade with Communist China is not the answer. If all restrictions were removed, we believe such trade would only slightly affect Japan's commercial deficit; and to the extent that Japan supplied strategic goods to augment Communist China's war potential—which is what the Chinese Communists want—Japan would be sowing the whirlwind. For above anything else, the Chinese Communists would like to undermine ,or overpower Japan.

It is also not enough to say that Japan can find a natural trading partner in Southeast Asia. Certainly Southeast Asia needs Japanese manufactured goods. It is buying them at the rate of several hundred million dollars a year. This amount could, of course, be increased by devices to tie Southeast Asia's economy to Japan. But these are out of the question. Japan's products must compete for markets on their merits. And other countries—notably Great Britain, France, the Netherlands, and the United States—are also seeking to expand their trade with Southeast Asia.

What then is the answer? Here is what the Japanese tell us. After noting that there are difficult and stubborn internal problems they themselves must solve, they say:

> The Japanese nation . . . can exert very little control over the elements which are shackling her foreign trade. These problems— underdeveloped or unavailable nearby supply sources, unstable export markets, inconvertibility of foreign currencies, tariff and export–import quota limitations—are primarily in the field of international relations and their solution is dependent upon the development of goodwill and cooperation between the sovereign nations of the free world. . . . The United States is the greatest economic power in the world today. Actions taken by the U.S. government, which appear to the average American situated in his powerful economy to be minor and unimportant, may have a tremendous effect upon the economies of other, less stable countries. Therefore, the foreign economic policy of the United States is of worldwide significance. . . .

I think we must admit the force of what the Japanese say. I might add one thing. I would say that what is most required, if the economies of Japan and other nations dependent on a large volume of foreign trade are to be viable, is a continuing rise in the purchasing power of the free world—and particularly, so far as Japan is concerned, in Southeast Asia. This can be accomplished by increasing capital investment and continued technological progress. Removing barriers to international trade will also in itself tend to increase the productivity and hence the purchasing power of the trading nations by encouraging each to produce those things which it can produce most efficiently. At the same time, this increased purchasing power will lead to further international trade.

February 6, 1954

❀ ONE IMPORTANT BYPRODUCT of the heavy American procurement spending in Japan that began during the Korean War, Herbert Bix argues, was the creation of a Japanese military-industrial complex similar to and linked closely with the American one. Increasingly in the late 1950s, Japanese arms manufacturers developed ties with their American counterparts through licensing agreements and through joint ventures to produce American-designed weapons under contract in Japan. Gradually, as the role of military expenditures in the economy increases, Japan is developing her own version of a "locked-in demand" for an armaments economy.

Until the term of Kishi Nobusuke as prime minister, however, Japan's long-term commitment both to continued arms production and to American security aims in the Pacific was somewhat uncertain. Kishi, staunchly pro-American, adopted an unequivocally "positive" policy toward the U.S.–Japan alliance and proved a dependable ally for America in Tokyo. Earlier hints by government leaders of desires for rapprochement with China and the Soviet Union ended with the Kishi cabinet. Moreover, Kishi's unshakable determination to renew the U.S.–Japan security pact in 1960, when it could expire (*see* "Politics, 1952–1960"), accurately demonstrated the commitment of the Japanese government to continued close ties with the United States.

HERBERT P. BIX*
Links with American Corporations

... Several features of the military-industrial nexus that emerged in the sixties under Kishi's successors, Ikeda and Satō, deserve particular attention.

There is a very tight relationship between American and Japanese defense industries. ...

1. Most of the top Japanese defense contractors are tied to the top 100 American defense contractors ... by licensing agreements and joint ventures. General Electric, for example, America's fourth largest manufacturer and its number two defense contractor, has licensing agreements with about sixty-five Japanese companies as well as a ten percent position in Tokyo Shibaura Electric, Japan's number three defense contractor. G.E., interestingly enough, is a frequent sponsor of academic gatherings and "scholarly" publications on Asia which support the Security Treaty system.

2. The major Japanese defense firms presently have a low ratio of defense output to total manufacturing output. But there are indications that this is now changing. Mitsubishi Heavy Industries, Japan's number one defense contractor and its largest manufacturing concern, for example, devotes ten percent of its output to arms and almost thirty percent to motor vehicles. This giant and other leading defense contractors are tending to move into defense production. As competition increases in consumer goods markets with the influx of foreign goods and the liberalization of investment opportunities for foreign firms, many Japanese industrialists are being tempted into the military hardware market where the state is the only buyer and foreign competition is less keen. After its recent tie-up with Chrysler Motors, Mitsubishi Heavy Industries separated out its automotive operations and announced its intention to plunge more heavily into defense production. The president of the number two defense contractor, Mitsubishi Electric Com-

* Herbert P. Bix, "The Security Treaty System and the Japanese Military–Industrial Complex," *Bulletin of Concerned Asian Scholars* II:2 (January 1970), pp. 37–41.

pany, at the time of his appointment as chairman of the Japan Weapons Industry Association in May 1969, stated that he wanted to see Japan's defense expenditures raised to four percent of GNP. The direction these leaders have taken is sure to be followed by the entire defense industry. One can see here how American business and government pressure on Japan for liberalization of investment terms is being met in Japan by increased investment in defense production.

3. In the process of nurturing the Japanese military–industrial complex, the U.S. government has frequently acted as broker for "private" American defense contractors. Thus in 1967 the American ambassador to Japan, U. Alexis Johnson, is alleged to have personally called on the Vice Minister of Foreign Affairs, Ushiba, to ask for the use of G.E. engines in building the TX (*i.e.,* the F4E Phantom fighter) plane. But the more common means of facilitating link-ups between the two military-industrial complexes are governmental bilateral agreements and memoranda, such as the November 1962 Data Exchange Agreement and the June 1968 "Memorandum on Military Research and Development" concluded between the Japan Defense Agency and the Pentagon. The July 1969 U.S.–Japan Aerospace Cooperation Agreement is another example of this kind. Valued by *Business Week* (September 13, 1969) as being worth at least $200 to $300 million to American defense contractors, it paves the way for American aerospace industry assistance in the seventies in the development of Japanese Q and N series launch vehicles—ICBM-type rockets which could be armed with nuclear tips rather than space research satellites. . . .

As the Japanese military–industrial complex enters the stage of self-sustaining growth during the 1970s, it is safe to predict that retention of the security treaty will not be necessary for either side. What is much more difficult to predict is whether a revived Japanese imperialism can remain integrated in the American imperial system. For the present, we should note that the strongest pressure for revision of the antiwar constitution, expanded defense production, liberalization of investment terms, overseas deployment of the defense forces, and strengthening of the security treaty comes from the leaders of heavy industry, finance, trade, and commerce—the class of monopoly capitalists. For reasons of their own there are also a number of Japanese "realist" intellectuals who espouse these same goals. To paraphrase Hobson one might say that imperialism and militarism, while irrational from the standpoint of the Japanese nation as a whole, today seem increasingly rational for certain classes and groups within Japan. . . . Just as there can be no question as to American efforts over the years to spur on Japanese rearmament, so today there can be no question as to the result: the existence in Japan of a locked-in demand for an armaments economy. This stems largely from the fact that the highly sophisticated technology of modern space and weapons systems and the job skills associated with such production are not readily transferable to civilian consumer production. The major steps to creating that demand were the Korean War weapons production boom, the 1951 military alliance with the United States, the 1954 Mutual Defense Agreement, and the decision of the Kishi government to build a modern aerospace industry under the co-production formula (*i.e.,* U.S.–Japanese joint arms production) in 1957. The existence in Japan of a military-industrial complex raises but leaves unanswered the question: Will it go on expanding until it is used?

Treaty of Mutual Cooperation and Security Between Japan and the United States (*January 19, 1960*)

Japan and the United States of America,

Desiring to strengthen the bonds of peace and friendship traditionally existing between them, and to uphold the principles of democracy, individual liberty, and the rule of law,

Desiring further to encourage closer economic cooperation between them and to promote conditions of economic stability and well-being in their countries,

Reaffirming their faith in the purposes and principles of the Charter of the United Nations, and their desire to live in peace with all peoples and all governments,

Recognizing that they have the inherent right of individual or collective self-defense as affirmed in the Charter of the United Nations,

Considering that they have a common concern in the maintenance of international peace and security in the Far East,

Having resolved to conclude a treaty of mutual cooperation and security,

Therefore agree as follows:

ARTICLE I

The Parties undertake, as set forth in the Charter of the United Nations, to settle any international disputes in which they may be involved by peaceful means in such a manner that international peace and security and justice are not endangered and to refrain in their international relations from the threat or use of force against the territorial integrity or political independence of any state, or in any other manner inconsistent with the purposes of the United Nations.

The Parties will endeavor in concert with other peace-loving countries to strengthen the United Nations so that its mission of maintaining international peace and security may be discharged more effectively.

ARTICLE II

The Parties will contribute toward the further development of peaceful and friendly international relations by strengthening their free institutions, by bringing about a better understanding of the principles upon which these institutions are founded, and by promoting conditions of stability and well-being. They will seek to eliminate conflict in their international economic policies and will encourage economic collaboration between them.

ARTICLE III

The Parties, individually and in cooperation with each other, by means of continuous and effective self-help and mutual aid will maintain and develop, subject to their constitutional provisions, their capacities to resist armed attack.

ARTICLE IV

The Parties will consult together from time to time regarding the implementation of this Treaty, and, at the request of either Party, whenever the security of Japan or international peace and security in the Far East is threatened.

ARTICLE V

Each Party recognizes that an armed attack against their Party in the territories under the administration of Japan would be dangerous to its own peace and safety and declares that it would act to meet the common danger in accordance with its constitutional provisions and processes.

Any such armed attack and all measures taken as a result thereof shall be immediately reported to the Security Council of the United Nations in accordance with the provisions of Article 51 of the Charter. Such measures shall be terminated when the Security Council has taken the measures necessary to restore and maintain international peace and security.

ARTICLE VI

For the purpose of contributing to the security of Japan and the maintenance of international peace and security in the Far East, the United States of America is granted the use by its land, air, and naval forces of facilities and areas in Japan.

The use of these facilities and areas as well as the status of United States armed forces in Japan shall be governed by a separate agreement, replacing the Administrative Agreement under Article III of the Security Treaty between Japan and the United States of America, signed at Tokyo on February 28, 1952, as amended, and by such other arrangements as may be agreed upon.

ARTICLE VII

This Treaty does not affect and shall not be interpreted as affecting in any way the rights and obligations of the Parties under the Charter of the United Nations or the responsibility of the United Nations for the maintenance of international peace and security.

ARTICLE VIII

This Treaty shall be ratified by Japan and the United States of America in accordance with their respective constitutional processes and will enter into force on the date on which the instruments of ratification thereof have been exchanged by them in Tokyo.

ARTICLE IX

The Security Treaty between Japan and the United States of America signed at the city of San Francisco on September 8, 1951, shall expire upon the entering into force of this Treaty.

ARTICLE X

This Treaty shall remain in force until in the opinion of the governments of Japan and the United States of America there shall have come into force such United Nations arrangements as will satisfactorily provide for the maintenance of international peace and security in the Japan area.

However, after the Treaty has been in force for ten years, either Party may give notice to the other Party of its intention to terminate the Treaty, in which case the Treaty shall terminate one year after such notice has been given.

❀ THE SECOND DECADE of the Japan–United States security treaty, 1960–1970, witnessed the continuing growth of Japan's economic power and the expansion of the Self-Defense Forces. With the escalation of the Indochina war in the mid-1960s, Japan became the main overseas market for American arms procurements, and the large U.S. military bases in Okinawa and Japan proved vital for the prosecution of the war. As with the Korean War, Japanese businesses profited handsomely from the conflict even though Japan was not itself actively involved in the fighting.

By 1969, however, sentiment inside Japan had built up around the issue of the return of Okinawa, a Japanese island held in trust by the United States since 1945. In addition to the nationalistic appeal of the issue, the island's return to Japan was demanded by groups opposed to the use of bases on Okinawa for support of the American war effort in Indochina.

Prime Minister Satō negotiated the return of this island to Japan (Okinawa came under Japanese sovereignty in 1972) in the Satō–Nixon Communiqué of November 1969. Simultaneously, however, Satō explained that Japan considered her obligations under the security treaty to have become considerably broader than previously acknowledged. For the first time, the Japanese government officially stated that both Taiwan and South Korea were important for Japan's security, and the Japanese prime minister publicly proclaimed the beginning of a "new order" in the Pacific based on the American–Japanese alliance. Satō later downplayed the implications of the communiqué following harsh domestic criticism and a virulent Chinese reaction.

The Satō–Nixon Communiqué now appears to have been the high-water mark for postwar Japanese–American relations. At the time of the communiqué the relationship was apparently as stable as ever, and Satō exuded confidence in both the communiqué itself and in his speech before correspondents in Washington. Opposition to Satō's position was expressed at the time in the Japan Socialist party organ, *Shakai Shimpō,* as well as in the statement of 165 prominent Japanese. Comparable to the widely based American feelings against the Vietnam war, this group provides one of the best expressions of Japanese sentiments on the issues of Okinawa reversion and Japanese complicity in the Indochina war.

PRIME MINISTER SATŌ*
The New Pacific Age

It is the third time that I am addressing you here at the National Press Club. On this occasion, it is my great privilege and pleasure to speak to you about the new development in international politics and the new relationship between Japan and the United

---

* Eisaku Satō, "Prime Minister Heralds the New Pacific Age," *Japan Report* XV:22 (December 1, 1969), pp. 5–8.

States—what can almost be called the New Pacific Age—which has been brought forth by the current talks between President Nixon and myself.

It is hardly necessary to mention that, for Japan, its relations with the United States are much more important than its relations with any other country. At the same time, I am firmly convinced, not only that the relations of mutual friendship and trust with Japan are immensely important for the United States, but also that the maintenance and promotion of such relations of mutual friendship and trust between Japan and the United States are indispensable conditions for the peace and stability of the Asian Pacific region. . . .

The biggest problem in the negotiations between Japan and United States for the return of the islands was nothing more nor less than the role that Okinawa was playing in the maintenance of peace. Japan and the United States agree in their basic recognition of the importance of United States military bases on Okinawa. The peacekeeping function of the bases on Okinawa must continue to be kept effective. However, the fact that our territory, Okinawa, and the one million Japanese who live there have been kept under the administration of the United States since the end of the war has left an unresolved feeling in the hearts of the Japanese people—in other words, it has remained in our thoughts as a symbol of defeat, and this mental block has been exerting a subtle influence on the relations between Japan and the United States. . . .

It is natural that, with the return of Okinawa, Japan should gradually assume the responsibility of the local defense of the islands. Japan's self-defense capabilities are already filling an important role in securing the primary defense of Japan and it is our policy to continue to consolidate such capabilities. For my part, it is my expectation and conviction that the United States, in response to the hopes of the free nations, will continue to maintain its function of deterring war in Asia along the lines of President Nixon's pronouncement at Guam.

In connection with this point, President Nixon and I both reaffirmed our intention firmly to maintain the Japan–United States security treaty. Of course, the first objective of Japan in continuing this treaty is to ensure Japan's own security by filling the gaps in its own capabilities through cooperation with the United States. However, in the real international world it is impossible to adequately maintain the security of Japan without international peace and security of the Far East. This is where the second objective of the Japan–United States security treaty comes to the foreground—the cooperation of Japan and the United States in the form of the use of facilities and areas in Japan by United States forces under Article VI thereof for the security of the Far East in a broader context. And it would be in accord with our national interest for us to determine our response to prior consultation regarding the use of these facilities and areas in the light of the need to maintain the security of the Far East, including Japan.

In particular, if an armed attack against the Republic of Korea were to occur, the security of Japan would be seriously affected. Therefore, should an occasion arise for United States forces in such an eventuality to use facilities and areas within Japan as bases for military combat operations to meet the armed attack, the policy of the government of Japan toward prior consultation would be to decide its position positively and promptly on the basis of the foregoing recognition.

The maintenance of peace in the Taiwan area is also a most important factor for our own security. I believe in this regard that the determination of the United States to uphold her treaty commitments to the Republic of China should be fully appreciated. However, should unfortunately a situation ever occur in which such treaty commitments would actually have to be invoked against an armed attack from the outside, it would be a threat to the peace and security of the Far East including Japan. Therefore, in view of our national interest, we would deal with the situation on the basis of the foregoing recognition, in connection with the fulfillment by the United States of its defense obligations. However, I am glad to say, such a situation cannot be foreseen today.

. . . The national goal that we have to pursue in the 1970s is to cooperate, in nonmilitary fields, with the Asian countries that differ in race, religion and culture, in their efforts to secure prosperity through mutual cooperation while preserving their freedom and independence. Since the United States plays the central role in preserving global peace and also holds great responsibility for the security of Asia, I believe that it is Japan rather than the United States that should take the leading role in such fields as economic and technical assistance toward the nation-building efforts of the Asian countries.

We have already set our goal for the 1970s to make it the decade for Asian development, but Japan alone cannot hope to secure the peace and prosperity of Asia. Along with the efforts of the Asian countries themselves, both the material and moral cooperation of the industrialized countries that have a great interest in this area are required. This is because in the construction of a new Asia, not only the material aspects such as the eradication of poverty, famine, and disease but the attainment by the Asian people of freedom and social justice must also become one of the goals. Here again I find the shape of a New Pacific Age, where a new order will be created by Japan and the United States, two countries tied together by common ideals.

The cooperation between Japan and the United States is not confined to our two countries or just to Asia. As this cooperation is one between the first and second ranking economic powers in the free world, it would extend over a wide range of global problems, such as the easing of general tensions, the strengthening of the function of the United Nations, arms control, and the realization of disarmament, the settlement of the North–South problem, the preservation of the free trade system and the securing of a stable international monetary system. . . .

From this viewpoint, I believe that our two countries should widen the range of policy options in both their bilateral and multilateral relations. It is desirable to maintain a state of affairs where it is always possible to engage in a broad and flexible dialogue.

If Japan and the United States can bring off this kind of cooperation, it is then that the New Pacific Age will become rich in substance. I personally have high expectations and strong belief in the future of this New Pacific Age.

It can be said that the two great nations across the Pacific, of quite different ethnic and historical backgrounds, are on the verge of starting a great historical experiment in working together for a new order in the world, on a dimension that transcends a bilateral alliance. Although this experiment has just begun, I have full faith that this experiment will surely be successful due to the goodwill, mutual trust and efforts of our two nations. I am especially pleased that it was President Nixon and I who set this experiment in motion by bringing about the return of Okinawa.

Satō-Nixon Communiqué*

President Nixon and Prime Minister Satō met in Washington on November 19, 20, and 21 to exchange views on the present international situation and on other matters of mutual interest to the United States and Japan. . . .

The president and the prime minister specifically noted the continuing tension over the Korean peninsula. The prime minister deeply appreciated the peacekeeping efforts of the United Nations in the area and stated that the security of the Republic of Korea was essential to Japan's own security. The president and the prime minister shared the hope that Communist China would adopt a more cooperative and constructive attitude in its external relations. The president referred to the treaty obligations of his country to the Republic of China, which the United States would uphold. The prime minister said that the maintenance of peace and security in the Taiwan area was also a most important factor for the security of Japan. The president described the earnest efforts made by the United States for a peaceful and just settlement of the Vietnam problem. The president and the prime minister expressed the strong hope that the war in Vietnam would be concluded before return of the administration rights over Okinawa to Japan. In this connection they agreed that, should peace in Vietnam not have been realized by the time reversion of Okinawa is scheduled to take place, the two governments would fully consult with each other in the light of the situation at that time so that reversion would be accomplished without affecting the United States' efforts to assure the South Vietnamese people the opportunity to determine their own political future without outside interference. The prime minister stated that Japan was exploring what role she could play in bringing about stability in the Indochina area. . . .

The prime minister emphasized his view that the time had come to respond to the strong desire of the people of Japan, of both the mainland and Okinawa, to have the administrative rights

* *Keesing's,* 1969, p. 23699.

over Okinawa returned to Japan on the basis of the friendly relations between the United States and Japan, and thereby to restore Okinawa to its normal status. The president expressed appreciation of the prime minister's view. The president and the prime minister also recognized the vital role played by U.S. forces in Okinawa in the present situation in the Far East. As a result of their discussion it was agreed that the mutual security interests of the United States and Japan could be accommodated within arrangements for the return of the administrative rights over Okinawa to Japan. They therefore agreed that the two governments would immediately enter into consultations regarding specific arrangements for accomplishing the early reversion of Okinawa without detriment to the security of the Far East including Japan. They further agreed to expedite the consultations with a view to accomplishing the reversion, during 1972, hopefully subject to the conclusion of these specific arrangements with the necessary legislative support. In this connection, the prime minister made clear the intention of his government, following reversion, to assume gradually the responsibility for the immediate defense of Okinawa as part of Japan's defense efforts for her own territories. The president and the prime minister agreed also that the United States would retain under the terms of the Treaty of Mutual Cooperation and Security such military facilities and areas in Okinawa as required in the mutual security of both countries. . . .

The president and the prime minister agreed that, upon return of the administrative rights, the Treaty of Mutual Cooperation and Security and its related arrangements would apply to Okinawa without modification thereof. In this connection, the prime minister affirmed the recognition of his government that the security of Japan could not be adequately maintained without international peace and security in the Far East, and therefore the security of countries in the Far East was a matter of serious concern for Japan. The prime minister was of the view that, in the light of such recognition on the part of the Japanese government, the return of the administrative rights over Okinawa in the manner agreed above should not hinder the effective discharge of the international obligations assumed by the United States for the defense of countries in the Far East including Japan. The president replied that he shared the prime minister's view.

EDITORIAL BOARD, SHAKAI SHIMPŌ, ORGAN OF JAPAN SOCIALIST PARTY*
On the Japan–U.S. Joint Communiqué

DOWNGRADING OF MAINLAND JAPAN
TO THE STATUS OF OKINAWA

The government asserts that as a result of the recent talks with the U.S. government it has succeeded in getting Okinawa returned to mainland Japan in 1972 "free from nuclear weapons" and "in the same status as mainland Japan." However, the Japan–U.S. joint communiqué shows not only that U.S. nuclear weapons will remain on Okinawa and be freely used by the United States even after its reversion to Japan, but also the fact that even the Japan mainland is going to be made a nuclear base for the United States from which it will be able to start military operations freely in exchange for Okinawa's reversion to Japan. . . .

Since the Satō government accepted from the first the U.S. desire to use its military bases on Okinawa freely even after its return to Japan, it was natural that the Japanese side could not carry through its demand to get Okinawa returned "free from nuclear weapons" and "in the same status as mainland Japan," nor did the United States accept such a demand of the Japanese side. . . .

It was the "flexible utilization of the prior consultation system" that was used as a trick to settle this contradiction, though superficially. By this flexible utilization, the U.S. armed forces will be able to start direct military operations not only from Okinawa but also from mainland Japan. Further, the United States will be able to introduce nuclear weapons into Japan. This is not elevating Okinawa to the status of mainland Japan but downgrading mainland Japan to the status of Okinawa.

. . . So far, Okinawa has been called the keystone of U.S. Asian strategy, but in the future, the whole land of Japan will be made the keystone. This is a too high price that the Japanese people will

* Editorial Board, "On the Japan–U.S. Joint Communiqué," *Shakai Shimpō,* 1970, pp. 3–5, 6–9, 14–18.

have to pay for the return of Okinawa, and will leave a grave root of calamity to the Japanese people. We cannot accept the Japan–U.S. joint communiqué which will bring the above mentioned consequences to the Japanese people.

DANGEROUS AIMS OF THE JAPAN–UNITED STATES SUMMIT TALKS

The joint communiqué clearly shows that the Japan–United States summit talks were held to make arrangements on joint Japanese and U.S. plans for the domination of Asia in the 1970s. The main purpose of the talks was to establish a cooperative setup to help the United States which has so far held undivided sway in Asia extricate itself from its military and economic deadlock—as is seen in its decisive defeat in the aggressive war in Vietnam—and to reorganize the anticommunist system of domination in Asia. This is clear from the emphasis laid on Japan–U.S. cooperation in the joint communiqué.

This naturally means that Japan is going to lighten the military and economic burden of the United States from off its shoulders, and it is certain that in the future Japan will take steps to increase its military power, on the one hand, and will move toward increasing its share in the joint defense responsibilities and sending its armed forces abroad, on the other. This is what we call the development of the present Japan–United States security treaty into a treaty covering the whole of Asia and backed by nuclear weapons. . . .

AN ANALYSIS OF THE FAR EASTERN SITUATION

The most important characteristic of the analysis of the Far Eastern situation in the joint communiqué is that the situation is analyzed only from the standpoint of anticommunism and positions of strength and that the keynote of the analysis is military confrontation with China, Korea, Vietnam, and other socialist countries. Nowhere in the joint communiqué is seen the attitude of improving relations with these socialist countries politically and diplomatically or of maintaining the peace of Japan and of Asia through restoration of Japan's diplomatic relations with China and promotion of friendly relations with Korea. The joint communiqué does not point to the easement of tensions or peace in Asia but to military confrontation and tension.

(1) TENSION IN THE KOREAN PENINSULA

The joint communiqué, stressing tension over the Korean peninsula, states that the prime minister stated that the security of the Republic of Korea was essential to Japan's own security.

1. This position is based on the stand of the community of the destinies of both Japan and the Republic of Korea and is very dangerous to Japan. It is unreasonable and dangerous to consider that the destiny of Japan is inseparably related to that of any other country, and the more so, since the Republic of Korea with which Japan's destiny is said to be tied, is no other than the Pak Chung Hi regime whose basic policy is to defeat communism by marching northwards and unify Korea by use of arms. After all, this stand calls for Japan's share in the defense of the Republic of Korea and inclusion of that part of Korea within the area of joint defense under the Japan–United States security treaty. This is also not unrelated to the fact that the so-called arguments of the Liberal Democratic party and the government for "Japan's independent defense" are not intended for Japan's defense but are based on the idea of joint defense between Japan and the Republic of Korea.

(2) STRENGTHENED POLICY OF HOSTILITY TO CHINA

The joint communiqué takes up a dispute in the Taiwan straits, and, though it does not touch upon the menace of China, there is no doubt that the China question, centered on "its nuclear menace," was an important focal point of discussion in analyzing the situation of Asia. . . . Since Taiwan is an integral part of China and since the Taiwan question is an internal affair of China, the fact that Japan openly promised to assume joint responsibility for U.S. domination of Taiwan and to intervene in a dispute militarily constitutes a serious intervention by Japan in the internal affairs of China and means a further escalation of Japan's policy of hostility to China. This will further increase tension between Japan and China and make it more difficult for Japan to restore diplomatic relations with it. . . .

Further, the joint communiqué states that "the prime minister said that the maintenance of peace and security in the Taiwan area was also a most important factor for the security of Japan," and makes clear Japan's stand that it shares its destiny with Taiwan as in its relations with the Republic of Korea and that Japan herself will intervene in a dispute over Taiwan. These facts show that the Japan–U.S. security treaty is linked with the U.S.–ROK and the U.S.–Taiwan mutual defense treaty, with Okinawa as the nodal point, and is integrated with them strategically, and that it opens the way for participation of Japan's self-defense forces in a dispute over Taiwan. . . .

(3) SUPPORT FOR THE VIETNAM WAR AND "RECONSULTATION"

The joint communiqué states that the Japanese side expressed understanding and support for the earnest efforts of the United States for the Vietnam war and that both sides agreed that "should peace in Vietnam not have been realized by the time reversion of Okinawa is scheduled to take place, the two governments would fully consult with each other in the light of the situation at that time so that reversion would be accomplished without affecting the United States efforts." This is an extremely important point.

. . . The joint communiqué says that in case the Vietnam war is continuing in 1972, the return of Okinawa itself may be a subject of discussion of reconsumption [reconsultation]. The fact itself that the return of Okinawa is complicated with the Vietnam war is unjustifiable, while this passage about "reconsultation" leaves a possibility of the return of Okinawa being postponed further to a future date.

DEVELOPMENT OF THE SECURITY TREATY INTO A NEW SECURITY TREATY

The joint communiqué says that "the prime minister and the president agreed that they highly valued the role played by the Treaty of Mutual Cooperation and Security in maintaining the peace and security of the Far East including Japan, and they affirmed the intention of the two governments firmly to maintain the treaty." It says that they further agreed that the two governments should maintain close contact with each other on matters affecting the peace and security of the Far East including Japan, and on the implementation of the Treaty of Mutual Cooperation and Security. This means that Japan and the United States will be jointly responsible for the security of Asia, in contrast to the fact that so far only the United States has been responsible for it and that as a result, the scope of Japan's share in defense responsibilities will be greatly expanded.

The joint communiqué also stresses the principle of "self-help" of Asian countries. The principle of "self-help," that is, the independent efforts of Asian countries to form an anticommunist military alliance, and Japan's leading role in it are the basis of the Asian policy of the Nixon administration. Further, the joint communiqué says that the president assured that, "without prejudice to the position of the United States government with respect to the prior consultation system, the reversion of Okinawa would be carried out. . . ." This passage is of great significance. . . .

FRAUDULENT NATURE OF "RETURN WITHOUT NUCLEAR ARMS"

. . . 1. There is no explicit statement in the joint communiqué about the return of Okinawa "without nuclear weapons." It does not make any mention of the removal of B52s engaged in patrolling flights with hydrogen bombs or of CBW weapons, which are weapons of mass extermination of populations together with nuclear weapons. The U.S. side merely expressed "deep understanding" of the policy of the Japanese government. This confirms the basic policy, followed by the United States, of not permitting any other country to interfere in the questions of nuclear weapons and shows that the U.S. side has a free hand concerning nuclear weapons in Okinawa.

2. The government says that Okinawa will be returned "without nuclear weapons." In the first place, the Japanese side has no right or authority to verify the removal of nuclear weapons from Okinawa. How can the government decide that the nuclear weapons have been removed? The prime minister revealed the truth about this question when he said in his speech at the National Press Club that nuclear weapons could be meaningful only when their whereabouts is not known. At the same time, this statement recognized

the continued presence of nuclear weapons in Okinawa pending its return to Japan.

3. When the government says that Okinawa will be returned "without nuclear weapons," the content and scope of nuclear weapons are not made clear. "Absence of nuclear weapons" means absence, not only of Mace B missiles and land-fixed nuclear weapons, but also of nuclear submarines, nuclear fleets, B52s and all the other sea and air movable nuclear weapons. This must be made clear particularly in the light of the fact that emphasis in nuclear strategy is being switched to the strengthening of movable nuclear weapons.

4. "Absence of nuclear weapons at the time of return" does not guarantee nonintroduction of nuclear weapons after the return of Okinawa to Japan.

Actually, . . . [a] high-ranking U.S. government official said in his explanations on the communiqué that the U.S. side had obtained the conviction that the Japanese government would agree to the introduction of nuclear weapons into Okinawa in time of emergency. The joint communiqué, which represents the understanding of the U.S. government, says that the president assured the prime minister that, "without prejudice to the position of the United States government with respect to the prior consultation system under the Treaty of Mutual Cooperation and Security, the reversion of Okinawa would be carried out." Particularly, since the wording "without prejudice to" means without "loss of already acquired rights" in diplomatic language, it is clear that the United States reserves the right to introduce nuclear weapons into Okinawa. In other words, this means that the Japanese side has promised to reply affirmatively to a United States request to permit introduction of nuclear weapons, and the way has been opened for bringing nuclear weapons into mainland Japan. . . .

TWO DIRECTIONS IN THE BUILDUP OF THE SELF-DEFENSE FORCES

As the joint communiqué clearly shows, the security treaty has entered on its third stage, the stage of an Asian security treaty, the first stage being the conclusion of the first security treaty in 1951 and the second stage its revision in 1960. In this setup, Japan's Self-Defense Forces will build up its fighting strength, on the one hand,

and will point to the direction of overseas dispatch, on the other. These two directions are mutually related and inseparable and will become gradually more marked. Already the government has decided on a defense plan for a period after the return of Okinawa in the name of "independent defense." It has also decided to strengthen conventional armament to a maximum under the fourth defense buildup program starting in 1972 so that Japan may effectively cope with local war, although depending on the United States in nuclear war. In the latter half of the fourth program, it is planned even to arm Japan with nuclear arms. Under these circumstances, it is certain that Japan will start serious efforts to nuclearize herself under the fifth defense buildup program.

As the Japan–United States security treaty is expanded into an Asian security treaty, Japan's Self-Defense Forces will be openly dispatched abroad. Since Japan is to take the place of the U.S. armed forces and to play a leading role in the Japan–United States security treaty, this is a natural conclusion. In future, the Japanese Self-Defense Forces will develop joint military operations with the United States in Asia. This clearly means Japan's revival as an imperialist, militarist state aimed at redomination of Asia. We should never allow Japan to walk the path of aggression again. . . .

The Socialist Party of Japan will thoroughly expose the dangerous intrigues of the joint communiqué in order to turn the "deceptive return" of Okinawa brought about by the Satō government into its genuine return, and will fight with might and main together with the people for the abolition of the security treaty and for immediate, unconditional and complete reversion of Okinawa to mainland Japan.

JAPANESE PROTEST*
Requesting the Demilitarization of Okinawa

The Extraordinary Diet Session, to be convened on October 16, is to decide on Japan's basic attitude on the question of the reversion of Okinawa. We take this occasion, prior to the opening of this

* U.S., Congress, Senate, Committee on Foreign Relations, *Okinawa Reversion Treaty: Hearings on Ex. J. 92–1*, 92d Cong., 1st sess., October 27, 28, and 29, 1971, pp. 105–107.

Diet session, to make clear, as regards this problem of the reversion, our fundamental line of thinking on which we, the undersigned, have agreed, and to submit concrete proposals to the National Diet and to the Satō government.

. . . The government claims that Prime Minister Satō obtained a promise from Washington, at the Japan–United States summit conference in the fall of 1969, that the island chain would be returned to Japan "without nuclear arms and with a status basically similar to that of Japan proper." Yet no confirmation of this pledge had been made at the time of the signing of the reversion agreement in June of this year. Actually, our suspicion is deepened that, through the negotiations, the reentry of nuclear warheads into Okinawa and free sorties by U.S. forces from Okinawa, as well as from Japan proper, might have been acknowledged. The reason that such ambiguity still remains in the government notion as regards the Okinawa reversion is due to its basic posture of seeking a mere "return of administrative rights" over the island chain without changing in any way the premise of maintaining the U.S. military bases there. . . .

Therefore, we hereby request the government to make public in full, at the forthcoming Diet session, the details of negotiations on Okinawa.

. . . As is explicit in the Satō–Nixon joint communiqué issued in Washington in 1969, the Satō government has tried to handle the Okinawa issue on the basis of a philosophy which assumed the continuation of hostile confrontation between United States and China and which bound them to the toeing of the line of Washington's policies. This is nothing more than an extension of the logic of Cold War which has consistently been maintained by the postwar conservative governments in Japan.

Against this policy, it has been our contention . . . that inasmuch as Japan has the responsibility and capability for the easing of tension in Asia—above all, through the reopening of diplomatic relations with China—the government should exert their efforts to the utmost in having Okinawa reverted to Japan as a "keystone of peace" in Asia; and for this reason we did oppose the government notion on the reversion of administrative rights over Okinawa. The clock of history moves, however. And now with an apparent policy switch of the United States, as reflected in the recent United States–China rapprochement, the basic premise of the government conception has been shaken from the bottom, and it is evident that a fundamental rethinking on their part is now called for. This new development provides a golden opportunity for Japan to widen the scope of its own choice as befits an independent nation.

What is the road which we Japanese people should follow at this juncture of history? We are convinced that the best alternative open to us is (a) to bring into effect the demilitarization of Okinawa, that is, to have the United States pledge herself to remove all the military bases from Okinawa, and (b) for the Japanese government to make unequivocably clear that Japan will not deploy any self-defense forces there.

Voices have been gaining ground lately of apprehensions over "the resurgence of Japanese militarism" among the peoples of China, Korea, and other Asian countries. In this context, the complete removal of American bases from Okinawa and the decision not to deploy Japan's own Self-Defense Forces there would be the best way to prove to the peoples of these nations Japan's determination that she neither follow the American Cold War strategy nor allow "the revival of Japanese militarism." . . .

Above all, the demilitarization of Okinawa would be an indispensable condition for the securing of peace and human rights for the people of Okinawa. It is their voice, more than any others', that shall have priority on matters concerning their reversion to Japan.

. . . For them, the basic aspiration intensely expressed in the slogan of "return to mother country" has been none other than this demilitarization of the island chain. The fact that the reversion agreement gives them little prospect of the removal of U.S. bases from Okinawa has caused the people of Okinawa a profound disappointment and distrust in the program of reversion to Japan. Moreover, the projected dispatch of the Self-Defense Forces is giving rise to a stronger resistance than to U.S. forces on the part of the island residents, which is a clear indication as to where their wishes lie. In other words, not only is the idea of demilitarization of Okinawa of great significance from the standpoint of international politics, but, more important, it meets the desires of the people of the Okinawa islands.

For the reasons stated above, we make the following proposals to the National Diet:

(1) The National Diet adopt a resolution proclaiming the

demilitarization of Okinawa, while at the same time (a) requesting the United States to remove her bases from Okinawa as soon as possible after the reversion agreement comes into force, and (b) pledging itself not to deploy the Self-Defense Forces on the Okinawa islands.

(2) The National Diet request the government that the latter shall reopen negotiations with the United States after making necessary amendments to the present text of the reversion agreement in accordance with the resolution under (1) above, and resolve that it will ratify the reversion agreement only after it will satisfy itself with the result of renewed negotiations.

We hereby urge that the National Diet and the government should start taking their actions for the easing of tensions in Asia in the manner befitting an independent nation, and through such actions meet the fervent wishes of the Okinawan people. The essential step to this, we believe, is to carry out immediately the proposals we presented above.

ASUKATA ICHIO,	Mayor of Yokohama
KURODA RYŌICHI,	Governor of Osaka
MINOBE RYŌKICHI,	Governor of Tokyo
NINAGAWA TORAZŌ,	Governor of Kyoto
FUKUTAKE TADASHI,	Tokyo University
IENAGA SABURŌ,	Tokyo University of Education
INOUE TAKESHI,	Kyoto University
MARUYAMA MASAO,	Tokyo University
MATSUMOTO SEICHŌ,	writer
NARAMOTO TATSUYA,	historian
NOMA HIROSHI,	writer
ODA MAKOTO,	writer
ŌE KENZABURŌ,	writer
OSARAGI JIRŌ,	writer
RŌYAMA MICHIO,	Sophia University
SUMIYA MIKIO,	Tokyo University
TŌYAMA SHIGEKI,	Yokohama City University
TSURUMI KAZUKO,	Sophia University
TSURUMI SHUNSUKE,	critic

October 7, 1971.

❀ THE JAPAN–U.S. security pact, implicitly revised by the 1969 Satō–Nixon Communiqué, came due for renewal a second time in 1970. It was widely predicted that there would be violent struggles as in 1960, but the treaty was routinely approved by the Liberal Democratic government. The third decade of the Japanese–American military relationship began with the withdrawal of most American ground troops from Indochina and the economic resurgence of the Japanese economy.

The most important questions regarding Japan's future rearmament revolve around the present level of defense spending and the military's possible future expansion, the problem of civilian control, constitutional legitimacy, and military secrets. Sharp disagreements exist on the significance of the present military budget, and the issue is often discussed in terms of the percentage of Japan's GNP currently spent on defense, as James Weinstein does below. Others, like Albert Axelbank, feel that Japan's present military establishment is already powerful and that increases proposed in Japan's fourth defense plan, even if measured in small increments of the GNP, would result in a Japanese military with significant offensive potential beyond its home islands.

JON HALLIDAY AND GAVAN McCORMACK*
Growth of Japan's Armed Forces

The military budget has consistently been estimated by the most flattering criteria, which have in fact been used to mask the speed of Japan's military growth and, above all, the specific characteris-

---

* Jon Halliday and Gavan McCormack, *Japanese Imperialism Today* (Baltimore, Md.: Penguin Books, 1973), pp. 80–84, 86–87.

tics of the Japanese forces. Before going on to look at Japan's military plans and the question of overseas action and expansionism, these characteristics must be outlined.

First, Japan has attained a degree of self-sufficiency in munitions manufacture which is unparalleled among the Western powers, with the possible exception of the U.S.A. By the end of 1969, Japan was making ninety-seven percent of its own ammunition and eighty-four percent of its aircraft, tanks, guns, naval craft and other military equipment. As of mid-1970 munitions production accounted for twelve percent of all machine-building production.

Japan has fought doggedly to ensure a high degree of self-reliance: during the visits of Laird and Connally to Japan in the latter half of 1971, intense pressure was applied to oblige Tokyo to buy more of its planes in the U.S.A.—both as part of a package to prop up the U.S. dollar, and to enforce Japanese dependence on America. The Japanese Defense Agency and arms industry, headed by Mitsubishi Heavy Industry (MHI), successfully staved off this demand. The new defense budget published in January 1972 shows that Japan is to start building at once twenty supersonic jet trainer-fighters, and to build some 200 over the next five years, even though these could be bought much cheaper in the U.S.A. Likewise, MHI has obtained a license to manufacture the McDonnell-Douglas F4EJ Phantom fighter aircraft (which will replace the F86 over the next few years). . . . The government was able to infiltrate the plane decision into the new budget as part of an overall plan to boost the domestic economy in the wake of the Nixon shocks.

Second, in the important area of technology, Japan is among the leading handful of countries in the world: it was the fourth to launch a space satellite, after only the U.S.A., the U.S.S.R., and France. Research on nuclear energy has been extensive: there has been what one American authority calls "technological preparedness for nuclear developments." In hardware, too, Japan has not exactly been lagging: already by 1967 it had the latest Type-61 tanks, heavy artillery, transport helicopters, F104 supersonic jet fighters, Nike Hercules antiaircraft missiles, and destroyer and destroyer escorts specially equipped for antisubmarine warfare.

Third, all three branches of the forces are heavily over-officered, which means they could be expanded at very short notice by perhaps four to five times; many of these officers, like the NCOs (also a big surplus), are battle-hardened veterans of the Pacific and Asian wars. . . .

Fourth, although Japan's armed forces are not—proportionate to population—on the scale of those of South Korea or Taiwan, they are not inconsiderable: they are already the seventh strongest in the world. They are approaching a point of maximum effectiveness and power, short of a leap to a full-scale offensive nuclear strategy.

The methods by which Western writers have computed the Japanese defense budget have to be criticized. As a percentage of GNP it is true that Japan's expenditure on its armed forces comes out lower than that of Britain or France. But:

> Relating Japanese military expenditures to percentage of GNP has little relevance in a country where annual economic growth rates are over 10 percent. Annual military expenditures have been increasing at a high rate despite a decrease in the percentage of GNP allocated to them. An increase in military expenditures to two percent would provide more money than can rationally be used unless Japan undertakes an ambitious nuclear weapons development program.

The total defense budget for fiscal 1970 came to ¥569,354 million ($1600 million): this was about seven percent of the general account budget, but this was a 17.7 percent increase over the 1969 defense appropriations, and rate of increase, in a moving situation, is the critical criterion. In April 1971 *The Times* correspondent wrote: "The fourth defense program, running from 1972 to 1976, will cost from £6000 million upwards—and the operative word is 'upwards.'"

The new defense budget unveiled in February 1972 ran to ¥802,000 million (about £1 billion)—a 19.6 percent increase over the previous year—*i.e.,* an even faster rate of increase than previously. . . .

Furthermore, the usual method of computing Japan's forces all in one lump is extremely misleading: as far back as 1967, while Japan stood only in twenty-second place as far as ground troops were concerned, it had the seventh strongest navy in the world and the sixth strongest air force:

> The level of defense spending is about seventh in the world, as is Japan's population . . . even the present rate of defense

'spending . . . will make Japan a significant military power. Not, to be sure, in land forces, where the lack of conscription and insular security, combined with the naval weakness of her neighbors, make it unnecessary. But in the more expensive aspects of naval and air armament, Japan's technological superiority and economic potential over her Asian neighbors will give her maximum advantage.

It is obvious that Japan's huge industrial potential makes purely static comparisons unsound.

To resume: to state that Japan has the seventh strongest armed forces in the world is too vague, as it stands. Japan has concentrated on the two key arms—the navy and the air force, in which it has vast technological superiority over all its neighbors, except the U.S.S.R. The armed forces have now grown to the point of *maximum* advantage, and further expansion of the land army is *unnecessary*. . . . All three forces could be expanded very fast, given the high proportion of officers and NCOs; the situation is very similar to that of the German army after Versailles, which was also highly overofficered and readily expandable. The army is highly mechanized for a land force, with one vehicle for every five men (as of 1968).

MARTIN E. WEINSTEIN*
Is Japan Changing Its Defense Policy?

The contention that the Fourth Defense Plan (1972–1976) is going to fundamentally or substantially alter Japan's military status rests largely on the undisputed fact that the plan calls for the doubling of Japan's defense budgets over the next five years. The Third Plan amounted to $7.5 billion, and the Fourth Plan calls for the expenditure of approximately $15 billion. The key word, *doubling,* has been taken to imply that Japan's military strength will be twice as great in 1976 as it was in 1972. More sophisticated analysts have eschewed this obviously oversimplified approach, but many argue that the planned increase in defense

* Martin E. Weinstein, "Is Japan Changing Its Defense Policy?" *Pacific Community* IV:2 (1973), pp. 191–193.

expenditures will significantly strengthen Japan's military capability, at least to the extent that by 1976 the Self-Defense Forces will be prepared to assume full responsibility for Japan's conventional defense.

The simplistic approach is worth examining for two reasons. Firstly, although obviously fallacious, it has the widest currency. Secondly, it raises the question of what the expenditures projected in the Fourth Plan do mean. I would suggest that the following brief table sets these expenditures in a reasonable statistical framework.

	Defense Expenditures in $ billions		Defense Expenditures as Percentage of GNP	
	1971	*1976*	*1971*	*1976*
Japan	1.8	4	0.8	0.9
United States	78.7		8.–	
Soviet Union	55.–		11.–	
China	8.–		10.–	

Japan's security environment is the Asia-Pacific region, and Japanese policy-makers operate in the belief that Japan's military security is a function of its relations with the United States, the Soviet Union, and China. The table indicates that Japan's defense budget in 1971, the last year of the Third Plan, was 2.3 percent of the United States, 3.3 percent of the Soviet, and twenty-two percent of Chinese defense expenditures. The United States, Soviet, and Chinese governments do not publish projected defense expenditures, but it is generally assumed that the American and Soviet budgets will remain relatively stable between now and 1976, while the Chinese defense budget is expected to increase to $11–12 billion.

Assuming that these forecasts are correct, in 1976 Japan's defense budget of $4 billion will be approximately five percent of the United States, seven percent of the Soviet and thirty-five percent of the Chinese expenditures. Thus, even these gross statistics indicate that the Fourth Defense Plan is not going to appreciably alter Japan's military position vis-à-vis the United States and the Soviet Union. And though the Chinese have been most vociferous in denouncing Japanese rearmament and militarism, it is highly unlikely the Tanaka cabinet is entering an arms race with China. If it were, it could equal or surpass the Chinese defense budget by increasing Japan's outlays from one percent to three percent of GNP. Rather, the expected narrowing of the difference between the Japanese and Chinese budgets (moving Japan from twenty-two percent to thirty-five percent of China), simply reflects the anticipated disparity in their economic growth rates, and the stability of budgetary allocations in Japan, where since 1960, defense expenditures have remained at approximately one percent of GNP, and seven to nine percent of the national budget.

Moreover, after examining the procurement schedule of the Fourth Plan, it appears to me that even the modest picture of Japan's improved military position posited in the above analysis is an exaggeration. I would estimate that Japan's relative military position during the period of the Fourth Plan will remain stable, or suffer a slight decline.

Among the principal items scheduled for procurement under the plan are:

Air Self-Defense Forces: 46 F4 Phantoms, 68 FST2 Japanese-designed jet fighters, 2 battalions of Nike ground-to-air missiles;

Maritime Self-Defense Forces: 2 small helicopter carriers (three helicopters each), fourteen destroyer escorts, five conventionally powered submarines, six high speed missile ships;

Ground Self-Defense Forces: 280 medium tanks.

It is these extremely expensive items that account for the bulk of the planned budget increases. It should be kept in mind, however, that these procurements are not pure augmentations to Japan's existing forces. Quite the contrary, the new aircraft, naval vessels and tanks are to a large extent replacements for obsolete F86 jet fighters being phased out of the inventory, and for overage ships and tanks scheduled for scrapping. Also, the doubling of the budget reflects the doubling of the cost of many of these items over the past decade.

Furthermore, apart from the establishment of a small garrison on Okinawa, to symbolize its reversion, the operational range of the Self-Defense Forces is not being extended. In fact, a larger carrier designed to support six helicopters was deleted from the plan and replaced by two smaller ones on the grounds that its greater range offered an unacceptable potential for operations beyond Japan's home waters. As envisaged in the plan, the Maritime Forces will continue to be limited to antisubmarine and minesweeping missions in Japan's coastal waters. The mission and capability of the Air Forces will not extend beyond Japan's territorial air space. The Ground Forces will continue to be responsible for the partial and temporary defense of Hokkaido, and for the maintenance of internal security. Although their manpower authorization may be increased by several thousands, it is unlikely that the actual strength of this volunteer force will increase in the face of the labor shortage in the Japanese economy.

And again, the comparative element must be considered. Because of the Sino-Soviet conflict, the Chinese are expected to push ahead energetically on the buildup of their nuclear missiles as well as their air and naval forces, while the Soviets will probably further reinforce their position in Northeast Asia by deploying additional units from Europe. After taking all these factors into account, I would surmise that in comparison to the probable Soviet and Chinese positions in 1976, the forces Japan is planning to build will be no stronger than they were in 1971. It is quite possible, depending on how far the Soviet redeployment is carried, that in comparison with Soviet naval and air forces, the Japanese will be less well equipped in 1976 than they were in 1971 or in 1966.

It seems to me, therefore, that in its present form the Fourth Defense Plan is the most convincing evidence that Japan is not changing its defense policy.

ALBERT AXELBANK*
Will Japan Rearm?

The main question is whether Japan, in its indomitable quest for equality and a world-leadership role as befits its industrial ranking, will also seek great military power, including nuclear weapons. Denials by Tokyo officials, as well as by various experts on Japan, that the country will ever again become militaristic are not entirely reassuring. . . .

Tokyo has a well-subsidized space program and is doing considerable research in rocketry, missiles, and nuclear energy for peaceful purposes. Japan has already launched a civilian nuclear-

* Albert Axelbank, *Black Star Over Japan: Rising Forces of Militarism* (New York: Hill & Wang, 1972), pp. 4–7, 16–17, 55.

powered vessel. It has joined that select group of nations which has lofted artificial satellites into space. Because of Japan's developments in rocketry, some experts say Japan will have a workable nuclear-weapons delivery system long before its possible possession of nuclear weapons.

The issues of rearmament and nuclear weapons are controversial in Japan and they are being debated with increasing frequency. One question that is often heard is: Can Japan really be independent if it continues to ask another nation to shoulder part of its defense? Under the Treaty of Mutual Security with the United States, Washington has assumed obligations to defend Japan against aggression. Leftists naturally wish to jettison the military alliance with the United States, but a majority of the citizens probably also feel uneasy about it.

Although not so critical of the alliance as the left, the right wing also sees some advantages in reducing or completely eliminating Japan's military dependence on America. The thinking is that the people would probably be more agreeable to a major expansion of the Self-Defense Forces if a big reduction took place in U.S. military bases in Japan. Presently, there are about ninety U.S. installations in Japan, not including Okinawa.

Another question that is often asked is: Should Japan remain under the American nuclear umbrella? An increasing number of Japanese, including many liberals, have begun to doubt the effectiveness of this protection, even though most Japanese citizens view nuclear weapons as anathema.

At the present time, Japan is rearming quietly without going through the politically painful process of amending the pacifist constitution under which rearmament is illegal.

Accompanying this quiet rearmament is the rising defense budget in Japan, which is a very important trend. Japan is now in the midst of its fourth five-year defense buildup plan (1972–1976). The cost of this plan is double the third, which was double the second, which was roughly double the first.

Specifically, the first defense buildup plan cost almost $2 billion; the second cost $3.6 billion; and the third $7 billion. By the time the fourth plan is completed, in 1976, the total cost is likely to be $16 billion, or a minimum of $3 billion each year. Some Japanese military analysts predict the fifth defense buildup plan will run between $25 billion and $30 billion. They also suspect that expenditures for nuclear-arms development may be included in the sixth buildup plan (1982–1986), if not the fifth. In any case, it may be said that Japan's defense budgets are showing a tendency toward boundless growth.

In the early 1970s, Japan's military budget was hovering near one percent of the nation's gross national product. This figure looked as if it would double by the end of the fourth buildup period and perhaps even triple by the close of this decade. The percentage of the GNP for the military seemed small. After all, in the same period (1971–1972) it was tiny compared with the United States (seven percent), Russia (twelve percent), China (8.5 percent), and Britain, France, and West Germany (each near five percent).

But it should be noted that Japan's GNP was the third largest in the world, and it was expected to rise to between $300 billion and $400 billion within six years.

Moreover, the military spending of these other powers, with the exception of West Germany, included large sums for nuclear forces.

Japan's total defense outlay in 1972 was about half of West Germany's. But West Germany had 100,000 more men in its army than Japan. It must also be remembered that West Germany has land boundaries with no fewer than nine countries, including Czechoslovakia and East Germany. By contrast, Japan's borders are absolute: next to them are only deep seas or channels.

Some critics charge that the Japanese defense buildup already goes beyond mere requirements for self-defense. The charge is immeasurably hard to prove. Nevertheless, Japanese government officials have frankly stated that Japan must have enough retaliatory power to strike back at enemy bases if an attack is launched against Japan. Meanwhile, the continuing defense buildup is creating doubt in the minds of some nations that Japan's military may not always remain defensive in character.

In the same vein, various neighboring nations are growing suspicious of Japanese proposals, usually informally made, to dispatch Japanese peacekeeping forces overseas to help other nations in an emergency, or to train military units of other countries that are friendly to Japan.

Japanese military officers say the Self-Defense Forces have seven or eight times the firepower of the defunct Imperial forces at the peak of their fighting excellence, around 1942. This means that individually, the Japanese soldier of today packs from seven to eight times the wallop of his 1942 counterpart. . . .

Nowadays, the most conservative of leaders stress the need to defend the maritime lifeline of Japan which, they claim, passes close to Taiwan and through the Malacca Strait, the strategic channel that connects the South China Sea with the Indian Ocean. This is sometimes referred to as the Malacca Strait Defense Line.

About ninety percent of the oil that feeds Japan's industries is shipped through the Malacca Strait—sometimes Japanese tankers pass through at five-minute intervals—and it is said that if this oil flow were suddenly stopped, the Japanese economy would be stifled within a month. But the fact is that no great power has threatened or is threatening to close the strait. China, if it were so inclined, does not have the warships to do it. In addition, it is apparent that if China or the Soviet Union were at war with Japan, the danger to Japan's industrial sinews would be of much closer proximity than the Malacca Strait. . . .

Interestingly, it was reported in 1972 that although Japan had reasonably offered to help deepen the Malacca Strait in order to permit supertankers to pass without danger, it had "acted so heavy-handedly that it seemed some degree of Japanese control would sneak in the side door." The words are from an April 10, 1972, column in *Newsweek* by William P. Bundy, former U.S. Assistant Secretary of State for Far Eastern Affairs.

There is another Japanese lifeline: the 38th parallel that divides North and South Korea. It is often called the first line of Japanese defense by officers of the Self-Defense Forces as well as military analysts and various politicians. Some of them speak of the "Red Flag at Pusan Theory." This theory maintains that if South Korea is communized, Japan will soon be caught in the same net. Pusan is the major South Korean port city in the southern tip of that country, about 120 miles from Japan. At the time of the greatest advance by the communists during the Korean War, Pusan remained within the small perimeter of land that was not overrun by the enemy.

Are these notions of lifelines perhaps signs of renascent Japanese ambition? Some observers say yes; others explain that it is only natural for a strong nation with massive industrial power to do whatever is required to protect its trade and other interests. . . .

The military buildup plans for the 1970s and 1980s call for emphasis on a big navy. At the present time, however, Japan is already the leading naval power in Asia, excluding the U.S. and Soviet fleets. China says it is forsaking superpower status. But Japan is not. The hawks in the ruling party and within the SDF often state such ideas frankly, if unofficially.

The Defense Agency's goal is a navy of 300,000 to 350,000 tons by 1980, a minimum of thirteen divisions for the ground forces, and an air force of 1200 planes. The one or two helicopter carriers, which will join the Japanese fleet around 1975, are said to be a substitute for a long-smoldering dream within the agency to build a 30,000-ton attack carrier. But some experts say that such an impossible dream may not be impossible for Japan in the years ahead.

At the beginning of 1972, Japan had approximately 130,000 tons of warships, about 920 aircraft, and 180,000 soldiers, in addition to a 36,000-man reserve force. Japan had nearly thirty destroyers, half that many frigates, and ten submarines. Most of these ships were new, built in Japanese shipyards, and some were equipped with the latest conventional missiles. The Defense Agency has plans to add nuclear-driven submarines to the fleet, probably around 1980.

☃ SINCE THE 1969 Satō–Nixon Communiqué, the diplomatic and economic bases for American–Japanese relations have been dramatically transformed. On July 15, 1971, the announcement of President Nixon's trip to Peking, without any prior consultation with Tokyo, proved deeply embarrassing to Satō's government. Then, on August 15, Washington devalued the dollar and unilaterally imposed a ten percent surcharge on foreign imports into the United States, with Japanese goods a principal target. These economic steps followed in the wake of the highly publicized and symbolic clash over textile negotiations, as the Americans sought "voluntary" restrictions on Japanese imports and greater freedom for United States investment in Japan.

Koji Nakamura traces the effects of these diplomatic and economic changes have had on Japanese–American relations. A *Mainichi* interview with Elly R. Caraway, Jr., President of Burlington Industries, the biggest American textile manufacturer, and a member of Nixon's Advisory Council on United States–Japan Economic Relations, discusses the implications of the textile dispute. George Ball, Under-Secretary of State under Lyndon Johnson, warns of the dangers in Nixon's new foreign policy and its consequences for Japan.

KOJI NAKAMURA*
Old Pillars Fallen

Less than two years ago, Japanese Premier Eisaku Satō completed negotiations in Washington for the return of the Ryukyus to Japan. The long aftermath of the defeat seemed over: on his return, Satō proclaimed the dawning of "a new era" in United States–Japan relations. The doubters feared only that Satō had agreed in return to toe the U.S. line in East Asia. And it was assumed this would hamper any positive initiatives toward Peking.

But now it appears that Washington was not the ball-and-chain round Tokyo's ankle it was thought to be—or, if it was, that it was only intended to ensure Washington got to Peking first. Not long ago Chinese premier Chou En-lai reportedly admonished Japanese visitors that it was "presumptuous" for Japan to attempt to build a "bridge" between Washington and Peking. But until last month, Japan believed Washington's pledge of mutual consultation was intended to apply to the China question—and to work both ways.

Neglected, insulted, and apprehensive, Japan finds itself today confronted by a challenge of greater dimensions than any it has faced since August 1945, when it had to accept or reject the Potsdam declaration. And the options are not even clear cut. China's invitation to President Richard Nixon, and his acceptance,

* Koji Nakamura, "Old Pillars Fallen," *Far Eastern Economic Review*, August 7, 1971, pp. 49–50.

open the prospect of a balance of power, global and regional, in which Japan's place could be uncertain and insignificant.

The whole basis of Japan's foreign policy has been upset, less than a year after Expo '70 seemed to put it on the international map and assure recognition of its important position in Southeast Asia's future. Its role as peacemaker between the United States and China . . . appears superfluous if not ridiculous. . . .

Tokyo's reaction to the July 16 announcement was slow and uncertain. Two things were evident: the government's genuine surprise that Peking and Washington could be contemplating détente at this stage, and its anger and sense of betrayal that Washington could, without warning, alter what was supposed to be mutual policy on China in a way which left Japan so conspicuously out in the cold. . . .

Satō's government has largely held that close United States–Japanese cooperation effectively isolated China—and that the China issue could be used by Japan as a lever to strengthen ties with Washington and to promote the importance of its role in Asia. From a conservative angle, confrontation with China actually served Japan's national interests.

The development most calculated to upset this policy has occurred. But observers here point out that Japan has probably always been much more "expendable" than it realized—both for Washington and for Peking. Earlier this year, LDP members who had frequently visited China were already saying: "Once China establishes contact with the United States, Peking can afford completely to ignore Japan." And Washington has not gone out of its way to mollify Tokyo since Nixon's announcement, stating only that "close contacts" would be maintained where "international problems" were concerned.

Three weeks have passed without the government enunciating any very clear policy. Satō and other ministers and officials have made fragmentary reference to Japan's readiness to "accommodate" itself to the new situation, and any enthusiasm for a "two Chinas" policy has vanished. . . . The government recognizes the public desire for drastic adjustments in Sino-Japanese relations. But it has difficulty not only in deciding what tune Washington has called, but even whether it wants to dance to it.

Over Taiwan, it probably wants to be let off the hook. If the

Taiwan delegation walked out of the United Nations, the absurdities of a policy which now claims to desire the seating of both Peking and Taipei yet which does not support "two Chinas" would disappear. And the Taiwan question could begin to create a situation which has never been true of modern Japan: a split between government policy and the activities of big business. While the government assured Chang Chun, senior adviser to Generalissimo Chiang Kai-shek who was attending the ill-timed Taiwan–Japan cooperation committee meeting in Japan at the end of July, of its desire that Taiwan remain in the UN, leading companies announced their decision not to attend the meeting, or the similar occasion annually arranged with South Korea.

This split is not new; it has been growing steadily ever since Chou first laid down his four principles governing trade with China. Japan Airlines, Nippon Steel, and Toyota, three of the firms which gave prominence to their nonattendance of the meetings, had already started cutting down on business with Taipei and Seoul early this year, and pressure on the China issue from business as a whole has been increasingly felt by the government. Satō mistakenly increased the impatience of business circles by announcing in February: "I will not settle the China question during my term of office." Nor, probably, will he, since settlement will be more difficult and his term of office possibly shortened. His reminder in a press conference after the Nixon visit was announced that he had always tried to separate business and politics may have been intended as self-justification. In the circumstances, it sounded more like a forlorn admission of defeat. The failure to decide whether China should be given preferential tariffs as a developing nation was another indication of Satō's reluctance to move more than an inch at a time.

He is still reluctant. While publicly admitting Nixon's visit to Peking would "amount" to recognition, he has hedged round the possibility of Japan recognizing China with the condition that "the problems of the past" must be "understood." . . . More significant, in the extraordinary Diet session which followed Nixon's bombshell, no member raised the question of reappraisal of the pro-Taiwan, anti-Peking guidelines of Japanese foreign policy. Perhaps it was so obvious as not to be necessary; perhaps the silence reflected general uneasiness at the way in which all pillars at once had collapsed.

America's hostility to Peking has been the central pillar—affecting patterns not just of trade and aid but of the whole defense structure. The security treaty between the United States and Japan envisaged Peking as number one public enemy. Now the force of this premise is so greatly weakened, Japan may start looking for a way of loosening its defence ties with America. Either it will draw closer to China, or the arguments of those who feel Japan should develop its own defence capability will be strengthened. The Washington–Peking détente could increase the possibility of a nuclear Japan.

Certainly this would horrify Peking. The United States attitude is less clear. Does Washington want a nuclearized Japan, or would it prefer Tokyo to remain under the American nuclear umbrella? The recent visit to Japan by Defense Secretary Melvin Laird did nothing to quell speculation that the Nixon Doctrine logically would entail reassessment of Japan's overall defense role.

KOJI NAKAMURA*
Straddling the San Clemente Fault

Never since the Pacific War has Japan been so bereft of equilibrium and unwillingly caught up in the changing power structure of the region. Never before have its allies treated it so harshly, or its adversaries appeared so attractive and potentially accommodating in their respective attitudes to Japan.

The national bewilderment created by the sudden exposure has faced Japan today with what could prove to be its most crucial choice in postwar years: should Japan attempt to exploit the new policies of Washington, Peking, and Moscow, trying to turn these to its own advantage; or should it cleave to the old line and attempt to maintain the equilibrium of the status quo? The latter choice would mean continuing to play second fiddle in the orchestration of power as conducted by Washington, with no one any longer sure of which tune the conductor will elect to play. The former choice would inevitably lead Japan into carving out a more

* Koji Nakamura, "Straddling the San Clemente Fault," *Far Eastern Economic Review*, March 4, 1972, pp. 27–28.

independent—and inevitably a more neutralist—role, in regional affairs. It would presuppose not only considerable diplomatic expertise on Japan's part but a new and firm political direction. It would mean a complete departure from all postwar policies, for Japan has not boasted a positive foreign direction of its own since the end of the American occupation.

Despite Nixon's shocks, the temptation for Japan to continue hiding under the American umbrella is considerable, for under this shield Japan has achieved the stability and security it boasts today. But its very economic success apparently has inspired some jealousy in the United States. The result—protectionism—has caused some rethinking in Tokyo about the advantages claimed for the complete identification of Japan's interests with those of the United States.

The last year has thus seen a series of trials and betrayals which have necessitated the basic reappraisal of Japan's foreign policies. The Nixon shocks (the sudden announcement of the visit to Peking, the severe economic measures which led to revaluation of the yen, the imposition of textile quotas and the success in persuading Japan to cosponsor the motion in the UN designed to retain Taiwan's membership) exposed the vulnerability of Japan's hitherto blind faith in Washington. When Nixon touched down in Peking, the Japanese people were rather brutally reminded that the United States (or any other major power for that matter) could ignore the interests of its most faithful ally in order to accommodate its most bitter opponent, if national (or personal electoral) interests so dictated. Japan had placed its trust in the 1969 joint communiqué marking Washington's agreement to return Okinawa to Japan's control. This pledged the two countries to consult fully on policy matters regarding China. To the extent that the trust has been betrayed, intense distrust has replaced it in Japanese breasts.

Following the July announcement of Nixon's intention to fly to Peking, distrust and doubt were multiplied with the announcement a month later of Nixon's economic measures which suspended dollar convertibility and imposed a ten percent surcharge on imports. They were evidently aimed primarily at Japan and naturally they threw the economy into confusion and put enormous pressure on the yen. It was, however, recognized in some circles that Japan could not plead totally innocent to the U.S. charge that it had followed an insular and selfish policy of jealously guarding its own business and industry while successfully penetrating the American market. Japan had not reciprocated the freedom in the U.S. and elsewhere which it has keenly exploited.

The fundamental issue, temporarily overlaid by these two moves, is the changing nature of the United States–Japan security treaty, which has been the lodestar of relations between the two countries. This crucial question has been comparatively neglected. Few in Japan paid attention to a statement, reportedly made either by Nixon or by Henry Kissinger at San Clemente in September 1970, that the security treaty aimed to police Japan against "turning communist or returning to militarism." More recently, James Reston asked Premier Chou En-lai last summer whether he agreed that the security treaty was an effective instrument in curbing any revival of Japanese militarism. Did Reston's question reflect new trends in American thinking about the treaty? . . .

The rationale behind the treaty, conceived twenty years ago as a strongly anticommunist bilateral military arrangement, appears to have changed and may even embrace a concern with Japan's internal political institutions which does not reflect its original intentions.

Why do the Japanese accept with so little question the continuance of an arrangement whereby a foreign military presence remains in Japan although the reasons behind the pact have altered so fundamentally?

From the American point of view, the ideal balance is a Japan strong enough to take over some of its regional defense commitments—but still very much under American control.

If Washington and Peking reach even a tacit agreement on containing Japan, Moscow probably would seek Tokyo's collaboration in its own efforts to maintain its influence in Asia. Hence the importance of Soviet Foreign Minister Andrei Gromyko's visit to Japan late in January, ostensibly to attend the second government-level meeting between the two countries—a meeting disrupted since 1967. The outcome: a pledge that talks will begin this year with a view to laying down terms for a peace treaty; promise of "further economic cooperation" between the two countries; and an invitation to Satō to visit Russia.

The "northern territory" issue will be the crucial aspect of the talks. When relations were resumed in 1956, Japan claimed four islands off Hokkaido which Russia occupied: Habomai, Shikotan, Etorofu and Kunashiri. Russia agreed "to return Habomai and Shikotan to Japan . . . after the conclusion of a peace treaty." Omission of the two Kurile Islands in that statement effectively prevented the opening of talks leading to a peace treaty. If agreement to do so has now been reached, it would seem the impossible has occurred—either the Soviet Union or Japan has given in, or at least indicated readiness to do so.

In promising increased "economic cooperation," Moscow reaches the heart of one of Japan's most acute concerns, which also has long been felt to have a bearing on its sense of security in military terms: the absence of diversified sources of supply of natural resources—above all, sources of energy. Moscow proposed joint development of the vast Tjumeni oilfields of West Siberia, whose output would be carried through 6000 kilometers of pipeline to Nakhodka and shipped to Japan. Tjumeni would, according to this plan, provide fifty million tons a year of crude oil with a low sulphur content for twenty years. The scheme would fit perfectly into Japan's program for diversifying its supplies of oil, currently concentrated in the Middle East which supplies ninety-nine percent of Japan's annual needs.

Substantial supplies from the Soviet Union would greatly improve Japan's position in the international oil market where, although it is the biggest importer of petroleum, it has almost no bargaining power. Such an economic arrangement would also create a counterweight in Japan's dealings with China—which reportedly is deeply concerned by the project, not least because of the boost it will give the Soviet military position in the Far East.

But to take any accord with Russia further, Japan must decide if it is prepared to detach itself from the American foreign policy structure with which it has been so deeply integrated. Japan might choose to embark on a major program of economic collaboration with Russia which would have strong political implications, given its anxiety over future relations with the United States and its uncertainty over China's attitude.

The question is whether this would strengthen Japan's chances of acting as an independent, neutral power; or whether it would be squeezed between three giants and fail to play each off against the other. The answer depends not so much on its economic strength as on its political resolve. The postwar political record is not conducive to optimism on this score; perhaps Satō's successor may strike a more positive note.

ELLY CARAWAY, JR.*
A Textile Executive's View

WORSENING OF RELATIONS UNAVOIDABLE IF JAPAN DOES NOT COOPERATE

CORRESPONDENTS. The meeting of the Joint United States–Japan Committee on Trade and Economic Affairs ended without producing any political or economic results for the United States this year. It is thought that, with this, United States–Japan relations will become still more serious. What do you think?

CARAWAY. The serious thing is the economic situation in the U.S. I do not know whether the Japanese people and the Japanese delegation fully understand this fact, but as far as I can see from reading the newspapers, Japan did not respond to U.S. requests at the Joint Economic Conference. President Nixon asked Japan for an upward revaluation of the yen, liberalization of imports, restricting of exports to the United States and the taking over of foreign aid. Japan was supposed to have been a good friend of the United States. Despite this fact, Japan did not help the U.S. As for Europe, it is criticizing the United States. No country in the world is willing to help the United States. With this, the economic situation in the U.S. will become still more serious, and United States–Japan relations will also worsen unavoidably. ... We are not aiming at shutting out imports from other countries. We are only trying to limit such imports. In the case of textiles, some types of Japanese products are monopolizing forty percent of the U.S. market. Furthermore, they are increasing at a tremendous rate. That is why we are trying to restrict them, by item.

CORRESPONDENTS. Do you mean to freeze the share of the market by imported goods by nation and by item?

* Elly Caraway, Jr., *Mainichi* Interview (American Embassy translation).

CARAWAY. That is exactly correct. The one and only way to settle the problem of injury to the United States from imported goods is the quantitative restriction on imports. For example, imports will be restricted by each country for all countries, such as restrictions by Japan, Taiwan, the ROK, etc. The Long-Term Agreement on Cotton Goods is the prototype for this.

CORRESPONDENTS. Setting aside the question of textiles for the time being, do you not think that the world will enter into a period of trade war if the United States were to restrict the imports of the products of all weak industries in the same way?

CARAWAY. A trade war has already started. The United States has been sitting quietly, in the midst of this situation, with its hands tied behind its back. The time has now come when we should demand the conclusion of government-to-government agreements, not only on textiles, but also on automobiles, iron and steel and electronic machines and instruments. The method for this should be not only the guaranteeing of the export amount in the United States market for a given product of a given nation at a certain base period, for example, 1970, but also the recognizing of a certain amount of increase each year for that product. This should be applied not only to Japan but also to all nations which have lower wages than even Japan, such as the ROK and India.

JAPAN'S ECONOMIC SETUP HAS STRONG COMPETITIVE POWER

CORRESPONDENTS. If your logic is followed, it means that until the wage levels in all nations, including Japan, rise to the same level as in the United States, import restrictions will have to be continued. . . .

CARAWAY. No, even that will not be sufficient. Even if the wage level in Japan were to become the same as that in the United States, Japanese industries will still maintain a position of advantage toward the United States. This stems from the difference in the U.S. and the Japanese economic setups. Japan has a very excellent economic setup, in the form of monopolization, which cannot be imitated by the United States. Therefore, even if the production costs in Japan and the United States were to reach the same level, Japanese products will still have the ability to win when competing with U.S. products in the U.S. market.

CORRESPONDENTS. Why does not the United States then amend its Antimonopoly Act and create a system which is the same as that of Japan?

CARAWAY. That is a very good question. However, there is very little hope for that. The economic setup in the U.S. is moving in a direction exactly the reverse of that in Japan. It attaches strict restrictions on mergers and it also prohibits talks between enterprises on prices.

CORRESPONDENTS. By the way, do you intend to reject the principle of liberal trade?

CARAWAY. I will answer in this way to that question. Is not Japan itself enforcing many import restrictions? Also, all other nations in the world are enforcing import restrictions. Consequently, except for the United States, there did not exist any liberal trade in the world anywhere. I have no intention at all of criticizing the fact that various nations of the world are enforcing import restrictions. What I wish to say is that there is no need for the United States alone to keep its market open.

ADOPTION OF TRADE PROTECTIONISM IS NEEDED

CORRESPONDENTS. Will you be angry if I were to call you a trade protectionist?

CARAWAY. I will gladly take the position of protectionism. That is because American industries are being driven into confusion by imported goods. The United States needs to take a protectionist stand to all nations, including Japan. Frankly speaking, President Nixon's new economic policy proposes protectionist measures toward the U.S. economy. The demand for the upward revaluation of the currencies of other nations and the import surcharge are measures to protect the U.S. economy. This is a very good thing. The meaning of protectionism, in the way I use the term, is to curb the exports of various nations of the world to the United States within a framework which is permissible for the U.S. Even if Japan were to liberalize its imports in exchange for the curbing of exports to the U.S., the results will not amount to much. According to tentative calculations made by experts, U.S. exports to Japan will only increase by 300 or 400 million dollars a year at the most. Rather than that, the more important thing for the U.S. international payments balance is to curb exports to the United States.

GEORGE W. BALL*
Needed: An Asian Policy

With the winding down of the war in Vietnam and the president's announced visit to Peking, we had better devise a long-term Asian policy if we are not to go riding off in all directions.

Obviously, such a policy must take primary account of the two great centers of power in that part of the world. China, with its huge and growing population and vast continental territory, has suddenly emerged from a long night of isolation. Japan, with a stabilized population, industrial competence and commercial vigor, is moving from economic strength to political assertiveness.

Thus, the first step in designing an Asian policy is to answer two key questions: how are relations between those two power centers likely to develop, and what should be the character and objective of our relations with each?

While it is far too early for a conclusive answer to the first question, the most plausible guess is that Japan and China will become competitive to the point of antagonism—caught up in a protracted struggle for dominance in Asia.

WIDE DIFFERENCES

It is not that they lack qualities in common. The peoples of both countries are extremely hard working, gifted, nation centered, and proud—equally disciplined within totally different systems. But in terms of political, economic, and military power they differ widely. Economically, China is laggard, moving at a ponderous pace toward industrialization. Much touted as a potential mass market, it is more likely to take the road toward autarchy than play a

* George W. Ball, "Needed: An Asian Policy," *Newsweek,* August 16, 1971, p. 45.

major role in world trade. Thus, its greatest asset is its vast population of incalculable potential, which exercises a powerful magnetic attraction for the rest of the world.

Japan's assets, less subtle in character, are easier to quantify. With a gross national product two and a half times that of China and with massive investments throughout Asia, Japan is the unchallengeable economic leader. Given its technology and industrial plant, it could become a modern military—even a nuclear—power in a shockingly short time.

Since the contrast is between potential and actual strength, Japan, in the next decade, will have far greater impact for good or evil. It follows then that, though we should develop relations with China within the narrow limits possible, our prime Asian objective should be to strengthen the ties with a Japan not yet solidly anchored to the West.

Today we are not doing that well. To fit the Japanese, with their special structure and history, into the industrialized trading world will require far more steadiness of purpose than is evident in our confusing demands that they liberalize their market while protecting ours. Nor is it a task we should be undertaking by ourselves in an abrasive bilateral context; instead we should enlist the other industrial nations to tackle it in common.

Need for Speed

Unhappily, we must move quickly if we are to halt the souring of relations on both sides, with the administration now openly bitter at the Japanese government's unresponsiveness to its restrictionist textile demands, while the Japanese, caught off guard by our abrupt about-face toward China, are apprehensive of an American withdrawal from Asia that could leave our defense commitments in doubt.

Thus, if we are not careful, we may critically weaken Japan's moorings to the West—particularly if we continue to talk out of both sides of our mouth. Feeling financially put upon, we have been reinforcing Japan's new lack of confidence in us by urging her to carry a greater share of the "defense burden"—or, in other words, to increase her own armed forces. But is that not reckless advice to a nation still uncertain of its own destiny—a nation still haunted by a samurai tradition it has rigorously sought to suppress—just when its manufacturers are quietly agitating for bigger armaments in a society uniquely structured for a military–industrial complex? Is it prudent, after all, for us, who forced Japan to renounce armies and war, to be urging her to rearm before the people are fully ready? For who can foretell what latent forces might be set loose by the very process of remilitarization—to stir old memories, revive old ambitions and deflect Japan from her present serene course? And how unsettling for other Asians still troubled by the nightmare of the rising sun!

❀ WITH ONE of the major justifications for the Japanese–American alliance—the "threat" of the People's Republic of China—no longer so viable, and with capitalist economic competition increasingly replacing partnership, Tokyo's traditional policy had all but collapsed. The resignation of Prime Minister Satō and the election of Tanaka Kakuei were partially in response to growing pressure for normalization of relations between China and Japan which was capped by the new Japanese prime minister's trip to Peking in September 1972. The search for a more independent position abroad for Japan is likely to intensify as further shocks weaken an already unsteady Japanese–American relationship.

Japan's future plans are thus not clear. Japanese–Russian relations have yet to be fully normalized since World War II, and continued United States–Japanese economic rivalry combined with the Washington–Peking diplomatic détente may reinforce efforts by Japan and the Soviet Union to improve their relations. In addition, Japan continues to be interested in developing the oil and gas deposits of Siberia which could help lessen her dependence (ninety percent) on Middle Eastern oil, still significantly under American influence.

INTERNATIONAL INSTITUTE FOR STRATEGIC STUDIES*
Japanese Trading and Investment Patterns

[The year] 1971 was difficult for Japan, in almost all respects. The euphoria of Expo '70 was slowly succeeded by a mood of disillusion and, as the year wore on and one disagreeable international development followed another, profound shock. The year ended with Japan on a more even keel again, but conscious that things were unlikely to be as easy in the future either at home or abroad as they had been in the past decade. . . .

Oil was, for much of the year, an anxiety. The Japanese government was deeply concerned at the new OPEC [Organization of Petroleum Exporting Countries] militancy which, building on the successes already achieved in 1970, led to further very substantial increases in host government "take" and thus in prices for the consumer, as a result of the Teheran oil settlement of February 1971. These events caused Japan—sensitive at the extent of her dependence on oil supplies beyond her control—to build up her oil stocks and undertake a complete reappraisal of her resources-procurement policies. Raw materials are much the most important import of Japan and her level of dependence on overseas supplies is greater than any other country's . . . .

Recent events have shown the political and, possibly, strategic implications of this dependence on overseas sources of supply. The predominantly American ownership of the international oil industry can mean that oil politics become yet another element affecting Japan–United States relations; the initial reaction in Japan to the Teheran settlement was thus (in some quarters) to blame the Americans for the higher costs. On the other hand, Japan is realizing increasingly the possible political implications of assuming direct responsibility for raw material procurement herself. The most notable recent example has been the friction with Australia

* International Institute for Strategic Studies, *Strategic Survey 1971* (London: IISS, 1972), pp. 58–62.

(and others) over Japanese suggestions that, because of lower production rates in Japan in 1971, lower delivery options, or other modifications, should be applied to the mineral supply contracts. It seems doubtful whether it can be politically acceptable for Indonesia to acquiesce indefinitely in a situation whereby three-quarters of her exports, nearly all of them raw materials, go to Japan. . . .

The possible strategic implications of this dependence center on Southeast Asia, partly because almost all Japan's oil at present passes through the Malacca Straits and partly because the area is itself intrinsically so important, not only for its supplies but as a market. Already Japan is concerned at the congestion and shallowness of the Malacca Straits and technical consultations have taken place with the states in the immediate area. Alternatives are not easy to find. The projected pipeline across the Kra Isthmus has not yet been established as feasible and the Lombok Straits, a route further south through Indonesian waters, although deeper, would mean a longer voyage and also include difficult and poorly charted waters. Political stability in the area is clearly of great importance to Japan and her policies, including aid and trade policies, are likely to be framed in such a way as to promote it. But should there not be stability—and should the United States and other outside governments decline to intervene to try to restore it—Japan would be presented with a serious crisis and would have to reappraise its whole posture abroad, political and possibly military. Of the great powers, only Japan has vital interests there.

FOREIGN TRADE PROBLEMS

Apart from the anxiety in the United States about the threat from Japan's economic dynamism, there was a widespread realization elsewhere of the possible effects of what one British politician called the Japanese "time bomb." The shrillest criticisms continued to come from China, which proclaimed that Japanese economic expansion was certain to bring military expansion. European countries were anxious lest Japanese exports, denied the same outlet into the United States, would be diverted into their markets (a sharp rise in steel exports in 1971 had already led to talks and an interindustry limitation agreement). . . .

The growing importance for Japan of trade with the developed world is clearly brought out, the picture in 1955 being broadly reversed by 1970. The excessively favorable balance of trade for Japan with certain Asian countries is notable; if continued unchecked it could lead to frictions. The figures show the reverse of this for the Middle East (because of oil) and indicate the *relatively* unimportant position occupied by mainland China. There was already a deficit of $315 million in Chinese trade with Japan in 1970—and it is unlikely that China could at present supply Japan with much that she needs, such as raw materials, with the possible exception of coking coal. Japan might be ready to import agricultural foodstuffs, for instance pork or beef, if China's production can be expanded and if the strong agricultural protectionist lobby within Japan can be appeased. There are impediments in the way of expansion but both sides are likely to make great efforts to see what each can supply.

Japan–Soviet trade has been marked by steady expansion, rising from $40 million in 1958 to $822 million both ways in 1970, when it constituted nearly half Japan's economic exchanges with communist countries. There has, however, been a persistent and large balance in favor of the Soviet Union, though this showed some sign of correcting itself in 1970. According to a new trade agreement in 1971, trade should nearly double again over the next five years. The economies of Japan and the Soviet Union are in many respects complementary, for Japan has the right location, finance, and skills needed to develop Eastern Siberia and the Soviet Far East, whereas these regions could offer her many of the raw materials she needs (though the distances and the harshness of the terrain and climate should not be underestimated). So far the mutual suspicions which have bedeviled Japan–Soviet political relations and an apparent overestimation by the Soviet Union of the urgency of Japanese needs have prevented development agreements, except for one large forestry project and a scheme for the construction of a new harbor on the Soviet side of the Japan Sea. The potentialities remain, however, very considerable. A Soviet political decision to woo Japan could, if accompanied by generous concessions over the Northern Islands and a more realistic attitude to economic cooperation, inject new elements.

V. SPANDARYAN*
The U.S.S.R. and Japan: Possibilities in Cooperation

Fifteen years ago, in October 1956, an agreement was reached on the normalization of relations between the U.S.S.R. and Japan. The time that has gone by since then has convincingly confirmed that there are a good many possibilities for the development of mutually advantageous cooperation with our Far Eastern neighbor, cooperation that corresponds to the interests not only of both countries but also of the cause of peace in the Pacific basin.

Soviet–Japanese trade doubled in the course of the fulfillment of the first five-year agreement on goods turnover and payments between the U.S.S.R. and Japan in 1966–1970. During this period, the volume of reciprocal deliveries totaled about 2,600,-000,000 rubles. In 1970 our goods turnover with Japan was more than 650,000,000 rubles. This autumn a new five-year trade agreement for 1971–1975 was signed with Tokyo; this agreement envisages a further steady growth in goods turnover between the U.S.S.R. and Japan.

The volume of reciprocal deliveries of goods has expanded substantially. Our exports to Japan consist mainly of types of fuel, raw materials, and industrial materials that are vitally necessary for Japan's economy: coal, petroleum and petroleum products, iron, chromium and manganese ore, potassium salts, asbestos, nickel, aluminum, pig iron, commercial timber, cotton, and other goods. In the past few years exports to Japan of Soviet machinery and equipment have also expanded.

Our imports from Japan are of great importance for our national economy and include various types of machinery and equipment, including complete sets of enterprises for the chemical, pulp-and-paper, food, textile, and machine-building industries, ships, forge and press equipment, machine tools and instruments, as well as such industrial materials as rolled ferrous metal and pipe,

---

* V. Spandaryan, "The U.S.S.R. and Japan: Possibilities in Cooperation," *Pravda*, October 20, 1970, in *The Current Digest of the Soviet Press* XXIII: 42, pp. 41–42.

chemical products, and other goods. In the past few years, there has been a substantial expansion in our purchases of Japanese consumer goods and raw materials for their production: knitwear and clothing, footwear, fabrics, haberdashery, woolen yarn, artificial silk, and synthetic fibers.

Firm ties are developing between Soviet economic organizations and Japanese business circles. The successes in the development of Soviet–Japanese trade are indisputable. But it should be emphasized that the possibilities for the further significant development of comprehensive economic relations between the U.S.S.R. and Japan are still far from exhausted.

The Soviet Union is consistently carrying out a policy of the accelerated development of the productive forces of the country's eastern regions, in particular the economic potential of the Far East. The development of the enormous fuel, power, and raw material wealth and the industrial and agricultural resources of these vast areas of the Soviet Union is of serious national economic importance. At the same time, this can facilitate the development of trade with the countries adjacent to the Pacific basin, including our neighbor Japan.

The most farsighted representatives of Japanese business circles have long appraised the possibilities that will open up for Japan in connection with the successful development of the economy of the U.S.S.R.'s eastern regions both from the standpoint of obtaining large orders for the delivery of Japanese equipment, machinery, and industrial materials and from the standpoint of the expansion of purchases in the U.S.S.R. of types of raw materials and fuel for which Japan has a great need.

The Japanese economy depends on foreign markets to a substantial extent, and for this reason Japan is very much interested in the development of its foreign economic ties. Suffice it to say that in Japan's total consumption of various items imports comprise the following percentages: petroleum, over ninety-nine percent; natural gas, seventy-four percent; coking coal, seventy percent; iron ore, ninety percent; copper ore, eighty-three percent; nickel, 100 percent; lumber, fifty-eight percent; and cotton, 100 percent. We may add that Japan sells a substantial portion of its industrial output in foreign markets.

In the postwar period, Japan's foreign trade has developed almost twice as fast as trade in the capitalist world as a whole.

However, in the past few years Japan has been increasingly running into difficulties in promoting its exports in the markets of the capitalist countries, above all in the market of the U.S.A., which accounts for almost one-third of Japan's foreign trade turnover.

In these conditions, Japanese business and public circles are more and more frequently appealing for a revision of Japan's one-sided foreign economic orientation to take into account the situation that is shaping up in world markets.

The movement in Japanese business and public circles for the further development of trade and economic ties with the Soviet Union is explained by economic necessity and corresponds to Japan's national interests. The Soviet Union, with its steadily developing economy and vast natural resources, especially in the eastern regions of the country, is one of Japan's most promising natural trading partners. This becomes especially obvious against the background of the undoubted successes in the development of Soviet–Japanese trade in recent years, as well as against the background of the continual economic tremors and financial storms that are shaking the capitalist world and undermining Japan's traditional foreign economic ties.

Japanese business and public circles are realizing more and more that for the development of broad economic cooperation with the U.S.S.R. a new approach is necessary, one that would include not only the usual trade exchanges but also a search for a more rational and mutually advantageous utilization of the advantages of the international division of labor and the geographical proximity of our countries, the organization of scientific and technical exchanges and the creation of appropriate credit and financial conditions.

What is involved here is a search for fundamentally new forms of economic interaction and cooperation between two industrially highly developed countries with different social and economic systems.

KOJI NAKAMURA*
Tanaka on Top

Tanaka often has indicated that Japanese participation in Siberian development programs (of which he has been the strongest proponent here) could reduce the "thick American shadow" over Japan. Observers feel Tanaka takes the view, too, that Washington needs a friendly rather than a critical Japan and that this situation could be fully exploited in Japanese relations with Peking—bilaterally or regionally.

The diplomatic strategy which Tanaka is expected to follow in his approach to Peking will also be applied to negotiations later this year to conclude a peace treaty with the Soviet Union. Where the impact of Tokyo's relations with Moscow on the Russo-Chinese and Sino-Japanese positions is concerned, Japanese involvement in Siberian development programs raises a delicate problem. As Satō's minister of international trade and industry, Tanaka was a strong proponent of increased involvement in the development of oil and other resources in Tjumen, Yakut, and Sakhalin; today he is well placed to picture this program's shadow over China.

In particular, the $3000 million Tjumen oil scheme—which involves construction of a 4300-kilometer pipeline—would bring pressure to bear on the sensitive Chinese mind. Running near the Sino-Russian border under paved highways, the pipeline would service the gigantic military complex which Moscow maintains in Vladivostok and other points in the Soviet Far East. If such Japanese involvement in Siberia could serve the current interests of the Soviet Union, there is reason to believe Moscow will forsake two of the Kurile Islands (Etorofu and Kunashiri) within the terms of a peace treaty with Japan.

One complicating factor in Russo-Japanese relations, however, is the recent positive U.S. approach to Russia for participation in

* Koji Nakamura, "Tanaka on Top," *Far Eastern Economic Review,* July 8, 1972, pp. 14–15.

322]   POSTWAR JAPAN: 1945 TO THE PRESENT

the development of Siberia. Apparently both Moscow and Washington believe it is in their interests to prevent an "overgrowth" of the Japanese presence in Siberia. Yet the Japanese presence there could be used effectively in bilateral negotiations with China. Peking might accommodate Japan if, by doing so, it could reduce Japanese tacit support for Moscow in its China policy. But it is possible, too, that a deep Japanese involvement in Siberia could backfire by increasing the extent of China's long distrust of Japan. Tanaka has no easy task.

2. Politics: 1952–1960

❁ THE JAPANESE DIET, whose decisions had real authority once the occupation ended, has been dominated by the conservatives up to the present day. The conservative base of the ruling Liberal Democratic party—the source of the seats they win consistently—is the countryside. Both the delay in some occupation reforms and the reversal of others permitted the conservatives to utilize their prewar organizations while building other organizations relevant to the new rural structures created by the land reform. The key is the *jiban,* the political machine in each district which R. P. Dore describes below.

The *jiban* organization of the Diet member is itself based on local community bosses with their own *jiban.* The description here by Dull is of one such boss, Maeda Shōichi, a real person given a fictitious name. While Maeda may be somewhat extreme *in toto,* his methods of manipulation and the providing of political favors are also techniques employed by Liberal Democratic members of the Diet to maintain their *jiban.* The ability to provide such favors to constituents is a principal explanation for the endurance of the conservative party for more than twenty years.

THE ECONOMIST*
The Japanese Diet Constituency System

The Japanese elect their House of Representatives neither by the single-member constituency, first-past-the-post system the British and Americans use, nor by any of the variations of proportional representation used in other countries. They have, as might be guessed, their own way of doing it. It is a mixture based on multi-member constituencies and nonproportional counting of the votes, and it produces one peculiar complication.

For elections to the House of Representatives, Japan is divided into a number of constituencies, each of which elects three or five members. But each voter in each constituency has only one vote. The parties put up their candidates, and the voter marks his ballot for the man—or, very occasionally, woman—he likes best out of the, say, three Liberal Democrats, two Socialists, one Communist, and one Kōmeitō man on the list. His choice may be guided by the party he wants to support, or by the faction inside that party he prefers, or simply by the candidate who attracts him most personally. The three or five candidates who get the most votes, according to the size of the constituency, are elected.

It sounds fairly easy. The complication it produces is that each party has to guess accurately in advance how many members it can reasonably hope to get elected in that constituency, and to put up that number of candidates. If it puts up three where it really has only enough votes for two seats, its supporters will split their votes between the three and it may end up with only one man elected, or conceivably even none. That is what happened to the Socialists in 1969. If it puts up two candidates where it might have tried three, on the other hand, those two will get in with whopping majorities but it will have thrown away the chance of a third seat. This imposes a double load on the party headquarters: first they must assess their local support very accurately, and then they must get the factions within the party to toe the line.

* "You Have to Get It Right," *The Economist,* March 31, 1973, p. 28.

RICHARD K. BEARDSLEY, JOHN W. HALL, AND ROBERT E. WARD*
Elections

Elections are also complicated by the extremely stringent regulations governing campaign tactics. Practically every aspect of campaigning is rigidly controlled in what is said to be an effort to minimize the advantages of large financial support and to equalize the terms of competition among candidates. Such matters as the following are precisely specified by law: the beginning and duration of the campaigning period; the identity and number of those permitted to campaign in a candidate's behalf; the types and, on radio and television, the number of speeches which a candidate or his supporters may make; the amount of money which may be spent by a candidate or his supporters for campaign purposes; the number, color, size, and distribution of newspaper advertisements, posters, election cards, and other publicity media which any candidate may use; the number of autos, trucks, or other vehicles that may be employed; the type of contacts which campaigners are permitted to make with the public (house-to-house canvasses, for example, are absolutely forbidden).

Under such circumstances the politician's life is not a happy one. Indeed, from the standpoint of practical politics, it would be an almost impossible one, if any substantial amount of attention were paid to these regulations. In practice, they are as freely and widely circumvented as the Hatch Act and similar legislation in this country [the United States]. This is particularly true in respect to political campaign funds. Most candidates will admit quite freely in private conversations that few if any candidates, themselves included, even come close to observing the legal regulations governing maximum expenditures.

* Richard K. Beardsley, John W. Hall, and Robert E. Ward, *Village Japan* (Chicago: University of Chicago Press, 1959), pp. 417–418.

PAUL S. DULL*
Maeda Shōichi—A Japanese Political Boss

Maeda Shōichi was born February 19, 1903, in Hei-ōaza, the second child and eldest son in a family of eight. His father and mother were of common rank (*heimin*). In 1921 his father died and Maeda inherited his father's domicile. He was not married until 1941 and there have been no children from this marriage, although a boy was adopted in 1942. In 1947, Maeda moved to a larger house in Hei-ōaza.

Maeda's schooling was scanty because he was unruly in the classroom and was often a truant. To this day he cannot write his name or count written figures—a lack most unusual in Japan. His personal characteristics do not commend him. He is taller and heavier than the average Japanese and his features are rather coarse. For months on end he wears the same rumpled and dirty Western-style tweed suit, of a loud pattern. Many say that on hot summer days he takes off his clothes in the office and conducts his business in that state. Apparently he is a coward and a bully. He is said to be afraid of drunks and to keep a sword under the mattress (*futon*). Unless he has friends with him he is seldom assertive or loud, but otherwise he is both. In his office and in the town legislature (*chōgikai*), he habitually beats down his opponents by shouting his arguments.

His criminal career started early. He was sentenced in 1921 by the Bo supreme court to one year and two months in the penitentiary for the crime of arson. In 1928, he was sentenced by the Kō district court to seven years in the penitentiary for the crime of illegal entry and burglary. His term was shortened to five years and three months by an Imperial amnesty to criminals. In 1944, he was fined twelve hundred yen by the Kō district court for violating the National Emergency Draft Law. In 1951, he was fined thirty

* Paul S. Dull, "Maeda Shōichi: A Case Study of a Japanese Political Boss," in Robert E. Ward, ed., *Five Studies in Japanese Politics* (Ann Arbor: University of Michigan Press, 1957), pp. 16–20.

thousand yen by the same court for violating the Essential Goods Regulation Law.

After his release from the penitentiary in 1943 he worked his small farm. The closing years of the war, however, brought Maeda his first opportunity to acquire wealth and use it for political ends, when the government rationing of essential commodities began to be enforced. At this time he engaged in black-market operations, gaining a sizable amount of capital. Shortly thereafter he started operating with the Suzuki family: the father, Jun, and two sons, Kaneo and Shige. These men had also been farmers but had branched out into dealing in goods made from *igusa*, a cultivated reed used in the manufacture of the mats which all Japanese have on their floors. Soon after the end of the war, Suzuki Kaneo and Maeda formed the Aison Kōgyō Kaisha, a company ostensibly engaged in making paper yarn, but actually a front for black-market activities. When the company was no longer useful for such purposes, there followed some complicated financial maneuvers, including a large loan from the Chūgoku Bank of Kō City. The firm soon declared itself bankrupt, however, and only half the loan was recovered by the bank. There is little doubt that Maeda himself came out of the transaction with more money than before.

At this time the same group gained control of the Naka-chō branch of the Kō Igusa Goods Cooperative. . . . Suzuki Shige became managing director and Maeda a director. The cooperative was effectively milked and eventually went bankrupt. Although the farmers brought in high-grade *igusa*, this was sold on the black market solely for the profit of the administrators, who then bought cheap *igusa* from which the cooperative made goods which were necessarily of the poorest quality. The farmers were credited only with the profit, if any, from the sale of the cheap goods. These manipulations, of course, contributed to the group's fortunes, but brought Maeda in danger of punishment. Indeed, the procurator wished to bring action against him but could not obtain any complaining witness fearless enough to testify in court.

During the food shortage of the last part of the war and the first postwar years, the cultivation of *igusa* was strictly regulated by the Japanese government in order to prevent farmers from growing this crop on land which could be used for rice. A third scheme of Maeda's was to take over the office of chief inspector of the Igusa

Inspection Committee, a governmental body which regulated the sale of *igusa* goods to keep them off the black market. There is no evidence as to how Maeda became chief inspector; his growing position as a dealer in *igusa* goods may have been a factor. There is no doubt that he used this position to promote his own black-market activities and to charge illegal fees for permitting others' *igusa* goods to be transported. As noted before, Maeda was eventually brought to trial for this extortion and fined a nominal sum of thirty thousand yen. According to the court records in this case, Maeda's gang attacked and beat those whom they caught trying to transport *igusa* goods without his stamp or, at the least, confiscated a good share of the goods before they would permit the rest to be moved. Inasmuch as the intercepted goods were often bound for the black market, the operation was essentially a hi-jacking one.

Out of these often illegal operations Maeda became relatively wealthy. He used his money next to build a political machine that would add to his power in the community. In 1946 he was a candidate for the office of director of the Nōgyō Nōchi Iinkai, a precursor of the present Nōgyō Kyōdō Kumiai (Farmers' Coöperative), but was defeated because of his personal unpopularity. Some of his henchmen, however, were more successful in gaining offices within the organization, and through them he appears to have controlled it until it too went bankrupt as a result of his use of the organization for his own ends. When its successor, the Nōgyō Kyōdō Kumiai, was organized he became a director, and later its managing director. Since that time he has used this cooperative as his primary tool for exercising political control over Naka-chō as well as for increasing his own fortune and that of his friends. Unlike most farmers' cooperatives it is not run for the benefit of farmer members. . . .

Manipulation of credit is carried out by Maeda by several methods. Most of the money available to the farmers' cooperative comes from Maeda, whose investment is some six million yen or eighty percent of the farmers' cooperative's total resources. Control of this group's funds enables Maeda to prevent loans which a farmers' cooperative would normally make. This is a considerable weapon against a farmer whose livelihood may depend on credit and who stands little chance of securing it from a commercial bank. If the farmers' cooperative lends money to an applicant who cannot obtain a loan elsewhere, interest rates are higher than usual. Observation of loan operations bore out the stories that loans were on a day-to-day and individual basis.

A Farm-Forestry Central Bank (Nōrin Chūō Ginkō) was established by the Japanese government to enable farmers to borrow money at 2.6 sen per day and thus buy the tools necessary to increase production. Funds from this governmental bank, however, are available only through village and town agencies. In Naka-chō, the farmers' cooperative withholds this money from its members. When applicants have asked for loans from this fund, Maeda has said that no funds were available, so that they would borrow money from him at a higher rate of interest. The informants did not know if Maeda had drawn Naka-chō's share of funds from the Farm-Forestry Central Bank. They suspected, however, that he had himself arranged for the use of this money at 2.6 sen per day and was then lending it out at 4 sen per day.

If Maeda exploits the farmers' cooperative and farmers' committee for his own profit and to threaten financial ruin for any who may oppose him, he also uses these groups to reward his supporters. They receive the advantage of low rice requisition figures, easy credit, and lower prices for oil and fertilizer. In addition, as chairman of the farmers' committee and head of the farmers' cooperative, Maeda controls employment within both agencies and distributes jobs to his henchmen. Many informants complained that the farmers' cooperative had too many employees, including some twenty clerks. A comparison based on observation of other farmers' cooperatives leads to the estimate that the number of employees of the Naka-chō Farmers' Cooperative was about four times more than normal. Although apparently well aware of practices which add to the expense of the organization and make its cooperative features less attractive, farmer members dare not complain or try to get a change of officers lest their rice requisition quotas be raised and their credit restricted.

Maeda has used the town government in this third technique of gaining profit and exercising control: manipulation of taxes. He first ran for the town legislature in 1947 and was elected. Since then he has controlled it absolutely, and at most sessions he is the only member of the legislature who speaks. In the rare instances when he is opposed, he shouts threats at the top of his voice to prevent any member from complaining of his management of the farmers' cooperative, his vulnerable point. The town mayor (*chō-chō*) is powerless, under the postwar system of local government, for he cannot secure legislation over the opposition of the legislature. The only proposals before this body are Maeda's.

Until the 1952 election the office of mayor was held by a supporter of Maeda. Gathering forces of opposition finally succeeded in defeating this man. However, although the new mayor opposes Maeda, his record shows him to be more anxious to capitalize on whatever power he can capture than to spearhead any reform movement. The tradition of bosses in Naka-chō does not seem to be losing vitality. . . .

There are many men like Maeda Shōichi in both rural and urban Japan. Some have criminal records; most do not. Their techniques of control vary with particular circumstances. Some make use of the institutions of the *oyabun–kobun* (literally, leader–follower); others use the *yakuza* (bullies). In some cases, their rule may result in a benevolent paternalism; in many instances, "bossism" results in a selfish accumulation of power and money at the common man's expense. If one accepts the idea that democracy would be a desirable thing for Japan, as was assumed during the occupation years, political bosses create a disturbing obstacle to its growth.

The so-called democratizing of local government in the Local Autonomy Law lessened the power of the home ministry and of executives in village, town, and city and increased that of local legislative bodies. Such a rearrangement of power did not guarantee a more democratic use of authority, as the case of Maeda illustrates, although the change made it possible for new faces to appear on the political scene. Democratic machinery of government provides no safeguard against bosses if the electorate is not aware of its responsibilities, or its power, and if it even thinks it improper to oppose politicians who are already dominant in the political hierarchy of Japan.

Attempts have been made to place the blame for postwar bossism in Japan on the Liberal party. This thesis seems difficult to support. Local politics seldom reflect the rivalries of the national parties. Bosses tend to ally themselves with the party in power and the Liberal party has been in power most of the time in postwar Japan. Maeda, it will be remembered, was a Socialist during

Katayama's cabinet and easily shifted to the Liberal party when Yoshida came to power again.

If a prognosis must be made for the course of this disease in Japanese politics, it would be that the trouble will remain chronic. It is not particularly susceptible to cure by manipulation of governmental machinery or by a change in parties. It is, in fact, too deeply imbedded in Japan's political mores for much immediate change to be anticipated.

R. P. DORE*
Rural Conservatism

To be elected, a candidate must have a *jiban*—literally a "ground base," but better translated a "machine"—which is just such an organized network of personal contacts designed to bring favorable personal influences to the maximum number of individual voters. The methods of nursing constituencies familiar to most democratic societies are carefully used. The candidate appears as often as possible at public gatherings in the constituency, or at least (since there are many large constituencies electing four or five members) that part of it which he chooses to cultivate. He seeks the presidency of local societies, makes sure that he heads as many subscription lists as possible, is kind and courteous to visitors from the constituency in Tokyo and may even entertain them lavishly. But a good *jiban* is something more. It is a network of personal acquaintanceship with large numbers of prominent persons in the villages each of whom is in a position to influence a larger number of votes personally himself.

Sometimes there may be some formal organization to make this easier. Particularly at, and just before, election time, numerous XY support societies spring up in the villages, formed by a few of the "powerful men" in each hamlet who are sympathetic to XY. A meeting is held in a local restaurant. Each member may pay a fee of 100 yen and get food and drink to the value of 200 or 300 yen

* R. P. Dore, *Land Reform in Japan* (New York: Oxford University Press, 1959), pp. 414–418, 419.

(the difference being made up, illegally, by the candidate). The sake flows and an enjoyable time is had. A member of the prefectural council who is a follower of the candidate and uses the same network of personal relations to secure his own election will probably be there, and take every opportunity to extol the candidate's qualities and detail the particular benefits he proposes to secure for the district. The candidate himself arrives and thanks them formally for their support. He joins in informal conversation with as many as possible, and tells off-the-record anecdotes of prominent politicians ("Of course, X was really after the foreign office") which give his hearers a glowing sense of "inside dope" contact with the great. The "powerful men" go back to their hamlet honored, grateful, and loyal. They may directly solicit the votes of neighbors, employees, or those dependent on them; even if they do not, the glowing accounts they give of their favorite at informal hamlet meetings can sway a good many votes. Even the mere word, spread around the village, that so-and-so, the mayor, the cooperative president, a respected "powerful man," "is for XY" may influence the votes of their admirers.

Connections built up in this way are sedulously maintained between elections. Local "powerful men" who are key figures in such a *jiban* can expect particularly careful hospitality when they go up to Tokyo, they can expect help in getting their sons into good jobs, they can be sure of getting New Year and midsummer cards from their member and picture postcards from foreign countries. . . .

All candidates try to build up a *jiban* of this sort. Conservative politicians are more successful than Socialists partly because they generally have more money to spend on entertainment and the like, but to a far greater extent because, hitherto forming the government party, they are able to promise tangible benefits to their constituents. . . . [A] large proportion of central government expenditure—thirty-one percent in 1956—is devoted to grants and subsidies made for specific purposes to local authorities, or sometimes, through local authorities and cooperatives, to individuals. Of this money the major proportion goes to rural areas, and the existence of this system is a powerful electoral weapon in the hands of government candidates.

In the making of these grants a large area of discretionary choice exists, and a member of the Diet is in a good position to exert pressure on the competent officials to see that his constituents benefit. When a new Diet is elected there is never any lack of volunteers for the standing committees for agriculture, transport, communications, education, etc., which command a high proportion of these funds. Large numbers of private members' bills are presented (they may contain financial provisions) to establish new types of subsidy which will be of particular benefit to the proposer's own constituency, and members of the government party combine to "log-roll" them through the Diet. The importance of these mechanisms to the politician is clear in the conflict which annually arises at budget-making time. The finance ministry, with the support of the industrial world, has for some years been running a campaign to reduce such expenditure, partly on general anti-inflationary grounds, partly on the grounds that the administration of these grants is costly, sometimes dishonest, and often productive of insufficient economic returns to justify the cost. The last-ditch defense of the grant-giving ministries has had the active and ultimately telling support of large numbers of the rank and file of government-party members. Some reduction has been made, from forty percent of the national budget in 1953 to thirty-one percent in 1956, but not as much as the advocates of retrenchment have demanded.

At election meetings and in written election addresses, sitting members frequently point to their achievements in the past. "I made them build a proper concrete school." "I proposed the law to give dairy farmers a subsidy for improving grass land." "I secured priority for the widening of the prefectural road." Even more important are promises of future benefits. The "powerful man" who comes back to the hamlet from the XY support society meeting with the news that XY has promised to get the village a subsidy for installing improved rice seed-beds is a much more useful supporter than one who does not.

Moreover, these devices enable conservative politicians to use existing rural organizations in their interest. A large number of these grants are channeled through village authorities and cooperatives. A promise may be personally made to a village mayor or cooperative leader, or at private district meetings of such officials. The mayor or the cooperative leader passes the word around that he is supporting X because he has promised to get the village such and such subsidy or to propose such and such a law, and indicates that the village's interest requires that as many votes as possible should go to X—not simply to ensure his election, but even more to demonstrate the village's support and so make it difficult for him to go back on his promise. In some districts with large irrigation networks depending on frequently flooding rivers in need of constant government-financed riparian works, the irrigation union is a particularly important channel for such influence. By these means Diet members and local officials mutually strengthen each other's position. The Diet member gets his votes, and the mayor, the cooperative president or the chairman of the Irrigation Union Committee has his ability to pull strings at the center to recommend him for relection.

The rural *jiban* is often spoken of as "feudal," a network of hierarchical relationships through which votes are mobilized by personal loyalties. Such many of them undoubtedly have been— the Inukai family's iron *jiban* in Okayama, from which Inukai Ki used to boast that he could be elected without spending a penny, is a famous example. But increasingly they are becoming the framework for purely calculating contractual relations of the sort described above. Opposition members can use them to a certain extent, insofar as they become members of the relevant standing committees, but their influence is small compared with that of politicians of the prospective government party. Not, then, until it is touch and go between the Liberal Democrats and the Socialists as to which will form the next majority will the Liberal Democrats lose this particular important advantage.

❀ AS THE OCCUPATION drew near its close in the early 1950s, General Matthew Ridgway, MacArthur's successor as Supreme Commander, granted the Japanese government the right to consider changing occupation reforms. The resulting moves accentuated the so-called "reverse course" and caused alarm to the opposition parties. Yet, divided after the peace treaty–security pact dispute, the right and left Socialist parties were frequently far apart on theory and strategy for dealing with such controversial laws as the Subversive Activities Prevention Bill, reminiscent of repressive prewar legislation. Only after the Korean War ended, crystalizing the issue of Japanese dependence on the United States, did the two wings of the party cooperate more successfully.

COLE, TOTTEN, AND UYEHARA*
Socialist Schism

Factionally and organizationally divided, the Socialists faced the new era of national independence in April 1952 with uncertainty. International events and domestic politics at times deepened the gulf and intensified the competition between the two main factions and then forcibly brought them closer together. The possibility of a conservative merger and recognition that, divided, the Socialists could never achieve a parliamentary majority slowly induced rapprochement....

The divided Socialists fought their first important legislative battle against the conservative government's Subversive Activities Prevention Bill—the first major measure proposed after the end of occupation controls. Although the ostensible aim of the bill was to curb Communist activities, Socialists in both main factions and labor unions unanimously opposed it. They were motivated not by compassion for Communists but by a deep-seated distrust of a revived political police. The left wing in Japan is not likely to forget its experiences under the notorious Peace Preservation Law, the interpretation of which had been extended to include all opposition groups. The Socialists labeled the new bill a postwar edition of the former hated law, merely clothed in democratic terminology. Despite their serious numerical handicap in the Diet (forty-eight out of 466 in the House of Representatives), the Socialists carried out a vigorous and partially successful campaign to embarrass the government and to force revisions of the bill. All left-wing elements opposed the measure, but there was considerable differ-

* Allan B. Cole, George O. Totten, and Cecil H. Uyehara, *Socialist Parties Postwar Japan* (New Haven, Conn.: Yale University Press, 1966), pp. 37–38, 40–43.

ence in the degree of their intensity. Possibly because more left than right Socialists had suffered under the prewar thought police, and also because the campaign against the bill served as a convenient rallying point for lukewarm Socialists, the left SDP and Sōhyō organized several waves of strikes (not all of them effective) and even threatened resort to a general strike. The right SDP and its supporting unions, while opposed to the antisubversive law, criticized the use of the strike as a political weapon. They warned against the possibility of JCP infiltration and accused the government of forcing the Socialists and their allies into taking such drastic measures. These were the most determined and coordinated opposition tactics since 1945. The controversial law was enacted but only after seventy-nine days of intermittent strikes, delaying parliamentary tactics, detailed interpellations, and a disastrous Communist-inspired May Day riot which greatly reinforced the government's rationale. Opposition to the bill not only illustrated essential differences between left and right Socialists in political strategy and tactics but also emphasized the continuing lack of confidence and common ground between the majority conservatives and the Socialists. The severity of this confrontation has been only slightly mitigated with the passage of years and has erupted into violence over several subsequent issues.

The Socialists were encouraged in their bid for leadership of the opposition when the right Socialist candidate in a Tokyo by-election in March 1952 was elected. Since this area was within right Socialist "territory," the left SDP had probably not intended to elect its candidate; but his electoral support was more than double that predicted by public opinion polls, suggesting the influence of supporting labor unions, particularly of Sōhyō. This marked the early resumption of effective results from close cooperation between left Socialists and labor unions and was a harbinger of Socialist revival.

Soon after this election, the peace treaty came into effect, and Japan regained exercise of its sovereignty. After having been premier since the fall of the Ashida cabinet in 1948, and having successfully guided Japan through the last years of a humiliating occupation, Shigeru Yoshida was expected to retire from political life. Instead, he dissolved the special session of the Diet in August 1952, even before it had convened, and called for elections on October 1. He hoped thereby to minimize the growing challenge to his authority resulting from the return of many prominent victims of the purge, notably Hatoyama, who had been purged in 1946 just before he was to have become premier; Yoshida then had become Liberal party president and prime minister. A reorganized second conservative party, the Progressives, had also been formed in February 1952, headed by Mamoru Shigemitsu, also previously purged.

The right Socialists campaigned for revision of the two treaties and the abolition of the administrative agreement implementing the U.S.–Japan Security Pact, for a planned economy, a stable balance of payments, and the use of foreign exchange accumulated from the Korean War boom to rebuild industry and to raise living standards. The left Socialists called for a struggle against Japan's "subordinate" position stemming from the two treaties. They opposed rearmament and the "reverse course," urged neutrality independent of both the free world and the communist camp, and rejected any joint struggle offers from the Communists. Sōhyō gave these policies unqualified support.

The electoral judgment was harsh on the Liberals, who barely maintained their majority. From 285 returned in 1949, they were reduced to 240 seats. The Progressive party obtained only 85. The Communists were totally unsuccessful; their leaders were mostly underground or in exile and their association with violent tactics in the public mind did them no good. It is estimated that many of their votes shifted to the left Socialists, who made the most spectacular advances—from a mere sixteen seats, when the SDP had split a year previously, to fifty-four seats and three and a half million votes, or 9.9 percent of the total. The right SDP increased its representation from thirty seats at the time of the schism to fifty-seven elected by four million votes, which comprised 11.4 percent of the total. An unstable political situation was thus created. The conservatives were not only divided into two parties but the separatist Hatoyama faction in the Liberal party held the balance. This indication of the popular will convinced the Socialists, especially the left SDP, that their arguments were valid and that they should intensify their opposition. The Socialists maintained their respective election policy committees in full operation. Another characteristic of this election was the large number of depurgees returned to the Diet. Out of 466 members, 140 were in this category. Only sixteen were members of the SDP—thirteen of them, including

Chairman Jōtarō Kawakami, being in the right SDP. This trend reinforced Socialist contentions that the domestic danger was not coming from Communists but from ultranationalists and that it was the mission of the SDP to correct the "reverse course."

This term became popular after General Ridgway, on May 1, 1951, announced that the Japanese government might reconsider occupation-sponsored laws and institutions. Premier Yoshida promptly formed a committee for this purpose. The conservatives were only too eager to "rectify" key democratization policies which they considered not to be in line with Japanese realities and traditions. They tried to classify all elementary- and high-school teachers as public officials to prevent strikes and political activities and to centralize controls. The Liberal government wanted particularly to curb the political effectiveness of the powerful Japan Teachers' Union which supported the Socialists. The attempt to increase and strengthen the control of the national police over rural and municipal police forces caused Socialists to risk the use of violence in the chambers of the Diet. Efforts were made to revive control over the press and other media of information. Abolition of the public election of prefectural governors in favor of centralized appointment (as in prewar years) was seriously considered. A law for registration of the citizenry was also passed. The conservatives wanted to enact tighter controls over the labor movement, reinstate the legal sanctions of the old family system, and above all revise the antirearmament constitution. After repeatedly overcoming stiff Socialist resistance, they scored numerous successes in their "reverse course" policies despite much factional bickering.

The administrative agreement was signed by the Japanese and American governments just before the peace and security treaties went into effect. It stipulated that Japan would provide military bases for United States security forces. The Socialists claimed that the agreement was unconstitutional, and they appealed unsuccessfully to the Japanese Supreme Court. The agreement proved to be closely linked to the Japanese national budget as it provided for annual Japanese defense contributions—an aspect of the agreement that later embarrassed the Japanese conservatives and the United States government. Japan's police reserve, created soon after the Korean War started, was to become a "peace preservation force"—another proof, in Socialist eyes, of the trend toward remilitarization.

The right SDP demanded that the stabilization of the national livelihood should come before any rearmament. Both wings insisted that military expenditures be eliminated from the national budget. The left was more drastic in proposed budgetary pruning. When, in the spring of 1953, the Japanese and American governments moved to extend United States military bases, as provided in the administrative agreement, the left Socialists, Sōhyō-affiliated labor unions, and the local populace organized intensive resistance movements. The best known of these were directed against new bases at Uchinada (Ishikawa prefecture), Asama (Nagano), and Myōgi (Gumma). On-the-spot demonstrations were coordinated with political opposition in the Diet. Socialist doggedness and insistence that the availability of military bases for a foreign power on Japanese soil only fostered world tension was encouraged by a growing anti-American feeling among the Japanese people and by the changing international situation.

❀ WHEN THE JAPANESE regained control over their own domestic affairs, the police decentralization reform was one of the first items to be reconsidered. Writing in the mid-fifties, Sugai analyzes the government efforts to recentralize the police, and the rationalizations given by conservative leaders. They spoke of the dangerous international situation and of the need for domestic order, but Sugai argues that in fact they represented the old prewar mentality of bureaucratic control. Opposition forces fought the changes strongly, fearing precisely the old thought-control style.

SHŪICHI SUGAI*
The Japanese Police System

Decentralization of the reorganized police system, it was claimed, had resulted in inefficiency, or weakening, of the overall police strength, alienating government and police, impeding coordination and cooperation, and fostering mutual distrust and jealousy among the different units. In addition there had developed increased expenses, corruption of municipal police units, obstacles to the exchange of personnel among different units, and so forth. These defects were not beyond amelioration by a voluntary cooperation of the different police units. But there was a suspicion that the necessary remedial measures along this line would be half-hearted at best—if they were not deliberately sabotaged—to create an excuse for reorganizing, recentralizing, and by some means restoring the old police system.

In the meantime, the international situation changed rapidly for the worse. Already in 1949 a bolstering of the Japanese police by an armed police force was reported to be under consideration in Washington, D.C. Then in June 1950 fighting broke out in Korea, and a month later the National Police Reserve of 75,000 men was hurriedly established to fill the gap left by the occupation forces being mobilized for the Korean front. This new force was to be under the prime minister's personal control, entirely separate from the ordinary police and free from interference by any public safety commission. It was to be equipped with American weapons, including mortars and machine guns, clothed in American-type uniforms, and drilled in army fashion. This seemed at first glance to solve the problem of strengthening the present Japanese police system, but later developments made it clear that further changes were desired.

In April 1951, General MacArthur was relieved of the office of Supreme Commander for the Allied Powers. On May 2, 1951, his

* Shūichi Sugai, "The Japanese Police System," in Robert E. Ward, ed., *Five Studies in Japanese Politics* (Ann Arbor: University of Michigan Press, 1957), pp. 7–11.

successor, General Matthew B. Ridgway, announced the policy of relaxing occupation control. For the Japanese government, this was a signal for revising the Police Law. In June of that year an amendment of the Police Law was submitted and passed through the Diet, authorizing smaller communities having their own municipal police units to decide by referendum whether they wished a merger with the National Rural Police. The first wave of referenda held between June and September of 1951 showed that nearly eighty percent of the total number of communities concerned, or 1028 towns and villages, favored the abolition of their own police forces and the surrender of their jurisdiction to the National Rural Police. The National Rural Police, by absorbing such municipal police forces, which totaled more than 13,000 men, considerably increased both its jurisdictional area and its numerical strength. Such referenda were repeated every year thereafter.

The next steps toward a return to the prewar police system were to abolish the remaining municipal forces, then bring about their absorption into National Rural Police, thus finally accomplishing a recentralization. The government and the National Rural Police were waiting only for an opportunity to take such steps. . . .

In line with the new policies adopted by General Ridgway, the Japanese government set up the Ordinance Review Advisory Committee which was to reexamine the ordinances and laws introduced at the behest of the occupation forces and report on the desirability of continuing their existence. In July 1951 this committee expressed its views in respect to the abolition of municipal police forces and their absorption into the National Rural Police and suggested that *all* agencies with police functions be unified under a ministry of public safety. . . .

In February 1953, the National Diet received a bill to revise the Police Law and to establish under a minister of state a national police board within the central government, which would relegate the National Public Safety Commission to the status of an advisory agency. In addition it was proposed to establish prefectural police forces, the chiefs of which were to be appointed by the chief of the National Police Board, which would supersede the National Rural Police and Municipal Police forces. Cities of more than 500,000 population, however, were to be allowed to retain their own police units. This bill was not passed by the Diet, because the National Rural Police and prefectures would not agree to the continuance of autonomous police units in these major cities, and because the weight of the Progressive party and the Socialists was opposed to the government at that time on a budgetary issue.

In January 1954, a new and more successful bill to revise the Police Law was submitted to the Lower House of the National Diet. This time the Progressives were more cooperative with the government; the National Rural Police and prefectures also approved this bill, because the municipal police forces were to be abolished altogether. The new bill provided that the National Public Safety Commission, headed by a minister of state, was to be the superior organ instead of the National Police Board as in the 1953 bill. The police board itself came *under* the said commission. The prime minister was to appoint the chief of the National Police Board with the advice (and not necessarily the consent) of the commission. Among other functions the National Police Board was to handle nationally important matters, such as major disasters and riots.

Further provisions of the bill called for the National Rural Police and municipal police forces to be abolished and replaced by prefectural police forces. The chief of the Tokyo-to police was to be appointed by the prime minister with the advice of the National Public Safety Commission. The chiefs of other prefectural police forces were to be appointed by the chief of the National Police Board with the advice of the National Public Safety Commission. The chiefs of the prefectural police forces were to appoint the personnel of their forces with the consent of the prefectural Public Safety Commission. With the exception of salaries to those police officers above the rank of superintendent, who were to be national rather than local officials, the expenses of the prefectural police were to be defrayed by prefectures, using local taxes and national subsidies. Communication, criminal identification, material equipment, and expenses for any other operations conducted on a national scale were to be financed by the national treasury.

The most controversial points in the new bill were the appointment of key officers by the prime minister and by the chief of the National Police Board, and the abolition of the police forces of the five major cities. In the Lower House, the bill was amended to conciliate the Progressives and the five big cities. The Progressives consented to the amended bill under the erroneous impression that since the current session was nearly over the Upper House would take no action, and the bill would be killed.

The amendments of the bill introduced two major changes: (1) The chief of the National Police Board should be appointed by the National Public Safety Commission with the approval of the prime minister. The chief of the Tokyo-to police should be appointed by the National Public Safety Commission with the consent of the Tokyo-to Public Safety Commission and the approval of the prime minister. The chiefs of prefectural police should be appointed by the National Public Safety Commission with the consent of the prefectural Public Safety Commission. This amendment meant that the National Public Safety Commission was restored to its former position instead of being demoted to an advisory agency. (2) The abolition of the police forces of major cities was so controverted between prefectures *pro,* and the five big cities *contra,* that a dilatory compromise, which was not a compromise at all, was offered, to the effect that the inactivation of the five municipal police forces should be put off for one year, or until July 1955.

The period of session of the National Diet was to expire on May 22, although the more important bills, including the revision of the Police Law, had not yet been acted upon by the Upper House. There the Socialists were bitterly opposed to the revision of the Police Law on three counts. They foresaw that the chairmanship of a minister of state in the National Public Safety Commission could be used as a bridgehead for a move to put the police under political influence. Further, they recognized the antidemocratic tendency of the bill, and, last but not least, they resisted the intended abolition of municipal police forces. Meanwhile the period of session had necessarily been extended again and again between May 22 and June 3.

On the night of June 3–4, the Socialist Diet members, pushed to the extreme, staged a riot to prevent the chairman of the Lower House from entering the assembly. A few minutes past the midnight deadline, still outside the doors of the meeting room, the chairman had to declare the resolution to extend the period two more days, the fourth of such resolutions. Feelings were running so high by this time that two hundred policemen had to be summoned to bring belated order to the House. Subsequently, the Socialists claimed the extension to be legally null and void and absented themselves when a fifth extension of the period finally resulted in a vote. On June 8, with no Socialist members present, the revision of the Police Law was passed by the conservative members of the House of Councilors.

The government's justification of the revision was stated in the Diet by Minister of Justice Inukai. In part, his statement reads:

The present Police Law which was enacted as one of the more important of the occupation policies, was, no doubt, an epoch-making and important legislation, reforming from the ground up the prewar Japanese police system and putting emphasis on the ideals of democratic police. However, being enacted in a hurry, reflecting the then-prevailing "international circumstances" [this is a Japanese euphemism for the occupation—S. S.], it had many points which were not suitable to our national circumstances and was not free from defects which in actual practice produced inefficiency and bad economy. It had been widely recognized from the beginning that sooner or later, a thoroughgoing revision would be necessary in order to cure and correct such errors and defects. That is to say, the present police system is dual, consisting of National Rural Police and City, Town and Village Autonomous Police units. The National Rural Police governing towns and villages has too much the character of national police without local autonomy of any kind, while the municipal police governing cities has, on the other hand, too great a measure of complete autonomy, lacking the character of national police. The consequence of this dualism is that there are police systems of different types in existence in cities on one hand and in towns and villages on the other, and that this dual system has some features which are not suitable to the operation of modern police functions, which should naturally combine both national and local characteristics. Furthermore, the City, Town and Village Autonomous Police, being organized and operated independently in each city, town, or village—despite the fact that functional areas of public safety are rapidly becoming broader and broader —the responsibility is divided among many units under this multiple police system and their organic coordination is obstructed to a considerable extent. Of course, in the past years, efforts were made to establish friendly relationships and to smooth mutual contact and coordination among different police units by personnel exchange and agreements of cooperation; but such finesse in maneuvering had limitations in view of the defects inherent in the structure itself, and the existence of blind spots, caused by the multiple division into different police units, has been hampering an efficient operation of the police. In addition to this, the fact that such shortcomings had a pernicious influence in terms of clearcut responsibility for national public safety is still fresh in the nation's memory from various "incidents" which have happened frequently in these years. On the other hand, from the point of view of a desirable reform in public administration and finance, the duplication of facilities and personnel of the National Rural Police and Municipal Police has unnecessarily introduced greater complexity and increased the economical burden, and consequently the necessity for fundamental reorganization is now being recognized in current public opinion. . . .

When, and if, this revision comes into force, it is expected that by a simplification of structure, 30,000 men in police personnel and nine billion yen in police expenses will be saved. . . .

This explanation enumerates the alleged defects of the 1947 police system and may be considered to epitomize the criticisms from the Japanese government's side, even to constitute an official epitaph to the occupation-sponsored policies on the police system. Actually it remains doubtful whether any sincere efforts had been made within the given framework to cure the defects which were not certainly incurable. It is also interesting to note that the official explanation implies that the 1954 system of prefectural police units constitutes a synthesis of the former two extremes of National Rural Police and Municipal Police. It was one of the issues raised when the new police bill was in debate in the National Diet—that is, whether the prefectural police units were nearer in nature to the Municipal Police or to the National Rural Police.

The National Public Safety Commission and the National Police Board are the national superstructures over the entire prefectural police forces and are purely national agencies in character. The National Public Safety Commission consists of a chairman, who is a minister of state appointed by the prime minister, and five commissioners who are themselves appointed by the prime minister with the consent of the two houses of the National Diet. The chairman convokes the commission, and votes only in case of a tie among the commissioners, whose quorum is three. While the commissioners have a guarantee of tenure, the minister of state as chairman holds the office during the prime minister's pleasure. The commission appoints the chief of the police board with the approval of the prime minister. The National Public Safety Commission in addition to national matters handles certain local affairs, such as major disasters and riots, which may be of national significance. That these agencies were regular national organs was beyond dispute, and the issue raised in the National Diet concerned for the most part the ambiguous nature of the prefectural police units.

The character of the new prefectural police forces is undoubtedly that of a nationalized police: (1) The chiefs of the prefectural police forces are, along with high police officers of those forces, national government officials, and the power of their appointment rests with the National Public Safety Commission, although the consent of the prefectural Public Safety Commission is required. (2) Theoretically the prefectural Public Safety Commission has the power of operational control over the prefectural police units, but control over the chief of the prefectural police is by nature one of general supervision and is only advisory, if not illusory, in view of past experience. (3) All of the more important police functions are regulated by national statutes, and very little is left to the initiative of the prefectural Public Safety Commissions. (4) The salaries, allowances, and like expenditures of police personnel are all governed by standards established by the central authorities; the prefectural assemblies have little to say about such disbursements although these expenses are defrayed by the prefectures themselves. (5) The authorized number of police personnel, their distribution in terms of the differentiation of ranks, the organization of police headquarters, the arrangement and location of police stations, etc., are all regulated by the standards established by the central authorities; here again the prefectures make only minor decisions. (6) One motive behind the 1954 reform was the desire to eliminate the weaknesses inherent in the municipal police systems forced upon Japan by the occupation. (7) The long-standing tradition of the national police system, which had been very effective since early Meiji, is still a very strong influence in the present approaches to the problem of police organization.

❖ ALTHOUGH THE OCCUPATION officially dissolved the old ownership patterns of the family-dominated corporations, large business concerns continued to exist; in fact, they had already recovered much of their preeminence in politics by the end of the occupation. They consolidated ownership under the Dodge Plan of economic austerity and profited from the relaxation of the Antimonopoly Law at the close of the occupation. Looking into the future, their basic concern was preservation of the status quo: a favorable and stable, hence predictable, environment; and, by the mid-fifties, the corporations were once again able to gain acceptance of their views by bureaucrats and politicians. They favored continued conservative rule but were ready to dispose of a conservative prime minister if he seemed unreliable in any way. Their greatest fear was a Diet majority of Socialist and Communist members, and to this end they supported a unified conservative party, what is now the ruling Liberal–Democratic party.

CHITOSHI YANAGA*
Big Business in Japanese Politics

QUEST FOR POLITICAL STABILITY

Among the expressed goals of organized business, political stability is assigned a very high priority. Indeed, it is near the very top of the list of objectives. As far as big business is concerned, political stability is achievable only under a strong conservative government, which alone can provide the optimal conditions under which business can prosper. The government must be equal to the task of preventing the reformist forces, namely, the labor unions and the Socialist and Communist parties, from gaining strength and upsetting the political status quo.

On June 8, 1954, the four economic organizations issued a joint statement, roundly berating the Diet for its outrageous behavior, which, they believed, had not only invited the distrust of the public but also caused loss of face abroad. Lamenting the adverse effects of such behavior on Japan's incessant efforts to improve her international payments position, it appealed to the political parties to

* Chitoshi Yanaga, *Big Business in Japanese Politics* (New Haven, Conn.: Yale University Press, 1968), pp. 68–70, 148–151.

do their utmost to rise above party interests and strategy in order to correct the situation.

Ever since the 1920s, big business and the conservative parties have looked upon the reformist parties as their deadly antagonists, bent on subverting the existing order. Their fear has been greatly intensified by the postwar emergence of the Communist party as a legitimate political organization under the Allied military occupation. In the Konoe memorial, which advocated the ending of the Pacific War, Prince Konoe, who had served as prime minister before the war, stressed that Japan's defeat in itself was not really a matter of grave concern. What was far more dangerous than defeat was the communist revolution that might accompany the defeat.

Most businessmen have viewed the fluctuations in the political fortunes of the conservative party with apprehension because of the heavy dependence of major business and industrial enterprises on government support and financing. It is clear that *zaikai*'s [large business interests] attitude does not make allowance for the fact that a degree of political instability is practically unavoidable, especially in times of rapid economic changes. Moreover, business itself contributes to some extent to this instability.

The only kind of political stability envisaged by the Japanese business community is predicated on maintaining the conservative party in power. The ruling conservative party must command no less than a two-thirds majority in the House of Representatives. It must be able to preserve the existing system, both political and economic, and to circumvent the efforts of the reformist parties to take over. With this in mind, *zaikai* furnished the powerful thrust which brought about the merger of the two conservative parties (the Liberal party and the Democratic party) in November 1955 into the present Liberal Democratic party. *Zaikai* was convinced that only a unified conservative party could effectively hold in check the growing power of the Socialists, who had won 156 seats in the House of Representatives. . . .

THE UNMAKING OF GOVERNMENTS

In Japan the power of organized business brings down a government when it concludes that the prime minister has outlived his usefulness and become a definite liability. Once organized business withdraws its support, the collapse of a government follows. There is no way it can be prevented against the will of the business community. Yoshida, Hatoyama, and Kishi all had no recourse except to yield to the irresistible pressure of organized business.

Prime Minister Yoshida, who came to power under the most fortuitous circumstances, was hesitant, almost reluctant, to accept the post offered him, but, by adroitly utilizing the power of the Allied military occupation, he succeeded in building a formidable power structure.... He counterbalanced the influence of the professional politicians by bringing in former bureaucrats to form a tight cadre of faithful followers and protégés. He carried out political purges with the backing of the occupation and at times exploited rivalries between factions within the party to strengthen his own position.

Once he was firmly entrenched, Yoshida doggedly refused to relinquish his post in spite of opposition from the public and organized business to his methods and policies. His arbitrary exercise of power, his refusal to heed advice, and self-righteous attitude—reinforced by his unusually strong elitist sense—had generated acrimonious attacks against him, yet he stubbornly refused to admit that he was no longer useful or wanted. *Zaikai*'s power prevailed in the end and he reluctantly resigned. *Zaikai* merely withdrew what it had given in the first place.

In spite of the support of organized business, the Hatoyama government, which followed the Yoshida government, lacked the strength necessary to cope with political problems from the very beginning. In the election of February 1955, which he himself called, Hatoyama failed to win a majority. Organized business was so disappointed that it became more determined than ever to push the merger of the two conservative parties. The merger, however, which came in November, failed to bring about the hoped for improvement in the political situation. By the late summer of 1956, organized business found the situation intolerable and for all intents and purposes made up its mind that a change of government was needed.

The prestigious *Asahi Shimbun,* on September 5, stated that both *zaikai* and political circles were agreed on the desirability of Hatoyama's retirement from the premiership. At a secret meeting of more than seventy *zaikai* leaders, held at the Tokyo Kaikan, a decision was made to demand the immediate restoration of a stable political situation by the Hatoyama government. *Zaikai* was convinced that the prime minister had reached his limits both physically and mentally. FEO [Federation of Economic Organizations] President Ishizaka bluntly stated that the "affairs of state cannot be entrusted to an invalid." On September 6, Ishizaka and Japan Chamber of Commerce and Industry President Fujiyama met with Liberal Democratic party Secretary-General Kishi, Executive Board Chairman Ishii, and Policy Committee Chairman Mizuta and presented what amounted to *zaikai*'s demand for the resignation of the Hatoyama government.

Meanwhile, the Hatoyama government's negotiations with the Soviet Union, which had been in progress for some time, bore fruit. In October the Soviet–Japan Joint Declaration was signed, restoring diplomatic relations between the two countries. Ishizaka, Kobayashi, and Sakurada had been opposed to the Hatoyama government's efforts in this direction and used the issue to demand the retirement of the prime minister. *Zaikai* regarded the government's Soviet policy as a clear deviation from, if not an actual violation of, established conservative party policy. This, rather than the prime minister's illness, was the real reason for *zaikai*'s demanding Hatoyama's resignation. *Zaikai* also viewed with considerable apprehension what it regarded as the high-handed and sometimes reckless methods used by Kōno, Premier Hatoyama's right-hand man, in getting things done.

At a news conference on November 2, Premier Hatoyama disclosed his intention to retire. In December he stepped down. Despite competition from Kishi and Ishii, Hatoyama's successor Ishibashi was elected to the presidency of the party at its national convention on December 14, mainly through the vigorous efforts of Matsunaga Yasuzaemon, the elder statesman of the electric power industry, who managed to raise the necessary funds and to win over a large number of delegates.

Kishi, who lost the bitter contest with Ishibashi, unexpectedly captured the prize that had eluded him when the latter was forced by illness to resign his premiership on February 22, 1957, after little more than two months in office. Premier Kishi secured the support of Fujiyama and other *zaikai* leaders in forming his government, which was, in fact, a continuation of the Ishibashi government, except for the inclusion of Ishii as state minister. The second Kishi government, formed in June 1958, was in reality a partnership of business representatives and former bureaucrats, but its strongly bureaucratic character proved to be its undoing. It succeeded in outraging public opinion more than any other post-war government, and Kishi was jettisoned by organized business after his inept handling of the security treaty in the Diet, which led to the riots of July 1960 and the cancelation of President Eisenhower's visit to Japan.

⚙ THE LIBERAL DEMOCRATIC PARTY, although ruling with an absolute majority in the Diet, was not invulnerable to organized public pressure on a given issue. The attempted expansion of police power in 1958 illustrates this. In October, the conservative government, headed by Kishi Nobusuke, introduced into the Diet a "law and order" bill, the Police Duties Law Amendment Bill. The opposition protested loudly, and, after the ensuing parliamentary maneuvers and public uproar, the bill was dropped. The bill would have expanded the powers of regular policemen. Particular provisions were debated at length, but the real issue was the extent of police power. The public debate shows both the desire of the LDP government to strengthen its control vis-à-vis any dissident activity, and the resistance of large segments of the population to this tendency.

D. C. S. SISSONS*
The Dispute Over Japan's Police Law

... [I]t is first necessary to describe the scope of the existing Police Duties Law (No. 43 of 1948). As its first article clearly states, it relates only to certain police functions (the protection of life, limb, and property, the prevention of crimes, and the mainte-

* D. S. C. Sissons, "The Dispute Over Japan's Police Law," *Pacific Affairs* XXXII:1 (March 1959), pp. 36–37, 43–45.

nance of the peace) and does not, for example, deal with such functions as the investigation of crimes, the arrest of suspects, or the regulation of traffic. It is the statutory authority which enables a policeman on his own initiative: to stop and question a person whom there are reasonable grounds for considering to be about to commit a crime (Section a.II); to take into temporary protective custody a drunken or mentally deranged person where he is likely to injure himself, other people, or property (a.III); to order other persons to take action necessary to avert impending damage from natural causes (a.IV); where a crime is about to be committed, to warn persons to desist and, if the crime endangers life or seriously endangers property, to take coercive action to prevent its commission (a.V); to enter premises open to the public to prevent the commission of a crime or to prevent damage to life or property (a.VI,2); and to enter private property to prevent immediately impending damage to life or property.

The amendment sought in addition to authorize a policeman on his own initiative: (1) to take into temporary protective custody persons about to commit suicide and youths whose conduct appears likely to endanger life or property; (2) to search persons before questioning them or before taking them into protective custody when there are grounds for suspecting that they are armed; (3) where a crime is likely to occur which is clearly likely seriously to violate public order, to take coercive preventive action and to enter private property where necessary for the performance of this duty. The last of these powers was naturally the most controversial.

The grounds on which the government sought to justify the proposed legislation are most clearly expressed in the manifesto issued by the prime minister in the name of the cabinet on October 27. This referred to the increase in juvenile delinquency and to "the concern felt by all good citizens over the succession of recent incidents in which groups of people have openly flouted public order and the fundamental human rights of the community." In particular it mentioned the Beppu gang warfare incident of the previous year and the very recent clashes between unions and police in the Oji Paper strike, the demonstrations against the teachers' efficiency rating system, and the picketing of ethics instruction courses. "For a long time [in the words of the manifesto] we have been hearing complaints that the police are too weak to provide security for democratic society in the face of this surge of disorder and violations of the fundamental human rights of the people. Under the existing law the police, even though they foresee collective violence, cannot take proper steps to prevent it and clashes involving large numbers of people cannot be avoided." . . .

The brunt of the opposition's attack, however, was directed not so much against the individual articles of the bill as against the dangers of the bill's being abused—by the police themselves or by the police acting under instructions from the government. The critics emphasized that the police continued to have a bad reputation for exceeding and improperly using their existing powers. (This is a doubly serious problem in Japan since the courts have on occasion held that it is criminal forcibly to resist a police officer even though he be acting unlawfully.) Government spokesmen were in the unfortunate position of not being able completely to deny this. The best answer the minister could make was "I propose to get to grips with this problem. It appears to be a question of educating the police. I propose to drive home to every policeman the points brought out in these debates." Nevertheless, embarrassing situations continued to occur around the time of the actual controversy over the bill: for example, on October 3 the Tokyo high court announced the very light sentence of "three months imprisonment suspended during good behavior" in a case where the accused was a policeman who had used violence to extort a false confession as a result of which his victim had been wrongly sentenced to five years imprisonment. The procurators had refused to prosecute the policeman whose case only reached the courts because it had been taken up by the local bar association. On October 30 the police authorities announced administrative punishments ranging from reprimands to pay-cuts on seventeen policemen in connection with assaults by police on reporters covering a students' protest demonstration on September 16. On December 27 the Tokyo district procurators decided not to indict any of these policemen on the grounds that (1) the police were tired at the time; (2) they had been angered by the insults of the demonstrators; (3) in the bad light the pressmen could not be distinguished from the demonstrators because their dress was identical; (4) the perpetrators were very sorry for what they had done and had been punished administratively; (5) the persons injured were not unduly insistent that punishment be imposed. On November 13 the press announced that a constable had been disciplined for taking three men to a police box for questioning when he overheard them discussing the bill.

The question of abuse of the new powers by the government was handled by the critics in two ways. First, they asserted that the amendments to the Police Law in 1954 made the police the servants of the government of the day. Secondly, they pointed to the prewar legislation to illustrate that citizens would be unwise to rely on government assurances. The *Sandei Mainichi* (a weekly mass circulation home magazine), for example, produced for its readers extracts like the following from *Diet Debates* during the enactment of the notorious Peace Preservation Law in 1925:

> MR. HARA. The discretion conferred is unlimited. Anything becomes punishable. . . .
> MR. YAMAOKA (Criminal Section, home ministry). The government denies this. . . .
> THE PRIME MINISTER (Mr. Wakatsuki). The government's purpose is to ensure that freedom of expression and publication is not violated. We respect these freedoms to the utmost. On the other hand, to refuse to take action against violations of these freedoms would be most unfortunate. That is why this law has been introduced. There are those who misrepresent it as designed to prohibit labor activities. There is no objection to labor activities directed toward the raising of the status of the worker and we have no intention of placing any restriction on such activities. This law places no restraints on labor activities.

In its earlier stages the opposition movement against the bill was very similar to that against the Subversive Activities Bill (1952) in that it centered on organized labor, the press, and the academic world. But even within these fields the opposition to the present bill was more extensive. According to the *Asahi* newspaper some four million people participated in the protest strike on November 5, a much larger figure than in the 1952 strike. Moreover, whereas in 1952 labor was disunited, in protesting against the Police Duties Bill the four rival labor federations (Sōhyō, Zenrō, Shinsambetsu, and Chūritsukei) were for the first time cooperating closely in a common effort.

As in 1952 the three major dailies (and indeed the large majority of newspapers) attacked the bill from the outset. As a press campaign it has been rivaled only by the "Taishō democracy" campaigns against the Katsura and Kiyoura cabinets (in 1913 and 1924). The most influential newspaper (the *Asahi,* which is said to have a circulation of more than four million) attacked the bill relentlessly not only in editorials but through its news items, special articles, letters to the editor, "education column," etc. Of the metropolitan dailies two (*Sankei* and *Nihon Keizai*) were at the outset inclined to support the bill, but after the Diet extension on December 4, they joined the others in vigorous denunciations of the government. Also as in 1952, declarations opposing the legislation were issued by such bodies as the influential Japan Science Council (Gakujutsu Kaigi), a statutory body of 200 members each elected on the basis of his published research, the Bungeika-kyōkai (the leading professional association of literary men), the Japan PEN club, and by faculty associations in many of the universities.

What distinguishes the recent movement from other protest movements was that it included many organizations which as a rule eschew politics. Notable among these were the YMCA, Shufuren (Federation of Women's Organizations) and several religious organizations (Christian, Buddhist, and Shinto). Such groups appear to have played a vigorous and independent part while being prepared to cooperate to make their joint protest effective. Apart from the publishing, motion-picture, and hotel industries the business world appears to have supported the government.

It now remains briefly to consider the significance of the bill and of its reception. Within the Liberal Democratic party the organ primarily responsible for studying policy on police matters is the Public Order Policy Committee (Chiantaisaku Iinkai). Among the eighty-five dietmen who are members of this committee, twenty are former police officials. According to the press this committee proposed the introduction of similar legislation in the June session of the Diet but this was resisted by the predecessor of the present minister. Obviously the wave of incidents in September provided the best opportunity to pass the legislation. Principal among the government's miscalculations may have been the attitude of the press which in the past has in the last resort come down on the side of the government when the opposition has attempted to prevent the passage of legislation. There are also some grounds for thinking that the government may have been relying on rivalry between the labor federations to render the opposition movement ineffective. Lastly, there is the unpredictable factor of changing factional alliances within the government party itself.

❧ IN 1955 first the Socialists, and then the conservatives, unified their divided blocs, creating a clear two-party division, organizationally as well as ideologically. Their mutual distrust was exacerbated by LDP efforts in the mid- and late fifties to recentralize education and police, change the election system to weaken the Socialists, and reintroduce ethics in the school curriculum. Kishi Nobusuke, prime minister beginning in early 1957, began the appropriation for the LDP of Socialist-sponsored welfare ideas, and simultaneously attacked labor. After the 1958 elections, the two parties continued to dispute about government policies on labor, police, and foreign policy.

COLE, TOTTEN, AND UYEHARA*
Frustrations of the Opposition

On January 18, 1955, the two Socialist parties in separate conventions solemnly pledged to reunite after the general election in February. The public was calling for a reunited SDP and had little patience with the details of relative Socialist power and factional feuding. The two parties adopted identical resolutions to reunite as "a class-oriented mass party," to put forward only one candidate for premier, to overthrow capitalism, to destroy fascism, to reject communism, and to achieve socialism through a democratic and peaceful formula. . .

In April 1955, two ten-member unification negotiation com-

* Allan B. Cole, George O. Totten, and Cecil H. Uyehara, *Socialist Parties in Postwar Japan* (New Haven, Conn.: Yale University Press, 1966), pp. 53–59, 61–63, 65–66.

mittees and two five-member subcommittees on policy, organization, and operations were created. These met at least three times a week until September, when they completed a draft program for a unified SDP. . . .

The basic platform or program for the reunified SDP was hailed as a triumph for the right SDP by the "bourgeois" press. Platform terminology was such, however, that each wing could easily interpret the formulae to suit its own convenience. The willingness of the cautious Nishio faction to accept the new platform, and the unexpected outbursts of indignation in the left SDP against it, roughly gauged the degree of concessions by that wing. Unable to quiet these voices without a full convention, the separate left held its last tense conclave on September 19–20, 1955. Although the new platform was eventually ratified, more than one-third supported a resolution demanding its revision. The right merely convened an enlarged Central Committee meeting on September 27–28 but was faced with an almost equally belligerent resolution to uphold the new platform.

On October 13, a unified convention unanimously adopted the "contractual" platform without debate. . . .

. . . Thus, after ten tempestuous years, the Social Democratic party of Japan completed another cycle of divorce and reconciliation—this time emerging as the second largest party in the Diet.

When the second Hatoyama cabinet was formed after the general election in February 1955, the Socialists did not immediately oppose the government, since it promised to restore relations with the Soviet Union and to carry out progressive housing, extended social security, and other welfare policies. This unusual situation was soon normalized by a tense confrontation. Japanese–American negotiations on Japan's defense contributions to be included in the national budget were regarded by Socialists as a prime example of blatant American interference in Japanese domestic affairs. The government's decision (in response to American requests) to enlarge five air bases and press forward with rearmament aroused the determined ire of the opposition and their organized labor support. Even though a minority, the Socialists were able to shelve two crucial government bills to create a defense council and another to revise the constitution. In July 1955 they declared full-scale opposition to the "reactionary"

Hatoyama government. When reunified in October, the Socialists by constitutional practice became heirs-apparent to the minority Hatoyama government. The specter of a Socialist government prompted the conservatives to overcome all personality conflicts in order to create the Liberal Democratic party on November 14, 1955. This signaled the opening of a new era in Japanese politics. Far from mitigating conservative–socialist antagonisms, development of a two-main-party system sharpened the confrontation, occasionally even to the point of limited violence.

After the fall of 1955—for the first time in modern Japan— political parties in the Diet, especially in the House of Representatives, were clearly divided between Socialists and Conservatives. Although two major parties had emerged, the ratio of power between them was two-to-one in the Lower House in favor of the Conservatives; Socialists were an even smaller minority in the House of Councilors. And there was less common ground between Socialists and Conservatives concerning basic political philosophy, world outlook, and political strategy than existed in Western two-party systems. If these parties were to alternate in office, the swing of the pendulum as regards policies would at first be very great. Furthermore, because of deep mutual distrust the Socialists have not been able to exploit the rampant factionalism among the Liberal–Democrats or to combine with LDP dissidents on common goals to any appreciable extent. Their suspicions of Conservatives, stemming in part from remembering how many of those leaders had helped to suppress the prewar socialist movement, has occasionally erupted; at other times chronic numerical inferiority has made Socialist leaders lethargic. . . .

Early in 1956, the SDP selected five points on which to challenge the Conservatives: (1) defense of the postwar constitution and rejection of the small constituency principle; (2) opposition to military bases; (3) restoration of relations with the Soviet Union and Communist China; (4) action to cause the downfall of the Hatoyama cabinet; and (5) capture of one third of the House of Councilors in the forthcoming election. As for the Liberal Democrats, they had voiced diametrically opposed policies described as "rectification of excesses" wrought in the course of occupation reforms. Aging Premier Hatoyama declared at a mass rally that he would like to revise the constitution even if he had to "reduce" (*gensatsu*) Socialist strength. . . .

Two of the numerous bills to revive old laws and to create new institutions particularly aroused Socialist ire in 1956: one to revise all electoral districts into small constituencies and another to make school boards appointive rather than elective. Although the Liberal Democrats denied political motivation, it was obvious that they hoped to reduce Socialist representation in the Diet below the one-third mark by adopting the small constituency principle. If a relatively nonpartisan rearrangement of· districts had been proposed, the Socialists would have been hard pressed in their opposition, and they would surely have lost many seats in one or more subsequent elections. It was generally accepted by the press and other informed opinion that the small constituency system *might* eventually lead to a more stable two-party system. But the conservatives overplayed their advantage. Their proposed rearrangement involved such blatant gerrymandering that even the press (referred to by left Socialists as "the bourgeois press") and a substantial portion of their own colleagues in and out of the Liberal Democratic party were dissatisfied. According to Socialist calculations, passage of this revision of the electoral law would nullify most of the opposition party's gains since 1952. To many of its leaders this was a problem of political survival. The gerrymandering would have most affected the younger left-wing SDP Diet members who relied upon labor union support. Many older Socialists, particularly in the right wing, were not against small constituencies but were compelled to oppose such gross manipulation which might at least temporarily shatter their party. The opposition accused the conservatives of attempting a "legalized coup d'état," and of trying to establish a "stable government" at the expense of popular respect for the fairness of the legislative process.

The Socialists utilized every parliamentary trick and tactic short of illegality. Although House Speaker Hidetsugu Masutani was a conservative, he was a member of the "out" group and was apparently not in favor of ramming the small constituency bill through the House. Fearing that public opinion might be repelled, the Socialists were persuaded, after bitter debate in their CEC and in caucus, to accept a modified version of the electoral bill without the appended electoral districts—a compromise suggested by the speaker. . . .

In the House of Councilors, the bill immediately became involved with another contest over the passage of a measure to make members of school boards subject to appointment by the usually conservative heads of local bodies. This change was aimed at reducing the influence which the politically powerful Japan Teachers' Union had gained in these boards during the previous decade; it was also intended to centralize control over education. . . . Eventually the president of the Upper House called for the assistance of 500 policemen and tried to convene a "surprise" plenary session, with few SDP members present, in order to pass the bill. This precipitated a scene of utter confusion and violence. The next day (June 2, 1956), amid an uncanny silence in the Diet chambers, the school board bill was passed, but other important measures, such as the small constituency bill, failed of enactment. . . .

The Socialist star continued to rise during the winter of 1956. The SDP had achieved two and parts of two others of its five aims mentioned earlier; its leaders apparently felt confident of soon assuming power, but their hopes were dashed when Premier Hatoyama resigned in mid-December after the Diet had ratified the Japanese–Soviet declaration restoring "normal" relations. Tanzan Ishibashi was chosen president of the Liberal Democratic party and, on December 23, 1956, he formed his cabinet, promising a 100-billion-yen tax reduction and 100-billion-yen for expanding the economy. Japan was then experiencing a major boom, and such a positive, expansive financial policy threw the SDP on the defensive. This was in contrast to its attitude toward Ishibashi when, as minister of finance in the first Yoshida government ten years earlier, he had been the prime SDP target as the evil genius of runaway inflation. Nine weeks after becoming premier, however, Ishibashi was forced to resign because of illness. Nobusuke Kishi, who succeeded him on February 25, 1957, appropriated more and more Socialist policies. He openly proclaimed a showdown (*taiketsu*) with the SDP and its supporters, particularly Sōhyō. . . .

In an attempt further to weaken union leadership and financial power, the government by ordinance withdrew from certain categories of civil servants the right to maintain union membership and prohibited automatic withholding of union fees from paychecks. In another attempt to reduce the influence of the Japan Teachers' Union, it instituted the "efficiency rating system" for promotion of teachers. The temporary law limiting the right of coal miners and electric power workers to strike was made permanent. Feeling ran high in conservative circles in favor of further circumscribing all types of union activities. . . .

Premier Kishi continued to keep the Socialists on the defensive but his position within his own party was becoming increasingly precarious toward the end of 1957. He carried out Ishibashi's expansive economic policies which soon drained Japan's foreign exchange reserves to a dangerously low point. Hurriedly he then had to resort to stringent economic policies. The Socialists accused him of befriending monopoly business interests at the expense of small and medium enterprises. The Kishi Plan to develop Southeast Asia with Japanese technical knowledge and American capital encountered skepticism both in Washington and in the region to be assisted. How to bolster his leadership as a national election approached was the problem confronting the premier.

Time was fast running out in the spring of 1958 for Premier Kishi to hold a general election under his own conditions. Since the last one in February 1955, Socialist and conservative forces had achieved mergers; the gavel had passed to four successive conservative cabinets without an electoral contest (except the partial Upper House election in 1956); the international climate had changed considerably; and Japan had begun to take a more active role in world affairs. The SDP emphasized its demand for an election in early 1958 by postponing its convention until February; the lobbying and pork barrel scars on the national budget passed by the Diet on March 31 also presaged an election. Only the date remained to be set. In line with his challenge to the Socialists, Kishi had hoped to call a sudden election but by this time all element of surprise had vanished. For the first time in Japanese political history, the premier and the leader of the opposition together "agreed to dissolve" the Diet and hold a general election: the date set was May 22, 1958.

On the domestic front, the conservatives had appropriated many SDP demands: increased social security, health insurance, and old-age pensions. They were bitterly opposed, however, on labor and educational policies. . . .

Contrary to expectations, the SDP increased its Diet representation by only eight seats, from 158 to 166. Thirty-five representatives, including many prominent Socialists elected in 1955, were defeated. The proportion of total votes cast for Socialist candidates was only 2.7 percent greater than in 1955. The press called on the SDP to reevaluate its policies; the party leadership reluctantly conceded its relative defeat and submitted to perfunctory self-criticism. Nevertheless, in number of votes the SDP had made its largest gains since 1952. While its support had increased by one million votes in each election since then, its most recent gain was by 2.2 million over the 1955 level. For the first time, the Socialists alone obtained thirty-three percent of the total vote. . . .

After the general election of 1958, confrontation between the two main parties gradually became more intense. As the majority party, the Liberal Democrats voted themselves the chairmanships of all committees in the House of Representatives. Previously these posts had been shared with the opposition. For several years the Conservatives had been attacking the political influence of the Japan Teachers' Union—one of the pillars of the SDP. As soon as the second Kishi cabinet was formed in June 1958, the minister of education declared that teacher efficiency rating would be instituted throughout the country. Although ostensibly an administrative move, the political intent was obvious: to weaken the Teachers' Union substantially, both as an organization and as a force in elections to the Diet. This change would correspondingly, though indirectly, weaken Socialist strength in the Diet.

The opposition, including leftist labor unions, were determined to do all in their power to challenge this new threat. Unions and students held rallies; demonstrators clashed with the police; the SDP attempted to mobilize members of Parent-Teacher Associations, housewives, and workers into a national joint-struggle organization; teachers and their pupils went on "mass leave."

As a corollary to the efficiency rating, the conservatives rammed through a bill to increase the "supervisory allowance" for grade- and high-school principals. The SDP and the Japan Teachers' Union regarded this as a deliberate attempt to alienate school principals from the union. In the House of Representatives the Socialists stalled, negotiated, forced votes on motions of nonconfidence, but could not prevent passage of the bill. They tried to take advantage of their control over the chairmanship of the educational committee in the House of Councilors, but their rivals forced a vote calling for an interim report and then a final tally.

Tension was aggravated when the Liberal Democrats instructed the schools to revive the teaching of "ethics" (*shūshin*). Socialists bitterly denounced this as an effort to reindoctrinate the Japanese people in outworn traditions invalidated by the war. Again and in vain they resorted desperately to defensive tactics which may have hurt them somewhat in elections to the Upper House in 1959.

⚓ KISHI NOBUSUKE assumed office in 1957 and resigned after the revised United States–Japan security treaty took effect in June 1960. The 1960 demonstrations were concerned not just with the security treaty itself, but in the end with Kishi, too. Many who supported the treaty's revision, including many important businessmen, opposed Kishi's handling of the affair. The description below traces Kishi's career as it rises and falls with Japan's fortunes in the twentieth century, and gives a striking picture of the man at the center of the storm.

GEORGE R. PACKARD III*
The Second Rise of Kishi

Revision of the security treaty became so tightly entwined with the ambitions and political fortunes of Kishi Nobusuke that we should pause here to look briefly at the background of this extraordinary, controversial politician.

Kishi was born in 1896 in a former samurai family in Yamaguchi prefecture, earlier known as Chōshū, which has produced more prime ministers (seven) than any other area in Japan. Educated in the orthodox channels for the elite, he graduated with distinction from the Tokyo First Senior High School and the Law Faculty at Tokyo Imperial University. He attended college (1917–

* George R. Packard III, *Protest in Tokyo: The Security Treaty Crisis of 1960* (Princeton, N.J.: Princeton University Press, 1966), pp. 47–51.

1920) during the period of social and political unrest that un-
settled Japan after World War I. The atmosphere was one of
excitement and confusion as new ideas from the West, such as
Wilsonian liberalism and Bolshevik Marxism, collided with traditional Japanese concepts. Students and scholars formed associations to study and spread the new thoughts. Some students, such as
Asanuma Inejirō at Waseda University, became attracted to the
cause of socialism during these uneasy postwar years. Kishi, on the
other hand, became a student of the nationalistic Professor Uesugi
Shinkichi and fought against the more liberal views of such men as
Professors Minobe Tatsukichi and Yoshino Sakuzō. He was also
deeply impressed, curiously, by the radical nationalist, Kita Ikki,
whose home he visited occasionally. For a time, Kishi was a
member of the Gokoku Dōshikai (National Protection Comrades
Group), which was set up to combat the radicals and their ideas
on campus. As a student, Kishi read the works of Marx and
Kautsky but rejected Marxism because, as he put it, "it goes
against human nature."

Kishi turned down an offer from Professor Uesugi to succeed to
his chair and chose instead a traditional career in the government.
He rose rapidly during the 1920s and 1930s in the ministry of
commerce and industry, where he came to be recognized as a
brilliant leader and a promising bureaucrat. From 1936 to 1939 he
served as second highest civilian official in the Japanese puppet
government of Manchukuo, responsible for planning the economic
development of the vast Manchurian empire. Returning to Tokyo
in 1939, he became vice-minister of the commerce ministry, where
he soon clashed with his superior, Commerce Minister Kobayashi
Ichizō, over his (Kishi's) plan for tighter control of the economy.
The upshot of this conflict was Kobayashi's resignation in April
1941; Kishi then became minister of commerce in the Tōjō cabinet
of October 1941. He was thus a cosigner of the declaration of war
against the United States in December 1941. In 1943 Kishi became vice-minister for military procurement, a post directly under
Tōjō, and minister without portfolio, where he played a major role
in holding together Japan's faltering economy during the war
years. In 1944, soon after the Japanese loss of Saipan, Kishi resigned with the rest of the Tōjō cabinet, reportedly helping to
topple Tōjō from power. After the surrender, he was held (without

trial) for three and a half years at Sugamo Prison as a Class A war criminal. Released in 1948, he took a job in the business of his close friend, Fujiyama Aiichirō, who was later to become his foreign minister. In 1952 he was depurged and began a new career in politics.

Kishi's comeback was as remarkable as the confused state of conservative politics after Japan's independence in 1952. Throughout much of the occupation and up to 1954, "One-man" Yoshida Shigeru had survived a series of crises and dominated the conservative camp. In December 1954, however, Yoshida was ousted by the aging (seventy-one) semi-invalid, Hatoyama Ichirō, and this set off a wild struggle among would-be successors, who expected the new administration to be short-lived (though it actually lasted until December 1956). Kishi began his meteoric comeback by joining Yoshida's Liberal party in 1953, but he soon combined with Miki Bukichi and Kōno Ichirō (and others) to support Hatoyama's rebellion against Yoshida and was expelled from the party in the same year. He thus played an important (some say decisive) part in forcing Yoshida into retirement in December 1954. In 1955, with the merger of the two conservative parties, Kishi became secretary-general of the new Liberal Democratic party (LDP) and a leading candidate to succeed Hatoyama.

The ailing Hatoyama stepped down from office in December 1956, having fulfilled his pledge to normalize relations with the Soviet Union. In the factional scramble to replace him, the three leading candidates were Ishii Mitsujirō (former member of the Yoshida cabinet), Ishibashi Tanzan, and Kishi. Kishi was still an "outsider" at this point, having no deep roots either in prewar party politics (like Hatoyama) or in the postwar "Yoshida school" of politics like Ishii. The latter, in Japanese political parlance, refers to the group of men drawn mostly from the ranks of the career bureaucrats, whom Yoshida brought into his successive cabinets. The "prize pupils" of this school included Ikeda Hayato, Satō Eisaku, Hori Shigeru, and Ishii Mitsujirō. One of the few constant factors in the shifting alignments within the LDP has been the enmity between the Yoshida and Hatoyama alliances.

Kishi was an outsider, but he had a foot in both camps: he was allied with Kōno Ichirō, a former Hatoyama man, and his younger brother, Satō Eisaku, was heir (along with Ikeda) to the Yoshida faction and loyal to Kishi. He also benefited from the sudden dearth of top conservative leaders in 1956 caused by the deaths of Ogata Taketora and Miki Bukichi and the retirement of Hato-yama. Thus, on the first ballot for LDP presidency on December 14, 1956, Kishi had a plurality, but he lost on a subsequent vote by the slight margin of seven votes when his rivals teamed up to back Ishibashi. The battle before and during this convention wracked the party and gave rise to charges of corruption and vote-buying. In the new Ishibashi cabinet of December 23, 1956, Kishi became deputy prime minister and minister of foreign affairs. After Ishibashi was forced by illness to retire in February 1957, Kishi moved into his place without a party contest and was voted presi-dent of the LDP as a formality on March 21, 1957.

In five years Kishi had risen from the status of a depurged war criminal to prime minister of Japan. In thirteen years he had moved from Tōjō's cabinet to leadership of the most important U.S. ally in the Pacific.

⌘ THE LARGEST MASS ACTIONS in Japanese politics since the threatened 1947 general strike took place in the spring of 1960. The issue was the proposed ratification of the revised United States–Japan security treaty. Signed in 1951, together with the peace treaty, the pact represented an earlier stage in the relationship of the two countries. Japan in 1960 was not equal, but no longer treated by the United States as a weak, defeated nation.

Business interests, however, saw in United States–Japan security arrangements a basic framework for their continued prosperity. In the late 1950s, when revision was being dis-cussed, this was especially important. Beginning with a bal-ance of payments deficit in late 1957, the Japanese economy went into a slump persisting throughout 1958. On the left, the revision issue was tied to larger issues. Diet Socialists originally had opposed the security pact, and when the issue arose again these feelings were stronger than ever. A unified People's Council was formed to counter the proposed treaty in a united-front forum, and the groundwork was laid for the greatest political crisis in postwar Japan.

GEORGE R. PACKARD III*
Protest in Tokyo: The Security Treaty Crisis of 1960

FORMATION OF THE PEOPLE'S COUNCIL

We have looked briefly at the four main groups behind the drive against the security treaty that began in 1959: the Socialists, verging on a new split and moving leftward; Sōhyō, gradually overcoming its qualms against open cooperation with the Communists; the JCP, backing a broad united front against U.S. imperialism; and Zengakuren, at odds with the Communists and straining for an immediate revolution of the proletariat. In early 1959 the leaders of these groups and other left-wing organizations sought to follow up their Police Bill campaign with a new and massive movement against the revised security treaty. The new coalition that finally developed was called the People's Council for Preventing Revision of the Security Treaty (Ampo Jōyaku Kaitei Soshi Kokumin Kaigi). . . .

ORGANIZATION AND ACTIVITIES OF THE PEOPLE'S COUNCIL

The new People's Council was officially inaugurated on March 28, 1959, at the National Railway Workers Hall. A total of 134 organizations (including the thirteen original sponsors) sent 620 representatives to this first meeting. Every conceivable type of "progressive organization" was represented: the Women's Socialist League, Japan Anarchists' League, Executive Committee of the Japan Group Singing Association, League for the Emancipation of Outcasts, Christian Peace Association, and so forth. The slogans

* George R. Packard III, *Protest in Tokyo: The Security Treaty Crisis of 1960* (Princeton, N.J.: Princeton University Press, 1966), pp. 105, 111, 113, 116–117, 134–137, 179–181.

adopted at the meeting reflected the nature of the new organization, covering the whole range of leftist grievances: opposition to nuclear weapons, foreign bases, "alliance" with South Korea and rearmament, and support for the "peace constitution," neutralism, and human rights. The Council's three stated policy aims were to prevent revision of the security treaty, achieve neutralism, and abolish the security system.

The thirteen original sponsors formed a thirteen-member board of directors. . . . This was the overall coordinating body, where the principle of unanimity applied to all decision-making. A secretariat with a director, two vice-directors, two secretaries, and several part-time students was set up to handle the daily business of the board of directors. In each prefecture, a regional joint struggle council (Kemmin Kyōtō Kaigi) was formed, made up of the particular "mix" of left-wing elements that prevailed in that area. Below the prefectural joint struggle councils were district joint struggle councils (*chihō kyōtō kaigi*), again formed of the local left-wing groups in towns and villages throughout the nation. By August 1, 1959, all forty-six prefectures and metropolitan areas (*todōfuken*) had regional councils, and, by July 1960, 1686 district councils had been formed. These local councils were coordinated from the center by instructions and "requests" from the board of directors in Tokyo and by occasional meetings of a National Representatives Council (Zenkoku Daihyōsha Kaigi) to which the local councils sent delegates. The National Representatives Council had no power of decision- or policy-making, but served rather as a forum for transmitting information and enthusiasm from Tokyo to the outlying districts. A Strategy Committee (Senjutsu Iinkai) was formed in April 1960 to resolve arguments over tactics among the Directors. This committee consisted of representatives from the JSP, JCP, Sōhyō, the Tokyo Joint Struggle Council, and the National Federation of Neutral Labor Unions. . . .

Some of the council's most important work went on in the countryside during 1959. The prefectural and district joint struggle councils formed rapidly in the spring of 1959, with Sōhyō playing a major role. By July 1959, forty-five of Japan's forty-six prefectures had set up joint struggle councils, and it is noteworthy that the headquarters for thirty-one of these councils were in Sōhyō offices, while eight were in JSP offices. These councils varied in name and composition, depending on the relative strength of the local leftist groups. Participation on the boards of directors of the local councils was sometimes determined by the amount of money (per capita) contributed by each member-group. Organizations, rather than individuals, were the units of membership in all the councils. Some of the types of organizations included were peace committees, women's associations, farmers' and teachers' unions, mothers' groups, child protection societies, and the like. A few new local elements, such as a civic group in Nerima Ward, Tokyo, and a shopkeepers' group in the city of Maebashi, attracted attention for their unprecedented participation in the leftist movement, but most of the organizations were long-time advocates of left-wing causes. The councils printed handbills and posters, arranged for antitreaty speeches by scholars and famous people in factories, and ran small meetings in the towns and villages. Most important of all, they helped organize and stir up enthusiasm in the local rallies and demonstrations and arranged for the sending of local delegates to Tokyo to join in the larger protest demonstrations.

The most important regional council was unquestionably the Tokyo Joint Struggle Council for Safeguarding Peace and Democracy. This council sat on the Board of Directors as one of the thirteen original sponsors, and also on the five-member Strategy Committee. It included Sōhyō's regional chapter, Chihyō, in Tokyo, which played a leading role in furnishing manpower for the demonstrations. The council's headquarters were provided by Sōhyō. . . .

THE ANTITREATY FORCES, 1959

The campaign against the revised security treaty began officially with the gathering of leftist forces under the People's Council in March 1959 and ran through the rest of the year in ten "united action" drives. . . . [T]hese drives were coordinated with the major Sōhyō campaigns and were almost identical with the traditional labor offensives of postwar Japan. There were two new features, however: a hardening of antitreaty sentiment among older organizations and the appearance of new groups set up specifically to oppose treaty revision. In both cases, the result was a vast outflow of antitreaty propaganda. The leftist campaign followed the basic principle that the attack on the treaty must be many-faceted: each leftist organization was instructed to support the attack in ways suited to its special concerns. In other words, pro-Peking groups would stress how the new treaty would damage Sino-Japanese relations; leftist lawyers would bring out the legal "defects" in the treaty; leftist scholars would use their prestige, publications, and influence to alert students and intellectuals to the dangers of the new treaty; and leftist journalists would publicize the antigovernment campaign.

Among the older left-wing organizations, Sōhyō led the way. At its 12th National Convention in August and September 1959, Sōhyō took its most radical line in recent years, voting down a motion to give exclusive support to the Japan Socialist party and pledging to ". . . lead all Japanese workers in their fight to crush the Kishi government's attempt to revise the Japan–U.S. security treaty." At this convention, Sōhyō launched an extraordinary fund-raising campaign, approving a special assessment of 45 yen (about 12 cents) per head which was designed to increase yearly revenue by 150 percent over the 1959–1960 total and bring 114 million yen (about $317,000) into its coffers.

The main theme of Sōhyō's antitreaty campaign was that the treaty lay at the heart of all the problems of Japan's laboring masses. The foremost labor problem in Japan during 1959 was the displacement of coal miners by the "energy revolution," and Sōhyō therefore used the discontented coal mine unionists in Tanrō as the spearhead of its antitreaty rallies and demonstrations in the fall of 1959. Politically active unions geared their particular protests into the antitreaty campaign. The Japan Teachers' Union (Nikkyōsō), for example, staged classroom walkouts on September 8, 1959— the day of the People's Council's 6th United Action—to protest the teachers' efficiency rating system. Other unions, such as those of the journalists and press workers, and railway and public enterprise workers, passed resolutions at their yearly conventions pledging to fight harder against the treaty. . . .

The attack on the treaty came in surprising strength from another quarter—from new "private" (*minkan*) organizations of "men of culture" (*bunkajin*) formed solely for the purpose of resisting treaty revision. Leading these groups were the "progressive intellectuals," including many of the famous professors and writers who had been bitter opponents of the alliance since 1951. These intellectuals had played an important role in fomenting the great national debate over the treaty in 1957 when they issued a statement on February 28 of that year (fifth anniversary of the signing of the administrative agreement) calling for a reexamination of the security treaty. As discussion and debate wore on from 1957 to 1959, a great variety of solutions sprang up; the more radical among them favored outright abolition of the treaty, while others were for negotiations with the United States to eliminate the most annoying features of the treaty.

Around mid-1959, however, opinion among the progressive intellectuals began to solidify into uncompromising opposition to treaty revision by the Kishi government. In December 1959 the influential Peace Problems Symposium (Heiwa Mondai Konwa Kai) issued a new statement opposing treaty revision and alleging that the Japanese government and people would have to take responsibility for any new treaty in the eyes of the Soviet Union and Communist China, whereas in 1951 they had been forced into signing. The group took the remarkable stand that the existing treaty had no definite term and *was therefore provisional in nature,* while the new treaty had a definite ten-year term and would thus lose its provisional character. Other defects in the new treaty, according to the statement, were that it would strengthen Japan's objectionable social and political structure, damage relations with Communist China, increase the chances of war, and lead to the buildup of the munitions industry in Japan. The group called for Japan to do away with the old game of power politics and rely for her security on the peaceful spirit of the constitution, thus following in the footsteps of her Meiji period ancestors and leading Asia on a new path to modernization. . . .

The revised security treaty was signed by Kishi, Herter, and others in the East Room of the White House at 2:30 P.M. January 19, 1960, with President Eisenhower looking on. The treaty was not, strictly speaking, a mutual defense pact, for though it went beyond the old treaty and explicitly obligated the United States to act "to meet the common danger" in case of an armed attack on either party *in the territories under the administration of Japan* (Article V) it did not obligate Japan to aid the United States in case the latter were attacked outside this area. Okinawa and other islands under the "residual sovereignty" of Japan but administered by the United States were thus excluded from the treaty area by the above language. The response of both parties to an armed attack in the treaty area would be limited by their respective constitu-

372]   POSTWAR JAPAN: 1945 TO THE PRESENT

tional provisions and processes. The new treaty, like the old one, granted the use of bases in Japan to U.S. forces for the purpose of "contributing to the security of Japan and the maintenance of international peace and security in the Far East" (Article VI). A new administrative agreement was to govern the use of these bases; this agreement relieved Japan of sharing in the cost of maintaining the U.S. troops (amounting to $30 million annually at that time) and made some of the wording more agreeable to the Japanese, but it did not limit in any essential manner the status of U.S. troops in Japan.

The new treaty removed two features that had been objectionable to Japan in the old one: it deleted the clause permitting U.S. forces to intervene at the request of the Japanese government in large-scale riots and disturbances and it eliminated the requirement for Japan to get prior consent from the United States for granting military rights to any third party. It also added an obligation for both parties to settle disputes in accordance with the U.N. Charter (Article I), a major improvement in the eyes of the Japanese government.

Article III obliged both parties to maintain and develop, subject to constitutional limitations, their capacity to resist armed attack, and Article IV provided for consultations in the event that the security of Japan or peace and security in the Far East were threatened. In the exchange of notes accompanying the treaty the United States agreed to consult with Japan beforehand on major changes in deployment, equipment (*i.e.,* nuclear weapons) and use of bases for military combat operations outside Japan. Either party could terminate the treaty after ten years by giving one year's advance notice to the other.

In the Joint Communiqué after the signing, both sides stressed the economic and cooperative aspects of the treaty, and mention was made of the forthcoming celebration of the centennial of U.S.–Japan relations in the "new era." The next day it was also announced that President Eisenhower and Crown Prince Akihito would exchange visits in 1960, and that the President would arrive in Japan around June 20. Few people—perhaps not even Kishi—were aware at that time of the enormous potential effect of this decision on Japanese politics.

Back in Tokyo the signing was greeted calmly. The treaty text and entire administrative agreement were carried in the newspapers. The People's Council rallied at Hibiya Park on the day of Kishi's departure and Sōhyō called for strikes and workshop rallies on the day of the signing. The Socialist party made a statement on January 19 to the effect that the hand that countersigned the Imperial Rescript to begin the Pacific War had now signed the new pact which might drive Japan into a new abyss. Sōhyō said that the government was going against the times and the new Democratic Socialist party observed that the treaty added to the apprehensions of the Japanese people and was unconstitutional. Zenrō deplored the treaty and urged the government to dissolve the House of Representatives.

No untoward incidents marred Kishi's return to Tokyo on January 24, 1960. The LDP saw to it that he received a "hero's welcome" and the nation settled back for the long and bitter debate over ratification in the Diet. The People's Council spoke ominously of large-scale strikes and demonstrations in mid-April, near the climax of the debate, but for the moment, at least, there were no new outbursts.

❀ WHEN THE REVISED security treaty and other relevant documents were submitted to the Diet for approval, the sides were already clearly drawn. The Socialists debated the issue thoroughly and also engaged in parliamentary obstruction. The debate was echoed outside the Diet in the media. The People's Council intensified its activities while newspapers, books, and magazines covered every detail of the controversy. The May 1 downing of an American U2 spy plane over the Soviet Union heightened the debate. Charges that similar planes flew from Japanese soil were made, and U.S. Air Force statements that they were weather planes did not relieve Japanese fears that their country could be dragged into war by involvement with the United States. Kishi, in this atmosphere, chose May 19 to force approval of the treaty through the LDP-dominated Diet. He could then look forward to having it officially pass the Diet on June 19, the day of President Dwight

Eisenhower's projected visit (it went into effect automatically after thirty days). But the cost was high, as his tactics accelerated the tempo of public demonstrations.

GEORGE R. PACKARD III*
The Great Debate

THE DEBATE OUTSIDE THE DIET

While the debate raged on inside the Diet, a campaign of gigantic proportions was being waged outside in the newspapers, magazines, books, radio, and television. Never since the war had a foreign policy issue so absorbed the nation; the Diet deliberations were carried by TV and radio into private homes, bars, and coffee shops, and phrases such as "scope of the Far East" and "prior consultation" became popular topics of conversation among housewives and office clerks. Between February and June 1960, hardly a day passed without some newsworthy development in the debate.

Both the older left-wing organizations and the new antitreaty groups intensified the attack they had begun in 1959. . . . Pamphlets, handbills, and posters poured off the presses carrying arguments that are by now familiar to the reader: the risk of war, the danger of alienating the Soviet Union and Communist China, the infringements on Japan's sovereignty, and the violation of the constitution. The parties added to the flow with pamphlets, "white papers," and articles stating their positions. What really distinguished this period from the earlier debate was the shift of moderate or "neutral" opinion against the treaty. This could be seen clearly in the attitudes of the major newspapers in Tokyo which claimed to be independent: until January 1960 the press, despite some misgivings, had generally welcomed treaty negotiations, but in that month the tone changed to one of outright

* George R. Packard III, *Protest in Tokyo: The Security Treaty Crisis of 1960* (Princeton, N.J.: Princeton University Press, 1966), pp. 214–216, 219, 238–245.

hostility. The *Asahi Shimbun* editorial of January 14, 1960, made four demands that, if they had been accepted, would have changed the basic character of the treaty. They sought to (1) replace the "prior consultation" clause with "prior agreement"; (2) limit the purpose of United States bases in Article VI to the maintenance of Japan's security only; (3) delete all clauses incurring doubts as to constitutionality (the meaning here is not clear); and (4) drastically reduce the ten-year term of the treaty. With Japan's leading daily thus opposed to core provisions of the treaty, and with the rest of the supposedly nonpartisan press growing more critical of the government by the day, Kishi was clearly headed for trouble.

Throughout the Diet debate the press remained critical of the government's handling of the interpellations and dubious of the treaty itself. The *Asahi's* editorial of April 15, for instance, accused the government of not showing sufficient "sincerity," and complained that the issues were not being "clarified." All the papers called on Kishi to "satisfy" the nation's doubts: "Even though the world outlook of the several political parties may be different, the nature of the problem is such that, for the sake of the nation and the people, the parties must get together and forge a mutually satisfactory policy."

To the Western reader, the *Asahi's* insistence on a "mutually satisfactory policy" seemed incredibly naïve in the context of the bitter partisan rivalry, the Cold War, and serious ideological gap between the parties in Japan. It can be explained in part, however, by the traditional belief that all disputes may be settled harmoniously by mutual accommodation of conflicting interests—that each side must yield slightly to preserve the unity of the whole. The press was also motivated in part by growing impatience with Kishi, by nationalist feelings that the treaty was too restrictive, and by its long history of opposition to the party in power which had become the measure of its "objectivity." . . .

Looking back on the public debate over the treaty in the spring of 1960 one is impressed less by the intensity of the attacks of the left wing than by the shift of moderates . . . to the opposition and by the relatively weak fight put up by those who claimed to believe in the treaty. There is no question that important segments of public opinion changed from apathy to opposition as a result of the debate in this period, and, though a majority of the nation still probably favored the treaty, the vigorous and determined minority, with its new allies from the center, became resolved more than ever to avoid a humiliating defeat in the Diet. . . .

On Thursday morning, May 19, 1960, the LDP formally proposed a fifty-day extension of the regular Diet session. House of Representatives Speaker Kiyose referred the matter to the Steering Committee, whose approval was required prior to a vote in plenary session. At about the same time (10:41 A.M.) the House of Representatives Special Committee opened its 37th meeting, with the Socialists carrying out their plan to present petitions and to stall. The LDP members tried to close the debate and vote on the treaty, but the session fell into disorder and the chairman had to call for a recess at 12:37 P.M. All afternoon the directors of the Steering Committee wrangled about the proposed extension and it was not until 4:30 P.M. that Chairman Arafune Seijirō could open a meeting. At this session there was further shoving and confusion, as JSP and DSP Committeemen stomped out shouting that the meeting was improper. The LDP members, now meeting alone, quickly approved the extension motion and an announcement was made that a plenary session would begin at 5:00 P.M.

Socialist Diet members and their burly male "secretaries" then staged a mass sitdown (*suwarikomi*) outside Speaker Kiyose's office to prevent him from reaching the rostrum. At this stage they were still unaware of Kishi's plan to vote on the treaty as well, and were seeking only to block the extension vote. There were skirmishes in the hallways as LDP members and their "secretaries" brushed with the Socialists. Kiyose, literally trapped in his office, used his telephone to call for mediation talks with party leaders.

The People's Council sent out an "emergency mobilization order" at 2:30 P.M. and assembled some 15,000 demonstrators around the Diet by early evening. The crowd, mostly Sōhyō unionists, chanted *"Ampo hantai"* ("Down with the treaty") and *"Kishi taose"* ("Overthrow Kishi") as rain began to fall. About 5000 policemen were on hand to guard the Diet building. At 6:00 P.M., Kiyose and House of Councilors Speaker Matsuno Tsuruhei ordered 2000 police into the Diet compound, but not into the building itself. More wrestling took place between Diet members outside the speaker's office. Just after 9:00 P.M. Kiyose began a series of appeals to the Socialists over the public address system: "Please stop the sitdown demonstration as it will only cause confusion and disorder." The LDP withdrew its members from the scene. Nishio and other DSP leaders stood by, hoping for a chance to "mediate."

At 10:25 P.M., with Speaker Kiyose still imprisoned in his office, the first bell rang for the plenary session. At this point, in the first surprise move of the day, Chairman Ozawa called for the Special Committee on the Treaty to reconvene, with members of all parties present. Nishimura Rikiya and Matsumoto Shichirō (both JSP) stood and presented nonconfidence motions to the chairman, and, at the same time, Shiikuma Saburō (LDP) proposed that the debate be ended and a vote taken. For the next two minutes there was so much confusion that the Diet proceedings do not record the events. The Socialists, shouting and harassing the chairman, walked out of the room as Ozawa announced closure, took the vote, and declared that the treaty and related bills were approved. The *Proceedings* contain only this brief notation:

> 10:25 P.M.
> CHAIRMAN OZAWA: Before the intermission . . . [Many people talk and leave their seats, confusion reigns, impossible to hear]. . . .
> 10:27 P.M.

Minutes later Kiyose issued a warning: "Break up the sitdown within fifteen minutes or I shall be forced to ask the police to enter the Diet building." At 10:35 P.M. the last bell for the plenary session sounded and LDP Diet members filed into the Diet chamber. Ozawa had on his desk the Special Committee's favorable report on the treaty. The antimainstream factions, claiming that this was the first time they had heard of Kishi's plan to vote on the treaty that night, left the chamber for hurried discussions; they decided to vote for extension but not for the treaty. . . .

At 10:48 P.M. Kiyose issued his final warning, but the Socialists, who were arrayed with locked arms on the floor between the speaker's office and the rostrum in the Diet chamber, refused to budge. At 11:00 o'clock Kiyose ordered 500 police officers to break up the blockade. During the next forty-five minutes each Socialist was carried bodily by three or four policemen (a process known in Japanese slang as *"gobōnuki"* or uprooting) out of the area amid popping flashbulbs and the glare of movie camera lights. This was the second time in the history of the Diet that police had actually entered the chamber. At 11:48 P.M., Kiyose, flanked by a squad of Diet guards, made his way through the melee to his seat on the dais; a minute later he opened the plenary session in the presence of LDP members only. The fifty-day extension was quickly approved, and Kiyose then announced that a new session would be convened "tomorrow"—just after midnight. The session ended at 11:51 P.M. and exactly fifteen minutes later, at six minutes past midnight, a new plenary session opened. Ozawa made his report, and Kiyose called for a rising vote on the treaty and related bills. The *Proceedings* record that "all present arose." Then there were the traditional *Banzai*'s and the stormy session adjourned at 12:19 P.M. This meant, of course, that, without any action by the House of Councilors, the new treaty would automatically receive the Diet's approval exactly thirty days later, on June 19, 1960.

Outside, the crowds, which had dwindled to some 5000, heard the news in darkness and went home. The next morning banner headlines in all the major papers proclaimed that the LDP had "unilaterally" approved the treaty; photographs showed LDP Diet members raising their arms for the *Banzai* next to rows of empty Socialist seats. The JSP declared on May 20 that the extension and treaty passage were null and void and began a boycott of all Diet proceedings. Japan was thus plunged into her worst crisis since the war.

REACTIONS TO KISHI'S SURPRISE MANEUVER

The Japanese people were well enough accustomed to rousing battles among their elected representatives, and they had long been aware of the impending clash, but the rapidity of Kishi's move, coming as it did after the disturbing events of the past few months, produced genuine surprise and shock. The *Asahi Shimbun's* morning edition for May 20 had gone all the way from Tokyo to Kamakura with a front-page editorial warning the parties against violence, when it had to be recalled, overtaken by events. The People's Council, which had planned a major rally for May 20 to block the treaty in the Lower House, had quickly to change its placards and slogans to protest against Kishi's "undemocratic" actions.

Surprise is odious in Japan, and people go to extreme lengths to avoid it. It was not so surprising that Kishi resorted to force, but the "slick" way in which he arranged to have the treaty pass the Diet automatically on the day of Eisenhower's arrival was more than many could take. There had been rumors, for several days before May 19, that he might try such a maneuver, but the stark accomplished fact was still a shock. After all, Kishi had specifically stated in the Diet on May 4 that there was no connection at all between Eisenhower's visit and ratification. Some felt that it was a neat trick and that the Socialists had been outwitted, but many more were repelled by what seemed to have been unnecessary deception in approving the treaty hard on the heels of the Diet extension vote. The column *"Tensei Jingo"* expressed a widespread opinion on May 21: Kishi might think he is presenting Ike with a bouquet on June 19 but "that is the thinking of a petty bureaucrat concerned with protocol. It is like a retainer performing tricks before his master. He seems to be forgetting the importance of the loyalty he owes to the people." . . .

The press quickly and uniformly condemned Kishi as if with one voice. The *Asahi* editorial for May 20, "The LDP and government's Undemocratic Act," said that the LDP's mainstream had placed a great strain on Japan's parliamentary democracy, and called on Kishi to "reflect" on his acts. It made no mention of the Socialists' prior use of force. The *Mainichi* said, "In view of the fact that doubts about the new treaty continue to exist despite more than 100 days of deliberations and that practically no debate had been held on the new administrative agreement which is so closely tied in with the daily lives of the people, we had repeatedly called for thorough deliberations through extension of the session and for the dissolution of the Lower House thereafter to ascertain the public's opinion." *Tōkyō Shimbun* said that Speaker Kiyose should have called a "summit meeting" of the three party heads to avert the disaster. The *Yomiuri* was indignant that hundreds of policemen had been called into the Diet: "When the government and government party so easily take such extraordinary measures, the prestige and power of parliamentary government cannot be preserved." Even the conservative *Nihon Keizai Shimbun* censured the LDP for taking "single-handed action." The theme of "tyranny of the majority" was common to all the discussions of LDP behavior. . . .

Kishi, who had never enjoyed the best of relations with the press, and was less than loved for his remark of January 16, 1960, that the only parts of Japanese newspapers worth reading were the sports pages, aggravated the press again by canceling his May 20 news conference on grounds that the situation was "too delicate." Then on May 25–26, he publicly censured the papers for their presumption that they alone represented public opinion. When he finally met reporters on May 28, he upheld his party's moves of May 19–20 and said he had no intention of resigning. "If we succumbed now," he added, "Japan would be placed in great danger." When a questioner suggested that the demonstrations against him were receiving very little public criticism, Kishi made a reply that was to become famous: "I think that we must also incline our ears to the voiceless voices. What we hear now are only the audible voices, that is all."

⊛ THE MONTH from May 19 to June 19, 1960, was the period of greatest tension in domestic politics since the end of the war. To the spokesmen for the *zaikai*—the large business interests—the lessons were ominous. Many saw the events as a battle in the Cold War and feared greater struggles in the future. *Zaikai* leaders were angry, too, at the press for their coverage of the struggle. At a meeting in July 1960 they attacked the media for one-sided coverage, and excesses were reportedly confessed to by newspaper and media representatives. Yet this should not be seen as a permanent division between government and business on one side, with the press on the other. In fact, the major press is a part of the Establishment in Japan just as papers like *The New York Times* are in the United States, despite differing opinions. Richard Halloran, once a correspondent for the *Washington Post* and now Japan correspondent for *The New York Times,* discusses the role of the press in Japan below, and argues that the coverage of the 1960 protests represented divisions *within* the Establishment, not antagonism against it.

RICHARD HALLORAN*
A Regulated Press

The Japanese press, like all others in the world, reflects the character of its society and fills a role peculiar to its nation. The press is part of the Establishment and a key element in the decision-making process. It originates some ideas and refines others as the nation moves toward the consensus that governs its actions. The Japanese press is not a mirror but a molder of public opinion on behalf of the Establishment. It dispenses the decisions of the Establishment and assists in persuading the public to follow. The press in Japan started as an independent force but was quickly brought under control by the nation's rulers and has remained so since. It has not developed a tradition of independence but has been subject to domination by the authorities or to their indirect influence. The enduring historical theme of the Japanese press has been the evolution of its relationship with the ruling elite. . . .

The Japanese press emerged from the occupation with its ninety years of tradition largely intact. The occupation washed over the press, as it did over many Japanese institutions, leaving all but the surface unchanged. The press, having never known genuine independence, groped along for a few years recovering from defeat and then resumed its function as the communications instrument of the national leadership. Wartime consolidations carried over, dividing the press into a well-defined hierarchy.

The press today is dominated by the *Asahi Shimbun, Mainichi Shimbun,* and *Yomiuri Shimbun,* which have the most space, the largest staffs, and the biggest circulations. They constitute the backbone of the national press, and blanket Japan with their multiple editions printed in several cities. The three major papers not only influence their readers but the rest of the newspapers as well as other media. Below them are several smaller and more specialized papers, such as *Nihon Keizai Shimbun,* a paper similar to *The Wall Street Journal;* local metropolitan papers like *Tōkyō*

* Richard Halloran, *Japan: Images and Realities* (New York: Alfred A. Knopf, 1969), pp. 159–160, 170–172, 174–177, 180–183.

Shimbun and *Ōsaka Shimbun;* and the provincial papers such as *Hokkaidō Shimbun* and *Nishi Nippon Shimbun.* Around the newspapers are a bewildering variety of political, economic, sports, ladies', and entertainment weekly and monthly magazines. The Japanese are the world's most literate people, and their consumption of reading matter is enough to stun the uninitiated. Radio and television, too, have reached into the remote hamlets of the land.

The major change in the press is that it is no longer subservient to the ruling elite but has been upgraded into membership in the Establishment. It has joined the Establishment as a result of its history, because a vacuum opened as the postwar power structure took shape and the press slipped in, and because the Establishment needed the press as its communicator and transmitter of information. Moreover, the press is considered part of the intellectual community and is obliged, in the Confucian tradition of benevolent service, to use its knowledge to serve the nation. The press also has more tangible ties with the Establishment. Owners and publishers, as businessmen, are Establishment members, and many newspapers have large loans from banks and carry an increasing amount of advertising from business. Some journalists have gone into politics and yet maintained contact with their former colleagues.

The press is thoroughly enmeshed in the Establishment's decision-making mechanism. Staffs of the big papers have trained and thoughtful specialists who have access to extensive research facilities to turn out thoroughly prepared articles on national problems. Some ideas originate with the writers and are presented for discussion and eventual action; for example, Kishida Junnosuke of the *Asahi* is a leading thinker on Japan's security questions and is widely respected for his original commentaries. Other articles seek to refine proposals under consideration. A debate in the press over reducing restrictions on foreign investments covered every thought and fact about the issue for three years. The press, by omission, assists the Establishment in avoiding questions it does not wish discussed. Japan has suffered from a roaring consumer price inflation for seven years, but the press has confined its coverage to dutiful, low-keyed reports of isolated statistics. Few hard-hitting analyses or editorial calls for relief have come out.

The press transmits information within the Establishment both publicly and privately. In the intricate process of reaching consensus, the Establishment needs a tremendous amount of information, not only about the question at hand but about the thinking and pressures coming from the different sectors of the ruling elite. The papers cover these down to the slightest nuance. When the Japanese economy runs into trouble, the finance minister, director of the Economic Planning Agency, and governor of the Bank of Japan begin holding press conferences in which they mention various economic trends. They drop, ever so gently, a hint that raising the central bank rate may be in the offing. This alerts the rest of the Establishment that trouble is at hand and opens a debate over measures to be taken, including the pros and cons of raising the bank rate and how much. It goes on for several months until the bank rate, inevitably, is raised—the warning sign having been plain for all to see since the day it was first mentioned.

. . . The main purpose of editorials and interpretive columns is to expose the thinking of the Establishment gradually to the public so that it may be eased into following the lead of the elite. The deliberate, cautious Japanese do not like surprises, nor do they care for rapid changes. Little in Japanese life turns sharp corners, but eases slowly around a wide bend. Editorials nudge these changes along by shades of nuance, not by thundering exhortation. Panel discussions, either in print or on radio and television, are akin to this editorial technique. Several prominent men get together with a press commentator to ruminate on the topic under consideration and expose to the public the thinking going on in the Establishment as it moves toward a consensus.

Japanese newspapers usually print a far larger amount of foreign news than most Western papers because they are freer to analyze and criticize this than they are domestic news. The Establishment often has no views on news from abroad or finds critical press articles helpful in its negotiations with a foreign power. Japanese correspondents in Vietnam have rather consistently filed dispatches critical of American policy that Japanese leaders have used to resist American pressures for moral and political support of the war. They contend that they cannot come out in public support of the United States because public sentiments are against it. The same is true of editorials on foreign affairs. The Establishment does not object if editorials use America as a whipping boy—so long as this does not damage Japanese exports to the United States.

POSTWAR JAPAN: 1945 TO THE PRESENT

The theoretically ideal role of the press is to foster harmony, but it is not always unified in its views and must make adjustments like other segments of Japanese society. The opposition of the press or a particular newspaper to a proposal in its formative stages does not mean that the press opposes the Establishment or the government. It is merely partaking in the endless discussion that is part of the process of reaching consensus. The closer to consensus the Establishment gets, the more the press falls into line. After a decision is reached, the press or a single paper may push for a revision, which is fair game, but it will not advocate turning back on the decision already reached.

Moreover, the Japanese press is sometimes viewed as pro-socialist or procommunist, which is an error. The press, either in print or in the personal opinions of newsmen, gives few indications that it wants drastic changes in Japan's form of government or its social order. Nor does the press give much sign that it wishes the conservative government turned out of office, though there are alley-cat fights to turn particular people out. The press, rather, has become highly nationalistic and often expresses this nationalism in anti-American terms. Taking an anti-American stance often means adopting a position that comes close to that taken by the left. But these positions are advocated within the framework of the existing order in Japan, not to overthrow it.

During May and June 1960, a turbulent debate over the security treaty with the United States ended in ratification of the treaty, the last-minute cancelation of President Eisenhower's visit, and the resignation of Prime Minister Kishi Nobusuke. Many students of Japanese affairs look on the 1960 events as evidence that the Japanese press is antigovernment. But careful study of the role the press played in those days shows that it acted as part of the Establishment and not as a reflector of public will against the government.

For several years prior to 1960, the Establishment had been unhappy with the security arrangements concluded with the United States at the end of the occupation. The Japanese considered these an unequal treaty and a reminder of Japan's defeat. The government negotiated a new treaty and presented it to the Diet for ratification in the spring of 1960. The socialists opposed the treaty because they wanted to see Japan break all military agreements with the Americans and force the United States to withdraw the military forces that remained in Japan. The socialists were supported by the communists, who wanted to break up the American defense system in the Western Pacific. Leftists in the Diet refused to deliberate the treaty, but Kishi forced a vote, which set off the turmoil. The press demanded Kishi's resignation primarily because the papers thought he had broken the rules of the game by not compromising and persuading the opposition to debate the issue. Kishi, in their view, had also ignored the demands and advice of the press in reaching a decision on the treaty, another fracture in consensus. The quarrel with Kishi was thus more of a fight within the Establishment over methods than it was a disagreement over policy.

During the two months of disruption, the press sometimes followed a course parallel to that of the leftist opposition, but for different reasons. When leftists demonstrated in the streets, the press first warned that the demonstrations should not be turned into mob violence. The newspapers then became somewhat ambivalent. They opposed the violence editorially but indirectly encouraged it by references to student uprisings earlier that year in Korea and Turkey. For one ten-day period the papers supported the demonstrations, so long as they were orderly. When President Eisenhower's press secretary, James Hagerty, who came to Japan in advance of the planned presidential visit, was mobbed near Haneda Airport and had to be rescued by helicopter, the press turned against the demonstrators and condemned their violence and the damage they had done to Japan's international prestige.

The press afterward split on the question of whether the Eisenhower visit should be canceled, some papers contending the original plan should be followed to improve Japan's international standing, others urging that it be canceled to keep the American president from becoming involved in Japanese politics. After the Kishi government decided to cancel the visit because it could not guarantee Eisenhower's personal safety, the press campaign against Kishi slacked off quickly. The papers knew he was on his way out and they had accomplished their objective in the intra-Establishment infighting. In all of this, public opinion had little to do with events, which were caused by the clash of the opposition with the government and by the efforts of Kishi's enemies, including the press, to force him to resign. . . .

The Japanese press is unique in the way it operates from day to day. Its physical arrangements alone are astounding. *Asahi,* for instance, publishes forty-two editions a day, fourteen in Tokyo and the rest in other printing centers. The paper has a staff of 7900 employees, making it four to five times the size of a comparable American paper. The same loyalties, lifetime employment, compensation, and other aspects of Japan's paternalistic corporate life, apply to newspapers as they do to other businesses. Decisions are made by consensus and newsmen, unlike their Western counterparts, work in groups, articles being the product of numerous reporters who feed information to a writer who turns out the completed story. A Japanese newspaper can smother a story with more manpower than any ten American papers. At a 1966 United States–Japan ministerial meeting in Kyoto, *Asahi* alone sent more reporters than the entire foreign press corps there.

The most distinctive feature of the Japanese press is the "press club," which is an association of reporters attached to every government agency at the national and prefectural level and often at the local level. It is also attached to political parties, business firms and industry organizations, labor unions, and educational and social organizations. The press clubs are the main, and usually only, channel into which news from a source moves through the newspaper to the readers. Before World War II, they were "organs for the adjustment of news and for regulating newsgathering activities," according to the 1967 annual review of Shimbun Kyōkai, the press association. The review contended that today the press clubs "maintain themselves as simple social organs with newsgathering activities left on a free and unrestricted basis." The most cursory observation will show that this is patently not the case. The press clubs are so powerful that they determine who is allowed to cover the news, what questions are asked, what information is released to the public, and generally how media conduct their news operations. An individual reporter has little say in these matters, which are decided collectively by the clubs. Enterprise or investigative reporting is pointedly discouraged. A leader of one press club explained that the main purpose of the club is to do away with "excessive competition" and "extreme enthusiasm" and to prevent "overzealous newsgathering." The press clubs are splendid examples of the Japanese preference for group action, collective responsibility, careful regulation, and conformity. They are also a subtle but effective form of censorship.

The press clubs are the main link between the Establishment and the press, and could not exist without the implicit approval of Japan's newsmakers. Some politicians contend that they go along with the press-club system only because they will be attacked in print if they fail to. But most are quite comfortable with the clubs because the system gives them tight control over the news that goes out into the public domain. Reporters assigned to cover a particular politician become so cozy with him that they rarely report anything critical about his activities—if they do, it is usually a slip-up. The politician sees that they are well informed on the understanding that they will report only what he wants to see in print, and then only in the manner that will serve him best. He keeps this arrangement alive with lavish entertainment and a constant flow of gifts, and often assigns a competent lieutenant to see that every wish of the club is met in arranging meetings, travel, and communications. The same is true with clubs covering government agencies. Because little independent reporting is done, a news report from the foreign ministry can be considered a policy statement or an authoritative explanation of the ministry's position even though a comprehensive set of facts might lead to another interpretation of what is really going on.

The prime minister's press club is the most important and meets with the chief cabinet secretary three or four times a day. The latter official is the official spokesman for the prime minister and the cabinet and is the chief source of pronouncements designed to persuade the Establishment and the public. The chief cabinet secretary tells the press club more than appears in the public prints, making the club privy to high government policy and, in effect, an extension of the prime minister's office. The press club, however, does not always defend the prime minister and can turn out to be his severest critic within the Establishment.

꙳ BY JUNE 1960 Kishi had not only earned the enmity of large segments of the Japanese public and the press, but, more dangerously, he had lost the support of the *zaikai*. They saw the great disturbances as a personal failure of Kishi's and

POSTWAR JAPAN: 1945 TO THE PRESENT

speedily produced a replacement. The opposition of the Socialists and street riots involving hundreds of thousands of ordinary citizens could not topple a prime minister; a lack of business support could. The life of Kishi's successor, Ikeda Hayato, demonstrates the benefits that *zaikai* sponsorship could bring to a bureaucrat's career.

CHITOSHI YANAGA*
Ikeda's Rise to Power

Nowhere has the power of organized business in Japan been more effectively used than in the making and unmaking of governments in the period since the end of World War II, especially since the merger of the conservative parties in 1955. The power of life and death over the government has been exercised by organized business overtly and dramatically at times, but quietly on the whole, unnoticed by the casual observer. No candidate for the premiership can be successful without the tacit, if not expressed, approval of the business community. Nor can a prime minister long continue in his post after he has lost the support of organized business. . . .

There is no doubt that good fortune contributed greatly to Ikeda's meteoric rise in the political world from a relatively obscure tax official in the finance ministry to finance minister and finally prime minister, an achievement he could not have aspired to or planned for except with the help of Dame Fortune. This smiling lady was none other than *zaikai*, which discovered him, rescued him from bureaucratic routine if not oblivion, and groomed him for the highest political post in the nation.

When the business tycoon, Nezu Kaichirō, president of Tōbu Railway Company, died intestate in January 1940, most of his large fortune went to the Nezu Educational Foundation and the Nezu Art Museum; the remainder went to his son and heir. To the surprise of the Nezu family and its executors, Ikeda, then director

---

* Chitoshi Yanaga, *Big Business in Japanese Politics* (New Haven, Conn.: Yale University Press, 1968), pp. 141–143.

of the Tokyo District Tax Office, imposed an inheritance tax of 36 million yen on the estate. In behalf of the Nezu family and the three executors, Yamamoto Tamesaburō, managing director and subsequently president of the Dai Nihon Beer Company and a close friend of Ikeda's, explained the situation and an understanding was reached whereby Ikeda reduced the tax to 8.2 million yen, less than one-fourth of the original assessment.

Miyajima, one of the executors of the Nezu estate and confidant of Prime Minister Yoshida, took a strong liking to Ikeda. He was favorably impressed by the decisiveness demonstrated by the finance ministry official in disposing of the Nezu inheritance tax problem. When Yoshida subsequently sought his advice regarding a suitable candidate for the post of vice-minister of finance, Miyajima remembered and recommended Ikeda. Ikeda's star was now definitely in the ascendancy. *Zaikai* liked what it saw in the promising government official and gave him support.

Ikeda ran for the Diet from his native prefecture of Hiroshima and won a resounding victory at the polls on January 23, 1949, garnering the largest number of votes in his election district. Less than a month later, on February 16, at the age of forty-nine, he was appointed finance minister in the third Yoshida government on the recommendation of Miyajima, who had been offered the post but had declined. Before making the recommendation, Miyajima had consulted Yamamoto and Sakurada, Miyajima's protégé and successor as president. In appointing Ikeda, the prime minister had deliberately flouted the practice of selecting cabinet ministers only from among veteran Diet members who had served at least three terms. Ikeda at the time was a brand-new freshman member of the Diet, who had been elected less than four weeks earlier. This was clearly a case of big business giving such powerful support to the man they had discovered that the prime minister accepted the recommendation without hesitation.

As Minister of International Trade and Industry in the Kishi government, which he joined in June 1959 at the time of a cabinet reshuffle, Ikeda was actually in a faction that was not congenial to the prime minister, but *zaikai* supporters were able to get the cooperation of this faction. There is no question that the untimely death of Liberal Democratic party President Ogata speeded Ikeda's rise to power. On July 14, 1960, after a bitter contest, Ikeda was elected to the presidency of the Liberal Democratic party, succeeding Kishi, but only after a tremendous amount of money had been spent by *zaikai* to ensure his victory. Five days later the Ikeda government was formed, superseding the Kishi government, which had been jettisoned by organized business.

3. Big Business in Postwar Japanese Politics

❀ PARALLEL WITH the reversal of other occupation reforms there came a rapid turnaround in the MacArthur program to deconcentrate industrial ownership and redistribute the holdings of wealthy families to a broader segment of Japanese society. This policy reversal came somewhat later than, for example, the clearly antilabor policies of the occupation. By the mid-fifties, according to Chitoshi Yanaga, however, the reemergence in new form of the traditionally powerful cliques—business, bureaucracy, and family—was complete. The only missing element from prewar days was the military, and the power of aristocratic families had been somewhat reduced. A new center of influence had also arisen, the university-based clique, whose impact was increasingly felt as science and technology became more important for reemerging industrial Japan. Yanaga below describes the reappearance of much of the prewar power structure, as well as the uniquely central character of the Japanese capital, Tokyo, which serves as the base for all of the decision-making elites.

CHITOSHI YANAGA*
Big Business in Japanese Politics

One of the characteristics of Japanese society is the existence of a number of rather exclusive groupings. . . . Such cliques or groups provide the oasis of the power structure. In the prewar period, power was exercised by three distinct cliques, the financial (zaibatsu), bureaucratic (*kambatsu*), and military (*gumbatsu*), but in the postwar period the military and the financial cliques have ceased to exist. Only the bureaucratic clique has retained its power. Zaibatsu has been superseded by *zaikai* (the business leader clique). Two other groups, already mentioned, have come into prominence, namely, the extended family clique (*keibatsu*) and the university clique (*gakubatsu*).

. . . Although no longer recognized as a basic legal unit, the family is still the touchstone of social success. The importance of family background or connections in achieving success in almost any field has not diminished. On the contrary, it seems to have increased greatly. More than ever, family status (*iegara*) and pedigree (*kenami*) are necessary qualifications for membership in high society and for achieving a position of prestige and influence in business and politics, even in academic life.

Candidates for important posts are judged on the basis of family ties. When a new governor of the Bank of Japan was appointed in late 1964, press and public approval was on the basis of the appointee's family background rather than on his ability, which was widely recognized. If one's pedigree is not the best, it is always possible to improve it by marrying into the right family. Such ties are widely sought, especially in the business community. Chances for such marriages are greatly enhanced for men who have acquired a quality education, such as graduation from the prestigious Tokyo University, which is open to all solely on the basis of ability. Bright young graduates of the best universities are always in demand as husbands for daughters of influential business and

* Chitoshi Yanaga, *Big Business in Japanese Politics* (New Haven, Conn.: Yale University Press, 1968), pp. 15–16, 20–21, 26–29.

political leaders. When one already has a good pedigree, it is possible to improve it socially and financially by acquiring a degree from an elite school. Marital ties are often established to enhance the position, prestige, and power of the families as well as the individuals involved. It is also possible to enhance the social status of the family through the centuries-old practice of adoption, which continues to flourish in Japan. . . .

UNIVERSITY AND SCHOOL CLIQUES (*Gakubatsu*)

The unique character of the university clique is responsible for the influence wielded by the graduates of Tokyo University in business, politics, and government as well as in higher education, science, technology, and medicine. Ever since its establishment in 1886, Tokyo University has inculcated in its students a strong sense of elitism and leadership. In light of the incredibly difficult entrance examinations, it is not surprising that its graduates feel superior, even though in many instances such an attitude is not justified in terms of academic achievement. The university was founded specifically for the purpose of training government officials. Upon graduation, its early graduates were given the privilege of immediate appointment, without examination, to the newly created higher civil service. This established a tradition of administrative elitism, and until the end of World War I the cream of the Tokyo Imperial University graduates went into government service. In no time the university had established undisputed supremacy in higher education. It attracted the best students from all over the nation, and students have been flocking to it ever since.

Tōdai—as Tokyo University is commonly known—is in a sense a most exclusive club, membership in which establishes eligibility for the highest positions in the realm. Of the ten postwar prime ministers between 1945 and 1965, seven were Tōdai graduates (Shidehara, Katayama, Ashida, Yoshida, Hatoyama, Kishi, and Satō). . . .

CONCENTRATION OF POWER IN TOKYO

One of the most distinctive features of Japan's power structure is the extraordinarily high concentration of power wielders in Tokyo. Here, in the world's largest city, a supermetropolis of over 11

million people and the seat of the national government, are located
the main offices of practically all the major corporations, making
it the business, banking, financial, transportation, communication,
publishing, and mass media center of Japan. All political parties,
labor unions, and trade associations have their national headquarters here. The leading universities, research institutes, mu-
seums, art galleries, theaters, radio and television broadcasting
systems, and the country's six largest newspapers are located in
Tokyo. All major political and economic decisions are made in
this city. It is as if Washington, D.C., New York, Chicago,
Philadelphia, Pittsburgh, Boston, and Detroit were rolled into one.

Such a concentration of power is unknown in the United States.
To create an analogous situation, it would be necessary to locate
the head offices of America's hundred largest corporations in
Washington, D.C., together with their presidents, board chairmen,
and directors, many of whom would be related by marriage not
only to each other but to influential political leaders and government administrators. Furthermore these top-level executives
would, for the most part, claim the same alma mater, belong to the
same country clubs, have ready access to government offices,
maintain daily contact with government officials by phone or over
the luncheon table, enjoy intimate relations with influential senators and congressmen, and also serve on government advisory
bodies and administrative commissions. The impact of this sort of
concentration of political, economic, and social power on the
governing process can indeed be far-reaching. . . .

Although there has been some discussion regarding an "establishment," no one has come up with convincing proof that such a
thing exists, especially one comparable to the Establishment in
Britain. There are power groups representing different segments of
society, to be sure, but they cannot be isolated easily. There seems
to be general agreement among students of Japanese politics that
the nation is governed jointly by organized business, the party
government, and the administrative bureaucracy.

As to which of the three groups is most powerful, there is no
agreement. Any judgment must necessarily be highly subjective
and is likely to be biased. Professional politicians believe that the
administrators are running the country. Businessmen are quick to
assert that the party politicians determine national policies. Ad-

ministrators are convinced that organized business, working through the party in power, is in control of national policies.

In terms of economic policies, it is easy to conclude that organized business rules supreme. The power of the administrative bureaucracy over organized business is quite apparent when it comes to power to regulate and control business, and to grant or withhold licenses, government loans, and subsidies. The party is no match against the power of organized business. Yet there have been instances where the party in power was able to exert a decisive influence over the bureaucracy. . . .

As presently constituted, organized business, the party government, and the administrative bureaucracy are the three legs of the tripod on which the Japanese political system rests. Functionally they are interdependent, even though they operate for the most part in distinct areas. Organized business initiates and proposes policies. It sponsors and supports the party in power. The party in turn forms the government and selects candidates for the Diet, who function as legitimatizers of government policy. The administrative bureaucracy proposes, drafts, modifies, interprets, and implements policies under the surveillance of the party and the government. The most important functions of the bureaucracy involve the protection and promotion of business and industry, in whose behalf it formulates long-term economic plans, makes forecasts, sets goals, and establishes priorities. Organized business provides members for the cabinet, the Diet, and government advisory councils and administrative commissions. It hires retired government officials as corporation executives and trade associations officials.

In return for political contributions by organized business, the party in power strives to create a political climate conducive to carrying on profitable business enterprises. In this role, the party in power is in effect the political arm of organized business in much the same manner that the Japan Socialist party is the political arm of labor. It is the party in power that selects the prime minister and the cabinet members who head the administrative departments and exercise decisive influence on budget formulation.

The spectacle of Japanese politics is in a sense a dramatic production, presented jointly by the business community, the ruling party, and the administrative bureaucracy. Organized business is the playwright as well as the financier. The ruling party, as producer, director, and stage manager, adapts the play and makes sure that the production meets with the approval of the playwright-financier. It is also responsible for picking the leading actor, who must be *persona grata* to the financier. The administrative bureaucracy utilizes its expertise in looking after the technical details as well as the business end of the production.

⊗ THE END OF direct family control over zaibatsu groups, ordered by the American occupation government, and the lessening of centralized rule by business, bureaucracy, and the military were threats to zaibatsu hegemony after World War II. Their outright destruction, however, was avoided, and the foundations were laid early for the rebuilding of "new-style" zaibatsu, distinguished from their prewar ancestors chiefly by the discarding of single-family ownership. Yanaga calls these *zaikai.*

Today, the old zaibatsu structures have reappeared effectively intact, as shown here in *Pacific Basin Reports.* The old Manchuria-based Nissan zaibatsu, for example, now produces Datsun automobiles. Furthermore, the Pacific War and the postwar reconstructing of the old zaibatsu empires led to a higher degree of monopolization in many economic sectors than existed before 1941.

CHITOSHI YANAGA*
What Is Zaikai?

... [A] new postwar term, *zaikai,* has come into wide use. It practically supersedes zaibatsu, which has ceased to have the

* Chitoshi Yanaga, *Big Business in Japanese Politics* (New Haven, Conn.: Yale University Press, 1968), pp. 32–35, 38–39.

original institutional meaning of financial clique, which is no
longer applicable to the existing economic structure. By inference
as well as usage the new term connotes big business power group.
It is frequently interpreted more broadly as a synonym for "business circles," "financial circles," and even "business community."
More inclusive than zaibatsu, it is nevertheless restricted to big
business. In journalistic usage it more often than not refers to the
leaders of big business, particularly to leaders who have the support of the powerful economic organizations—closed circle of
organization-based, powerwielding activists. *Zaikai* also denotes the
place where the craving for political power is openly expressed and
gratified—that hypothetical arena in which big business influences
the government, or even society as a whole, by the collective
strength and "unified will" of its economic organizations. Most
frequently identified with the term *zaikai* are the top executives of
four big business organizations (Federation of Economic Organizations, Japan Federation of Employers' Associations, Japan
Committee for Economic Development, and Japan Chamber of
Commerce and Industry) and executives of the Japan Industrial
Club whose board of directors consists of the presidents of the key
organizations and the elder statesmen of business, industry, and
finance.

"*Zaikai* literally presides over Japanese society." These are the
words of a Tokyo University economics professor who believes
that, of all interest groups, *zaikai* "has the greatest opportunities
and plays the most decisive role." This power is manifested in a
variety of ways—in the legislative program, in the choice of prime
minister (not to mention cabinet members), and in the makeup of
the government's advisory councils and administrative commissions. *Zaikai*'s power of life and death over governments has been
dramatically demonstrated time and again. Candidacy for the
premiership is unthinkable without its tacit approval, and the prime
minister's days are numbered if his policies or methods no longer
meet with its approval.

Zaikai, however, is by no means a monolithic structure any
more than is the conservative Liberal Democratic party, which
champions its cause. Pluralism characterizes the business community as it does the world of politics, as the existence of trade
associations testifies. The diversity of attitudes, motives, and interests that characterizes *zaikai* has made the cooperation of the large

key organizations indispensable in achieving consensus and in presenting a united front on issues and problems.

In the negotiations with the Soviet Union for the restoration of normal diplomatic relations, conservative *zaikai* elders of the Federation of Economic Organizations, especially President Ishizaka, urged the government to go slow, whereas leaders of the fisheries industry, who are vitally interested in favorable relations with the Soviets, especially in the North Pacific, pushed vigorously for an early resumption of diplomatic relations. On the problem of relations with Communist China and North Korea, the majority of the men connected with *zaikai,* which is pro-American, often disagree and clash with the Kansai spinning interests and the fertilizer industry, both of which are interested in expanding their markets into communist countries.

Even though business leaders belong to all four peak organizations, as well as the same conservative party, they are by no means of one mind nor are their interests identical. Diverse groups are formed on the basis of special interests and on the basis of the distance between these groups and the seat of political power. The most important and influential group is that which is closest to the government. The next most important group is made up of men who are no longer very active. Finally, there is the group which feels an affinity with the political contender who lost the race for the premiership.

Business leaders are also identified and labeled on the basis of their foreign policy attitudes. The pro-American group is "all out" for close collaboration with the United States. The internationalists favor trade relations and close collaboration with the countries of Asia, including Red China. An intermediate group, taking a more balanced, long-term view of international relations, regards either extreme as unwise and prefers a middle-of-the-road policy. . . .

One of the most revealing statements ever to come from a political leader regarding business-government relations was Prime Minister Ikeda's matter-of-fact assertion that "the government is the captain and *zaikai* the compass of the ship." The implication is unmistakable. The government follows faithfully the direction indicated by *zaikai.* Ikeda did not mention, however, that while *zaikai* indicates the destination, it is the responsibility of the captain to take the ship through the stormy sea of politics and safely into port. If he fails to do so, the captain is usually relieved of his command, promptly and often unceremoniously. As a matter of fact, *zaikai* casts about for a replacement the moment the captain is seen to falter.

The role of big business in this triumvirate is unquestionably far more important today than before the war. The business community shapes the basic trends and direction of Japanese politics as well as the economy. As the largest and most dependable source of funds for political parties, big business is a *sine qua non* of success for political candidates. Business is well represented on the cabinet, advisory councils, the Diet, and the party. Moreover, through the effective use of mass media, some of which it controls, organized business exerts a powerful influence on society as a whole. . . .

ENTERPRISE GROUPS

Unlike the old zaibatsu, which dominated the prewar economic scene under a system of highly centralized family control through holding companies, the new postwar big business structure is composed of enterprise groups. These groups are of two kinds: those organized around the former zaibatsu and using the old names (Mitsubishi with thirty-eight separate corporations and a research institute; Mitsui with twenty-two corporations; Sumitomo with fifteen corporations) and those held together by large banks (Fuji, formerly Yasuda; Dai Ichi; and the Industrial Bank of Japan, through which the enterprises in both groups manage their financing).

These groups, known as *keiretsu,* cannot be described in American business terms. They are not really monopolies, since they compete with each other strongly and no one group completely dominates a given field. Actually they are horizontal groups of companies, each group containing many varied industries as well as a bank, a trust company, insurance companies, a trade company (or companies), and a real estate company. Member companies tend to cooperate with other companies within the group and to compete with companies outside the group. When entering new fields such as atomic energy or petrochemicals, where investment requirements are beyond the capability of any one company in the group, several or most members will combine to finance the venture jointly. The groups vary in cohesiveness. Within each group, the bank is the primary though not the sole source of banking support. The group's trading company handles the sales, particularly export trading, and the purchase of raw materials, but not exclusively. Policy coordination is achieved through presidents' clubs, which meet periodically.

These enterprise groups represent the postwar restructuring of big business on the basis of common interests, the better to cope with common problems in such fields as production, sales, and financing. . . .

PACIFIC BASIN REPORTS*
The Reaches of Zaibatsu Power

Trying to understand the workings of modern Japanese capitalism without understanding the zaibatsu combines is like watching a football game where both sides are wearing the same uniform and none of the players has a number. Political decisions at the highest levels, foreign investment, loan capital, military contracts, information, personnel—all tend to flow along the channels carved by the half-dozen major financial–industrial groups that dominate Japanese life, as surely today as they did in the years before World War II.

Today the same big names—Mitsubishi, Mitsui, and Sumitomo —flash in neon from marketplaces in Japan and the capitals of Southeast Asia. Once again these three, together with the Fuyo group, Dai-Ichi Kangyō group and Sanwa group (descendants of other prewar Japanese combines) are the main organizers of Japanese industry, commerce, and finance. Allied with the six zaibatsu . . . are seven big integrated konzerns with familiar names— Nippon Steel, Tōshiba-IHI, Hitachi, Toyota, Nissan, Matsushita, Tōkyū.

These thirteen groups . . . represent an unprecedented concentration of economic power in Japan, exceeding even that of the zaibatsu at the close of the Pacific War.

* "1972 Handbook of Japanese Financial/Industrial Combines," *Pacific Basin Reports,* April 1, 1971, pp. 1–4.

WHAT IS A ZAIBATSU?

... The contemporary zaibatsu ... differ markedly in form from their World War II era predecessors, in which all member firms were closely controlled by family holding companies. Nevertheless the modern zaibatsu continue to bear the marks of their past, and in this respect differ from financial–industrial groups found in the United States. Whereas U.S. groups tend to be loosely organized, zaibatsu are characterized by more centralized control, and more open and formal coordination (including formal monthly planning meetings by the top executives of member companies).

Secondly, group control in Japan, even more than in the United States, stems from the power of the big lender rather than the big stockholder. Equity capital plays a relatively small role in corporate financing, with the average Japanese corporation relying on loans for seventy to eighty percent of its capital (and on equity financing for twenty to thirty percent)—roughly the reverse of the average debt-to-equity ratio in the United States. As pointed out in *The Industrial Review of Japan,* the fact that the big zaibatsu banks "have overwhelming influence on their client enterprises is one of the characteristics of Japan's financial structure."

A third characteristic distinguishing zaibatsu from their counterparts in other countries is the central role of those uniquely Japanese institutions, the general trading companies, in extending group control at home and abroad. The top eight houses (all zaibatsu-affiliated) handle half of Japan's foreign trade; act as investment bankers as well as traders; mobilize and coordinate the flow of capital, raw materials, and finished products, especially overseas but also within Japan.

Member companies are bound to a zaibatsu by multiple ties, including ownership, credit, supply and marketing, and sometimes (but not always) management ties. A good, if incomplete, description comes from Hiroshi Okumura, of the Osaka Securities Company Economic Research Institute. A zaibatsu group, says Okumura, "is not the result, merely, of functional or transactional ties between independent businesses, but is rather *an organic entity* formed through interlocking stockholdings and personal linkages." ...

In addition to the six contemporary zaibatsu discussed in this report, zaibatsu-like groups exist around the Tokai Bank (in the

Nagoya area) and around the politically powerful Industrial Bank of Japan. . . .

THE ZAIBATSU AND KONZERNS IN JAPAN'S ECONOMY

By the end of World War II, the four zaibatsu (Mitsui, Mitsubishi, Sumitomo, Yasuda) held a position of unchallenged dominance in the Japanese economy, accounting for 24.5 percent of the total paid-up capital in Japan. The top ten business groupings accounted for 35.2 percent of paid-up capital.

Today's figures are not strictly comparable. But they do indicate that the six modern zaibatsu and seven konzerns enjoy a dominant position in the economy at least on a par with that of their 1946 forbears. For example:

• *In finance,* zaibatsu firms account for half the paid-up capital of fifty-five leading financial institutions. (In 1946 the four zaibatsu accounted for 49.7 percent of the paid-up capital of all financial institutions.)

• *In heavy industry,* considering only companies with yearly sales over $100 million, the members and allies of the six zaibatsu and seven konzerns today account for ninety-two percent of the paid-up capital. (In 1946 the four zaibatsu accounted for 32.4 percent of all paid-up capital in heavy industry; the top ten business groupings accounted for forty-nine percent.)

Comparison of absolute figures shows that the giant modern zaibatsu and konzerns not only have a share of the pie comparable to that of their 1946 predecessors, but the size of the "pie" itself has increased manyfold. In 1946 the top ten business groupings, including the four zaibatsu, accounted for $760 million in total paid-up capital at then prevailing exchange rates. As of March 1970, members and allies of the six zaibatsu and seven konzerns accounted for a bare minimum of $8,149,000,000 in paid-up capital. Making liberal allowance for currency depreciation, the evidence is clear that today's handful of combines controls the greatest concentration of productive forces in the history of Japan.

⊛ SOON AFTER WORLD WAR II, business leaders developed informal means of cooperation—the business federations described below. Roughly equivalent to the American National Association of Manufacturers, these lobby groups in Japan are far more powerful, acting essentially as the policy-making center for both business and government. Far from the American model of relative "pluralism" of business, labor, and other interests, they represent a centralization of business power unequaled in other capitalist countries.

The 1970s have seen the emergence of a new business group, the Sanken, or Industrial Problems Study Council. According to *Pacific Basin Reports,* Sanken, which has assumed leadership from older groups like Keidanren, the Federation of Economic Organizations, represents the development of an ever-increasing oligopoly in the Japanese economy.

CHITOSHI YANAGA *
Japanese Business Federations

... Under the zaibatsu system, representatives of Mitsui, Mitsubishi, and other great houses met, deliberated, and made policy decisions that were immediately transmitted to the various enterprises in their far-flung economic empires and were promptly carried out by hundreds of corporations throughout the country. With the zaibatsu gone, the business world no longer was in command of an effective, unified organization. Business leaders keenly felt the need for an overall organization to bring together the widely scattered, uncoordinated trade associations.

* Chitoshi Yanaga, *Big Business in Japanese Politics* (New Haven: Yale University Press, 1968), pp. 41–43, 46–52.

Zaikai leaders met on September 3, 1945, the day after the surrender documents were signed aboard the *U.S.S. Missouri,* at the official residence of the minister of commerce and industry, Nakajima Chikuhei, to discuss how to control the national economy, reestablish a business structure, and bring organizational strength and unity to the business world. Most urgently needed was an organization to represent the entire business community in presenting its desires to the occupation authorities.

FEDERATION OF ECONOMIC ORGANIZATIONS

The Federation of Economic Organizations (FEO) was set up in August 1946 under the aegis of the government and the occupation. It is an all-inclusive, powerful organization that functions as the supreme coordinating body of big business. Its main purpose is to maintain close contact with all sectors of the business community for the purpose of adjusting and harmonizing conflicting views and interests of the various businesses and industries represented in its huge membership. . . . It is the front office of the business community and is in effect a partner of the government. It is not a pressure group in the usual sense of the term, for its activities are extensive and its influence so great the results are obtained without resorting to ordinary pressure techniques.

FEO's regular membership embraces more than 100 major national trade associations and over 750 large corporations. In addition there are five special association members and fifty-one individual honorary members, all respected elder statesmen of the business world. Unlike the Federation of British Industries, forty percent of whose membership is made up of firms employing less than 100 workers, the FEO excludes small and medium enterprises and speaks exclusively for big business.

The federation is unique in that, although it is an organization for private business, its corporate membership includes both public and quasipublic corporations such as the Japan National Railways, Japan Monopoly Corporation, Japan Telegraph and Telephone Corporation, Japan Development Bank, Japan Export-Import Bank, Bank of Japan, National Finance Corporation, Medium and Small Enterprise Finance Corporation, Central Bank for Agriculture and Forestry, Central Bank for Commerce and

Industry Associations, Overseas Economic Cooperation Fund, Japan Public Highway Authority, Capital Rapid Transit Authority, and Japan Air Lines. Obviously, the inclusion of government and quasigovernmental agencies in the membership has helped greatly to reinforce the intimate business–government relationship.

The close relationship between the government and FEO is seen in the presence of cabinet ministers at the general meetings. It has become customary for them to extend greetings to the federation on such occasions. At FEO's 15th General Meeting on May 6, 1955, for example, the governor of the Bank of Japan, the minister of finance, the minister of international trade and industry, the director of the Economic Planning Agency, and the ministers of welfare and construction extended their greetings in person.

The president of FEO is regarded as the "prime minister" who presides over the *zaikai*'s "invisible government." In the performance of his duties he is assisted by five vice-presidents, one of whom is the full-time "deputy prime minister." This office has been held by Uemura Kogorō, dynamo and kingpin of the organization. . . .

JAPAN COMMITTEE FOR ECONOMIC DEVELOPMENT

A completely new economic organization without any prewar antecedents came into existence in April 1946 before FEO was actually launched. A few months after the surrender, in the early spring of 1946, even before the rubble of war had been cleared away in Tokyo, a small group of determined and dedicated junior executives gathered in a small room of the Industrial Club. Most of them were in their thirties and forties. A handful were still in their twenties. After several meetings they concluded that a new kind of organization was badly needed to give direction to the reconstruction of the economy, to the democratization of management, and to the modernization of business enterprises. They were thoroughly convinced that the new era demanded a new spirit, new ideas, and a new sense of unity and social responsibility on the part of the managerial class. The twenty-nine directors initially chosen to lead the new organization known as Keizai Dōyūkai—or, in English, the Japan Committee for Economic Development (JCED)—were in their forties. They were managing directors of corporations, although there were a few presidents among them. Dissatisfied with the status quo, they were determined to find new directions for the nation's economy.

The old zaibatsu attitude of putting profit ahead of everything else, they felt, was not only out of date but harmful and could not possibly contribute to the building of a strong and viable economy or really serve the national interest. They saw that an effective economic organization for spiritual regeneration and mobilization was imperative if economic recovery were to be achieved in the face of the confusion that gripped the nation. One of JCED's sponsor-founders, in recalling its early role, called it the "Youth Corps for cleaning up the rubble of war."

Speaking for the thirteen sponsors at the inauguration of JCED, Fujii Heigo deplored the instability and sterility of politics as demonstrated by the government's ineffectiveness and lack of policy, its failure to grasp the essence of democracy, and its preoccupation with democratic form and trappings. He was highly critical of those business leaders who were intent on preserving the old capitalist order under the guise of democracy and liberalism. . . .

The JCED differs from other economic organizations in that its membership of some 1500 is made up entirely of individuals who are bound together by common interests and goals and dedicated to promoting the healthy growth of the economy. Like its American counterpart, the Committee for Economic Development, it is a nonpolitical, nonprofit organization devoted to research that would make free enterprise fully compatible with economic growth and stability. It does not represent or speak for any particular group or corporation. Its major concern is overall national economic well-being. Especially significant from the point of close government–business relations is the fact that JCED membership includes the presidents, vice-presidents, or directors of public corporations such as the Japan Development Bank, Japan Export-Import Bank, Japan Housing Authority, Japan Public Highway Authority, and the Bank of Japan. . . .

Although it has been known as a "thinking" economic organization, JCED was not just a thinking group, even in the beginning. It was also an action group. While it served definitely as an ideological arsenal, advocating revised capitalism, democratic management, full employment, and increased productivity, it was active on management's front line, coping with labor problems and trying to rebuild the national economy through labor–management collaboration. After the Japan Federation of Employers' Associations was formed in 1948, JCED withdrew from activities in the labor field and concentrated its energies on policy matters.

JAPAN FEDERATION OF EMPLOYERS' ASSOCIATIONS

The Japan Federation of Employers' Associations (Nihon Kei-eisha Dantai Remmei), or JFEA, was founded in April 1948 to achieve industrial peace and increase productivity. As management's headquarters for labor policy, it devotes its energies almost entirely to labor problems, coping with the demands of labor unions, and promoting labor legislation. In terms of operational effectiveness, it is regarded as the most powerful and unified of the four organizations under discussion. Its voice is powerful enough to be a decisive factor in the government's choice not only of the minister of labor but even of heads of bureaus or sections within the ministry.

In a functional sense, it is similar to the FEO, except that it deals primarily with labor problems. Its greater cohesiveness and decisiveness of action is due to the fact that there is greater agreement in the business community in its confrontation with labor than in almost any other aspect of economic activities. FEO and JFEA are complementary. Their memberships are almost identical, with considerable overlapping of leadership. The two organizations may be regarded as the two sides of the same *zaikai* coin. Three public corporations, Japan National Railways, Japan Monopoly Corporation, and Japan Telegraph and Telephone Corporation, are members of JFEA, as are the trade associations. Presidents of the Japan Development Bank, the Japan Public Highway Authority, the Capital Rapid Transit Authority, and Japan Air Lines are on its board of directors. There are two general categories of membership: (1) national trade and employers' associations and (2) prefectural and local employers' associations. Small and medium enterprises are also included among the 30,000 companies that make up the membership. Member associations and their constituent corporations represent the whole range of industry and commerce, including construction, transportation, and mass media.

Since the JFEA must cope with labor's periodic offensives,

emphasis is on its tactical and operational functions. Its actions have frequently been aggressive and, at times, reactionary. The organization is highly sensitive to the activities of labor and the reformist parties, especially the Communist party, which is the *bête noire* of big business. It fights to assert the rights of management and, in its efforts to initiate and revise labor legislation, makes no bones about management's demands that its wishes be reflected in government policy. It has sent seven members, representing employers, to the government's Labor Legislation Council.

It maintains close liaison with the Ministries of Labor and Welfare, the Social Welfare Committees of both houses, and the Labor Subcommittee of the Policy Committee of the Liberal Democratic party. In addition, it holds frequent informal meetings with government leaders to discuss and communicate its views and wishes. It usually invites the Ministers of Labor and Welfare and the prime minister to its general meetings. It makes more effective use of mass media to influence public opinion in the interest of employers than any of the other three organizations. It has actually gone into the mass media industry and now finances a daily newspaper (*Sankei Shimbun*), a television outlet (Fuji Television), and a radio broadcasting company specializing in cultural programs (Bunka Hōsō).

In the immediate postwar years it was known as the "fighting Nikkeiren," since its main function was to fight off the labor offensives that were waged relentlessly against employers, but emphasis is now on the promotion of cooperation between management and labor. To maintain the expansion and growth of enterprises in the present era of trade liberalization, JFEA is exerting greater efforts toward increasing productivity, reducing costs, and training employees. It is prodding management to improve the quality of managerial personnel and to provide conditions favorable to the ready assimilation of technological innovations. It also places increasing emphasis on the social responsibilities of management.

JAPAN CHAMBER OF COMMERCE AND INDUSTRY

The oldest of the four economic organizations we have been discussing is the Japan Chamber of Commerce and Industry. It dates back to March 1878, when Japan was struggling to establish herself economically in the face of domination by foreign merchants. With eight businessmen as sponsors (among them, Shibusawa, Ōkura, Masuda, and Minomura) a Chamber of Commerce was founded in Tokyo at the instance of Minister of Industry Itō and Minister of Finance Ōkuma. Three years later it became the Tokyo Chamber of Commerce with Shibusawa as president.

Organized on a strictly geographical basis, the Japan Chamber of Commerce and Industry is a federation of 445 local and regional chambers in various cities throughout the country. It represents all business activities, large and small, manufacturing and financial, trades and services. It is the only one of the four organizations which includes medium and small enterprises as members and devotes much of its energies to strengthening them. But large corporations are also members, and their voice grows stronger with the passage of time. This is particularly the case with the Tokyo Chamber of Commerce, which virtually dominates the parent organization.

The activities of the Japan Chamber of Commerce and Industry are more or less similar to those of the other three economic organizations. They include dissemination of the views of the business community, presentation and proposal of policies to the government, the compilation and publication of statistics, education, and publicity pertaining to important issues and problems, the improvement of technology and management techniques, maintenance of standards in commerce and industry, the promotion of trade and tourism, and arbitration and mediation of differences arising in international trade.

The chamber is particularly active in the promotion of export trade, the improvement of the nation's balance of international payments, and international economic cooperation. On the domestic front, it concentrates on the development of the regional economy, increased consumption, and price stabilization. It maintains close working relationships with the ministry of international trade and industry, the foreign office, the ministry of transportation, and the Japan Foreign Trade Association.

It has been the practice of the Chamber to speak up on important political matters, frequently admonishing or prodding the government. In the spring of 1953 it expressed its dissatisfaction and displeasure at the government's failure to enact the proposed budget bill and other important pieces of economic legislation. Like the other three organizations, it invites cabinet ministers and the prime minister to its discussions of important matters. In 1961 it invited Prime Minister Ikeda, the minister of international trade and industry, the director of the Economic Planning Agency, and the postal affairs minister to its general meeting, at which a resolution was adopted calling on the government for a tax reduction.

PACIFIC BASIN REPORTS*
Zaibatsu and the Corporate State

> ... It is said that the Japanese economy, in the decade of the 1970s, is in the process of changing from an era of "competitive oligopoly" to one of "cooperative oligopoly." ...
> —Editorial, *Asahi Evening News,*
> January 11, 1972

The financial–industrial elite has a preponderant influence in the government of all the leading Western countries. But in Japan that influence is increasing to a point that borders on direct rule. The locus of power is the *zaikai,* defined by the *Mainichi Daily News* as "a politico-economic group of wealthy financial leaders who can exert tremendous influence on the government and politics." And when one talks about *zaikai,* one is talking first and foremost about leaders from the six zaibatsu, the seven konzerns, and the Industrial Bank of Japan.

The *zaikai*'s highest body for collective decision-making is the "Industrial Problems Study Council" [Sangyō Mondai Kenkyū]— or Sanken, as it is known. Innocuous sounding to the uninitiated, the Sanken evokes for Japanese businessmen what a similar body consisting of J. P. Morgan, John D. Rockefeller, Andrew Carnegie, and two dozen of their peers might have in the United States. Three-fourths of the Sanken's twenty-four members represent either zaibatsu or the top konzerns. Particularly influential in the Sanken are the Fuyo group and the Industrial Bank of Japan,

* "1972 Handbook of Japanese Financial/Industrial Combines," *Pacific Basin Reports,* April 1, 1971, pp. 11–12, 14–16.

although Mitsubishi, Sumitomo, and Mitsui groups are also well represented. Nippon Steel sends its two top executives to the Sanken, as do all four of Japan's leading business policy organizations. . . .

It was only in late 1970 that the Sanken assumed the role of "Big Business GHQ," as *Japan Stock Journal* tentatively describes it; or "Supreme Command of *zaikai* . . . strongest pressure group . . . a superpowerful organization that 'can even buy Japan',' in the words of the *Mainichi Daily News.* Until then the undisputed leadership of the business world fell to Keidanren, or Federation of Economic Organizations, a kind of super–Chamber of Commerce dating from the thirties and also dominated by zaibatsu. Until that time neither Keidanren nor Nikkeiren, which supervises labor relations for the *zaikai,* were represented on the Sanken, and for basic reasons.

There was a struggle over basic strategy, culminating in 1970, and Keidanren lost. The disagreement between Keidanren and Sanken was over how best to rationalize an oligopolistic economy and its relationship to the state; and this difference was personified in the chiefs of the two organizations, Taizō Ishizaka, long head of Keidanren, and Kazutaka Kikawada, of the Sanken.

Ishizaka, an old Mitsui group man known for years as "prime minister of *zaikai,*" had a reputation as a stout believer in laissez-faire—which meant, in the context of modern Japan, a believer in "competitive oligopoly." He and most Keidanren officials believed the various business groups should "coordinate their opinions" but not "establish a united leadership"; contend for indirect influence in the government, not combine to rule directly; preserve competition among them (along with cooperation) as essential for a healthy economy. This school of thought opposed the trend toward vastly increased state intervention in the economy.

Sanken chief Kikawada, on the other hand, believed the various business groups should unite and speak with one voice, rather than contend; should divide markets, rather than compete; directly control government policy, rather than influence it indirectly. Government, in turn, should play a "major policy role" in planning the economy. The logical outcome of the policies advocated by Kikawada is a system of "cooperative oligopoly," closely tied in with the government; the direct exercise of state power by a united business leadership—in a word, the corporate state.

In the fall of 1970, Keidanren essentially capitulated. Ishizaka's successor as Keidanren president, Kogorō Uemura, was obliged to join Sanken under humiliating circumstances—and Nikkeiren's chief executive Sakurada also joined—thus demonstrating to all that Sanken was now supreme. Kikawada, who only four years earlier had helped organize Sanken (along with Nakayama of the Industrial Bank and Iwasa of Fuji Bank), was now recognized as the new "prime minister" of a united *zaikai*. . . .

Four items from studies in the Japanese press illustrate in concrete terms the consequences of this important shift in business–political relationships.

• *"Zaikai*'s 'old boys,' with Ishizaka topping the list, remote-controlled politics by means of political donations. . . . When necessary to have *zaikai*'s intentions incorporated in national policy, [Ishizaka] did exert pressure on the government but by simply submitting petitions or recommendations. . . . He openly criticized politicians and bureaucrats. . . .

"Sanken is different. It gets into direct contact with the government's policymaking organs and arranges with them to have its intentions reflected in the policy they map out." One mechanism for direct control is the "policy board system"—long advocated by Kikawada and his group—whereby key *zaikai* leaders meet regularly to make state policy and inform the prime minister and cabinet of their decisions. Ten of these "deliberative councils" are already in existence, covering different phases of state policy.

• "Prime Minister Satō attends at least eight regular monthly meetings with *zaikai* leaders," including the Itsuka-kai, Kitchō-kai, and Sansui-kai, in addition to numerous informal contacts and the meetings of the ten deliberative councils.

• Kikawada "holds so much power that the Economic Planning Agency officials are afraid of displeasing him only to incur what they call the 'K purge.' Thus he never fails in having *zaikai*'s intentions reflected in the government's economic policy."

• The new nakedness of *zaikai* control came out during the furor over a proposed industrial pollution control law, when leaders of the ruling Liberal Democratic party (LDP) were faced with an overwhelming public demand for stiff controls. LDP officials met with *zaikai* leaders on November 19, 1970 and ". . . asked for 'greater than previous' financial aid from Keidanren so as to win the [mid-1971 House of Councilors] election. . . . On the occa-

sion Keidanren took up the environmental pollution issue." Both
Keidanren and Kikawada's influential Keizai Dōyūkai warned
against criminal penalties for industrial pollution. ("We shall have
none willing to work as factory managers," said a Keidanren
spokesman. "Factory management itself might become impractical
in some cases," warned a staff member of Keizai Dōyūkai.) LDP
whip K. Tanaka told newsmen that evening with unaccustomed
explicitness, *"Zaikai* is unanimously opposed to the environmental
pollution control law bills." Shortly thereafter, the government and
party cut all enforcement provisions out of the bill, rendering it
harmless.

In the realm of economic policy, the assumption of leadership
by the Sanken group is already beginning to have far-reaching
effects. Here is a look at some recent actions in this perspective:

1 ₌ Economic Relations with the United States—1971 witnessed
a stunning series of reversals of Ministry of International Trade and
Industry (MITI) guidelines on capital liberalization, drastically
speeding up the timetable for allowing foreign direct investment in
autos, computers, integrated circuits, and other industries. The
year also saw decisions to extend (in both time and scope) existing "voluntary restraint" agreements on textile and steel exports to
the United States, and to apply similar principles of "orderly
marketing" to other export industries.

Behind the decision to ease the tension in Japan–United States
relations—even if it meant "sacrificing" the textile industry, for
example—were the dominant voices of the steel, auto, and electric
appliance industries, which depend heavily on export sales to the
United States, and were willing to accede to U.S. commercial
"blackmail" to hold that market.

What emerged was a dual position: on one hand more speed in
opening Japanese industry to foreign investment; on the other
hand, assenting to limited U.S. protectionist measures so as to
safeguard a smaller-than-hoped-for but still healthy share of the
U.S. market. *Mainichi Daily News* described this stance of the
ruling *zaikai* in Tokyo as "acting from the 'utmost state interests'
viewpoint— *i.e.,* motivated by the 'collective capital of the Japanese economy' "—even if it meant the opposition of the textile
manufacturers of Osaka. "What is important here," the paper

concluded, "is that the government and the political world are taking action in accordance with the opinion of *zaikai*."

2. *Nippon Steel Merger*—Sanken saw it as

> essential to break through at a single stroke . . . the Antimonopoly Law bulwark. . . . When the Yawata–Fuji amalgamation plan was announced, there arose one movement after another opposing the proposed merger among the fellow steelmakers and principal users who would have to bear the brunt. Soon afterwards, however, the statements of *zaikaijin* [top business leaders] criticizing the merger plan disappeared completely from newspapers. That showed that Sanken did not waste time in arranging with each and every division of the national economy, where it kept an able liaison officer, to iron out the differences and consolidate the united front throughout *zaikai*. Against such united front of *zaikai*, the dissident scholars and government officials, especially the Fair Trade Commission staffers, could only make a futile resistance. *Zaikai* thus challenged the Antimonopoly Law and won the battle.

3. *New Steel Cartel*—In December Japan's Fair Trade Commission (FTC) authorized formation of an "antirecession cartel" by the six major steelmakers. *Asahi Evening News* in an editorial noted the formula for holding down production under official guidelines—"a cloak to hide what in effect is a cartel"—and statements of steel industry leaders that they intend to jack up crude steel prices by an average 5000 yen per ton. The newspaper inquired how the FTC intends to prevent steel price rises stemming from production cutbacks. The paper editorialized that the FTC action, together with "voluntary restraints" on steel exports to the United States and Europe, ". . . thus completes the intricate network of cartels that now grips the Japanese steel industry and markets, both domestically and externally. . . . The major changes that have taken place in the situation of the steel industry, which is one of Japan's basic industries, go so deep that they cannot help but create intensive repercussions in the structure of the overall Japanese economy."

4. *Holding Company Revival?*—In late 1969 a study group of Keidanren began drafting a plan for the rebirth of Japan's presurrender system of zaibatsu holding companies. The main argument for it was the vulnerability of sections of the economy to foreign takeover as a result of capital liberalization (a program, it

should be added, that is most energetically pushed by the very same *zaikai*). "The move seems to be much to the liking of the zaibatsu groups," said *Oriental Economist*. Mitsubishi Bank Chairman Tajitsu commented: "It would, in fact, be extremely convenient if we had a holding company," and many believe the new Mitsubishi Development Company will in fact be it. In such an event, the Antimonopoly Law—already sorely compromised—would suffer its final *coup de grâce*.

❀ THE GOVERNMENTAL BUREAUCRACY is another factor which ensures centralization of power. As Yanaga notes, "executive supremacy" continues to have a more important part in the governing process than the parliamentary Diet and political parties. The bureaucracy functions as the actual main decision-making body at the national level, with day-to-day influence supreme in most areas of government. In effect, the bureaucracy not only runs the government, but retains a veto over policies with which it disagrees. Usually the influence of the bureaucracy is exerted on behalf of the *zaikai*, and the bureaucracy's interests are seen in most cases to be identical with those of big business. Such a congruence of interests is further ensured by the continued control over the bureaucracy by a self-perpetuating administrative elite, men from similar backgrounds and the same schools, who are cultivated by businessmen often with the same educational and social background.

CHITOSHI YANAGA*
Role of the Bureaucracy

The government was the sole source of capital in the immediate postwar period, and the administrators were in control of the

* Chitoshi Yanaga, *Big Business in Japanese Politics* (New Haven, Conn.: Yale University Press, 1968), pp. 96, 98–99, 102–106.

allocation of funds to business and industry. Consequently, the top administrators held in their hands the power of life and death over various enterprises, and *zaikai* was at the mercy of those who dispensed the desperately needed funds. As promoter, protector, and spokesman of business and industry, the bureaucracy worked to advance the interests of private monopoly. Government officials were constantly on the lookout for effective policies for maintaining the economic system, often anticipating needs of business before *zaikai* itself was aware of them. The formulation of policies designed to meet the needs of business is still regarded as a responsibility of government ministries. . . .

Before World War II the Finance Ministry, which enjoyed the greatest prestige among ministries, managed to attract the best university graduates every year. Yet it was the Home Ministry that exercised the most extensive powers in administration, particularly through the use of its police powers. Until it was abolished after World War II, the Home Ministry was manned by more politically ambitious and power conscious individuals than any other ministry. A large number of these men went into politics in the 1950s.

With the government devoting most of its energies since the end of the war to ensuring healthy economic growth and prosperity, the Ministry of International Trade and Industry and the Ministry of Finance have come to exercise a decisive influence in the shaping of national policies. These two ministries and the Bank of Japan are now the first choice of the top graduates of the leading government universities, especially Tokyo University.

Because of the nature of the functions they perform, bureaucrats are experienced in planning, organizing, and drafting bills. They are good at administrative work and especially good at figures. These are skills highly prized by political parties as well as private business. Consequently, both the conservative Liberal–Democratic party and business are on the alert to secure their services, and bureaucrats have no difficulty in finding desirable positions after they retire from government service. . . .

Politicians and businessmen have little difficulty in establishing close relationships with civil servants. Corporations ply them with lavish entertainment and treat them as very important persons, which many of them undoubtedly are. Some companies have personnel assigned to government offices whose sole function is to secure the approval of applications by developing friendships with appropriate civil servants. Entertaining officials at mah-jongg parlors and teahouses has become standard procedure for corporation executives.

EXECUTIVE SUPREMACY

Japan's tradition of executive supremacy of nearly two thousand years' standing does not as yet seem to have lost its force, in spite of the new constitutional provision stressing the principle of legislative supremacy, which makes the Diet the highest organ of state power. On the contrary, the power of the executive branch appears to have increased in the period since the end of World War II.

The traditional concept of the government official as lawmaker, administrator, and judge, all in one, is no longer legally valid. An independent judiciary now exists, and a structural separation of the executive and legislative functions has been achieved. In practice the supremacy of the executive branch is quite evident. One can argue that administrative power in principle is strictly functional and its leadership derivative rather than primary, but this does not alter the fact that administrative officials exert a powerful and often decisive influence in making and implementing policy.

The Diet actually functions as a sounding board—a national forum for conducting debates and airing views—but, lacking a system of loyal opposition, it is becoming a mere rubber stamp, a ratifying and legitimatizing body under the domination of ex-bureaucrat members, who, perhaps unwittingly, are causing the legislative branch to play a minor, if not impotent, role. Its standing committees are more often than not headed and controlled by former bureaucrats, partial to the ministries in which they once served. These men work constantly to increase budget allocations to their former ministries, instead of trimming such budgets in the interests of economy.

The influence of the bureaucratic brotherhood—past and present civil servants who are active in government service, in politics, and in private business, interest groups, public corporations, and peripheral quasigovernmental bodies and organizations —is indeed pervasive. It reaches into virtually every nook and cranny of national life. In this context, its influence is certainly as great as, if not greater than, that of the business community.

There is hardly any aspect of Japanese life today which is not in one way or another the concern of the national government. The administrative bureaucracy of some three-and-a-half million persons exerts a powerful influence on the course and shape of national development. The central administration is the chief guardian of the public interest. It decides where the public interest lies. The decision as to how the nation's economy is to be ordered or structured rests with the administrators who formulate the budget, offer administrative guidelines for business to follow, let government contracts, and allocate and distribute subsidies, loans, investments, and purchases in ways favorable or unfavorable to certain industries and enterprises. In other words, the government through its administrators promotes, protects, controls, regulates, and often manages economic activities.

As society becomes ever more complex, due to undreamed-of advances in science and technology, the role of government becomes more crucial. The variety and complexity of government functions require specialization, with the result that the legislative branch tends not only to lose control of the executive but to rely heavily on the expertise of the bureaucracy. Lawmakers often find matters handled by the administrators beyond their comprehension. . . .

The administrative bureaucracy holds the key position in the legislative program submitted to the Diet by the cabinet. The various ministries prepare the bills. More than ninety percent of the laws enacted are government bills. Even bills sponsored privately by members of the Diet are usually drafted with the help of the bureaucrats in the ministries. The Diet therefore functions merely as a hopper through which bills must pass in order to obtain the stamp of legitimacy before they become laws.

Unlike the practice in the United States, where enabling legislation is enacted by the Congress, and administrators exercise discretionary powers within a given framework, the Japanese system delegates the formulation of enabling regulations to the administrators. The administrators in the economic ministries are in constant touch with representatives of economic organizations, enterprises, and corporations, who know better than the party in power what policies are needed in their own behalf. Consequently, the party also delegates the technical aspects of economic policy-making to the bureaucrats.

Once policy decisions have been made, the administrators are given wide latitude in execution. It is impossible to formulate regulatory details in advance. In the mind of an administrator in the Japanese system, the dividing line between the making and the execution of a policy is by no means clearly drawn. He applies policy or regulation as he sees fit or not at all.

Ministers may come and go and the party in power may have its ups and downs, but top-echelon administrators function without interruption and formulate policies according to their judgment. In the United States there is approximately an eighty percent turnover among the 700 to 800 top-level policy-making administrators every four or eight years. In the Japanese system there is practically no turnover except through the normal process of retirement. Only cabinet ministers change with considerable frequency, but in the postwar period there has not been much alternation of parties. There is no lateral entry into the administrative bureaucracy from private life. This continuity strengthens the strategic position of the bureaucracy, and enables its members to maintain continuous liaison with the lawmakers, who are themselves former civil servants.

The bureaucrats, according to Professor Fujiwara, are in effect subcontractors in the government's policy-making structure. Legislation on public safety, for instance, is normally proposed to the ruling party by the Japan Federation of Employers' Associations (JFEA) or initiated by the party itself. In the latter case, former civil servants of the defunct Home Ministry are usually the active participants and initiators of the legislative proposal. As for the actual work of drafting the bills, the JFEA and the party's Policy Committee both rely on officials in the Labor Ministry and the National Police Agency.

The bureaucratic fraternity is characterized by solidarity born of common experience and *esprit de corps*. It utilizes the complex ties, both horizontal and vertical, which form a vast network of influence and power. This is the basis of the strength of this extensive group, which is composed of not only present officials but also those who have retired and are in politics and serving as Diet members or cabinet ministers and those who have become top executives in large private and public corporations, government banks, public authorities, and quasipublic bodies.

Their political masters, including the cabinet ministers, decide only the broadest outlines of policy, leaving implementation en-

tirely to the permanent administrators. The higher civil servants
are therefore the "permanent politicians." They effectively control
the administrative machinery and are intensely jealous of their
autonomy. They brook no interference. Politicians often lay down
policy regarding the status, composition, and operations of an
administrative agency, but its execution is left to the civil servants,
who always have the last say and who invariably get their way.
Their power is inviolable when it comes to matters of internal
organization. Their ability to resist and frustrate attempts at reductions in force is a convincing demonstration of the power they
possess. . . .

DESPITE THE IMAGE of Japanese industry projected abroad
—one of giant factories operating in totally automated fashion—Japanese industry in reality is more than half composed
of small- and medium-sized enterprises. This "dualism" in
industry, a persistence of near-feudal industrial relations side
by side with the most modern plants, is explored below by
Hubert Brochier, a professor at the University of Paris. Far
from being an anachronism, Brochier explains, the dual structure has clear advantages for large corporations. It provides a
cushion of "expendable" small subcontracting firms and re-
dundant employees during recessions, dependable cheap subcontracting of parts, and a guaranteed reservoir of relatively
cheap labor. The lower cost of labor in smaller firms is particularly important given the higher wages paid by the corporations, and given the large part of their labor costs that are fixed
due to the permanent employment system for core employees.
For a contrary view of the relationship of the permanent employment system to labor costs, see the selection by Koji Taira
in the following section: "The Japanese Labor Movement
since 1952."

In effect, the giant corporations grow at the expense of the
small and medium firms, whose role is thus central to the
successful functioning of the Japanese economy. While the

origins of industrial dualism lie in "traditional" production—
Japanese crafts and handmade goods—small enterprises have
become integral to such modern manufactures as electronic
goods through the subcontracting of transistors, circuits, and
tubes.   ·

HUBERT BROCHIER*
Principal Characteristics of Small Firms†

Let's try, first of all, by means of a few statistics, to define the
importance of small- and medium-sized firms in the national
economy. According to the 1960 census, which uses the legal
definition of the small firm (a total capital of not above ten million
yen and less than 300 employees), small firms . . . employ eighty-
five percent of the work force. However, this is an overall figure
which throws together several different sectors, including the service with the industrial. It would be more accurate to use more
limited statistics, dealing only with manufacturing industries.

If we limit the examination to industry alone and set the upper
limit for small- and medium-sized firms at 200 employees, we
notice that, in 1960, small firms employed about sixty-six percent
of the labor force, as opposed to 41.3 percent in the United States
and 39.4 percent in Great Britain. These figures are derived by
setting the lower limit for large firms at 200 employees, but,
because of technical considerations, the small- or medium-sized
firm must be redefined for each branch of production. After this
correction is made, we see that small- and medium-sized firms
employ nearly seventy percent of the work force. It has been estimated, furthermore, that they produce more than fifty-eight percent of manufactured goods, and account for more than one-half
of all exports. . . .

How are all these small firms divided up among the various
branches of production? One set of statistics, from the "Survey of

* Hubert Brochier, *Le Miracle économique japonais, 1950–1970* (Paris:
Calmann-Lévy, 1970), pp. 110–113, 119, 126–128, 130–131, 133–134.
† Translated by People's Translation Service.

Small and Medium Sized Firms," ... gives the portion of total added value attributable to all firms by branch. This allows us to determine those areas in which small businesses predominate.

We find that in about half of the branches, small firms account for the lion's share of production. How did this division of labor come about? We can see that small firms are primarily concentrated in two areas: "native" industries like porcelain, food production, textiles, and traditional clothing; but also in a certain number of fields in the modern sector: precision instruments and spare parts for various complicated machines. We shall see that these two groups correspond to two special types of firms, the historical origin and present function of which are profoundly dissimilar. . . .

The essential characteristics of the small firm sector have now been approximately described and defined. The basic problem is how to provide an explanation for their survival. How is it that a backward sector of this size can survive in the midst of such a highly evolved capitalist economy? How does one explain the survival of often wretched and very poorly equipped workshops in the face of modern firms which should have competed them out of existence? How, in a word, does one explain the persistence of such a pronounced duality in an economy whose competitive ability is recognized and even feared by the great industrial powers? The answer to this question, by destroying the implicit assumptions that give rise to it, will show us that Japanese economic dualism is in fact, or has been up to now, an aid to competitiveness, and that to a certain degree, Japanese economic growth has been founded on it. . . .

The practice of subcontracting is . . . a direct consequence of the systems of permanent employment and wages according to seniority. Both are well established within the large firms and give them a very rigid labor cost structure. Because they cannot freely increase or decrease their own labor force, they use subcontracting as a stabilizing mechanism. This permits them to get around the difficulties imposed by traditional employment practices. But on the other hand, the lack of mobility of the work force in large industry provokes a transfer of the risks and costs of economic fluctuations to the unprotected small firm sector in which labor is much more mobile. Small firms, for their part, can if necessary slough off surplus labor into the semi-activity of worthless agricultural work. Thus, the solidarity of peasant families is what finally bears the social costs of the system. In an economy where, in what would appear to be an irreconcilable contradiction, a rigid system of employment coexists with violent economic fluctuations in time of crisis, the articulation of large firms to small firms to agricultural labor absorbs the oscillations. But at the same time as it stabilizes oscillations, it also transmits them from the sector in which they originated (owing to fluctuations in demand either inside or outside the sector) to the "regulator valve" sector, which is composed of a chronically overabundant agricultural population, into which are added the unlucky souls who have been thrown out of work by the great industrial recessions.

In order to draw up a complete balance sheet on the "advantages" of small firms, or at least on the reasons for their survival, we should bring out their extraordinary adaptability. Because of the small amount of capital investment required for these firms, because of the rudimentary nature of the equipment and materials involved, and under the pressures of necessity, small firms have been able to show a remarkable adaptability to fluctuations in demand. When silk isn't selling well, they switch to the production of nylon stockings. If the bottom falls out of the market for wooden sandals, they make plastic ones. If toys just won't sell, they launch into production of spare parts for automobiles.

However, this elasticity, this adaptability of small firms, which testifies to the quality of the management and the technical acumen of the workers, is gradually lessening because of their growing dependence on big companies and the increased specialization that goes with this.

This general picture covers a broad spectrum of specific situations. In some cases the position of small companies improves under the hegemony of the big firms, while in others they are hurt by it.

First of all, the degree to which big firms have recourse to subcontracting varies in different industries. If one calculates on the basis of the proportion of total costs going to subcontractors, one sees that the industries that subcontract heavily are shipbuilding, the automobile industry, machine tools, electric power, radio and television. In addition, one must remember that the actual amount of labor provided by the subcontractors is in excess of the proportion of costs attributed to them, since they pay particularly low wages. . . .

This brief analysis of the market structure in which small firms are called on to provide their services helps us to understand the deep reasons for their dependence on larger industry. We should add that this dependence is often grossly exploited by the large companies, which take advantage of their position to make a maximum profit on their production cost. This is because they themselves determine how much they pay to the smaller subcontracting firms. It can even be said that a whole series of social mechanisms exerts permanent pressure on the small firm to reduce its prices, even if the power of the large firms is left out of account. Furthermore these pressures make it difficult or impossible for the smaller firms to modernize.

Credit conditions, for example, work against them. In spite of various government attempts to improve the situation and in spite of the existence of certain institutions specializing in loans to small firms, they do not have an easy time finding the funds they need for short, medium, and long-term investments. Big companies, on the other hand, get preferential treatment from the bank that belongs to their group. Generally speaking, they also have the advantages of greater solvency and larger assets.

This inequality with respect to credit is felt particularly during periods of tight money. Loans to small firms (*i.e.,* loans that carry the greatest risk and the least commercial interest) are the first to be axed when decisions of the monetary authorities bring about a restriction of credit. Small firms are then caught between two equally dramatic perils, since on the one hand credit restrictions normally slow up demand, thus drying up their markets with the big firms, and on the other hand they often prevent the small firm from meeting its own obligations. The number of bankruptcies among small firms thus increases considerably every time there is a recession. In 1964, for example, the number of small firms declaring bankruptcy rose to the high figure of 4200, and in 1967 and 1968, which were *prosperous* years, the number rose to 8000 and then 10,000. It would seem clear that the process destined to liquidate the small firm has now been set in motion.

In many cases, the larger firms exert pressure on the small firms, which depend heavily on them, and make them into unwilling financial auxiliaries. All it takes for this to happen (and it is common practice) is for the big firm to pay the small firm by means of long-term drafts which fall due seven or eight months after delivery. Thus the financial clout of the larger firms allows them to pass on to subcontractors the burden of their financing, especially during periods when they are having great difficulty meeting their own obligations. . . .

Inasmuch as small firms form the major part of "native" industry, they have played an important role in the industrialization of Japan and especially in its development up to the Second World War. They made possible the low cost production of traditional consumer goods and this, in turn, permitted low salaries and a corresponding growth in savings, which were then invested in the development of heavy industry and war production. Furthermore, excess production became available for export. If, from that moment on, economic development had brought with it a general increase in salaries, it is likely that the structure of consumption would have taken on more modern forms and a portion of investments would then have had to be reoriented, away from heavy industry and export production and toward internal consumption. The growth process then would probably have been slowed down.

Today the role of small- and medium-sized firms is different but nonetheless vital. Since their employees constitute a huge "industrial reserve army," they make it possible for large-scale industry to take advantage of highly developed machinery and up-to-date technology, without creating too much unemployment in the country as a whole. In addition, small- and medium-sized firms contribute to the significant lowering of overall production costs by integrating low cost elements into the modern production process. The low salaries and poor working conditions explain their low cost.

Finally, these firms act as a mechanism regulating fluctuations in the market. By transmitting the effects of market fluctuation to archaic sectors of the economy, they enable large-scale firms safely to avoid the negative consequences of recessions. Thus the economic system of Japan benefits both from modern technology and from cheap labor. Obviously, this is what makes Japanese products so competitive on the international market. . . .

❃ IN ADDITION to its other unique features, Japanese capitalism has benefited from a rate of domestic savings unequaled in any other advanced industrial nation (and in few developing countries). Explanations for this phenomenon usually begin from the supposedly "natural" propensity of the Japanese people toward thrift. A few theories have even attempted to endow the Japanese with an Oriental variety of Protestant ethic, drawn from the Confucian tradition. Japan is thus seen as the "only" non-Protestant nation to industrialize, except, of course, for Catholic France and Italy and Orthodox Russia.

Another explanation is given here by Hubert Brochier. While not entirely denying native thrift, he attributes the rate of savings at least partially to structural factors in Japanese society, for example, less expenditure than in any other industrial countries on social security, welfare, and public services for which the Japanese have to provide for themselves. Moreover, he explains, a good part of "saving" turns out to be direct investment by owners of small- and medium-sized enterprises, who are often unable to obtain loans from either commercial banks or the government.

HUBERT BROCHIER*
Japanese Frugality†

As is widely known, the Japanese are one of the most savings-minded peoples in the world, in spite of a quite low per capita income. In 1968 private consumption came to only 52.5 percent of the GNP, compared to 63.7 percent in France. An independent

* Hubert Brochier, *Le Miracle économique japonais, 1950–1970* (Paris: Calmann-Lévy, 1970), pp. 228, 232–235.
† Translated by People's Translation Service.

study made in 1963 . . . showed that the proportion of personal savings to individual income was 22.5 percent in 1961, considerably higher than that in all the other industrialized countries (comparative figures are: Germany 12 percent; Great Britain 10.7 percent; France 8 percent; U.S. 7 percent). . . . Between 1951 and 1957, savings by individuals varied from 10.6 percent to 19.1 percent of national resources, considerably higher than the corresponding figure in France. The origin of these savings also reflects specifically Japanese tendencies. For instance, savings percentages in agricultural families are much lower than those of urban households, and, naturally, than those of owners of businesses or factories. . . .

Other statistics show that in 1964, 60 percent of the total yearly savings of urban workers came from bonuses, and that 55 percent of the summer bonus and 48 percent of the end-of-the-year bonus were saved. . . .

It should be added that until recently the practice of buying on credit has been very little developed and the only way to purchase one of those "consumer durables" (such as transistor radios, TV sets, and various appliances) that flood the shops was to save the money in advance. Thus the rate of private savings is boosted on a long-term basis by a series of national traditions or habits. . . .

To these structural considerations we should add, of course, the influence of a set of circumstances due to the war and its effects on family property. The need to "rebuild reserves" clearly played an important role in the growth of savings after the war, whether this was done by rebuilding the family dwelling or by building up reserves of money in all its forms.

Yet the phenomenon has deeper implications. First, it is linked to the principal characteristic of the economic structure of Japan: economic dualism, or the persistence of a broad sector of small, individually run firms, poor in capital, underequipped, and hard put to find funding on the capital market. Since, as we have seen, these firms are, for all that, no less an integral part of the industrial structures of Japan and are thus being carried along by the growth process, they can meet their equipment needs only through the personal savings of their owners—unless they can obtain funding from specialized institutions. The large number of firms in the service sector operate in a similar way and make a similar demand on the personal savings of the owners: it is admitted that more than half of all savings are accumulated by the owners of small firms (not including farmers). Thus, it is the numerical importance of small firms that explains, at least in part, the volume of private savings.

❀ FOR FOREIGNERS, the most visible result of Japan's unique business–government system is the impressive volume of Japanese exports—a seemingly endless cornucopia of cars, tape recorders, and television sets—backed by a domestic economy expanding at unbelievable rates: nine percent per year in the 1950s, ten percent during the sixties, and over thirteen percent in recent years. Japan's aggressiveness and competitiveness in selling consumer goods abroad are well known.

James Abegglen, a business advisor for the Boston Consulting Group, below examines some of the mechanisms which business and government utilize to ensure that exports continue to grow. Among these are government assurance of corporate debt and open encouragement of trade cartels—the latter forbidden in some international law. In addition to close cooperation between corporations, the government has an agency, JETRO, whose function is to facilitate exports.

Not all foreign observers find this system completely admirable, however. In the excerpts below from *Fortune* Louis Kraar reveals business practices used by Japanese firms that might be considered unscrupulous elsewhere. He views as particularly scandalous the agreements between prominent trading companies to divide markets rather than compete for them, unlike American exporters. He also notes a general willingness to forego immediate profits for the purpose of establishing "beachheads" in foreign markets in anticipation of profits later, also a practice not commonly followed by American corporations.

Yet despite this apparent success in marketing goods abroad, the Japanese economy, surprisingly, is less dependent on exports than any Western industrial nation except the United States, as the table from Brochier shows. In addition, the composition of Japan's exports has changed radically since the 1930s, when textiles were fifty percent of total exports. Today, more than seventy-five percent of Japanese goods sold abroad consist of technically advanced manufactures: steel, chemicals, cars, electronic manufactures, ships—none of them subject to the serious market fluctuations often suffered by textiles and raw materials.

JAMES ABEGGLEN*
The Economic Growth of Japan

... Japan is the only non-Western country that has become industrialized. It has not become Western in the process, and Japan's business system and practices are quite different from those of any Western economy. The differences have tended to obscure understanding in the West of the nearly ideal conditions Japan has created for economic growth. There are three key elements that determine the Japanese system: unusual methods of financing growth, a unique relation of government and business, and special ways of using labor resources.

The first requirement for growth is capital. A large part of the capital requirement of Japanese companies is supplied by bank loans—a practice that would be extremely dangerous and indeed unthinkable in most countries. In Japan it works, and it is a source of much strength. A massive debt goes into the capital structure of Japanese corporations, nearly eighty-five percent of whose capital is obtained by this means. The "net worth ratio" of Japanese corporations is therefore extremely low compared with European and U.S. companies in all industries. For example, the leading domestically owned petroleum company, Idemitsu, has a debt-to-equity ratio of about eleven to one. Debt ratios on this order mean that Japanese companies need not finance their growth out of re-

* James Abegglen, "The Economic Growth of Japan," *Scientific American* 222:3 (March 1970), pp. 31, 33–35.

tained earnings. Once they earn enough to cover the interest on their debt there is little financial constraint on growth.

How can Japanese business assume the level of risk associated with such heavy debt? The main reason is that the government stands behind the debt position of major Japanese companies. In so doing it not only makes possible the financing of growth through debt; it also ensures for itself a central role in determining the pace and direction of that growth.

The commercial banks are aggressive lenders, with almost 100 percent of their deposits out on loan. This makes them in turn extremely dependent for funds on the central bank (the Bank of Japan). In addition to bringing to bear the usual monetary tools (discount rates, open-market operations, and reserve requirements) the Bank of Japan determines the availability of funds for commercial bank loans by imposing penalty rates on borrowings from it by individual banks in excess of certain limits. The central bank in effect stands as guarantor to the commercial banks and thus ultimately to the borrowing corporations. By channeling funds through the commercial banks to specific companies on specific conditions, the Bank of Japan can save companies that are in trouble or can put them out of business. No major company's loan is ever likely to be called unless the central bank wants it called.

... Perhaps "Japan, Inc.," the label a Japanese businessman recently applied to his country's economy, best indicates how the system functions. In this analogy the Japanese government corresponds to corporate headquarters, responsible for planning and coordination, long-term policy formation, and major investment decisions. The country's large corporations are thus analogous to corporate divisions: they have a good deal of autonomy within an overall policy framework, are free to compete with one another, and are charged with operating responsibility. . . .

For the government, long-range plans are put forward by the Economic Planning Agency. These plans carry no legal sanctions for their enforcement; they are advisory, intended to indicate in what directions the economy can most efficiently move. Actual policies are worked out in the ministries, notably the Ministry of International Trade and Industry and the Ministry of Finance, and specifically through the work of some 300 consultative committees of businessmen and officials. Quite apart from formal committee meetings, there is constant interaction between business and government personnel, giving industry representatives an opportunity to learn how officials react to their investment proposals and plans and also to negotiate informally for assistance and favors.

Virtually all sectors of Japanese business are organized into trade associations that represent an industry before government agencies and in the community. The associations, in turn, make up a federation of economic organizations, Keidanren, which speaks for industry as a whole in major policy matters and in relations with counterpart groups in other countries. Keidanren cannot be compared to the Chamber of Commerce or National Association of Manufacturers; its prestige and real power are far greater. Similar business representation is accomplished with regard to trade union matters by a federation of employers' associations, Nikkeiren, which speaks for management in national policy decisions on labor and in confrontations with nationally organized trade unions.

Neither Japanese government nor Japanese business is monolithic. The ministries vary in their approaches, and different sectors of industry have different needs and objectives. Policies tend to represent compromises among various special interests. In general any substantial shift in product, investment, pricing, or distribution policy of a major company is at least informally reviewed by one or more government officials. Similarly, government decisions on new laws or regulations affecting business are preceded by detailed discussions with the businessmen likely to be affected. As implied by the phrase "Japan, Inc.," there is a basic assumption that the objectives of government and business are the same: the maintenance of Japan's economic health and the promotion of the nation's interests. Whereas a real corporation's head office can ultimately issue orders to its divisions, however, the Japanese government does not. To a remarkable extent the entire system operates by consensus.

There are several peculiarly Japanese reasons why this is so. One is the long history of government leadership in business, beginning with the Meiji era's drive toward industrialization and continuing with the drive toward military supremacy in the 1930s. Second, there is the strong sense of national identity that pervades Japan, derived in part from island geography, the long exclusion of foreigners, the single language, the homogeneous culture, and the sense of ethnic identity. Finally, there is the common background in education and training of leaders in government and in the large corporations, most of whom go to the same universities and have similar early career experiences.

The upshot of all these factors . . . is a national economy that behaves as one huge corporation. Moreover, "Japan, Inc.," is a special kind of corporation: a conglomerate in U.S. terms. A conglomerate can channel cash flows from low-growth to high-growth areas and apply the debt capacity of safe, mature businesses to capitalize rapidly growing but unstable ventures. It can move into a dynamic new industry and bring to it financial power that no existing competitor can match. It can increase capacity quickly. The result is that the conglomerate is in a position to dominate a new industry by setting prices so low that existing competitors cannot finance adequate growth. Its costs are so low, compared with the competition's, that it can sell at the going price and earn large profits. In all these senses "Japan, Inc." is indeed a conglomerate, a zaibatsu of zaibatsu. The Bank of Japan is the financial center, and with the bank's help each rapidly growing industry can incur more debt than it could on its own; the borrowing power of the entire portfolio—Japan itself—is available to each industry. Hence the economy as a whole funds new enterprises, holds prices down, competes successfully in the world market, and earns large profits.

LOUIS KRAAR*
How the Japanese Mount That Export Blitz

To hard-pressed competitors around the world, Japan's export drive is taking on the overtones of a relentless conspiracy to invade and dominate every vital international market. Almost everywhere, from North America to Southeast Asia, the Japanese are steadily increasing their already enormous share of sales. The very rhetoric

* Louis Kraar, "How the Japanese Mount That Export Blitz," *Fortune* XXXII:3 (September 1970), pp. 127–130, 170, 172.

of Japanese businessmen reinforces the image of a hyperaggressive trading power—with talk of "advancing" into a new area, "forming a united front" against foreign rivals, and "capturing" a market.

Moreover, this thrust comes from a nation that firmly shields its own market against foreign competitors, who are thus doubly provoked and are now threatening economic warfare. . . .

The trade clash is even more intense in the United States, which buys nearly a third of Japan's exports and is its largest single customer. Tokyo's refusal to adopt long-term "voluntary" limits on textile exports has prompted a reluctant Nixon administration to support stringent legislation setting quotas. And atop this significant American retreat from a free-trade stance, protectionist forces in Congress are pressing for even broader restrictions on other products. "The present economic image of Japan in the United States is not poor; it is bad," observes Philip H. Trezise, Assistant Secretary of State for Economic Affairs.

Japanese manufacturers of television sets are facing a major showdown with American competitors, who have accused the Japanese of dumping—*i.e.,* selling below recognized market prices —a charge on which a U.S. Treasury ruling is soon expected. While the Japanese TV set makers firmly deny dumping, other Japanese manufacturers openly acknowledge that they often use cut-throat export prices for market penetration. To establish its air conditioners in Western Europe, for example, Hitachi, Ltd., deliberately sold below cost for three years. As a company executive puts it, with surprising candor: "If you get a better price in some countries, then you can sell to others for a 'dumping' price. As long as the unit production cost is low, the company still has an overall profit from its total sales. We sold at a loss in Europe to break into the market, and now we're making a profit there."

Such practices fall somewhere in the gray shadows of the General Agreement on Tariffs and Trade, and the argument will doubtless continue as to whether they are in actual violation. Meanwhile, Japanese exports are expected to keep right on soaring. They are now projected to reach nearly $42 billion by 1975, producing a staggering trade surplus of $12 billion, a prospect that leads Assistant Secretary Trezise to warn: "I seriously question whether the international system can stand a Japanese global trade balance of $12 billion in 1975."

The starting point for this trade offensive is an economy of phenomenal strength, directed wholeheartedly toward growth rather than immediate profit. Over the past decade the Japanese gross national product has increased by an average of more than sixteen percent annually, and from this ever broadening base, exports have also been rising by an average of sixteen percent a year—about twice as fast as the growth of world imports. The entire economic system is, inherently, a powerful export-promotion apparatus. Always anticipating growth, corporations routinely expand manufacturing facilities to optimum size, pushing excess production onto world markets at profit margins that competitors find cruelly low—when they exist at all. Now Japan is preparing to move on to new trade peaks by emphasizing exports of entire industrial plants. As befits an insular industrial giant, it is also making long-term deals overseas to assure a stable supply of raw materials for use in the ever greater expansion of its export position. Within five years the Japanese expect a 123 percent rise in exports, enough to seize at least ten percent of the global market.

Hit with the full impact of this aggressive export drive, rival industrial nations are now beginning to ponder the singular, and devastatingly effective, tactics being employed by the Japanese. The program has some highly original features that will be hard to match:

• The export offensive is commanded by Premier Eisaku Satō in person; he heads the Supreme Trade Council, where top business and government leaders quietly slice up the world market and set annual goals for every major product and country.

• To boost exports, the government backs corporations with an arsenal of help—credit at preferential rates, attractive tax incentives, and even insurance against overseas advertising campaigns that fail to meet sales targets.

• Cartels of exporters meet regularly to fix prices and lay plans for overwhelming foreign competitors.

• A large and growing foreign aid program is, at heart, another export-promotion device, fueled with long-term credit and direct investments.

• Giant general trading companies spearhead the export drive. Their tireless sales forces abroad are backed by the full force of Japan's banks and government ministries.

• A government-owned company, JETRO, operates on a global basis to promote Japanese products and arm companies with export intelligence.

EXCEEDING TARGETS IS A DUTY

The key to the entire program is intimate, effective teamwork between corporate executives and government officials at every level. United by a group spirit that makes the Japanese behave like a tight-knit family, businessmen and bureaucrats cooperate to promote continuing growth. . . .

Detailed strategy for the export drive is developed through the Supreme Trade Council, a thirty-member body that brings together the country's elite from key ministries dealing with the economy and from the major private industries. . . .

To carry out expansion plans, the Ministry of International Trade and Industry (MITI) constantly confers with company representatives about allocation of resources. Through "administrative guidance" (which is almost always obeyed), MITI even sets minimum sizes for industrial plants when it feels economy of scale is vital. The Ministry of Finance, through the Bank of Japan, funnels funds to areas with the highest growth potential. By backing an extremely high use of corporate debt to finance growth, this ministry and the central bank play a key part in setting the pace and direction of expansion. This government structure stabilizes a Japanese business system devoted to high growth—the launching platform of the export offensive. . . .

The system enables companies to use highly flexible market penetration tactics. Two Japanese auto makers—Nissan Motor Company and Toyota Motor—established footholds in the United States by offering dealers higher commissions than were given on other imported cars, as well as unusually generous advertising support. . . . Other Japanese companies readily acknowledge that they forego profits to break open new markets. "When there's sharp competition and we want to introduce our products, then in the initial sale we make a sort of sacrifice hit," declares Morihisa Emori, managing director of Mitsubishi Shōji Kaisha, Ltd., the general trading company with the largest total sales. There is a distinctively Japanese motive behind such tactics, he explains: "In America top management people are big stockholders and are more defensive about maintaining profits. For us, growth is most important."

Such penetration pricing is not only a significant competitive device, but also sets the base for handsome future profits. The rapid growth of production facilities at the sacrifice of high immediate returns cuts unit costs; this steadily leads to large profit margins at the same time that it allows highly competitive prices to squeeze out rivals. Until three years ago, Japan's shipbuilding industry operated at almost no profit margin for exports, according to a highly qualified Tokyo accountant; now Japanese yards have heavy backlogs of orders, turn out half the annual ship tonnage of the world, and report tidy earnings. Norihiko Shimizu, a Japanese economist with the Boston Consulting Group, declares: "Japan's pricing policies can in no way be termed dumping. They constitute a powerful competitive weapon in capturing and holding market share." . . .

TANKERS AND INSTANT NOODLES

The uniquely Japanese *sōgō shōsha,* general trading companies, add a number of effective touches of their own. As the principal sales agents for all products, these mammoth companies mobilize the combined forces of manufacturers, banks, and government and are the day-to-day leaders in Japan's assault on world markets. The ten largest trading houses are responsible for some fifty percent of the country's exports and sixty-five percent of imports. Together with smaller, specialized firms, the traders make more than seventy percent of Japan's total foreign sales.

. . . The trading firms thrive on a traditional form of Japanese economic cooperation. Most manufacturers concentrate entirely on production, assigning to traders both the buying of raw materials and the selling of finished products at home and abroad. As middlemen, the large trading companies earn their profits (with margins as low as 0.5 percent) on massive turnovers. In return for commissions, trading houses assure manufacturers of growing markets and come to their aid with timely infusions of credit. . . .

Since any major international transaction must be cleared, at least informally, with MITI, the Japanese government is able to guide trading-house teamwork in directions that will expand markets. One result is an easy blending of official aims with private business interests—as when Japanese trading firms signed a five-year contract with the Soviet Union in 1968 to import $163 million worth of lumber from Siberia in exchange for exports of machinery and textures valued at the same amount. Japan sorely needs lumber, while its manufacturers are always seeking new outlets. . . .

The government works closely with the trading companies, too. An association of fourteen top trading companies meets every other month, often with government officials present, to discuss foreign-trade tactics. Inevitably, such gatherings of supposed competitors fortify cooperative bonds. When mainland China's Premier Chou En-lai announced in April that Peking would not trade with Japanese companies dealing with Taiwan and South Korea, the major trading companies reacted as though they had arranged a division of labor. Some firms chose to stick with China, while others decided to maintain business with Taiwan and Korea. But the overall result so far has been to ensure Japan's continued access to all those coveted markets. . . .

Although carried under the banner of "economic cooperation," nearly half of Japan's total $1.2 billion assistance to developing countries last year consisted of export credits for the purchase of Japanese products. Private companies handle most of these sales with government financing, actively seeking out and signing deals that are officially called foreign aid. . . .

Lumped into the aid package are direct private investments (totaling $144,100,000 last year), which also stimulate Japanese exports. Overseas joint ventures, carefully coordinated with the government, open up fresh markets for Japan. With combined financial help from major trading companies, banks, and the government, Nippon Steel has established joint-venture mills in Malaysia, the Philippines, and Brazil. The mills are considered "foreign aid" even though all are equipped with Japanese machinery, and the Philippine mill buys semiprocessed hot coils from

Nippon Steel. None of the foreign affiliates competes in Japan's principal markets in highly industrialized countries. By spawning manufacturing affiliates for textiles in underdeveloped countries, Japanese companies benefit both from cheaper labor and from new outlets for petrochemicals required by the foreign factories. . . .

Surprisingly, in view of the tremendous overseas sales effort, Japan's economic strength is relatively independent of trade. Exports account for only about nine percent of GNP, in contrast to nineteen percent for West Germany and thirty-five percent for Holland. While Japan naturally must export to pay for foreign purchases of raw materials, its relative dependence on imports is shrinking. Technological advancement has reduced reliance on imports of machinery, and the more advanced heavy and chemical industries require proportionately less in the way of imported raw materials. . . .

Ultimately, long-repressed domestic demands could slacken the pace of export growth. Despite its emergence as the third-largest economic power in terms of GNP (after the United States and the Soviet Union), Japan still faces widespread deficiencies in housing, social services, and roads, as well as a choking environmental pollution. The industrious work force has lately been demanding—and getting—wage increases that outpace productivity gains.

EXPORTS AND IMPORTS AS A PROPORTION OF GROSS NATIONAL PRODUCT IN 1966 (CURRENT PRICES) IN SEVERAL INDUSTRIAL COUNTRIES*

	Exports	Imports
The Netherlands	44.2%	45.3%
Belgium	36.3	37.4
Switzerland	30.8	30.0
West Germany	20.9	19.4
United Kingdom	18.4	18.9
Italy	17.9	15.8
France	14.5	14.3
Japan	11.5	9.8
United States	4.9	4.8

* Source: Hubert Brochier, *Le Miracle économique japonais, 1950–1970* (Paris: Calmann-Lévy, 1970), p. 244.

COMPOSITION OF JAPAN'S FOREIGN TRADE BY CATEGORY OF PRODUCTS*

	1934–1936	1953	1963	1967
EXPORTS				
Textiles	50%	36%	23%	16%
Metals and metallurgical products	7	15	30	17
Machines	6	15	27	42
Chemical products	3	5	6	17
Nonmetallurgical products	2	4	4	4
Food products	9	10	5	4
Others	23	15	5	–
	100	100	100	100
IMPORTS				
Food products	22	26	16	16
Raw materials and fuel	57	58	61	58
(including raw materials for textiles)	(32)	(20)	(13)	(8)
Manufactured goods	21	16	23	26
	100	100	100	100

* Source: Hubert Brochier, *Le Miracle économique japonais, 1950–1970* (Paris: Calmann-Lévy, 1970), p. 245.

4. The Japanese Labor Movement Since 1952

⚜ MOST OF the Japanese labor movement is organized in "enterprise" unions. The enterprise union consists of the workers in a given company or plant and is roughly comparable to a local of an American union. It crosses trade and skill lines, often including both blue- and white-collar employees. The enterprise unions of an industry, for example of coal miners, in turn belong to the "national union" of coal miners. However, such national unions are not at all analogous in power to a union like the United Mine Workers or the United Auto Workers. As the discussion below indicates, the national unions have virtually no money, no staff, and no economic power. In Japan it is the enterprise unions which make decisions about wages, strikes, and other economic issues.

At a higher level, unions generally belong to one of the national labor federations. There are two major ones, Sōhyō and Dōmei. Except for an annual "spring wage offensive," their function is largely political. Sōhyō provides major financial and manpower support to the Japan Socialist party, Dōmei for the right-socialist Democratic Socialist party. Sōhyō began in 1950 as an anticommunist federation after the Red purge, but it soon moved somewhat to the left. Dōmei is a recent federation, organized in 1964. However, it was a merger of three older groupings long oriented toward right socialist politics. The first was Sōdōmei, which had roots going back before World War II. The other two, Zenrō and Zenkankō, grew out of the dissident groups from Sōhyō. During the

1960s somewhat less than half of the unionized work force was affiliated with Sōhyō, while Dōmei and independent federations were smaller. And as late as 1964 almost one-third of all unionized workers were not affiliated with any national federation at all.

The "dual economic structure" of Japan greatly reduces the potential power of unions. Union activity is confined to the large firms, as well as to public and quasipublic corporations (which operate railroads and telecommunications in competition with private firms). This means that unions extend to only about one-third of the *total* work force; the other two-thirds is in small- and medium-sized enterprises, the less "modern" sector of the Japanese economy. The smaller firms pay less, and employees there have less status. This structure is weakening, but how fast it will break down and what it will mean is unclear.

SOLOMON LEVINE*
Enterprise Unionism

The reasons for the emergence of enterprise unions in Japan have been fully explored elsewhere and may be quickly summarized here. Economic, political, cultural, and ideological factors all contributed to their development. As mentioned, in the immediate postwar years, enterprise employees, blue- and white-collar alike, were threatened equally by the ravages of rampant inflation and dire shortages. Their economic interests suddenly merged. Since open labor markets did not exist, the greatest assurance of economic security for a worker lay in gaining recognition of permanent attachment to his enterprise. By pooling their bargaining strength together, white- and blue-collar workers could extract employment guarantees from management, weak as the latter were in this period of economic chaos and mindful of occupation

* Solomon Levine, "Unionization of White-Collar Employees in Japan," in *White-Collar Trade Unions,* ed. Adolf Sturmthal (Urbana: University of Illinois Press, 1967), pp. 235–240.

directives. For economic reasons alone, the manualists depended on their alliance with the white-collar workers, and vice versa.

In addition, the white-collar workers were in key positions to know about and understand the technical operations and financial conditions of their enterprise. With management sorely harassed by the occupation and in peril of being purged, the manual workers in many cases looked to the white-collar members for leadership in presenting bargaining demands, organizing the union, and oftentimes actually administering the company. In a sense, white-collar leadership replaced management in looking out for the welfare of the firm's employees. A chief motivating force was to preserve the enterprise as a source of livelihood for all the permanently attached. . . .

Enterprise union structure . . . was accompanied by two distinct levels of activity in the newborn Japanese labor movement. At the enterprise level, particularistic activities prevailed with almost exclusive attention given by the enterprise union to problems immediately affecting the enterprise. At the national level, the primary preoccupation of the union leaders was with ideological and political issues. . . .

But for the most part, this meant that the enterprise unions would be primarily concerned with problems at the local level and would give little heed to the needs for integrating and developing the labor movement at the national level. A vigorous but narrowly confined collective bargaining system developed, centering mainly on the career guarantees for permanent workers and wage advances geared to length of service within the particular enterprise. The enterprise union usually secured union shop and dues checkoff guarantees for its members, provision of office space on company premises, and some share in the management-sponsored welfare program. Only in a few instances—such as in shipping and to some degree in coal mining, textiles, and private railways—did multiple-enterprise bargaining emerge. Moreover, negotiations were handled strictly by the enterprise union's officers; neither they nor management particularly welcomed participation of "outsiders" from national union organizations to which the enterprise unit affiliated. Finally, the bargains made usually applied to the entire regular work group, white- and blue-collar alike, in the form of blanket wage increases and bonus payments. The stake of the white-collar employee thus was tied to the blue-collar worker. In some agreements the distinction between *shokuin* and *kōin* was formally abolished, and in the early years there was a noticeable closing of the wage differential between the groups. Little attention was given to job evaluation and classification plans, the bargainers preferring to rely mainly upon factors of age, education upon entry, length of service, family size, and other nonproduction related elements. . . .

Under these arrangements, there has been no decline in white-collar membership within the enterprise unions, and there have been relatively few instances of permanent breakaways (with the exceptions to be noted) of the white-collar elements from them. Management, it may be added, probably has not been wholly displeased with the combined union structure, since, if unionism there must be, the enterprise form serves to strengthen the ties of the workers to the enterprise, and enterprise-union white-collar leadership often moderates union demands upon the management (who often consider such experience for white-collar employees as good training for promotion up managerial ranks).

Widespread development of enterprise unions almost immediately raised questions of employer interference and company-dominated unionism, primarily because of the prominent leadership role exercised by white-collar members. Both the new Trade Union Law of 1946 and the Constitution of 1947 guaranteed workers the right to organize unions on virtually whatever base they chose. The problem, of course, was how to draw the line between worker and manager in organizations where the distinctions between the two were highly blurred because of Japanese methods of administration, allocation of authority, and decision-making. While the Trade Union Law was finally amended in 1949 to eliminate management representatives from union jurisdictions, many of the unions opposed the changes partly out of fear that their leadership would be weakened and bargaining strength reduced at the enterprise level. Some of the most active organizers of the new unions have been white-collar employees. For example, a survey in 1947 found that in the metal industry close to half the active organizers had been drawn from *shokuin* positions, and of these half had come from the ranks of *kakarichō* (subsection chiefs). It was also found that sixty percent of the *kōin* organizers actually were senior first-line work leaders who were likely to be the closest subordinates of *kakarichō*.

The revised law now excluded from the protection of the labor relations legislation any worker organizations "which admit to membership officers, workers at the supervisory post having direct authority to hire, fire, promote, or transfer, workers at the supervisory post having access to confidential information relating to the employer's labor relations plans and policies so that their official duties and obligations directly conflict with their loyalties and obligations as members of the trade union concerned and other persons who represent the interest of the employer" (*sic*). The administrative task of drawing the line between those eligible and not eligible to become unionists was left to the tripartite Labor Relations Commissions established by the act, through a set of provisions for examining trade union qualifications. At least sixty percent of all unions before the 1949 amendments had permitted higher management functionaries to serve as officers. As a general rule, the commissions now drew the line to include *kakarichō* provided they were not engaged in labor relations or personnel functions. This has meant that most of the new recruits into the unionized enterprise or organization, even though destined to rise into management ranks, still almost inevitably become union members. Some of these, young university graduates imbued with a sense of reformism or even radicalism, keep alive the white-collar militancy originally exhibited among the enterprise unions. Those who do rise into management ranks usually can boast of earlier trade union ties and are often able to continue in close contact with the enterprise union leadership.

ALICE H. COOK*
Industrial Unionism

National unions in Japan are, with a very few notable exceptions, federations of enterprise unions. The national union has no individual members. Its administration serves mainly to coordinate the work and programs of the enterprise unions by providing a meeting ground where, at annual or more frequent intervals, the

* Alice H. Cook, *Japanese Trade Unionism* (Ithaca, N.Y.: Cornell University, 1968), pp. 63–66.

representatives can arrive at consensus on a variety of matters only indirectly concerned with union–management relations. . . . [L]eaders of the enterprise unions do not seek nor do they rely upon assistance from the national unions in any of their day-to-day affairs.

The national union's resources are slender. Its power in every respect is limited. It undertakes, almost always, only indirect economic activity. It provides the most general guidelines ("Raise wages to the level of Western Europe!") and, with the few exceptions to be noted, does not participate in bargaining. It rarely sets up strike funds, and where these so far have been established they are inadequate. National unions are only now in some few instances beginning to develop mutual benefit programs. Their research and education sections exist in the person of a single nonprofessional member of the central executive committee who has neither the finances nor the know-how to provide significant services (nor do the enterprise unions seek such services), except for the publication of a union journal.

Yet these bodies are genuine entities within the labor movement. Labor leaders generally see a great need for them and project their development into organizations somewhat like the national unions of the United States or even of Germany. . . .

The model toward which Japanese national unions strive is commonly referred to as "industrial unionism." Achievement of industrial unionism in Japanese terms would mean that the national union could accumulate and administer a strike fund; participate with the enterprise officers in bargaining; set up benefit programs, provide research, educational, and organizational services for its regional and enterprise affiliates, exercise discipline over its subordinate units and over its members, and in general look and behave like an American industrial union. My consistent attempts to discover what steps were being taken toward realization of this goal yielded pitifully few and faltering examples, a reflection presumably of the entrenched power of the enterprise union system in Japan. It is unlikely that Japanese trade unions can become industrial unions in their own definition of this term short of a radical change in the whole industrial system in Japan. These possibilities will be discussed at a later point. Suffice it to say here that the unions' progress toward centralized power is everywhere strongly proposed but only haltingly and half-heartedly undertaken. To be sure, certain unions are setting up benefit programs. The hope is that these programs will turn the attention of the member to his national union, attaching him to it by strands of obligation, gratitude, and loyalty. Similarly, a number of national unions in private industry are taking the first halting steps to establish strike funds. In all these undertakings, without exception, the problem as has been noted above is to persuade enterprise unions and their members to divert any substantial additional funds to the national office programs when the enterprise unions may be already operating their own benefit programs and administering their own strike funds.

Levine has long contended that since "the role of the national unions in the Japanese collective bargaining process is obtuse and indirect," they devote their energies for the most part "to political strategy and the ideological struggle—and the more they concentrate upon these activities, the less qualified they become to handle bargaining issues at the enterprise level." In other words, "the national unions and centers perform the universalistic political functions of the labor movement; the enterprise unions, particularistic economic functions." While I largely agree with Levine's contention I would nevertheless maintain that the national union, despite its absence at the bargaining table, exercises important influence on the list and levels of demands, on consultations which precede settlement, on scheduling of strikes and coordination of other pressures on employers, and even on the level and nature of final agreements—in a word, its economic function and influence are far from insignificant. While, so far as political policy and activity are concerned, the national union clearly plays an important role, the enterprise unions are also politically active, particularly in local elections, so that here too the functions of coordination and leadership of the enterprise affiliates are at least as important in the national union's political activity, as is direct liaison of the enterprise unions with a political party. . . .

Shirai, in his study of union finances, notes that the national union may by no means receive all the per capita nominally due to it.

The relationship between individual union members and a national union or [center] is quite weak, and a national union cannot give much material return to individual members except in a few cases in terms of strike benefits, relief benefits, and mobilization of assistance for picketing. Therefore the national union's share of dues represents, so to speak, an abstract "cost of unity" or "expenses for united activities." Under such circumstances, enterprise unions report and pay on a number of members which is often less than the actual membership. This will vary depending on the degree of unity among affiliated enterprise unions, their capacity for industrywide concerted action and for industrywide bargaining. In other words, *the actual sum of dues paid the national union will vary with the attitudes of the affiliated enterprise unions toward industrywide concerted action* and the degree of autonomy each claims to have. . . . *Thus the determination of a national union's share of dues is a highly political matter and differs with the tradition of each national union.*

Thus the problem of where and how to attack the weakness which has its source in income is increased by the circularity of the problem. Low income means little staff and power. Little staff and power mean little service either to the enterprise union or its members. The effect of having few and only restricted services available from the national union is to throw the enterprise union back upon its own resources and thereby to strengthen the vested interests which develop under local autonomy. Several important unions, of which the chemical workers is a good example, are determined to establish at least central strike funds in the national treasury and have begun to do so in a small way. The problem is that of raising the per capita or other income of the national union. A decisive breakthrough depends on the national's being able to offer substantial benefits in a critical strike of unlimited duration. This, in turn, is difficult to do without some initial accumulation of a capital nest egg. The chemical workers have begun not only by slightly raising per capita dues but by borrowing, *i.e.,* holding, some of the welfare and strike funds of the enterprise unions. Such a solution is only possible, however, when the affected enterprise unions are not immovably jealous of their own autonomy in these matters.

HUBERT BROCHIER*
The Great Trade Union Confederations:
Sōhyō and Dōmei†

The present situation is characterized by the division of trade unions into two rival confederations, Sōhyō and Dōmei, and by an important percentage of trade unions that are either independent or whose affiliations fluctuate.

Sōhyō

In 1968 Sōhyō was by far the most powerful organization. Its membership was 4,191,000 (forty-five percent of unionized workers).

The most important unions in Sōhyō are public employees' unions: city and county employees (Shichirō, 840,000 members), teachers (Nikkyōsō, 550,000), national railroad system (296,-000), post office (228,000), and telephone workers (186,000).

In the private sector Sōhyō includes the private railroad workers unions (253,000), metalworkers and machinists (213,000), day laborers (153,000), steelworkers (209,000), chemical workers (160,000), and coal miners (61,000).

Workers in the public sector are more numerous than those in the private sector; they also have a prevailing role in the leadership of the organization. Since their salaries are fixed by the government, Sōhyō has to launch campaigns in the fall (when the national budget is being prepared) or in the spring (when the budget is voted by the legislative assembly), which is not necessarily convenient for the private sector.

The political philosophy that inspires Sōhyō is usually based on Marxism, at least within the leadership and in the official proclamations. But most unions reject orthodox communism and communists have been excluded from the leadership. Sōhyō invokes the concept of class struggle and endeavors to fight "capitalist

* Hubert Brochier, *Le Miracle économique japonais, 1950–1970* (Paris: Calmann-Lévy, 1970), pp. 165–167, 169–172.
† Translated by People's Translation Service.

monopolies." Since the confederation has little influence so far as collective bargaining is concerned, it is essentially oriented toward political action. This tendency is reinforced by the fact that a good number of its members, being civil servants or public employees, do not have the right to strike or to express their demands directly; they consequently tend to express them on a political level. In addition, there are powerful ties, personal and institutional, between the union and the Socialist party (a great number of the Socialist members of the Diet come from Sōhyō, which provides financial support for the activity of the party).

The political program of Sōhyō is largely oriented toward foreign policy: it is at present centered around an active participation in the peace movement. Since its second congress in 1951, Sōhyō has advocated "four principles of peace":
—the settlement of a universal peace treaty
—the neutrality of Japan
—the refusal of all military bases
—the refusal to rearm
This attitude provoked the split out of which came Zenrō (the leading wing of the rival confederation, Dōmei. It also led Sōhyō to refuse to join the International Confederation of Free Trade Unions [ICFTU] and to oppose, at times violently, American policy in Japan. Sōhyō expresses strong hostility to the idea of rebuilding the Japanese army (even if solely for self-defense purposes). The consequence of its principle of neutrality is a quite definite anti-American attitude; but this does not mean that Sōhyō is connected with the Communist party. . . . In fact, Sōhyō has excluded old Communist leaders from its leadership and from all important bodies, and it seems much closer to a left-wing socialist organization without any international discipline. . . .

However, it would be a mistake to exaggerate the "politicization" of Sōhyō and to imagine that it does not have an economic impact: on the contrary, it has been marked by the development and the increasing success of "spring offensives" (*shuntō*), which aim at salary increases. These offensives constitute a much more systematic technique for making wage demands than the "rendez-vous" [between workers and management] of the French trade unions. The tactic of spring offensives is now ten years old. The number of union members who participated in them was more than 1.4 million in 1955 and reached 6.5 million in 1964, with regular yearly increases. The importance accorded to the economic struggle is indicated by the ascension of Kaoru Ōta to an important position of union leadership. It can be said that the united action of the great majority of Japanese unions in the struggle for pay raises has become an institutionalized practice.

The unions have recognized that this tactic is the only one that allows them to obtain high pay raises and to tip in the workers' favor the scales usually balanced in favor of the employer. Furthermore, the tactic avoids the situation where pay raises are granted in proportion to the scale of business of the particular firm, whereby raises would be lower in the sector of small- and middle-sized industry. It is apparent that the method of the spring offensive, which brought about mediocre results between 1956 and 1960 (five to nine percent annual raises), has had greater success since that date. Since 1961, pay raises recorded during the course of the spring movements have usually been in excess of ten percent, in spite of the growing opposition of Nikkeiren (the employers' federation). This success is doubtless due to the fact that specialized manpower has become progressively scarcer in a large number of areas, and perhaps because today the organizations playing a strategic role tend to be the most powerful unions in the private sector, not, as was the case before 1961, organizations in the public sector, which are more vulnerable legally. In the spring of 1965, the recession did not prevent the pay offensive from achieving a marked success, since the settlements were based on the 3000 yen increase obtained after a two-day strike by the employees of the privately owned railroads. More generally, it can also be said that the role of the steelworkers' union (Tekkōrōren) has increased significantly.

The spring offensives, by permitting workers to profit from advances in the leading sectors and by guaranteeing substantial pay raises to the weaker ones, also contribute to eliminating economic dualism by making social "segregation," in which small industry employees were caught, more and more difficult.

Dōmei

The Japanese workers' movement has witnessed numerous attempts to create, outside Sōhyō and against it, a powerful center for union activity more moderate in its conception and methods.

The latest of these attempts was marked by the regrouping of the two most powerful rival organizations, Zenrō and Sōdōmei, first into a confederation with rather loose ties and then into a single organization—the Zen Nihon Rōdōkumiai Sōdōmei—in short, Dōmei (Japanese Workers' Confederation), in November 1964.

Zenrō was made up of organizations that had broken with Sōhyō after the launching of its neutralist campaign. Sōdōmei represented the old reformist tradition of the Yūaikai. The new organization wanted to form a center to rival Sōhyō, which was considered "leftist" and unrealistic. . . .

Dōmei's power does not appear negligible; it claims 1,800,000 members. Its strength is to be found in private industry: the maritime union . . . textile union . . . electrical union . . . and metal workers' union. . . . Although the total number of members in this new center is but half the number of Sōhyō members, its influence can only increase, since it controls a certain number of organizations representing the most profitable industries in the private sector. However, a large number of affiliated unions (especially those that come out of Zenrō) also represent medium-sized industries, a particularly weak sector in the Japanese economy, which must bear directly the brunt of changes in the economy. That is why Dōmei generally approaches wage questions very cautiously, taking into account the "possibilities" of each firm.

From an ideological point of view, Dōmei has inherited the orientation that was common to Sōdōmei and Zenrō. It makes use of reformist socialism with particular reference to British laborism. It also rejects economic analysis and Marxist politics, and insists on the democratization of union organization by trying to eliminate struggles between factions. In short, it advocates "industrial democracy" not only in the form of negotiations between employers and employees (both parties are assumed to be equals), but also in the form of worker participation in controlling and directing the firm.

We can say that the attitude of Dōmei, harking back to that of Zenrō, is one of complacency vis-à-vis the structure of Japanese capitalism or at the very least is open to compromise.

This moderate attitude is explained by the concern to be different from Sōhyō and by the structurally moderate character of the principle Dōmei unions (maritime and textile workers); besides, since it has no important civil servant unions, Dōmei can avoid making demands on the level of violent political struggle.

Dōmei can thus have a more autonomous strategy and appear less "politicized." It resembles American unions in its desire to frame all demands in terms of wages and standards of living.

☯ THE JAPANESE "long-service" wage system (*nenkō*) determines wages primarily by seniority and age. To those accustomed to the idea of paying according to skill, this may seem strange, yet the structure of Japanese employment makes *nenkō* a very efficient system for the employer. Wage by seniority encourages a worker to stay at the same job. Thus he may gain enough work experience that he is a better worker than someone with a nominally higher skill level. By comparison, a worker in an American plant is paid largely according to his skill level, rather than by seniority alone.

The *nenkō* system is fundamentally not conducive to labor militancy. If seniority is a major basis for wages, and the seniority system itself makes changing jobs difficult, then a worker is naturally hesitant about risking his job. The *nenkō* system includes the possibility of promotions, but there are also effective techniques for getting rid of unwanted or radical workers, so workers have an incentive to please their employer, not to confront him.

ROBERT E. COLE*
Seniority System

JAPANESE WAGE-RATE STRUCTURES

The wage system in Japan is called *nenkō joretsu chingin;* the term explains the dominant role played by length of service and age in wage determination. This wage system is part of a still larger

* Robert E. Cole, *Japanese Blue Collar* (Berkeley and Los Angeles: University of California Press, 1971), pp. 75–81, 101–104, 119–121.

system called *nenkō seido,* which denotes both the system of promotion and employment tenure. . . .

The basic wage is the most important element (fifty-six percent) and is a common feature of Japanese wage-rate structures. In the manufacturing sector the basic wage averages 86.3 percent of the monthly contract wages (excluding overtime, shift differentials, and holiday work). Generally, the basic wage consists of the starting wage plus annual increments *(teiki shōkyū)* and a portion of the yearly "base up" *(besu appu).* The unskilled blue-collar worker receives the starting wage on entering the firm after graduating from middle or high school. It is determined by market factors. In the past, the starting wage in Japanese factories was close to the monetary earning ability of the agricultural labor force from which industrial manpower has been supplied. The annual increments to the starting wage, the second element in the basic wage, are determined, in order of their importance, by length of service, age, and rating assessment of superiors. The emphasis on length of service in the firm obviously puts experienced workers, who enter the firm later, at a disadvantage.

Takei [diecasting company] makes rating assessments of workers twice a year. The foreman makes the initial assessment which is passed on to the supervisor and section chief for their comments. Foremen reported that they based their ratings on: diligence, seriousness, lack of absence and lateness, productive performance, and cooperation with fellow workers. They believed upper management sometimes altered their assessments by weighing union activity, political affiliation, and loyalty to the company. The assessment is not open to worker scrutiny or a matter for worker grievance. Differences in pay among workers resulting from these assessments are not large but may add up over the years.

Differences in annual increments may seem small to outside observers and unlikely to serve as incentives, but they are important. Takei workers discussed and compared their annual increments with great intensity. The annual increments are a reflection of daily competition among workers in terms of production and winning the favor of superiors. Workers have quit in both the diecast and auto parts company when they learned that other workers of the same age and with the same length of service received slightly higher increments.

The third element of the basic wage is the yearly "base up."

Japanese unions negotiate for the lump sum of the total wage cost of the firm which is then divided among the total number of regular workers (temporary workers are not covered by the union) either in the form of a fixed cash increase or a percentage increase. It is called *besu appu*. The union will usually bargain with the firm over its distribution. Generally a portion is divided equally among all employees and another is paid on the basis of age and length of service. . . .

RELATION OF FACTORY PERFORMANCE TO WAGES

That wages and wage increases are determined by length of service, age, and education and not factory performance or job competence has been of particular interest to Western observers. To some, this implied a wage system that falls outside economic rationality as it is understood in the West. But this view cannot be sustained if we recognize that one of the main reasons for payment by age and length of service is that with growing age and lengthening service the worker acquires skill and experience and, therefore, increases his value to the firm. A rough check of wages by occupation reveals that, generally, skilled jobs are associated with higher length of service and higher wages and semiskilled jobs with lower length of service and lower wages. . . .

The Japanese company does not leave to chance the young worker's acquisition of skill and productive capacity. The young worker entering the company directly after school graduation is untrained. If he shows promise, he is gradually led through "stages of difficulty." In the beginning he will be assigned relatively simple jobs and then gradually be introduced to increasingly difficult ones over the years. This often involves a complicated system of job rotation. In this way, it is expected that the employee's value to the company increases. It is true, the wage fit with factory performance is not as tight as that found in an American factory. Nevertheless, a clear correlation between wage and factory performance exists, and, if it is not as tight, it is because the practice of permanent employment makes it less necessary. That an employee's rewards must be calculated to match exactly his present productive contribution is not relevant in a system of permanent employment. In the major firms a large retirement allowance is designed to help the employee after he retires and to reward him for long years of productive service. In an American firm, where the young worker may quit the next day, it is unavoidable that he be paid for the preceding day's production. But the large Japanese firm, operating with the assumption (not always true as we shall see) that the worker will continue with the firm until retirement, need not reward the worker at the exact moment he makes his contribution and with the exact amount corresponding to his contribution. This suggests that low interfirm mobility is responsible for introducing economic rationality into the *nenkō* wage system. If we may assume that the employee's productivity rises rapidly until somewhere between thirty and forty, after which it gradually declines, it seems that the *nenkō* wage system underpays young and overpays older workers. The element of rationality is introduced because, presumably, management seeks to cancel out the overpayment of older workers by underpaying young ones. This is achieved by having workers spend their entire career in one company. Building this attachment permits the company to collect on its training investment. A worker separating at an early age costs the company its training investment. Similarly, it is expensive for an older worker to separate from the firm, because his productivity does not justify his high wages and he will have difficulty finding another job at equivalent wages. Only if the worker stays with the company throughout his career will his high wages in later years provide economic justification for the underpayment in his youth. . . .

An integral part of the *nenkō* wage-rate structure and one of the basic rewards open to blue-collar workers is the system of promotion. Promotion to foreman means not only additional wages but also a release from the work routine, a chance to exercise authority over subordinates, and high status in the shop.

Incorporated in the *nenkō* concept are payment by age and length of service and promotion on the basis of age and length of service. Even regular blue-collar workers—but not workers classified as temporary—with normal skill qualifications, leadership abilities, and demonstrated loyalty can expect some form of promotion under *nenkō*. Like the wage system, the promotion procedure is not inherently irrational. Based on the assumption that with increasing age and length of service, not only job skills but skill in human relations, ability to lead people, and status in the shop will have increased, the *nenkō* approach does not necessarily turn out incompetent supervisory personnel. The *nenkō* promotion procedure controls and channels tensions over promotion aspirations in an equitable way among workers who have relatively little access to the market.

The importance regular workers attach to promotion aspirations offers Japanese managers great possibilities for worker manipulation. A common occurrence in the two companies was to suggest to workers that their chances for promotion will increase if they agree to various changes such as job transfers. Because promotion by age and length of service is, in practice, selective (that is, not everyone gets promoted) and because the timing is flexible, management can pick and choose and so make workers compete for its favor.

This practice has important consequences for social change. Given the highly crystalized age-grading characteristics of Japanese firms, young subordinates must wait a long time for positions of power and responsibility. If they display attitudes or behavior that deviates from the expectations of their superiors, they will not reach even the bottom rungs on the promotional ladder. Conformity to such vertical structures and acceptance of the rewards and duties defined by superiors restricts social change initiated from below. Advance in a particular business firm entails acceptance of the existing order. Innovation occurs within this framework. "Success reinforces the way in which success has been achieved." Similar situations are by no means unknown in the West. But the highly crystalized age-grading characteristics of Japanese firms, low interfirm mobility, and the transmission of traditional authority relationships give the *nenkō* pattern its particular configuration and strength.

As an age-grading system, the *nenkō* approach to wages and promotion has important consequences for individual worker motivation. This is critical to the understanding of the economic rationality within *nenkō*. . . . At the diecast firm, I was told, worker interest in foreman promotion became especially pronounced at age thirty-five. Generally, this gradual increase in promotion expectation with advancing age must have profound consequences for increasing work satisfaction, reducing alienation, and providing effective work incentives.

The gradual increase in promotion expectation combined with the practice of permanent employment leads many blue-collar workers in large firms to view their job as a stage in a career. In other industrial societies, like the United States, it is reported that careers apply only to a small elite of the labor force. If it is correct that Japanese blue-collar workers, particularly those in large firms, look upon their jobs as stages in a career, this is of major importance. Careers are said to be a major source of stability in modern societies. Every organization must recruit and maintain its personnel as well as motivate job performance. The prospect of continuous predictable rewards, a feature of careers, creates willingness in workers to train, to achieve, and to adopt a long view and defer immediate gratification for the later payoff. Provided that expectations are met, career patterns may serve as a major stabilizing influence on a society. Apparently this has been the result of *nenkō* wage and promotion, and the practice of permanent employment in the postwar period. It suggests that the so-called docility and high work motivation of Japanese blue-collar workers must be understood in the context of their career commitments. . . .

Managers generally said that they would not fire workers except under the most exceptional circumstances. Westerners have been particularly impressed with Japanese management statements such as "We have the right to fire but it would not be right to do so." These views, however, are subject to considerable modification depending on the company, industry, and economic climate.

Management tries to screen out incompetents during their trial period before they become regular employees. Once the probation period is past, a number of other devices are available for dealing with regular workers should they become undesirable. An employer may simply transfer undesirables and incompetents to harmless positions where they do not interfere with production. This was not uncommon in the diecast plant, particularly at the supervisory level. Devices designed to make workers quit are numerous. This is not to say that Japanese executives are lying when they explain to their foreign visitors that they do not fire as a general rule. In part, this is a problem of translation. Managers will reserve the term *kubikiri* or *kaiko* for firing or discharge. They would prefer, however, in many cases to use the term *yamete morau,* which literally translated means that the company has "received the quitting [of someone upon its request]." This is a euphemism for firing when the company leaves the worker no alternative but to quit. . . .

There are many techniques for getting an employee to quit. For example, a professor had been looking for a way to fire his secretary. One day he came into the office and found she was absent without telling anyone in advance. He saw his chance and feigned great anger in front of the office girls. The next day when the secretary came to work she heard from the other girls that the professor was upset. Embarrassed that the professor did not think more highly of her, she said, "Well, if that's the way he feels about it, I quit." The following day the girls announced that the secretary had quit. Undoubtedly, the professor would have said the same. By choosing such an indirect way of firing, he avoided a lowering of morale in his office staff. Though this may strike the Westerner as a terribly inefficient and circuitous way of getting things done, it probably comes as second nature to the professor.

The above device is less likely to work in a factory, where, with their livelihood at stake, workers cannot afford to be as sensitive. To give an extreme example, an oil refinery worker employed at a major corporation is not likely to quit because his feelings are hurt when he knows that he cannot obtain another job at the same high wages. One of the characteristics of the Japanese dual economy is that employees who quit large firms are less likely to be employed at other large firms. Instead they will often end up working at a smaller firm for lower wages. For example, of the 118,400 employees who left their jobs in firms with over 500 employees between January and June 1965, only nineteen percent were re-hired in firms employing over 500. At the big firms, this is a powerful incentive for not quitting over relatively minor matters. In short, the availability of alternative employment at similar wages and working conditions is a key factor in determining worker response to such management tactics. The worker's need to maintain his livelihood normally outweighs the consideration of losing face, notwithstanding Western stereotypes to the contrary.

There are still other devices used by management to get workers to quit. Constant job transfers or the threat of them, assignment to dirty, low-status jobs, making it known to the worker that he has no chance for promotion, or that his yearly pay increment will be lower than his fellow workers', are some of the more common techniques. Working in a low-prestige job under the eyes of one's former colleagues can be so humiliating that the worker will soon decide to quit. This is particularly true if the worker is young and skilled (*i.e.,* the labor market situation is favorable for him). The mere threat of such tactics by management may be sufficient to significantly increase work performance. . . .

It is clear, then, that a variety of devices fall short of direct firing but nevertheless may force the worker to quit. In such a way, management may rid itself of incompetents, agitators, and, to some extent, surplus personnel. In extreme cases, however, such as existed in the postwar coal industry or the reorganization of the auto industry in 1955, large-scale direct firing may take place.

❀ THERE ARE differing views on the origins and meanings of the permanent employment system. Hubert Brochier notes that it parallels the persistence of "feudal" social relationships, and may in fact have been caused by such relationships, which continue to govern much of Japanese life. He also sees it as a very stable, even rigid, system that encompasses virtually all employees in the large corporations.

Koji Taira takes issue with both these conclusions. He finds the origins of permanent employment in the special conditions of the labor market and the union movement after World War II. Further, a complex salary system of bonuses for the permanent employees, use of temporary workers within the plant, and extensive subcontracting have combined to give the employer all the flexibility he needs. The selection by Tsuda Masumi serves to illustrate the organization of the labor force within the large plants Brochier and Taira are concerned with.

HUBERT BROCHIER*
Permanent Employment†

Although at first sight nothing resembles a French or American firm so much as a Japanese one, the sociological realities within

* Hubert Brochier, *Le Miracle économique japonais, 1950–1970* (Paris: Calmann-Lévy, 1970), pp. 47–50.
† Translated by People's Translation Service.

are profoundly different. The archaic nature, or at any rate the originality, of Japanese economic life appears most clearly in the system of industrial relations on which it is founded.

This originality is due to one essential and distinctive characteristic, which carries with it numerous consequences: the custom of permanent employment—*shūshin koyō*—the lifelong commitment of the worker to only one firm. When the new employee, be he laborer, engineer, or salaried employee, enters the service of a firm, he is committing himself to that firm for his whole working life. He knows that the company will not dismiss him, even temporarily, unless he has committed a particularly serious error or under the pressure of exceptional circumstances. He, on the other hand, will not try to leave the company—in search of higher pay, for example. Indeed, such an ambition is totally foreign to him and the very idea that he could better his own situation by going from one firm to another is presently inconceivable to the average Japanese employee.

This stability can be understood statistically by comparing the personnel turnover in comparable firms in Japan and abroad. The greatest difference in this respect is between Japanese and American firms, but that between Japanese and French firms is also very significant. . . .

One aspect of the Japanese industrial structure, however, has an attenuating effect on this rigid social bond. I am referring to the existence of numerous bonds that subordinate one firm to another or tie their managements together. Thus it is possible to effect personnel transfers between two firms in the same group, or between a firm and its subcontractors. But normally such transfers are tolerated only in the uppermost echelons of the hierarchy; blue-collar workers who wish to be transferred generally run into serious obstacles. . . .

It should be pointed out, furthermore, that the permanent employment system is a good example of those socio-economic mechanisms that provide their own rationale. Since the Japanese worker is fired only in extreme circumstances, it follows that it is quite difficult for him to find new work, especially if it is known that he has been dismissed (and his age is sufficient testimony to that).

For example, it has been estimated that in 1960 (the year the rate of increase of national income shot up thirteen percent and management began to complain about a scarcity of labor), only half of the workers above thirty years of age who had lost their jobs were able to find paid work. For those lucky ones, furthermore, the new position was, in most cases, not as good as the old one. They worked as clerks, guards, or errand boys. Others went back to the land and either worked on their parents' already ridiculously unproductive farms or swelled the ranks of temporary or day-laborers. This explains why a firm hesitates to dismiss an employee, as it knows that his dismissal will undoubtedly bring about his social and economic downfall.

One might think that these explanations are nothing more than *ex post facto* rationalizations of a situation that can be traced back to the beginnings of Japanese industrialization. Unlike what occurred in Western countries, industrialization did not proceed from the wholesale destruction of feudal structures and construction of a bourgeois society based on an individualistic creed. Although the feudal system was *politically* abolished in the first years of the Meiji revolution, feudal values and behavior patterns remained and formed the basis for the new nationalist ideology on which modern Japan has been built. These values have therefore coexisted alongside and intertwined with industrialization. It is precisely the tenacity of feudal-type social relations, penetrating right into the most modern firms, that provides us with the most profound explanation of such an openly anachronistic employment system.

To be more specific, the owner treats his workers like the old Japanese daimyō used to treat his servants or children. This application of *oyako* (system of family-type relationships) goes way beyond employment policies.

KOJI TAIRA*
Non-Permanent Employment

The 1949–1950 deflation was ... instrumental in introducing an important structural change in enterprise unionism which weakened the power of unions to affect the wage level of the firm. The enterprise union as a rule included in its membership all the

* Koji Taira, *Economic Development and the Labor Market in Japan* (New York: Columbia University Press, 1970), pp. 180–187.

employees of an enterprise except for the managerial personnel, but the 1949–1950 deflation made it clear that it was not always practicable for the union to protect its members against the loss of jobs. The realization of this fact led to a union policy that limited membership to a size at which the absolute security of uninterrupted employment would be possible at all times. Any worker employed to be a permanent regular employee automatically became a union member. In exchange for this kind of union shop for regular workers, management acquired unrestrained freedom in hiring and firing "temporary workers" in response to changes in the business conditions of the firm and in paying whatever was necessary to obtain their services. The Japanese firms already had an experience in this kind of arrangement during the 1930s. Indeed, the early 1930s and the early 1950s were similar in one respect, that is, the excess-supply labor market. How similar market conditions give rise to similar institutional solutions is striking indeed.

In this connection it should be noted that "permanent" and "temporary" workers in the Japanese official statistics after the war tend to understate the extent of "temporary" workers. A firm's work force is first classified into "casual" and "regular" workers. The "casual" worker is employed on a day-to-day basis or for less than thirty consecutive days. The "temporary regular" worker is employed for more than thirty consecutive days but with a specific term of contract. The "permanent regular" worker is one with an indefinite term of employment. According to the Census of Establishments of 1954, the "casuals" were 6.5 percent of the "regulars" in manufacturing. According to the monthly labor surveys of manufacturing establishments with thirty or more "regular" workers made by the ministry of labor, the "temporary regulars" were 7.4 percent in 1956 and 7.7 percent in 1959. The proportions of "temporary regulars" to all "regulars" were higher in industries like primary metals (9.8 percent), machinery (11.0 percent), electric equipment (14.1 percent), and transportation equipment (10.6 percent). The "casuals" and "temporary regulars" together may have accounted for more than a fifth of all workers in these industries in 1959.

But these were official statistics. There is reason to believe that the official definitions of "temporary" and "permanent" workers vastly understate the proportions of workers who in the custom of each firm are hired as "temporary" subject to inferior wages and working conditions, and without being entitled to intrafirm welfare facilities. An independent research suggests that in the transport machinery industry the ratio of "temporary" to total employment rose from twenty-five percent in March 1960 to thirty-one percent in March 1961 and that, in all manufacturing, the increase in this one-year period was from seventeen to nineteen percent. For the same period the Ministry of Labor statistics reported 11.5 percent in December 1960 and 12.1 percent in December 1961 for the transport equipment industry, while the figures for all of manufacturing were 8.3 and 7.9 percent respectively....

The interfirm profit structure was also in disequilibrium during the 1950s.... Since the large, high-wage firms were not necessarily enjoying high profit rates on capital, this influenced the direction of capital flow in favor of more profitable smaller firms, raising the demand for factors in these firms proportionately more than in the large firms. Some of the manufacturing firms even shifted parts of their productive activities to smaller firms through subcontracting relations to siphon out some of the profits smaller firms were capable of making. Tokutarō Yamanaka observes: "The power of unions has grown to such an extent that it is hardly possible to make wage cuts.... In striking contrast, there has been hardly any progress in the unionization of workers of small-medium industries. This explains why more and more large industries have come to find it profitable to subcontract work to small-medium firms. By establishing such relationships, the large industries can take advantage of the 'cheap labor' of small businesses...."

The mutual accommodation of unions, managements, and the labor market is nowhere more marked than in the wage–employment relationship between different size groups of firms.... Given the wide disparity of wages between large and small firms at the beginning of the 1950s, the smaller firms had acquired a comparative advantage of labor cost relative to the larger ones. Thus, from 1951 to 1954, employment tended to increase in the smaller firms relative to the larger ones. The strength of demand for labor in the smaller firms tended to arrest the lagging of wages behind larger firms. With the passage of time, however, the stabilization of wage increases in the larger firms increasingly tended to enable these firms to employ more labor. Finally, during recent years (after 1957) the prosperous economic conditions and the stability

of wages in the larger firms relative to those in the smaller ones
have resulted in considerable increases in employment of labor by
the larger firms. . . .

THE INTRAFIRM WAGE STRUCTURE

Another consequence of the mutual accommodation of labor and
management in the postwar labor market was the emergence of an
intrafirm wage structure which showed a steep rise in wages corresponding to the age of the worker. When the average earnings for
different age groups were compared around 1955, for example, the
older workers' earnings were considerably higher than those of the
younger ones in almost all skill categories. The range of apparently
age-related increments in pay in each skill category was so wide
that the earnings of a janitor after many years of service could be
higher than, say, those of a young starting engineer. . . . Why does
age alone make so much difference in a worker's earnings? One
might be tempted to answer that it is becuase age itself is something highly valued in the traditional culture of the Orient. Upon a
closer look, however, the situation is completely different. . . .

It is much more natural to suppose, than to resort to cultural traditions, that the postwar age-related wage system as well
as the absolute job security for permanent workers was brought
about upon trade unions' insistence. Once established, the age-
related pay system within the firm was maintained through subsequent wage increases obtained by the enterprise union supported
by the firm's hiring policy. By the end of the Second World War
the level of wages had sunk very low, and wage differentials of all
kinds had nearly disappeared. Workers in the larger enterprises
took to unionism in this milieu, and it was necessary for them to
be bound by exceptional solidarity in order to survive these
difficult years. Solidarity above all required equality of status of all
the fighting members and an equitable distribution of gains made
by collective efforts. Workers of all descriptions, male and female,
young and old, skilled and unskilled, white-collar and blue-collar,
contributed their utmost efforts and sacrifices toward the common
goal of survival. A high degree of intraunion democracy was
thereby achieved; each contributed according to his ability and
strength, and each shared in the gains according to his needs. The
age-related pay structure was born of the trade unions' homespun

notion of equity, democracy, and solidarity. It was derived from the concept of "living wage."

The need for survival brought about the concept of "living wage" evidently as an emergency concept until the restoration of normal socio-economic conditions. The "living wage" principle was given the first explicit formulation by the Electric Industry Workers' Union in the fall of 1946. . . . Employers denounced it as a worst form of egalitarianism. . . . The Electricity Formula was revolutionary in that it abolished pay differentials and differences in wage payment methods by education, status, and sex. The total pay was the sum of two components: (a) the "living wage" and (b) additions for skill, work, and length of service. The "living wage" in turn consisted of three elements: (1) the basic wage roughly geared to the physical strength and mental agility of the worker so that it was scaled up to reach its maximum for the age bracket of twenty-six to thirty-five years and scaled down thereafter, (2) allowances for the number of dependents, and (3) cost-of-living differentials by geographical area. The proportion of the living wage component was more than seventy percent at first but had decreased to sixty percent by 1955. The average earnings of a worker when the formula was adopted were calculated to reach their maximum at forty-five years of age. This pioneer wage system was adopted in many other industries and firms under the pressure of trade unions. The collective agreements which established these intrafirm wage systems for the first time in these firms have since been honored as The Original Agreements (*genshi kyōtei*).

For the whole manufacturing sector, the pay gradient by age became steeper on the whole until 1958. This was due to the interaction of two forces; the annual wage increases won by the union members who were by definition already in the firm and the excess-supply conditions of the labor market which pressed down the starting (hiring) wages of young workers. Although the wages of the new recruits were fixed as low as the market would bear, the workers after joining the firm and the union shared in the subsequent rounds of wage increases. But significant differentials were already made between new recruits and established workers, and these were maintained through the years. So long as the excess supply of labor persisted, the starting wages increased far less rapidly than the average wages of the established workers who continued to win wage increases through collective bargaining. Low starting wages and subsequent wage increments on that base, repeated over many years, had produced an impressive gradient of wages by length of service in the firm by the middle of the 1950s. It was at this point that people began to speak of the peculiarity of the intrafirm wage structure in which age did seem to be most prominent among the correlates of individual earnings. A little amount of historical perspective and analytical imagination would have saved many of them from entertaining a patently false proposition that the observed peculiarity of the age-earnings correlation was a specialty limited to Japan.

. . . From the point of view of the worker who was fortunate enough to pass the tight hiring standards of a large, high-wage firm, it would have been an extremely foolish action for him to leave his job in the labor market context of the 1950s. Thus, if the workers of these firms were considered in isolation, they appeared to be permanently committed to their current employers.

But the unions had left the employers with a lot of room for their maneuver. In search of greater flexibility of production and labor cost, the large firms during the 1950s made use of subcontractors and a class of workers known as *shagaikō* (extra workers), in addition to temporary and casual workers. The "extras" were brought into the parent firms by the subcontractors who worked on portions of the production process. The core of permanent employees within a given firm was thus surrounded by rings of temporary, casual, and extra workers inside it and by bands of subcontractors and their workers outside it. In the early 1960s it was found that thirty percent of total employment in the engineering and chemical industries was in the "nonpermanent" category.

In addition to the limitation of the "permanent" work force to a necessary minimum, the firm made its cost as flexible as was compatible with changes in the state of business. This was effected by the method of wage payments, which divided the total pay into two broad components, one of which was regularly paid and somewhat rigid, and the other was paid as a bonus or allowance adjustable to the state of business. Thus, contrary to an expected consequence of lifetime commitment—that labor is a fixed cost "not susceptible to adjustment as conditions require" (Abegglen) —it seems that Japanese firms have on the whole maintained labor

and wages as variable as conditions and economic calculus require.
One would indeed suspect that, by acceding to the unions' demand
for job security, the employers might have obtained a greater
degree of flexibility in production plans and work force management than possible otherwise.

*TSUDA MASUMI**
Japanese Wage Structure

The framework of current Japanese labor relations was established
in the 1930s. The labor management policy then adopted may be
called "divide and rule." It is a policy under which the employees
were to be separated into the following groups.

A. THE COMMITTED STANDARD WORKER

The standard workers are . . . the employees employed immediately after their graduation at their respective school levels. From
the first day on which they report to the company they are thrown
into the company training school for up to three years as trainees,
and each employee, after completing the course, is placed in an
appropriate job. Junior high school graduates are placed in production and maintenance jobs and college graduates are allocated
to white-collar jobs. It is the principle of the company that their
basic wage periodically increases and that these standard workers
are employed until their retirement age. After their retirement, the
company usually takes care of them in some way: introducing
other jobs for them from subsidiary companies, loaning them out
for the opening of small shops, etc. These employees are called
"standard workers" or "model employees" because their starting
wages, wage increases, transfers, and promotions constitute the
basis on which those of other employees are determined. They are
also called "key employees" because they are committed to their
company for almost all of their economically active life. Their
commitment is thus called "lifetime commitment," and their wage

* Tsuda Masumi, "Japanese Wage Structure and Its Significance for
International Comparisons," British Journal of Industrial Relations III:2
(July 1965), pp. 193–195.

is referred to as a "lifetime maintenance wage." The latter name came into use after World War II when the retirement compensation plans of companies were applied to the production and maintenance workers.

B. The Committed Nonstandard Worker

Because of sudden expansion of business, an enterprise occasionally finds it necessary to increase the number of semiskilled and skilled workers. The major supply of such workers, in addition to standard workers, comes from smaller companies. Big enterprises can attract workers from smaller companies with better compensation because of the existence of a dual economy. After their employment, such workers also become "committed" employees, but their wage increases, transfers, and promotions are less than those offered to the standard worker and they may be discharged if the company finds it absolutely necessary to reduce the number of its committed employees.

They are not standard workers because they are not hired immediately after their school graduation but are employed at the halfway stage of their economically active life. They are, in principle, employed until retirement age. They are thus called "nonstandard committed workers."

C. Temporary Workers

The two groups mentioned are called "permanent" or "regular" workers because of their "commitment." Besides these, a big enterprise hires a considerable number of temporary workers whose employment tenure depends upon the needs of the enterprise. They are usually allocated to lower-level jobs, but some of them work on the same high-skilled jobs as the permanent workers. Their basic wage is less than half that of a permanent worker and it is not periodically increased. The supply and mobility of these temporary workers is related to the mobility of the employees of smaller companies.

D. Outside Workers

Another group of workers work within the premises of big enterprises. Many of them work in construction and transportation departments and some of them work on the same production and maintenance jobs as the permanent worker (especially in the shipbuilding industry). They are formally the employees of subcontract or labor-contract companies. The big enterprise, as their master company, pays their wages directly to those contract companies who, in turn, pay these outside workers. The big enterprises use these workers because of their skill and because they are paid a lower wage. The mobility of these outside workers is closely related to the mobility of the employees of smaller companies and of the temporary workers.

The composition of employees in Japanese enterprises is illustrated in the following diagram.

The Employee Composition

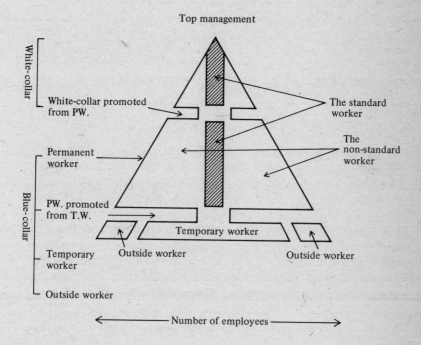

🌸 SUMIYA MIKIO describes the *nenkōsei* and the attendant phenomena of permanent employment and temporary workers more as outgrowths of technological impact than remnants of feudal times. He argues that post-World War II technological change has simplified job content to the extent that young, inexperienced, and, most important, cheap labor can be used. This development has destroyed the rationale for *nenkō* and permanent employment. Industry's trend toward hiring policies that allow for easy layoff or firing of employees will, as Sumiya sees it, likely drive the union movement toward industry-wide organization as the weaknesses of enterprise unionism become more apparent.

SUMIYA MIKIO*
Implications of Technological Change in Industrial Relations

. . . Japan, in the middle of the nineteenth century, was technologically backward; its industrialization was brought about by the transplantation of modern technologies from Western countries. Consequently, it was faced with the need to create an effective management which could make these technologies operational, not to speak of the need for recruiting, committing, and disciplining a labor force. This certainly led to the destruction of conventional labor relations, but it should be emphasized that an effective management and the whole apparatus of new industrial relations was created entirely separately from the preexisting industrial relations. The skilled workers at this time had a high labor market mobility and sold their skills to any employer. There existed a

* Sumiya Mikio, "Implications of Technological Change in Industral Relations in Japan," *British Journal of Industrial Relations* III:2 (July 1965), pp. 210–218.

nationwide labor market on the basis of each craft. On this basis they had, by the end of the century, organized craft unions.

Then, after the turn of the century, or more specifically because of the impact of the Russo-Japanese War in 1904–1905, the scale of production, on the one hand, became larger, and, on the other, large enterprises made big advances in the introduction of new technologies. Leaders in the heavy industrial sector were especially enthusiastic about introducing Western technologies, and as a result industrial relations were influenced drastically in this area.

First, the new technologies demanded more precise and exact skills. Machine operations were continually improved and at the same time, a systematic training of labor became necessary. Parallel to this development, the compulsory education system was expanded and the period of compulsory attendance was extended from four years to six. Meanwhile, it gradually became commonplace for companies to establish their own training program facilities, to recruit those who had completed their compulsory education requirement, and to train them as the skilled workers which each company was requiring. Thus, in Japan, it was the companies that instituted and financed programs for the development of skills.

It was quite natural, therefore, that the companies, who took full responsibility for such training, should want to use those trained in their own companies for as long as possible. Thus, this gave rise to a type of worker who was "raised within a company from his youth" (*kogai*), and, in turn, it led to a family-type relationship between the company and the worker.

On the other hand, since the latter half of the nineteenth century, an apprenticeship system had been built up in Japan, with skilled workers serving as masters. These skilled workers were, however, not well prepared and were too few in number to undertake the systematic training of new apprentices. As a result, apprentices were promoted to the rank of ordinary workers before their training was completed, and eventually acquired the necessary skills on the basis of practical experience at their work. Therefore, in Japan, as is often the case in developing countries, the level of skill was measured by the length of experience. This situation, together with the lengthening of service time in a specific company, which was endorsed by that company, led, after World War I, to the establishment of *nenkōsei* (length of service reward system)—one of the characteristic features of Japanese industrial relations. *Nenkōsei* itself served to enforce a lengthening of service which, in turn, eventually gave rise to the practice called *shūshin-koyō* (lifetime employment). Once the group of such permanent employees, who were committed to a company for their wage-earning life, was formed, there appeared—as a parallel development—a group of *rinjikō* (temporary workers), who served as cushions in adjusting supply to demand. By 1930, these three cornerstones of Japanese industrial relations were laid (though incompletely) in the way described above.

POSTWAR CHANGES IN LABOR RELATIONS AND TECHNOLOGY

This system of industrial relations underwent drastic changes after World War II. One of the most important of these changes was the widespread organization of trade unions. In the period when the practice of lifetime employment and family-type labor relations were being established in large-scale enterprises, the trade unions had been unable to penetrate these major centers of employment. After World War II the lifetime employees were prepared to organize unions in the specific enterprises for which they worked. These enterprise unions emphasized a class struggle approach and they seriously undermined traditional industrial relationships. On the other hand, enterprise union activity, by the very nature of its own structure and functions, led to union members strengthening their ties with their respective enterprises. For instance, in the process of postwar reconstruction, union activities designed to prevent the discharge of workers had the additional effect of bolstering the lifetime-employment relationship. Therefore, the lifetime-employment system can be said to have been completed after World War II—for the first time—as a result of the unions making an issue of securing employment for the workers. Thus, employees' enterprise unions were organized in a different way from what had been the case with European trade unions; that is, Japanese unions were organized by building on and yet transforming preexisting industrial relations practices. It is true, of course, that enterprise unions are members of nationwide federations, but the locus of trade unionism existing at the enterprise union level makes for a characteristic feature of Japanese labor organizations.

In 1953–1954, with the end of postwar disorder and turmoil, technological innovation and change once again became a matter of concern, as it was necessary to rehabilitate the nation's economic structure so that Japan could regain a place in the international economy. The increased capital accumulation made possible by the Korean War provided a strong stimulus for economic rehabilitation. Conflict had commonly arisen between the labor movement and those who sought to institute technological change; and Japan was no exception. The problem took a specific direction in Japan, however, by virtue of the trade unions being organized at the enterprise level. The unions strongly opposed technological change, fearing that it would weaken previously acquired union control in the workshop. In addition, they expressed the fear, often felt in other countries, that rationalization, under the name of technological change, might bring about mass unemployment. It is true, in fact, that management, despite the strong opposition of the unions, did succeed in expanding their control over workshop labor relations in the process of their promotion of technological change. In this respect, technological change has had a decisive impact on labor relations.

... [T]he most dreaded consequence of technological change by the trade unions was the threat of unemployment arising from its labor saving effects. Economic development was, however, so rapid, with "investment attracting investment," that the result was not unemployment but a labor shortage, as had been the case in many European countries. The number of employed workers jumped from 17 million in 1955 to 25 million in 1963, that is, an increase of some fifty percent in eight years. ...

Certainly, the increases in productivity were remarkable, but the increase in total production exceeded that of productivity, and, as a result, the total employment expanded. It is true, of course, that such an increase in employment varied according to industry. Indeed, in coal-mining where employment actually decreased to half in the past five years, the amount of production remained stable as productivity per man increased. In the textile industry, where both production and productivity achieved little progress, employment remained stagnant. Automobile production showed great advances, but so did the productivity level; thus, employment did not expand much in this sector. ...

TECHNOLOGICAL CHANGE AND LABOR RELATIONS

The fact that the labor shortage came to the fore in a period of technological change does not mean that there was no redundancy in many of the companies which promoted technological change. In a case such as the chemical industry, especially, there appeared a surplus of experienced middle- and old-aged workers as the result of the company having discarded its obsolete equipment. In the case of these workers, their old skills and experience rapidly became obsolete. If this situation had occurred in a Western country these workers would have been discharged and become unemployed, with the possibility of being hired by another company. In Japan, however, where the lifetime employment system is rigidly enforced, such a discharge cannot be carried out without risking a severe conflict with the trade union. Therefore, in many cases, the company chooses to transfer such workers to other jobs rather than discharge them. Moreover, the retraining of these workers for a new job is done within the company at the expense of the company. This is in sharp contrast to the general practice in Western countries.

It is generally true that younger workers adjust more easily in retraining for a new job than do older workers. As a result, the advancement of technological change means that the past structure of age-status and experience determining skill level loses its basis. Long experience counts for less, in the face of technological innovations. *Nenkōsei,* one of the basic cornerstones of Japanese industrial relations, has as one of its *raisons d'être* the strong correlation between length of service and skill, and so the obsolescence of accumulated experience serves to shake *nenkōsei* at its very foundation.

For example, it is common that the *nenkō*-based wage structure results in the wages of workers between forty and fifty years old being four times as high as the seventeen- to eighteen-year-old age group. . . . But the irrationalitiees of such a set-up became apparent under increasing technological change and in recent years an occupationally based wage system is being increasingly relied upon.

Technological change not only makes obsolete the experience acquired by older experienced workers but also destroys traditional skills by simplifying the content of work. Skilled workers gradually lose their places on the production line. This tendency has had a specific effect on labor demand, given the context of the *nenkō*-type wage structure. Since wages were cheaper for younger workers, the companies tried to use as many younger workers as possible with the advent of more simplified work content deriving from the new technologies. This goes a long way toward explaining the recent shortage of young workers. Hence, in Japan so far, the shortage of labor deriving from technological change is, to be precise, not an overall labor shortage but rather that of young workers. Despite the "labor shortage," there still exists a certain amount of redundancy among middle- and older-aged workers.

In addition, the present labor shortage is stimulating the development of higher labor mobility, especially among younger workers. This, as would be expected, has an important impact on labor relations through its weakening of the lifetime employment practice—an impact which had not earlier been foreseen. For example, the close tie between management and labor, which had come into existence through the lifetime employment practice, cannot be found among young workers who are willing to change companies. In such a situation, the trade union movement has recently been making conscious efforts to base its driving energy and forward motion upon this group of workers.

It is not reasonable for companies to use experienced workers at higher wages when their skills are not required for jobs whose content has become simplified. The same problem would arise in the future, were the companies to employ the present-day young workers as regular employees. It is for this reason that, in such industries as automobile and electrical machinery where the simplification of job content is far advanced, great use is being made of temporary workers. Another alternative which management has resorted to in recent years has been the greater utilization of sub-contract laborers—in such industries as steel where various kinds of miscellaneous jobs exist. These temporary workers and sub-contract laborers have working conditions which are considerably inferior to those of the regular workers. In addition, these workers cannot join the union since the union is only for regular employees. The temporary and sub-contract laborers are subject to an unstable employment relationship, and they lack the sufficient conditions necessary to establish an enterprise union. In contrast to this, the regular employees are becoming a privileged group who are moving toward a strengthening of their tie with the company as technological change proceeds.

An important technological innovation has been the recent proliferation of the "continuous production" process with its high speed of operation. Under such a process, shutting down or interrupting production is a costly action potentially involving great losses for the company. Therefore, the companies are now more sensitive than before about the stability of labor relations at the workshop, and they are making enormous efforts to bring about increased labor control.

It has already been noted that in Japan, where the trade unions are organized by enterprise and their activities are carried out within the enterprise—specifically at the workshop—enforcement of labor control within the enterprise by the company means a direct confrontation with the union and a checking of its activities. As a result, the companies and the unions have struggled to see who would establish control over the workers at the workshop. The company has been the winner.

A notable feature of this situation is that, the higher the level of technological advancement in an industry, the less likely will the unions of that industry be affiliated to a national confederation such as Sōhyō. The unions in industrial sectors such as oil refining, chemicals, and automobiles tend to be mostly independent unions, cut off from the mainstream of Japanese trade unionism.

Thus, technological change, while shaking the foundations of existing labor practices, does not reach a point where it succeeds in transforming the nature of Japanese enterprise-based labor relations. It seems, rather, that the effect of technological change . . . is to strengthen the tightening thread of control over the workers within the enterprise.

LABOR ORGANIZATIONS INSIDE AND OUTSIDE THE ENTERPRISE

As we have seen, the trade unions took up a hostile attitude toward technological change. Even today, "antirationalization" remains an important slogan for the national unions. At the level of the enterprise union, however, the situation is quite different. When competition among the large enterprises reaches a high level, the enterprise unions cannot ignore it. For an enterprise union to oppose technological change in such a situation is to weaken the competitive ability of its company and consequently to act against its own interests as the representative of the employees of that company. As a result, enterprise unions find that it pays them to cooperate with their companies in the introduction of technological innovations. If the unions were organized industrywide, it might be possible to check the trend toward technological change to some extent. But enterprise unions are in no position to do this, being bound to support their own enterprise in the face of severe competition within the industry.

Excessive attachment to their respective companies on the part of the enterprise unions, however, inevitably leads to their transformation into company unions. How, then, have the trade unions sought to avoid such development? For the last ten years, Japanese trade unions have been searching for an appropriate course to pursue, in face of the fast tempo of technological change. In some cases, they have sought to solve the problem by strengthening the regional cooperation of enterprise unions. In other cases, they have considered the reorganization of the enterprise-based unions into industrywide unions. None of these, however, have proved to be the solution.

At present, the unions are tending to organize combined action throughout the industry in the direction of strengthening the federal organization of enterprise unions and using this to resist the tightening thread being woven by the company around union activities within the enterprise. For example, the basis of national union activities for the last ten years has been *shuntō* (spring struggle) and most of the 9 million organized workers have joined this movement. *Shuntō* was born of the idea of making industrially standardized demands and struggling with a unified time schedule in order to realize the unions' demands. This implied the recognition that the achievement of wage increases had become possible only by utilizing the standardization of demands by the individual enterprise union.

In short, the Japanese enterprise union has now come to grips with the need for strengthening organizational structure and activities outside the enterprise in order to ensure an effective movement capable of meeting the challenge of technological change. Initially,

Japanese industrial relations were based upon enterprise unionism; now the process may be entering a new state which is oriented toward industrywide organization and activities.

❀ THERE ARE some built-in differences among workers in Japanese unions. One basic cause is that the enterprise structure leads to a mix within unions of blue- and white-collar workers. In spite of the higher social status and pay of the office workers, and their generally separate social life, in the union they have sought to reduce some of the differences between themselves and blue-collar workers. In both blue- and white-collar groups, women work in large numbers but for much less pay. They work for fewer years and less money, and rarely are regular employees.

In spite of these differences, age is probably a more divisive factor among the workers. The seniority system, the age of marriage and family responsibility, and, finally, the desire for employment after retirement all tend to make older workers less militant.

ROBERT E. COLE*
Unity and Cleavage Among Workers

A major cleavage exists between male and female workers. The treatment of female workers and their work cycle is different enough from that of male workers to demand special attention, especially since discussions of blue-collar workers generally deal with male blue-collar workers and ignore the increasingly large category of female blue-collar workers.

Women play a large role in the economic life of the nation. They accounted for 18,830,000 or close to forty percent of the

* Robert E. Cole, *Japanese Blue Collar* (Berkeley and Los Angeles: University of California Press, 1971), pp. 147–148, 154–155, 158–164.

total employed labor force in 1965. In the manufacturing sector, it is estimated that they account for approximately one-third of all production and related employees. Today it is considered normal for girls to take a job after graduation. Most, however, stay in the labor force only until they marry or give birth. Consequently, the average length of service for women is 4.1 as compared to 7.7 years for men, and their average age is 26.3 years as compared to 32.8 years for men. The younger age combined with shorter service means less access to skill and leads to more limited chances for promotion as well as to lower wage levels for women. It is estimated that their average wage level is still less than half that of male workers.

The shorter service of female workers is partially based on company retirement policies. A ministry of labor survey in 1965 reported that 9.4 percent of the firms investigated had formal rules requiring the retirement of women once they were married. Another 7.5 percent of the firms, though lacking a formal rule, indicated that they followed it in practice. Some 27.9 percent of the firms reported the existence of a separate retirement age system for women; this means generally earlier retirement ages for women. Given the age-seniority system of wage increase and promotion dominant in many Japanese firms, separate retirement ages for women prevents their use in responsible positions and contributes to their low wage level.

In 1966, the district court of Tokyo ruled against the retirement age system of Sumitomo Cement Company on the grounds that it violated the provision of the constitution guaranteeing equality between men and women and the freedom of marriage. This may well mean the gradual disappearance of separate retirement age rules for women. Recent manpower shortages also work in that direction. In 1968, for the first time in the course of Japanese industrialization, the number of ever-married women in the labor force exceeded the total number of single women. This does not mean that the employment status of women is automatically raised. Few married women employees achieve regular employee status. Particularly noticeable in recent years is the increase of part-time workers, most of them married women.

The lowly status of women employees was seen at Takei Diecast. Those working on the shop floor were generally married women in their late thirties, who took the jobs to supplement family income. Despite their age and length of service, which was often three or four years, they were paid under 20,000 yen a month—little more than an eighteen-year-old boy earned on entering the company after graduating from high school. Women's jobs on the shop floor were concentrated in low skills such as the inspection line, packing section, and hand-breaking of excess metal from castings. At Takei, the work rules specified the retirement age for women as fifty; this contrasts to fifty-five for men. The auto parts firm fixed the retirement age for women at thirty as opposed to fifty-five for men. . . .

Age was a major source of worker cleavage and coalition in the two firms studied. In all rapidly changing industrial societies, we expect generational differences to develop and mutual understanding to be difficult to achieve between young and older workers. Where pay is according to the nature of work or work achievement, coalitions are more likely to be formed along skill levels. Where strong industrial unions have reduced wage differentials, we expect generation differences to be held somewhat in check. But in Japan, where payment is explicitly according to age and length of service with marked wage differentials developing between young workers and older workers, the break between generations is heightened. It is not only the different wages but the uneven spread of expenses throughout a worker's career that makes a meeting of minds difficult. The economic obligations felt by workers in bachelorhood are quite different from those of the married worker, who is generally over thirty, has children to support, and is thinking of saving for retirement. The differential incomes by age and length of service and the differential obligations create different life styles. In Japan, in the middle sixties, the gap was further accentuated because of different educational experiences. Young workers are participating in the expanding educational system of an advanced industrial society. This isolates them from the adult population and contributes to a significant cultural cleavage. Blue-collar workers over thirty-five received their formal education in prewar schools and were shaped by community and family attitudes which are in many ways strikingly different from the postwar experiences of young workers. Young workers did not know the hardships of war and the immediate postwar period. They were raised in a more democratic environment with a freedom to experiment seldom seen in the prewar period. They are not caught as tightly in the web of social obligations as older workers. They are more oriented toward the expanding consumer economy. These differential experiences intensify young workers' identification with others of the same age with similar wages, values, and life styles. . . .

Most Japanese workers marry late. In the firms studied, the proper age for getting married was estimated by blue-collar workers to be twenty-eight or twenty-nine, with the wife being twenty-five. . . .

Workers explain late marriage in terms of the low pay to young workers. They believe they cannot afford to get married until their late twenties, when their wages rise and they have had time to accumulate savings. Generally, age thirty as the time of marriage and child-bearing sees the sharpest rise in financial obligations in the work career. It is a time at which the fit between rewards received and actual needs is worst. . . .

The time for marriage and child-bearing coincides with another very important change in the worker's life. . . . [I]t is extremely difficult to change jobs after thirty. Even if a job change is possible, it often means lower wages, which workers are not willing to accept once they have family responsibilities. This is a time for settling down and thinking of the future. The worker becomes more concerned about the financial position of the company and is more susceptible to management appeals. Company benefits are lopsided in favor of those over thirty and if the worker does not step out of line he can cash in on them.

The forces impinging on the worker around thirty require the most crucial adjustment since he first entered the factory. It is a time for scaling down of the high ideals of youth and adjusting to supporting a family on factory wages. Company loyalty and family ties are strengthened at the expense of worker solidarity. The amount of leisure time spent with fellow workers declines as more time is spent with the family or working overtime to support the family. The shift in worker loyalty to the company with increasing age is not unique to Japan but has also been reported in the United States. What is unusual is the convergence of the various forces noted to make the shift around the age of thirty sharp and decisive for Japanese blue-collar workers.

The shift from worker solidarity to company loyalty moves the worker into competition with his fellow workers as he seeks to demonstrate his loyalty. This competition becomes stronger as workers approach their late thirties and early forties and aspirations for promotion intensify. Friendships, which were a key factor in the young worker's attachment to the company, decline in importance relative to a more direct attachment to the company. As might be expected, worker attitudes and behavior toward their union often change radically. Workers are less willing to support the union in making strong demands on the company. Given the difficult economic circumstances which confront the worker after thirty, one would expect them to press their union to demand higher wages. On the contrary, the difficulty of finding another job and the promise of security and economic benefits in the long run turn them in the opposite direction. If there is a militant left-wing union, the workers are particularly susceptible to behind-the-scenes company maneuvering to organize a second union more sympathetic to management. Whether it actually happens, however, depends on a variety of factors, such as type of management, age composition of the entire work force, economic position of the firm, and relations between blue- and white-collar workers. In particular, the demographic structure of the firm—the result, at a given point in time, of recruitment, turnover, and biological aging —strongly conditions the degree of worker militancy. The unusually low age of the Japanese labor force must always be kept in mind when seeking explanations of contemporary worker behavior.

The shift from worker solidarity in the under-thirty category to a preoccupation with family and orientation toward the company is most noticeable among the left-wing union leaders. The thirty-one-year-old leader of the right-wing socialist faction, advocating a more cooperative attitude toward Takei, only four years earlier had been a leading member in the shop of Minseidō, the communist youth group. A large number of foremen and supervisors in the Tokyo plant had also been former left-wing union leaders but had undergone similar conversions around age thirty. The simplistic notion that age turns young radicals to mature conservatives is far from adequate in explaining this behavior. I have tried to identify the structured pressures in Japan which produce a sharp break around age thirty. . . .

The majority of firms (about eighty percent) set their retirement age at fifty-five; the number of firms raising the age to fifty-six, fifty-seven, and sixty has increased in recent years, how-ever. Company retirement allowances may be paid to those who leave the company before retirement age, but the total allowance is usually constructed on the basis of final base pay so that it strongly favors those with long service. The retirement allowance encour-ages commitment to the firm. Generally, the allowances are lower for blue-collar workers, because their base pay is lower.

In the present-day average blue-collar family, the children will be twenty-five and twenty-three years old when their worker father reaches the retirement age of fifty-five. At best, the worker will be fifty when his second child graduates from high school, which leaves him five years to concentrate on saving for retirement, assuming none of his children go on to higher education. The difficulties of saving before retirement, the leveling off of the wage increase curve in the later years, the inability to rely on children for aid or support, low old-age pensions, increased life-span, and the low retirement pay in small and medium firms, mean that most blue-collar workers continue to work after the official retirement age. At Takei Diecast, blue-collar workers said they could not rely on the pension, did not expect to retire at age fifty-five, and would probably "work until I drop." They expected to work as special employees at Takei or some other company. In either case, they were likely to have much reduced income and irregular employ-ment. Gujo Auto Parts made it a practice to rehire favored retired employees at lower wages to man their welfare facilities such as their canteen and employee discount store. The practice of select-ing favored employees undoubtedly contributes to employee com-petition to demonstrate their loyalty to the company and works against resistance to the company by older employees. The cir-cumstances at the two firms were quite typical. For example, a recent ministry of labor survey of workers who had reached retirement age reported: seventy-four percent were still working as employees, eight percent were self-employed, and eighteen percent were without regular employment. Of those still working as em-ployees, seventy-six percent received an income lower than that before retirement. Blue-collar workers, it is estimated, are receiv-ing only seventy-five percent of their preretirement income. Almost half of those employed after retirement age were forced to move to smaller firms to earn their livelihood. An examination of the employment structure of nonagricultural industries by age and size of enterprise reveals that the overwhelming number of employees over fifty-five are working in firms with fewer than 300 employees. Essentially, the larger firms "rationalize" their enterprise by dumping their older labor force onto small and medium companies.

{} SINCE THE ENTERPRISE UNION has a great deal of autonomy and is limited to one enterprise or firm, it is susceptible to manipulation by management. The policy of "mutual understanding" (*sōgo rikai*) between management and union is one technique for doing this. Cole describes below how this operated in the auto plant where he worked while studying Japanese labor. In that factory, management was more powerful than labor, so "mutual understanding" worked to the disadvantage of the workers.

If management has to deal with a union, it also has the option of promoting a second union. A second union may grow naturally out of a split in the original union, but, since the pattern has been for the second union to be more conservative, it clearly benefits management most. Major union splits such as the Sōhyō–Dōmei division heighten this situation, as Alice Cook suggests, for Dōmei wants to increase its number of adherents and it is achieving this at least partially at the expense of Sōhyō. Often these two federations have fought for control and influence over enterprise unions, thus contributing to the weakening of the labor movement as a whole.

ROBERT E. COLE*
Union-Management Cooperation

The policy of mutual understanding was based on mutual trust (*sōgo shinrai*). It was another slogan used by the auto parts

* Robert E. Cole, *Japanese Blue Collar* (Berkeley and Los Angeles: University of California Press, 1971), pp. 259–262.

company. Management emphasized that it gave confidential information to the workers and the union to build this mutual trust. On a personal level, the relations between union leaders and management personnel were carefully cultivated. The union leaders had free access to the hotel the company management used for entertainment purposes. The union was also brought into the formal operation of the company's recreation program. On all levels there was an attempt to integrate the union with the company's administrative structure for the control of workers; this made it difficult to develop union autonomy to any great degree. Rather than union autonomy, company cooptation seems to have been the dominating characteristic of this case. Mutual understanding based on mutual trust works in the interests of workers and democracy only if the power between management and labor is fairly evenly balanced. When the company holds a commanding edge, as is so often the case in Japan, mutual understanding is little more than a front for company domination.

Union leaders explained that worker criticism of the policy of mutual understanding meant that additional education was required. Besides the question of elitist control, this explanation poses yet another issue.... [Jonathan Swift] made the following observation in *Gulliver's Travels:* "When they [human beings] are supposedly governed by 'love or reason,' he [the individual] is under continuous pressure to . . . behave and think in exactly the same way as everyone else." The workers at Gujo Auto Parts are ostensibly governed by a view in which mutual understanding is the only reasonable course; all other approaches are officially absent. The official line is that higher production will in the long run insure higher wages and so eradicate any incipient problems. To voice other views is to endanger one's job security or promotion prospects. The totalitarian tendency is inherent when workers, though not compelled to do anything, are "exhorted," "advised," and "educated." Industrial democracy, however, means recognition of different roles and interests for the managers and the managed and cooperation where interests and roles overlap. Such a situation permits expression and regulation of conflict. The attempt to wipe out lines of conflict by instituting an ideology of harmony and unity may increase rather than decrease the potential for violent conflict. Particularly intense conflicts, which are not susceptible to the ideology of harmony and unity, are likely to explode violently, for they lack legitimate channels for their expression. This may be a factor in the nature of Japanese strikes; though most are usually short, some are extremely long, intense, and violent.

The situation at the auto parts firm is not representative of all Japanese unions. But the meaning that mutual understanding, union democracy, and union autonomy took on there reflects a crystalization of tendencies which is present in most Japanese firms. This is true of unions that explicitly assert a policy of mutual cooperation as well as those that purport to follow a leftist ideology. The common characteristics of Japanese union are excessive identification with the interests of the firm, a desire to avoid conflict, enterprise unionism, and subordination to the authority of management—all rooted in worker and management consciousness.

The dual meaning of the policy of mutual cooperation was best symbolized by worker reference to the union as a gear in the company. This implied a strong criticism of a weak union that lacked autonomy. However, the workers also said that they drew advantages from the union being a gear in the company. They believed the union had a say in many more matters than would be the case if it adopted a more militant posture.

The union, by virtue of its acceptance by management, had access to inside happenings, which provided workers with an all-important predictability. They had a degree of security and knowledge of future developments. This does not necessarily mean workers influenced developments except in a passive sense: by relying on management to do the right thing. Above all, the mutual cooperation approach to labor–management relations was a path that minimized conflict and maximized harmony, an all-important consideration in the semiclosed corporate world of the Japanese firm.

The success of this approach in the long run hinges on an economic bargain between union and company. The union gives over to management control in the shop, including even the right to fire under extreme circumstances. In return the union is promised that its members will share in the economic benefits that will result. The nature of the bargain and whether it is kept by the company depends on such factors as market conditions, size of the enterprise, amount of labor mobility, growth rate of firm and industry, and the good will of the company and strength of the union. However, union strength tends to be compromised because it becomes a victim of its call for mutual cooperation. The ultimate weapon, the strike, is inconsistent with the avowed policy of mutual understanding.

The good will of the company in keeping its end of the bargain does not arise from intrinsic kindness but from enlightened self-interest. Japanese companies learned much from the history of the postwar period with its legacy of militant left-wing unions. By keeping their bargain, they buy insurance that present unions will not be replaced by more militant ones. The unions making this economic bargain depend for their existence on the threat created by more militant unions that might replace them.

ALICE H. COOK*
Second Unions

... Japan has no concept, legal or otherwise, of exclusive rights for a dominant union. When harmony is no longer possible within a single organization, the dissidents, often in the name of democracy, withdraw to form a second union. Probably no Japanese would fail to understand this kind of behavior as a compelling necessity for any group no longer able to be heard or to have its views taken into consideration in the final policy around which consensus is achieved. In this sense both Sōhyō and Zenrō were breakaway second unions from the original bodies with which they were affiliated.

But second unionism in Japan has another, more ominous, implication. Within the enterprises, when movements of this kind occur, the second union usually and rapidly becomes first in point of view of size and significance. If this happened spontaneously perhaps objections would be absorbed. But evidence is general that many of these breakaways are abetted and sponsored by the employers who encourage disaffected oldsters in a union led by radical young men, or a group of craftsmen who have been short-

* Alice H. Cook, *Japanese Trade Unionism* (Ithaca, N.Y.: Cornell University, 1968), pp. 97–98.

changed in a recent division of the "base up," or an "anti–main current" faction, to form a second union. The most noted cases of second unionism in the recent past occurred after long strikes which had dragged on for months, notably at the Miike Mines in 1960 and two years before at Ōji Paper, strikes which, in the opinion of many observers, were early doomed to defeat at the hands of the stronger employers. But the formation of a second union at such a juncture in a bitterly fought strike is as treasonable in Japan as it would be in the West. Particularly when viewed by the leaders and loyal followers of the first union, the persons or organizations responsible for the organization of second unions are nothing short of immoral. In every case to date, it is the Sōhyō union which has suffered, while in most instances the second union has been immediately chartered by a Dōmei affiliate. Thus the problem of second unionism is mainly one for which the Dōmei unions have to have an answer.

꧂ THE DISPUTE at the Miike coal mine illustrates the effect of enterprise unionism and second unions in practice. Lasting about a year, from the fall of 1959 to the fall of 1960, the struggle was over layoffs, partly political (Miike was known for its militance), and partly technological in nature. The *enterprise* union in this case was Sankōren, the union for all Mitsui Company coal miners. Miike was the largest of the Mitsui coal mines; the Miike local was the largest in Sankōren. When the local struck—without much support from Sankōren —there were splits in the union. The white collar workers split; then a second union formed among the miners, which soon affiliated with the right Socialist Zenrō federation (later part of Dōmei). Tanrō, the *national* coal union, supported the strike, but the weakness of national unions showed itself, and Tanrō eventually had to agree to an unfavorable settlement. The enterprise union, Sankōren, was the *least* helpful to the local, to the point that the Miike local took the unprecedented step of withdrawing from the enterprise union. The strike ultimately showed that labor unions lacked the power to protect their members from increased layoffs.

BENJAMIN MARTIN*
Japanese Mining Labor: The Miike Strike

The Shakespearian line, "One sorrow never comes but brings an heir," provides a fitting commentary on recent events in Japanese labor relations. The extraordinary turbulence accompanying the Diet ratification of the Japanese–American Security Pact was to be succeeded, several weeks later, by a climactic turn in the Miike coal mine strike, Japan's most serious labor dispute in modern times.

The Miike mine, Japan's largest and most modern colliery, is the hub of industrial activity for the Kyushu city of Ōmuta (population 250,000). Its five principal factories which produce chemicals and nonferrous metals, rely on the mine for their large coal requirements. Both the mine and the industrial enterprises are important subsidiaries of the Mitsui concern—Japan's foremost financial and industrial combine (zaibatsu). Ōmuta is also a stronghold of the left Socialist Japan General Council of Trade Unions (Sōhyō) and its affiliated Japan Coal Miners Union (Tanrō). During 1960 the mine was the scene of a bitter conflict engendered by the severe depression in the Japanese coal mining industry and the irregular background of labor–management relations. The outcome of this struggle is having repercussions throughout Japan's troubled labor movement.

Long the weak link in the country's industrial development, the coal mining industry suffers from low-quality deposits, surplus manpower, low productivity, and excessively high extraction costs. . . .

On the advice of experts the industry is drastically reducing labor overhead and raising productivity. A reduction of 60,000 mine employees was planned during 1960, and by 1963 approxi-

* Benjamin Martin, "Japanese Mining Labor: The Miike Strike," *Far Eastern Survey* XXX:2 (February 1961), pp. 26–30.

mately one-third of the present industry complement of 300,000 will be eliminated. These cuts are to come primarily from the larger unionized mines which hitherto have not been as severely affected as the smaller and largely unorganized collieries. The discharge of employees is regarded as an abandonment of traditional employer obligations. The paternalistic relationship which pervades so much of Japanese life is present in industry in the form of far-reaching employer responsibilities for the welfare of his employee wards. From the time an employee is granted permanent status within the enterprise the customary practice is for the management to assure him of continuous employment until he reaches retirement age. Along with this, the strong pressures of Japan's huge labor surplus and the unwillingness of the larger, better-paying establishments to engage (on a permanent basis) a worker who has been previously employed elsewhere (whatever the reasons for his discharge or resignation) make dismissal tantamount to a life sentence of unemployment and poverty. Appropriately, the Japanese refer to such an event as *kubikiri*— having one's head cut off. Personnel retrenchments consequently are the major cause for the most bitterly contested industrial disputes since the end of the war.

The Mitsui Mining Company owns six of the country's biggest and best collieries. Its 35,000 employees constitute the Mitsui Coal Miners Federation (Sankōren) which is the principal affiliate of the Japan Coal Miners Union (Tanrō). The Miike Mine union with a membership of 14,000 is the largest in both Sankōren and Tanrō and its preeminence in numbers is matched by its renown as Japan's most powerful local union. . . .

Backed by the prodigious power of the Mitsui concern, the management decided on a showdown. In August, 1959, it proposed to Sankōren the voluntary retirement (with severance allowances) of approximately 5000 of their 35,000 employees, including more than 2000 from the Miike mine. . . .

Initially Sankōren opposed the company plan, but after repeated bargaining sessions, the federation tacitly agreed not to interfere with the company's enlistment of voluntary retirements. The Miike local, however, remained adamant. The required number of volunteers were obtained at the five mines while only 1000 were secured at Miike. In November the company issued dismissal notices to 1277 additional Miike employees, including 300 union activists who were termed "production obstructionists." In retaliation the Miike union ordered its members to strike on Tuesdays and Fridays.

The respective positions of the disputants had crystalized: the company contended that the discharge of the 1277, including numerous union leaders, "was necessary for the reconstruction of the Mitsui Mining Company," while Tanrō termed "the unilateral discharge by nomination" as an unfair labor practice which aimed at "total destruction of the union." . . . Assured of financial support the mine executives were prepared to carry on an endurance contest with the strikers. Japanese unions have slender financial resources, and for that reason strikes are usually short. To provide adequate support for 14,000 strikers over an extended period was a near-impossible undertaking, yet the tenacity and sacrifice of the miners, for a time, proved to be an overriding factor.

Before long the dispute mushroomed into a nationwide confrontation between labor and capital. The Miike battle became the focal point of the controversy between Tanrō and the coal operators over industry cutbacks. The ubiquitous Japan Federation of Employers' Organizations (Nikkeiren) mobilized national employer support while operators of the major collieries agreed to supply coal to the Miike customers during the strike. The government-controlled coal price had been reduced at this point, but a number of important industrial and power companies continued to pay the former high rates, the difference (averaging 70¢ per ton) going to the Mitsui Mining Company to help finance the lockout. Employers recognized that to inflict a serious defeat on Tanrō, labor's most powerful industrial union, would weaken the entire labor movement. . . .

As the strike developed into a stalemate, fissiparous tendencies (an almost inevitable concomitant of severe union crises) made their appearance. The Mitsui White Collar Employees Federation (Sanshokuren), an affiliate of Tanrō and Sankōren, voiced its dissatisfaction with the Miike union policies and announced its intention to bargain separately with the company. (It was to secede from Tanrō several months later.) Subsequently a dissident faction emerged in the Miike local which advocated a cessation of the strike and a resumption of bargaining with the company. Sankōren's membership at the five other mines was suffering from suspensions of seasonal bonuses (an integral part of the wage structure), and delays in wage payments. This, plus the impression that the Miike struggle was doomed, forced Sankōren to make similar proposals to Tanrō headquarters. Following a rebuff at the March 11 meeting of the union's executive board, the opposition seceded and on March 17 announced the formation of a second union. The company promptly recognized the rival organization, which recruited about 4500 of the 14,000 employees. A back-to-work movement was organized which, in spite of bloody clashes with mass picket formations, managed to smuggle 2000 workers into the mine. Nevertheless the strikers continued to prevent resumption of coal shipments.

Not unexpectedly the right Socialist Japan Trade Union Congress (Zenrō Kaigi) publicly announced support of the splinter organization, dispatching manpower and funds to its aid. . . .

Following the unexpected defections, Sankōren's refusal to participate caused Tanrō to cancel plans for an April industrywide twenty-four hour strike aimed at further reducing the dwindling coal reserves. As the situation grew increasingly critical, Sankōren pressed the Tanrō officers to arrange for a rapid resolution of the Miike deadlock. For the first time in its existence the organization was forced to request the Central Labor Relations Commission to undertake mediation of the strike. Beyond some minor modifications the CLRC mediation plan upheld the company position. The term "voluntary retirement" was substituted for "discharge," but the list of 1277 workers selected for dismissal remained unchanged. Severance pay was increased by 10,000 yen ($22.00). The company readily agreed to the proposals.

To establish the union's stand on the mediation plan Tanrō scheduled a special two-day convention for April 8. At the outset the officers of Tanrō were inclined to accept the harsh provisions of the plan in the interests of organizational unity. Although by now in a more compromising mood, the Miike local demanded its rejection while the Mitsui Federation (Sankōren) insisted on its acceptance. As the tormented, emotionally charged convention seesawed back and forth between mutually unacceptable alternatives, the conference was extended to ten days. Finally by a large majority the delegates voted to reject the mediation proposal. Incensed, the Sankōren representatives walked out declaring themselves no longer bound by Tanrō decisions. The coal miner's union seemed to be disintegrating. After the conference the internal situation continued to deteriorate. Sankōren ceased its important financial assistance to the Miike strike fund and the Miike local withdrew from Sankōren. Thereupon Sankōren entered into negotiations with the company and agreement was reached on a voluntary retirement plan as well as what amounted to a wage cut of approximately 3000 yen ($8.00)....

Following the successful entry of the mine by strikebreakers, the strikers concentrated on the mass picketing and control of the Mikawa mine hoppers, without free access to which the company was unable to resume coal shipments. An injunction was requested from the Fukuoka district court to force the pickets to clear this section of the mine. After some weeks of legal sparring and unsuccessful attempts by bailiffs to clear the hopper area, the court issued an injunction and ordered its enforcement, thereby bringing the dispute to its climax. Both sides grimly prepared for the showdown. The control of the hoppers was a matter of survival for the strikers. To reinforce their defiance of the injunction order, Tanrō and Sōhyō sent 15,000 supporters to bolster the picket lines; the central government dispatched 13,000 police to Ōmuta.

A few days prior to the injunction deadline the Ikeda cabinet was sworn in as successor to the Kishi regime. Prime Minister Hayato Ikeda and his newly appointed labor minister, Hirohide Ishida, moved quickly to forestall bloodshed at Miike. Such an event would be a highly inauspicious beginning for the new cabinet, not to speak of the effect it might have on the forthcoming Diet election in the fall. Ishida contacted the leaders of the business world and convinced them of the necessity for arranging a truce at Miike.

Weakened by internecine divisions and financially exhausted, Tanrō readily assented to the truce proposal. There was the possibility that the new mediation formula might help Tanrō out of its agonizing dilemma by softening the company's stand. Initially the Mitsui Mining executives were unwilling to agree as, in their estimation, a conclusive rout of the strikers was in the offing. However, too much was at stake for those who supported the ruling conservative party. A truce was arranged at the end of July while the Central Labor Relations Commission prepared a revised mediation formula which, this time, both sides were committed to accept. On August 10, the CLRC made public its findings. To the consternation of the strikers and Tanrō, the company position was again almost completely vindicated: the 1277 discharges were to become "voluntary" for those who consented to resign within a one-month period, and those cooperating were offered the added inducement of a 20,000 yen ($55.00) "special livelihood fund." The commission further recommended government assistance to workers seeking employment opportunities and in providing retraining for those discharged.

Tanrō was left with no alternative but to submit. As before, the Miike strikers were defiant but the material and moral means with which to continue resisting had been exhausted. Again discord and reluctance made necessary the extension and reconvening of a special Tanrō convention. In the end, however, the disconsolate delegates voted unanimously (on September 6) to end the year-old Miike dispute through acceptance of the mediation formula.

. . . The most immediate consequence of the defeat was its effect on the coal miners. The weakening of union power is encouraging coal operators to meet the economic crisis at the increased expense of their employees. The leading daily of north Kyushu observed editorially that managements of the large coal mines seem to equate industry modernization with the discharge of miners. Just how far the deterioration of working conditions and job security will go is still to be seen. That they will decline significantly is a certainty.

Tanrō's past achievements have been exemplary: it has been the only industrywide organization with sufficient centralized authority successfully to invoke the united action of its affiliates; it was unique in its ability to order an industrywide shutdown and to expect full compliance. Industrywide bargaining, the aspiration of every union in Japan, exists only in the coal and maritime industries. Its retrogression is now an actuality.

With a total membership surpassing 7 million the Japanese labor movement is one of the world's largest, though paradoxically it remains one of the weakest in terms of economic power. Its numerical impressiveness is due, in large measure, to postwar occupation reforms which were, however, incapable of nullifying the tenacious influence of employer paternalism, the pressures of a closed labor market, and the traditional attitudes of loyalty and subservience. Despite a growing union consciousness among its adherents, Japanese trade unionism remains insufficiently rooted to resist the pressure of organized capital. . . .

5. Politics: 1960-1973

POLITICS AS USUAL

§ LABOR UNIONS and the socialist parties are theoretically separate, but in practice their relationship is very close. Sōhyō has been tied to the Japan Socialist Party (also called the Social Democratic party, or SDP). Zenrō and Sōdōmei, later united in Dōmei, have been allied to right-wing Socialists, both when they were in the JSP and when they split off as the Democratic Socialist party in 1959. A major dispute between them has been how much emphasis to place on political versus economic demands. In general, Sōhyō has been more political, but in particular labor issues it has also been more militant. The selection below discusses the factors tending to create a more political orientation in labor federations.

COLE, TOTTEN, AND UYEHARA*
Labor and Electoral Support

Two principles regarding union—party relations have been most widely accepted and abused in postwar Japan. In theory, labor organizations and leftist parties are supposed to be independent of each other; they should cooperate, but neither should seek domination over the other. And the corollary has been that union members, in voting and other political actitivites, should be free to support parties according to individual choice. . . .

* Allan B. Cole, George O. Totten, and Cecil H. Uyehara, *Socialist Parties in Postwar Japan* (New Haven, Conn.: Yale University Press, 1966), pp. 313, 315–317, 319–322.

496] POSTWAR JAPAN: 1945 TO THE PRESENT

The Social Democratic party, having a tiny membership and shallow rootage in union locals, depending on labor organizations for mobilizing voters and financial support, is susceptible to union pressures. Morover, the main leftist labor federations have often managed political struggles which have carried them deeply into party activities. Since 1947, labor leaders have been the largest special interest group among SDP Diet members in both houses. Labor leaders, particularly those of a more conservative stripe, have reacted against divisive communist manipulation of the early postwar labor movement, and party (SDP or JCP) attempts to control unions. On the other hand, national leadership of the leftist Sōhyō has, since SDP unification in 1955, more frequently called for expansion of Socialist party membership in unionized shops. The National Liaison Council for Socialist party members in Sōhyō, founded by party and union leaders in August 1961, coordinated ten such councils in industrial unions. Although many members are reluctant to be publicly labeled as to party, a marked majority of leaders of labor federations connected with Sōhyō tend to be SDP members. At the 17th Sōhyō Convention in August 1961, more than sixty percent of the delegates were politically so identified, but SDP party members among the rank and file are few. On the other hand, about half of the executives of local SDP federations are from unions. . . .

Differences between left and right Socialists on the one hand and Sōhyō and Sōdōmei–Zenrō on the other concerning necessary political action boiled down to the degree to which such activities should be limited to tactics to promote the economic ends of organized workers. Leftists insisted that against the focused political influence of monopoly capitalism there would be only amorphous national opinion unless the labor movement mobilized purposeful numbers to offset those forces and, hopefully, to achieve a socialist order. This turned into a vicious cycle with the conservative interests of organized employers interreacting with labor's tendencies to transform economic into political struggles.

The decisive prize, of course, has been control of the regulative and once oppressive state. Its policies affect not only the rights which can protect or break the labor movement; they can also exert decisive influence toward inflation or deflation, with consequences for the real income and job security of workers; the state determines the distribution of tax incidence as well as policies like rearmament and the liberalization of tariffs which have significance for workers' interests. This outlook had considerable appeal as long as Japanese society provided workers with little stake except subsistence employment in the capitalist system.

Profound changes, especially since 1957–1959, have been affecting Japan's industrial relations and the environment of proletarian politics. Technological innovations and spectacular economic growth have impelled industrial shifts affecting employment. They have accentuated rewards and new semimanagerial statuses available for those with recent specialized training, so that new professionalization is expanding in larger factories. Labor–management relations are being modernized, and paternalism as well as the seniority system are being modified, the latter by increasing distinction in wages according to type of work. The productivity of labor is being greatly increased. More representatives of labor have been added to governmental commissions. Drastic liberalization of the tariff structure has further affected business organizations and job security. Retraining and reemployment services for workers have received more emphasis. There have even been scattered labor shortages.

Though Socialists maintain correctly that profits from economic growth have not been equally shared, still, the incomes, consumption, and welfare of most workers have been significantly improved. Of course, analogies with the conditions and attitudes of workers in the United States and Western Europe could be misleading, but, as we shall see, there are many recent signs that in Japan, too, better levels of living and the proven fact that regulated capitalism need not cause continual shrinkage of purchasing power and chronically expanding productive surpluses have tended to moderate the temper of workers. Japanese union leaders and Socialist politicians have noted the very practical impact of these changes and have had to develop responses.

Another causal dimension of labor politicism in Japan is to be found in the structure of union organizations. In the sector of large private industries, populous national labor federations have been constructed of enterprise union components which tenaciously control their own bargaining with management. Mobilization for political struggles as extensions of economic demands often constitutes the principal self-justifying strategy for national leadership and central organs. Thus, among leftist unions a premium is placed on militancy, and a tradition with emotional and philosophic implications has developed. Furthermore, during the early postwar chaos, the weaknesses of industries imposed objective limitations to feasible bargaining demands of unions, while after 1950 the relative power of unions dwindled in the face of resurgent managerial strength. Thus many unionists have preferred political activism to the apparent alternatives: lethargy and company union docility.

The other more vigorous sector of the labor movement is composed of unionized workers in governmental services and monopoly corporations. Their loss of strike and, on the part of the former, collective bargaining rights has left them little but political demonstrations and limited dispute tactics. Of course, the employer toward whom their struggles are directed is the government, and for this reason successive councils of national and local government workers' unions have found it useful to ally with Sōhyō and the left Socialists. It was, however, chiefly Communist leadership which tried to mold these unions into a striking force in 1947–1948 to attain a so-called "people's government." Indeed, it has been observed that almost any widespread strike is bound to assume political significance, and short strikes are usually used to reinforce any extraordinary political demonstration.

Finally there are views and interests of union leaders and the rank and file which induce politicism. Among veteran leaders are some who, as intellectuals-turned-labor-elite between the world wars, were imbued with Marxist doctrines and became accustomed to combinations of unions being in most respects, except electoral numbers, congruent with prewar parties. Even more numerous are leaders of the younger and now often more boldly radical postwar generation. It is difficult for such men to return to industrial jobs and union offices after a term in the national Diet. Other aspirants crowd up the union ladder, and labor–SDP legislators with the support of their organizations usually try to be reelected. One of their perpetual problems is to keep in close touch with labor constituents. Some but not all labor Diet members have behaved as though they were aware that they represented more interests among their complex constituencies than just those of organized workers.

Though there is such a natural entente between trade unions and the Socialist parties, organized workers comprise a minority of the electorate, even if industrial and service employees are added to white-collar and governmental functionaries. The proportion of those organized has slipped with the faster growth of the labor force to less than thirty-five percent. Labor leaders confess that the party receiving official union support cannot depend on a tight discipline binding its members as the conservative parties can rely on traditional prestige and sanctions wielded by rural patriarchal bosses. Many of the urban leaders as well as the rank and file have become somewhat disillusioned with politicians and the ballot box, while others feel that, lacking the massive, disciplined union membership of its British counterpart, the party alone cannot conduct effective struggles outside the Diet. Thus, and especially when economic grievances were acute, members often responded to the political strategies urged by leaders of national industrial and general federations. At both union and Socialist party conventions criticisms are often heard to the effect that party–union relations are confined to elites of party and union national headquarters. This is somewhat less true in prefectural and municipal politics.

❀ MOVING INTO THE 1960s, the Socialists were faced with the need to reevaluate their policies or to remain a permanent minority party in the Diet. A slogan was coined to the effect that they had reached an insurmountable "barrier of one-third." Their political line—basically arguing that socialism through political action was the first priority—was not appealing to workers whose standard of living was rising. Further, if they were ever to march past their steady position of one-third of the seats in the Diet, their votes had to come from the middle strata of Japanese society which comprised over half of the population.

One possible solution to this dilemma was "structural reform," the doctrine adopted by the JSP in 1961 under the leadership of Eda Saburō. Later branded as reformism following its lack of immediate success, it came under attack, and Eda was forced out of the party chairmanship. But the problems that the structural reform doctrine represents still exist, and thus it is still an issue in the Socialist party.

It is not clear, however, that a reformist Socialist line *would* gain more votes. The right Democratic Socialist party has one, and it has not been picking up Diet seats. LDP losses in elections up through 1969 went instead to Kōmeitō, the Clean Government party. Kōmeitō is the political party of the Sōka Gakkai, the religious Value Creation Society. In the 1969 Lower House elections, Kōmeitō garnered a surprising eleven percent of the popular vote. Yet overall electoral trends suggest only a slight change from the stable "one-and-a-half parties" system to one with one-and-seven-eighths parties. The seven-eighths, of course, continues to be splintered among the left-wing parties and Kōmeitō, with the Liberal Democratic party in firm control, even though it now polls less than fifty percent of the national votes.

R. P. DORE*
The Japanese Socialist Party and 'Structural Reform'

The Japanese Socialist party has a new policy, or at least a new "doctrine" and a new slogan—"structural reform." Henceforth the party is to press for piecemeal modifications of the more objectionable features of contemporary capitalist society—to demand full employment, minimum wage legislation, shorter working hours, better social security, restriction of monopoly price control, state regulation of basic industries. In this way it will hasten the establishment of socialism by a gradual accumulation of changes in the structure of society and by giving the workers, in the process of demanding these reforms, the experience in group action necessary for the final struggle. . . .

* R. P. Dore, "The Japanese Socialist Party and 'Structural Reform,'" *Asian Survey* I:8 (October 1961), pp. 3–5.

In Japan, as in Western Europe, conservative governments have learned how to avoid major depressions, and they have learned the electoral value of welfare programs. Labor unions have gained in power and secured for their members a share in the rewards of rising productivity. Indeed, if ability to produce be the criterion, capitalism has nowhere been more buoyantly successful than in Japan—not many economies can register a sixteen percent increase in the Gross National Product in one year as Japan did in 1959. And the statistics which show a rise in real wages of more than fifty percent between 1951 and 1959, even granted a discount for official optimism, remain impressive. With television sets now in at least four out of every ten Japanese homes, their commercials daily extolling the virtues of bigger and better cameras, washing machines, electric cooking pots, and soon popular cars, it is not surprising that a conservative prime minister who promises to double incomes in ten years—as Ikeda did at the last election— has more appeal than a party which seeks a major rearrangement of society. . . .

The new doctrine, or rather its acceptance by the party convention in March 1961, owes a great deal to Eda Saburō, the energetic, and on television very personable, general secretary of the party who took over the leadership after Asanuma's assassination and earned considerable respect for his direction of the election campaign. Eda himself has explained the background to the new doctrine. The party has, he says, lacked any clear policy by means of which it could positively work for the achievement of power. It had consequently been forced into a negative, defensive posture, concentrating solely on "opposition" to each new initiative of its opponents. The result was the predominance of three equally sterile views in the party; there was the "poverty revolution theory" of those who looked to war and economic depression as the objective conditions for revolution; the "piecemeal revolution theory" of those who overlooked the importance of gaining power and imagined that the revolution could be accomplished by an accumulation of pressure for reform in the Diet; and finally there was the "spinelessness of those who had lost their determination to gain power and were willing to accept the role of eternal opposition."

The theme recurs that somehow the Socialist party must find a way to make the running. The unions, too, despite their well-known penchant for political activity, had in fact taken part only in campaigns of *opposition* and *resistance* to government measures. Structural reform is to be something more positive. . . .

The partial reforms for which the party will press include improvements in living standards—shorter hours, higher wages, better social security and so on; changes in the industrial structure—restriction of monopoly prices, planning controls over basic industry and industrial location, tax reforms and the strengthening of small enterprises by cooperative organization; and a change in the structure of external trade—the expansion of trade with the communist bloc and the elimination of military alliances which prevent it.

COLE, TOTTEN, AND UYEHARA*
Socialist Support from Middle and Other Strata

Long before emergence of the two–main party system, many a Socialist campaigner had become fully aware of the importance of support by voters who belong neither to Japan's most potent elites nor to the industrial working class. Relative to Japanese society and defined in these sweeping terms, people in the middle strata comprise some sixty to seventy-five percent of the population. More narrowly and occupationally defined, they constitute about one-quarter of the total population and nearly one-half of all city-dwellers. . . .

Japanese Socialists emphasize their special affinity with industrial laborers, especially with those organized into trade unions. But when referring to "the masses" they generally mean most of society other than the "ruling class." With respect to middle strata there is disagreement, yet almost all recognize political opportunities among the many highly educated citizens with a sense of alienation and in the hardships and grievances of the massive petty bourgeoisie. Moreover, they hope for future growth in part because a significant majority of youth are expected to vote

* Allan B. Cole, George O. Totten, and Cecil H. Uyehara, *Socialist Parties in Postwar Japan.* (New Haven, Conn.: Yale University Press, 1966), pp. 418, 446–447.

for "progressive" parties, and because most of Japan's growing population is being absorbed into the urban labor and lesser middle strata. The chief obstacles for the SDP in this regard are conservatism, apathy, and difficulties in organizing cohesive middle-class groups for political action. Some leftist ideologues have long predicted that much of the weaker middle strata will or should be proletarianized, while most Socialists think that only in the long run, and gradually, could the least economical enterprises be absorbed into state-operated corporations.

The controversy between left and right in the party over "class party" versus "national party" in essence asks whether SDP gains between 1952 and 1965 have maximized the support available from the more readily organized labor sector and whether, if there is to be continued growth toward a ruling majority, there must be more efforts to attract middle-class votes. Except for the cultivation of the leftist intelligentsia, disproportionate attention has been given to organized labor. This was natural, for during the democratization period there was no great organized surge of middle-class forces comparable to that of the labor movement. White-collar workers, it is true, did organize, but for reasons already explained their unions usually identified themselves with labor. A combination of circumstances in and after 1953 caused leaders and factions of the SDP to pay more attention than before to middle-class interests. As reunification became possible and the two-main-party pattern emerged, strategic imperatives accentuated competition for the support of middle strata. Since 1957, the rapid growth of the Japanese economy has made observers generally more aware of the increased significance of these social elements. However, it is not so easy to interpret the import of this trend for practical politics. "Structural reformers" within the SDP have had such changes in mind in proposing more moderate tactics, but related polemics have impeded development of a concerted strategy to attract middle elements and "break the barrier of one-third" strength in the national legislature. One might expect that the Democratic Socialists would make the most effective overtures to the middle strata, but in this they have so far not notably succeeded. Meanwhile the militant Sōka Gakkai has attained the third largest bloc of seats in the House of Councilors. Its appeal is to economically and psychologically insecure people; it builds, chiefly within Japan's sprawling urban agglomerates, inner communities with apostolic solidarity, voluntary welfare systems, and a sectarian hierarchical ladder for advancement and recognition. There could be no more graphic indication that all of the national parties have been conspicuously remiss in neglecting the needs and latent responses of the petit bourgeois and lowest classes.

⚙ THE LATE 1960s gave birth to a new, nonsectarian left group in Japan, Beiheiren (Japan "Peace in Vietnam!" Committee). Beiheiren's activities have expanded from opposing the Vietnam war to helping U.S. soldiers desert, to concern with pollution, Okinawa, and Japanese imperialism. In the interview below on the results of the 1969 elections, *Ampo*, Beiheiren's English-language publication, discusses the Japanese political scene with Mutō Ichiyo, political commentator and head of Beiheiren. His analysis concentrates on the moribund nature of the Japanese left-wing parties and unions. He sees current Japanese politics as unstable and suggests new possibilities.

MUTO ICHIYŌ*
The December 1969 Elections: An Analysis—
AMPO Interviews Mutō Ichiyo

AMPO. I want to ask some questions about the recent victory of the Liberal–Democratic party in the elections, but, before we get into this specific election. I think it's worth explaining some things about the power of the LDP in general. Since most of our readers have never lived under a one-party system, probably many of them don't know how a single party keeps itself in power in this way. For example, one thing that many people might not know is the

* Mutō Ichiyo, "The December 1969 Election: An Analysis—AMPO Interviews Mutō Ichiyo," *AMPO* 3–4 (March 1970), pp. 12–20.

fact that the LDP spends approximately ten times as much in an election as its opposition parties.

MUTŌ. In fact, the LDP has kept in power since 1955, after the different conservative parties were unified. You can understand what it is like when you think of the American two-party system. Either the Democratic or the Republic party is in power there, and they follow nearly the same policy on all issues. So in Japan, the Japanese "Republicans" and "Democrats" are unified. That's the basic thing. And you mentioned money spent for the elections. That is very important, but more important is the fact that the Liberal–Democrats have been holding state power for a long time, and the money spent not specifically during the election campaign but all round the year, in the form, say, of subsidies, in the form of investment and loans from the government . . . these things consolidate the solid social base in support of the party. And all organizations thus created were mobilized in the recent election. . . . Well, that is the system of bourgeois society itself, which has constantly, in day-to-day activities, been organized to support the LDP.

And so you could have the same picture if you put the two American parties together, and thought in terms of that. You will find that American voters, who theoretically have any option, and could have voted for Black Panthers or anybody, will always support . . . most of them, at least . . . either of the two major parties, which are the same thing.

AMPO. It's as if America had a single party called the "Democratic–Republican Party."

MUTŌ. Yes, exactly. There used to be a Liberal and a Democratic party, and they merged, and they maintain slight differences. Not the original difference, but the party itself is a coalition of factions, each of which is in itself a small party representing different, *slightly* different, political tendencies.

AMPO. Well, let's move on to the recent election. Despite widespread protests, including even street-fighting and strikes and other kinds of opposition to the LDP, the results of the election seemed disappointing. The LDP gained in seats, the Socialist party seems to have suffered its worst defeat ever. How do you explain this election?

MUTŌ. Well, first of all, the election itself was a well-planned tactic of the Liberal–Democrats. The timing, and the way it was

held, these things were completely coordinated by the Liberal–
Democrats, without the protest of any of the major opposition
parties . . . without any of the opposition parties seeing through the
design and trying seriously to prevent it. The election was held
between Christmas and New Year—that means, in the busiest time
of the year. And in the preceding month, in November, Satō went
to Washington and signed the joint statement. And the election
was designed hastily and was held before the people had time to
have doubts about the joint statement. And as you know there was
great press propaganda, praising Satō and his great deed of bringing about the return of Okinawa to Japan. And as for the nature
of the return of Okinawa to Japan . . . it was something alien to
the interests of the Japanese people, the Okinawan inhabitants, in
particular. Still, it was bombastically played up in the press and
TV that Satō did something very good for the Japanese people,
and Satō chose the date of the election in consideration of this
fact.

And . . . the Joint Statement was in fact the conclusion of the
1970 security treaty, a new security treaty. And we must remember that in 1960 the original security treaty was first signed, then
put to the Diet for debate, and then demonstrations followed
which led to the resignation of the Kishi cabinet. Knowing that, the
Satō cabinet just reversed the order of the political process. They
started with the Diet in August, through which the University
Control Law was railroaded. And there was no debate at all about
the treaty and the Satō visit. Only New Left forces stood up and
protested and tried everything to prevent him from going. Then the
Joint Statement was signed, and it did not need to be put to any
Diet debate. It was so designed. And then, after the administrative
act of signing the treaty, the virtual treaty, the Diet was dissolved,
without permitting the people to give any consideration to the
significance of the treaty. And so the time was chosen, and the
order of the political process was chosen . . . unilaterally by the
Liberal–Democrats. That partly explains the victory of the LDP.

In that respect we must note that the rate of abstention was very
high—second highest since the war. Only sixty-odd percent of the
eligible voters went to the polls. . . . I'm sure that all the New Left
forces boycotted the elections. That means that in this election a
new tendency among students and young workers has become
clearly apparent . . . a change of political thinking. Formerly they

voted for the Socialists as the opposition party number one. But now they're just despairing of all the parties and of the parliamentary system itself, because it is so completely manipulated by the Liberal–Democrats. The high abstention rate shows partly the growth of that tendency. And under these circumstances the Liberal–Democrats could win only thirty percent of the eligible voters. And the percentage of votes gained by the party to the total of the votes cast fell by more than one percent. Yet the party could increase its seats.

So the victory was a victory of political tactics, and doesn't indicate any stability under the new Liberal–Democratic government.

AMPO. One of the things that was also widely noted about the election was the shift in the opposition parties: the Socialist party lost many, the Kōmeitō gained, and the Communist party made the greatest gains it has in recent years. Do you have any comments about that?

MUTŌ. The best way to approach that question is to ask, did the recent election represent any change in the political map of postwar Japan? I would say, yes. It is very important . . . not the election result itself, but the trend which has produced this election result. We are talking about the end of the postwar democracy period; that period was ended with the signing of the Joint Statement.

Well, this means that the traditional pattern of political antagonism between the LDP as the only government party and the JSP as, not the only, but almost the only significant opposition party . . . with these two forces split over the interpretation of "peace and democracy" . . . that pattern has ended.

The Socialist party is a small party in terms of its membership; it has only thirty thousand members, according to today's newspaper. Yet it garners more than ten million votes. That is a strange party. It has been able to operate as the major opposition party because there was a widespread atmosphere of "peace and democracy" among the Japanese voters, which was the main ethos of the postwar Japanese population . . . workers and working people. "Peace and democracy" . . . that was the only criterion by which people passed judgment on the government policy. That "peace and democracy" was the slogan of the LDP too. The political struggle in Japan has been fought around the issue of "peace and democracy." For example, the government pledges support for the prohibition of nuclear weapons, and the Socialist party says the same thing. So basically they follow the same system of values but have completely opposite opinions about concrete facts. For example the LDP says, "This is no introduction of nuclear weapons," while the JSP says, "That is the first step toward introduction of nuclear weapons." This style of antagonism lasted for nearly twenty years.

But that sentiment of the people has been undermined in the process of rapid economic expansion. People still say they are for peace and they are for democracy . . . everybody says so: Liberal–Democrats, Socialists, Social Democrats, Communists, everybody. But the content of that has become so vague, has come to be so far from their daily lives that the "peace and democracy" slogan has ceased to be a *mobilizing* slogan, and instead has become a slogan for the maintenance of the status quo. And so since the JSP depended mainly on that sentiment of the people for votes, young people came to find no interest in the party, nothing attractive in the party, because it is with the status quo that they are dissatisfied. Only people over the age of thirty-five, who experienced the bitterness of the postwar period, remained as solid supporters for the party.

On the other hand, the JSP depended also on the organized votes of Sōhyō, and Sōhyō as a whole acted as the political branch of the Socialist party. . . . But a change has been taking place inside the Sōhyō movement since 1960 or so in the wake of economic expansion. In the newly established industries, such as the chemical combines, electronics factories—there the workers came from rural areas, or workers who had no political experience, and Sōhyō failed to organize them under their own wing. Dōmei organized them better than Sōhyō, but most of these workers in key industries remain politically blank . . . or, that is to say, politically subordinate to bourgeois influence. And their thinking is influenced primarily by the company. And in the major Sōhyō-affiliated unions there are splits from the right wing, and labor control has been greatly strengthened. Sōhyō has failed to combat effectively these offensives, which are connected mostly with technological innovation and so-called "rationalization" of industry. And so Sōhyō strength and the independence of Sōhyō workers from the enterprises has been weakened. It has lost its political grip even on its member workers; political influence of the Sōhyō Socialist leadership has declined.

So the Socialists lost not only vague public support, but also organized support because of the undermining of the position of Sōhyō. That is what is reflected in the receding of the Socialist party influence.

This is something which cannot be reversed as long as the JSP is essentially a party of "peace and democracy" which by its abstract nature has lost its support . . . has lost its attractive force . . . among the workers: on the one hand the workers who are being influenced by the management and on the other hand among the workers who are being radicalized.

The Communist party is emerging basically as a substitute for the Socialist party. The Communist party gained in influence at the expense of the Socialist party . . . it is clear everywhere. That means that in the process of increasing its influence the JCP became social democratic so that it could base itself on the same constituency on which the JSP had been based for many years. The party has become bound and restricted by the atmosphere of its constituency, which is "peace and democracy" long emptied of its postwar contents. It is the decreased reproduction of the Socialist party in the Communist party, in the body of the Communist party. The Socialists had 134 seats and the Communists only four. Now the Communists have fourteen seats, but this is still far smaller than the Socialists' number. And now we can call the CP *almost* a social democratic party of the JSP pattern (if not of a German SPD pattern) with the difference that the JCP has a more solid organization and a far larger number of members, and more discipline.

AMPO. What about Kōmeitō?

MUTŌ. Well, Kōmeitō is organized on an entirely different political principle. As you know its political platform is enigmatically vague and allows various interpretations. Sometimes it is close to the Socialists and sometimes it resembles that of the Liberal–Democrats. The identity of the party is not in its political posture but in its special way of organizing people. As you know it's a religious party, and its creation and development in itself is a reflection of the confusion in the political thinking of the current stage of development. We are now in a transitional period, and many people who supported the LDP are now disappointed, as are many people who supported JSP, and yet they cannot find any political channel through which they can express themselves. Kōmeitō gives a substitute . . . not a real political substitute, but a quasipolitical entity. . . .

In a period of transition such an organization can take a pseudopolitical form, can operate as a political party even without a clear political outlook. And, since the Kōmeitō and JCP share almost the same constituency, there is a great competition between them. That is, the great body of Kōmeitō supporters are not rich people but proletarians, people who are not satisfied with the present society. . . .

Within the Socialist party no consensus exists, but some important union leaders are advancing a specific proposal, and successfully. Well, I will explain that. Sōhyō is in a very serious condition, and Dōmei is extending its influence rapidly. And there is a third sector of workers who are not unionized or, even if unionized, have no workers' consciousness. Those are the three divisions of the Japanese working class. Dōmei is the traditional right-wing union, just like AFL in America. Sōhyō centers on government employees and public corporation employees, including National Railway workers. Dōmei operates mainly on the basis of textile workers, seamen, and electrical industries. Most of the private enterprise workers, which are most important in the present Japanese class structure, are outside of either of the two trade union centers.

In this situation there is a proposal which has been put forward for several years by some of the Sōhyō leaders and some of the independent trade union leaders, and supported by Dōmei and ICFTU, the International Confederation of Free Trade Unions. It is a sly way, a clever way, of swaying the whole Japanese labor movement to the right. Instead of emphasizing affiliation with Dōmei, or with ICFTU, they propose "unification of the labor front." And the first step toward that unification was achieved when IMF-JC, the International Metalworkers Federation, Japan Committee, was established by some of the Sōhyō, Dōmei, and independent union leaders. They claim that it has nothing to do with politics, that it is an organization only for the achievement of the workers' economic demands. And, by the bye, that movement is connected with the labor departments of the important workshops and enterprises.

In the case of the steel workers this is most conspicuous. Soon there will be a merger between Yawata and Fuji iron and steel companies and Nippon Steel Corporation will be established as the second biggest giant company in the world, following U.S. Steel. Well, in the process of the growth of the steel industry, the union, which is affiliated with the Federation of Steel Workers Unions, which is again affiliated with Sōhyō, has been completely, you know, emasculated from within. The company strengthened its attack on militant workers and completely isolated them. And the company managed to exclude even Socialists from the leadership. And now the Yawata leadership is held not even by Socialists, not basically by Social Democrats, but by representatives of the company. Well, the union organization was thus undermined. The Steel Workers Union and the federation itself moved further and further to the right, without leaving Sōhyō. This was all the worse. Within Sōhyō, a powerful right-wing axis came to be formed around the Steel Workers Union and the Postal Workers Union.

Now they are again advocating strengthening the unification movement by calling various semiprivate meetings for "promotion of productivity," participated in not only by union leaders from various union centers, but also by business representatives, and even government, you know. These are called *kondankai,* and there are various *kondankai* held. And now the split of the labor front, allegedly for the unification of the labor front . . . unification on the right-wing principle . . . is being prepared. And sooner or later the right-wing tendency of the JSP will have to choose whether or not to ally with part of this right-wing movement. And already Mr. Takaragi, a powerful advocate of the labor front unification proposed that there must be a Japan Labor party, to replace the Japan Socialist party.

Well, under these circumstances, the JSP will be split into three parts. One is that part, the right wing; the second is the middle-of-the-road part, which is of the traditional Mindō (League for the Democratization of Unions) orientation. (Mindō has been the group which has led Sōhyō since its establishment, and Mindō has now split, but the main current remains with Sōhyō leader Iwai.) And the third group is the new movement of young new left radical workers, represented by the Antiwar Youth Committee.

Well, the present scene is characterized by polarization between right and left, and assuming that the party should have remained a major political expression of the Japanese working class, the Socialists' failure in the elections represents the fact that the party was too conservative to depend on the resurgence of the consciously proletarian wing emerging from this polarization.

. . . [T]here was a survey of the unionist opinion held last year. It shows that among the workers below the age of thirty, almost thirty percent have no faith in parliamentary democracy; instead they declare that they will choose direct action to achieve their demands. And Sōhyō, and its traditional leadership, just can't understand what is taking place among these workers, and have no words for dialogue with them. And so, theoretically there is a way of reorganizing the JSP, to organize on a class basis instead of a "peace and democracy" basis. But that would be impossible for the Socialist party as a whole. If so, there is no rescue for the party as a whole.

AMPO. So the only thing is for it to split in some way or . . . some part of it could be saved, perhaps if it split.

MUTŌ. That's why I say that the elections showed that the period of reorganization of the political map is approaching. On the one hand the Liberal–Democrats won, but its basis is not secure . . . it has no stability. Second, among the opposition parties, the Communist party made a great advance, but there is an absolute limit for the advance of the party because it is stepping into the area evacuated by the Socialist party. And, third, there is a general polarization in the labor movement, and although under the present circumstances the forces of the right wing, the right-wing polarization, is stronger, everywhere there will be reorganization around the pole of left-wing radical ideology. And so there is a very clear task for all the new left groups, and that is to find a real political expression, a radical political expression, for the Japanese working class, and to basically reconstruct the Japanese labor movement on a class basis. There is every possibility to do that.

❀ WHEN IKEDA HAYATO replaced Kishi as prime minister following the 1960 security treaty crisis, the Liberal Democratic party began to operate in a more moderate political style. Ikeda's Income-Doubling Plan was one result of this

shift; it replaced Kishi's more hard-line and repressive methods with economic pacification techniques. R. P. Dore in 1961
discusses the effects of the LDP's extraordinary length in
power and the increasing costs of electoral campaigns in Japan.

R. P. DORE*
Japanese Politics and the Approach to Prosperity

If there is little complacency, one would not infer, from accounts
of last year's massive demonstrations and occasional riots against
the passage of the Japanese–American Security Treaty, that there
was much political apathy either. It is significant, however, that
this was a dispute in part over foreign policy, in part over the use
and abuse of parliamentary procedure; not a dispute over domestic
policy. And it is significant that the widespread support which the
Socialist party gained in its demands for Mr. Kishi's resignation in
June was not reflected in any substantial increase in the Socialist
vote in October. At least it is clear that there is not the kind of
increase in economic dissatisfactions within Japan which is likely
to help left-wing parties.

This is a situation which, as in England and Western Germany,
has the most serious consequences for the Socialist party. But the
growing prosperity is having some effects on the conservatives too.
They have held power in Japan for the last twelve years; since
1955 within the framework of a single party, the Liberal Democratic party. The party holds more than 300 of the 467 seats in the
Lower House of the Diet and can count on the support of two-
thirds of the members of the House of Councilors. With some
justification they have come to look on themselves as the permanent government. There is a growing self-confidence in the party
which expresses itself in two contradictory forms.

In one section of the party it has led to an increased determination to "get tough" with the left. In concrete terms this means, in
part, stronger measures to curb the power of trade unions, revision

* R. P. Dore, "Japanese Politics and the Approach of Prosperity," *The
World Today* XVII:7 (July 1961), pp. 290–294.

of the liberal labor laws enacted during the American occupation, restrictions of the right to strike, and a much greater willingness to use police power and court injunctions to break strikes. In particular it means more positive measures to break the power of the Teachers' Trade Union, the wealthiest and, in its leadership at least, the most extreme of the left-wing unions, which has long been feared by the Liberal–Democrats as a channel for the diffusion of left-wing ideas among the younger generation. It is significant that the present minister of education, the foremost exponent in the present cabinet of the advantages of an aggressive policy, declared on his assumption of office that, unlike his predecessor, he intended under no circumstances to hold talks or negotiations with the Teachers' Union. A second concern of the "get tough" school of the party is to introduce legislation to give the police greater powers to restrict political demonstrations. . . . The Liberal–Democrats should, according to this school of thought, be prepared to make much more ruthless use of their parliamentary majority to force their measures through the Diet, whatever tactics the Socialist opposition adopts.

So far, however, this school of thought has not succeeded in dominating the Liberal–Democratic party since Mr. Ikeda's succession to the leadership, and the premiership, last July. He seems to have taken seriously the threat to Japanese parliamentary institutions implicit in the deep divisions which developed over the security treaty and to have decided to avoid measures or tactics likely to provoke the kind of Socialist opposition which would once again require the use of police and tear gas in the precincts of the Diet. It has not been easy for him to maintain this "low posture" policy, as the Japanese press calls it, and in May and June of this year he has twice been forced by pressure from the party to apply closure procedure and force bills through the Diet in the teeth of strong Socialist opposition, which has once again taken the form of boycotting Diet sessions and the organization of street demonstrations. In neither case, however, are the issues involved big enough for the Socialists to carry their opposition to extreme lengths, and it does seem that as long as Mr. Ikeda remains in control of his party more fundamental provocation will be avoided. His willingness to hold his hand and wait patiently until opposition has spent itself is, of course, the other, more considered, expression of the party's mood of self-confidence. As long as the boom continues and the parliamentary system is maintained, conservative supremacy is unlikely to be threatened.

How long Mr. Ikeda will remain in power depends in part on his own skill in maintaining public support, in part on a complex balance of forces within the party. The Liberal–Democratic party is in effect an alliance of factions, each of which is united around one or two leading politicians who could possibly harbor reasonable ambitions of becoming prime minister. Some eight main factions divide between them almost the whole membership of the party. They have faction offices, and they usually have some semiformal procedures for holding meetings and reaching decisions. They have official titles and they are registered formally as political organizations. As such they report their financial affairs to the ministry of self-government, and it says something for the importance of these factional organizations that during the first six months of 1960, during which time Mr. Ikeda was campaigning actively for the presidency of the party, his factional organization (the Broad Lake Society, "lake" being a pun on the name Ikeda) spent thirty percent more than the total expenditure of the Liberal–Democratic party organization itself.

In an indirect way the new prosperity is having the effect of strengthening these factional divisions, chiefly because elections are becoming increasingly expensive to candidates. At each succeeding election in the last ten years costs have spiraled. The formula frequently repeated in the newspapers as the basis of calculations for Liberal–Democratic candidates at the last election was: "three you're in and two you're out," meaning that an expenditure of 30 million yen (£30,000) would always guarantee election, while the candidate who spent only 20 million yen would be almost sure to lose. There is doubtless some journalistic exaggeration here, but there can be no doubt that many candidates spent sums of that order, and, since the legitimate forms of expenditure in posters, leaflets, meetings, and advertising are carefully regulated in quantity, a good deal of it is spent in illicit ways. One candidate was reported to have loaded a fleet of forty taxis with consignments of underwear which were distributed to the villages in his constituency the day before polling day. Another sent out truckloads of sugar. Most of it, however, goes into the pockets of election-brokers, people who approach the candidate's agent with expressions of their admiration of the candidate, promises of their fervent support, and boasts of their ability to marshal votes. They often make off with a sizable "gift," not because the agent believes in their vote-getting powers but because he fears their ability to scare off voters by malicious rumormongering should they be disappointed.

This inflation of electoral costs is a natural result of increasing prosperity, given the nature of the Japanese electoral system. The two main parties compete in constituencies each of which elects from three to six members. This means that Liberal–Democrat candidates are competing for the electors' single vote, not simply with Socialist candidates (who are usually poor) but also with each other. The result is that at each successive election there is a hardening of the lines of factional division within the party. Each faction vies with the other for the limited number of nominations as official party candidates. Prominent politicians campaigning in constituencies other than their own are enthusiastic about their own protégés, but often lukewarm in their support of members of other factions. A more important form of indebtedness, tying the faction member to his leader, is financial. Liberal–Democratic candidates are reported to have received only £1500 each from central party funds at the last election. The rest they had to raise themselves, but the ability of the ordinary rank-and-file candidate to raise money from business friends is obviously much more limited than that of a prominent faction-leader, and a good many candidates have to rely on support from that quarter—support which must, in duty bound, be requited in loyalty to the faction and its leader.

Drawing his support from a party constituted in this way, a prime minister has to tread very warily. The patronage at his disposal usually makes it possible for him at least to muster the strongest faction for himself, but he has to make sure, in choosing his cabinet, that each faction is given a sufficient share of the offices available to prevent it from becoming a center of disaffection. It also means, paradoxically, that the party organization, as the organization within which the conflicting claims and policies of the various factions are resolved, comes to rival the cabinet as an organ for the formulation of policy, particularly in matters involving sectional interests with which various factions might be differently involved. During a recent doctors' strike against the national health service it was the party secretariat, rather than the Minister of Health, which played the main role in negotiating a settlement.

The increasing cost of elections has other consequences than the hardening of factional divisions. The publicity given to the less savory type of electoral practice induces a general mood of cynicism about the electoral process in particular and the parliamentary system in general. (The total number charged with offenses against the election laws at the time of the last elections was 31,000, of whom over 27,000 were accused of bribery or related offenses.) Moreover, there is a very real danger of increased corruption in government, inasmuch as the businessmen who provide their political friends with these large sums of money are likely to expect in return something more concrete than the mere maintenance of a climate favorable to business.

❀ TANAKA KAKUEI became prime minister in 1972, ending the nearly eight-year term of Satō Eisaku. In contrast to the usual LDP prime ministers, Tanaka had relatively few connections to the zaibatsu and he was not a graduate of prestigious Tokyo University. His accession to power was also marked by acrimonious debates within the LDP on foreign policy. Satō had been viewed as almost obsequiously pro-American, and Tanaka made good use of Satō's reverses in China policy and economic policy (Nixon did not inform his close ally Satō of his trip to the People's Republic, and the revaluation of the yen forced on Japan by the United States contributed to Satō's demise). The succession battle won by Tanaka is described below by Elizabeth Pond, and Mutō Ichiyo comments on the changes, or lack of them, produced by Tanaka's administration.

ELIZABETH POND*
Succession: A Japanese Game of
Intricate Political Subtleties

Thursday, December 2, 1971

What does a succession struggle look like in a consensus society
where there is no consensus?

The description is a bit stark. But there is an unusual confluence
of uncertainty in Japan in 1971.

The old—some call it abnormally close—relationship with the
United States is over. It was shattered by President Nixon's China
demarche "over the head" of Japan, by the new American tough-
ness on economics, and by American arm-twisting over textiles. . . .

Almost as an afterthought, Okinawa, with its development
problems and its implicit strategic questions for Japanese security
beyond the home archipelago, is coming back to Japan after a
quarter-century of American occupation. . . .

As it happens, under the catalyst of the Nixon shocks, a new
economic consensus has already begun to jell with surprising swift-
ness. There will be some grumbling, but the emphasis is moving
inexorably away from a blinkered expansion of production and
exports to social investment and social balance.

The political word, however, has yet to find its consensus, either
in policy or in leadership. Policy is a matter for the future, to be
hammered out by the traditional triumvirate of business, the
bureaucracy, and the politicians, once a new prime minister is
invested. Leadership is a matter for the urgent present, to be decided by the politicians, subject to the nods or frowns of business.

There are certain parameters to Mr. Satō's succession, of
course. Most fundamentally, the field is limited to the Tory establishment, which here as perhaps nowhere else in the world still
enjoys unchallenged political and social authority.

The Liberal Democratic party, which has ruled Japan for two

* Elizabeth Pond, "Succession: A Japanese Game of Intricate Political
Subtleties," *Christian Science Monitor*, December 2, 1971.

decades, has been losing votes steadily, until its strength now totals less than fifty percent of the electorate. And with the flux of population away from the conservative countryside into the politically less predictable cities, the LDP has now exhausted the possibilities of favorable manipulation of multiple-Dietman districts.

Yet the opposition parties have proved unable to seize any benefit from the LDP decline and the nonvoting apathy of a third of the electorate. Their attempts at unification have so far proved abortive. And, curiously, they have grown more fossilized than the LDP, if age of members is any criterion. The bright young men just out of the university may rail against what they consider an archaic LDP—but they still join it. They know where power lies.

Within the LDP the succession struggle comes down to a contest of personalities rather than policies. There are some differences in policy between the contestants, and some issues—such as China— play a prominent role as weapons in skirmishes. But policies are really minor. The important thing is the leader—his faction, his power, his contacts, his money, his ties of obligation.

In the past the candidates for the party presidency—and thus for the prime ministership—have been cut out of the same Tory mold: without charisma, skilled in backroom maneuvers, adept at filling the party coffers, clever and cool enough to face down the barrage of questions by the opposition in the Diet without ever divulging any policies. This year, however, the scene is different. Two candidates fit the tradition; three do not.

The typical candidates are Foreign Minister Takeo Fukuda and Dietman Masayoshi Ōhira. The atypical ones are International Trade and Industry Minister Kakuei Tanaka, Dietman Takeo Miki, and chairman of the LDP executive council Yasuhiro Nakasone.

Until the Nixon shocks Mr. Fukuda was considered a shoo-in. He and Mr. Tanaka were Mr. Satō's mainstays; and, while Mr. Satō avoided naming any preference between them, he was universally regarded as favoring the sixty-six-year-old Mr. Fukuda.

Certainly Mr. Fukuda had (and has) impeccable credentials for Japanese politics. He graduated from the law faculty of Tokyo University, joined the prestigious Ministry of Finance, rose rapidly in the bureaucracy, turned politician, got elected to the House of Representatives eight times, took over the key party post of secretary-general, and finally returned to the Finance Ministry as its chief. . . .

Masayoshi Ōhira doesn't have quite as traditional a record as Mr. Fukuda, for he graduated not from Tokyo University but from the unrelated Tokyo University of Commerce (now called Hitotsubashi University). He has been in the center of mainstream LDP politics for two decades, however, as a close associate of the late Prime Minister Hayato Ikeda.

Mr. Ōhira began his political career as secretary to the then Finance Minister Ikeda, then became Chief Cabinet Secretary and later Foreign Minister under Prime Minister Ikeda.

He is credited with the low-posture course that got the government safely through the turbulent 1960 demonstrations against renewal of the U.S. security treaty and also through the controversial normalization of relations with South Korea.

One of the sixty-one-year-old Ōhira's prime assets is his lack of enemies. He acceded to leadership of his sixty-two-man faction only last April, so he doesn't have a long history of muscling there. He was never secretary-general of the party and thus never had to shake down reluctant companies for funds on a grand scale. He is regarded as cautious and dependable, if secretive to a degree unusual even for Japan. . . .

A SELF-MADE LEADER

Of the five major candidates, Mr. Tanaka, who is only fifty-three, is the most unusual.

His outspokenness is just the opposite of Mr. Ōhira's extreme reticence. Alone among leading LDP politicians he is a self-made man, without benefit of any formal education beyond a technical high school. As a youth he started his own construction company and made enough money to launch himself in politics. In this new game he quickly showed an instinctive flair that matched or even surpassed his proven administrative ability.

Before long he rose to become the young head of that Tokyo University preserve, the Finance Ministry. In that post in the early sixties he presided over the takeoff years of Japan's economic miracle. In the latter sixties he became LDP secretary-general and managed the successful Okinawa-reversion election of 1969. He also collected and distributed, it was said, even more money than his predecessor, Mr. Fukuda.

Mr. Tanaka's ties with the business community are said to be good but specialized. Mr. Fukuda has more support—and access to funds—from the traditional business community, whereas Mr. Tanaka draws support and funds from the newer, more innovative, industries. This means that Mr. Fukuda can perhaps attract more money over the long haul, while Mr. Tanaka can pull in more contributions for specific, directed campaigns. As a political financier, Mr. Tanaka has a reputation for meticulous, unstinting payment of debts. . . .

The fourth candidate, Takeo Miki, in the protocol-conscious LDP, is a bull in a China shop. His unorthodoxy stems less from his background (graduation from an American college followed by graduation from Meiji University) than from his bucking of the party leadership past the accepted point.

For the last decade he has criticized the government's China policy for its pro-Taipei coloration. In '68 and '70 he challenged the incumbent Eisaku Satō for the LDP presidency and actually gained votes in the later election, though he did not unseat Mr. Satō.

With no love lost between them, Mr. Satō last July reduced the cabinet share of the Miki faction (which is now sixty strong) from two to one. With this and with the subsequent American-Chinese détente, Mr. Miki has increased his public criticism of Mr. Satō. . . .

Yet in the end Mr. Miki is still a follower of LDP club rules. He is a former cabinet member (Foreign Minister) himself. And, whatever his flirtation with the opposition parties, he has so far refrained from cooperating with them in a move to oust Mr. Satō. He is a party man with higher party aspirations, and he knows that he would be cut off from all other LDP factions if he did go outside the party to topple Mr. Satō. . . .

The last candidate, Yasuhiro Nakasone, at fifty-three, is the same generation as Mr. Tanaka. He is not considered a serious contender in the coming party election, but is regarded as sure to be a major candidate for leadership in the next decade.

A graduate of the law faculty of Tokyo University, Mr. Nakasone entered politics early and was first elected to the Lower House at the age of twenty-nine. He started as a lone wolf, but before long joined Mr. Satō's cabinet as Director General of the Defense Agency.

In that capacity he devised plans for the current fourth defense buildup and also at one point proposed revision of Japan's constitution, which bars Japanese military forces. Youthful looking, he is handsome, and popular among women voters, and in the early sixties he cut a deliberately Kennedy-like figure.

MUTŌ ICHIYO*
Nothing to Offer:
Kakuei Tanaka Steps into Power

In an extremely corrupt intraparty election highlighted by a fierce factional feud, Kakuei Tanaka, Minister of International Trade and Industry of the Satō cabinet, on July 5 replaced Eisaku Satō as president of the ruling Liberal Democratic party, and thus became prime minister of Japan on July 6. The change of prime minister was an imperative for the ruling class, centering on business magnates, because Satō has become useless after completing their strategic design of Okinawa "reversion." They feared that, if Satō should continue, his extreme unpopularity might undermine the position of the Liberal Democratic party as business's irreplaceable ruling system. Moreover, they judged a "new face" could better solve the unprecedentedly knotty and difficult problems they face: the change in the Asian situation, the precarious economic situation and protracted recession in Japan, the crumbling international monetary system, economic contradictions with the United States, and the social contradictions stemming from the Japanese "economic growth." . . .

In a way, Tanaka may be likened to Hayato Ikeda who stepped into power after the notorious Kishi cabinet was overthrown in a popular upsurge against the Japan–United States Security Treaty (Ampo) in 1960 in that both had to emphasize "the need for people's support" as their gesture of offsetting their predecessor's wrongs. Tanaka on July 5 said: "I will stay always with the

* Mutō Ichiyo, "Nothing to Offer: Kakuei Tanaka Steps into Power," *AMPO* 3–4 (May–July 1972), pp. 3–4.

people." The difference is that Ikeda in 1960 had his "income-doubling program" to woo the people while Tanaka in 1972 has nothing to offer save that he is fifty-four years old (a young prime minister!) and that he is "from among the common people" (he graduated only from primary school). The illusion of grandiose prosperity promising people material felicity was still valid in 1960, but now Tanaka has no such magic wand.

Tanaka, in his first press conference as president of the Liberal Democrats, first of all paid homage to his predecessor Satō, pointing to Satō's "three great deeds"—the conclusion of the Japan–South Korea Treaty, the railroading through the Diet of the special law of repression on students' revolt, and the Okinawa reversion treaty. Tanaka is very proud of these three accomplishments—the dirty tricks that prepared the way for Japanese imperialism. Note that Tanaka was the major person who, under Satō's guidance, plotted and staged these political intrigues.

What Tanaka wants to impress as his original political program is his plan to "overhaul the chain of the Japanese islands," a crazy plan to plant factories all over the country, especially in sparsely populated districts. While this is the 1972 version of Ikeda's "high-tempo economic growth," the announcement of the Tanaka plan came just when "prosperity" and "GNP" were sufficiently exposed for what they were worth. People know by now that these mean pollution of innumerable strange kinds (photochemical smog, cadmium, oil, etc.), demolition of nature, unquenchable inflation, annually increasing public utility charges, attacks on union organization, police state, to say nothing of its external version—imperialist expansion to foreign lands. Long a Minister of International Trade and Industry (a government agency completely in the service of big business in Japan, Inc.), Tanaka is determined to "solve" these problems in the interest of monopolies. He had this to say in his first press conference as president of the Liberal–Democratic party: "I will bring factories into rural areas, and then farmers can have jobs there. . . . You people are egoistic, you complain when we want to do anything positive. Look at the airport trouble [meaning the Sanrizuka struggle]." One thing he does not know is that what once (twelve years ago) projected a positive image now forecasts for the people only another vast disaster.

On top of it all, Tanaka's position in the ruling party is miserably precarious. He won the presidential election by means of

money and an alliance of three groups led by himself, Masayoshi
Ōhira (new foreign minister), and Takeo Miki (a state minister),
defeating his rival Takeo Fukuda and his faction. The *Sankei
Shimbun,* a newspaper often regarded as an organ of the Liberal
Democratic party, reported that, before the presidential election,
votes were purchased by the four presidential candidates at
30,000,000 yen each. Tanaka won over his rival Fukuda by a vote
of 282 to 190, but Fukuda and his followers, notorious supporters
of Taiwan and South Korea, are hanging tough against Tanaka,
declaring they control forty percent of the party members. Immediately after Tanaka announced the list of his candidate members to the press, the Fukuda faction withdrew its two members
from the Tanaka cabinet, simply to humiliate the new prime
minister!

Thus, the objective situation characterized by the semicrisis of
the Japanese ruling class ("semi" because it has so far not been
forced on them by the struggle of the Japanese people) deprives
Tanaka of any option other than following the line laid down by
Satō . . . and Nixon, probably with a bit more opportunism. He
has announced that he will fly to Washington to confer with
President Nixon before he begins any moves to restore diplomatic
relations with China. While "young, agile, and quick to act" is the
public image he wants to create of himself, he has too many bosses
to be so. His original plan of crazy "overhaul" is indeed disastrous
to the people, but the likely outcome of the synthesis of all forces
at work would be no less ominous for the people—and disappointing to the ruling class. All in all, the Tanaka cabinet will have to
out-Satō Satō in its repressive nature. Look at his cabinet members—Nakasone as Minister of International Trade and Industry
(the man known for advocacy of Japan's own nuclear arms) and
Shūzō Inaba as Minister of Education (notorious right-winger and
founder of the Self-Defense Forces, who after becoming minister
declared his intention to deprive universities of their autonomy,
talking scornfully about professors).

๛ SOON AFTER BECOMING prime minister, Tanaka tried to
parley political advantages from his new foreign policy initiatives into electoral results. In fall 1972 he changed Japan's

policy toward China, previously support of the Chiang Kai-
shek regime on Taiwan and hostility to the People's Republic,
to one of accommodation with mainland China. Hoping to
make the most of this shift and encouraged by public opinion
polls, he subsequently traveled to Peking and then called an
immediate election for December 1972. The outcome, discussed here by Albert Axelbank, was a startling reverse for
the LDP and gains for the Socialists and Communists. Most
surprising, perhaps, was the serious defeat suffered by the
right Democratic Socialists and the Kōmeitō, the Clean Government party. Although Tanaka had been expected to do
much better, the election results continued the trend of erosion of LDP support evident since the late 1950s.

ALBERT AXELBANK*
Leftward Turn in Japan

The quick, flashy smiles of Japan's plutocrats and ultraconservative leaders have vanished. Prime Minister Kakuei Tanaka is no
longer the beaming "computerized bulldozer," the sobriquet
coined by the mass media. His Liberal Democratic party and its
chief pillar—big business—under whose rule Japan has become an
economic superpower, albeit at the expense of the environment
and the people's livelihood, admit they are deeply worried about
the recent advance by the left-wing parties.

These parties made notable gains in the general elections of
December 10. Especially spectacular was the Communist showing,
their best in the postwar period. The Japan Communist party
(JCP) increased its seats in the 491-seat Lower House from
fourteen to thirty-eight. Its popular vote rose to 5,500,000 from
3,200,000 in the previous election in 1969. The proportion of the
popular vote for the party also jumped, from 6.8 percent to 10.5
percent.

* Albert Axelbank, "Leftward Turn in Japan," *The Progressive*, February 1973, pp. 10–11.

The Socialist party also gained, rising from eighty-seven to 118 seats, while two middle of the road opposition parties suffered disastrously, allowing the Communist party to leapfrog over them to become the number two opposition party. Of course, the ruling Liberal Democrats are in no immediate danger of being toppled. They still hold a commanding lead in the Lower House, a majority of 284 seats.

What implants fear in the hearts of the conservatives is that the Communists' publicized dream—leading a coalition regime in Japan before 1980—is now a step nearer attainment. If this event should occur, the main planks of the conservatives would be instantly torn up: the security pact with Washington would be scrapped, the Self-Defense Forces disbanded, the emphasis on GNP growth changed to emphasis on a welfare state.

Probably the Communist successes at the polls give them a right to be confident. Veteran JCP leader Sanzō Nosaka, who fled to China in World War II and engaged in propaganda work against the Japanese armies, says the election returns have strengthened the possibility of a "unified front" and "democratic alliance government" to be achieved within the 1970s. By "democratic alliance government" is meant a coalition of the left-wing parties holding a majority in the Diet (Parliament), which has been the chief quest of the JCP.

There is considerable resentment by many citizens against the long-time rule of Japan by the conservatives, almost unbroken for a quarter of a century. One result of the "industry first" policy of the conservative regimes is that Japan now has probably the world's worst pollution and population problems.

Tanaka's "plan to remodel the Japanese islands," which was much ballyhooed as a panacea for all of Japan's domestic ills, has actually cost the prime minister some voter support because the plan has accelerated land speculation and inflationary trends throughout the nation. Critics have also claimed the plan would merely disperse pollution all over Japan. As a result, many citizens who are not Marxists at all voted for the Communists as a protest against ruling party policies.

In response to left-wing gains, Tanaka on December 22 formed his new cabinet, loading it with men well experienced in confrontation with the left. With but a few exceptions, its members are conservative, nationalistic, uncompromising, anticommunist. To achieve "unity" in his own party, Tanaka shook hands with his rivals and put a few of them in his cabinet, some of them from the extreme right wing of the party. In a real sense the new Tanaka cabinet is a "crisis cabinet."

Confrontation is likely to come soon on the explosive issue of militarism. The left wing vigorously opposes buildup of the Self-Defense Forces (SDF). They challenge the necessity of the Fourth Defense Buildup Plan (1972–1976)—which will cost more than $15 billion—in the face of decreasing tensions in Asia. Yet, in the new cabinet, Tanaka has at least four men who favor stepped-up rearmament. Some of them favor creation of a national militia to supplement the SDF. Two ministers do not believe in the reliability of America's "nuclear umbrella," a disbelief that lends itself to approving future possession of Japan's own nuclear arsenal. At least two ministers favor changing the present "peace" constitution, although many citizens regard it as a bulwark against full-scale militaristic revival.

This issue—militarism—will probably accelerate as the expected confrontation between the Tanaka administration and the left wing expands. Indeed, only a few days before 1973, the defense agency, against the wishes of Tachikawa residents, dispatched airborne units to Tachikawa Air Base, in Western Tokyo, to take up permanent positions there. Meanwhile, on December 26 the defense agency director-general—a cabinet official—hinted that SDF units transferred to Tachikawa might be used to "maintain public peace and order" if police were unable to cope with the job.

The restlessness of Japanese citizens under the present regime seems to suggest that they have learned before their leaders the lessons that a richer gross national product can mean a poorer quality of life for the people, and stepped-up rearmament less real security for the nation.

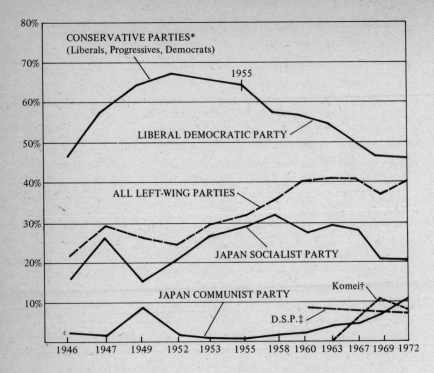

Key:
*In 1955 the Liberals, Progressives, and Democrats were united as the Liberal Democratic party.
†Komei party (Clean Government party) was formed initially as part of the religious Sokagakkai (Value Creation Society).
‡The Democratic Socialist party formed as a splinter from the Japan Socialist party; after 1960 it is listed separately; until 1958 it is included in the JSP vote.

EDUCATION

✿ Along with the abolition of the wartime Thought Police and most of the militaristic societies, the reform of education was a notable success of the American occupation. However, the return of sovereignty in 1952 soon saw attempts to reverse many of the educational reforms. Areas in which this first occurred were the reassertion of appointment of boards of education by the government and the certification of school textbooks. The main thrust of the occupation in education had been to decentralize and thus democratize the Japanese school system previously under direct control of the ministry of education. Gradual erosion of educational reforms, whose course is sketched here by R. P. Dore and Marius Jansen, can thus be seen as recentralization by the conservative government toward prewar forms. Opposition to such attempts has been led by one of the largest unions, the combative Japan Teachers' Union (Nikkyōsō), which is on the political left. To date, however, Nikkyōsō efforts have slowed down the "reverse course" in education but not stopped it.

R. P. DORE*
Reforms in Postwar Education

The year 1945 marked the end of the ethics course and of attempts to achieve standard production of loyal and obedient patriots in

* R. P. Dore, "Education: Japan," in *Political Modernization in Japan and Turkey*, eds. Robert E. Ward and Dankwart A. Rustow (Princeton: Princeton University Press, 1964), pp. 195–199.

the elementary schools. But after half a century in which these had been central concerns, it was impossible that primary education should lose its political significance. The schools have continued to be a major source of political conflict to the present day.

The changes introduced under the occupation regime were radical. Textbook production was turned over to free enterprise with only loose certification by a central authority. Locally elected education committees assumed powers over staff, curriculum, and textbook choice which had formerly been concentrated in the ministry. Ethics disappeared from the curriculum along with history and geography, and the social studies course which took their place was supposed to teach an objective and critical knowledge of the nature and history of Japanese institutions. History was written to make students mindful not of the glorious reigns of former emperors but of class divisions, of economic exploitation, and of struggles for freedom and equality in the face of oppression and despotism. The teachers became organized in a powerful trade union dominated by radical left-wing leaders, and were able in many districts to secure sympathetic majorities on local education committees.

The decade since the ending of the occupation has seen steady pressure by the conservative parties controlling the government to "correct the excesses" of these reforms, and legislation seeking that end has been responsible for some of the tensest political crises of the period. Particular sources of controversy have been the bills to prevent teachers from joining political parties and to prohibit their union from disseminating political literature, the bill to replace elected by nominated education committees, an abortive bill to restore central control over textbooks, the institution of a new course of moral instruction, and the introduction of a merit-rating system increasing the teachers' liability to discipline on political as well as on other grounds. Perhaps no other educational system in the world is so continuously and so earnestly fought over. In part the struggles have been struggles for power between the government and a union fighting to retain its organizational cohesion and the privileges of its members. It is much more, however, than a mere dependence on that union's funds and organization which has prompted the Socialist party to resist these measures with every constitutional and unconstitutional means at its disposal. Socialists have seen in these measures a conscious attempt by the conservatives to restore thought-control of the prewar sort, and university intellectuals even of moderate political views have shared their fears—as witness the public protest by a group of university presidents against the abolition of education committee elections in 1956. . . .

The "reverse-course" has proceeded slowly, if steadily, perhaps most effectively by means which have not required legislation and so have not attracted much attention. The gradual tightening of central ministry control by fiscal and other measures has now given the advisory circulars of that ministry the authority of directives, and the system of textbook certification has been slowly tightened. Thanks to the latter expedient, the more single-minded interpretations of Japanese history in the light of class warfare have now been expunged from the textbooks, but the Japanese child still gets a version of his country's past much less partisan and much closer to the canons of academic historians than his counterpart in most industrial countries. The new morals course reminds children of the duties as well as the rights of democratic citizens, but in terms which would have counted as pernicious and subversively individualistic before the war. If it is no longer as certain now as it was ten years ago that an overwhelming proportion of the rising generation will cast their first votes for the Socialist party, it is by no means certain, either, that they would fall easy victims to mass totalitarian appeals of any complexion. The content of education apart, there seems to have been a considerable change in the atmosphere of postwar schools. There is greater freedom of classroom discussion and less disposition on the part of teachers to maintain an aloof dignity. . . .

. . . Quite apart from the enervating effects of intensified competition for higher education and a career, the political neutralization of postwar education may well have made the new generation as a whole less politically conscious than its parents. The young man who left an upper elementary school in 1935 may not have thought himself entitled to an opinion about what Japan's foreign policy should be, but at least he thought he ought to read the newspapers with care and concern. The modern young man may well be more concerned to get a transistor television set. It is as difficult to find conclusive evidence for trends towards "apathy," "privatization," "mass-media hypnosis," or "consumption orientation" in Japanese as in Western societies, and the evidence of polling statistics is ambiguous. The point is that in these respects Japan now differs little from Western societies.

One final point deserves mention. Since the war, women have been given the vote and all higher education has become coeducational in principle, even though the majority of female university students still in fact attend segregated women's colleges. The proportion of women voters has climbed steadily with each postwar election—the female voting ratio being fifteen percent lower than the male in 1946, only seven percent lower in 1958—and there is evidence to suggest that the female vote is not simply part of a family vote. The fact that civics and morals courses at all levels are now taught in a coeducational context should further promote the integration of women into the active political community. In a country where there has been a sharp divergence between the values and personalities of men and women, politics are likely to change as they become less exclusively an all-male preserve.

MARIUS B. JANSEN*
Education, Values, and Politics in Japan

Children's textbooks in the social sciences tend to reflect accurately the values of a society. Since their lessons and morals are set forth in direct and simple language, they indicate in bold outline the things which the society, or part of it, thinks it important for the young to absorb. In Japan today such textbooks show a striking contrast to those used before the surrender of 1945, and they deserve attention as evidence of the rapid change of values that has taken place in some parts of Japanese society.

Recently the new textbooks have come under sharp attack. The debate over educational policy is one of the most important and least publicized struggles in contemporary Japan, and the controversy furnishes an excellent opportunity for judging the nature of change in Japanese society. That change has been sectional and uneven, differing in quality between those who teach and those

* Marius B. Jansen, "Education, Values, and Politics in Japan," *Foreign Affairs* XXXV:4 (July 1957), pp. 666–672.

who govern. There is a particular contrast between the way in which segments of the intelligentsia interpret the new moral basis of Japanese education and the way in which the political leaders, the liberals and moderates of prewar years, cling to the old ethic of their younger days.

The struggle focuses sharply on who is going to write the textbooks. Since Japanese society has been open and free in recent years, the textbooks in use today reflect the values and concerns of the intellectuals, or at least of the articulate and representative minority which gives the broader group its tone. To be sure, the intellectuals are not a united or clearly definable group, and neither are the so-called "conservatives." Yet there is a large area of agreement within each group. Each is convinced the other is determined to destroy its influence by alienating the minds and affections of Japan's 20 million lower-school pupils.

The education controversy also throws light on reforms effected during the American occupation. One can see where these fell short, where form was confused with substance, and one can also see where they satisfied long-standing needs. One is also struck by the way institutions can serve purposes other than those for which they were designed. Certification of textbooks, for instance, installed by occupation planners to eliminate nationalistic and militarist indoctrination, has been continued by Ministry of Education officials who now utilize the system to ward off excessive antimilitarist and antinationalist teachings. The government leaders have discovered the possibility of putting old wine into new bottles.

Any doubt that the education system is in the forefront of the political struggle in Japan today should have been removed by the behavior of the House of Councilors in late May of 1956. The Hatoyama cabinet had sponsored legislation making the boards of education appointive instead of elective. The Socialist minority, responsive to the appeals of the powerful Teachers' Union, fought to prevent final action by all the methods known to other parliamentary bodies and by some of its own devising. In answer, the government mobilized 500 policemen in and around the chamber. The outnumbered Socialists were then unable to prevent action on the bill, which passed June 1 amid scenes of wild disorder.

This marked the first substantial change in the organizational pattern which had been instituted during the American occupation. Many Japanese liberals concluded that local politicians would now be able to warp the education system back to some of its prewar themes. Others, however, pointed out that the elective boards of education had not been outstanding successes and that the same liberals had complained earlier of their domination by local political bosses. Perhaps all that can be said is that there is no longer the possibility that the boards can become effective elective bodies. . . .

A bill affecting the manner of selecting textbooks in lower schools which failed to pass the 1956 Diet was in many ways much more important than the changes which affected the boards of education. It would have altered the machinery of textbook certification to allow for greater bureaucratic control. This is a matter which could immediately affect the content of education, and it is the more significant in view of the history of Japanese textbooks.

Before the end of World War II, schools in all parts of Japan used uniform textbooks prepared by the Ministry of Education. The system of national textbooks was instituted in 1903. Loyalty and duty, taught in ethics (*shūshin*) textbooks and reinforced by lessons in history, geography, and language, were the core of the value structure. The ideology had been given its definitive statement in the Imperial Rescript on Education of 1890, which cites loyalty and filial piety as "the glory of the fundamental character of our empire, and . . . the source of our education." The principal revisions in the national textbooks came in 1910, after the annexation of Korea; in 1918, after World War I; in 1933, after Manchuria; and in 1941, on the eve of Pearl Harbor. Except for the 1918 version, each revision tended to strengthen the nationalist content of the textbooks. Information about the outside world, names of famous foreign figures, and descriptions of other social systems diminished, to be replaced by increasing emphasis on the benefits of Japan's family state. As symbols of that state, the Imperial Rescript and the Imperial portrait were the center of reverence at school ceremonies. The textbooks provided most of the content of Japanese education. Teachers expounded them, and for the pupils they represented ultimate truth. . . .

Occupation reformers set to work to change this system of sacrosanct textbooks. They had the advice of leading American educators as well as the enthusiastic cooperation of Japanese educators—for the intellectuals, unlike the landlords, militarists, zaibatsu, and politicians, were eager to help in reforming themselves. Under the new Fundamental Law of Education of 1947 it became the duty of the education system "to contribute to the peace of the world and the welfare of humanity by building a democratic and cultural state." Education was to strive for "the full development of personality," and peace, democracy, and international cooperation were to become the themes for the new system.

Basic revisions of the curriculum followed. The old training in ethics was ruled out, and in the lower schools history and geography disappeared as separate subjects. Henceforth, the new laws stated, efforts were to be made "to develop a proper understanding of the actual conditions and traditions both of children's native communities and of the country, and further to cultivate the spirit of international cooperation." Out of this came new courses in social studies, with textbooks bearing titles like *Akarui Shakai* ("The Enlightened Society") and *Shakai no Kōzō* ("The Structure of Society"). In content and approach these differed sharply from the previous eulogies of samurai and emperors.

Japan's postwar textbooks have been produced privately. The system works as follows: The Education Ministry provides course-of-study outlines for each age level and indicates the material that should be covered. Each November and December publishers present drafts to the ministry, which then refers them to five readers selected from a list of qualified educators. These men judge the work against the curriculum requirements and determine whether or not it is neutral in politics and religion and in harmony with the Fundamental Law of Education. In other words, the drafts have to support internationalism, peace, and democracy. The readers do not know whose manuscript they read, and their verdicts are reported anonymously. The next step involves a review by a committee of sixteen, also appointed by the ministry, which reconsiders the manuscript in case of sharp disagreements among the original readers. Until recently this committee verdict, identified as "Opinion F," was a formality.

If the manuscript is approved, the publisher can list his book. He now sends sample copies to one thousand textbook exhibits which are held throughout Japan in late June. Representatives of schools and school boards come to these exhibits, make their selections, and file their orders. The publishers then print the required number of copies. As before the war, parents buy the text for their children. The textbooks are no longer uniform and standard, and since they change constantly and are poorly bound and disintegrate rapidly they have become a major form of private enterprise. Many jobs are involved; in 1955, ninety-two textbook publishers printed over 230 million textbooks. A sixth-grade teacher had a choice of 173 books. . . .

But the real struggle is over content. In August 1955 the Democratic party issued a pamphlet entitled *"Ureubeki Kyōkasho no Mondai"* ("The Problem of the Dreadful Textbooks"). This was prepared by a party commission which drew on records of a House of Representatives committee as well as on many popular attacks on textbooks. It tried to link the Teachers' Union with the Japanese Communist party and charged that union leaders were writing misleading and slanted texts which were poisoning the minds of the young as well as emptying the pockets of their parents. The attack was badly overdone. Education Ministry officials denied ever having seen the pamphlet, and the press was quick with charges of McCarthyism. But the pamphlet had some results. It probably convinced some of its readers, since it was issued all over the country through party offices. It frightened the publishers, who the following year quietly withdrew most of the textbooks attacked. And it convinced the intellectuals, if they needed convincing, of the depravity of the Liberal–Democratic leaders.

Those leaders next prepared the bill changing the system of certification which failed to pass the 1956 Diet. Since then, administrative measures have been taken to achieve some of the same results. Beginning with junior high school, social science textbooks are again to be divided into sections on history, geography, and current problems. The committee of sixteen readers will now be drawn from a panel of eighty, so that specialists can judge each subject. New policies toward "controversial" textbooks have gone into effect, and "Opinion F" now plays a more active role.

A particularly striking case was the rejection of a junior high school text called *Nihon no Shakai* ("Japanese Society") which had been a nationwide best-seller with a half-million sales. "Opinion F" rejected a revision of the book on grounds that it was overly partial to the new constitution, unbalanced in its treatment

of basic human rights, and portrayed World War II in excessively
dark colors.

. . . It is clear that the ministry, whether or not it gets its way
with proposed legislative changes, has enough power to keep textbooks from going too far to the left. It can revise curricula and
force a review of current texts at any time. It is equally clear that
many of the textbook writers are deeply concerned by what they
see as a trend back toward old-style patriotism. Symbolic of their
position is the refusal of elementary-school teachers in several
cities to lead their pupils in singing the national anthem, on
grounds that its reverence for the Imperial family is out of harmony with the new democracy. Meanwhile, there is the ironic sight
of the elderly conservatives who sit as judges of what the young
shall read, to see that it is in harmony with laws which they did not
make, do not like, and seek to change.

♢ THE ISSUE OF school textbook certification, smoldering
since the mid-1950s, became highly controversial in recent
years. In 1965 Ienaga Saburō, a well-known Tokyo University
Professor of Education, after long strugggles with the Ministry
of Education to get a textbook officially accepted, sued the
government on grounds of censorship. Below, R. P. Dore explains the complicated development of the Ienaga case, and
Ienaga himself outlines the importance of the textbook lawsuit, drawing from his personal experience before World
War II. The result of the suit, a startling defeat for the ministry and a vindication of Professor Ienaga, is given by Dore in
an excerpt from the judge's opinion. It is still unclear, however, if this case marks a halt to the recentralization of education by the Japanese government or whether the Ienaga suit
will prove only a temporary setback to that policy.

R. P. DORE*
Textbook Censorship in Japan: The Ienaga Case

The Tokyo district court recently handed down a judgment which is generally considered to have considerable importance for the future of primary and secondary education in Japan. It concerned the operation of the system whereby the Ministry of Education (*Mombushō*) examines all textbooks used in primary and secondary schools and permits only those which are approved to be used in schools as textbooks. . . .

In 1963, following a further *Mombushō* directive, local authorities established "combined textbook areas." That is to say, the education committees of neighboring communities established joint committees (usually including teachers) to choose the same textbooks for common use throughout the area. Tokyo has forty-seven such areas, but in the extreme case of Aomori prefecture, which has only one, a single committee for each subject chooses the textbook which shall be used throughout the prefecture. In other prefectures where there are several textbook areas there is also a certain measure of centralization effected by the power of the prefectural education committee (which frequently contains former *Mombushō* officials) to offer advice and guidance to local committees. The *Yomiuri* of July 14, 1970, offers, as an example of such centralization of control at the prefectural level, the case of a Japanese-language textbook, the particular feature of which was that it included many examples of schoolchildren's own compositions and placed great emphasis on the stimulation of creativity. Immediately before the introduction of the "textbook area" system it accounted for nearly one-third of the textbooks sold for Japanese-language courses in Gifu prefecture. Immediately afterwards it sold none at all and total sales fell from 1,200,000 to 700,000. . . .

An *Asahi* article on July 14 reports publishers' complaints concerning the operation of the system. If a textbook is considered faulty but not beyond redemption, they will be told what points

* R. P. Dore, "Textbook Censorship in Japan: The Ienaga Case," *Pacific Affairs* XLIII:4 (Winter 1970–1971), pp. 548–555.

must be changed if the book is to be approved, and secondly what it is "advisable" to change. And if they do not take the advice, they fear for the fate of later textbooks which they may present for inspection. If the textbook is considered beyond redemption, they will be given examples of what is wrong with it, but no overall assessment. In either case the information and advice is orally given, and no obligation rests on the committee to explain its reasons for rejecting a textbook. The article goes on to describe how publishers, as a result, have come to exercise a tight self-censorship—or rather a censorship over their authors. It adds, however, that the self-censorship works also in the opposite ideological direction. A new factor in the situation since 1965 is the regular publication by the Japan Teachers' Union (JTU) of a critique of current textbooks. Publishers are also concerned not to be condemned by the JTU as purveying a reactionary militaristic textbook, and this is why such nineteenth-century military figures as General Nogi and Admiral Tōgō do not appear in modern history books.

The tightening of the approval system and the moves toward centralization of the textbook choice procedure are generally seen as part of a general trend toward centralization of control over the content of education. This trend toward centralization is variously interpreted: (a) as simply a nostalgic throwback toward the prewar period (when many senior administrators began their official careers and when Japan had one of the most highly centralized educational systems in the world); (b) as simply part of the power struggle between the Ministry of Education and the Japan Teachers' Union. Whether, as the JTU claims, it seeks freedom and diversity in education in contradistinction to uniformity and centralization, or whether, as its critics claim, it seeks an equally centralized—though antigovernmental—control over the content of education, the fact remains that the power struggle exists clearly in the perception of both parties, and it is hard for those engaged in education in Japan to be neutral. There are a large number of education committees in Japan—some would say the vast majority—where either the Ministry of Education has decisive influence and the JTU has none, or vice versa. Few can maintain a truly independent position vis-à-vis both sides.

On the underlying reason for this power struggle, there are three by no means contradictory views. The first is that, whatever the original points at issue, the battle now is sustained by its own momentum as a "pure" struggle for power between two irreconcilably opposed bodies. The second is that it reflects a conflict between opposing sets of deeply held ideological beliefs—whether, for instance, the teaching of history should concentrate on the miseries of the nation's past or on its glories, whether it should emphasize the doings of the rulers or of the ruled, whether it should inculcate the values of patriotism and dedication to national progress or of resistance to authority and the establishment of individual rights. The third is that behind this ideological conflict lies a political party conflict: the JTU supports opposition parties and the type of education it favors is thought likely to inculcate critical attitudes toward the established government, whereas the Ministry of Education, like any other ministry, is subject to the political direction of the Liberal Democratic party which has held power in Japan for the last fifteen years.

These issues have recently come to public attention by the lawsuit brought by Professor Saburō Ienaga of Tokyo University of Education, a well-known Japanese historian. His textbook on Japanese history was rejected in 1963. In 1964 it received conditional acceptance. Professor Ienaga agreed to the conditions under pressure from the publishers and made the necessary changes. In 1965 he brought a civil suit against the Ministry of Education, claiming damages for loss of royalties (due to the nonpublication of the book in the previous year) and mental distress (due to his being forced to relinquish some of his views in order to be able to publish the text). This suit is still pending. In 1966 he resubmitted his textbook in its original form and it was rejected. This time he brought an administrative suit against the ministry asking for reversal of the decision on the grounds that it was illegal and unconstitutional. It was on this complaint that judgment in his favor was delivered in the Tokyo district court on July 17. The trial attracted great public attention and each of its twenty-eight hearings was reported in detail in the press. Seventeen witnesses appeared for Professor Ienaga, including such notables as Professor Nambara, former president of Tokyo University, and fourteen for the Ministry of Education, including such notables as Professor Morito, chairman of the Central Council for Education. Supporters' societies were formed to rally support for each side.

Professor Ienaga's house was the scene of frequent demonstrations and he had occasionally to ask for police protection. The judgment was reported in the evening papers on July 17 under some of the biggest banner headlines that had been seen for months, together with pictures of the jubilant demonstrations of Professor Ienaga's supporters. The disputed passages in the textbook were as follows:

1. Each historical period was introduced with an illustration. The examiners had objected to the choice of illustrations and to the captions. (In 1964 when the book was published the final compromise was to retain the illustrations and remove all the captions.) Each caption was headed "The people who supported history" or—the phrase is hard to translate—"The people on whose labors history was built." As an example, the illustration for the Tokugawa period showed peasants delivering rice to samurai intendants, and the caption read: "It was the productive labor of the peasants which supported feudal society. As this picture shows, the rice produced by the sweat of the peasants' brow passed into the hands of the warrior class." The objection raised was that "supported" was a difficult concept for children to understand. Moreover, the fact that four of these introductory pictures were of the same type (steel workers for the Meiji period, craftsmen for the Heian period and a stone-age mask) seemed rather one sided; it would be better to take material representing all classes.

2. The following passage concerning Japan's earliest chronicles of the seventh century: "Both the Kojiki and the Nihongi begin with stories of the 'Age of the Gods.' *Not only the stories of the 'Age of the Gods,' but also those relating to the first several generations after the [first human] Emperor Jimmu were all invented after the Imperial family had united the country in order to justify the Imperial family's rule over Japan,* but they are intermingled with a variety of myths and legends told among the magnates and the common people, and they constitute a precious record of the ideas and the arts of ancient times." The examiners required the clause underlined to be deleted on the grounds that it did not adequately represent the ideas and intentions of the people of the period.

3. The following passage dealing with the Russo-Japanese Non-aggression Pact: "In April 1941, in order to strengthen her

strategic position for a southward advance, Japan concluded a nonaggression pact with the Soviet Union." The examiners required insertion of the phrase "at the suggestion of the Soviet Union."

The following is a summary of the court's judgment:

Article 26 of the Constitution states that every child has an equal right to receive an education adapted to his abilities as the law shall provide, and every parent has the duty to see that children receive a basic education.

This is to be interpreted as meaning that, in a democratic society which respects individual dignity, every citizen has the duty, not only toward his own children, but toward the whole of the next generation, to help them to develop their own personalities, to transmit to them the cultural heritage, and to develop them as individuals capable of sustaining a healthy society and a healthy world.

This fundamental notion may be called, in contrast to the concept of the state's right to educate, the concept of the people's (or of the nation's) freedom to educate.

The role of the state is primarily to assist the people to perform their duty to educate their children, and accordingly the powers entrusted to the state in this regard do not require involvement in the content of education, but only the provision of the necessary facilities.

The provision "as the law shall provide" indicates that education is not a matter for control by administrative action not specified by law. But the scope of legislation is also limited. While the provision of the external conditions for education should be legally regulated through the representative parliamentary system, this does not apply to matters of content. These are matters which do not easily consort with the principle of majority decision influenced by party politics. They are to be worked out in the personal contact between teacher and pupil: teachers, through their own study and efforts at self-improvement, should seek to embody the rational "will to educate" of the people as a whole, and, owning a direct responsibility to the people as a whole, to fulfill the task which the people have entrusted to them.

Concerning the guarantee of academic freedom contained in Article 23 of the Constitution: this naturally includes the right of scholars freely to publish the results of their academic work, including their theories and opinions as scholars, and the publication of textbooks is naturally included as one form of such publication. It is a particularly appropriate form of publication inasmuch as (Fundamental Law of Education, Article 1) it is one of the purposes of school education to foster an eagerness for the pursuit of truth which is also the function of university research.

A further guarantee of the right to publish is contained in Article 21 of the Constitution which forbids censorship. It is accepted that the freedom to publish may in some circumstances be limited by considerations of public welfare, but the essence of the ban on censorship is that where the ideological or philosophical content of a work is at issue, it is forbidden for public authority to be used to prevent publication, even in the name of public welfare.

The requirement (School Education Law, Article 21) that all textbooks should be approved by the ministry before they may be published as textbooks therefore constitutes censorship insofar as, and only insofar as, ideological and philosophical judgments enter into the decision to approve or not to approve.

Ideological and philosophical judgments should be understood to include not just political views, but everything relating to the life of the spirit, naturally including theories and opinions which scholars might hold as a result of their research. In the case of history textbooks this means not only a general philosophy of history or the evaluation of particular historical events, but also such matters as periodization insofar as they reflect a view of history.

Insofar as it is designed to provide an education adapted to each child's stage of mental and physical development and to secure equality of educational opportunity, and insofar as it does not involve censorship in the terms above defined, the licensing system itself is not an infringement of the constitution.

But, given also that it is the role of the state to provide the external facilities for education and in the matter of content to confine itself to guidance and advice, the only considerations involved in the examination of textbooks should be misprints and clearly recognizable objective errors; the physical makeup of the book and other technical matters, and whether the content falls within the broad outlines of the indicated curriculum.

An examination of the three points at issue and of the arguments advanced by both sides suggests that in none of these cases was any clear error of fact involved and that they were all points involving a personal perspective on history. The rejection of the textbook therefore constitutes censorship and represents an impermissible use of the licensing system.

In his *obiter dicta* the judge went on to distinguish between "educational freedom," which means the right of the individual citizen to educate, in contradistinction to the state's right to educate, and the "freedom of the teacher." The latter is basically guaranteed by Article 23 of the Constitution, concerning academic freedom. Hence, he stated, it is not permitted for the state unilaterally to require teachers to use certain textbooks, or to limit the participation of teachers in the choice of textbooks, or to give legal force to its curriculum guides and so circumscribe the teacher's activity in detail.

Newspaper editorial comments were in a guarded way mostly favorable to the judgment. Most pointed out that the ministry was bound to appeal and that it would be many years before a final judgment was given, but that meanwhile certain changes ought to be made. A *Mainichi* columnist (July 18) gave one of the most positive expressions of support for the judgment, pointing out that most of the countries of Western Europe and America have nothing like the Japanese system of control over textbooks; by contrast communist countries have national textbooks like prewar Japan, and it was ironical that Japan should in this regard be more like the communist countries than the rest of the free world.

. . . The Association of Constitutional Legal Scholars had, in fact, during the course of the trial passed a resolution supporting the view taken by the judge, and it is said that the ministry had had difficulty in finding an expert on constitutional law to testify on its behalf. In addition there were various comments from other scholars and educators, and symposia including members of the ministry of education in all the major newspapers. Some of the points made are as follows:

MINISTER OF EDUCATION, MR. SAKATA: . . . It is a mistake to consider the "freedom of the teacher" and "academic freedom" as the same thing. . . . Academic freedom as guaranteed in the Constitution—the freedom to do research and to publish the results —is permitted in universities, but it is a mistake to try to apply this principle from primary schools up. Professor Ienaga's contention, as a university professor, that what is permitted in universities should apply also to lower schools ignores the need to adapt education to the mental and physical development of the child. It inevitably will lead to the idea that Article 8 of the Fundamental Law of Education concerning the (political) neutrality of the educational system can simply be ignored. If academic theories of a political partisan nature are allowed in the classroom it will cause great disquiet. The Fundamental Law is based on the Constitution, the School Education Law on the Fundamental Law, and the ministry's curriculum outlines are based on the School Education Law. Of course one ought not to circumscribe the teacher in the classroom in every little detail; there's got to be some free discretion allowed. But the judgment takes a big leap. . . . There seems to be a logical gap in the judgment in the discussion of how the people's "right to educate" is entrusted to the teacher. . . . To take Mr. Ienaga's own case: on the first draft of his textbook submitted there were over 300 problem passages. Of these he accepted the criticism made in the case of a hundred of them. On the rest there was argument back and forth, and in the end only the passages he complained of in the court case were left. By accepting the criticism in a hundred cases he was admitting the value of the licensing system [*Mainichi,* July 18].

MR. SAKATA [in response to a question whether teachers ought not to be more respected]: Yes, but at the same time the education they give ought to be worthy of respect. For example, it is absurd to discuss the relative merits and demerits of socialism and capitalism in primary and middle schools. In a university, when teachers propound an academic theory one assumes a certain critical faculty on the part of the student. But in the schools, whatever a teacher says the children implicitly believe. [*Asahi,* July 18.]

DIRECTOR OF THE BUREAU FOR PRIMARY AND MIDDLE SCHOOL EDUCATION, MINISTRY OF EDUCATION, MR. MIYAJI: . . . The judgment is contradictory. On the one hand it says that textbooks should be treated like any other books. On the other it says that the ministry may correct factual errors in textbooks. Then why not factual errors in ordinary books? . . . The judge says that the content of education is not to be determined as a political matter by majority decision. And yet he takes his stand on the Fundamental Law of Education which depends on majority decision. . . . Professor Ienaga says that we can leave the content of textbooks to authors, but, just because a professor believes deeply in the truth of his theory, what will happen if he insists on putting it in a textbook? Do you really want to have biased textbooks coming out? There's a difference between teaching academic theories in a university and teaching them in a school. Education must be geared to children's mental and physical development. The mere thought of the disorder which would arise if the ministry did not prescribe standards sends shivers down my spine. [*Asahi,* July 18.] . . . [If the judgment goes in favor of Professor Ienaga:] It would not just be a terrible thing for the Ministry of Education, it would be a terrible thing for everyone. Anything could become a textbook—comic books, pornographic books, anything the teacher likes to choose. To put it in Ienaga style, thanks to the ministry's licensing powers it's impossible to give detailed sex education to little girls of seven or eight. Education has got to be geared to the child's development. If you yourself were asked by your own child: "Where do babies come from?" would you tell him? It's not a matter of telling the truth under all circumstances. As the proverb says: "trim your sermon to the listener." [*Mainichi,* July 15.]

IENAGA SABURŌ*
The Historical Significance of the
Japanese Textbook Lawsuit

It cannot be denied that the educational reform carried out amid Japan's large scale democratization, which began with the defeat in August 1945, owed much to the orders and leadership of the American occupation army. But one cannot conclude that the reform was merely the result of compulsion by the occupation. Although for the Japanese government which was making every effort to preserve the *ancien régime* the reform seemed "forced," Japan's intellectuals, reflecting on the causes of the greatest catastrophe in Japan's history, believed that uniform education imposed by the central political authority bore a heavy responsibility; realizing the necessity of fundamental reform in education for the rebirth of Japan, they proceeded to carry this out. The Fundamental Law of Education (1947) is a law enacted from a draft prepared independently by Japanese; it was not something "imposed" by order of the occupation forces. In particular, Article 10 of the Fundamental Law of Education, though in indirect language, placed limits on educational administration, assigned it the duty of arranging external conditions of education, and prohibited it from interfering politically in the content of education.

The Ministry of Education became entirely a "service" institution; and educational administration was placed largely under the jurisdiction of publicly elected local boards of education. As for the content of education, the Ministry of Education was to set standards and the curriculum, but the "course of study," which concretely expresses educational content, was offered only as a guide when a teacher actually conducted his class and was not meant to be binding. Government-compiled textbooks were abolished. It was decided that primary schools and the new-style middle and high schools would temporarily use textbooks certified by the Minister of Education, but that the certification would be

* Ienaga Saburō, "The Historical Significance of the Japanese Textbook Lawsuit," *Bulletin of Concerned Asian Scholars* II:4 (Fall 1970), pp. 5–8.

transferred to local boards of education as soon as sufficient paper could be supplied. Certification was extremely lax until the 1950s, and there were almost no cases in which textbooks which disagreed with government ideology were excluded. The contents of textbooks were of course markedly changed as compared with the prewar period. Principles of democracy and peace were extolled instead of the emperor-system morality. Textbooks on Japanese history no longer began from the tales of the "age of the gods" but from life in the stone age. As the emphasis shifted from emperor-, nobility-, and warrior-centered history to broader fields of society, economy, and culture, Japanese history gave much more space to activities of the common people.

It became possible to deal with such anti-Establishment movements as peasant revolts, the labor movement, the socialist movement, pacifism, and the truth about the Korean annexation and the invasion of China. Postwar historical education set out with the new aim, not of history as a means of cultivating antiforeign or nationalist feelings, but of looking unflinchingly at both the bright and dark sides of a people's past, and of trying to help in the creation of future history.

Unfortunately, postwar reforms in education began to crumble in a few short years. Along with the intensification of the Cold War, the American occupation army abandoned the policies of democratization and demilitarization and began reviving Japan as part of the anticommunist camp. Japan's conservative government, which has maintained a semipermanent majority of seats in the National Diet, welcomed the military alliance with the United States and pressed forward with policies of rearmament, undoing the democratic reforms and restrengthening monopoly capital. These have been the fundamental factors in bringing about the abandonment of democratization in educational content.

The government "course of study" has undergone repeated retrogressive revisions, and, as time has passed, democratic, pacifistic, and scientific hues have faded and such things as the obligation of serving the country, rearming, or approving of military cooperation with the United States, and unscientific, "emotional" patriotism, have come to be emphasized. Although in the beginning the Ministry of Education's course of study was nothing more than a practical guide for classes, from 1958 it took on the binding power of law. Certification of textbooks became strict, and cases occurred one after another in which textbooks which did not agree with the Ministry of Education's ideology were either not certified or revisions demanded (and not certified so long as such revisions were not made). Uniformity was again imposed upon education by an arbitrary power from above.

Not only were the contents of textbooks made uniform by certification, but also the adoption of textbooks in the schools— that is, their selection—gradually reached the point in many areas where the teacher did not independently choose books; instead they were uniformly chosen by local school boards. With the adoption in 1963 of measures to supply state-purchased textbooks to children in primary and middle school, a system was begun which completely deprives teachers of the freedom of choice. Through a process of dual selection, whereby books adopted by teachers are chosen from those already selected by certification, an arrangement is made which keeps textbooks considered undesirable by the government out of the hands of children. (This system also involved the strengthening of the Ministry of Education's supervisory authority over textbook publishers and their employees.)

Such a system of government control must be seen in the context of other measures which have been taken to deprive teachers of their independence—for example, the denial to teachers of freedom of political activity in 1956; the abolition of public election boards of education in 1956 (they later became appointive); the enforcement of ratings of teacher performance (the important point here is that rating sessions are closed and the person rated has no right of appeal); and enforcement of a national achievement text (the Ministry of Education prepares the questions and conducts the test simultaneously at schools throughout the country to determine whether or not classes are being conducted according to the government curriculum). Measures to strengthen the power of educational administration, which have been advanced one after another in spite of strong opposition from teachers' unions, intellectuals, and others, have moved in the direction of government control of education.

Why have such policies, which run counter to the ideals of postwar educational reform, been steadily achieved? The basic reasons must be sought in such broad historical conditions as the continuation of the conservative government's firm rule, the establishment of the Japanese–American security treaty system, and the people's loss of political concern due to "economic prosperity" within this system (no matter how rent with contradictions and false that "prosperity" may be). But if we consider the problem within the limits of law, many laws and administrative regulations have been enacted which violate the fundamental idea of renouncing war in the Japanese Constitution and the guarantee of fundamental human rights. One can thus see in the field of education indications that the Constitution is becoming essentially a dead letter. For the Japanese people, who until 1945 had lived for many years under a system of a state-controlled education, it was difficult to understand the idea of "freedom of education" contained in the Constitution and in the Fundamental Law of Education. . . . The interest of legal and judicial circles in educational problems is slight. What might be considered theoretical or administrative research on laws concerning education is almost nil, and this is one cause of the lack of legal criticism of administrative legislation which violates the Constitution and the Fundamental Law of Education. This disinterest has weakened the will to prevent enforcement of such administrative legislation.

To understand why I had to file the textbook certification suit, the first of its kind in the world, it is essential to understand fully the conditions of Japan's peculiar educational administration, as related above. This suit was filed to challenge directly the hard facts of continuing state control of education, which lasted so many years from the latter part of the nineteenth century, and of restrengthening educational control amid circumstances of world history intensified by the Cold War. The ultimate aim is to return "freedom of education" to the hands of the people.

THE CIRCUMSTANCES OF MY PERSONAL EXPERIENCE WITH TEXTBOOK CERTIFICATION

I entered elementary school in 1920, and the old-system junior high school in 1926. My education was based on the authorized morality of the emperor system described above. Since entering the university, from which I graduated in 1937, I have been studying Japanese history.

Neither on campus nor after graduation was there any security for academic freedom until the defeat of 1945. Especially during the wartime period, which lasted for fifteen years from 1931, any scientific study of Japanese history was extremely difficult because of the harsh restrictions on freedom of thought and expression. There were taboos in all fields. Presentation of our studies and even the acquisition of historical materials was greatly restricted. During this period, my thought and knowledge had been narrowly limited, partly because of the difficulty in overcoming my own prejudices resulting from the education received since elementary school, and also due to the prohibition on freedom of scientific study.

The acquisition of freedom of thought, expression, study, and the like, which came with the end of the war in 1945, wiped out at one blow numerous taboos which had been barriers to the study of Japanese history and paved the way for its rapid progress. This situation enabled me to extend my field of vision and enrich my thought.

Looking back at the undemocratic, militaristic, and nonscientific historical education which I had received, I seriously desired to provide our next generation with an "education of scientific Japanese history" appropriate to the new Japan. In accordance with my ideal plan I wrote a textbook of Japanese history for high schools. This textbook has been used constantly for almost two decades since being approved by the education ministry in 1952. The revisions which I have made on several occasions, each requiring certification by the Education Ministry, gave me a chance to take a close look at the process of certification of textbooks. The certification has become stricter year by year, as I saw in 1952, 1955, and 1957. The strictness of these certifications reached a peak in 1963 and 1964. In 1963, when my textbook failed to be approved, an official of the Education Ministry verbally notified the publisher and me of the reasons for its rejection. Reluctantly, I altered some points in the book and submitted the draft, which was then approved in 1964 on the condition that I modify almost 300 items. Of these items, if I refused to modify those which the Education Ministry thought very important, then I was repeatedly urged to modify them until finally in many places I was forced to make changes against my will. If I had continued to refuse their modifications, my textbook could not have been approved and published in time for the academic year.

Looking at all the items used as the pretext for the rejection and demanded modification, we can clearly see the tendency of the Education Ministry to control the content of historical education through the enforcement of state certification. . . .

✿ FOR MOST WESTERNERS, knowledge of the Japanese student movement has come exclusively from the sensational newspaper stories of recent years, in which violent groups of Japanese youths appear on front pages throwing Molotov cocktails and battling with riot police. Invariably, these guerrilla bands are said to be led by the Zengakuren, a group sometimes identified as "Maoist" and "Communist"-inspired. Zengakuren, however, is not a unified student organization, but a loosely used word for the movement as a whole, which is splintered into a bevy of ideologically opposed factions. Gavan McCormack traces Zengakuren from its founding in 1948, through the 1960 security treaty crisis—its high-water mark—to its current fragmented state. There are today three main groupings: one favorable to the Japan Communist party, an independent Trotskyite faction, and a coalition of all the rest, sometimes cooperating, sometimes bickering, but ranged generally against the JCP. As in the United States and Western Europe, student activity in Japan increased dramatically in response to America's war in Indochina, and similarly it subsequently transferred its attention and energies to the universities themselves. Currently quiescent, the Japanese student movement in the past has been able to mobilize enormous popular support for certain issues, but its future development is uncertain.

GAVAN McCORMACK*
The Student Left in Japan

STUDENT MOVEMENT: ZENGAKUREN AND THE JCP

Zengakuren, the All-Japan Federation of Student Self-Governing Bodies, was founded in 1948 on a program surprising now for its relatively moderate, democratic tone—opposition to the reemergence of fascism in education, absolute freedom of organizing in the student movement, etc. . . . It was not until 1958, however, that the student movement made decisive steps away from JCP domination as the party made clear its commitment to revisionist moderation. In that year emerged the League of Communists (Kyōsandō or Bund), and shortly afterwards the League of Revolutionary Communists (Kakkyōdō). However, despite the plethora of organizations which sprang up to outflank it on its left, the JCP continued and continues to command considerable strength, principally today through the Democratic Youth League (Minsei) founded in 1964. . . . Recent estimates give Minsei control of the self-governing committees of about ninety-eight universities with an enrollment of 453,000 students. At the base there are perhaps 12,000 militants, and they can rely on the backing of 38,000 irregulars. Militant anti-JCP students control about 440,000 students, but that control is divided in practice between many factions.

It should be explained here . . . that by the Japanese system all students are automatically inscribed on the autonomous committee of their faculty, whichever group happens to be controlling it. The system has the unfortunate effect of enhancing factionalism, and indeed, nowadays, the very word Zengakuren has come to have very little meaning. . . . Over the past decade, the self-governing committees of the nation's departments and universities have been aligned broadly in three separate and generally hostile groups: the pro-CP Minsei; the independent and go-it-alone Kakumaru or

* Gavan McCormack, "The Student Left in Japan," *New Left Review* 65 (January–February 1971), pp. 41–45, 48–50, 52–53.

Revolutionary Marxists, who have some juridical claim to be the authentic successors of the original Zengakuren; and the group of factions known in the past first as Sampa (Three-Faction), then Goha (Five-Faction), then Happa (Eight-Faction) Alliance—which, upon developing to include many nonorganized radicals in a remarkable break from traditional factional exclusiveness, was in late 1969 reorganized as Zenkyōtō, the All-Japan Federation of Joint Struggle Committees. . . .

Broadly speaking, the spectrum of the non-JCP left groups includes quasi-Trotskyist, Maoist, "Structural Reformist," and Anarchist groups. The principal quasi-Trotskyist organizations are Chūkaku or Core and Kakumaru or Revolutionary Marxists. Both, or their parent organizations, Bund and Kakkyōdō, were founded in opposition to international communism's post-1956 revisionist line. . . . Both groups insist they are anti-imperialist and anti-Stalinist, but Kakumaru insists it is much more anti-Stalinist than Chūkaku is, and identifies Ho Chi Minh among others as a Stalinist. However, Kakumaru is also extremely elitist and sectarian, insisting that it alone is the legitimate Zengakuren and refusing to participate in united front actions, as it regards compromise with anarchists and others as unprincipled. . . . Over the past year or so there have been frequent battles—with staves, iron pipes—between Kakumaru and other student groups, especially Chūkaku. [For] example: at Waseda, a major private university in Tokyo of about 40,000 students, the first half of 1969 passed with Ōkuma Hall, the symbolic founder's hall, under occupation by Kakumaru, while the original site of contention at Waseda, the newly built No. 2 Student Hall across the road from it, remained under occupation by the other factions of the left alliance; the roadway between was the scene of intermittent battles between the two, the injured ending in a nearby hospital. On the rare occasions, as for the "Liberate America" July fourth demonstration of 1970, when both groups have attended the same event without fighting, it has been because of the placing of the Citizens' Peace in Vietnam Committee between the hostile factions. . . . Chūkaku now controls some thirty-six self-governing committees with a membership of 67,800 students, of whom 2000 are activists and 6500 irregulars, while Kakumaru controls thirty self-governing committees with a membership of 66,000, of whom 1800 are activists and 3500 irregulars. . . .

The Maoists came together in 1963 with the formation of the League of Marxist-Leninists (ML), out of remnants of the old Bund, and was greatly expanded after 1966 with the formal expulsion of Maoists from the JCP. From 1968 the organization was formally constituted as the Japan League of Marxist-Leninists (ML) and its student section as the Student Liberation Front or SFL. . . .

The Anti-Imperialist group of Zengakuren, formed in 1968 after the breakup of the former "Three-Faction" Zengakuren alliance, is a major cluster of student organizations, made up of breakaway, revolutionary elements from the Socialist Party's youth and student struggle sections against the 1960 security treaty renewal, known variously as the Socialist League, Internationalists; Anti-Imperialist Student Council; Proletarian Military Group, together with the Maoist SFL. Between them this group controls 144,800 students, of whom 2800 are activists and 8300 irregulars.

Then there are the "Structural Reform" groups, generally breakaways from the JCP of 1961 vintage, followers of Gramsci and Togliatti, who stand for auto-gestion in industry; the 4th International; the Preparatory Committee for an armed uprising, and various anarchist groups.

. . . "[U]nited front"–style organizations have emerged in recent years to coordinate activity not only on the student level but also on that of workers and of citizens generally. . . . [I]n the student case the organization is Zenkyōtō, or the Joint Struggle Committee. This organizational form came to maturity in the course of the long Tokyo University struggle in 1968, was subsequently copied elsewhere, and was expanded into a national federation in September of 1969. Its major significance is that for the first time the university movement spread from the ranks of the militant sectarian cadres to those of the student masses, to nonaligned radicals many of whom, formerly "non-poli," became in the turmoil of 1968–1970 a major force of activity. Faction-fighting remains a serious problem between Zenkyōtō and the two factions which remain outside and militantly opposed to it, the JCP's Minsei, and Kakumaru, but notwithstanding this the new federation was a big step forward.

Contrasting with the old Zengakuren, centralized and somewhat hierarchical in structure with its built-in disadvantage of factional competition between both faculties and universities for control of the apparatus at every level, Zenkyōtō in essence arose in the course of the struggle and reflects very clearly the antiauthoritarian, antibureaucratic, egalitarian camaraderie of the world behind the barricades in which it was conceived. . . .

STRUGGLES: STATE AND PRIVATE UNIVERSITIES

This new, perhaps in the Japanese context radically new, kind of organization emerged in the course of struggles at Tokyo and Nihon universities. The former, at the alma mater of the nation's elite, developed from the January 1968 protests over the feudal and exploitative conditions under which medical graduates served a one-year unpaid compulsory hospital internship, through the now-familiar stages of occupation, unyielding stand by the authorities, bust by riot police, to a massive expansion which in the end paralyzed the entire university for a year. The latter developed with similar momentum (indeed as the universities are physically close their development was complementary) in the huge and corrupt private Nihon University after students found that the university authorities had embezzled £2 million of university funds. The university president, a close friend of Premier Satō, had been using the money to build himself a mansion, to buy gifts for university officials, and for donations to the coffers of the ruling Liberal Democratic party. The student enrollment was 100,000, the university had long been known as Nihon University Co., Ltd., because of the way it was run. . . .

The disputes of Tokyo and Nihon universities, mentioned here briefly, are in a sense representative of the problems of Japanese universities in the years 1968–1969. Some of the issues elsewhere were—control of a student hall (notably Waseda), drastic fee increases (Keiō, Meiji, Tokyo Women's), or the poor, mass-production quality of the education in others. The major distinction is between state and private universities. There are nearly 400 private universities in Japan, often with enrollments of 50,000–100,000, where fees are usually over £200, education always inferior to the state-run, low-fee (£12–15 a year) elite universities, and where certain characteristics are almost universal—emphasis on the spirit of the founder, which seems never to have been interred with his bones, promotion of a college song and flag, and existence of a college mafia. Thus the initial issue in private universities tended to be more concrete—fee increases, overcrowding, control of student facilities, demand for free speech rights, while in state universities fees were low anyway, the quality of education much superior, and free speech more or less assured; so protests were more likely to be explicitly ideological, or to develop quickly, as in Tokyo University, into an attack on the university itself as a bastion of privilege and linchpin of an oppressive, reactionary system.

. . . The organizational forms developed in the past few years, Zenkyōtō for the students, the Citizens' Peace in Vietnam Committee, the workers' Antiwar Youth Committee, may continue and develop further, but somehow a new way must be found to expand the basis of the struggle. Perhaps it will be by relating directly to the most oppressed of the Japanese masses, the two million or so ex-untouchable *eta,* the half-million or so almost as severely discriminated against Korean minority, or the fifty million or so still thoroughly dominated and exploited women; perhaps by expanding and politically organizing the present tremendous concern over the destruction of the environment; perhaps in consequence of some at present unforeseen crisis developing in the economy, or by the government trying to push too far too fast in the remilitarization of Japan and its reorganization in the interests of monopoly capital. . . .

AGRICULTURE, ECONOMIC DEVELOPMENT,
AND ECOLOGY

❀ SINCE 1972 the new administration of Prime Minister Tanaka Kakuei has been notable for further major relocation plans for industry to rural areas. Tanaka's "remodeling Japan" scheme, published in a best-selling book, calls for rural development considerably more drastic than that proposed in the New National Composite Development Plan (*Shinzensō*). Its general contours and its rapid adoption by business are outlined below by Louis Kraar in a *Fortune* article. Seemingly, Tanaka's bold plan would attempt to halt the rural exodus to the cities, or possibly reverse it, but there has been a surprising amount of local opposition to such development. Viewing a village coalition that opposed the establishment of a huge oil refinery in Kagoshima prefecture, Kobayashi shows the tenacity with which Japanese farmers, fishermen, and other local residents have opposed damaging industrial schemes. Perhaps more significant than this conservationist approach is the political fallout in rural Diet constituencies which have routinely voted conservative but now feel threatened by the government's plans. Though part of a more general trend of urbanization in rural areas, the Liberal Democratic plans could eventually trigger political changeovers to the Socialist and Communist parties in a variety of places.

R. P. DORE*
Beyond the Land Reform: Japan's Agricultural Prospect

Ten years ago few people were prepared to be optimistic about the prospect for Japanese agriculture. The postindependence government had enacted a revised Agricultural Land Law in 1952 designed to fix the post-land-reform status quo, prescribing low rentals on the small remaining portion of tenanted land, keeping the rigid restrictions of the occupation legislation on landlords' right to repossess, and maintaining the low ceiling restrictions which limited holdings in every prefecture except Hokkaido to less than five (in some prefectures less than two) hectares. But there were Jeremiahs enough to argue that no legislation could thus fly in the face of nature. The laws of supply and demand, village feudalism, and the insidious political machinations of the landlords would all conspire to bring the old system of tenancy back before long.

Five years later critics were slowly beginning to admit themselves confounded. These legal bulwarks against the revival of landlordism, reinforced by the postwar apparatus of price supports, agricultural cooperatives, and government-supported credit facilities, seemed firm enough. Pessimism now shifted to other grounds. So the peasants were likely to hold on to their tiny plots of land, but what would it profit them? There was little leeway for increases of productivity in Japan's horticulturally intensive agriculture; would not agricultural incomes simply stagnate while other sectors offered a steady rise of living standards—given (what seemed the truth) that industry was never likely to absorb workers from the farms fast enough to reduce the agricultural population and leave more land for those who remained behind? Today it is these modified arguments for pessimism which are in turn being proved false; agricultural productivity has indeed been rising at a rapid—some would even claim a spectacular—rate. And the labor

* R. P. Dore, "Beyond the Land Reform: Japan's Agricultural Prospect," *Pacific Affairs* XXXVI:3 (Fall 1963), pp. 265–271.

demands of the industrial sector have been expanding so fast that, for the first time in Japanese history, the prospect of a rapid decline in the agricultural population leaving a smaller number of viable farming units seems real enough.

A few figures will indicate the scale and nature of productivity increases. Rice remains the major crop, and the efficiency of its production is still the biggest determinant of agricultural productivity. There may have seemed little scope for improving yields given the high levels already reached in the early fifties, but better seeds and fertilizers, better drainage, new methods of forcing seedbeds, and above all, a rapid diffusion of new methods of pest control have enabled Japanese farmers to do better than ever before. Average yields at the beginning of the century were about 250 kilograms per acre. Steady improvement had raised the figure to an average of 284 for the years 1925–1928, and to 316 for the years 1949–1951. Ten years later the average for 1960–1962 had reached 396. At the same time an expanding urban market for what were hitherto luxury foods has enabled farmers to earn more by diversifying their production and switching to higher income–yielding crops. . . . The overall estimates of the total value of agricultural production for the crop year 1960–1961 show a twenty-five percent increase over the 1952–1957 average, a rate of increase which few other countries can match.

The other side of the equation—the decline in the agricultural labor force—is as yet not so easy to document. Between the two censuses of 1950 and 1960 the total number of farm households declined by less than two percent, though the population living in those farm households fell by more than nine percent as more underemployed, younger sons and cousins left for the cities. The real spurt in out-migration, however, belongs to the recent boom period beginning in 1959. According to sample survey figures, for instance, the number of males in farm families aged 15–19 declined by eight percent in the single year 1960 to 1961.

So far this has produced only a slight decline in the number of farm families. The pattern of migration has been the traditional one. Urban employers prefer to recruit young school-leavers; few married farm households find the opportunity to move to the towns and take their families with them. Consequently it will take time for the recent outflow of single young men to be reflected in a decline in the number of farm operating units. That this will surely happen, however, if the present industrial expansion continues, seems to be the clear implication of the results of an excellent sample survey of school-leaving farm sons conducted in March 1962. . . .

The significant point of these figures is that, whereas hitherto throughout the period of industrialization, the migration flow has never been strong enough to take more than the increase in the rural population—leaving one son, usually the eldest, to replace his father on each family farm—now in a good many families all the children are leaving. Only four percent of the eldest sons of farmers with the smallest farms—those cultivating less than half a hectare—work on the farm after leaving school (assuming that the nineteen percent who have gone on to a university are unlikely to come back). Even assuming that the four percent of younger sons who have stayed at home intend to inherit the farm (and the postwar abolition of primogeniture inheritance makes this a plausible assumption), and also assuming that a fair proportion of that thirty-eight percent of eldest and thirty-three percent of younger sons who now commute from home to other jobs will try to keep the farm going on a part-time basis and that a small proportion of the thirty-five percent of eldest and fifty-five percent of younger sons who have left home for jobs in the towns will find the prospect of inheriting half a hectare attractive enough to bring them back, it still seems likely that a quarter or more of these farm units will disappear as soon as this generation's parents become too old to work their farms and, for want of a son at home to leave them to, sell up and follow their children to the towns or else live in retirement in the villages on the remittances of dutiful migrant sons.

The picture is somewhat different on the bigger farms. Some fifty-five percent of the eldest sons of families with more than one-and-a-half hectare of land stay to work at home after leaving school and will presumably carry on the farm when their parents retire. (It is worth remarking, too, that the majority of these eldest sons are high-school graduates; the next generation of managers of these one-and-a-half–hectare farms is going to be not merely literate but well educated.) But even here a quarter of the eldest sons have already left home. . . .

Already, however, the outflow of labor has clearly reduced underemployment in agriculture and increased labor productivity.

According to the ministry's calculations, compared with the 1957–1959 average, the physical volume of agricultural output in 1961 had risen by six percent and the labor force declined by eight percent, giving a rise in labor productivity of nearly sixteen percent. Farm mechanization is only in part determined by labor shortage (in part it is a reflection of farmers' ability to buy themselves more leisure and relief from backbreaking toil and in part of their keenness to be up-to-date), but the spread of powered cultivators (from some 80,000 in 1955 to over a million by the end of 1961) is a significant sign of the times. Now one farm household in six owns one of these machines and over a half of the farmers had their land plowed by them in 1961.

Nevertheless, Japanese agriculture still presents policy-makers with a problem—no longer a problem of stagnation but one of relatively slower growth. While labor productivity in agriculture was sixteen percent higher in 1961 than the 1957–1959 average, the comparable figure for manufacturing industry was fifty-seven percent. Industrial wages have not been rising quite as fast as productivity but they have not lagged far behind, and, if recent trends continue, there is bound to be a growing gap between farm and nonfarm income—a politically dangerous gap for a Liberal Democratic government which largely relies on farmers' votes.

So far the problem has not become serious. The differential which established itself in the mid-fifties, with farm incomes per family member running at about seventy-five percent of the figure for urban worker families, has remained fairly constant. Average farm income per family member increased by more than thirteen percent from 1960 to 1961, and, although the cost of living rose too, the external signs of greater well-being are obvious enough in the villages—television sets in every other farm house by February 1962, washing machines and electric rice-cookers in every fourth home, and even refrigerators in about seven percent of households. There also seem to have been similar improvements in the diet and an increase in savings. By 1962 even in Kagoshima (a southern prefecture not noted for its prosperity or for its enthusiasm for education) over a half of the children who have completed compulsory schooling were going on for an extra three years of senior high school.

The paradox of slower increases in agricultural productivity and faster improvements in farm incomes has a dual explanation. In the first place government supports have kept agricultural prices from falling and even—for political rather than for economic reasons—raised them a few points. . . . The second factor is the increase in opportunities for nonagricultural earnings. In 1955 about thirty-five percent of the income of farm households came from outside agriculture; in 1961 the figure was forty-eight percent. In part this transfer out of agriculture of the labor of farm household members appears in the figures for the decline in the farm labor force already quoted, but, apart from those who commute regularly to full-time jobs from their farm homes, there are also a good many farmers who find increasing opportunities to supplement their income with seasonal work in construction and the like. By 1960 only thirty-four percent of farm households were classified as full-time, compared with fifty percent in 1950, and of the remainder thirty-two percent (as opposed to twenty-two in 1950) spent more of their working time outside agriculture than in it.

Here, then, lies the kernel of the present problem for Japanese policy-makers. Farm household incomes must not be allowed to fall too far behind urban incomes. At the same time the use of costly price supports to prevent that happening comes to seem increasingly irksome. In a booming Japan experiencing a great surge in the "will to economize" and confident of its ability to expand exports enough to cover any amount of food imports, it seems absurd to go on paying Japanese farmers $110 a ton for Japanese wheat when foreign wheat of better quality can be had for $70 a ton, unloaded at Yokohama. Moreover, Japan is under increasing pressure (from countries it wishes to persuade to liberalize restrictions on Japanese exports) to relax the import controls which protect high price levels—especially of meat and dairy products. Yet the possibility of moving to lower levels of price supports seems politically remote. A bill to introduce a new system of price-fixing for barley and naked barley which would allow the government enough flexibility to discourage farmers from producing these overpriced and overabundant grains was finally abandoned in 1962 after it failed to get through two Diet sessions. Meanwhile the farmers' alarmed reaction to violent swings in the price of meat and dairy products (and, to be fair, the alarm of the consumer, too, when the price of pork rose sharply) added a new act to the statute book in 1961 which included these in the list of price-supported products.

The farm support costs, therefore, cannot be reduced unless, by compensation, farmers' incomes are visibly and materially raised by the other factors. Of these the most hopeful is the withdrawal of labor from agriculture and a sharp rise in labor productivity. But how should this withdrawal of labor proceed? By outright migration, a fall in the number of farms and larger acreages per unit? Or by a further increase in the number of part-time farmers?

There is no doubt what the ministry of agriculture wants. An increasing proportion of part-time farmers is a messy solution, implying—and the point is made by charts in its reports showing the "feminization and gerontization of the farm labor force"—that agriculture is left with the least active and least enterprising workers. Weekend and womenfolk farmers do not have their heart in farming and are loath to invest money in it. Only the full-time operators of large holdings can begin to reap economies of scale and to afford the experiments and the risk-taking which alone can make agriculture a viable industry.

One might have expected that conservative Diet members would have had other ideas and seen political advantages in keeping as large a part of the industrial labor force as possible tied to little bits of land property—just as Le Play saw this as the best solution for the subversive anomie of the industrial proletariat in nineteenth-century France. But, if they do, they seem not to have succeeded in articulating their views. It is the outright migration solution which is now the official policy goal.

It is this situation which has made the Land Law begin to seem out of date. The 1952 act was designed with the overriding purpose of preventing the revival of landlordism. . . . [I]t has been so successful in making the leasing of land a discouraging and unprofitable occupation that tenancy has been steadily declining since the end of the reform. Since this has happened despite the fact that one of the major punitive restrictions—rent control—is unenforced and unenforceable, it could be plausibly argued that the availability of other more profitable forms of investment (stocks and bonds absorbed nearly ten percent of farm savings in 1962) and the general loss of confidence in ownership rights divorced from actual cultivating possession, mean that even if the present controls were removed no one would any longer buy land for the purpose of leasing it out.

This might be disputed. It could be argued that the really discouraging feature of the law is the tenant's absolute security of tenure and the stringent restrictions on the landlord's right to repossess, that this is enforceable and is in fact largely enforced, and that without the law the whole situation would change, particularly if a depression made alternative forms of investment less profitable and the chance to cultivate land more precious.

Whatever the value of the law as a defense against landlordism, there seems no doubt that certain features of it have operated as an actual hindrance to the emergence of the government's visionary pattern of the agricultural future. . . .

LOUIS KRAAR*
Japan Sets Out to Remodel Itself

Driven by a deep sense of national purpose, Japan has attained remarkable economic growth, a tremendous export surplus, and a commercial prowess that is the envy of the rest of the world. But gradually the Japanese are coming to realize that they have paid heavily for these achievements. Tokyo, Nagoya, and Osaka are megalopolitan nightmares, hopelessly congested and permeated with choking fumes. The atmosphere is killing the famed cherry trees in Tokyo, and in nearby Kawasaki it is killing people as well. In a nation that ranks among the top economic powers, only fifteen percent of the homes are connected to sewers.

Now Japan is at last beginning to change course. The obsession with ever-rising production and high-pressure exporting is giving way to a fresh national goal. The Japanese are mobilizing to undertake a vast restructuring of the entire nation and its economy. To check the horrendous pollution and urban congestion, factories will be dispersed to the countryside and dozens of new towns will be created and linked by networks of superhighways

* Louis Kraar, "Japan Sets Out to Remodel Itself," *Fortune* LXXXVII:3 (March 1973), pp. 98, 100–102.

and express railways. Above all, the objective is to improve the quality of life.

The ambitious effort, which the Japanese call "remodeling," will require an estimated investment of $1 trillion in public and private funds. . . .

Prime Minister Kakuei Tanaka has made remodeling the focus of his new regime, and he is a forceful, practical man capable of directing a national transformation. Unlike most Japanese politicians, who plod upward through the government bureaucracy, he came into politics after a lucrative career as a building contractor. The youngest postwar premier, Tanaka, fifty-four, is far more venturesome than his predecessors. Witness the ambitious target date he has set for completion of the entire transformation—1985.

Last June, Tanaka presented the grand design for social and economic change in a book, *Remodeling the Japanese Archipelago,* which became a best-seller and helped boost him to power. Although the concept is now generally termed "the Tanaka Plan," the ideas have actually been taking shape for several years within the cohesive government–business establishment. Thus there is already a consensus on the basic thrust. And while many practical problems and inevitable resistance to some features are still being overcome, both the bureaucracy and private corporations are already starting on a path to transfigure the nation.

A gradual evolution in public opinion underlies the change and makes it possible. "While our factories are the most modern, we have shabby homes, heavy pollution, and not-so-good living conditions," notes Dr. Saburō Okita, an influential government adviser, who is president of the Japan Economic Research Center. "People suddenly became aware of this." Indeed, communities have become so agitated over the ill effects of *kōgai,* as the Japanese call environmental disruption, that many industries find it impossible to overcome public resistance to the building of new plants. Complaints about pollution and lawsuits against corporations have risen dramatically in the past few years. The ever-worsening traffic snarls and dangers of driving in Tokyo and other big cities have reduced many proud car-owners to merely displaying their autos in front of their homes, rather than risk driving them. And lately the Japanese have been troubled to find that urban children, who are accustomed to playing on apartment steps and dodging cars in back streets, often don't know quite what to do when they are taken out to the countryside. They just sit on the grass and play cards. . . .

The main trouble is that much of Japan's industry and a third of its population—some 35 million people—are crammed into barely one percent of the country's total area. To relieve the congestion in the urban belt along the Pacific coast and to end the economic stagnation of underpopulated rural areas, the government recently formed the Corporation for the Relocation of Industry. It is headed by Keiichirō Hirata, a former Vice-Finance Minister, who also serves as chairman of the Comprehensive National Development Council, an influential group of economists and business leaders that sets Japan's economic priorities. Hirata boasts that the redevelopment plan "will give us a new Japan."

The relocation corporation has designated zones in relatively open areas covering seventy-five percent of the country, and it is beginning to lure factories into these regions from the overcrowded cities. . . . The government offers financial incentives both to the companies that relocate and to the communities into which they move. Tanaka estimates that these subsidies will have totaled from $7 billion to $10 billion by 1985. So far, dozens of companies have applied for loans to cover their moving costs, for accelerated depreciation on vacated buildings and equipment, and for other government assistance. Those considering a move out of Tokyo include Azuma Steel, Meidensha Electric Manufacturing, and Mitsubishi Steel. Nippon Aluminum and Yammaru Diesel are planning to leave Osaka. To encourage outlying communities to accept industry, the government offers them grants to build parks and pollution-monitoring facilities. Later, Tanaka hopes to add a "factory-expulsion tax"—a special surtax on factories that remain in congested cities.

If relocation succeeds, about half the wretched industrial jungles around the cities of Tokyo, Nagoya, and Osaka will be razed, making way for parks and housing. At the same time, existing rural towns will be painstakingly developed into model communities, each with some 250,000 people, verdant industrial parks, and strict environmental controls. Sites have been selected for more than seventy such new towns and detailed design is swiftly going ahead. The government plans to invest an average of $1.8 billion in each new town. . . .

LAND-GRABBING AND POLITICS

Many companies, seeking quick profits from the national remodel-ing, have invested so heavily in real estate as to pose a threat to the plan itself. The land-buying spree began right after publication of Tanaka's book, and it has pushed prices up by as much as fifty percent in some places. The government anticipated a twelve percent increase in land values in the fiscal year ending March 31, but prices shot up an average of twenty percent in the first half. Hideo Edo, president of Mitsui Real Estate Development Co., says with great dismay: "In the past, increases were mostly in a few big cities. Now they extend from one part of the country to another." Much of the speculation involves land earmarked for new towns and factory sites, but astronomical land prices could sabotage many remodeling projects.

The land-grabbing has stirred public controversy over the Tanaka Plan. During recent parliamentary elections, opponents accused the premier of personally profiting from land deals. They also attacked the plan as favoring the interests of big business and charged that it would merely spread pollution around the islands. The Communist party of Japan, which directed its campaign at discontented city-dwellers, gained seats in the election, and the Japanese press now makes a habit of calling Tanaka's leadership "disappointing."

But this judgment overlooks the fact that most of the changes Tanaka has popularized are already beginning to happen. Tanaka's Liberal Democratic party, which has ruled since its formation in 1955, has retained its overwhelming absolute majority. Moreover, since the impetus for remodeling comes from the tight-knit Japa-nese establishment, the plan's support and success are independent of Tanaka's political future.

. . . The dispersal of industry to the countryside promises to bring about some profound political changes that will make Japan less protectionist and benefit its consumers. Some 7,600,000 Japa-nese, nearly sixteen percent of the labor force, work on farms, many of which are small and inefficient. Japan produces rice, to name one major crop, at three times the U.S. cost. A staunchly protectionist voting bloc, the heavily subsidized farmers bitterly oppose food imports. But, in the long run, remodeling offers the government a way around this tough domestic pressure group. As manufacturing plants and new communities locate in rural areas, many farmers will be lured from the land by real-estate agents offering handsome prices and by factory jobs. Already over half the earnings of agricultural workers come from nonagricultural sources, such as seasonal employment in industry.

*KOBAYASHI YASUHIRO**
Judging Tanaka's "Remodeling Japan" Theory†

There has been an undeniable boom going on everywhere in the Japanese islands ever since Prime Minister Tanaka's announcement of the proposed "development" of various areas. Lately, however, the angry residents of these regions have forced the government to listen to their views on the projects. In fact, the "remodeling" theory could almost be called a "conflict theory for Japan." At the *Asahi* newspaper we have received factual reports on the state of many of these local conflicts, and here we will . . . show some of the details [in one area].

THE POWER WHICH DROVE THE LOCAL DEVELOPMENT PLAN INTO BECOMING A "REJECTED BILL." SHIBUSHI, KAGOSHIMA PREFECTURE.

Shibushi Bay. There is a beautiful crescent-shaped shoreline which makes one wonder if the figure of speech "white sand and green pines" wasn't made for this place. One part of the bay is designated a national park.

The New National Composite Development Plan (*Shinzensō*) chose this seashore as its victim for a large-scale development scheme for southern Japan to rank with Mutsu Ogawa prefecture of the north. Then Kagoshima prefecture drew up the New Osumi Development Plan in December 1971. And finally this summer [1972], after scarcely more than eight months, the government

---

* Kobayashi Yasuhiro, "Judging Tanaka's 'Remodeling Japan' Theory," *Asahi Jānaru* XIV:41 (October 10, 1972).

† Translated by Tomoko Moore.

announced that it would reconsider the project and the proposal became a "rejected bill." What caused this to happen was the resourcefulness and strength of the residents' movement in Shibushi, which has been called "the strongest antipollution group in Japan at the present time." This is how the New Osumi Development Plan started.

"We will fill in Shibushi Bay to a depth of two meters offshore, then we will encourage new industrial development, including such types as food processing, heavy machinery, and oil refineries which would include a million-barrel Nissan installation. Making this large-scale industrial project the primary force, we aim at making great strides in the whole prefecture. Furthermore, we will consult the residents, and we will not approve the location of pollution-causing industries, an unprecedented step and one that can serve as a model for the era of the seventies."

In these boastful words the governor of Kagoshima prefecture announced the plan with self-confidence. Obviously, he believed that, if he brought factories to poor villages, everyone would surely be happy about it.

Osumi Peninsula is a barren plateau covered with white sandy soil known to the residents themselves as "the land of sweet potatoes," meaning that the soil yields only sweet potatoes. Per capita income in Kagoshima prefecture is the lowest in Japan, and the income of people living on the Osumi Peninsula is only slightly more than eighty percent of the prefectural average.

The expectation of the prefecture government, not unnaturally, was that an offer to improve income by large-scale industrial development in such an impoverished area would meet with few objections. Yet this plan went astray from the start.

"UMEBOSHI [PICKLED SOUR PLUMS] RATHER THAN BEEFSTEAK"

Immediately after the announcement of the plan, the documentary television film *"Ayamachi"* ["A Mistake"]—about the famous pollution problems of Yokkaichi City—was shown locally in Kagoshima. Shown in succession on the screen are images of dashing oil company executives, and children writhing in an asthma attack. In the background a poem of Ishigaki Rin flows across the screen:

> Wondering if eating beefsteak under smoggy skies is good,
> the people of Isozu have begun thinking they want
> to eat pickled plums once more under clear skies.

Among the people gathered in the village meeting hall to watch the program there were sighs of "That's so, that's so," and from that day on the residents insisted, whether to the governor or to cabinet ministers, that they "wanted to eat pickled plums under blue skies rather than beefsteak in the smog."

In late February four fishermen came as representatives from the village of Kazenori to encourage the people of Shibushi and related their own tale of a fierce struggle to prevent a new plant of the Osaka Cement Company. "Our struggle is not a mere anti-pollution fight. Before considering the problem of whether or not there will be pollution, we are opposed to reclamation itself. Fishermen are derided, but we have pride in fishing." The similarly derided fishermen of Shibushi Bay listened to the talk and tears came to the eyes of many. By the end of the meeting, the fishermen and their wives decided that they had to transform what had been only a movement against pollution into a fight for the right to their livelihood, coining the slogan "Defend the fishing grounds."

The fishermen began to study furiously. Ui Jun came to lecture about the logic of antidevelopment, high-school instructor Nishioka attacked the falsity of the word "scientific," and in April Professor Miyamoto Ken'ichi spoke at the "Shibushi Rally for the Defense of Nature in Kyushu." [Shibushi is located on Kyushu.] The rally was the occasion for an exchange of opinions among groups from all parts of Japan—residents' groups, scholars, and conservationists. Political parties and researchers all cooperated with the Shibushi group, which even sent representatives as far as Yokkaichi to see the results of development and pollution with their own eyes.

Their actions were not confined to study and observation. The villagers attended their town meeting and prefectural assembly. They also bargained collectively with the town's mayor and the governor and issued invitations to a public inquiry, demanding a "dialogue."

All their activities produced no change, however, and finally their angry voices were heard at the regular June prefectural assembly. They even surrounded the assembly building three times, in siege fashion, and the last time the police tactical squad

was called in, resulting in four residents being injured. In the middle
of this turmoil, the Liberal Democratic party leaders in the assembly forced through a bill canceling the national park designation of the bay to accelerate the development plans.

Yet the exclusion of the residents from the decision had the
opposite results from those intended by the fast move. Widespread
distrust was planted among the population in Kagoshima, and
eventually, as a consequence of their haste to push the project
through, the authorities were compelled by public opinion to
reexamine the development plan.

A central figure in bringing about the victory of the Shibushi
villagers was Director Koyama of the Environmental Office, who
visited the area in August and criticized the administration of
development. Saying that "the prefecture's ways are wrong,"
Koyama promised the residents that "neither reclamation nor the
cancelation of the national park will be permitted." Applause and
tears greeted his words.

DOCTORS AND PRIESTS

By the end of September there were eleven opposition organizations on the coast of Shibushi Bay, including fishermen's groups
and local labor unions. All of them belonged to the Shibushi Bay
Antipollution Liaison Committee. The committee chairman, Tōgo
Sōbei, sixty-four, runs a large hospital of internal medicine and
psychiatry in Shibushi and is a haiku poet as well. In March 1971
he organized the town's most prominent residents into the Association to Prevent the Pollution of Shibushi Bay and became its chairman. Formation of this association, more than half a year before
the submission of the development plan, provided a spark for the
other groups. In high spirits Chairman Tōgo says, "Even if I
become the only one involved, even if I have to take this business
to court, I am determined to prevent the development of Shibushi
Bay."

Vice-Chairman Teruoka Yasutami, sixty-three, is a Buddhist
priest of the Kongō Temple. He comments that "the teaching of
Shinran [a famous Japanese Buddhist figure] was to try to rescue
the people from suffering. Now the mission of the priest is indeed
to rescue the people from pollution." Teruoka calmly proselytizes
the townspeople, even those in the faction favoring development,

proclaiming that "if pollution enterprises come it will be hell, if they don't it will be paradise."

The chairman and vice-chairman of the Association for the Realization of Absolute Opposition to Oil Combines in Kawara, Iwashige Koei (forty-three) and Yasumatsu Toshihide (forty-three), are also a doctor-and-priest combination. Chairman Iwashige notes that the victory over the plan "was blessed by circumstances, such as a series of judicial decisions on pollution, the reworking of the New National Composite Development Plan, and the rising public opinion on pollution." However, it was not, of course, only thanks to "circumstances."

Chairman Tōgo cited as one of the factors making possible their success "the loose solidarity of all the groups." People participating in the movement come from various backgrounds, from nature conservation groups to labor unions, fishermen's cooperatives, and local self-government associations. Additional strength was gained by making the most of business connections and by having local notables act as mediators, since the influence of such old men is still considerable in the villages. Behind the mediators followed young people, fishermen's action corps, uncompromising housewives. All performed their duties to the fullest.

Furthermore, the movement consistently followed the "Kagoshima formula"—that a resident should stand at the head in dealings with the existing political parties and organizations. That this formula was followed from the beginning was confirmed both by Chairman Kotani of the prefectual Sōhyō labor council and others. This meant, for example, that even in street demonstrations the representatives of the labor unions and political parties walked behind the residents. Thus no one was disturbed when the authorities claimed that "you are being made to dance by the political influence of one party."

Bureaucrats in the Kagoshima prefectural government explained to Environment Office Director Koyama that they would prepare a second draft of the plan, incorporating drastic revisions, but the contents of the second draft were not made public. Moriyama Kazuhiro (thirty), a barber in Kawara and head of education and publicity for the Association for Realization of Absolute Opposition, shows fighting spirit on the subject. "Whatever the contents of the second draft may be," he says, "the *real* battle to come will be over the *Nihon Rettō Kaizō-ron* ["Remodeling Japan"]. That is next."

People are also beginning to say: "I have been a member of the Liberal Democratic party, but I will never vote for the LDP again." Vice-chairman Teruoka is himself a classmate of Cabinet Secretary Nikaidō and had once served as a local representative for the LDP. Now Teruoka, too, has swung around and has joined the movement to defeat Nikaidō.

Comments Chairman Tōgo, "We will try to bring together a united Socialist–Communist alliance, but if that does not work we are prepared to put up our own candidate." Traditionally conservative constituencies [*jiban*] are slowly beginning to be shaken by these aroused villagers who started with nature conservation and antipollution.

UI JUN*
Pollution: Basic Theory of Kōgai

... Japan has the worst problem of environmental pollution of any country in the world. ... It is difficult to express the severity of this pollution quantitatively, but it was in Japan that various new diseases fatal to man, and coming from water pollution, first appeared. Minamata disease appeared in two places in Japan in rapid succession, and it has been reported that there has been a third, less severe, outbreak in Finland. And it is almost certain that *itai-itai* disease (*itai* means "pain" in Japanese), which is cadmium poisoning, first appeared at Toyama, and then later at Tsushima. And *yubimagari* disease (*yubimagari* means "twisted fingers," which is one of the effects of this disease), which is suspected to be a kind of poisoning by cadmium and other heavy metals, has appeared in a number of places in the country. And now *itai-itai* disease has appeared in a third place, also in Japan. ...

It is often said that *kōgai* is a side effect of, or a distortion of, rapid economic development. But I think that this is a notion that

* Ui Jun, "Pollution: Basic Theory of *Kōgai*," *AMPO* 9–10 (n.d.), pp. 17–21.

comes from the side of the producers of *kōgai*. But as far as I can see, *kōgai* is *not* such a trifling thing as just a side effect or a distortion of rapid economic development. To say that it is "distortion" is to say that if economic development were carried on rightly, or managed to follow a natural course without distortion, *kōgai* would not appear. But the fact is that *kōgai* is one of the most powerful factors *of* rapidly developing economies. Japanese economists have pointed out a number of factors in the success of Japan's capitalist economy, and the things most stressed have been low wages and trade protection. Now I am adding to these a third: the neglect of *kōgai* . . . the permitting the economy to dirty its own clothes. The problem of *kōgai* is an essential part of the structure of the capitalist economy of Japan. . . .

Steel engineers say that the most important factor in the rapid recovery and modernization of Japan's postwar steel industry has been the Oxygen LD furnace. We are familiar with the multi-colored smoke that comes from the chimneys of steel mills, which is a necessary product of this LD furnace. In Europe or the United States this kind of furnace cannot be used unless its smoke is cleaned in a dust collector. But, if this dust collector is taken into account, the LD furnace is not particularly cheap. This dust collector and the necessary connecting ducts are several times larger than the furnace itself. Of course we cannot judge their cost just from their size, but they cost at least thirty percent of the whole setup . . . and the small furnace itself is already very expensive. In Japan it has been possible to operate this furnace without the cooling duct and dust collector. Thus the steel companies in Japan have profited some thirty percent on each furnace, a profit which can be turned to more profit, and so on. . . .

The problem of *kōgai* also involves a problem of social discrimination. We can point out various ways in which *kōgai* creates social segregation. One is given a disease from pollution, becomes poor because of the disease, and then is discriminated against because of the poverty. The reason why one group of Minamata patients accepted the humiliating compromise plan for compensation was that it was the only way to escape this discrimination. Until then they had been in the position of depending on "sympathy" payments from the corporation, and being treated by the townspeople as moneygrubbers; now at least the compensation is official, even though it is not enough. And in Tsushima, an agreement was made among pollution victims to keep out scholars who came from outside to investigate, because if it became known that there were victims of *itai-itai* disease no members of their families could marry or get a job. . . .

There have been many cases in which Tokyo University has taken sides with the polluters, sought to obscure the causal relation, or has even oppressed honest researchers. Perhaps the people who did these things were caught up in the system of Tokyo U., and subjectively did not intend to commit such acts. Perhaps this university by its nature is built in such a way as to lead those who start with good intentions into the position of the assailant. . . .

And you are already aware that today's capitalism makes profit even from *kōgai,* and that the *kōgai*-preventive industries are now the stars of the stock market. Some students of, for example, electronics, will say that they have no connection at all with *kōgai.* However, according to some computer manufacturers, one of the best customers for middle-range computers is *kōgai*-monitoring centers. So most of the divisions of the Technological Department at Tokyo U.—which is to say, most engineers in Japan—have something to do with *kōgai,* and most of them are making money from it.

When this monitoring by computers or the setting of "environmental standards" is discussed, the question always comes up: Why is it that we never touch the source which is *producing kōgai?* If we did, we could *eliminate kōgai* before we *measured* it. But present preventive techniques can not do that. Our way of attacking the problem is organized in such a way as to leave the source alone, and to consume as much money as possible in "preventive measures." The procedure that has become orthodox, growing out of the technological point of view of Tokyo U.—where all of us make our livings—is to monitor *kōgai* with computers. But the present technological system *itself* is necessarily producing *kōgai,* and cannot be separated from *kōgai.*

Chronology: 1945-1973

1945: Atomic bombs destroy Hiroshima and Nagasaki; Japan accepts Allied Potsdam Declaration and surrenders; Gen. Douglas MacArthur, as SCAP, establishes Occupation Headquarters in Tokyo; Yasuda Plan for dissolving zaibatsu announced

1946: International Military Tribunal for the Far East, 1946–48; first postwar election returns many wartime leaders to Diet; SCAP reforms begin; land reform gets under way

1947: New constitution; MacArthur bans February 1 general strike; socialist Katayama cabinet formed without Diet majority; purge widened

1948: Katayama replaced by more conservative Ashida cabinet; "reverse course" begins, erasing many reforms, amid American criticism of occupation; Yoshida Shigeru is prime minister

1949: Elections give Japan Communist party nearly 10% of votes; Yoshida is still prime minister; "Red purge" begins; severe deflationary Dodge Plan results in massive unemployment; reparations removals halted

1950: Korean War; National Police Reserve created; SCAP bans public demonstrations; communists purged from politics and mass media

1951: Rehabilitation of wartime leaders; Gen. Matthew Ridgway replaces MacArthur as SCAP; San Francisco peace treaty not signed by Soviet Union, India, China

1952: Peace treaty in effect, Japan regains sovereignty; U.S.–Japan administrative agreement; Safety Agency assumes duties of National Police Reserve; Yoshida remains prime minister

1953: Negotiations between Japan and the United States for defense pact; elections give socialists more votes, but Yoshida remains prime minister

1954: Mutual Defense Assistance Agreement signed, implementing 1951 security pact between U.S. and Japan; Safety Forces renamed Self-Defense Forces, Safety Agency becomes Defense Agency; Hatoyama is prime minister

1955: Hatoyama remains prime minister after elections; socialists re-unite bickering wings; Liberal Democratic party formed from merger of conservatives

1956: Japan–U.S.S.R. formal diplomatic relations, without agreement on peace settlement; Japan admitted to United Nations; Ishibashi prime minister

1957: Kishi Nobusuke replaces Ishibashi as prime minister; negotiations start on revision of U.S.–Japan security pact

1958: General elections return conservatives, but Socialists win one-third of popular vote; Kishi still prime minister; informal trade relations broken off by People's Republic of China after Nagasaki flag incident

1959: Mounting opposition to renewal of U.S.–Japan defense treaty; Socialists split over issue of opposition to renewal

1960: U.S.–Japan security pact signed; Democratic Socialist party formed by right-wing split-off from JSP; riots against ratification of treaty; Eisenhower visit is canceled; JSP leader Asanuma assassinated; Kishi resigns and is replaced by Ikeda as prime minister

1961: Emphasis on economic improvement; Ikeda "income-doubling plan"

1962: Civil administrator appointed to head military government on Okinawa

1963: Elections return Ikeda and LDP, but left-wing parties gain over 40% of popular vote; trade agreement between Japan and U.S.S.R.

1964: Tokyo Olympics; Satō succeeds Ikeda as prime minister; Kōmei party formed by Sōka Gakkai religious association

1965: Japan and South Korea normalize diplomatic status, sign basic agreement

1966: Large American arms procurements within Japan following escalation of Vietnam war

1967: General elections give Liberal Democrats less than 50% of popular vote for first time, but LDP retains control of Diet

1968: Student turmoil widespread; occupation of buildings by students paralyzes Tokyo University

1969: Satō–Nixon Communiqué; return of Okinawa negotiated; riots against use of Okinawa as American base for Vietnam war; elections give new Kōmei party 11% of votes

1970: U.S.–Japan security pact renewed a second time; Osaka World's Fair; farmers battle police at Sanrizuka for land confiscated for new Tokyo jetport

1971:   Dollar devaluation and 10% surcharge on American imports aimed largely at Japanese exports to U.S.; Nixon China diplomacy undercuts Satō

1972:   Okinawa returned to Japanese sovereignty, but American bases are left; Tanaka replaces Satō as prime minister; Tanaka visits Peking, establishes diplomatic relations with China; Communists win 10% of vote in general elections

1973:   Tanaka enunciates "remodeling Japan" ideas; yen floated in international money markets; after upward revaluation, Japanese per capita income put at around $3,000; election of Nagoya mayor gives control of Japan's five largest cities to socialist/communist coalition

Further Reading

Books listed here are useful for more detailed information in several areas; some literature is included. Books used in *The Japan Reader* are not included. Starred titles (*) are available in paperback.

1. The American Occupation, 1945–1952

* Dazai Osamu, *The Setting Sun* (New York: New Directions Publishing Corp., 1956).
* John W. Dower, "Occupied Japan and the American Lake, 1945–1950," in Edward Friedman and Mark Selden, eds., *America's Asia* (New York: Pantheon Books, 1971; paper—New York: Vintage Books, 1972).

John W. Hall and Richard K. Beardsley, eds., *Twelve Doors to Japan* (New York: McGraw-Hill Book Co., 1965).

Kawai Kazuo, *Japan's American Interlude* (Chicago: University of Chicago Press, 1960).

Owen Lattimore, *Solution in Asia* (New York: The John Day Co., 1949).

Helen Mears, *Mirror for Americans* (Boston: Houghton Mifflin Co., 1948).

* Minear, Richard, *Victor's Justice: The Tokyo War Crimes Trial* (Princeton, N.J.: Princeton University Press, 1971).

2. The Politics of Prosperity, 1952–1973

* Zbigniew Brzezinski, *Fragile Blossom: Crisis and Change in Japan* (New York: Harper and Row, 1972).
* George DeVos and Hiroshi Wagatsuma, eds., *Japan's Invisible Race* (Berkeley and Los Angeles: University of California Press, 1966).
* R. P. Dore, *City Life in Japan* (Berkeley and Los Angeles: University of California Press, 1958).
* Robert Guillain, *The Japanese Challenge* (New York: Harper & Row, 1970).

* Nobutaka Ike, *Japanese Politics: An Introductory Survey* (New York: Alfred A. Knopf, 1956).

* Donald Keene, *Modern Japanese Literature: An Anthology* (New York: Grove Press, 1956).

Solomon Levine, *Industrial Relations in Postwar Japan* (Urbana: University of Illinois Press, 1958).

Richard H. Mitchell, *The Korean Minority in Japan* (Berkeley: University of California Press, 1967).

Ivan Morris, *Nationalism and the Right-Wing in Japan: A Study of Postwar Trends* (London: Oxford University Press, 1960).

* Ōe Kenzaburō, *A Personal Matter* (New York: Grove Press, 1968).

* Ezra Vogel, *Japan's New Middle Class* (Berkeley and Los Angeles: University of California Press, 1963).

Yoshida Shigeru, *Yoshida Memoirs* (Boston: Houghton Mifflin Co., 1962).

Periodicals

The following periodicals regularly include useful articles on contemporary Japan.

AMPO* (Tokyo)

Asian Survey (Berkeley)

Association for Radical East Asian Studies* (London)

Bulletin of Concerned Asian Scholars* (San Francisco)

Far Eastern Economic Review (Hong Kong)

Japan Quarterly (Tokyo)

Journal of Asian Studies (Ann Arbor)

Le Monde (Paris)

Pacific Affairs (Vancouver)

Pacific Basin Reports* (San Francisco)

* Starred publications are available in a few university libraries, but may be ordered directly from the publishers: *Ampo,* P.O. Box 5250, Tokyo International, Japan; *Association for Radical East Asian Studies,* occasional papers, 6 Endsleigh St., London W.C. 1, England; *Bulletin of Concerned Asian Scholars,* 604 Mission Street, room 1001, San Francisco, Ca. 94105; *Pacific Basin Reports,* Custom House, Box 26581, San Francisco, Ca. 94126.

Notes on Contributors

JAMES ABEGGLEN is an economic analyst for the Boston Consulting Group.

GEORGE ATCHESON was the Political Officer for the U.S. State Department during much of the American occupation of Japan.

ALBERT AXELBANK is a correspondent for *The Nation* and *Progressive* and lives in Tokyo.

HANS H. BAERWALD teaches political science at U.C.L.A.

GEORGE W. BALL is a former State Department diplomat and well-known foreign policy analyst.

W. MacMAHON BALL, an Australian, was British Commonwealth representative to the Far Eastern Commission in 1946–1947.

RICHARD K. BEARDSLEY teaches anthropology at the University of Michigan.

T. A. BISSON taught at Yenching University in Peking in the late 1920s, published *America's Far Eastern Policy,* and worked during the occupation of Japan with the U.S. Strategic Bombing Survey and the Government Section, SCAP. He taught at the University of California, Berkeley, from 1948 to 1953. He was a major figure in the controversy over the Institute of Pacific Relations in the 1950s, and is currently preparing a memoir of the occupation period.

HERBERT P. BIX teaches history at the University of Massachusetts, Boston.

HUBERT BROCHIER is a professor of political economy at the University of Paris and also teaches at the École des Langues Orientales.

ELLY CARAWAY, JR., is President of Burlington Industries and served on Nixon's Advisory Council on United States-Japan Economic Relations.

ALLAN B. COLE teaches at the Fletcher School of Law and Diplomacy, Tufts University.

ROBERT E. COLE is in the Sociology Department and the Center for Japanese Studies of the University of Michigan.

ALICE COOK teaches at the New York State School of Industrial and Labor Relations at Cornell University.

R. P. DORE teaches sociology at the Institute of Development Studies, University of Sussex, England.

JOHN W. DOWER teaches history at the University of Wisconsin, Madison.

PAUL DULL is Professor of History at the University of Oregon.

MIRIAM FARLEY worked for the Institute of Pacific Relations and was an editor of *Far Eastern Survey* in the late 1940s.

FUKUTAKE TADASHI is Professor of Sociology at the University of Tokyo.

MARK GAYN was a journalist in Tokyo during two years of the American occupation and has reported on China for Canadian newspapers since then.

ANDREW GRAD traveled extensively in Japan in the 1930s. During the American occupation he worked in the Government Section of SCAP as head of the unit dealing with prefectural affairs, and carried out research on land reform in all parts of Japan.

ELEANOR M. HADLEY worked in the occupation bureaucracy in the 1940s, wrote a Ph.D. dissertation on the zaibatsu dissolution program, and is currently Professor of Economics at Smith College.

JOHN W. HALL is Professor of History at Yale University.

JON HALLIDAY, author of *Japanese Imperialism Today* (1973), is preparing a history of Japanese capitalism since the Meiji Restoration. He is also a member of the editorial board of *New Left Review*.

RICHARD HALLORAN is the Tokyo correspondent of the *New York Times*.

IENAGA SABURŌ is Professor of History at Tokyo University of Education. His *A Cultural History of Japan* has long been used as a standard text in Japanese schools.

MARIUS B. JANSEN is Professor of History at Princeton University.

WILLIAM F. KNOWLAND, former owner of the *Oakland Tribune,* was U.S. Senator from California in the 1940s and 1950s and a leading figure in the American "China Lobby."

KOBAYASHI YASUHIRO is a newspaper writer in the Kagoshima branch office of the *Asahi Shimbun,* Japan's largest daily newspaper.

GABRIEL KOLKO teaches foreign relations at York University, Toronto, Canada.

JOYCE KOLKO received her training in political science and international relations.

LOUIS KRAAR is a writer for *Fortune* magazine.

SOLOMON LEVINE is a specialist in postwar Japanese industrial relations at the University of Wisconsin, at Madison.

JOHN M. MAKI teaches political science at the University of Massachusetts, Amherst.

BENJAMIN MARTIN wrote his article on the Miike strike as a researcher for the United Mine Workers.

GAVAN MCCORMACK teaches Asian history at Leeds University, England.

MEI JU-AO was the representative of the Republic of China on the Far Eastern Commission, the eleven-nation group which theoretically had authority over the American occupation of Japan.

MUTŌ ICHIYO is head of the Japan Peace in Vietnam Committee (Beiheiren) and edits the Japanese English-language magazine *AMPO.*

KOJI NAKAMURA is the Japan correspondent for the *Far Eastern Economic Review.*

GEORGE R. PACKARD III was an embassy official of the U.S. State Department during the 1950s and during the security treaty crisis in 1960. Today he is managing editor of the *Philadelphia Bulletin.*

EDWIN PAULEY, a California business executive, led the first major American mission to survey Japanese industrial capacity for the purposes of reparation and removal to nations Japan had invaded in World War II.

ELIZABETH POND is Asia correspondent for the *Christian Science Monitor.*

WALTER S. ROBERTSON was Assistant Secretary for Far Eastern Affairs during the Eisenhower administration.

KENNETH C. ROYALL was Secretary of the Army during the Truman administration.

D. C. S. SISSONS teaches politics at the Australian National University, Canberra.

KURT STEINER is Professor of Political Science at Stanford University.

KOJI TAIRA teaches Asian studies at the University of Illinois, Urbana.

SUMIYA MIKIO is Professor of Economics at the University of Tokyo.

GEORGE OAKLEY TOTTEN III is Professor of Political Science at the University of Southern California.

TSUDA MASUMI is Professor of Economics at Musashi University, Tokyo.

CECIL H. UYEHARA works for the Agency for International Development, Department of State.

ROBERT E. WARD is Professor of Political Science at the University of Michigan.

MARTIN E. WEINSTEIN is a specialist in American-East Asian relations at Columbia University.

CHITOSHI YANAGA is Professor of Political Science at Yale University.

Index

Acheson, Dean, 254
aerospace industry, 271, 292, 297–8
agriculture and rural areas (occ.),
72, 78–9, 139, 140, 187–218, 247,
558; Agricultural Association,
59, 64; cooperatives, 208, 211,
217, 328–9; food shortages and
distribution, 16, 44, 45, 58, 71,
72, 94, 95, 114, 145–7, 149–50,
187, 217, 254; land reform, 4,
14, 15, 59–60, 62, 74, 99, 123,
126, 186–93, 196, 200–17 *passim,*
218–23, 558; local government
and politics, 205–18; Nichinō
(Japan Peasant Union), 193–8
passim; peasant unions, 35, 59,
63, 193–200, 207, 210, 218, 222;
Zennichinō (All-Japan Peasant
Union), 193, 198–200; Zennō,
193, 197–8
agriculture and rural areas (postocc.), 218–23, 317, 329, 423,
427, 439, 558–64; food shortages
and imports, 266, 317, 439, 562,
567; labor force, 369, 423, 461,
558, 559–60, 561, 563, 567; local
government and politics, 220,
221–2, 223, 228, 323, 326–34,
448, 499; Tanaka Plan for rural
industrial development, 523, 526,
557, 564–73
Akihito, Crown Prince, 61, 372
Allied Council for Japan, 122, 144,
150–1, 165, 234

armed forces and defense, 223, 227,
228, 231, 233–4, 235, 238, 239–
40, 244, 252–3, 257–307, 313,
314, 340, 357, 497, 527; constitutional prohibition of, 18, 20, 21,
23, 227–8, 232, 239, 242, 253,
254, 261, 265, 298, 371, 374,
549; constitutional revision proposed, 262, 270, 291, 338, 357,
522, 527; demilitarization and
purge during occupation, 3, 6, 7,
9–10, 10–11, 12, 14, 20, 21, 23,
28–32 *passim,* 38, 41, 49, 51, 57,
77, 78, 107, 109–10, 122, 232,
233, 234, 263–4, 265, 529; Mutual
Defense Assistance Agreement
(with U.S.), 261, 271; National
Police Reserve, 239–40, 244, 260,
338–9; opposition to military
buildup and rearmament, 229,
231, 235, 238, 240, 241, 243,
253, 254, 255, 256, 265, 275,
281–7, 298, 302–9, 316, 337,
338–9, 357, 358, 449, 526, 527,
556; overseas deployment of Japanese forces, 270, 282, 289,
296; prewar military clique, 43,
77, 90, 265, 391, 392, 431; Self-
Defense Forces, 227, 244, 257,
258–9, 261, 274, 286–7, 289,
290, 293–301 *passim,* 526, 527;
U.S. forces and bases in Japan,
233, 235, 236, 238, 241, 242–3,
253, 265, 266, 273, 274, 277,

280, 281, 298, 307, 338, 339,
372; U.S. forces in Bonin Islands,
232; U.S. forces in Okinawa, 235,
237, 274, 276, 280, 281, 284,
285, 288, 289, 290, 298, 371;
U.S. forces in Ryūkyū Islands,
232, 237. *See also* military-industrial complex; nuclear weapons;
security treaty
Asahi Shimbun (newspaper), 381,
382, 386; on economic decentralization, 131; on economy in
1970s, 410; on Hatoyama's retirement, 349; on Police Law
revisions, 354, 355; on security
treaty (1960), 375, 378; on steel
cartel, 414; on Tanaka Plan, 568;
on textbook certification and
Ienaga case, 538–9, 545; and
union, 156–61
Asanuma, Inejirō, 364, 501
Ashida, Hitoshi, 39, 393; as prime
minister, 68, 73, 167, 168, 170,
173
Atcheson, George, 11; on Allied
Council, 144, 150–1, 165
Australia, 3, 241, 315–16
automobile industry, 400, 413, 423,
429, 435; labor, 459, 473, 475,
476

Baba (publisher of *Yomiuri*), 154,
155, 156, 159, 160
Baker, Frayne, 153, 156, 158
Bank of Japan, 416, 430, 432, 435
banking and finance (occ.), 5, 42,
51–3, 69, 70, 74, 79, 91, 101–4,
109, 128, 210, 215; foreign investment in Japan, 120, 137–8
banking and finance (postocc.), 228,
270, 394, 397, 399–400, 401–2,
424–30, 432, 434, 435, 436, 437;
domestic savings, 425, 426–8;
foreign investment by Japan, 227,
312, 400, 401, 434, 437; foreign
investment in Japan, 269, 270,
301, 382, 413
Beiheiren (Peace in Vietnam Committee), 504, 553, 556
Bisson, T. A., 24, 90, 92–3
Bonin Islands: U.S. forces, 232
Bradley, Omar, 238

Brines, Russell, 234
Bundy, William P., 300
Burma, 241
business and industry: antimonopoly
legislation, 62, 74, 79, 100, 128,
132–3, 347, 414, 415; military-
industrial complex, 227, 257–63
passim, 268–71, 274, 291, 292;
prewar and wartime, 77, 90, 392,
399, 401, 403, 406, 470–2. *See
also* banking and finance; economy; foreign commerce and
trade; labor and labor movement;
shipping; zaibatsu; *zaikai*
business and industry (occ.), 3, 5, 6,
12, 13, 14, 62, 65, 72, 77–138,
175; Draper-Johnston Mission,
106, 119–21, 128; and politics,
41, 56, 217, 218, 346–7; purge,
3, 28, 29, 30, 36, 37, 63, 64, 65,
67, 75, 79, 85–94 *passim*, 109,
124–5, 126–7; reparations, 4,
82–5, 93, 94, 119, 120–1, 123,
127, 260; U.S. business critical of
policies, 93, 98, 99–100, 106, 119–
21; Yasuda Plan, 79–82, 89
business and industry (postocc.),
227, 228, 229, 230, 270, 348–51,
380, 382, 388–439; enterprise
groups, 399–400; Japan Chamber
of Commerce and Industry, 350,
397, 408–10, 411; Japan Committee for Economic Development, 397, 405–7, 411; Japan
Industrial Club, 397; Keidanren
(Federation of Economic Organizations), 262, 350, 397, 398,
403, 404–5, 411, 412–13, 414,
431; and labor 484–6, 497; and
labor—Nikkeiren (Japan Federation of Employers' Associations),
397, 407–8, 411, 412, 419, 431,
450, 491; and politics, 347–51,
366, 387–400 *passim*, 403, 405–
19 *passim*, 428, 429, 430–1, 434,
435, 436, 437, 522, 523; pollution
problems, 230, 412–13, 438, 504,
526, 564, 565, 566, 567, 569, 572,
573–5; Sanken (Industrial Problems Study Council), 403, 410–
15; small and medium-size firms,
420–5, 441, 458, 463, 484; Tanaka Plan, 523, 526, 557, 564–

metallurgical industry, 439; labor,
178, 448, 451, 510. *See also* steel
industry
Miike Mine strike, 488–94
Miki, Bukichi, 365, 366
Miki, Takeo, 519, 521, 524
military-industrial complex, 227,
257–63 *passim*, 268–71, 274, 291,
292
Mimpo (newspaper), 154
Minobe, Tatsukichi, 364
Minsei (Democratic Youth League),
552, 554
Mitsubishi (family and business
holdings), 80–2, 86, 96, 100, 117,
269–70, 292, 399, 400, 402, 403,
411, 415, 436, 566
Mitsui (family and business hold-
ings), 80–2, 86, 100, 117, 399,
400, 402, 403, 411, 488, 490,
567; Miike Mine strike, 488–94;
Ōji Paper strike, 90, 352, 488
Mori, Kotarō, 200
Morita, Tatsuo, 197
Muto, Ichiyo, 504
Mutō, Takeo, 179
Mutual Defense Assistance Agree-
ment (Japan and U.S.), 261, 271
Myerson, Michael, 172

Nagoya: urban problems, 564, 566
Nakajima, Chikuhei, 404
Nakasone, Yasuhiro, 519, 521–2,
524
Narahashi, Wataru, 19, 21, 23–4, 39
National Police Reserve. *See* armed
forces and defense
navy. *See* armed forces and defense
Netherlands, 267, 438
New York Herald Tribune, on Japanese labor disputes, 176
New York Times, on Japanese labor
disputes, 179, 180
New Zealand, 241
newspapers, 16, 57, 58, 64, 65, 131,
148, 196, 266, 338, 357, 359, 362,
379–87, 394, 567; labor, 57, 58,
145, 155–61, 176, 370; Police
Law revisions, opposition to,
354–5; press clubs, 386–7; and
security treaty (1960), 370, 373,
374–5, 378, 379, 380, 385. *See*

also communications industry;
individual newspapers
Nezu, Kaichirō, 388
Nichinō (Japan Peasant Union),
193–8 *passim*
Nihon Keizai Shimbun (newspaper),
381; and Police Law revisions,
355; on security treaty (1960),
379
Nihon University, 555
Nikkeiren (Japan Federation of Employers' Associations), 175, 397,
407–8, 411, 412, 419, 431, 450,
491
Nippon Steel Corporation, 304, 400,
411, 437–8, 511
Nippon Times (newspaper), 131
Nishi Nippon Shimbun (newspaper),
382
Nishimura, Rikiya, 377
Nishio, Suehiro, 357, 377
Nissan Motor Company, 396, 400,
435
Nixon, Richard M., 257, 263–4, 524;
economic policies, 301, 306, 309–
13 *passim*, 316, 517; Peking trip
and China policy, 288, 301–6
passim, 314, 517, 518; and Satō,
Communiqué, 275, 276, 278–91
passim, 301, 506
Nosaka, Sanzō, 526
nuclear weapons: Japan has industrial base for, 228, 259, 292,
297–8, 313; Japanese opposition
to, 243, 281, 282, 285–6, 287,
288, 298, 368, 508; possible Japanese use of, 287, 297, 299, 305,
524, 527

occupation (SCAP), 228–44; Allied
Council for Japan, 122, 144,
150–1, 165, 234; Basic Initial
Post-Surrender Directive, 6, 7–11,
77, 78–9, 87, 90, 122, 123; Far
Eastern Commission, 3, 23, 94,
100, 111, 113, 114, 118, 123, 128;
financial cost, to U.S., 4, 31–2,
93, 96, 110, 117, 127; policies
and reforms, 3–4, 13, 14, 28, 29,
67, 92, 97–8, 106, 123, 125, 232,
234–5, 323, 334, 338, 391;
policies and reforms, criticism of,

and Japan, 3, 15, 227; desire for improved relations, 260–1, 262, 268, 307–8, 314, 317, 318–20, 350, 357, 358, 360, 398; disputed territory, 307, 308, 317, 321; peace treaty, 231, 236, 241, 246, 307, 308, 321; trade, 307, 308, 317–22 *passim,* 437. *See also* Allied Council for Japan; Far Eastern Commission

Union of Soviet Socialist Republics and the United States, 150–1, 165, 321–2, 373; U.S.S.R. viewed as threat, 4, 97, 106, 124, 183, 233, 245, 246, 247, 257, 264; U.S. in Japan viewed as threat, 237–8. *See also* Cold War

United Nations: Japanese backing, 249, 278; Japanese membership, 244, 252, 253; Nationalist China, 304, 306. *See also* Korean War

United Nations Charter: Japanese backing, 271, 272, 273, 372

United States and China, Nationalist, 277, 279, 284, 306, 310; communism in Asia viewed as threat, 4, 97, 106, 124, 134, 183, 233, 235, 237, 244, 245, 246, 247, 254, 257, 262, 263, 264, 267, 282, 547 (*see also* Cold War; Indochina war; Korean War); defense spending, 295, 299; GNP, 438; and Korea, South, 284, 310; labor, 421, 445, 452, 454, 457, 481

United States and China, Communist, 279; China viewed as threat, 4, 97, 106, 124, 134, 231, 235, 237, 254, 257, 267; Nixon trip and détente, 288, 301–6 *passim,* 314, 517, 518; U.S. in Japan view as threat, 237–8, 259–60

United States and Japan: Eisenhower trip and cancellation, 351, 372, 373–4, 379, 384, 385; Nixon-Satō Communiqué, 275, 276, 278–91 *passim,* 301, 506. *See also* occupation (SCAP)

United States and Japan—armed forces and defense, 227, 241, 244, 252–3, 262, 357; lend-lease agreement, 261; Mutual Defense

Assistance Agreement, 261, 271; U.S. forces and bases in Japan, 233, 235, 236, 238, 241, 242–3, 253, 265, 266, 273, 274, 277, 280, 281, 298, 307, 338, 339, 372; U.S. forces in Bonin Islands, 232; U.S. forces in Okinawa, 235, 237, 274, 276, 280, 281, 284, 285, 288, 289, 290, 298, 371; U.S. forces in Ryūkyū Islands, 232, 237. *See also* armed forces and defense; peace treaty; security treaty

United States and Japan—business and economics, 262, 268–71, 292, 301, 306, 308–14 *passim,* 316, 517, 518, 522; occupation policies criticized by U.S. business, 93, 98, 99–100, 106, 119–21; textile dispute, 301, 302, 306, 309–310, 313, 413, 433, 518; trade, 229, 301, 302, 306, 309–13 *passim,* 320, 413–14, 433, 518

United States and the Union of Soviet Socialist Republics, 150–1, 165, 321–2, 373; U.S.S.R. viewed as threat, 4, 97, 106, 124, 183, 233, 245, 246, 247, 257, 264; U.S. in Japan viewed as threat, 237–6. *See also* Cold War

Vietnam war. *See* Indochina war
Voorhees, Tracy, 237
voting. *See* elections

Walsh, E. C., 131
war criminals and war crimes trials, 10, 14, 24, 26, 121–2, 123, 156; Emperor Hirohito considered as war criminal, 11, 16, 20, 26
welfare services and programs, 356, 357, 361, 426, 438, 501, 504, 526. *See also* social security
West Germany, 299, 438, 445
Whitney, Courtney A., 37, 45; and constitution (1946), 19–23 *passim*
Willoughby, Charles, 159, 233
Woll, Matthew, 172, 173
women, 556; education, 532; in labor force, 478–80; Police Law revi-

About the Editors

JON LIVINGSTON did his graduate work in Japanese studies at Harvard. He is coeditor of *China Yesterday and Today* and a staff member of the Bay Area Institute of San Francisco.

JOE MOORE works in modern Japanese history. He has been a congressional assistant, and is currently studying at the University of Wisconsin.

FELICIA OLDFATHER did her graduate work in Asian studies at Washington University, St. Louis, and at the University of California, Berkeley. She is an editor of *China! Inside the People's Republic*.